THE HISTORY
OF CHRISTIANITY IN
BRITAIN AND IRELAND

THE HISTORY
OF CHRISTIANITY IN
BRITAIN AND IRELAND

From the first century to the twenty-first

Gerald Bray

APOLLOS (an imprint of Inter-Varsity Press)
36 Causton Street, London SW1P 4ST, England
Email: ivp@ivpbooks.com
Website: www.ivpbooks.com

First published 2021

British Library Cataloguing-in-Publication Data
A catalogue record for this book is available from the British Library.

ISBN: 978–1–78974–120–9
eBook ISBN: 978–1–78974–118–6

Set in Minion Pro 10.75/13.75pt
Typeset in Great Britain by CRB Associates, Potterhanworth, Lincolnshire
Printed and bound in Great Britain by TJ Books Ltd, Padstow, Cornwall

Produced on paper from sustainable sources.

Inter-Varsity Press publishes Christian books that are true to the Bible and that communicate
the gospel, develop discipleship and strengthen the church for its mission in the world.

IVP originated within the Inter-Varsity Fellowship, now the Universities and Colleges Christian
Fellowship, a student movement connecting Christian Unions in universities and colleges
throughout Great Britain, and a member movement of the International Fellowship of
Evangelical Students. Website: www.uccf.org.uk. That historic association is maintained,
and all senior IVP staff and committee members subscribe to the UCCF Basis of Faith.

Contents

List of tables   x
Preface   xi

Introduction   xv

1 In the beginning (to AD 597)   1
   The shadow of Rome   1
   Pelagius   4
   Ireland   6
   The Anglo-Saxons   9
   Wales   11
   A Celtic church?   13
   King Arthur and the end of Roman Britain   15

2 Between Ireland and Rome (597–871)   20
   Scotland   20
   The Roman mission to the English   22
   Monastic influences   31
   The Anglo-Saxon church   33
   The role of women   41
   The Viking invasions   43

3 One church in four nations (871–1154)   47
   Decline and revival in England   47
   The transformation of the English church and state   52
   The parish system   62
   Wales   67
   Ireland   68
   Scotland   74
   Anselm of Canterbury   77
   Church and state   80

4 The High Middle Ages (1154–1307) 83

The French connection 83

Thomas Becket 85

The universities and sacramental theology 87

The friars 92

The tithe regime 95

Ecclesiastical courts and canon law 97

The institutional church 102

Clerical taxation 104

Wales and Scotland 106

Post-invasion Ireland 108

The reign of King Edward I 112

5 The crisis of Christendom (1307–84) 115

Crown and mitre 115

The clergy 120

Scholastic theology 123

The Black Death 128

John Wyclif 130

Popular devotion 136

The Celtic fringe 140

6 New wine in old wineskins (1384–1485) 145

Redefining heresy 145

The state of the English church 149

Scotland and Ireland 155

Baptized paganism? 158

Public worship 162

Private piety 169

7 Tudor church reform (1485–1571) 176

The crisis of the monarchy 176

Martin Luther 180

The English church on the brink? 184

The 1529 Parliament 187

England's Lutheran moment? 191

Contents

	Thomas Cranmer's reformation	202
	The revival of Catholicism	208
	The Elizabethan Settlement	215
	Reform in Ireland	224
	Pre-Reformation Scotland	227
	The Scottish Reformation	232
8	**The calm before the storm (1571–1625)**	**243**
	The rise of Puritanism	243
	The Catholic opposition	257
	The Church of England: a fragile consensus (1571–1603)	261
	The Reformation in Wales	267
	Scotland between England and Geneva (1572–1603)	271
	The union of the Crowns – and churches? (1603–25)	277
	Britain on the European stage	283
	Developments in the Church of England	287
	Ireland at the crossroads (1571–1625)	295
9	**Sowing the wind (1625–53)**	**303**
	The world is turned upside down (1625–40)	303
	The Scottish crisis	314
	Onward Christian soldiers (1640–49)	320
	The Westminster Assembly	329
	The sectarian fringe	342
	Faith versus reason?	354
10	**Reaping the whirlwind (1653–1717)**	**360**
	Puritanism triumphant	360
	The Great Schism	369
	Throne and altar	376
	Liturgies of non-comprehension	386
	The light of reason?	389
	The Dissenters	403
	Presbyterian Scotland	408
	The world of the parish	412

Contents

11 An age of faith (1717–1832)   **416**

  A reasonable religion   416
  The religious Establishment   420
  The Evangelical Revival   424
  The sound of music   434
  The Welsh Revival   438
  Daughters of Zion   441
  Transforming the nation   442
  Moderates and Evangelicals in Scotland   448
  The Irish conundrum   453
  The dawn before the darkness?   456

12 Faith in crisis (1832–60)   **462**

  The death of the old order   462
  Scottish exceptionalism   471
  Apocalypticism   474
  The assault on the churches   478
  The Oxford Movement   481
  The revival of the convocations   489
  Tragedy in Ireland   491
  1859   494

13 The Victorian mirage (1860–1914)   **504**

  From faith to morality   504
  Disestablishment?   508
  The Catholic threat   514
  The American Revolution   519
  Politicization   523
  The Social Gospel   529
  The dying of the light   534

14 The decline and fall of 'Christian Britain' (1914–80)   **549**

  The edge of the abyss   549
  Waiting for God   555
  Post-war revival?   566
  The reckoning   574

Contents

15 The rivers of Babylon (since 1980) **588**

 A tale of two cities 588

 Carried into captivity 596

 Singing the Lord's song in a strange land 609

Bibliography 629

Index of names and places 659

Index of subjects 681

Tables

2.1 English dioceses, AD 597–1094   30

3.1 English dioceses, AD 883–1133   61

3.2 The medieval Welsh dioceses   67

3.3 Irish dioceses established between AD 1028 and 1192   72

3.4 The pattern of Scottish dioceses and their foundation
from AD 623 to 1192   76

4.1 Diocesan periods of anglicization from AD 1181 to 1533   109

5.1 Petitioners between 1342 and 1366   118

6.1 Convocations during the reigns of English kings from 1337 to 1461   151

12.1 English and Welsh dioceses in 1835: episcopal stipends   467

12.2 Examples of educated people who forsook their former beliefs,
1840–1860s   499

13.1 New dioceses created from 1836 to 1927   510

14.1 The Anglo-Catholic congresses, 1920–1933   556

15.1 Church membership of UK prime ministers since 1979   593

Preface

Writing a one-volume history of Christianity in the British Isles is a daunting task, but it is also an increasingly necessary one. No factor has been more influential in shaping the destiny of the peoples of Britain and Ireland than the gospel of Jesus Christ, and the history of these islands cannot be understood apart from it. At the same time, this unifying force has revealed itself in great diversity, contributing much to the distinctive identities of the nations that inhabit the North Atlantic archipelago and the divisions within them. The development of British and Irish Christianity contains many different stories that both converge and diverge from one another. Historians have done much to explain the details of how the church has evolved in the separate nations of England, Ireland, Scotland and Wales, but a synthesis of the whole has rarely been attempted. Yet the evolution of one nation cannot be understood properly without involving the others, and some attempt must be made to situate individual narratives in an overarching framework. This is what the present book attempts to do.

The past generation has witnessed an explosion of academic studies on the history of Christianity in the British Isles. Every aspect of it has been studied, often in great detail, and the cumulative results far surpass the capacity of any one writer to master. Most historians are more comfortable in some centuries and geographical areas, and many will feel largely ignorant of the others. A work of this kind must rely heavily on the labours of a wide range of scholars and will inevitably reflect their interests and bias to some extent, although fortunately the volume of research is such that a reasonably objective consensus is often possible. The days when an author's personal convictions determined his or her approach to the subject are now happily over, although it is often still the case that many Catholics gravitate towards medieval subjects and Scotsmen confine themselves to events north of the border. That is only to be expected but, with few exceptions, confessional or nationalistic concerns are far less important now than they were in the past.

The downside of this is that British and Irish society, at least in its academic and intellectual dimension, has secularized to an extent that many who study it have no faith commitment of their own, and may be quite insensitive to the factors that shape the Christian mind and have governed the behaviour of Christian people down through the ages. They may chronicle the theological and ecclesiological debates of the past without really understanding why they occurred, or why those who engaged in them took them seriously. Modern believers may sometimes share their puzzlement, but they are more closely engaged with the subject and more likely to feel the effects of this complex history as a living part of their own heritage. This volume is written from the standpoint of Christian faith, and makes no apology for that. Christians are sinners saved by grace through faith in Jesus Christ. We make no claims to perfection or to omniscience but, at the same time, '[we] know whom [we] have believed, and [are] persuaded that he is able to keep that which [we] have committed unto him against that day' (2 Tim. 1:12, KJV). Christians cannot be indifferent to matters of life, death and eternal salvation, and we believe that the events of the past, present and future will one day be judged by the justice and mercy of the eternal God. To write our history is to confess our sins before him, but it is also to reaffirm that it is through much tribulation that we shall enter the kingdom of God (Acts 14:22). We do not know when the consummation of all things will come, but we believe that it will, and we write with that perspective in view.

That the present time is one of trial for Christians and for Christianity in the British Isles is beyond dispute. The smug complacency of the Victorian era is gone beyond recall, and the immediate future is not encouraging. The UK is in greater danger of falling apart than it has ever been and the secular belief that peace and harmony will flow from shared material prosperity and religious indifference has been shown to be hollow. It is certainly true that at one level the peoples of the British Isles have become virtually one and, apart from local accents and folklore, the inhabitants of Cork, Aberdeen, Swansea and Cheltenham now share a common culture and mental outlook. But this homogenization has also produced a countervailing tendency that emphasizes 'the narcissism of petty differences', which threatens to sow division and bitterness among those who are fundamentally alike. In that climate a reminder that what we have in common is far more important than what separates us is more necessary than ever, and our Christian heritage provides us with a foundation for doing this that nothing else does. If this book can help us understand who we are, where we have been and where we may be going, it will have served its purpose. Of course, our faith is bigger than the British Isles – it embraces the whole of Europe and stretches across the entire world. But within that bigger picture the peoples of Britain and Ireland constitute a definable and distinguished unit. For better or worse, it has bequeathed to us a legacy that is our responsibility to embrace and hand on to generations yet unborn, until that day when our Lord will come again in glory. It is to encourage both an understanding of that inheritance and an acceptance of it that this book has been written.

The pages that follow reflect a wide-ranging involvement with both the history and the historians of British and Irish Christianity, and I am deeply indebted to the dedicated work and precious insights of many who have laboured in the field. My debt to them will be obvious from the ways in which I have made use of their work. More immediately, I am grateful to Alan Mordue, then of SPCK, who took an interest in this project while it was still an idea in the author's mind, and to Philip Duce, Senior Commissioning Editor at Inter-Varsity Press, who agreed to take it on under the wider SPCK umbrella, and to Eldo Barkhuizen, for his meticulous and much appreciated copyediting. It is my hope that their confidence in me will not go unrewarded, and that this volume will provide both enlightenment and inspiration to those who have been called to take up their cross and follow Jesus Christ in our generation. As he said to his disciples, 'Fear not, little flock, for it is your Father's good pleasure to give you the kingdom' (Luke 12:32).

Gerald Bray

Introduction

A few years ago I stepped off a train at Waterside Station in Londonderry. Derry, as the city is more commonly known, is now the last outpost of the UK, sitting at the mouth of the River Foyle only a few kilometres from the Irish border. But small and remote as it may be, Derry encapsulates the history of British Christianity to a degree that few other places do. It was from here that the monk Crimthann, better known to us as Columba, set out to establish a monastery on the island of Iona, from where he and his companions would evangelize the north of Britain. Centuries later the walls of Derry withstood a siege and helped defeat the armies of the Catholic King James II, thereby ensuring that Britain would remain a Protestant country. In our own time it was in Derry that the 'troubles' between Catholics and Protestants broke out in 1968 – a latter-day reminder of the religious fault line that runs across western Europe and has done so much to determine the destiny of both Great Britain and Ireland.[1]

There is another Derry of course, and it too has left its mark on us. It was here that Cecil Alexander, gazing out of the window of the bishop's palace and moved by the lush green hills of Inishowen that form the backdrop to the city, penned her well-known Easter hymn:

> There is a green hill far away
> Without a city wall
> Where the dear Lord was crucified
> Who died to save us all.

Mrs Alexander can be faulted on her geography – the hills outside Jerusalem are not nearly as green as the ones outside Derry are – but her effortless fusion of the local landscape with the atoning work of Christ betrays an intimate connection between her world and God's plan of salvation that has characterized British Christianity from the beginning.

---

[1] To prevent continual repetition, the words 'British' and 'Britain' will often be taken to include 'Irish' and 'Ireland', unless otherwise indicated. This is not altogether satisfactory, but no convenient composite terms exist.

Crossing the River Foyle to enter the city, I could not help but notice a large Union Jack on the far side of the bridge. People in mainland Britain seldom see the flag flying and few stop to think about it when they do, but Northern Ireland is different. Here the flag is a sign of conquest, of commitment and of defiance. Its centrepiece is the red cross of St George, standing for England, the nation that has long been the centre of the UK. Radiating out from it are the saltires of Scotland and Ireland, to remind us that England does not stand alone but is supported by sister nations that circle around it. The red-and-white banner of St Patrick is something of an artificial invention, but Patrick was a real person – an ancient British man who spent his life evangelizing Ireland and is now commemorated as its patron saint. St Andrew, after whom the flag of Scotland is named, was also a real person, known to us as the apostle and brother of St Peter, although he never came anywhere near Britain and might never have heard of it. Yet in being reminded of him we are taken back to the very beginnings of Christianity in the gospel preached by Jesus and his disciples, something that remains fundamental (and irreplaceable) in our own spiritual life.

In stark contrast to Patrick and Andrew, St George, the patron saint of England, is a figure of legend who is supposed to have slain a dragon somewhere in Syria or Armenia, but who probably never existed and certainly had nothing to do with Britain. Missing altogether from the flag is our fourth patron saint, David of Wales, who was not only a real person but the leading evangelist of his native country. His banner is not on the flag because Wales is a principality formally annexed to England, and so has been swallowed up by St George. What a tale this simple piece of bunting tells! In one flag we have a link to the New Testament and the origins of Christianity, a reminder of how it came to the British Isles through the work of intrepid missionaries, and a strange sense that distant myths (St George) can claim precedence over facts (St David) and assert themselves as the dominant thread of what we call history. The flag would not be what it is if it were not for Christianity, whose symbolism gives it meaning and coherence, nor would the country it represents make sense otherwise. Fictitious St George might have been, but the blood-red cross associated with him tells its own story. It is the cross of Christ, the cruel tree on which he shed his blood for the salvation of humankind. Over the centuries it has been appropriated for causes both good and bad, but its basic message transcends them and beats in the heart of all who follow the Saviour:

In the cross of Christ I glory
Towering o'er the wrecks of time

All the light of sacred story
Gathers round its head sublime.

The hymn strikes a chord in the heart of every believer who sings it, but how many know it was written by John Bowring (1792–1872), a Unitarian who once quipped that 'Jesus Christ is free trade and free trade is Jesus Christ'? Bowring was an archetypal Victorian – a liberal reformer at home, where he pushed for greater democracy and for modernization, including the adoption of a decimal currency, but a classic imperialist abroad. He went to China, where he played a key part in establishing that country's finances on a firm footing before becoming the fourth governor of Hong Kong, where he created a botanic garden and where his name is still commemorated in Bowrington Road. The achievements and contradictions of his time can be found in him in equal measure, reminding us that the story of British Christianity is larger and more complex than most people realize.

Its legacy comprehends men and women who were pillars of the church alongside many whom Winston Churchill once described as 'flying buttresses': those who (like himself) do not belong to it but who support it from the outside. It is a tradition that continues to this day. Alongside the saints and heroes of the faith are agnostics and even outright atheists who write church music, support the Salvation Army for purely secular reasons and sometimes pontificate on spiritual matters in ways unknown (and unacceptable) else-where. Comprehensiveness is the boast of the Church of England, celebrated by some and reviled by others, but a reality that no amount of preaching and teaching has ever managed to change.

Christianity is part of the warp and woof of Britain, but it is greater than any one country or nation. There have been people who have tried to maintain that the British are a chosen race, that God is an Englishman, that the peculiarities of the ancient Celtic church or of modern Anglicanism set us apart from others. This is false. The Christian faith was a foreign import, brought to our shores by unknown Roman traders or soldiers. It gradually took root but, as it did so, it reached out in mission to others, in particular to the still unevangelized tribes of Germany and northern Europe. Wynfrith of Crediton, virtually unknown in his homeland, became the great St Boniface, the man who did more to win the Germans for Christ than any other individual. Centuries later the teachings of the English John Wyclif were eagerly absorbed in Bohemia, where they helped to provoke a national uprising against an oppressive church and state.

Later on the flow went the other way. The British churches as we know them today were shaped by the theology of Wittenberg, Zurich and Geneva. In the seventeenth century, Dutch influence was so strong that Britain and the Netherlands were almost one country, as they briefly became in the time of King William III (1689–1702). Georg Friedrich Händel came to England from his native Germany and, although he never fully mastered English, he left us some of the greatest and most beloved oratorios in our language. More recently, British Christians have fanned out again, to North America, South Africa and Australasia as settlers, and to much of the rest of the world as missionaries. They have taken the Christianity of their homeland and planted it on almost every imaginable foreign soil. To some this smacks of colonialism, and in our post-imperial age there are constant appeals for 'indigenization', a process meant to strip this Christianity of its British roots and transform it into something more in keeping with the local culture. But this pressure is frequently resisted, not by latter-day metropolitan colonialists but by those who have received their faith in this form. Many Africans and Asians are unbothered by this supposed foreignness and are happy to take it on board, often with the English language too, and who are we to say them nay? After all, British Christians worshipped in Latin for nearly a thousand years before switching to their mother tongue, so inculturation is hardly the most salient characteristic of our faith.

Today, thanks to a combination of empire and technology, British Christianity is more influential on the world scene than it has ever been. A time may come when it loses its original identity and is regarded as no more British than Roman Catholicism is Italian. That day is not yet. Britain remains the centre of a cultural sphere that is still growing and spreading into places where it has never gone before. The hands that bring this culture may be American, as they often are, but the voice is mostly still British, whether it comes across as Anglican, Baptist, Methodist or Presbyterian. The great hymns, the theological confessions and the traditions of church government all betray the same unmistakable origin, and anyone who wants to understand world Christianity today has to come to terms with that.

Within the British Isles a certain pride of place has to be given to England. This is not only because England is the largest country of the archipelago, although it is that – more than 80% of the population lives there, a higher proportion than it has ever been. The English have given their language, their laws and their literature to the other nations, and have done so for centuries. We are not so naive as to think that England and the UK are synonymous, in the way that many foreigners do, but England's influence on the surrounding Celtic countries cannot be denied. Wales, Scotland and Ireland have become what they are because of their interaction with England, not with one another, and their identities can be understood only in that context.

For similar reasons a prominent place must be given to the Church of England and its Anglican cousins in Wales and Ireland, as well as to the established presbyterian Church of Scotland. Anglicanism is a peculiarly British phenomenon, as is the denominational diversity that has grown out of reactions to it. The Methodists, Baptists, Presbyterians and even the Catholics all have their own stories to tell, but they are what they are because they have separated from (or refused to become) Anglicans. We may wish that things could have been otherwise, but they have not been, and any history of Christianity in the British Isles must respect that reality.

For British people the variegation and worldwide spread of British Christianity may be a source of pride, but we must be modest about this. The purposes of God in human history are beyond our understanding and we must not presume that there is any virtue in us that has earned us the place we now occupy on the world stage. Rudyard Kipling (1865–1936), often hailed (or reviled) as the great poet of empire and a man whose relationship to Christianity was ambiguous, understood the need for humility very well. Asked to compose a poem for the Diamond Jubilee of Queen Victoria in 1897, he stuck his neck out and resisted the spirit of the age. In the words of his famous 'Recessional':

The tumult and the shouting dies
The captains and the kings depart
Still stands thine ancient sacrifice
An humble and a contrite heart
Lord God of Hosts be with us yet
Lest we forget, lest we forget!

The Union Jack still flies on the walls of Derry, but there the tumult and the shouting have never quite died. Questions of faith and identity still haunt the far corners of the land, even as the chattering classes of the big cities wish they would go away and leave us in what they call a post-Christian era, something that to them is a mark of progress and enlightenment. Church leaders often seem helpless before what appears to be a rising tide of unbelief, and the future looks bleak and uncertain. But the ancient sacrifice is still there, the humble and contrite heart that regards its own righteousness as filthy rags and turns to the cross of Christ as its only hope of salvation. The fire of faith may seem to be smouldering in embers but at any moment it may burst forth in glorious flame and sweep all before it. The scoffers of this age have their day but they will fade away like the morning dew when the sun shines on it. Believers know it is through much tribulation that we shall enter the kingdom of God. We do not surrender to the siren call of so-called modernity but listen instead to the still small voice that speaks to us from beyond the boundaries of time and space. We go on our pilgrim way, as John Bunyan so famously challenged us:

He who would valiant be
Gainst all disaster
Let him in constancy
Follow the Master.
There's no discouragement
Will make him once relent
His first avowed intent
To be a pilgrim.

British and Irish Christians are pilgrims on a journey that has not yet come to an end. It is the aim of this book to plot that journey so far, holding before our eyes the cross of him who died for us and trusting in his mercy that in his good time we shall arrive safely at our destination.

1
In the beginning (to AD 597)

The shadow of Rome

In the Roman year 802, better known to us as AD 49, the emperor Claudius issued a decree banning Jews from the capital city. They had been rioting over an obscure figure called Chrestus, who was almost certainly Jesus. The incident is known from the Roman historian Suetonius, and is obliquely mentioned in the New Testament, which tells us that two of the expelled Jews turned up in Corinth, where they hosted the apostle Paul on one of his missionary journeys.[1] Six years earlier, the same Claudius had authorized the invasion of Britain, an island first visited by Julius Caesar a hundred years before. Caesar had managed to impose a tribute on the tribes living along the southern coast, but had not attempted a permanent invasion. That was left to Claudius, who was able to parade in triumph at this latest acquisition to the still growing empire. As the Romans expanded their holdings in the decades that followed, so the Jewish followers of 'Chrestus' implanted themselves more firmly across the imperial provinces, eventually reaching as far as the remote island Rome had half conquered.

Nobody knows when the first Christians reached Britain's shores. There is a legend that says Joseph of Arimathea, a wealthy Jew who allowed Jesus to be buried in his tomb in Jerusalem, made his way there and settled in the south-west, where he supposedly founded the monastery of Glastonbury.[2] Given that the legend first appeared more than 1,200 years after the events it narrates, we may assume that it is a fable, but does it contain a tiny grain of truth? It is quite possible that the first Christians in Britain were traders not unlike Joseph, and

---

[1] Acts 18:2.

[2] See Matt. 27:57–60. This legend, and others of a similar nature, was published from original sources by D. Wilkins, *Concilia Magnae Britanniae et Hiberniae*, 4 vols. (London: Various presses, 1737), 4:685–707. Modern historians regard almost all as later inventions. The evidence for this period was collected and published by A. W. Haddan and W. Stubbs, *Councils and Ecclesiastical Documents Relating to Great Britain and Ireland*, 3 vols. (Oxford: Clarendon Press, 1869–78). The first volume covers the ancient British church (200–681), the church of Wales (681–1295) and the church of Cornwall (681–1072). The second volume covers Ireland and Scotland (350–1188) and the third deals with the English church. It was meant to cover the period from 595 to 1066 but never got beyond 871. On the arrival of Christianity in Britain, see 1:22–26.

it may even be that they went to the south-west, where the tin mines of Cornwall had long attracted people like them. Whether they reached such a remote province within the lifetime of the apostles is certainly doubtful. Paul wrote to the Romans about AD 57, telling them he intended to travel westward to Spain, where (we assume) there was still no Christian presence at that time, and Britain was a good deal further than that.[3]

It is more likely that the first Christians to reach Britain arrived sometime in the second century, although that can only be a guess. Christian traders might well have established themselves in Londinium (London) and worshipped relatively inconspicuously in that tiny metropolis. The church of St Peter, Cornhill, claims to have been founded in AD 179, which may seem improbable but is not necessarily fanciful. By that time there could well have been a Christian community in Britain, doing its best to proclaim the gospel in difficult circumstances. The first mention of Christians in Britain comes from Tertullian of Carthage (around AD 200), who claimed that the name of Christ had already conquered 'parts of the Britons unreached by the Romans', although given that this reference appears in a catalogue of distant regions where he claimed that the gospel had been preached, it is hard to know what to make of it.[4] Rhetorical flourish or historical fact? We cannot say. Similar statements can be found in Origen, writing in the early third century, although he was more cautious about the success of the mission, if indeed there had been one.[5]

If Christianity was not brought to Britain by traders, it might have arrived with soldiers in the Roman legions. Britain was a highly militarized province, and some of the soldiers posted there might have been Christians, but it is unlikely that they would have been able to set up a church. As soldiers they would have sworn an oath of allegiance to the emperor as the son of a god, which went against Christian principles. There is also the fact that before Christianity was legalized in AD 313, the church took a dim view of military service and discouraged its members from joining the army.[6] But there is a story that tells of how a Roman soldier met a Christian presbyter and was so impressed by him that he became a Christian himself. When the presbyter was

---

[3] See Rom. 15:24.

[4] Tertullian of Carthage, *Adversus Iudaeos* 7. The Latin phrase is *Britannorum inaccessa Romanis loca, Christo vero subdita*.

[5] Origen, *Homilia IV in Ezekiel, Homilia VI in Lucam* 1:24. Both echo Tertullian, but *Homilia XXVIII in Matthaeum* 24 says that the British, along with the Germans and other remote peoples, had not yet been reached for Christ.

[6] See J.-M. Hornus, *It Is Not Lawful for Me to Fight: Early Christian Attitudes Toward War, Violence and the State* (Scottdale, Pa.: Herald Press, 1980).

arrested and sentenced to death, the soldier took his place, thus becoming the first martyr for the new faith to die on British soil.[7]

The truth behind this account is hotly disputed, but it has a better claim to historicity than either the Joseph or Cornhill legends do. The tale was certainly embellished over time, but the earliest mention of it occurs only a century or two after the events it describes, by which date a cult of the martyr was in existence. We know him as Alban, or Albanus, and the site of his death is supposed to have been a hilltop just outside the Roman city of Verulamium, a day's march north-west of Londinium. A shrine to his memory was erected there that became the nucleus of the modern city of St Albans, which preserves his name to the present day. What we do not know is when Albanus might have been put to death. There were periodic persecutions of Christians in the third and early fourth centuries, and his martyrdom could have occurred at any time before AD 313. A date between 251, when Christians suffered under the emperor Decius, and 305, when the great persecution under Diocletian came to an end, would seem most likely, but from this distance in time it is impossible to say for certain. From our perspective it scarcely matters. What counts is that a Roman soldier was put to death for professing the Christian faith, and that he was later venerated – a plausible, if unprovable, historical foundation for the pious legends elaborated later on.

What is certain is that by 313 there were already several churches in Britain organized along lines common elsewhere in the Roman Empire. They could hardly have appeared overnight and might well have been in existence for a generation or two already. What we know is that three British bishops, Restitutus of Londinium (London), Adelfius of Lindum Colonia (Lincoln) and Eborius of Eboracum (York), together with Arminius, described as a deacon from Lincoln, attended a synod held at Arles in 314, where they participated in the condemnation of the Donatists. If we except Albanus, they are the first identifiable British Christians known to us. The Donatists were a new and rigorous North African sect that rejected any compromise with the godless Roman state and insisted that any bishops who had handed over Christian books to the persecuting authorities a decade earlier should be deposed. This was felt to be too extreme, and Donatism was rejected by the wider church. The Synod of Arles also recommended that Easter should be celebrated on the same day throughout the world, an important point that would later become

---

[7] Wilkins, *Concilia*, 4:707.

a matter of dispute in Britain, and that every bishop should be consecrated by at least three of his fellows.[8]

How much of what happened at Arles resonated with the British delegation is hard to say. There were certainly no Donatists in Britain, nor do we hear of anyone there who had handed over sacred texts to the imperial authorities. Perhaps the rule (or canon) that meant the most to them was the one that demanded the presence of three bishops every time a new one was consecrated. Acceptance of this suggests that there must have been more British bishops at that time than the three who went to Arles. If there had not been, the canon would have been inapplicable in Britain and its envoys might have opposed it for that reason. But they did not, and so we must conclude that the British churches were in step with their counterparts elsewhere, although they did not suffer from the internal divisions common among Christians in other parts of the Roman world.

The fourth and fifth centuries were a golden age for Christian theology, as the worldwide church debated the great questions surrounding the being of God as three Persons in one Substance and the Person of Jesus Christ, who was fully God and fully man. The Roman Empire was rocked by controversies over these and other matters, and its unity was more than once stretched to breaking point. But, as far as we can tell, Britain stood on the sidelines and merely acquiesced in the great theological decisions taken elsewhere.[9] This is hardly surprising. The province was remote from the scene of action, which mostly took place in the Greek-speaking eastern Mediterranean, and wandering theological disputants were unlikely to turn up in such a backwater. If any did, they have gone unrecorded and we can safely assume that the British church never experienced the divisions caused by the great Christological debates of the late Roman period.

Pelagius

There is however at least one, somewhat curious, indication that British Christianity might not have been in step with mainstream opinion elsewhere. A well-educated British monk called Pelagius made his way to Rome sometime

---

[8] Ibid. 708–710 contains the acts of the synod and the names of the bishops who attended it. 'Eborius' of Eboracum sounds a bit suspicious; it may not have been his real name, but one that was supplied from the name of the city he represented.

[9] Apparently there were British bishops who hesitated to affirm that Christ was 'consubstantial' (*homoousios*) with God the Father, but if so, their reluctance had no long-term consequences for the British church. See Haddan and Stubbs, *Councils*, 1:9–10, for the evidence.

around AD 400, where he became a popular preacher and teacher.[10] He wrote commentaries on the New Testament that were so good they were preserved after his fall from grace and recycled as the work of Jerome or of Cassiodorus. Only in the nineteenth century was their true author revealed, allowing scholars to arrive at a more favourable view of Pelagius than had been possible before that time. Where Pelagius got his learning from is unknown, but if it was somewhere in Britain it shows that the level of theological education available there in the late fourth century was comparable to anything that could be found in the Latin-speaking West.

When Alaric the Goth captured Rome in 410 and sacked the city, a stream of refugees fled to North Africa, among them Pelagius himself and many of his followers. There they encountered the formidable Augustine, Bishop of Hippo, who was already well known as a scourge of the Donatists. When Augustine heard what the Pelagians were teaching, he turned his ire on them, and it is largely thanks to his unremitting opposition that we know so much about them today. It seems that Pelagius was saying that fallen human beings were not entirely sinful. Somewhere in the human mind and will there remained an ability to turn to God and to cooperate with him in the process of salvation. Pelagius did not believe that people could save themselves entirely by their own efforts, but he thought they had a free will that could respond to the calling of God and work alongside him to get rid of their sinfulness. Augustine countered this idea by saying that humankind's fall into sin was total and irreversible. No human being, however good or moral, can voluntarily respond to God or cooperate with him in that person's salvation. That is possible only by the free gift of God in Christ, which is given to those who have been chosen to receive it. Human beings can do no more than confess their sins, hoping that God will hear their cries and be merciful to them, but even that is possible only if God gives sinners the grace to repent of their wrongdoing.

It was not long before Pelagius was condemned for heresy and had to flee North Africa. He went to Palestine and then to Constantinople, where the controversy he had stirred up was unknown and he could live in relative peace. Perhaps he had no idea why his teaching was wrong, and people in the East appear not to have reacted to it in the way Augustine did. We hear no more of Pelagius after this, but traces of Pelagianism survived in western Europe and they had to be stamped out. Germanus, a fifth-century Bishop of Auxerre, was particularly active in this enterprise, and in 429 he visited Britain in order to eradicate whatever Pelagianism might be lurking there. His mission was

---

10 The name Pelagius may be a Graeco-Roman translation of the native British 'Morgan'.

successful, but was there much Pelagianism for him to find? That we cannot tell. It is possible that Pelagius was supported by kinsmen and old friends from his youth in Britain, who were loyal to him personally without being consciously committed to his doctrine, which they might not have fully understood. Certainly Germanus did not have to spend long in Britain, so the roots of the heresy could not have been very deep.[11]

Ireland

Germanus was thorough, and he left nothing to chance. He had heard that there were British Christians in Ireland, where they were surviving like sheep without a shepherd. To remedy that situation, he sent them Palladius, a missionary bishop whose task was to organize the first Christian churches in the emerald isle.[12] Who these Christians were, how they had got to Ireland and whether they had been influenced by Pelagianism is unknown. They might have been merchants who had gone there and stayed, or refugees from the Saxon invaders who were raiding the eastern shores of Britain and beginning to settle permanently on the island. Perhaps they were slaves who had been captured by Irish raiders. They might have been a mixed multitude of different origins and even included a few native Irish converts – we do not know. Archaeological evidence and a few place names suggest that whoever they were, they were concentrated in the east and south-east of the country, but even that cannot be proved. All we can say for sure is that Palladius reached Ireland in 431 – the date that marks the beginning of recorded history there. How long he stayed and how successful his mission was is unknown, but for reasons that will become apparent, he was probably not there very long and his efforts were soon largely forgotten.

It was in the twilight years of Roman Britain that Irish raiders stepped up their activities and transported many Britons to Ireland as slaves. One of them was a 16-year-old boy called Patricius (Patrick), who stayed in captivity long enough to learn the language of the country and to develop a passion for evangelizing his captors. After seven years Patricius managed to escape and return home, where he was ordained into the Christian ministry. What sort of training or education he had is unclear, although we know from his surviving writings that his Latin was not particularly good. After his ordination, Patricius returned to Ireland, where he spent the rest of his life preaching the gospel far and wide, although probably not as extensively as later legend would claim.

---

[11] Haddan and Stubbs, *Councils*, 1:16–17.

[12] The most detailed study of the introduction of Christianity into Ireland is T. Charles-Edwards, *Early Christian Ireland* (Cambridge: Cambridge University Press, 2000).

Most of his activity seems to have been in the north and west of the island, although it is impossible to pinpoint his activities with any degree of precision. What we do know is that Patricius was not supported by his British countrymen as much as he might have hoped, and that he had to counter their opposition by explaining his motives to them. Ironically, it is thanks to that unhappy circumstance that we have the first written testimony to the spread of the gospel across the British Isles and we can glimpse the kind of world in which that evangelization took place.[13]

Who opposed Patricius and why? He himself tells us that when he was 15 he committed a 'grave sin', and evidently some thought it serious enough to bar him from ministry in adult life. There were others who apparently believed that he went to Ireland in order to enrich himself, although it is hard to see what basis they had for making that accusation. We know only one side of the story, and at this distance in time it is impossible to arrive at a balanced conclusion, but experience of similar situations elsewhere suggests that what might have happened is depressingly familiar. Patricius might well have been impatient in his zeal for evangelism, and this might have struck his superiors as unjustified arrogance. At the same time it is not hard to detect a spirit of jealousy in his accusers – the reaction of lesser men when confronted with someone whose passion (and success) was considerably greater than theirs.

Patricius died in Ireland and was probably buried at Downpatrick, a place that preserves his name. It is quite likely that he passed away on 17 March, which is still celebrated as his feast day, but in what year? We cannot say. What is certain is that his reputation as a missionary rapidly eclipsed that of Palladius, so much so that the work of the latter was absorbed into the legend of the former. Later generations claimed that Patricius went to Ireland in 432, only a year after Palladius, although there is no evidence for that. Some have even said that Palladius was also called Patricius, thereby creating a 'second Patrick' and making it easier to confuse the two men. Modern scholars generally agree that Palladius was the first Christian bishop in Ireland, sent there with the authority of the Roman church behind him, and that Patricius followed later, although how much later is uncertain. Richard Hanson believed that he was born about 390 and died about 460, which would make his mission almost contemporary with that of Palladius, but most others have preferred a

---

[13] For a translation of Patrick's works, see T. O'Loughlin, *St Patrick: The Man and His Works* (London: SPCK, 1999). For a comprehensive list of the sources for church history in medieval Ireland, see J. F. Kenney, *The Sources for the Early History of Ireland: Ecclesiastical*, 2nd edn (New York, N.Y.: Columbia University Press, 1968; repr. Dublin: Four Courts Press, 1997).

later date.[14] The Irish annals are of little help, since they give dates for Patricius's death that range from 457 to 493, all of which seem to be guesswork on the annalists' part. What is agreed is that Patricius lived and worked in the fifth century and he did not evangelize Ireland on his own. How is it then that he has been given the credit for the conversion of the Irish people?

Perhaps the main reason for this is that Patricius was an innovator in the field of mission, who succeeded in creating a permanent Christian presence in Ireland in a way Palladius had not. Ireland lacked cities, which in the Roman world had been the centres of the church. To make up for this, Patrick established monastic communities, which became the bases for evangelizing the many tribes that lived in the country. Each tribe, or clan, had to have its own church and bishop, who was almost always a monk and often the abbot of the local monastery. As far as possible, these monasteries reflected their local communities and control of them often passed from father to son. Odd though it seems to us, Irish abbots were allowed to marry and bequeath their monasteries to their descendants, a pattern that in some cases would survive until the sixteenth-century Reformation.[15] It was a situation unique in the Christian world and an anomaly as far as monasticism was concerned, but it worked. It appears that individual monks established their cells in strategic locations across the island, and these cells developed into churches. That must have happened early on, before the initial 'c' of the Latin word *cella* softened to a 'ch' sound, since it is recorded in Irish place names as Kil-. Their frequency (Kildare, Kilkenny, etc.) bears witness to the widespread influence this evangelistic method had. Within a hundred years Ireland had been Christianized, and the Irish were set to embark on missions of their own – not least to those parts of Britain where the gospel was unknown or where the church had been wiped out by barbarian invasions from the east.

The heroic age of Irish missionary activity came later, but the names of the so-called 'twelve apostles' of Ireland have been preserved for us and they

---

[14] R. C. Hanson, *Saint Patrick: His Origins and Career* (Oxford: Clarendon Press, 1968). The Irish annals record the death of Maucteus (Mochta) in 535 (or 537), who claimed to have been one of Patrick's disciples. If that was the case, the date of 493 for his death is more likely. See D. Ó Cróinín, *Early Modern Ireland 400–1200* (Harlow: Longman, 1995), 27. James Carney went so far as to date Patrick's mission from 5 April 456 to his death on 17 March 493, but such precision has been eschewed by more recent commentators. See J. Carney, *The Problem of St Patrick* (Dublin: Dublin Institute for Advanced Studies, 1973). On the other hand R. Flechner, *St Patrick Retold: The Legend and History of Ireland's Patron Saint* (Princeton, N.J.: Princeton University Press, 2019), argues that Patrick might have gone to Ireland (as a merchant) before the collapse of Roman rule in Britain, at least partly in order to escape the burden of taxation, and that 'spreading the gospel' was a respectable excuse for more worldly motives. It is a bold, revisionist thesis, but one that is unlikely to command much support.

[15] See A. Gwynn and R. N. Hadcock, *Medieval Religious Houses: Ireland* (London: Longman, 1970), for a complete inventory of Irish monasteries.

played an important part in the conversion of the island, especially in the south-west, where it seems that neither Palladius nor Patrick ministered. Some of the earlier ones might have been trained by Patrick himself, but even if they were not they carried on his methods and guaranteed that their own successors would be well equipped for wider service elsewhere. Taken in order of their presumed deaths (since we do not know when most of them were born), they were Ciarán of Saighir (d. *c.*530), Ninnidh of Lough Erne (d. *c.*530), Senán of Inis Cathaigh (d. 544), Mobhí of Glasnevin (d. 545), Columba of Terryglas (d. 552), Laisrén of Munster (d. 564), Brendan of Birr (d. 573), Brendan of Clonfert (d. 577), Ruadháin of Lorrha (d. 584), Columba of Iona (d. 597) and Canice of Aghaboe (d. 600). Brendan of Clonfert was a legendary navigator who was said to have sailed the Atlantic in his coracle and was thought to have discovered the Islands of the Blessed to the west, although whether these were the Faroe Islands, Iceland, Greenland or North America is unknown. Brendan's account is primarily an allegory of the Christian life, although apparently Christopher Columbus used it as a guide to the prevailing winds and currents of the ocean he later crossed. Of Columba of Iona, the only one of the twelve to evangelize beyond Ireland, we shall hear much more. The others remain obscure and wrapped in legend, but they serve as reminders to us that the conversion of an entire country is seldom if ever the work of a single individual. Patrick may get the credit for it nowadays, but the devoted labours of his host of disciples and successors confirmed his work and their contribution must not be forgotten.

The Anglo-Saxons

By the end of the fifth century the survival of once-Roman Britain was becoming increasingly precarious. The Roman legions left in 410, leaving the island's defence to the locals. For a while they were remarkably successful at this, but gradually the remains of the Roman province were worn down and fell into the hands of rival warlords, who weakened it still further by their internecine squabbling. It seems that one of them, a man called Vortigern, appealed to some Germanic raiders for support against his British enemies, and that they took advantage of this by establishing a permanent settlement along the eastern seaboard. That is supposed to have happened around AD 449, after which the post-Roman province rapidly descended into anarchy.

The Romano-British people were largely Christianized by this time, but the Germanic invaders who were settling in the east of the island were pagans. Most of the British regarded them as illegal immigrants and wanted them to go home, but they kept on coming – the Angles from a region of southern Denmark that was shaped like an angle, the Saxons from what is now north-western Germany and the Jutes, probably from mainland Denmark, which is known as Jutland to this day. They spoke a series of closely related dialects that strongly resemble Frisian, a minority tongue still used in parts of the Netherlands and Germany. When they got to Britain, they fused naturally into a single ethnic group, as they maintained a sense of their original tribal identities. We call them the Anglo-Saxons (the Jutes having been absorbed by the Saxons), and claim them as the immediate ancestors of the English people of today.

Our only written source for this invasion is a tirade against the shortcomings of the Britons and their treacherous rulers, written by a British monk called Gildas. The title of his book, *The Ruin of Britain* (*De Excidio Britanniae*), tells us all we need to know about his approach to the subject.[16] We are not sure when or where Gildas lived, but it was probably in what is now south-west England, sometime in the first half of the sixth century. Gildas was not primarily interested in writing a chronological history of his times, with the result that, although he mentions many different events, we cannot be sure when they took place. Nor, given his purpose, is it easy to separate fact from polemic. What we can say is that a century after the Roman legions had left Britain it was still possible to get a good classical education in some parts of the country, since Gildas had obviously had one. It is also clear that by his time the upper classes identified themselves as Christians and were familiar with the Bible, because Gildas peppered his account with biblical references his hearers would have been expected to recognize. Most intriguingly, from our point of view, Gildas (and presumably his readers) saw themselves as God's chosen people, the new Israel suffering for its sins in just the same way as the old Israel had done. It is a theme that would recur in later centuries and that has still not entirely disappeared, although in more recent times it has generally been pressed into service in support of Britain's supposed greatness, and not as an explanation for its failures, as it was with Gildas.

It used to be thought that the Anglo-Saxons drove the Britons out and pushed them into the hills of the west and north, where they survived in what became Wales, Cumbria and Cornwall. But while there may be some truth in that, we now know that the process was more complicated than historians once made it appear. DNA testing has revealed that a large number of Britons

---

[16] For the text, see Haddan and Stubbs, *Councils*, 1:44–107. An English translation is available in M. Winterbottom, *Gildas: The Ruin of Britain and Other Works* (London: Phillimore, 1978).

remained in Anglo-Saxon-held territory, where they were eventually absorbed by the newcomers. British place names survive all over England, although the English language was not much influenced by British. It is possible that the progressive tenses of English (e.g. 'I am coming', etc.), which do not exist in the other Germanic languages, are the result of British influence, as is the word 'dad' for 'father', but beyond that there is not much to report. The Britons' name for themselves (Cymry) survives in Cumbria, but we now call them Welsh – a Germanic word for Romanized indigenous people that pops up across Europe as Wallonia in Belgium, die Welschschweiz in Switzerland (la Suisse Romande in French) and even as Walachia in Romania. Roman Cornubia likewise became Cornwall in English – the Cornish Wales! Nothing speaks more clearly than this of the extent of Germanic dominance, since the natives were no longer known by their own names but by ones their conquerors chose to give them, and those who survived in occupied territory were almost completely assimilated by the invaders.

Wales

But what of British Christianity? Did it survive the invasions in some form or was it completely rooted out? This is impossible to say for sure. It is conceivable that it went underground, being preserved in folk rituals passed on from British mothers to mixed-race children, and the memory of former churches was preserved here and there. But as long as the Anglo-Saxons remained officially pagan, there was no organized Christian religious activity and certainly no form of education that might have preserved it. The British churches seem to have been deficient in this respect – for the acquisition of classical learning one had to go to Ireland, where such learning was not only maintained but propagated to a degree that equalled the best in western Europe at that time. Admittedly, the bar was low, but the Irish achievement should not be under-estimated, and it would be from there, as much as from anywhere else, that the culture of the Latin world would re-enter Anglo-Saxon England.

Meanwhile many of the inhabitants of post-Roman Britain emigrated to the European continent, where they founded Little Britain, or Brittany as we now call it. They took their British church with them, where it maintained a distinct existence at least until 818, when at the Council of Vannes the Breton church submitted to the Archbishop of Tours and its imported British customs were gradually forgotten or replaced with Gallic ones.[17]

---

[17] For the evidence, see Haddan and Stubbs, *Councils*, 2:69–101.

Back at home, the later sixth century was a difficult time for the Britons, who lost control of much of what is now England. They remained dominant in the remoter parts of western Britain, and the contours of what we now call Wales and Cornwall began to take shape.[18] They lacked political unity and their lands were subdivided into a number of petty kingdoms, most of which are little known and proved to be ephemeral. However, it does seem that every king had his own bishop and that the church was organized accordingly.[19] This was the world in which a young man called Dewi (David) gradually rose to prominence. Dewi was probably born in what is now Pembrokeshire, sometime early in the sixth century, and apparently died on 1 March (now his feast day), which is supposed to have been a Tuesday. That limits the options as far as the year of his death is concerned, and 589 is a popular guess, but we have no way of knowing for sure. In any case he was active in the 560s, when he spoke at a synod held at Brefi (now Llanddewi Brefi) and at another one that met at Caerleon some years later. On both occasions he is said to have spoken out forcefully against Pelagianism, the condemnation of which was why the synods were summoned in the first place, but the details are obscure. What 'Pelagianism' would have meant to Dewi is impossible to say and it might have been no more than a general term applied somewhat indiscriminately to anyone who seemed suspect for whatever reason.

What we do know is that the British church was still appointing bishops in the areas under its control and that, thanks to his performances in the synods, Dewi was recognized as the most outstanding of them. After his death he became the patron saint of Wales and his supposed career was regularly cited by much later churchmen as evidence that the Welsh church had once been (and therefore ought again to be) independent of the Church of England, with its own archbishop and provincial synod. It was a cause that would be frustrated for centuries and only became real in 1920 – in circumstances very different from anything Dewi could have imagined. His bones were laid to rest at the site where a cathedral was later erected and named after him, and the settlement thus established is called St David's to this day. With under 2,000 inhabitants, it is the smallest city in the British Isles.

What happened in Cornwall is much less clear. A British church survived there as long as the Cornish remained independent of the English, but how it was governed is unknown. A man called Kenstec appears as its bishop, but not

---

[18] See S. Victory, *The Celtic Church in Wales* (London: SPCK, 1977).

[19] B. Yorke, *The Conversion of Britain 600–800* (Harlow: Pearson, 2006), 149–151. It seems that the four bishoprics which survived the Norman Conquest were those of the four Welsh kingdoms still in existence at that date.

until the mid-ninth century, after which there was a succession of Celtic bishops for a century or so. However, after 959 they were all Anglo-Saxons. The see of Cornwall maintained a shadowy existence for another hundred years, until it was finally merged with Exeter in 1050. It remained there until 1877, when the modern bishopric of Truro was created, but by then all trace of ancient Cornwall and its language had disappeared.[20]

A Celtic church?

When Germanus of Auxerre visited Britain in 429, the island was still in regular contact with the European continent and keeping in step with developments in the wider world. But a generation later, barbarian invasions and the upheavals associated with them had made contact more difficult and the British church, now with an Irish offshoot, gradually drifted out of the Continental orbit. This had particular consequences for fixing the date of Easter. The Synod of Arles in 314 had already proposed a common date for the celebration, and the first Council of Nicaea in 325 had enacted canons that were intended to give effect to that proposal, but it took time for the new calculation to be adopted. Local churches often continued to use the systems they had grown accustomed to, or even devised new ones that did not take the Nicene canons into account. Rome did this about 410, and again in 457. The British church accepted the 410 decision but not the later one, of which it seems to have remained ignorant for quite some time.

The discrepancies were not great, but they occasionally led to different results and the churches found themselves celebrating Easter on different days. Rome gradually conformed to the Nicene pattern, but the Celtic churches of Britain and Ireland did not. There were occasional discussions about this, but the Celts felt the Roman methods were less scientific than theirs and resisted pressure to conform to what they saw as an inferior system. As long as the two churches had little contact with each other this made no difference and the question lay dormant, although with the passage of time both traditions acquired an air of authority in their respective spheres, running the risk of making any future adjustment look like a surrender of one side to the other.

Along with the Easter question a number of minor liturgical and practical differences set the Celts apart from the Romans. For example, Roman monks tonsured their hair by shaving the middle of the scalp, whereas the Celts

---

[20] See Haddan and Stubbs, *Councils*, 1:671–704. The last known Cornish speaker, Dolly Pentreath, died in 1777. There have been attempts in recent years to revive the language, and a Bible has been published in it, but this is the work of enthusiasts and is not a widespread popular movement.

shaved the edges instead. To illiterate people, variations of that kind were easily assumed to reflect differences of belief, which they did not. In other ways however, the Celtic churches maintained Roman traditions and ways long after the empire had disappeared. In particular they continued to use Latin for worship and for most other purposes too. Latin had been a spoken language in Roman Britain, but it seems to have been confined to a minority and did not long survive the departure of the legions. Unlike Gaul, Iberia or Italy, Britain never developed a Romance vernacular language but preferred the Celtic dialects that had once existed in those other countries but had died out by the end of the imperial period. As a result, the Celts worshipped in a recognizably foreign language, which helps to explain why they were such good scholars – they had to pay careful attention to every word of the Bible and the liturgy.

The many quirks that resulted from this situation led some nineteenth-century romantics to suggest that there had once been an independent Celtic church more spiritually minded than its Roman counterpart and more 'primitive', both in relation to the New Testament and in the context of early medieval culture. Reconnecting with one's Celtic roots was interpreted as returning to the early days of Christianity, and affirming a British (or Irish) version of the faith that was more authentic than its chief rivals. Pseudo-Celtic festivals were invented by romantic nationalists and the ancient druids were recycled as poets who could be (and often have been) Christian in every respect that matters, although of course they could claim to be neo-pagans as well. Celtic script and the Celtic cross became easily recognizable symbols of this 'revival' and many such symbols are still familiar, having been taken up by various strands of the 'New Age' movement in recent years. Celticism is now often promoted as being more mystical and spiritual than its English or Anglo-Saxon equivalent and therefore, in the eyes of its devotees, superior to it in every way. Its Christian form is decidedly non-dogmatic and anti-Augustinian, celebrating barbarian innocence and deprecating such uncongenial ideas as sin and human depravity.

The truth (alas!) is more prosaic. There never was a Celtic church in any real sense of the word, and the notion that there was a distinctive Celtic spirituality is largely a modern invention. Clare Downham's assessment is fair:

Perceptions of early Irish churches have been greatly influenced by romantic notions of 'otherness'. Ireland's place on the margins of Europe has led its early Church to be regarded as separate from the mainstream, with greater continuity of pagan traditions and possessing a less worldly outlook than the Church in other lands. Such stereotypes can only be maintained through a very selective and partial reading of the primary sources.[21]

There were certainly monks and hermits scattered across the Celtic world who lived in close communion with nature, but this was true of Christianity everywhere. Their mythical exploits are paralleled by similar tales from the eastern Mediterranean and elsewhere and belong to a recognizable genre of hagiography. The mixture of pre-Christian customs and Christian themes – 'baptized paganism' – detectable in the Arthurian legends can also be found in *Beowulf*, the Icelandic sagas and so on. There is nothing particularly Celtic about any of this, and the notion that there was once a self-consciously Celtic church that was closer to true Christianity than its Roman counterpart must be discarded. Romantics may be disappointed, but sober historians cannot be held captive by myth makers, however attractive some of their imaginative creations may be.[22]

King Arthur and the end of Roman Britain

The intersection of history and myth is at its most powerful in the legends associated with King Arthur. Who was he? If such a figure ever existed, he must have been the leader of the British forces that apparently halted the Anglo-Saxon advance across southern Britain sometime around the year 500. There was apparently a great battle at a place called Mount Badon, which may be Badbury (Wiltshire), where the Britons inflicted such a defeat on their enemies that they were left in peace for a generation. The core of this story need not be doubted. There probably was such a reverse in the Anglo-Saxon conquest, which represented a victory for Christians against their pagan foes. This spiritual aspect of the battle would have appealed to the Britons at the time and it was to have a long history ahead of it. Fighting for the sake of Christ became an integral part of medieval Christianity, in particular its British variant, and has remained so into modern times. Arthur and his knights of the round table were celebrated as archetypes of Christian manhood, whose testosterone-fuelled aggressiveness was a divine gift to be used in the service of the gospel. They were warriors consecrated to Christ, noblemen who lived and fought for

---

[21] C. Downham, *Medieval Ireland* (Cambridge: Cambridge University Press, 2018), 114.

[22] Particularly egregious in this respect is T. Cahill, *How the Irish Saved Civilization* (London: Hodder & Stoughton, 1996), a popular but grossly exaggerated account of what actually happened. For a good account, see L. Gougaud, *Christianity in Celtic Lands: A History of the Churches of the Celts, Their Origin, Their Development, Influence and Mutual Relations* (Dublin: Four Courts Press, 1992).

the glory of the holy city. The Arthurian legends called it Camelot, but it was really a picture of the New Jerusalem that would come down from heaven. 'Onward Christian Soldiers' may be a relatively modern hymn, but its roots go back a long way.

So too does the chivalric tradition associated with such figures as Sir Lancelot, Sir Galahad and Sir Gawain. The quest for the holy grail (the cup used by Jesus at the Last Supper) may be a fiction, but it strikes a chord with those who believe it is part of their Christian duty to protect the weak and fight for truth and justice. It goes without saying that the men were strong and the women and children weak and in need of defending, but this was not an exercise in male chauvinism. On the contrary, it gave aggressive masculinity a saving purpose and responsibility that denied the concept that 'might is right' and made service to others the crowning human virtue. Militancy in the name of the gospel is nowadays denounced by many as a perversion of the message of the Prince of Peace, but the Arthurian tradition gives it an appeal that has never been extinguished, despite every attempt to debunk the tales on which it is based. Arthur belongs to the 'matter of Britain', so much so that even the English have adopted him as a national hero.

There is a delicious irony in this of course, because if there ever was an Arthur, his fame rests on his success in keeping the English at bay, but logic has seldom been allowed to interfere with a good story. Camelot lives on as a fairy-tale-blessed society, and in that world Arthur is not dead. The wounded king has been taken to the isle of Avalon to recover, and when his country needs him, he will return and give it victory. Avalon is now the name of the eastern peninsula of Newfoundland, the first place in the new world that the English discovered and claimed for their own in 1497. It remains as testimony to the attempt of Henry VII (1485–1509), the first Tudor monarch, to turn the Arthurian myth into reality and thereby legitimize Henry's dynasty; but, as we know, the attempt failed. Henry VII called his eldest son Arthur, hoping that he would usher in a new golden age, but Arthur died before he could ascend the throne, and the legend, in so far as it had any chance of coming true, seems to have died with him. Henry VII's second son, Henry VIII (1509–47), would certainly change the religious face of the British Isles, but not in the way his father had envisioned or that the Arthurian tradition would have recognized.

Wrapped in legend spiced with myth, late Roman and post-Roman Britain remains tantalizingly hard to pin down. Leaving aside Pelagius, who made his career elsewhere, the only British Christians whose voices can still be heard are Patrick and Gildas. How typical was Patrick of the people from whom he came and to whom he went? He was at least a third-generation Christian, which was not unusual among the Romano-British upper class in the early fifth century, although his zeal for evangelizing the Irish sets him apart. His Christian convictions were undoubtedly sincere and there is nothing to suggest that he was less than fully orthodox according to the standards of the time, but the quality of his devotional life is hidden from our eyes. He was a man of action rather than a contemplative theologian, but that was what was required in the circumstances, and had he been a more reclusive figure we would probably never have heard of him. He wrote only when he had to – to explain his mission and dispel misconceptions in danger of hindering his work. What we have from his pen is valuable because it is unique, but nobody would claim that it is a classic of Christian literature. Much the same can be said of Gildas, who lived a generation or two later. His prophetic zeal, while beyond question, by its very nature can hardly be said to have been typical. If it had been, Britain might have been in a much better state than it was.

The authentic voice of Christian piety, as it would have been expressed by more ordinary converts to the faith, is almost impossible to track down – with one remarkable exception. This is the Old Irish poem known to us as 'St Patrick's Breastplate'.[23] It is unlikely to have been composed by Patrick himself, since it is doubtful whether he would have possessed the necessary poetic skill in a foreign language, and it reflects an outlook that would have been alien to a man educated in classical Roman culture. But it can be dated to a time more or less contemporaneous with him and it breathes the spirit of people who had recently passed from tribal paganism to the light of the gospel of Christ. It is best known to us in the versified translation done by the indefatigable Mrs Alexander in the late nineteenth century, which is still sung in our churches. Making allowances for the inevitable losses incurred in translation and the somewhat sanitized Victorian sensibilities of the translator, we can still feel the pulse of a poet who has one foot in his traditional culture, even as he embraces the divine revelation he has received:

I bind unto myself today
The strong name of the Trinity
By invocation of the same
The Three in One and One in Three.
I bind this day to me for ever
By power of faith, Christ's Incarnation.

---

[23] For the complete text and an English translation, see Haddan and Stubbs, *Councils*, 2:320–323.

His baptism in the Jordan river
His crucifixion for my salvation
His bursting forth from the spiced tomb
His riding up the Heavenly way
His coming at the day of doom
I bind unto myself today.

Here we see how Christian commitment is expressed in terms of oath-taking to a powerful Lord, who can ward off evil spirits and protect the one who confides in him. The mysteries of the Trinity and the incarnation take centre stage, precisely because they are signs of a mystical strength that can defy the mere logic of the material world and save it from destruction. Christ is worshipped, not for his teaching but for his miraculous deeds. His baptism was the moment of consecration to a life of service and suffering on our behalf. His crucifixion was the atoning sacrifice required for our salvation, but death could not hold him. He rose again in a triumphant display of his indomitable power and rode on like a mighty warrior to his heavenly destiny. He will come again in glory to judge the living and the dead and his servant (the poet) will be on the right side of that victory. This is the Apostles' Creed as confessed by a noble savage – simple, straightforward and to the point. Here was a man who knew where he was going and who understood how to get there. If the ordinary Christians of Britain and Ireland were anything like him, they were on the right track, and we should not be surprised that their labour and dedication produced lasting fruit in the conversion of their tribes and nations to Christ.

How should we evaluate the Christianity of late Roman and post-Roman Britain today? In one sense the Anglo-Saxon invasions obliterated it almost completely, leaving no unbroken tradition we can now claim as our own. The facts are hard to come by, and the legends that have filled the vacuum are dubious at best and fanciful at worst. Our only reliable link with the Roman period passes through Patrick and Ireland, and that too is covered in embellishments that make the truth difficult, if not impossible, to recover. And yet British Christianity as we know it now would not be the same if the Roman period had not existed. The Roman conquest stopped short of what we now call Scotland – Hadrian's Wall remains the symbolic, if not actual, boundary between two nations that did not exist when it was in use. South of that wall, what is now England is subdivided into north and south, based respectively on York and London. By historical accident the church has long been officially centred on Canterbury, but the archbishop lives in London, where his palace is located in the borough of Lambeth. Many ancient cathedral cities of England are built on Roman foundations – Lincoln, Chichester and Exeter, to name but three, and other Roman sites, like Chester and St Albans, were pressed into service as episcopal seats in later centuries. The Irish monastic tradition, first developed in late Roman times, has left its mark all over England (not to mention the Celtic countries of Britain), which cannot be understood without it. And last but not least, the very mystery that surrounds the period has provided fruitful inspiration to later generations, who have made of it what they would. The recreated afterlife of Roman Britain may be largely fictitious, but it has been influential nonetheless, and we cannot fully appreciate our spiritual inheritance unless we take it into account.

2
Between Ireland and Rome (597–871)

Scotland

It was in 563 that the Irish monk Crimthann, better known to us by his monastic name Columba, set out from Derry to establish a monastic outpost off the western coast of Scotland. The area had been raided and settled by Irishmen for some time, and their name – Scoti – was eventually given to the country as a whole. In the sixth century the southern Hebrides formed part of the Irish kingdom of Dál Riata, which included a sizable portion of what is now Northern Ireland. Columba was therefore not going as a missionary to a foreign land but to his fellow countrymen across the water.[1] The site he chose for his monastery was the small island of Iona,[2] hidden away and hard to reach for anyone coming by land, but of easy access by water, and the peoples who lived in the Western Isles went most places by boat. Iona is perhaps best described as a base camp from which the Christian mission reached out to the surrounding areas. We do not know many of the details, but within a relatively short time Christianity had spread, and been accepted, over wide areas of northern Britain. Beyond the Irish-speaking Scoti were the Celtic people we call the Picts, a Latin word meaning 'painted' because they covered their bodies with tattoos, and to the south of them the Britons, who still occupied Strathclyde and had been at least partially Christianized in late Roman times. It seems to have been a fifth-century king of Strathclyde, one Ceredig or Coroticus, who received a blistering letter from Patrick, complaining that his men had enslaved some newly converted Irishmen and sold them to neighbouring Picts, whom Patrick described as apostates from Christianity who had retreated back into their original paganism.[3]

---

[1] Unfortunately, like Patrick before him, Columba was not spared the attacks of his fellow clergymen back in Ireland, perhaps for similar reasons. See C. Downham, *Medieval Ireland* (Cambridge: Cambridge University Press, 2018), 126.

[2] More correctly 'Ioua'. The 'n' is due to a scribal error.

[3] T. O'Loughlin, *St Patrick: The Man and His Works* (London: SPCK, 1999), 93–105. On the Picts, see T. Clarkson, *The Picts: A History*, rev. edn (Edinburgh: Birlinn, 2010).

The conversion of the southern Picts to Christianity is associated with the activities of a certain Ninian, who is supposed to have come from Ireland and erected a monastery in Galloway called Candida Casa in Latin, or Whithorn in English. Ninian has acquired a considerable reputation as the first evangelist to north Britain, but his identity is elusive. He was probably the same person as Finnian of Movilla (in County Down), with a mistake in transcription accounting for the different initial and last letters of his name, which was really Uinniau. This Uinniau was a native of Britain who had gone to Ireland sometime in the early sixth century and become a master of novice monks, among whom was the young Crimthann. If that is so, the story that 'Ninian' preached the gospel in south-west Scotland must be a later invention, even though it was recounted by Bede in the early eighth century and dated to a period not long after AD 400.[4]

What is certain is that there was an ecclesiastical Establishment at Whithorn in the fifth century that eventually became a bishopric and remained attached to York until 1359. Whithorn might have been founded by Irish monks, perhaps under the direct oversight of St Patrick himself, and probably in his lifetime. But any connection with 'Ninian' can be ruled out, and it is just as likely that the Christian presence at Whithorn came overland from Roman Britain, as was the case in southern Scotland generally. The population south of the Clyde–Forth line was mostly British and the region's links to the south were strong, making the spread of Christianity from that direction all the more likely, and reinforcing the claims of York to jurisdiction over the churches in the area. Yet again we find that the absence of contemporary records and the confusion (or silence) of later chronicles have combined to produce an impenetrable fog of pseudo-information, made even denser by the exaggerated claims of 'Ninian's' enthusiastic, but ill-informed, modern devotees.

What we do know is that Columba and his monks succeeded in evangelizing the Picts, who lived north of Strathclyde, thereby creating a band of Christian territory stretching from Iona to the Severn Valley and embracing virtually all the Celtic peoples of Britain. By this time the still pagan Anglo-Saxons were already solidly implanted east of the Pennines, and the Irish monks were poised to go to them as well. The Anglo-Saxons had managed to establish a powerful kingdom of Northumbria, which stretched from the River Humber to the Firth of Forth, which was an obvious target for missionary endeavour. But before the Irish could get there, a different Christian mission had reached

---

[4] Bede, *Ecclesiastical History of the English People* (London: Penguin Books, 1990), 3.4. For a recent assessment of the evidence, see J. E. Fraser, *From Caledonia to Pictland: Scotland to 795* (Edinburgh: Edinburgh University Press, 2009), 68–72.

Northumbria from the south and the kingdom would soon be torn between rival brands of the new faith.

The Roman mission to the English

Columba died on Iona on 9 June 597, barely a fortnight after a group of monks who had set out from Rome nearly two years before finally landed on the shores of Kent. It was some time before the two missionary movements made contact, but the conversion of England would be marked by the activities (and rivalries) of both. The mission to southern England had originated with Pope Gregory the Great in Rome. Gregory I (590–604) is nowadays recognized as the last of the Latin Fathers of the church and the first of the medieval popes. As that reputation indicates, he lived at a time of transition, when the legacy of the Roman Empire was finally fading in western Europe and a new historical era was dawning. Gregory knew that the great days of Rome were long gone, but he had no way of foreseeing what the future would bring. As a man of great learning and energy, he wanted to restore the glories of the past, and in particular the reach that Catholic Christianity had enjoyed two centuries before his time. In 589 the third Council of Toledo had reconciled the Visigothic kingdom of Spain, which had previously accepted the Arian heresy as its official religion, to the Roman church. So when Gregory ascended to the papal throne, the climate for further conquest (or restoration) was particularly favourable.

Gregory knew that Roman Britain had been Christianized, and old maps told him that the country had once been divided into two provinces, one based at London (Britannia Superior) and the other at York (Britannia Inferior). He knew little about the survival of Christianity among the British and less about the Irish mission, which had gone beyond the ancient boundaries of the empire, but he was aware that the bulk of the old provinces had been conquered and settled by pagan Germanic tribes. There was nothing surprising or unfamiliar about this. Italy had fallen to the Ostrogoths, Spain to the Visigoths and Gaul to the Franks, who gave the country their name. All these had been converted to Christ in due course, so Gregory knew that their cousins in Britain were not beyond redemption. It seems that he planned to go there himself, but when he became Bishop of Rome he was no longer free to do so and had to send others instead.

What Gregory knew about the Anglo-Saxons is hard to say. There is a delightful legend that puts this question into plausible, if unproved, historical perspective. Wandering through the Roman slave market one day, Gregory is said to have caught sight of two young boys who were up for sale. He was struck by their blond hair, blue eyes and fair skin, which to the darker Mediterranean peoples made them seem like visitors from another world. When Gregory asked who the boys were, he was told that they were Angles. 'Not Angles, but angels,' he is said to have replied. 'What kingdom do they come from?' enquired Gregory. 'From Deira,' was the reply, Deira being one of the petty Anglo-Saxon kingdoms later absorbed into Northumbria. On hearing that, Gregory immediately made a play on words – in Latin *de ira* means 'out of wrath' – and he exclaimed 'Out of wrath they have been called into the light of Christ.' 'And who', asked Gregory, 'is their king?' 'He is called Aelle,' was the answer. 'They shall sing Alleluia in the land of Aelle,' replied Gregory, and from that day onwards he was determined to win the English for the Saviour.[5]

It is a story that can still bring a lump to the throat of an Englishman, who sees in this exchange not only the love of Gregory for an unknown people in a strange land, but also the hand of God at work, delivering an entire nation from the grip of Satan's slavery and setting it on a course that would lead it to praise the Lord of heaven and earth from that day to this. Whether it is true or not is a secondary consideration. The historian Bede (673–735), to whom we are indebted for the record of this exchange, was doubtful on that score, but he mentioned it because it was the tale that had been handed down to him and there was no better account available. For centuries the English would revere Gregory and pay special honour to the Roman church that had sponsored the Christian mission to them.[6] Even after the break with Rome in the sixteenth century, the sense that the English were a chosen nation, delivered from the wrath to come by a gracious God who had set them apart for better things, remained in the English consciousness, where to some extent it still abides. By recounting this story and outlining its consequences, Bede became the true founder of the English nation, long before it achieved the political unity it enjoys today. By giving them a sense of their divine destiny, Bede gave the English their soul, reminding them that they owed their national identity to their calling to receive the gospel of Jesus Christ for themselves and to transmit it to others far and wide.[7]

---

[5] Bede, *Ecclesiastical History*, 2.1.

[6] For a good overview of this long and complex history, see C. H. Lawrence (ed.), *The English Church and the Papacy in the Middle Ages*, rev. edn (Stroud: Sutton Publishing, 1999).

[7] The literature on Bede is immense. There is a detailed commentary on his *Ecclesiastical History* by J. M. Wallace-Hadrill, *Bede's Ecclesiastical History of the English People: A Historical Commentary* (Oxford: Clarendon Press, 1988). See also H. Blair, *The World of Bede* (Cambridge: Cambridge University Press, 1970); B. Ward, *The Venerable Bede* (London: Geoffrey Chapman, 1990); G. H. Brown, *A Companion to Bede* (Woodbridge: Boydell & Brewer, 2009); S. DeGregorio, *The Cambridge Companion to Bede* (Cambridge: Cambridge University Press, 2010).

Bede's account of the settlement and conversion of the Anglo-Saxons is much more detailed than any other source and almost contemporary with the events he describes. While not comprehensive, it is generally accurate enough and continues to shape the historical narrative today. One somewhat perverse result of this is that modern scholars sometimes feel the need to point out Bede's shortcomings and provide alternative interpretations, often based on archaeological or other evidence that can be read in different ways. There is no doubt that Bede had his prejudices, nor that he had to rely on sometimes inaccurate second-hand reports for things that had happened before his time and outside his native Northumbria. His scope was also limited. His intention was to recount the story of the conversion, and so other matters receive little emphasis: nobody would read him for the economic history of early England, for example. But these flaws, if that is what they are, are hardly unique to him and his modern detractors are not immune to similar faults of their own. Bede must be read on his own terms and appreciated for his remarkable achievement. Whatever else we may say about him, he remains one of the greatest, if not the greatest, Englishman who has ever lived. For a man who spent most of his life in a monastery on Tyneside and never travelled further than York, that is no small accolade.

Bede tells us that Gregory organized a mission team, headed by his own chaplain Augustine (not to be confused with Augustine of Hippo), that included a number of monks to assist him in his task. Augustine went first to Arles, the city that had been the centre of the Prefecture of Gaul at the time the synod of 314 was held there, and which Gregory evidently assumed would continue to act in that capacity as far as the mission to the English was concerned. Augustine and his companions were initially afraid to set foot in a strange and still-pagan country, but Gregory wrote them a letter of encouragement and instructed Etherius, the Archbishop of Arles, to do all he could to help them on their way. With this assurance, the party landed at Thanet on 26 May 597, the date that marks the beginning of the English church.

The England that greeted Augustine and his companions was a country subdivided into a number of kingdoms, largely based on tribal identities but occasionally showing traces of earlier Roman and British territorial divisions that had survived in popular consciousness. Many of these 'kings' were little more than tribal chiefs who gathered their followers around them – the word 'king' is related to 'kin' and reminds us that many of these statelets thought of themselves as extended families.

Among these many rulers a few stood out and appear to have exercised some sort of lordship over the others. One of these was Aethelbert, king of Kent from sometime in the 580s until his death around 616. Aethelbert had married Bertha, a daughter of the Frankish king, who was already a Christian. As part of the marriage settlement she had been permitted to bring a bishop by the name of Liudhard with her and establish Christian worship in Canterbury, the old Roman site that served as Aethelbert's capital. It is very probable that she and Liudhard did some quiet evangelism at court, although as long as the king remained a pagan there would have been no open conversions there. Yet after Augustine and his party landed, it was only a matter of months before Aethelbert was baptized, and within a year or so large numbers of his subjects had followed his example, which strongly suggests that the ground had been prepared in advance. Liudhard however played no part in these events and had probably died shortly before (or not long after) Augustine landed.

Today we are familiar with this pattern of mass conversion, which has been replicated in many African and Asian tribal societies, and there is no reason to suppose that what happened in Kent was unusual or insincere. The king was the head of the family, and the conversion was a kind of household baptism, albeit on a bigger scale. It probably could not have been otherwise. Just as nobody would have converted without the king's approval, so nobody would have resisted conversion once he had given the signal to go ahead. This was political loyalty, to be sure, but it was more than that. The bonds between the king and his subjects were deep and all-embracing, and were to remain so.[8] To a remarkable extent, British Christianity would be shaped by the piety and policies of its secular rulers, a tradition still not extinct. The faith of the monarch is no longer compulsory, but neither is it an entirely private matter; even today the connections between church and state are mirrored in the bonds between sovereign and people that transcend the more mundane political alliances of the moment.

After his initial success, Augustine went back to Arles, where Etherius consecrated him as bishop to the English. Augustine then wrote to Gregory, informing him of what had happened, and enquiring about how he should proceed with the practicalities of conversion. Bede includes a set of questions Augustine asked Gregory, along with the replies he received.[9] The questions are worth considering in detail, since they reveal what kinds of problems Augustine had to deal with and how the church of his day answered them (my paraphrase of the original Latin).

---

[8] See A. E. Redgate, *Religion, Politics and Society in Britain, 800–1066* (Abingdon: Routledge, 2014), 63–97.

[9] Bede, *Ecclesiastical History*, 1.27.

'1. Q: What is the relationship between a bishop and his clergy? How should the people's offerings be apportioned? What are the functions of a bishop?

'A: Guidance should be sought in the Pastoral Epistles, especially 1 and 2 Timothy. Revenues should be equally distributed to the bishop and his household for the purpose of hospitality, to the clergy, to the poor and to the upkeep of churches.

'2. Q: Why do customs differ from church to church when we all hold the same faith?

'A: No one church has the fulness of truth, and Augustine should feel free to take what seems good from whatever church he finds it in, so as to advance the kingdom of God among the English.

'3. Q: How should those who rob churches be punished?

'A: Punishment must depend on the circumstances. Some people rob churches out of necessity, and they should be treated more leniently. Others must be punished more severely, but with an aim to correct them rather than to destroy them. Every thief must restore his ill-gotten gains to the church in question.

'4. Q: Can two brothers marry two sisters as long as there is no blood relation between them?

'A: Yes.

'5. Q: What degrees of affinity should prevent a marriage? Can a man marry his step-mother or his sister-in-law?

'A: Affinity should stretch to the fourth generation. To marry a step-mother or sister-in-law is forbidden, because it is a form of incest, the women in question having become one flesh with a man's father or brother. Englishmen so married before their conversion are to be allowed to keep their wives, but the practice must be forbidden to those who are already Christians.

'6. Q: Given the difficulties of travel, can a bishop be consecrated without other bishops being present?

'A: This is permissible as a temporary measure where there are no other bishops, but when enough bishops have been appointed in a given region, no consecration should take place unless three or four other bishops are present.

'7. Q: How should we relate to the bishops of Gaul and Britain?

'A: You have no authority over the bishops of Gaul, and any questions relating to them must be referred to the Archbishop of Arles. On the other hand you have authority over all the bishops of Britain.

'8. Q: Can an expectant mother be baptized? How old should a child be before receiving baptism? How soon should a mother be brought back to church after giving birth? When should a husband resume conjugal relations with his wife? Can a menstruating woman attend church and receive Communion? Can a man receive Communion after having intercourse with his wife, if he has not yet washed?

'A: Women should not be barred from attending church for the reasons stated, nor should the baptism of an infant be delayed. A man should not resume sexual relations with his wife until the child is weaned, and after intercourse he should purify himself before receiving Communion.

'9. Q: Can a man receive Communion, or a priest celebrate it after having a wet dream?

'A: Not all wet dreams are the result of lust, and in those cases there is no bar to Communion or to celebration. However, men must examine themselves in this matter. If lust is involved, they must purify themselves first before receiving or celebrating Communion.'

As the above catalogue demonstrates, Augustine's concerns ranged all the way from international relations to intimate sexual matters, which were apparently the most pressing pastoral problems he had to face. They reveal the gulf in perception between the erstwhile pagan Anglo-Saxons and the Roman church Establishment and show us how much traditional ways would have to change once people became Christians. Modern observers are liable to find some of these questions intrusive and even obsessive in their quest for ritual 'purity', but such was the nature of conversion in an illiterate tribal society. It comes as no surprise though, to discover that the church's success in changing established practices was very uneven, and it would take a long time before significant progress in that direction would be discernible.[10]

Along with these illuminating replies, Gregory sent Augustine reinforcements, some of whom are named by Bede – Mellitus, Justus, Paulinus and Rufianus.[11] According to the initial plan of evangelization, Augustine should have gone on to London and established himself there, but London was a border town between Kent and the still unconverted East Saxons, so it was not a safe place for the head of the English church to be. Instead of going there himself, Augustine sent Mellitus, who thus became the great city's first bishop. He also consecrated Justus as Bishop of Rochester, although Paulinus had to wait until 625 before he was made Bishop of York. As it happened, he was consecrated by Justus, who by then had become the fourth Archbishop of Canterbury, having succeeded Mellitus, who had been elected to the see following the death of Laurence, Augustine's immediate successor.

---

[10] For a detailed study of this process, see B. Yorke, *The Conversion of Britain 600–800* (Harlow: Pearson, 2006).

[11] Bede, *Ecclesiastical History*, 1.29.

About the same time as he sent Mellitus to London, Augustine made contact with the surviving British church in Wales, but cooperation with it proved to be impossible. The Britons had little interest in evangelizing the Anglo-Saxons, and even less in submitting to the authority of Rome, represented by Augustine and his mission.

Augustine was supposed to send another of his companions to York, but this did not happen during his lifetime. When Paulinus finally got there, he was able to win King Edwin of Northumbria for Christ and baptized him in 627, but his support base was weak and when Edwin died in 633, he fled south, becoming in due course Bishop of Rochester. York remained without a bishop until 664, by which time the political and ecclesiastical situation was changing once more.

After a brief period of uncertainty, the new Northumbrian king Oswald (634–42) invited the Irish monks of Iona into his kingdom. The man who accepted this challenge was Aidan, who went to Lindisfarne, where he established his monastic headquarters. Aidan died in 651, but by then Lindisfarne, also known as Holy Island, had become a major evangelistic centre and the local Anglo-Saxons were well on the way to becoming Christians.[12] One of these was a young man named Cuthbert, who claimed to have had a vision on the night Aidan died, which persuaded him to become a monk. Cuthbert eventually became the Prior of Lindisfarne in 665 and twenty years later its bishop, but by then his life was drawing to a close. He resigned his see and died in 687.[13] Today he is remembered as the patron saint of Northumberland. In later times his remains were moved from Lindisfarne to Chester-le-Street and then to Durham, where they remain to this day, along with those of Bede. Cuthbert thus enjoys the distinction of being the first English Christian whose earthly remains are both preserved and identifiable.

The conversion of the rest of the English took place in stages during the course of the seventh century. The West Saxons were won over in the 630s by the missionary efforts of Bishop Birinus, who had been sent from Rome and consecrated by the Bishop of Genoa. As Bede tells the story, Birinus was allowed to establish himself at Dorchester, but before long there was a period of reaction against the new faith. Even when that was overcome, the West Saxons were reluctant to accept bishops who had come from abroad and Birinus's successor, Agilbert, was forced to resign and return to Gaul, where he became Bishop of Paris. Finally this opposition was overcome and in 670

---

[12] Ibid. 3.5.
[13] Ibid. 4.27–29.

Agilbert's nephew, Leutherius, was consecrated as bishop and moved his seat from Dorchester to Winchester, which after Canterbury and London remains the third most important see of the southern province.[14]

While this was going on, King Earconbert of Kent (640–64) removed the last traces of idol worship from his kingdom, marking a further step in the evangelization of southern England.[15] The conversion of East Anglia was promoted by its King Sigbert, who had been baptized in Gaul before becoming king sometime around 630. Sigbert was so devout that he gave up his throne to become a monk, although not before he had established a school for the training of future clergy along the same lines as the one in Canterbury.[16] Unfortunately Sigbert and his successor, Egric, were both killed in battle by Penda, the pagan king of Mercia (the English Midlands), which did not accept Christianity until 653. The cause of this was a royal marriage. Peada, the son of Penda, wanted to marry Alchfled, the daughter of Oswy, king of Northumbria, but Oswy would not agree to that unless Peada became a Christian. He duly submitted to instruction in the faith and the Mercians were rapidly converted. Interestingly, Irish monks played a major role in this, even though they were still celebrating Easter according to a different calendar from the one in use at Rome.[17]

Meanwhile the East Saxons, who had initially received Christianity from Mellitus, reverted to their pagan ways and had to be re-evangelized sometime around 653 by Cedd, a monk from Lindisfarne who had taken part in the Mercian mission.[18] Unfortunately that was not the end of the story. An outbreak of plague caused the East Saxons to revert to paganism once more, and it was not until 665 that they were finally won over by Bishop Jaruman, who had been sent to them from Mercia.[19] Sometime after that, probably in the late 670s, the South Saxons were converted thanks to the efforts of Wilfrid, who had been exiled from Lindisfarne (see below), and in 686 the Isle of Wight, the last pagan stronghold of the English, finally succumbed.[20] With that, the official Christianization of England was complete, although there was still much to do to make the new faith truly indigenous.

The church was organized along diocesan lines, as had become the pattern all over western Europe, but the dioceses were somewhat fluid and several

---

[14] Ibid. 3.7.
[15] Ibid. 3.8.
[16] Ibid. 3.18.
[17] Ibid. 3.21.
[18] Ibid. 3.22–23.
[19] Ibid. 3.30.
[20] Ibid. 4.13, 16.

Table 2.1 English dioceses, AD 597–1094

Year founded	Diocese	Year dissolved/transferred/monasticized
597	Canterbury*	Monastic from about 997
604	London	
604	Rochester*	Monastic from 1083
626	York	
630	*Dunwich*	870
634	*Dorchester*	660 (revived 869–1067; transferred to Lincoln in 1067)
655	*Mercia*	667 (transferred to Lichfield)
660 (670)	Winchester*	Monastic from 964
665	*Lindisfarne*	883 (transferred to *Chester-le-Street*)
666	*Ripon*	679
667	Lichfield	1075 (transferred to Chester temporarily)
672	*Elmham*	869 (revived 955–1094)
676	Hereford	
678	*Hexham*	821
678	*Lindsey*	875 (revived 953–1011)
680	Worcester*	Monastic from about 974x977
681	*Selsey*	1075 (transferred to Chichester)
681	*Whithorn*	803
705	*Sherborne*	1078 (transferred to Salisbury)
706	*Leicester*	888 (transferred to *Dorchester*)
823	*Cornwall*	1050 (transferred to Exeter)

proved to be ephemeral, although others have survived to the present day. In addition a number of cathedrals were monasteries, or were soon converted into monastic houses. To get a picture of this, see Table 2.1.[21]

From this list it will be seen that the most ancient foundations survived more or less intact, whereas of the sixteen founded from about 630 to 706 only four are still in existence, although the number rises to nine if transfers are taken into account. After 706 there were no new foundations for 200 years, Cornwall being only an apparent exception.[22]

---

[21] Sees that no longer exist are in italics. Many of the dates are approximate. Monastic cathedrals are marked with an asterisk (*).

[22] There was probably a bishop in Cornwall well before 823, but we have no record of him.

Monastic influences

It is hard to exaggerate the fame and influence of Iona and Lindisfarne on the development of Christianity in Britain, especially in the north. Their monks were renowned for their piety and self-discipline as they endured the hardships of the northern weather and terrain in their determination to win people for the faith of Christ. They were an inspiration to younger generations, who followed them with equal determination – Cuthbert's vision was but one among many callings to the monastic life. The monasteries themselves were centres of learning, where precious manuscripts were collected, preserved and copied. The Book of Kells, now on display in Trinity College, Dublin, which is the most famous illuminated manuscript produced at Iona, and the Lindisfarne Gospels, now in the British Library, speak for themselves. Both are copied in a fine scribal hand, but it is their magnificent illustrations, which combine Celtic, Roman and other styles, that make them unique.

The Irish monastic tradition made no claim to originality, which its exponents would have deprecated as heresy, but it preserved and transmitted to later generations a scholarly corpus that might otherwise have been lost. It is too much to claim that the Irish 'saved civilization', but their faithfulness and scrupulosity in copying the received body of learning deserves our praise and puts us in their debt. No doubt most of what they transmitted would eventually have come from southern Europe, but Britain did not have to wait that long to receive its legacy. Instead it was home-grown monks who supplied what would otherwise have been missing and who have bequeathed to us the memory of a time when remote and largely barren islands off the British mainland were major centres of learning and Christian faith.

But if the main pattern of monastic activity flowed from Ireland to Britain, there was also movement in the opposite direction. An interesting example of that was the mission of Bishop Colman, an Irishman from Lindisfarne who could not accept the decision of the Synod of Whitby to conform to the Roman calculation of the date of Easter. To escape that, he took a mixed group of English and Irish monks with him to Iona and then to Inishboffin, off the west coast of Ireland. What happened next is worth recording:

A dispute arose among them because in summer the Irish went off to wander on their own around places they knew instead of assisting at harvest, and then, as winter approached, came back and wanted to share whatever the English monks had gathered. Colman sought a remedy for this dispute, and after searching near and far, discovered a site suitable for a monastery on the Irish mainland, a place which the Irish call Mayo.[23]

The result was that two monasteries were created – one at Inishboffin for the Irish, and another at Mayo, for the English. It was the first example of a division that was to characterize Ireland and the Irish church for centuries, and whose effects can still be felt. The interplay between the native Irish and the immigrant English is impossible to miss – the Irish come across as lazy and feckless, the English as industrious and hardworking. It is a caricature that was to have a long future ahead of it.

The lasting contribution of the Irish mission in Britain was the creation of what came to be known as the minster church. 'Minster', a corruption of the Latin *monasterium* (monastery), was the name given to a number of large churches in England that were built around a monastic community and run along those lines. Some became cathedrals, but many did not, and even today there are churches scattered up and down England that bear witness to that tradition – Beverley Minster in Yorkshire, or Wimborne Minster in Dorset, for example. How important the minster churches were in the evangelization of England is hard to say. They undoubtedly exercised considerable influence in the areas where they were established, but there were many smaller churches where a single priest did his best to reach out to the neighbourhood, as well as unmanned chapels where services were occasionally held. The chief significance of the minster churches lies in the example they gave to others. Their organization and way of life set a standard that was widely respected and copied as much as possible. Several of them acquired privileges and exemptions from the control of the local bishop, establishing what are known as 'peculiar jurisdictions', which lasted until most of them were abolished in the mid-nineteenth century (1836–52).[24] The ones that survive have special functions, like the various royal chapels and the chapels of Oxford and Cambridge colleges, which are outside their local diocesan structures.

Minster churches also served as models for cathedrals as the diocesan structure of the Church of England became more closely defined. Instead of following the usual pattern, where cathedral functions were assigned to different dignitaries who had their own incomes, monastic cathedrals pooled

---

[23] Bede, *Ecclesiastical History*, 4.4. The English monastery was still going strong in Bede's day and so must have been attracting new recruits from across the water. It remained active (and English) until the Viking raids of the mid-ninth century put an end to it.

[24] For a history of the ones attached to the see of Durham, see F. Barlow, *Durham Jurisdictional Peculiars* (London: Geoffrey Cumberledge for Oxford University Press, 1950). This remains an under-researched area in English church history.

their resources and appointed church dignitaries from within their ranks. This not only saved money but also encouraged a community life intended to give the cathedrals a more vibrant spirituality. In most cases an existing monastery became the headquarters of a bishop and thus a monastic cathedral, but that was not always the case. Rochester, Durham and Norwich were pre-existing cathedrals that were given a monastic chapter, but after 1066 two new dioceses were created – Ely (1109) and Carlisle (1133), both built on existing monastic foundations. Carlisle was exceptional in that whereas the other monastic cathedrals were all Benedictine foundations, it was based on a priory of Augustinian canons, a religious order of recent origin. Canterbury, Winchester and Worcester, all of which were founded before the Norman Conquest, made up the remainder, but York was not among them. The cathedral is frequently called York Minster but it was never a monastic foundation: the name seems to have been assigned to it after the origins of the minsters had been forgotten. To complete the picture, in two cases it proved to be impossible to merge the cathedral with a local monastery, and so they were twinned instead. Coventry Abbey and Lichfield Cathedral were united in this way until 1877, whereas Bath Abbey and Wells Cathedral remain connected to the present day.

The Anglo-Saxon church

As the conversion of England progressed, it was only a matter of time before the Celtic churches and Roman mission would be stepping on each other's toes. As often happens in such cases, that led to bad feeling, especially on the Roman side, where there was a tendency to feel superior to the Celts and even to accuse them of heresy. One of the more prominent actors in this drama was Wilfrid (633–709/710), a Northumbrian monk who began his career at Lindisfarne but then went to Rome, where he learned that the customs he had practised at home were rejected, if not openly regarded as schismatic. Wilfrid was converted to Roman ways, and when he went back to England he did his best to impose them on his countrymen. He was probably the first Englishman to adopt the Rule of St Benedict as the basis for monastic life, and he founded monasteries that followed it, rather than the traditional customs that prevailed elsewhere. Eventually the entire monastic Establishment would come around to the Benedictine pattern, and in this respect Wilfrid's policies were to have a long-lasting impact.[25]

---

[25] The standard guide to monasteries in England and Wales is D. Knowles and R. N. Hadcock, *Medieval Religious Houses: England and Wales*, 2nd edn (London: Longman, 1971).

Wilfrid is chiefly known, however, for his vigorous advocacy of the Roman method for calculating the date of Easter. In 664 he attended a council at Whitby, which the king had called in order to determine which system should be followed, the Roman or the Celtic. A debate was held in the presence of the King of Northumbria, whom Wilfrid persuaded to adopt the Roman rule as being the one of more universal purchase. After that, the Celtic churches gradually switched over, the last ones in 768.[26] Wilfrid's cause would undoubtedly have triumphed in the end, for the reasons that persuaded the Northumbrians, but unfortunately he seemed unable to defend his ideas without lapsing into invective against the other side. That did not prevent him from becoming a bishop and being declared a saint after his death, but it left a bad taste in the mouth and contributed to an unfairly negative attitude towards the Celts. Fortunately Bede, who recounts the details of the controversy, was sympathetic to the Irish even though he supported Wilfrid, and so was able to transmit a more balanced picture of events to posterity.[27] In fact, as we have already seen, Irish customs put down lasting roots in England, where the united church that emerged after the Synod of Whitby retained much of the vigour that had been inspired by men like Aidan, one of Bede's heroes.

In 668 the fledgling English church acquired a new and highly gifted archbishop, Theodore of Tarsus, who went from Rome to Canterbury and stayed there until his death in 690.[28] As a Greek, Theodore was somewhat suspect to the Romans, but his effect on the English church was both extensive and salutary. As Bede tells us, he was the first archbishop to exercise real authority over the whole of England, and did so with considerable effect. He toured the country, doing his best to raise the standards of education and introducing music into the liturgy of the churches, something previously restricted to Kent. When he discovered irregularities, he put them right, most notably in the case of Chad, Bishop of Lichfield, an itinerant preacher who had done much to spread the faith in the west midlands and had a lasting reputation for personal holiness.[29] Chad had stepped in to fill a gap in the church's administration after the previous bishop's death but, rather than depose him, Theodore reconsecrated and confirmed him in his office. It was an approach

---

[26] A. W. Haddan and W. Stubbs, *Councils and Ecclesiastical Documents Relating to Great Britain and Ireland*, 3 vols. (Oxford: Clarendon Press, 1869–78), 1:203–204. There were some holdouts among the Welsh even later than this, and it was not until the early ninth century that the Celtic Easter was finally laid to rest.

[27] Bede, *Ecclesiastical History*, 3.25.

[28] Ibid. 4.1–2.

[29] Ibid. 4.2–3.

that would be typical of his episcopate and won him widespread support among the English.

Theodore also summoned the first national synod of the English church, which met at Hertford on 24 September 673. The synod issued ten canons, prepared in advance by Theodore, which were intended to regulate practice across the country. The celebration of Easter according to the Roman custom was the first priority, since unity on this subject was essential for the health of the church as a whole. Most of the other customs regulated the conduct and mission of the bishops, priests and monks. Each order of the clergy was to be given a specific sphere of responsibility and was expected to stick to it: there was to be no trespassing or interference in the affairs of others. An annual synod would be held at Clovesho, a place we can no longer identify but that was probably not far from Hertford, and provision was made for the appointment of more bishops as the church expanded. Somewhat remarkably, given the concerns of Augustine seventy years before, only one of the canons was devoted to marriage, and its main purpose was to forbid unjustified divorce.[30]

There was some opposition to Theodore's reforms, but he nipped it in the bud. When Bishop Wynfrid of Mercia refused to comply, Theodore deposed him and sent him back to his monastery, where he apparently led an exemplary life until his death. This shows us that personal sanctity was not enough for holding high office in the church: bishops had to be team players and obey the directions of the archbishop and synod if they were to exercise a public ministry.[31]

Theodore's episcopate was also notable in that for the first time we find the English church openly professing the Catholic faith decided by the great ecumenical councils of the universal church. Word had reached Theodore that a new heresy was troubling the eastern churches, and in order to counteract it he summoned a synod to meet at Hatfield on 17 September 680. There the English church affirmed its allegiance to the decisions of the five imperial councils that had been held up to that time – the first Council of Nicaea (325), the first Council of Constantinople (381), the first Council of Ephesus (431), the Council of Chalcedon (451) and the second Council of Constantinople (553). It also subscribed to the Lateran Council of 649, which bound the western church but had not been received in the east.[32] The third Council of Constantinople (680–81) was summoned to condemn the heresy known as 'monotheletism', the belief that the incarnate Christ had only one will, and not

---

[30] Ibid. 4.5.
[31] Ibid. 4.6.
[32] Ibid. 4.17.

two. This was in direct contradiction to Matthew 26:39, where Jesus, praying in the Garden of Gethsemane the night before his crucifixion, distinguished clearly between his human will (to live) and the will of his Father, which was that he should die. Since the divine will of the Father was also the will of the Son, it was obvious that Jesus had two wills, and that the apparent conflict between them was resolved by the submission of his human will to his divine one. No English bishop attended the council at Constantinople, but Wilfrid of York, who was in Rome defending his episcopal title, signed the preliminary document prepared by the Roman church for submission to it, appointing himself (in effect) as the representative of all the churches of the British Isles.[33] It was the first time that an English voice was heard in an international ecclesiastical forum.

Theodore possessed a classical and theological learning that was unrivalled, and he established monastic schools to further it wherever he could. Thanks to him, the Tyneside monasteries of Wearmouth and Jarrow acquired some of the best libraries in existence at that time. It was there that the young Bede was sent and where he spent the rest of his life. Today Bede is best remembered for his history of the English people, but there was much more to him than that. As an amateur astronomer, he wrote extensively on the calendar and in particular on the calculation of the date of Easter. He did not invent the Christian era of dating, which had first appeared at Rome over a century before he was born, but he used it in his history and did much to popularize it across Europe.[34]

In a very real sense what has now become the universally accepted 'common era' system of dating goes back to him, but that is not all that he achieved. He also wrote biblical commentaries and was the first person to tackle the entire canon in a systematic way. Much of what he said was copied from elsewhere, of course – originality was not regarded as a virtue in those days – but he performed an invaluable service by systematizing information gathered from a number of different sources. He also filled in gaps that had been overlooked by earlier commentators, who had often treated individual books (or groups of books) independently of the scriptural canon as a whole. Bede's encyclopedic treatment of the subject ensured that his commentaries would become (and remain) standard fare until the Renaissance, when the rediscovery of ancient manuscripts and the invention of printing led to a revival of the genre of commentary writing. In the process, Bede's contribution was eclipsed and largely forgotten, but his greatness remains undiminished. After all, how many

---

[33] Haddan and Stubbs, *Councils*, 3:140.
[34] See F. Wallis, *Bede: The Reckoning of Time* (Liverpool: Liverpool University Press, 1999).

biblical scholars can claim that their work is good enough to become the standard textbook for seven or eight centuries?

Bede was the glory of the English church in later times, but he lived in an age of giants. As he was writing in Jarrow, others were taking the gospel to Continental Europe, and in particular to the Germanic lands that had not previously been evangelized. Together with a number of Irish monks, these Anglo-Saxons established churches and monasteries all over what is now Germany, the Netherlands, Switzerland and eastern France. Few British people know it, but Boniface (d. 754), hailed as the 'apostle to the Germans', was originally Wynfrith of Crediton, whose evangelistic zeal took him to his still pagan Saxon cousins across the sea. Nor was he the first Englishman to go that way. An initial attempt to convert the Germans in the time of Theodore had failed, but before long Willibrord (d. 739), who had been born in Northumbria around the same time as Bede, and had trained in an Irish monastery, was sent to Friesland, where he became the founder of the local church.[35] He died and was buried in Echternach, and is still venerated as the patron saint of both the Netherlands and Luxembourg. Here the English were following (at some distance) in the footsteps of the Irish, whose earlier successes had owed much to the rising power of the Franks. The Franks had originally accepted Christianity under their great king Clovis in 497, but the hard work of evangelizing the nation was done by Irishmen like Columbanus (c.540–615) and Gallus (550–646), after whom the Swiss city and canton of St Gallen are named. By the mid-eighth century, the Franks were poised to become the major power in western Europe, and it was under Charles the Great (768–814), or Charlemagne as we know him, that this long gestation flowered in what has come to be known as the Carolingian Renaissance. Central to this movement was Alcuin of York (d. 804), a Northumbrian monk who had been invited to the Frankish court in order to improve the standard of education there and who soon became the most influential of all the Anglo-Saxon missionaries sent to the European continent.

The Continental missions undertaken from Ireland and Britain were a tribute to the progress Christianity had made in the islands in a relatively short time. Peoples who had no recorded pre-Christian history were sending out bishops and pastors of high quality at an astonishing rate. Furthermore, they were backed by a reputation for learning that was second to none. We cannot trace the origins of all those involved, and many will be for ever anonymous, but those who have been recorded are eloquent testimony to what must have

---

35 Bede, *Ecclesiastical History*, 5.10.

been a high degree of religious fervour and commitment. Both the Celts and the Anglo-Saxons knew that by accepting the faith of Christ they had been delivered from darkness into light. They did not look back on their pagan past with nostalgia, even if there were occasional relapses in the second generation after the initial conversion. They did not always forget that past, but when they recalled it they did so with the aid of Christian filters. This comes across very clearly in the greatest epic poem of the period, the famous *Beowulf*. We do not know who composed it or when, but it seems to date from a fairly early time, perhaps the seventh or eighth century, and the events it describes were set in the pre-Christian (and pre-British) past. But the poem is larded with biblical references and the struggle between good and evil in which Beowulf was engaged is presented in Christian terms. Most subtly, Beowulf, although basic-ally a hero fighting against evil forces, has something of that evil latent in himself. The poet knew that there is no neat distinction between good and bad, that all have sinned and come short of the glory of God. Pagan heroes may appear to be on the side of the angels, but are nevertheless scarred by original sin. Without Christ there can be no salvation, and so in the end even the hero dies unavenged.

The bards and poets sang of the deeds of the great warriors of old, but they were not slow to transfer their talents to sing the praises of Christ, and in particular of the cross on which he died. One of the most imaginative and most beautiful poems in Old English is the *Dream of the Rood* ('rood' means 'cross'), 156 lines of verse preserved in part on a stone cross from Ruthwell (Scotland) and in full in a manuscript of Old English texts now deposited in the library at Vercelli (Italy). The stone cross dates from about 750, which presumably means that the poem is older than that, although by how much is impossible to say. It might well have been composed during the lifetime of Bede, although no author can be securely identified. The *Dream of the Rood* belongs to a genre of Old English verse known as 'dream poetry', in which the poet goes to sleep, has a dream and then recounts it. It is the oldest example of this genre still extant and unique in the sense that the words of the poet give way to those of the cross itself, which tells the story of how it was made to suffer by bear-ing the body of the man who bore the sins of the world for the sake of our salvation.

There is no other literary work in any language that is like this one. The cross is made to speak for itself, and we are given a unique perspective on the death of Christ. The cross tells of how it started life as a living tree, only to be cut down and reshaped so that it could perform the historic task for which it was being prepared:

It was long since – I yet remember it –
that I was hewn at holt's end,
moved from my stem. Strong fiends seized me there,
worked me for spectacle; cursed ones lifted me.
On shoulders men bore me there, then fixed me on hill;
fiends enough fastened me. Then I saw mankind's Lord
come with great courage when he would mount on me.
(Lines 28–34)

The cross had no choice but to bear the suffering of the one it bore, firm in the knowledge that this was the way of salvation God had prepared for his people:

The young hero stripped himself – he, God Almighty –
strong and stout-minded. He mounted high gallows,
bold before many, when he would loose mankind.
I shook when that Man clasped me. I dared, still, not bow to earth,
fall to earth's fields, but had to stand fast.
Rood was I reared. I lifted a mighty King,
Lord of the heavens, dared not to bend.
With dark nails they drove me through: on me those sores are seen,
open malice-wounds. I dared not scathe anyone.
They mocked us both, we two together. All wet with blood I was,
poured out from that Man's side, after ghost he gave up.
(Lines 39–49)

The Saviour's loyal followers came to take his body down, but the cross lay abandoned until someone noticed it lying on the ground. Then they picked it up, covered it in gold and silver, and honoured it as the one that had been with Christ in the darkest hours of his suffering. Now the cross is lifted high, a sign of the salvation that Christ has won for his people, and a challenge to his followers to take up their own cross and follow him:

He asks before multitudes where that one is
who for God's name would gladly taste
bitter death, as before he on beam did.
And they then are afraid, and few think
what they can to Christ's question answer.
(Lines 112–116)

The poem ends with some reflections from the poet, who confesses that he is waiting for the time when God will come to deliver him from his present suffering, and unite him with the heavenly banquet where Christ and the saints celebrate his eternal victory. As he puts it, 'He loosed us and life gave, a heavenly home' (lines 147–148a). Or, in the words of the psalmist:

> Weeping may tarry for the night,
>   but joy comes with the morning.[36]

Here, in this remarkable poem, we see the experience of the true believer, who is united with Christ in his death but who will one day be honoured and raised up to the heavenly places, where he will rejoice with joy everlasting. The voice of the cross is the voice of the Christian in whom Christ dwells and for whom he died. 'I have been crucified with Christ,' said the apostle Paul. 'It is no longer I who live, but Christ who lives in me.'[37] The *Dream of the Rood* is the mystical experience of the Christian and proof positive that the message of the gospel had indeed sunk in to the poets of Anglo-Saxon England, and through them to the wider public.

Another feature of the early Anglo-Saxon church is the strong emphasis on miracles and other supernatural happenings, which Bede and others believed lent credence to the new faith. This emphasis, by no means unusual in stories of conversion, needs to be highlighted in an age when scepticism has replaced credulity as the default position in society as well as in the church. The distance between the modern world and that of Bede can be seen clearly in the account he gives of the English mission. When Augustine held a conference with the British bishops at which he implored them to submit to his authority, Bede does not hesitate to tell us that Augustine performed a miracle by restoring the sight of a blind man.[38] That was not enough to persuade the British, but they immediately became culpable in Bede's eyes, since they had obviously rejected the power of God at work in their midst. This kind of thing runs through Bede's history as its dominating theme. Mellitus, for example, extinguished a fire at Canterbury by the power of prayer.[39] King Edwin of Northumbria was moved to convert to Christianity by a heavenly vision he had when still in exile.[40] King Oswald was a particularly productive miracle-worker, being

---

[36] Ps. 30:5.
[37] Gal. 2:20.
[38] Bede, *Ecclesiastical History*, 2.2.
[39] Ibid. 2.7.
[40] Ibid. 2.12.

credited with a number of healings both during his lifetime and after his death.[41] The same can be said of Cuthbert, whose relics were especially precious for that reason.[42] Another great miracle-worker was John, Bishop of Hexham (687–706) and then Archbishop of York (706–14). Here we are dealing with a man whom Bede would have known personally, and Bede's testimony is not dependent on the credulity of others.[43] Nor were the visions and miracles confined to men – women, and especially nuns, were prominent actors as well.[44]

What should we make of all this? No doubt interpretation plays a large part in Bede's account. What to him (and others) might have seemed miraculous might just have been unusual, although timing and attribution also play a role. Not everyone was capable of such feats – only those who were especially holy or blessed were credited with these supernatural achievements. We would dearly like to examine the evidence, interview those involved and test the psychology of both the givers and the recipients of the reported blessings, but we are unable to do so. Our judgment must be suspended, but we should be careful not to surrender to unreserved scepticism. From the New Testament onwards, miracles appear in the context of evangelism and who are we to deny that God confirms his word with signs following?[45] We are dealing here with spiritual matters that go beyond the limits of human reason, and while gullibility ought to be avoided, we cannot close our minds to the possibility that the Lord of heaven and earth can do things that go beyond the limits of our understanding.

The role of women

One feature of Anglo-Saxon Christianity that is often overlooked, but stands in sharp contrast both to what was going on elsewhere at the same time and what was to come later in England itself, is the prominent part played by women in the founding of monastic houses and the propagation of the gospel. One reason for this is that Anglo-Saxon women could own property and were free to bequeath it to whomever they wished, including the church. But they were not merely benefactresses. Many of them took vows of chastity and became prominent figures in their own localities. Hilda (614–80), for example, who was

---

[41] Ibid. 3.2, 9, 11–13.
[42] Ibid. 4.28, 31–32.
[43] Ibid. 5.2–6.
[44] Ibid. 4.7–10.
[45] Mark 16:20; Heb. 2:4.

of royal lineage, became a disciple of Aidan and the first Abbess of Whitby, where the great council that decided the future orientation of the British churches was held during her time there. A little later Frideswide (650–727), a daughter of the king of Mercia, is supposed to have founded a monastery in Oxford that later became the basis for Christ Church. Even before that, Queen Etheldreda (630–79) took a vow of perpetual virginity, even though she was married to the King of East Anglia, and is credited with the foundation of the abbey that would eventually become Ely cathedral. Frideswide and Etheldreda later became the patron saints of Oxford and Cambridge universities respectively, an interesting circumstance given that both universities remained exclusively male until the mid-twentieth century.[46]

Etheldreda has another claim to fame, in that her name, corrupted to Audrey, came to be associated with an annual fair at which substandard goods were sold. Because of that they were known as 'tawdry' (St Audrey), and a new word entered the English language. Etheldreda had a younger sister called Sexburga (d. *c*.699), who was Queen of Kent until 664 and then a nun at Ely. Then there was Werburgh (650–700), now the patron saint of Chester, and Ebba (615–83), a Northumbrian princess who is remembered in church dedications across England. It is obvious of course that these were wealthy and well-connected women, but they used the opportunities their status afforded them to establish the church of Christ on a firmer foundation than it had previously enjoyed. The great century of conversion was a time of unparalleled women's missionary outreach that has not been equalled since. They are little known today and their achievements have been overshadowed by those of their male colleagues, but their extraordinary contribution deserves to be celebrated and remembered as one that gave added lustre to the great age of the Anglo-Saxon church.

One woman who belongs in a category of her own was the founder of Walsingham Abbey. According to legend, this was Richeldis, who was Lady of the Manor of Little Walsingham in 1061, when the Virgin Mary is supposed to have appeared to her on no fewer than three occasions, and revealed the dimensions of the house in Nazareth where she had received the annunciation of the birth of Jesus from the angel Gabriel. Richeldis then set about reconstructing this 'holy house', which eventually became one of the greatest pilgrimage sites, not only in England but in Europe. The shrine was destroyed in the sixteenth century Reformation, but enthusiasts rebuilt it in the early

---

[46] Their feast days are celebrated respectively on 17 and 19 October, with St Luke, the patron saint of learning, commemorated on 18 October – a three-day feast of academia.

twentieth century, and it is now once again a shrine of Marian devotion that attracts pilgrims from far and wide.

Who this Richeldis was is uncertain. A woman of that name was Lady of Little Walsingham in the mid-twelfth century, and it may be that the legend refers to her, making the date of 1061 at least two generations earlier than the historical record would support. But it may also be that 'Richeldis' is an alternative name for Queen Edith the Fair (or Swanneck), the first wife of King Harold II who was slain at the Battle of Hastings, making the traditional founding date more plausible. Whatever the truth may be, there can be little doubt that the story is completely fictitious and that the devotion that has accrued to the site is not based on any objective fact. It is a reminder to us that the human imagination is often stronger than (and impervious to) mere historical fact, and a warning that piety based on myth does not confirm the truth of the Christian gospel but is rather a hindrance to it. Richeldis, whoever she was, has a lot to answer for, as do those who perpetuated her 'vision' in the past and who continue to deceive the gullible.[47]

The Viking invasions

When Bede died in 735, his monastic brethren could look back on the success of Christianity in the British Isles and entertain great hopes for the future. By then all the various tribes and nations had accepted the gospel and most had conformed to the Roman dating of Easter, a visible sign of their communion with the wider church. All over Britain and Ireland church life continued more or less routinely, with regular synods in England to take care of everyday administration, and virtually nothing of any significance to report from elsewhere. Then, all of a sudden, the heavens opened and the British Isles were battered by a tempest that would change them for ever.

Virtually unknown to the ancients, the Scandinavian peoples were suddenly on the move. Travelling vast distances in longboats, these Vikings, as we call them, made their presence felt all the way from the plains of Russia in the east to the mysterious islands of Iceland, Greenland and eventually even Newfoundland in the west. The British Isles were a prime destination for them, both because they were easily accessible from the sea and because they were rich and fertile, at least by Scandinavian standards.

The first Viking raids on Lindisfarne and Iona took place in 793 and 794 respectively, and caused shock waves through the islands. Even Alcuin of York,

---

[47] See B. Flint, *Edith the Fair: Visionary of Walsingham* (Leominster: Gracewing Press, 2015).

by then safely ensconced in Aachen as Charlemagne's right-hand man, was deeply distressed to learn of the disaster. After 800 there was a pause for nearly a generation, but then the raids increased in frequency and intensity, with the result that many of the great monasteries were plundered and eventually abandoned. Iona was deserted in 849 and Lindisfarne in 875, by which time the old order was dying or dead. The Anglo-Saxon synods that had been held with impressive regularity from about 600 onwards came to an end in 845, almost certainly because the disturbed state of the country made it impossible for them to continue. What happened in Scotland and Ireland at that time is hard to say because of the lack of contemporary records, but decline seems to have been the rule everywhere. Even in England only about three books were published between 835 and 885 – half a century with almost nothing to show for it.

The monks of Iona relocated to Kells in Ireland, taking with them the beautiful illuminated manuscript that is now on display in Trinity College, Dublin. In England the relics of St Cuthbert were moved from Lindisfarne to Chester-le-Street and eventually to the safe fortress of Durham, taking Cuthbert's bishopric with them. The Vikings' initial impact was disruptive and destructive. In 867 they captured York, bringing the powerful kingdom of Northumbria to an end and replacing it with rulers of their own. East Anglia succumbed to them in 869 and much of Mercia was overrun as well. By 870 the independent Anglo-Saxons were reduced to the south and west of England, where they were regrouping around the kings of Wessex, by then the most powerful of the surviving kingdoms and the one destined to unite the whole of England for the first time.

Meanwhile the Vikings occupied about half the country, north and east of a line drawn from London to Chester and corresponding to the old Roman road that we call Watling Street (now the A5). This came to be known as the Danelaw, and traces of its existence can still be detected. Unlike the Anglo-Saxons three centuries before, the Vikings did not displace the existing inhabitants. Those who settled in the Danelaw accepted Christianity and became English, even though they contributed a substantial portion of their own vocabulary and grammar to the local language. Words like 'take' and 'back' come from Old Norse, as do many features of what we now associate with Scottish or northern English dialects. These include words like 'bairn' (child) and 'beck' (stream), as well as forms in 'k' that standard English replaced with 'ch', 'kirk' instead of 'church' being an obvious example. Place names ending in 'by' are of Norse origin, so that in Lancashire, for example, Kir(k)by can be found alongside the Anglo-Saxon Eccleston, both meaning

'Churchtown' in modern English. The two peoples and their traditions lived side by side for centuries but eventually blended, and today it is only through DNA samples that we can see how clumps of erstwhile Danes and Norwegians continue to inhabit significant tracts of the British Isles. One way of detecting them is to look for churches dedicated to St Clement, a favourite Viking saint. St Clement Danes in London is a good example of this, but there are many others. Even in the highland town of Dingwall, whose name is a corruption of the Old Norse word for 'assembly' (*thingvellir*), the parish church is dedicated to St Clement, a living reminder of its Viking origin.

In the Celtic lands of the north and west the Vikings did not integrate as easily as they did in England, but nevertheless soon established a working relationship with the local inhabitants. They set up a kingdom in Orkney, which from their point of view was the gateway to the rest of Britain. They also established a kingdom in what they called the 'Southern Isles', known to us as the Inner Hebrides, and the Isle of Man. In Norse the Southern Isles were called *suðre øyar*, a phrase later anglicized as 'Sodor'. When they became Christians, these Vikings naturally established a bishopric in their kingdom. The vicissitudes of time and politics were eventually to separate the two halves of this diocese, but the church in the Isle of Man never forgot its Viking heritage, and to this day its bishop claims the title of Sodor and Man.[48] In earliest times this diocese, like that of Orkney, was tied first to Lund and then to Trondheim, but when the Viking kingdoms collapsed these dioceses were absorbed into the Church of Scotland, apparently without any formal transfer.

The Norsemen had a genius for organization that the peoples they conquered (or settled among) apparently lacked, but they were flexible enough to blend in with the natives and soon lost their original identity. In Ireland they clustered along the coasts and built towns like Dublin and Wexford, making them bastions of Germanic language and culture that would later become bridgeheads for the anglicization of Ireland. In northern France they created the duchy of Normandy, which still bears their name, and which was to play a key role in later British history. The Norsemen arrived there in 911, but by the time they invaded England in 1066 they had become thoroughly 'Frenchified', despite some residual links that they retained with their Scandinavian origins. Most remarkably of all, these same Normans reached the Mediterranean, where they were able to establish a kingdom in Sicily and

---

[48] For the early history of the Manx church, see D. S. Dugdale, *Manx Church Origins* (Lampeter: Llanerch, 1998). See also R. A. McDonald, *The Sea Kings: The Late Norse Kingdoms of Man and the Isles, c. 1066–1275* (Edinburgh: John Donald, 2019). Sodor's more recent claim to fame comes from Thomas the Tank Engine, who lives in the semi-mythical island of Sodor; i.e. Man.

southern Italy that would retain its identity (if not its Norman heritage) until the unification of Italy in 1860. Although they were slow to recognize it, and did not always welcome it, the peoples of Britain and Ireland were being drawn into a network that stretched far and wide, and that was to have some surprising implications for the future development of their churches.

3
One church in four nations (871–1154)

Decline and revival in England

Sometime in the middle of the ninth century the momentum engendered by the years of conversion began to falter. By the year 800 then, there were no parts of the British Isles that had not heard the gospel, although there would soon be Viking settlements that were not yet converted. Although the arrival of the Vikings disrupted the old order, it was not long before they embraced Christianity; but the church was more preoccupied with survival than with thoughts of expansion. In fairness it should be said that what was true of Britain and Ireland was also true of most of western Europe. The papacy, in particular, fell into the hands of rival street gangs in Rome and was unable to offer any kind of lead to the church as a whole. The Carolingian Empire fell apart and the renaissance sponsored by Charlemagne fizzled out. This was the true dark age of western Christendom and lasted for the better part of two hundred years. During that time, the face of Anglo-Saxon England was transformed.[1] The many kingdoms that had existed before the Viking raids were progressively eliminated until only one was left – Wessex, centred on Winchester, which was too far from the Danelaw to be conquered by the Norsemen. It was there that the Anglo-Saxons regrouped and that a mini-revival of learning occurred under the auspices of King Alfred (871–99), the only English monarch to be accorded the accolade of 'Great'.[2]

Alfred was a dedicated supporter of the church, and under his leadership efforts were even made to translate the Scriptures into Old English. It was a

---

[1] For the details, see A. E. Redgate, *Religion, Politics and Society in Britain, 800–1066* (Abingdon: Routledge, 2014).

[2] Alfred's 'greatness' has often been exaggerated and misunderstood. He is best characterized as a good 'all-rounder' rather than as a genius in any area. As such, he attracted the admiration and loyalty of the English people without having done anything extraordinary himself. See A. Smyth, *Alfred the Great* (Oxford: Oxford University Press, 1995), for a major revision of the mythical Alfred in the light of historically verifiable fact.

sign of the king's desire to reach out beyond the elite of educated clergy who knew Latin and to catechize ordinary people in the rudiments of the faith. Alfred sponsored a translation of Gregory the Great's *Pastoral Rule*, which (as its name indicates) had the same catechetic aim in view, and under his patronage even such difficult texts as Boethius's *Consolation of Philosophy* and Augustine's *Soliloquies* were translated into accurate, if sometimes stilted, English. Alfred also encouraged a sense of Englishness by promoting an (abridged) translation of Bede's *Ecclesiastical History*, and it was in his reign that the vernacular *Anglo-Saxon Chronicle*, the major source of our knowledge of the later Anglo-Saxon period, was begun.[3] Alfred's piety has been exaggerated by his admirers but it was sincere, and there was a genuine, if somewhat limited, revival of spiritual life during his reign. Above all, Alfred survived and strengthened his kingdom, making significant expansion and development possible in the next generation.

Alfred's son Edward 'the Elder' (899–924), and even more his grandson Athelstan (924–39), were able to build on his legacy, and by the time Athelstan died England was united under a single monarch.[4] It was not the end of the Viking threat, but although there was a brief attempt in 1016 to divide the country once more between Danes and the English, it failed. For the past thousand years, England has remained a single state with its capital at London, something that was not achieved in Scotland for at least another 300 years and has never occurred in Ireland (or in Wales). Athelstan also made the shires, creating the counties that have endured, with some modifications, to the present time.[5] The church benefited from this new stability and before long was embarking on a transformation of its own. Alfred the Great had established schools to train young clergy, and the fruits of his labours became apparent in the years after Athelstan's death. Typical of the new breed of clergyman was Dunstan (909–88), who became Abbot of Glastonbury (940–56) and Archbishop of Canterbury (960–88). During his time at Glastonbury, Dunstan turned the monastery into a powerhouse of reform, training bands of young monks in the Rule of St Benedict and sending them out to found new monastic houses across England. Aethelwold, who had been one of Dunstan's colleagues at Glastonbury, became Bishop of Winchester in 963 and promptly set about reordering the cathedral along monastic lines. Within a couple of years, fifty

---

[3] The *Chronicle* survives in several different manuscripts, one of which continues to 1154. For a composite edition and translation into modern English, see M. Swanton, *The Anglo-Saxon Chronicle* (London: J. M. Dent, 1996).

[4] See S. Foot, *Athelstan: The First King of England* (New Haven, Conn.: Yale University Press, 2011).

[5] There was a major overhaul of the counties in 1974 but the ancient pattern is still largely discernible.

new monasteries had been founded under his direction, all of them following the Benedictine rule in a form that had been adapted for English use.

A third significant monastic reformer was Oswald, Bishop of Worcester (961–92) and concurrently Archbishop of York (972–92). Oswald eventually managed to turn Worcester into a monastic cathedral, but not York, which retained its secular constitution throughout the Middle Ages. Dunstan also began the process of transforming Canterbury into a monastic cathedral, but success was not achieved until 997, nearly a decade after his death. By then England was covered with monasteries that would be vastly influential in subsequent centuries. Peterborough was founded in 966, Ely in 970 (the earlier foundation having been destroyed by the Vikings), Thorney in 972, and so on.[6] What is significant about this development is that it was a concerted effort by bishops, monks and kings, all three groups working together for the restoration and expansion of the English church. There were occasional hiccoughs, it is true, like a reaction against the growing power of the monasteries that occurred after the untimely death of King Edgar in 975, but they were brief and soon overcome. The conflicts between Crown and church, and between bishops and monks, that would become common in later times were absent from the late tenth century, and the standard of episcopal appointments was remarkably high. Scholars look in vain for signs of bad or negligent bishops during these years, and several holders of the office were later canonized as saints in recognition of their outstanding holiness. It was even the case that most of the archbishops of Canterbury made the arduous and time-consuming pilgrimage to Rome in order to receive the papal pallium that was the distinct badge of their metropolitan office.[7] Such devotion to duty shows that standards were high and that for the most part those called to rule the church proved themselves to be worthy of their appointment.

It was in the time of King Edgar (959–75) that the first systematic attempts were made to regulate the church's finances. Sometime early in his reign he issued a law code ordering people to pay tithes to the church and giving detailed instructions about how this was to be done.[8] Tithing, a practice that went back to the Old Testament, had been practised from the beginning of the English church, although apparently on a voluntary basis. With Edgar we have the beginning of a pattern of church revenue that was not finally wound up

---

[6] See H. R. Loyn, *The English Church 940–1154* (Harlow: Longman, 2000), for the details.

[7] The pallium was a lambswool scarf that archbishops wore. The last archbishop of Canterbury to receive one from the pope was Thomas Cranmer in 1533.

[8] For the code issued at Andover sometime between 960 and 962, see D. Whitelock, M. Brett and C. N. L. Brooke (eds.), *Councils and Synods with Other Documents Relating to the English Church I, A. D. 871–1204*, 2 vols. (Oxford: Clarendon Press, 1981), 1:95–102.

until 1936.[9] It would become much more sophisticated and efficient in later centuries, but Edgar's code marks the transition from what was essentially a freewill offering to a tax obligation, which over time would not only transform the finances of the church but also the way in which people related to it as an institution.

Perhaps the most outstanding bishop of this period was Wulfstan (950–1023), who became Bishop of London in 996 and then of Worcester (1002–16), which he held concurrently with York (1002–23).[10] Born in the Danelaw and trained at the newly refounded abbey of Ely, Wulfstan was well placed to bridge the various fault lines that characterized the English church of his youth. He became an important counsellor to King Ethelred (978–1016) and then to the Danish King Cnut (1016–35), who gave him the platform he needed to bring widespread reform to the church. In 1014 he drafted a law code that he would later revise and issue sometime around 1020 in the name of Cnut.[11] This code gives us a detailed outline of ecclesiastical law as it stood in the early eleventh century. It covers tithes, the order of worship and the right of sanctuary in a church building, among many other things. It is the last of these that reveals to us that there were different categories of churches – great minsters, medium-sized minsters, small minsters and 'field churches'. Violation of sanctuary in the first of these would incur a fine of 5 pounds, whereas the same offence in the last three would be punished on a scale of 120, 60 and 30 shillings respectively.[12]

Wulfstan was also the author of a tract that is usually known as the *Institutes of Polity*, in which he outlined what he regarded as the daily routine of a bishop.[13] In addition to the usual emphasis on private prayer, study and the leading of public worship, Wulfstan advocated manual work as good for the soul, and said that a bishop was expected to preach the Word of God at every opportunity. In particular, bishops were to prevent unseemly behaviour and the idle gossip that so easily crept into feasts at court. The *Institutes* dealt not only with bishops but covered all eight orders of ministry in the church,

---

[9] Even then, a sixty-year period of commutation was authorized, so that the last tithe payments were made in 1996, more than 1,000 years after they were first introduced.

[10] See M. Townend (ed.), *Wulfstan, Archbishop of York: The Proceedings of the Second Alcuin Conference* (Turnhout: Brepols, 2004).

[11] For the 1014 text, see Whitelock et al., *Councils and Synods*, 1:387–402, and for that of 1020, ibid. 471–486.

[12] Ibid. 390 (sect. 5.1 of the code). This scale also reveals that the value of the shilling was less than it would become under the Normans. It appears that there were only five pence to the shilling instead of twenty, making the fine in the case of a middle-sized minster exactly half of that for a great minster.

[13] Wulfstan, *Die* Institutes of Polity, Civil and Ecclesiastical, *ein Werk Erzbischof Wulfstans von York*, ed. K. Jost, 2 vols. (Bern: Francke, 1959). There is no satisfactory modern English translation.

each of which was to be held by men who were equally dedicated to the service of God.

Wulfstan knew that there was a hierarchy of offices in the church, but regarded them all as important, because in his mind they reflected something of the biblical revelation.[14] He began at the bottom with the gatekeeper (*hostiarius*), whom he compared to the man who locked and unlocked Noah's ark (a symbol of the church), before and after the flood.[15] Next came the reader (*lector*), whom he connected to Isaiah's prophecy of the Holy Spirit.[16] After that came the exorcist, whom he compared to Jesus when he cast the seven devils out of Mary Magdalene,[17] and then the acolyte, who received the candlestick and taper from the archdeacon at his ordination as a sign that it is Christ who has brought light into the world.[18] Then came the subdeacon, whom he connected to Christ's miraculous changing of water into wine at the wedding feast of Cana,[19] the deacon, who was linked to the miracle of the loaves and fishes,[20] and the priest, who represented the sacrifice of Christ on the cross.[21] Finally there was the bishop, who imitates the risen Christ who blessed his apostles before ascending into heaven.[22] It is easy for us to see that this explanation of the church's offices is fanciful, but Wulfstan was concerned to show that every minister in the congregation reflects some aspect of the gospel and that his role, however humble it may appear to outsiders, is a calling from God to proclaim the message of eternal salvation. We would express this differently today, but can still resonate with the spirit of what Wulfstan was trying to say.[23]

By all accounts, Wulfstan lived up to his ideal of what a bishop should be, and his faithfulness gave an added weight of authority to the numerous law codes produced under his guidance, which were to remain the basis of English church law for the next century or more. The Norman Conquest of 1066 would bring considerable changes to the English church, but to a great extent they were changes that built on the foundations laid by Wulfstan and the saintly bishops of late Anglo-Saxon England.

---

[14] Ibid. 1:24.

[15] 1 Peter 3:20–21.

[16] Isa. 32:15; 61:1.

[17] Mark 16:9; Luke 8:2.

[18] John 1:9.

[19] John 2:1–11.

[20] Matt. 14:13–21; Mark 6:30–44; Luke 9:10–17.

[21] Heb. 5:1–10.

[22] Luke 24:51; Acts 1:7–8.

[23] See J. T. Lionarons, *The Homiletic Writings of Archbishop Wulfstan: A Critical Study* (Woodbridge: Boydell & Brewer, 2010).

Another important churchman and contemporary of Wulfstan was Aelfric, Bishop of Winchester (972–87) and then Abbot of Cerne (987–1004) and of Eynsham from 1004 until his death sometime after 1020.[24] Like Wulfstan, Aelfric was determined to communicate the gospel to ordinary laypeople, which meant doing it in English, not in Latin. Between them they either produced or sponsored a whole library of works, including lives of saints, commentaries on the Bible and doctrinal tracts, as well as on more secular subjects like grammar and philosophy. Particularly impressive are their sermons, which were clearly designed to stir up lethargic or complacent congregations. The collapse of the English state following the death of King Edgar and the rise of a renewed Danish threat was ascribed to the wickedness of the English, who had abandoned the worship of God for all kinds of mischief. This is Gildas all over again, although with a different foe in view. It is hard to know what to make of this material as far as judging the state of the church goes, since there is undoubtedly a large dose of homiletical hyperbole in the surviving sermons, but they at least show that the bishops were concerned not only for the clergy but for the laypeople in their care. Exaggeration is sometimes necessary to wake people up, and the fact that their homilies were preserved shows how valuable they must have been in getting ordinary worshippers to take their faith more seriously.

The achievement of these men stands out even more when we realize that it would be another four hundred years before anything similar would be attempted in the spoken tongue, and that there was nothing comparable to their activities in any other European country at that time. In the work of pastoral care England stood out both for quantity and quality, and it is a matter of regret that so little of that material, although well edited in the original versions, is available in modern English translations. The unfortunate result of that neglect is that one of the great generations of the English church has virtually disappeared from popular consciousness.

The transformation of the English church and state

King Cnut brought a much-needed stability to England and allowed men like Wulfstan to put their policies for church reform into practice. He looked back to the reign of King Edgar as a golden age and was careful to maintain ties

---

[24] See B. Thorpe (tr.), *The Homilies of the Anglo-Saxon Church*, 2 vols. (Cambridge: Cambridge University Press, 2013).

with Rome, despite the sad condition of the papacy during his reign. After his death there was an interlude (1035–42) when his two sons ruled England, but their early deaths paved the way for the restoration of the line of Alfred in the person of their half-brother, King Edward the Confessor (1042–66).[25] Edward was the son of King Ethelred and his Norman wife Emma, who later married Cnut. He was born sometime between 1002 and 1005, and spent his formative years in Norman exile, where he became familiar with Continental ways. His reign also coincided with a revival of the papacy, spearheaded by the monks of Cluny (Burgundy). The Cluniac monks had a programme for the renewal of the whole of western Christendom and were determined to use the existing church structures to achieve their aims. Edward was caught up in this, and did what he could to put their principles into practice in his kingdom. It is hard to say how successful he was, because his reforms were subsumed under the much greater changes that came after the Norman Conquest in 1066, but there are indications that he prepared the way for what was to come, and perhaps made the changes more palatable to the English than they would have been had they been introduced by the Normans. As his nickname suggests, Edward was a particularly pious king and his great legacy to us is Westminster Abbey, the church that he founded and that was to become the focal point of national religious celebrations, which it still is.[26]

After the Romans and the Anglo-Saxons, the third great invasion that was to determine the future of the British Isles was the Norman Conquest in 1066. So significant was it that the date has become the one every schoolchild knows, even if the rest of our history is largely forgotten. The Romans brought what is now England into the wider world, the Anglo-Saxons ensured that lowland Britain would be Germanic-speaking, with a Celtic fringe around the edges and in Ireland, and the Norman Conquest set the seal on patterns of society and government that have endured to the present. Similarly, the Christian church, which first appeared under the Romans, was transformed by the Celts and Anglo-Saxons and then structured by the Normans in ways that have likewise been enduring. But where the Romans and Anglo-Saxons never got much further than what is now England, the Normans eventually penetrated to the far ends of the islands, establishing themselves first in Wales and Ireland, and then in much of Scotland, ensuring that a cultural unity and continuity

---

[25] See F. Barlow, *Edward the Confessor* (Berkeley and Los Angeles, Calif.: University of California Press, 1970), for the best modern study of this king and his reign.

[26] See D. Cannadine (ed.), *Westminster Abbey: A Church in History* (London: Paul Mellon Centre and Yale University Press, 2019).

would bind the four diverse nations together and create the wider British world we know today.

When Edward the Confessor died at the beginning of 1066, it was unclear who should succeed him. In the absence of an obvious candidate an ambitious nobleman, Harold Godwineson, who was related to Edward by marriage, seized the throne and secured the allegiance of the nobility.[27] Harold soon had to face attacks, one from Scandinavian rivals who invaded the country from the east, and the other from William, Duke of Normandy, who believed that his claim to the English throne was as strong as, if not stronger than, anyone else's. William sought the support of the papacy before setting out on his expedition to England and received it, perhaps because other Normans were invading Sicily and southern Italy at the same time and the pope did not want to give them an excuse for turning on Rome. In return for his support the pope asked William to introduce the Cluniac reforms into the English church, which William agreed to do. Chief among these was the 'separation' of church and state. To modern ears this sounds like a strengthening of the state at the expense of the church, but in medieval times it was the opposite. Most states were small and weak, but the church was universal and commanded the allegiance of the entire population of western Europe, which made it potentially far more powerful than the state.[28]

In Anglo-Saxon England, bishops often sat in the king's councils and served as judges in the courts, alongside the courtiers who specialized in the law. They all judged cases indiscriminately, since there was no clear demarcation between secular and ecclesiastical laws. The Cluniac reformers who had taken over the papacy wanted to separate the two jurisdictions. As they saw it, the clergy (including monks and nuns) formed an autonomous estate of the realm that was entitled to its own laws and judicial system. Those who belonged to this estate were 'spiritual persons' who could be judged only by their peers. In other words the clergy administered their own laws to their own people, independently of the king's courts. It was once claimed that William effected this reform in an ordinance of 1072, but that has now been shown to be an exaggeration. What he did was to forbid the bishops from hearing cases brought against them (or the church in general) in the hundred courts, where secular justice was administered in the localities.[29] In fact it appears that William's decree

---

[27] Harold was the founder of Waltham Abbey, where he was supposedly buried after his death at the Battle of Hastings in 1066.

[28] For the details of the papal reforms and their impact on England, see H. Mayr-Harting, *Religion, Politics and Society in Britain 1066–1272* (Harlow: Pearson, 2011), 22–28; Z. N. Brooke, *The English Church and the Papacy from the Conquest to the Reign of John*, 2nd edn (Cambridge: Cambridge University Press, 1989).

[29] A hundred is a unit of land larger than a parish but much smaller than a county.

was only partially effective, not least because the church did not yet have a functioning system of courts capable of handling the business that would be coming their way. The issue resurfaced in the following century, as church and state battled it out for jurisdiction over a wide range of issues, but by then a workable system of church courts was being set up and an effective separation of church and state became possible. In the short term the church won, and its courts and legal system were recognized as being separate from those of the king, but in the longer run it was to be the secular state that would prevail. Modern people can ignore the church if they wish, but not the state, which claims authority over them whether they like it or not.

At its root the conflict between church and state was bound up with the definition of a Christian society, to which both sides in principle subscribed. Membership in this society was determined not by birth but by baptism. Those who were not baptized, like Jews for example, were aliens and lacked any sort of civil rights or recognition. Jews were never numerous in Britain but they were there, and often occupied an important place in trade and banking, as they did elsewhere in Europe. But when King Edward I decided, as an act of piety, to expel them from the country in 1290, they had no recourse. Out they went, leaving only a few place names as evidence of their former presence, and they were not to be readmitted – in very different circumstances – until 1656. The real question that faced medieval society was the need to decide what the status of the church and its full-time 'spiritual persons' was in relation to the rest. They were not aliens like the Jews, and therefore they were subject to the king and his laws. But they were a special corporation with their own rules that were quite different from those of the general public. To what extent did this entitle them to govern themselves?

The church did not want to be tied down to the dictates of secular rulers, not least because the latter were local whereas it was universal – at least within the limits of western Europe. It its view, kings were members of the church charged with the responsibility of governing the temporal aspects of society – property rights, warfare and so on. Kings ruled *Dei gratia* (by the grace of God), as the present queen still does. The kings accepted that, but did not believe that the grace of God meant submission to the pope or his representatives. Initially the church tried to enforce its view by establishing the rite of coronation. From 973 onwards, every legitimate ruler had to be crowned by the Archbishop of Canterbury (or equivalent), and his reign did not begin until then. As time went on however, it was accepted that a king acceded to the throne the moment his predecessor died, so that there would be no hiatus in government. The coronation ceremony then ceased to have any legal significance but it remained a powerful indicator of legitimacy in the popular mind. An 'uncrowned king' was possible but not desirable – a situation that still prevails – and the coronation was (and is) largely a religious ceremony.[30]

But if the kings ruled by the grace of God, then that grace was sufficient to give them full authority within their proper sphere, or so they claimed. In other words the clergy and the church as an institution were both subject to the laws of the state in so far as those laws determined matters that were within the state's competence. The kings could not ordain clergy or decide questions of theological doctrine, but if a priest committed a crime was he immune to royal justice? What did 'trial by one's peers' mean in the case of a priest or a monk? Could the church claim a kind of diplomatic immunity for its staff and try them in its own courts instead?

The difference between the king's courts and those of the church may seem unimportant to us, but it was highly significant because the legal systems under which the two jurisdictions operated were quite different.[31] The king's courts functioned under what we now call 'common law', a system based on precedent and on the all-important assumption that a man is innocent until proved guilty. The church courts, on the other hand, operated under a modified form of Roman law, which had been codified by the emperor Justinian I in the sixth century. According to that system, cases were decided by legal maxims that could be interpreted in different ways but that did not accept precedent as an overriding legal principle. It was also the case that a person accused was guilty until proved innocent, which sounds very unfair to us. There were numerous other differences between the two systems that produced different outcomes and made one seem better or worse than the other. Living with two sometimes incompatible legal systems was not easy, and in the end a compromise had to be found. What happened was that certain matters, largely connected to what we now call 'family law', were reserved for the church courts. In particular this meant that questions relating to marriage, divorce and inheritance were regarded as ecclesiastical matters, and were judged accordingly. On the other hand property and criminal cases were secular questions, and the king's courts handled them.

Laymen and clergy could be summoned before either type of court, but in the nature of things it was more common for laypeople to have to deal with

---

[30] See H. Everett, P. Bradshaw and C. Buchanan, *Coronations Past, Present and Future*, Alcuin Club and The Group for Renewal of Worship Joint Liturgical Studies 38 (Cambridge: Grove Books, 1997).

[31] For the history, see R. H. Helmholz, *The Oxford History of the Laws of England*, vol. 1: *The Canon Law and Ecclesiastical Jurisdiction from 597 to the 1640s* (Oxford: Oxford University Press, 2004).

ecclesiastical courts than for clergy to be summoned to the secular ones. However, the clergy would be treated differently in the king's courts if they could prove that they were in holy orders. Since the clergy were assumed to be literate in ways that laypeople usually were not, it was thought sufficient to ask whether they could sign their own name as proof of their status. If they could, they were granted 'benefit of clergy', which assured them of a more favourable hearing in the king's courts and better treatment generally. At a time when punishments often included bodily mutilation and people were sentenced to death for relatively minor crimes, 'benefit of clergy' was no small matter. The church objected to what it believed were the barbaric penalties of secular courts, which it was powerless to alter, but at least it did what it could to protect its own clergy from the negative effects of royal justice.

Having said that, 'benefit of clergy' was to have a long and inglorious history in England. Because of its perceived leniency, it was soon being abused on a massive scale, as laymen who could barely read and write were persuaded to claim their 'clergy', whether they were ordained or not. It could even be applied to laywomen, which was a clear abuse of the original intention, but so tenacious was its hold that it was not abolished until 1827. As long as it survived there was a legal distinction between clergy and laypeople that did much to shape popular consciousness of what the 'church' was, a consciousness that has still not disappeared. Wrong though they are, many people think that the 'church' is a body of religious professionals that a layperson can 'enter' by being ordained. The notion that everyone who is baptized has a claim to be a member of the church has simply not entered their minds.

In some respects the Norman Conquest acted as a catalyst for developments already taking place but whose importance had not been properly appreciated in late Anglo-Saxon times. One of these was the great expansion of monasteries and religious houses in general. After the Viking depredations of the ninth century, both English and Celtic monasticism went into decline, but after the unification of England in the reign of Athelstan this situation began to change. The monasteries that were then revived all followed the rule laid down in the sixth century by Benedict of Nursia. But by about 1100 there was increasing discontent across Europe with what was perceived as their growing worldliness, and various reform movements began to make themselves felt. Before long they were establishing themselves in Britain and Ireland and soon overtook the Benedictines in size and importance.[32] For the most part they originated in

---

[32] See D. Knowles and R. N. Hadcock, *Medieval Religious Houses: England and Wales*, 2nd edn (London: Longman, 1971). For the heads of these houses, see D. Knowles, C. N. L. Brooke and V. C. M. London (eds.), *The Heads of Religious Houses: England and Wales, I. 940–1216*, 2nd edn (Cambridge: Cambridge

what is now France – the Cluniacs in Cluny (Burgundy), the Cistercians in Cîteaux (Burgundy), the Carthusians in Chartreuse (near Grenoble) and the Premonstratensians in Prémontré (near Laon). There were also the Augustinian canons, who claimed a tenuous link with Augustine of Hippo (354–430) and followed his rule.

All of these new orders established themselves in the British Isles, but particular importance must be given to the Cistercians and the Augustinian canons. Founded in 1098, the Cistercians dedicated themselves to the cultivation of an inner spirituality that stood in sharp contrast to the liturgical splendour that had come to characterize so many Benedictine houses. They also had a strong sense of vocation, which manifested itself both in the way in which they developed their community life and the concern that they had to reach out to the wider world. They were soon expanding at an enormous rate and reached England in 1129, where their impact was soon felt. Some of the most majestic monastic ruins in the country today are of Cistercian foundations, notably Fountains and Rievaulx abbeys, both in Yorkshire. The popularity of the Cistercians was greatly influenced by Bernard of Clairvaux (1090–1153), who soon became their most prominent member. Bernard, recognized as one of the great spiritual leaders of western Europe in his own lifetime, has exercised an enormous influence ever since, not least on the Protestant Reformers, who regarded him as one of their forebears. This impression has been confirmed in recent years by Henry Mayr-Harting, who has written:

> the Cistercians were the Protestants of the twelfth century. Everything we have said about them – the interiority of their religion, the stress on vocation to salvation and vocation in this world too, the saving of time in the over-elaborate liturgy in order to accumulate wealth by working in their fields, and much else besides, all fit perfectly to the Protestant Ethic as famously described by Max Weber. The moral conditionality which they attached to the exercise of papal and episcopal authority . . . was part of this 'Protestantism'.[33]

(note 32 *cont.*) University Press, 2001); D. M. Smith and V. C. M. London (eds.), *The Heads of Religious Houses: England and Wales II. 1216–1377* (Cambridge: Cambridge University Press, 2001); D. M. Smith, *The Heads of Religious Houses: England and Wales III. 1377–1540* (Cambridge: Cambridge University Press, 2008).

[33] Mayr-Harting, *Religion, Politics and Society*, 150. He refers to Max Weber, *The Protestant Ethic and the Spirit of Capitalism* (Oxford: Oxford University Press, 2010). Originally published in German in 1905, the book was first translated into English in 1930.

The Augustinian canons traced their origins to the papal reforms of the late eleventh century, and their popularity in England was aided by the patronage of Henry I, who installed them in the newly formed cathedral of Carlisle in 1133. Another important centre was St Frideswide's in Oxford, a minster church that became Augustinian in 1122. St Frideswide's soon had a number of dependent churches in the city, including St Aldate's and St Ebbe's, which still reflect the evangelistic impulses that drove the Augustinians in their early days. In the sixteenth century St Frideswide's was converted into a university college, now known as Christ Church, which also serves as the cathedral for the diocese of Oxford, created in 1542.

The only major order of English provenance was the one established by Gilbert of Sempringham (c.1083–1190), who lived to be well over 100 years old and who, uniquely, established houses in which men and women lived alongside each other. Gilbert's initiative stands out and reminds us that England was in some ways more accepting of women working in ministry together with men than other countries in Europe were. There were also religious houses reserved for women, although they were always poorer and fewer in number than those for men. The evidence of church councils suggests that nuns were frequently the victims of sexual abuse, usually from laymen who did not respect the nuns' vocation, but the kings did what they could to counteract this. They were particularly keen to protect widows and women who had deliberately chosen the monastic life, often in defiance of relatives who wanted them to marry. Generally speaking, in medieval society they were more restricted than men, but in the context of the time had an unusual degree of freedom and were often able to live remarkably independent lives.[34]

At first the Norman Conquest did not affect the church in England because its Anglo-Saxon bishops and clergy remained in place, but that situation did not last long.[35] There was resistance to the Normans among the defeated English, and the church hierarchy was suspected, rightly or wrongly, of aiding and abetting it. In 1070 the Anglo-Saxon Archbishop of Canterbury was replaced by Lanfranc, the Abbot of Bec in Normandy, and a thorough reorganization of the church was set in train. No more English bishops were appointed, and the future abbots of the leading monasteries were also foreigners. To some extent this transfer of power was mitigated by continuities here and there. London had had a Norman bishop, William, since 1051 and he made use of the Conquest to extend the reach and riches of his diocese. At the

---

[34] See Redgate, *Religion, Politics and Society*, 159–168.
[35] See Mayr-Harting, *Religion, Politics and Society*.

other end of the spectrum, Wulfstan of Worcester, who had been consecrated in 1062, retained his see until his death in 1095, and his patience with the Normans was eventually rewarded by his canonization as a saint (1203).

The high quality and relative longevity of the Norman bishops also made them more acceptable to the English than they might otherwise have been. An example of this was Bishop Gundulf of Rochester (1077–1108), a Norman who showed respect for Anglo-Saxon traditions and established a fraternity at his cathedral that embraced both nations. It is significant that a large number of those who contributed to the establishment of this fraternity were English, a sure sign that they accepted the new Establishment and were in turn accepted by it.[36] The Normans initially tended to look down on the Anglo-Saxons as country bumpkins, but that attitude soon changed. By 1100 Anglo-Saxon saints were being honoured with new church and abbey dedications like Bury St Edmunds, named after a king of East Anglia who had been martyred on 20 November 869 for refusing to abjure his faith when he had been defeated by Viking invaders. Histories of the church of England were commissioned with the express aim of continuing the narrative of Bede. It would be some centuries before the two nations would merge into one, but even in the second generation, it was the Normans who were calling themselves English, not the other way around.

In 1070 a dispute over primacy erupted between Canterbury and York when Lanfranc insisted that the newly appointed archbishop of the northern province had to swear allegiance to Lanfranc, who was his superior, a view that was confirmed at a council held in Winchester on 8 April 1072. It was not the end of the dispute however, which resurfaced from time to time over the next century or more.[37] In the end the Archbishop of York was recognized as 'primate of England' while his Canterbury colleague was to be 'primate of all England', a decision that has been maintained to the present time.[38] A few new dioceses had been created in late Anglo-Saxon times, but from 1050 onwards they were either dissolved or transferred to different sites. The Normans speeded up this process and even created two new dioceses, as seen at the bottom of Table 3.1.[39]

It will be seen from this list that there was a definite trend towards the creation of monastic cathedrals after the Norman Conquest; but strong as this trend was, it never became universal. Several of the larger and more important

---

[36] Loyn, *English Church*, 78–79.
[37] For the details, see Mayr-Harting, *Religion, Politics and Society*, 29–31, 56–65.
[38] For the dispute, see Whitelock et al., *Councils and Synods*, 2:586–607.
[39] Sees that no longer exist are in italics. Monastic cathedrals are marked with an asterisk (*).

Table 3.1 English dioceses, AD 883–1133

Year founded	Diocese	Year dissolved/transferred
883	*Chester-le-Street*	(transferred to Durham, 995)
909	*Crediton*	(transferred to Exeter, 1050)
909	*Ramsbury*	1058
909	Wells	(joined to Bath, 1090)
995	Durham*	(monastic from 1083)
1050	Exeter	(transferred from Crediton)
1067	Lincoln	(transferred from Dorchester)
1075	Chichester	(transferred from Selsey)
1078	Salisbury	(transferred from Sherborne)
1085	*Chester*	(transferred to Coventry, 1102)
1088	Bath*	(with Wells)
1094	Norwich*	(monastic from about 1100)
1102	Coventry*	(with Lichfield)
1109	Ely*	(new diocese)
1133	Carlisle*	(new diocese)

cathedrals remained secular in their constitution, with an Establishment that functioned according to statutes that had been crafted for them. Such cathedrals were headed by a dean (as opposed to the prior in the monastic ones), who was supported by a series of dignitaries – the subdean, the chancellor, who took care of legal matters, the precentor, who organized music and worship, the treasurer and at least one archdeacon.

Within a cathedral, ministerial functions were performed by a college of canons. In monastic establishments these canons were monks, as were the dignitaries, and they functioned according to the rules of their monastic order. Secular cathedrals were more complicated. Their revenues were not held in common, as they were in the monastic ones, but apportioned to the clergy associated with the cathedral. Each of these received a grant of land (or other revenue) associated with a particular parish within the diocese. This grant was called a 'prebend' and its holder was a 'prebendary'. There could also be canons who did not have a prebend, and there was a further division between those who were residentiary and those who were not. In contrast to the monastic cathedrals, where everyone who served in them was essentially equal, the secular cathedral establishments contained gross inequalities of income. The prebendaries were almost always better off than other canons because they had a designated source of income, but some prebends were far more lucrative than others. It was by no means uncommon for a dignitary to hold a prebend in addition to his office, and a few were even wealthier than some bishops. Furthermore, once a man was appointed to a prebend, it was virtually impossible to remove him and absenteeism could easily become a major problem. In later times this pattern was regularized to some extent, as university lecturers and senior civil servants might be given a prebend as their chief source of income, with little or no expectation that they would ever serve in the cathedral itself. In this way the excess wealth of the cathedrals was put to other uses, but at the same time the nature and purpose of the cathedrals was obscured and their complex finances became targets for accusations of corruption.[40]

The advantage of the prebendal system for the cathedral was that it anchored the prebend in the diocese, since each prebendary had a direct relationship with the parish in which his prebend was located. It was also a way of gaining the support of important people outside the diocese, who could receive the gift of a prebend in the expectation that they would then support the interests of the cathedral in the wider church. So entrenched did the system become that it survived for centuries and was not wound down until 1840, when future appointments became merely honorary. As a result, although prebendaries still exist, they no longer receive any revenue from their prebends, which are merely symbolic reminders of the way things used to be.

The parish system

While all this was going on, further changes were coming to church government in England that would gradually seep into the Celtic borderlands as well. For some time the churches of western Christendom had been developing a parish system, by which villages and localities were grouped into units around local churches. These churches were the focal points of their respective communities and served to identify them to the wider world. There is some evidence that this process was occurring in Britain, especially in Anglo-Saxon England, as early as the tenth century, but it was not comprehensively organized.[41] Normandy was further advanced in this respect, and it seems that the Normans transported their system to England during the course of the twelfth century, from where it spread fairly quickly to Scotland and Wales.[42]

---

[40] See E. U. Crosby, *Bishop and Chapter in Twelfth-Century England: A Study of the* Mensa Episcopalis (Cambridge: Cambridge University Press, 1994).

[41] Redgate, *Religion, Politics and Society*, 108–111.

[42] See M. Aubrun, *La paroisse en France des origines au XVe siècle* (Paris: Picard, 1988). On its development in England, see N. J. G. Pounds, *A History of the English Parish* (Cambridge: Cambridge University Press, 2000).

Britain was gradually subdivided into manageable areas and, where they had not existed before, churches were built to serve their populations. In theory everyone ought to have been able to attend weekly worship on foot, although this ideal was not fully realized in the hillier and less populated regions of the north and west. How parish boundaries were demarcated is unclear, and there were frequent disputes over the details. The only way these could effectively be resolved was by claiming possession, and so parishes developed the practice of 'beating the bounds' every year to make sure their boundaries were respected.[43]

Two different traditions contributed to the formation of the parish network. The first was the minster church pattern, whereby a mother church was responsible for a number of dependencies in the surrounding area. As these daughter churches matured, they were often separated from the mother church and erected into parishes of their own. The other tradition was represented by what we now call the 'manorial' church. Landowners were encouraged to build churches on their properties and to endow them as best they could. The landowners were then recognized as 'patrons' of these churches and obtained the right to present to the bishop the priest whom they wanted to serve them. This right was called the 'advowson' (*advocatio* in Latin), and it still exists in the Church of England. In some cases the bishop himself, or members of the cathedral chapters, would build a church, and when that happened, they would become the holders of the advowson. It is important to understand that advowsons were regarded as private property that could be bought and sold quite independently of church control. The sale of advowsons was stopped in 1925, but they can still be given away, and in recent years many private patrons have surrendered their rights to the local bishop or to a church society that undertakes to fulfil the duties of a patron. There is a wide range of these, with only about a third of the total number of advowsons being in the bishop's hands. The rest are held by the Crown, by universities and colleges (especially Oxford and Cambridge), by a number of other dignitaries like the Lord Chancellor and by private individuals. Patronage is now coordinated and supervised by the dioceses to a degree that was previously unknown, but private patrons still play an important role, and in the case of church societies have often stamped their own image on the parishes in question.

The appointment and service of parish priests in the earliest phase of their existence are hard to determine. Parishes that belonged to monasteries would

---

[43] This habit still persists in some places, although it no longer has any legal significance.

be supplied by them, although not necessarily with monks. Private patrons could nominate anyone they liked, subject to the bishop's approval, which would normally be given to any qualified candidate. What the priests did is hard to determine. Obviously they conducted worship and officiated at the rites of passage – baptism, marriage and burial – but how far they were involved in other matters, like education or the writing of wills, is impossible to say. Many were married and fully integrated into their local village community, but celibacy was increasingly encouraged and became compulsory after the First Lateran Council in 1123. How long it took for that to become the norm we do not know, although the trend was certainly towards greater strictness. It is fair to say that by 1150 celibacy had become the expected standard, although concubinage continued and was not finally eliminated until clerical marriage was made legal again in 1549.

One aspect of the parish system that is easy to overlook is the impetus it gave to the building of churches. There had of course been numerous church buildings in Anglo-Saxon times, ranging from simple country chapels to a few magnificent urban basilicas, but the Normans tore most of these down and built afresh. The great age of cathedral building was still to come, but Durham made an impressive start and there was a veritable explosion at parish level in the early twelfth century. With rare exceptions, these Norman churches are the oldest intact places of worship in the British Isles and, although many have been extended and repaired over the centuries, they remain a silent but eloquent witness to the piety and enthusiasm of the immediate post-Conquest generations.

The parish system, designed to provide pastoral care to the entire country, was remarkably successful. There were however some places that got over-looked because nobody wanted them – swamps, thick forests and scrubland. These 'extra-parochial areas', as they came to be called, were not numerous but they played a significant part in medieval English society, because those who lived there (or who took refuge in them) escaped the heavy hand of the law. By far the best known of these areas is Sherwood Forest, bolt hole of the legendary Robin Hood, the tales of whom describe life in medieval England in much the same way as the Arthurian legends convey to us the spirit of late Roman Britain. In both cases impressions matter more than facts and, if properly understood, tell us much about a society that is otherwise hidden from our eyes. From the administrative point of view they were a headache, since the king's writ did not run in them, taxes were not collected there and even the church passed them by. But for the free-spirited, the unfortunate and the misfits in an increasingly ordered state they were a breath of fresh air, a refuge where the freedom (or anarchy) of an earlier age was allowed to continue unchecked. That freedom has long since disappeared of course, but extra-parochial areas still exist and remind us of a time when it was possible to escape the constraints of an ordered society without leaving the country.

The emergence of the parish system was facilitated by other developments that were to have long-term consequences. One was the subdivision of dioceses into archdeaconries. Archdeacons had existed in Anglo-Saxon times, although they do not seem to have functioned much outside the bishop's immediate circle. The Normans changed that by appointing them as administrators of the dioceses – the 'eyes and ears' of the bishops, as they came to be known. It was the archdeacons who supervised the parish clergy, made sure that the churches were kept in good repair and even examined candidates for ordination – all in the name of the bishop. For the most part, archdeaconries were designed to coincide with counties and were named after them. Every diocese had at least one, but the larger ones could have four or five and Lincoln, the largest diocese of them all, had no fewer than eight. Archdeaconries became mini-dioceses in their own right, and it is significant that when a new diocese was created it was by detaching an archdeaconry from an existing one. Thus the Lincoln archdeaconry of Cambridge became the diocese of Ely in 1109, and the great reordering that occurred in 1540 proceeded along the same lines.

Another development was the emergence of collegiate churches in different parts of the country. Some of these were minster churches that did not become ordinary parishes, but others were new creations that resembled both the minsters and the non-monastic (secular) cathedrals. They were staffed by a number of clergy, who constituted the 'college', and the revenues were divided among them. Each collegiate church had its own way of doing that and some became the centres of extensive networks of parishes under their care. They had remarkable powers of survival, and most of them did not disappear until the great reforms of the 1840s and 1850s, when they were finally reduced to the status of ordinary parishes.

Another feature of the Norman church was the establishment of 'rural deaneries', sometimes known as 'deaneries of Christianity', a word that was used to mean the generality of church members. These were small groupings of parishes, headed by a rural dean, who was usually the incumbent of one of them, which oversaw the implementation of administrative measures at local level and tried to maintain existing church buildings and the services conducted in them in good order. Rural deaneries appear to have faded out in the later Middle Ages and we know little about them. They were however revived in the nineteenth century and now play an important part in the administrative framework of the Church of England.[44]

The parish system also made it easier for the so-called 'peculiar' jurisdictions to expand. Very often bishops would acquire parishes in other dioceses and then claim a kind of extra-territoriality for them. One such peculiar belonged to the Archbishop of Canterbury and was based at the church of St Mary-le-Bow in the City of London. Because of that, it came to be known as the Deanery of the Arches (bow = arch), and over time its dean became the archbishop's principal legal officer.[45] This arrangement was formalized in the early sixteenth century and remains in place, so that the Dean of the Arches still presides over the ecclesiastical courts that (after having been displaced for many centuries) once again meet in the crypt of St Mary-le-Bow church.[46]

In the northern province rivalry between York and Durham created a kind of competition for peculiars in the other diocese, a competition that most people would agree was won by Durham. Large tracts of Yorkshire, centred on Northallerton and Howden in particular, were alienated from the diocese and run as semi-independent fiefs, which had their own separate representation in the provincial synod (convocation). Even the single parish of Crayke was effectively filched by Durham from York, apparently because it was a convenient staging post on the bishop's frequent journeys to London! The York–Durham rivalry was important because the northern province had only three dioceses (the third one being the much smaller and poorer Carlisle) and was therefore effectively riven in two. Every time a provincial synod was held, the Durham delegation would protest that it was not subject to it (although in practice it was), a tradition that was not abolished until 1862. One long-running dispute involved control of the revenues of the see of Durham during vacancies between bishops. The Prior (later Dean) and Chapter of Durham claimed these, but so did the Archbishop of York. In practice it was the chapter that administered them but the archbishop always protested his claimed right. This dispute became the longest-running one in church history until it was finally resolved in the year 2000 – by removing the claims of the dean and chapter and vesting the right in the archbishop, although he had never previously exercised it.[47]

---

[44] In some urban dioceses they are now known as 'area deaneries', but the principle is the same.

[45] F. D. Logan, *The Medieval Court of Arches*, Canterbury and York Society, vol. 95 (Woodbridge: Boydell & Brewer, 2005).

[46] M. Hill, *Ecclesiastical Law*, 4th edn (Oxford: Oxford University Press, 2018), 44–45.

[47] For the history of this controversy, see B. Till, *York Against Durham: The Guardianship of the Spiritualities in the Diocese of Durham*, Sede Vacante, Borthwick Papers 84 (York: Borthwick Institute, 1993).

Wales

It was in the course of the twelfth century that the four Welsh dioceses (St David's, Llandaff, Bangor and St Asaph) were reorganized and attached more firmly to England than they had been before. Wales was not at that time part of England, but its church was in the province of Canterbury and because of that the four Welsh bishops represented the country in the English Parliament for centuries before the country was turned into shires and integrated into England (1536). Attempts were periodically made to make the Welsh bishops and cathedrals as 'English' as possible but, as in Ireland and Scotland, the Celtic tradition was very strong and prevented wholesale assimilation. Before the arrival of the Normans, the most important churches in Wales had resembled the minster churches of England, but were known as *clas* churches, from a Welsh word (probably derived from the Latin *classis*) that meant 'community' or 'gathering'. These churches were usually controlled by a small group of people who resembled a kind of guild that passed responsibilities on from one generation to the next. The introduction of Anglo-Norman ways threatened this pattern and broke the stranglehold that the *claswyr* (clas-men) had on the churches. This happened first in St David's, but the change was incomplete and the cathedral did not acquire a dean until 1831! Llandaff resisted the longest, losing its *clas* only towards the end of the thirteenth century. There was also a tendency in Wales for the canons of the cathedrals to share out the revenues among them, rather than to establish prebends with a fixed income that could vary enormously from one to the other. In this way the Welsh church remained more 'egalitarian' and retained a pattern that had prevailed among the Celts in pre-Norman times.

The medieval Welsh dioceses are shown in Table 3.2. There were no further creations until after disestablishment in 1920.[48]

Table 3.2 The medieval Welsh dioceses

Year (re)founded	Diocese
1092	Bangor
1107	Llandaff
1115	St David's
1143	St Asaph

[48] The diocese of Monmouth was created out of Llandaff (1921), and that of Swansea and Brecon out of St David's (1923).

Ireland

Meanwhile a parallel development was taking place in Ireland. The church there, organized along traditional tribal lines, was difficult to keep in order. Monasteries played a more central role than they did elsewhere, and bishops often lived in or around them. Occasionally they doubled as abbots, making it difficult to know how far the episcopate was independent of monastic norms. Our understanding of the situation is complicated by the fact that the surviving evidence tends to stress the spiritual quality required of the bishops, abbots and monks rather than give any detailed instructions as to how the church should be organized and administered. This was probably because there was a flexibility in Ireland that either did not exist elsewhere or was being stamped out in favour of greater standardization. For example, Irish monasteries could be left in the charge of so-called 'coarbs' or 'erenachs', who might be laymen whose authority rested on their claim to be the inheritors of the saints who had founded the monasteries in the first place.[49] The offices of coarb and erenach were often hereditary, and given to men who were deeply rooted in their local communities, making it difficult to regulate them from outside. There is no evidence that these positions were abused by their holders, but the system was unfamiliar outside Ireland and therefore bound to be suspect in the eyes of reformers who wanted the church there to be more firmly integrated into western Christendom. The dilemma the Irish church faced was that the features which connected it most closely to the people it was called to serve were often the ones the most dedicated churchmen were trying to eliminate. Which of these two forces would prove to be the stronger was one of the great questions of Irish history for the rest of the Middle Ages and beyond.

Unfortunately our knowledge of the period between the conversion of Ireland and the beginning of the second millennium is patchy and we are overly reliant on what later generations had to say about these hidden centuries. That tends to be negative since those who commented on them were seeking comprehensive reform and therefore had a vested interest in portraying the Viking era as a time of both spiritual and institutional decline. There were undoubtedly losses here and there, but the church seems to have come out of this period in a healthier state than later reformers were inclined

---

[49] The word coarb comes from Irish *comarba* (heir of a saint); erenach is a corruption of *airchinnech* (church leader). They were not necessarily interchangeable, but the flexibility of Irish church order makes it impossible to distinguish them in any consistent way. See C. Downham, *Medieval Ireland* (Cambridge: Cambridge University Press, 2018), 132. At least one coarb still survives on the island of Lismore (Scotland), where the local laird is recognized as the inheritor of the ancient monastery of St Moluag, which was dissolved at the Reformation.

to admit.[50] What is clear is that by the time of the Norman Conquest of England, there were stirrings in Ireland that would lead the church there to seek closer ties with the outside world, and therefore integration into an ecclesiastical system that had evolved a long way since the time of Columba. The first datable indication of change came in 1074, when the Dublin clergy asked Lanfranc, Archbishop of Canterbury, to consecrate their bishop-elect, Patrick. Lanfranc did so and strengthened a link between Ireland and Canterbury that would last for half a century and linger in the memory long after that. All parties to the events of 1074 agreed that the Canterbury connection had been established at some point in the past, but they did not specify when that had been. The best guess is that Patrick's predecessor, a man called Dunan (Donatus), was consecrated at Canterbury as the first Bishop of Dublin sometime after 1028, the year when Sitric, the Norse king of the city, visited Rome, but there is no solid evidence for this.

Bishop Patrick had been a monk of Worcester, and his successor, Donngus (1085–95), was even then living as a monk with Lanfranc, who used this Irish connection to boost his claim to be primate of the whole of Britain and Ireland. In that context Dublin provided a useful excuse for Canterbury to claim primacy over York, a claim that was more immediately enforceable, but the potential importance of the link between Canterbury and Dublin should not be underestimated. Both Lanfranc and his successor, Anselm, did what they could to tighten discipline in the Irish church, particularly with respect to what they saw as its rather lax approach to marriage. Irishmen apparently divorced their wives and remarried more or less at will, with no reference to the church, where there was endemic corruption in the appointment of bishops and even in the ordination of the lower clergy, who were buying their way into the ordained ministry.[51] Clerical celibacy was still not the rule anywhere in western Europe but, given the deeply monastic structures of the Irish church, higher standards in this area might have been expected. Instead the Irish clergy frequently married and calls for celibacy were ignored, even long after it had become the canonical norm elsewhere.

The offending details might well have been exaggerated and the abuses complained of were probably less frequent than our knowledge of them suggests, but they were felt nonetheless and the pressure for greater discipline could not long be resisted. In 1101 a council was held at Cashel that is generally regarded as the first major step in that direction. The council issued canons

---

[50] See Downham, *Medieval Ireland*, 138–144.

[51] See J. Watt, *The Church in Medieval Ireland* (Dublin: University College Dublin Press, 1998), 5–7, for an example of a letter that Lanfranc sent to Turlough O'Brien, King of Munster, in 1074.

that attempted to get the Irish church to conform with the rest of western Christendom on matters like clerical celibacy and lay marriage, but with limited success.[52] One interesting point about it is that the local bishop, Maol Muire O Dúnáin, presided not only in his capacity as the chief bishop of Munster but also as papal legate, a clear indication that Ireland was at last entering the wider church at a time when major reforms were taking place all over Europe.[53]

The Council of Cashel was only a beginning of course – traditional habits could not easily be uprooted and Irish marriage customs remained sufficiently eccentric as to merit comment from outsiders right through the medieval period. Some progress was made however, in that a move to insist that abbots of monasteries ought to be celibate priests was successful in ensuring that Celsus, the hereditary abbot of Armagh and recognized successor of St Patrick, was forced to remain celibate when he was consecrated as chief bishop of Armagh in 1106. Soon afterwards there was a similar success in the consecration of the Anglo-Norman Gilbert as the first Bishop of Limerick. Gilbert succeeded Bishop O Dúnáin as papal legate, and in that capacity presided over the Synod of Ráith Bressail in 1111, which marked a new and important stage in the reform of the Irish church.[54]

The Synod of Ráith Bressail created a territorial church organization in Ireland along the same lines that Gregory the Great had originally envisaged for England. There were to be two provinces, Armagh in the north and Cashel in the south, each with twelve dioceses. Soon after this, Ireland witnessed a significant revival of monasticism that is closely associated with the name of Malachy (1094–1148). Born into a church family in Armagh, Malachy seems to have been destined for an ecclesiastical career from an early age. He came under the influence of Irish monks who saw that the church needed serious reform, and as soon as he got the opportunity he introduced Roman customs into the church at Armagh, including a sung liturgy and the regular practice of confirmation and penance. In 1123 he became Abbot of the still unreformed monastery of Bangor (County Down), and a year later was consecrated as Bishop of Connor. His attempts to introduce reforms in both the monastery

---

[52] For the text in both Irish and English, see G. L. Bray (ed.), *Records of Convocation*, 20 vols. (Woodbridge: Boydell & Brewer, 2005–6), 16:79–81.

[53] On the Irish church in the twelfth century, see A. Gwynn, *The Irish Church in the Eleventh and Twelfth Centuries* (Dublin: Four Courts Press, 1992); M. T. Flanagan, *The Transformation of the Irish Church in the Twelfth Century* (Woodbridge: Boydell Press, 2010). For the church in the Irish Middle Ages in general, see Watt, *Church in Medieval Ireland*; K. W. Nicholls, *Gaelic and Gaelicized Ireland in the Middle Ages*, 2nd edn (Dublin: Lilliput Press, 2003), 105–130.

[54] An English translation of the records of this council can be found in Bray, *Records of Convocation*, 16:81–84.

and the diocese met with opposition however, and by 1127 he was a refugee in Lismore, where he was able to gain the support of the local aristocracy. In 1132 he was consecrated Archbishop of Armagh but his plans for reform were frustrated and he soon resigned, choosing the less prominent see of Down instead. This gave him the freedom to travel, and in 1139 he went to Rome for the Second Lateran Council. On the way he met Bernard of Clairvaux, the most prominent monastic reformer of his time and the leading promoter of the newly founded Cistercian order. Malachy and Bernard became close friends, and when the former returned to Ireland in 1142 he founded the first Cistercian monastery at Mellifont.

While in Rome, Malachy had been commissioned as papal legate to Ireland, which gave him the authority he needed to introduce widespread changes to the church there. These took the form of establishing a network of Cistercian abbeys, reinforced by a number of Augustinian priories and the installation of Augustinian canons in several Irish cathedrals. In the course of this work Malachy gained a better appreciation of the needs of the Irish church, and in particular of the claims of both Dublin and Tuam to a status similar to that of Armagh and Cashel. In 1148 he convened a synod at Inis Pátraic, near Dublin, at which he put forward his plan for a reorganization of the Irish dioceses, which was promptly approved by the assembled delegates.[55] Malachy then undertook to go to Rome to seek papal approval for this, but on the way he stopped at Clairvaux and died there on 2 November 1148.

His cause did not die however, and the pope agreed to send a legate, Cardinal John Paparo, who in 1152 presided over a national synod at Kells, which was soon transferred to Mellifont.[56] The scheme proposed by Malachy was adopted more or less as it stood and in essentials has remained unchanged ever since. The Irish dioceses established in this way are listed in Table 3.3 (pp. 72–73).

The old tribal structure was not completely abandoned but was contained within a more recognizable western order. The biggest problem was that Irish dioceses were mostly very small and too poor to support a bishop in the style customary elsewhere. A further complication was that Ireland was not politically united and the church found it hard to maintain both its unity and internal order when the secular authorities were unable to create the conditions of peace and good government it needed to flourish.

The Irish themselves soon realized this, and when the Anglo-Normans invaded the country two decades later many of them were prepared to accept

---

55 Ibid. 16:84.
56 Ibid. 16:85–87.

Table 3.3 Irish dioceses established between AD 1028 and 1192

Year founded	Diocese	Ecclesiastical province
1028	Dublin	Dublin
1096	Meath	Armagh
1096	Waterford	Cashel
1098?	Killaloe	Cashel
1105	Armagh	Armagh
1106	Limerick	Cashel
1107	Derry	Armagh
1111	Ardcarn	Armagh (united to Ardagh, 1152)
1111	Ardfert	Cashel
1111	Cashel	Cashel
1111	Clogher	Armagh
1111	Clonfert	Tuam
1111	Clonmacnois	Armagh
1111	Cloyne	Cashel
1111	Connor	Armagh (united to Down, 1453)
1111	Cork	Cashel
1111	Down	Armagh
1111	Duleek	Armagh (united to Clonard, 1171)
1111	Elphin	Tuam
1111	Emly	Cashel
1111	Ferns	Dublin
1111	Glendalough	Dublin (united to Dublin, 1218)
1111	Kells	Armagh (united to Kilmore, 1216)
1111	Kildare	Dublin
1111	Killala	Tuam
1111	Killaloe	Cashel
1111	Leighlin	Dublin
1111	Lismore	Cashel (united to Waterford, 1363)
1111	Raphoe	Armagh
1111	Tuam[a]	Tuam
1136	Bréifne[b]	Armagh (became Kilmore, 1152)
1152	Achonry	Tuam
1152	Ardagh	Armagh
1152	Ardmore	Cashel (soon dissolved)
1152	Kilfenora	Cashel
1152	Kilmacduagh	Tuam

Table 3.3 Irish dioceses established between AD 1028 and 1192 *(cont.)*

Year founded	Diocese	Ecclesiastical province
1152	Kilmore[c]	Armagh
1152	Mayo	Tuam (united to Tuam, 1202)
1152	Ossory	Dublin
1152	Rathlurensis	Armagh (soon dissolved)
1152	Roscrea	Cashel (soon dissolved)
1152	Ross	Cashel
1152	Scattery Island	Cashel (dissolved by 1467)
1179	Annaghdown[d]	Tuam (united to Tuam, 1253)
1192	Dromore[e]	Armagh

[a]   Apparently combined, or confused with, a diocese of Cong, which is not otherwise known.

[b]   Foundation date uncertain. It might have been created in 1111 or shortly thereafter, but there is no bishop recorded until 1136.

[c]   Known officially as Tirbrunensis from Tír mBriúin.

[d]   Created by a synod at Clonfert.

[e]   Created by a synod at Dublin.

the result as God's provision for the church, even though they would not have asked for (or expected) it in advance. There is some controversy about whether the pope issued a bull in 1155 (*Laudabiliter*), giving the king of England permission to invade Ireland and claim lordship over it, but that is what Henry II (1154–89) did in 1171, using the papal bull as his authorization.[57] Henry II called a synod to meet at Cashel in 1172, where it was determined that the church of Ireland would be constituted along English lines under Henry's sovereignty and protection.[58] Unfortunately, Henry II lacked the resources to make good his claim, and the English were unable to fulfil their promise until the early seventeenth century, by which time the political and religious landscapes had both changed beyond recognition. But the ideal first expressed at Cashel was never lost sight of, and even today there are voices in Ireland that would like the country to be as much like England as possible. The church would never go that far, but despite the many ups and downs and furious denials of Irish nationalists, there can be no doubt that the country is today anglicized in a way that would have seemed incredible to Henry II, and to that extent the promise of Cashel is closer to reality now than it has ever been.

---

[57] The authenticity of the bull has been questioned, but most scholars now seem to accept it as genuine. See Downham, *Medieval Ireland*, 212, 252, 281.

[58] Bray, *Records of Convocation*, 16:91–95.

Scotland

Gregory the Great had originally planned for the whole of northern Britain to come under the sway of York but this never came about. For a while York was able to exercise some jurisdiction over the country as far as the Clyde–Forth line, and after a hiatus of several centuries revived the see of Whithorn (Galloway) in 1128 and appointed its bishops for the next two centuries, but its influence over the rest of Scotland was never very great and diminished over time. Even in Gregory's day the north-west was being evangelized from Iona, and church organization there followed the looser Irish pattern. York made periodic attempts to assert its primacy but these were often rebuffed, particularly as the Scottish kingdom grew stronger. No Scottish king could be happy with a church that looked abroad for its head, but Scotland was not powerful or rich enough to afford its own archbishop. The result was that the country found itself in ecclesiastical limbo, a situation not properly addressed until the late twelfth century and not resolved even then.

The peculiar situation of Scotland was made more difficult because the papacy, to which the Scots appealed for recognition of their independence, was tied to the ancient decision of Gregory the Great concerning the two provinces of mainland Britain. Documentation for the early period is virtually non-existent, so it is impossible to discover what the situation on the ground was, but we do know that King Macbeth (1040–57) visited Rome about 1050 and presumably became aware of the reforms to church government that were just then being promoted at the heart of the Christian world. We also know that Macbeth and his wife were generous benefactors of the church in Scotland, and that they took a genuine interest in improving its standards.[59] Modern readers are surprised to discover that Lady Macbeth was a supporter of church reform, but there we are – as so often, truth is stranger than fiction!

The Normans never conquered Scotland, but its kings intermarried with their English counterparts and were steadily influenced by them. One important influence at this time was Queen Margaret (1045–93), an Anglo-Saxon princess who married King Malcolm III around 1069, after her homeland had been conquered by the Normans. She founded and endowed a number of churches and religious houses, laying the foundations for the expansion and consolidation that occurred after her death. Her fourth son, who reigned as David I (1124–53), became a close friend of England's King

---

[59] A. W. Haddan and W. Stubbs, *Councils and Ecclesiastical Documents Relating to Great Britain and Ireland*, 3 vols. (Oxford: Clarendon Press, 1869–78), 2:151–152.

Henry I (1100–35) and picked up Norman ways during his stays at Henry's court. In his reign the church was firmly established along English lines. As in England, a parish system was set up and dioceses with their own bishops and cathedrals were created, or at least stabilized. There is evidence that many Scottish church foundations went back several centuries, in some cases as far as the original mission from Iona, but only in the twelfth century did the church as a whole acquire the institutional framework already in place in England and elsewhere. The Western Isles and adjoining mainland had been the strongholds of the Celtic church, but were devastated by the Viking invasions and by the twelfth century were no more than a shadow of their former selves. The Celtic monastic houses that survived were almost all in the hands of the so-called *céli Dé* (spouses of God), anglicized as 'Culdees', monks who belonged to a reform movement that had originated in Ireland in the eighth century. They were a tenacious group, and at least eight of their houses survived into the thirteenth century, one of them being the cathedral at St Andrews, from which they were not excluded until 1273. Scotland had one other monastic cathedral, at Whithorn, but as that was under the jurisdiction of York until 1359 it hardly counts. Brechin Cathedral was another Culdee foundation, but the Culdees there were gradually replaced by secular canons after 1219.[60]

It was in the course of the twelfth century that a distinct church of Scotland began to take shape. By 1150 or so, Scottish bishops were less often consecrated by the Archbishop of York, although they were still expected to swear canonical obedience to him. A crisis occurred in 1133 when King Henry I of England created the see of Carlisle, which the Bishop of Glasgow claimed belonged to him. A few years later, Carlisle was occupied by the Scots, but the English bishop seems to have carried on happily until his death in 1156 or 1157. Carlisle reverted to English control at about the same time, but the see was not filled until 1204, for reasons that are not entirely clear. By then however, the boundaries between England and Scotland were becoming fixed, and Glasgow made no further claims to jurisdiction over Cumbria.

King David I continued to press for the elevation of St Andrews to the status of an archbishopric for the whole of Scotland, and his cause was apparently taken up by Cardinal Paparo, who visited the country on his way to and from Ireland. David's plea was unsuccessful however, partly because of the papacy's commitment to the supremacy of York and partly because the popes did not

---

[60] See D. E. Easson, *Medieval Religious Houses: Scotland* (London: Longman, 1957), for a comprehensive inventory of Scottish monastic institutions.

Table 3.4 The pattern of Scottish dioceses and their foundation from AD 623 to 1192

Year founded	Diocese	Year dissolved/transferred
623	Iona	986
660	Kingarth	689
681	Abercorn	685
700	Ross	
721	Abernethy	(transferred to Dunblane?)
865	Dunkeld	
1012	Mortlach	(transferred to Aberdeen, 1132)
1028	St Andrews	
1035	Orkney	
1104	Moray	
1109	Glasgow	
1109	Skye	1134
1128	Whithorn (Galloway)	
1132	Aberdeen	
1134	The Isles	
1150	Brechin	
1151	Caithness	
1155	Dunblane	
1192	Argyll	

want to offend the Normans, who had occupied Sicily and southern Italy at the same time as they conquered England, and posed a potential threat to Rome. English pressure on Scotland increased after the accession of Henry II, but this went too far and in 1174 Pope Alexander III consecrated Jocelin as Bishop of Glasgow and exempted him from the jurisdiction of York by placing him under the Pope's own 'special protection'. That opened the door to a solution that was to be unique in the British Isles, if not in western Christendom as a whole.[61]

The Scottish dioceses were officially detached from York by Pope Celestine III in a bull known as *Cum Universi*, issued in 1192, but were not organized into provinces along the English and Irish models until much later. Instead of that, they were directly subjected to Rome and governed as exceptional cases. It was

---

[61] For the details, see R. Oram, *Domination and Lordship: Scotland 1070–1230* (Edinburgh: Edinburgh University Press, 2011), 334–346.

not until 1472 that an archbishop was set up in St Andrews (Glasgow was to follow in 1492), finally giving Scotland the kind of organization England had already had for over 800 years. The historic weakness of its episcopal system would become apparent at the time of the Reformation, less than a century later, when it was to prove much more difficult to retain it than it was in England.

Table 3.4 shows the pattern of Scottish dioceses and their foundation. In sharp contrast to what happened in England, the earliest Scottish dioceses almost all disappeared,[62] some within a generation. The most productive period for the creation of new ones began in the early eleventh century, and most survived until the disestablishment of episcopacy in 1690. By the time the Scottish church gained its independence from York, all the dioceses (except possibly Argyll) had been created, and Argyll soon followed.[63]

Anselm of Canterbury

One thing the Norman Conquest did was to bring the church of England into the mainstream of western Christendom. The Anglo-Saxons had not ignored their European neighbours, but once their missionary efforts had succeeded, ongoing contact was limited. With the coming of the Normans however, the church found itself part of an international network that stretched as far as southern Italy, and interaction became much more frequent. For better or worse, the English church began a relationship with western Europe that was to endure more or less unchanged for nearly half a millennium.

The great symbol of this new reality was the appointment of Anselm, Lanfranc's successor at Bec, to follow him to Canterbury. Anselm of Canterbury (1033–1109) is without question the most renowned figure ever to have occupied the throne of St Augustine, and the only Anglo-Saxon churchman who can hold a candle to him is Bede. But in what sense, if any, was Anselm English or British? There is no doubt about Bede, who was an Englishman to his fingertips, anti-Welsh prejudices and all. But Anselm had not set foot in the country until he became archbishop, and even then his disputes with the king (William II) forced him to spend a number of years in Italian exile, where he wrote some of his most important works. As far as we know he did not speak a word of English and had no need to learn it, since he moved exclusively in a Norman environment. He did take his duties at Canterbury seriously, and even exercised some jurisdiction in Ireland, but nobody now remembers him

---

[62] Shown in italics in Table 3.4.

[63] There would eventually be a diocese of Edinburgh as well, but it was not created until 1633.

for that. His claim to fame rests on his literary output, which was of seminal importance for the revival of theology in western Europe and was to be of great, although largely indirect, influence on British Christianity from the sixteenth century onwards. We are left with the paradox that the glory of the see of Canterbury was not really an English churchman at all but a living example of what was to become a widespread phenomenon of the High Middle Ages – an international figure with English connections, and in that sense the forerunner of much that was to come.

Anselm's theological genius was something new in the western church, and not just in England. There had been periodic revivals of learning in the past, most notably at the court of Charlemagne in the late eighth and early ninth centuries but, important though they were, they had not produced theology of the first rank, which had effectively died out with Gregory the Great. It was Anselm who would move things on further. The church of his time had more or less settled the Christological controversies of the late Roman period, the results of which are familiar to us from the words of the Nicene Creed, which entered the church's liturgy in the time of Charlemagne. As far as the western church was concerned, it had been decided that Jesus Christ was one divine Person incarnate in two natures, one divine and the other human, but two questions remained unexplored. One was what theologians now call the 'work' of Christ. Why did the Son of God become a man, and what did he accomplish by doing so? The other was the personhood of the Holy Spirit, the third member of the Trinity. What exactly was his relationship to the Father and the Son?

The second of these questions had recently come to the fore because it was a matter in dispute between the western and eastern (mainly Greek-speaking) churches. Limited contact between these two branches of Christendom had kept the controversy at bay for a long time, but with the advent of the Crusades in the late eleventh century, the question could no longer be ducked. It was no accident that Anselm found himself in southern Italy, which at that time was still largely Greek-speaking (and had been part of the Byzantine Empire as late as 1071), just as the First Crusade was making its way overland to Palestine, creating a love–hate relationship with the eastern church as it went. The result was that he put his mind to the problem of the Holy Spirit's relationship to the other persons of the Godhead and produced a treatise that was at once more biblically based and more theologically sophisticated than anything that had been written on the subject before his time. He defended the view that the Spirit proceeds equally from the Father and from the Son, the western position that had been articulated centuries before by Augustine of Hippo and that had finally been incorporated into the Latin version of the Nicene Creed around 1014.

This addition consisted of a single Latin word (*Filioque*, 'and from the Son'), which has since given its name to the controversy as a whole. The eastern church rejected this for a variety of reasons, of which the most important was that John 15:26, from which the Nicene doctrine was derived, speaks only of the procession of the Spirit from the Father. By a careful analysis of the wider Gospel text, Anselm demonstrated that the role of the Son in this procession could not be excluded, even if it was not clearly stated in a single verse. Anselm went beyond simple 'proof-texting', as quoting isolated Bible verses is called, to a more intricate theological argument based on the deeper meaning of a text that could be teased out only by careful exegesis and argument. This was the beginning of what would later be known as 'scholastic' theology, because it would be the theological method taught in the schools founded after Anselm's time.

To this debate, which was of particular immediacy at the time, Anselm added another, which was coming to the surface within the western church. This concerned the purpose of Christ's death on the cross. What did his sacrifice achieve? Everybody knew that it had something to do with salvation from the power and effects of sin, but how did this work and why did the Son of God have to become a man and die in order to accomplish it? To answer these questions Anselm set up a dialogue between himself and his disciple Boso, whom he cast as a well-meaning but ignorant enquirer. When Boso asked why the Son of God had to become a man and die for our sins, Anselm replied that it was the only way God's honour and justice could be satisfied. As we have been created in his image, our sins are too important to be ignored, but we have no way of getting rid of them. Only a perfect man can do that, by taking our sins upon himself and paying the price for them – and that price is death. This is what the Son of God did when he suffered and died in his human nature. But because he is God, death could not hold him, and so he came back, victorious over the just punishment he received on our behalf and now able to open the gates of heaven for us. What is more, because God is infinite, his sacrifice in Christ knows no bounds – there is nobody who has sinned in a way that Christ's sacrifice is unable to pay for. This, the so-called 'satisfaction theory' of atonement, was to become the standard western view until it was reworked by Martin Luther in the sixteenth century. Reworked, but not entirely replaced. The British churches no longer hold exactly the same doctrine that Anselm taught, but his influence is still visible in the way that we think about Christ's sacrifice, an achievement of which few theologians can boast and that reveals the full stature of this remarkable man.

Church and state

There can be no doubt that the church grew in strength in the centuries of monastic revival and that by 1150 it was in a position to rival the authority of the king. In Anglo-Saxon times there had been close cooperation between the secular and ecclesiastical establishments, and bishops were effectively nominated by the kings, to whom they then swore fealty. This was a common pattern all over western Europe, but the revival of the papacy in the mid-eleventh century changed all that. In particular the popes waged a long-running battle with the Holy Roman emperors over the investiture of bishops in the empire, but this controversy had little or no resonance in England or elsewhere in the British Isles. The first Norman kings continued the policy of their Anglo-Saxon predecessors and regarded episcopal and abbatial appointments as their prerogative. Even Anselm paid homage to William II in 1093, although his subsequent exile made him more aware of the conflict and more determined to limit the king's role as much as possible. That was easier said than done, but in 1107 the papacy worked out a compromise with both England and France. The kings would no longer invest bishops or abbots with the seals of their offices, in recognition of the fact that their appointments were spiritual and not temporal in nature. But the newly appointed prelates would still be expected to do homage to their secular ruler, who would also have a say (behind the scenes) in who was nominated. It was a sensible compromise and there was little trouble after that.

To modern minds it seems wrong that a secular ruler should take part in appointing church leaders, but we must remember the nature of medieval society and the place of the church in it. Even in a relatively sophisticated country like England, those in power all knew one another and were often related. It was simply not possible to contemplate a situation in which familial rivalries might spill over into the church, and no king could be happy at the thought that he would face powerful and entrenched opposition from one or more of his bishops. The kings never tried to adjudicate the spiritual suitability of the candidates for high office, which was clearly beyond their competence, but they could not be indifferent to an institution that owned at least a quarter of the land and that claimed the allegiance of the entire population. They were also wary of the possibility that litigation involving the church might be appealed to Rome, and were therefore reluctant to allow bishops to leave the country without permission. Even when the pope summoned the bishops to a council of the whole western church, as he did in 1123 and again in 1139, the kings allowed only a small number of them to attend, much to their resentment it must be said. Possible conflicts of interest therefore made it inevitable that there would be some degree of royal involvement in church appointments; the challenge was to ensure that such involvement would not compromise the overall mission of the church.

In England church–state relations became more complicated during the reign of King Stephen (1135–54). When Henry I died, he left only a daughter, Matilda, as his heiress, and it was by no means agreed that a woman could rule in her own right. Stephen of Blois, a nephew of Henry I, hastened to London as soon as he heard of Henry's death and had himself crowned in Westminster Abbey, an act that guaranteed recognition of his claim by the church. It also helped that his brother, Henry of Blois, was Bishop of Winchester (1129–71) and already a prominent figure in the English government. Unfortunately, Stephen did not fully understand the weakness of his claim to the succession, and instead of courting the church, on whose support he had to rely, he bit the hand that fed him. Before long he managed to fall out with several of the bishops, who then turned against him and supported Matilda instead. The result was a civil war that lasted from 1139 to 1143, during which Stephen was captured and imprisoned by Matilda's troops (1141).[64]

In the end the church managed to increase its power by acting as the honest broker between the two rivals. It recognized Stephen as king, but not his son Eustace as his successor. Instead it left the door open for Matilda's son, another Henry, to inherit the throne once Stephen was dead. Conflict was averted when Eustace drowned while trying to cross the English Channel, and in November 1153 an agreement was reached by which Henry would succeed Stephen, as he duly did in the following year. Throughout this process, the church flexed its muscles and increased its authority to a degree not previously known in England.

A large part of this was due to the growing importance of the papacy in English affairs. England had always shown deference to the popes, but they were far away and had little to do with the internal affairs of the English church. But by the mid-twelfth century that was changing dramatically. The reform of the papacy was bearing fruit, and the legal system of the church brought Rome and England closer together. The popes began to appoint English bishops and archbishops as their legates, giving them authority to apply the canons of the church in the secular sphere. They also negotiated with the kings to ensure the regular payment of a tax to the papacy, popularly known as 'Peter's Pence'. Financial donations to Rome had been part of English

---

[64] See E. King, *King Stephen* (New Haven, Conn.: Yale University Press, 2010); C. Hanley, *Matilda: Empress, Queen, Warrior* (New Haven, Conn.: Yale University Press, 2019).

life for centuries, but with the advent of the Crusades after 1095, the needs of the papacy became greater and the demands for money more insistent. Peter's Pence was now formally recognized, and remained payable until Henry VIII abolished it in 1533.

It might be thought that the English would resent 'foreign' interference in their affairs, but the papacy at that time was heavily influenced by English churchmen, one of whom, Nicholas Breakspear, became a cardinal sometime before 1149 and was subsequently elected Pope as Hadrian IV (1154–9), the only Englishman ever to have enjoyed such an honour. It was a sign, and a reminder, that the medieval church was an institution that transcended national and state boundaries. Nobody in Rome objected to being ruled by an Englishman, and so we should not be surprised to discover that nobody in England objected to being subject to a Roman bishop either.

4
The High Middle Ages (1154–1307)

The French connection

The appointment of men like Lanfranc and Anselm to the see of Canterbury was the tip of the iceberg that was the Norman invasion of England and the takeover of its church. In the course of the twelfth century the links between England and France, aided by Norman rule over the whole of the former and about half of the latter, were to intensify considerably, and not least at the intellectual level. Few Frenchmen ventured into England, but a number of Englishmen made their way to Paris, where they played a distinguished part in the renaissance of learning going on there at that time. The founding of the Abbey of St Victor in 1108 acted as a magnet for talent, and many famous names could be found there over the next two generations. Richard of St Victor (d. 1173) was one of the most outstanding theologians of his time and came from the Scottish borders, which were part of the ecclesiastical province of York.[1] Andrew of St Victor (d. 1175) was another Englishman who did pioneering work on the Old Testament and even learned Hebrew for the purpose. His biblical commentaries took their place alongside those of Bede as some of the most remarkable and influential interpretations of the Old Testament that the medieval church produced.[2]

The Abbey of St Victor went into decline towards the end of the twelfth century, but Paris remained a magnet for aspiring English churchmen. One of the most outstanding of these was Stephen Langton (1150?–1228), who became a renowned teacher in the Parisian schools and was still there when they received a university charter in 1200 – the oldest university in Europe. Langton was a biblical scholar and is credited with having created the chapter divisions that our Bibles still use.[3] Later on, he got caught up in politics when he was

---

[1] See L. Schumacher, 'Richard of St Victor', in D. Fergusson and M. K. Elliott (eds.), *The History of Scottish Theology*, 3 vols. (Oxford: Oxford University Press, 2019), 1:25–38.

[2] The best study of this is B. Smalley, *The Study of the Bible in the Middle Ages*, 3rd edn (Oxford: Basil Blackwell, 1984).

[3] Verse divisions did not appear until 1550, and the first English Bible to have them was printed ten years later.

elected Archbishop of Canterbury in 1207, much to the annoyance of King John, who refused to accept him. The church responded to this challenge by suspending its services until Langton's election was recognized, but it took the better part of five years for that to happen. Langton continued to be out of favour with the king until the latter's death and even afterwards could not return to Canterbury for some time. Eventually he was able to spend what would be the last decade or so of his life exercising his pastoral ministry, and during that time convened the important Synod of Osney (17 April 1222), which issued canons that are still part of English church law – the oldest of their kind.[4]

Another Englishman who studied in France was Thomas of Chobham (1160?–1233?), who was a disciple of the Parisian master Peter the Chanter (d. 1197). Thomas returned to England after Peter's death and became Subdean of Salisbury Cathedral around 1208. He seems to have returned to Paris in the 1220s, where he taught for a few years, but he remained Subdean of Salisbury until his death. Thomas wrote a highly influential manual on penance, but for modern readers his most interesting work is his *Summa de Arte Praedicandi*, one of the very few handbooks on the art of preaching, which was enjoying a renaissance in his time. Thomas explained that preaching is 'the proclamation of the Divine Word for instruction in faith and behaviour' and he set out how a sermon should be prepared. Good preaching involved three steps. The first was *lectio*, or what we would now call 'exegesis'. This involved determining the meaning of the biblical text that would be the subject of the sermon. Next came *disputatio*, or what we would call 'exposition'. This included the theological significance of the chosen text and how it should be understood. Finally there was *praedicatio*, the preaching or application of the text to the needs of the congregation. Thomas believed that sermons should be simple, designed with the spiritual edification of the hearers in mind. At a time when rhetoric was often a way in which the speaker would show off his own learning and abilities, this was a refreshing departure from the norm. Thomas's method was soon being imitated all over Europe and it was the model on which Reformers like John Calvin based their own teaching and practice, even if they no longer subscribed to the allegorical interpretations Thomas and his contemporaries took for granted.[5]

---

[4] See F. M. Powicke, *Stephen Langton* (Oxford: Clarendon Press, 1928). The canons of Osney (Oxford) are in F. M. Powicke and C. R. Cheney, *Councils and Synods with Other Documents Relating to the English Church II, A. D. 1205–1313*, 2 vols. (Oxford: Clarendon Press, 1964), 1:100–125.

[5] The Latin text of Thomas's work was not edited or published until 1988 and has never been translated into English. See G. R. Evans, 'Thomas of Chobham on Preaching and Exegesis', *Recherches de Théologie Ancienne et Médiévale* 52 (1985), 159–170.

In Langton's time Parisian learning began to spread to England itself, as scholars started migrating to Oxford (about 1180) and from there to Cambridge (in 1209). The two ancient English universities were thus founded only slightly later than Paris, and Oxford in particular was soon to gain a great reputation all over Europe. There can be no doubt that the French connection facilitated this precocious growth, which in the course of time was to become foundational for the English church.

French influence was strong in twelfth- and early thirteenth-century England, but traffic occasionally flowed the other way as well. One example of that is the *Ancrene Wisse* or *Ancrene Riwle*, a manual written in English for the guidance of three women who wanted to live as anchoresses.[6] Who wrote it remains a subject of controversy, but the use of English is probably accounted for by the fact that it was addressed to women, who would not have had enough education to be able to read Latin, or even French. But the work achieved such fame that it was soon translated into those languages and thus it represents an interesting example of how a tiny number of English women could make an impact on the universal church.[7]

Thomas Becket

Henry II was an energetic monarch who was determined to correct what he saw as the corruption that had crept into the English church during the reign of Stephen, but the path to reform was not always easy. Trouble arose soon after Thomas Becket, the king's chancellor, was made archbishop in 1162.[8] For a while Becket and the king maintained friendly relations, but these soured when the archbishop began to argue over important matters of principle that had been festering for some time. One of these was the special status of the clergy in the law courts, and another was the right of the king to tax church property. In order to settle these and other contentious issues, Henry II decided to turn what had previously been understood as custom into written law. In 1164 he composed what came to be known as the Constitutions of Clarendon, a document that outlined the various points in dispute and determined them in ways that favoured the state over the church.[9]

---

[6] An anchoress was like a hermit, but could not leave her cell, which was usually attached to a parish church.

[7] See E. J. Dobson, *The Origins of the* Ancrene Wisse (Oxford: Oxford University Press, 1976).

[8] On Becket, see A. Duggan, *Thomas Becket* (London: Bloomsbury Academic, 2004); H. Mayr-Harting, *Religion, Politics and Society in Britain 1066–1272* (Harlow: Pearson, 2011), 74–94.

[9] For the Constitutions and a commentary, see D. Whitelock, M. Brett and C. N. L. Brooke (eds.), *Councils and Synods with Other Documents Relating to the English Church I, A. D. 871–1204*, 2 vols. (Oxford: Clarendon Press, 1981), 2:852–893.

Among the issues raised was the status of advowsons, which the king regarded as secular property but which the church wanted to control, at least to some extent.[10] Other matters included the degree of freedom the church might have in making appointments and in its relations with Rome, where the interests of the clergy were often quite different from the wishes of the king. Most problematic of all was the status of 'criminous clerks', those clergymen and monks who were guilty of secular crimes. Should they be tried in secular courts like every other subject, or were they entitled to be heard in a church court, where they would be judged by their peers? In general Henry II wanted to restate the customs in force in his grandfather Henry I's time, although inevitably there were additions that were intended to reinforce the king's power. Archbishop Becket baulked at this but eventually accepted the Constitutions, at least in principle. One big difference between Henry II's time and that of his grandfather was that now the pope wanted a say. The Constitutions were forwarded to him and he rejected several of them, including the demand for the secular trial of criminous clerks. Becket was reprimanded for his willingness to concede too much to Henry II – he was caught between the king and the pope, an awkward position that almost inevitably propelled him in the latter's direction.

Henry II was pleased with the Constitutions but they solved nothing. The disputes merely got worse, and by the end of 1164 Becket had fled into exile. This was dangerous for Henry II, because Becket quickly attracted the support of Louis VII of France, hardly one of Henry's best friends, and was effectively backed by the church outside England. It was therefore advisable for him to come to terms with the archbishop, which he did after six years of strenuous negotiations that included a failed attempt to coerce the other bishops into supporting him.[11] Becket finally returned to England in 1170, just as Henry was invading Ireland, but there was no real reconciliation between the two men. What exactly happened is disputed, but it seems that in a moment of exasperation Henry asked out loud who would rid him of this troublesome priest (as he apparently called Becket). Four of his knights in attendance heard this and rushed off to Canterbury, where on 29 December they murdered the archbishop at his own altar in the cathedral.

---

[10] The church lost on this one and advowsons have always been regarded as part of the common law.

[11] This occurred as late as October–November 1169. See Whitelock et al., *Councils and Synods*, 2:926–939. In September 1170 the pope learned that Henry II had had his son Henry crowned as co-ruler, and responded by excommunicating the bishops responsible – London, Salisbury and York. Becket, who was now back in England, circulated the pope's letters, an action that seems to have been the immediate cause of the king's anger that led to Becket's murder.

This incident shocked not only England but the whole of Christendom. Wittingly or not, Henry II had made a martyr of Thomas Becket and neither he nor his successors would be allowed to forget it. The king was forced to do penance for his crime but, more importantly, a shrine to Becket's memory was erected in Canterbury cathedral, which thus became an important pilgrimage centre. How important it was can be seen from Geoffrey Chaucer's *Canterbury Tales*, a series of cameos written more than 200 years later, that bring the pilgrimage to life and give us an unrivalled literary portrait of the whole range of English society at that time. By then, Becket was a canonized saint and national hero, a permanent reminder of what church–state relations ought to be like, and of what might happen if things went wrong. Needless to say, it was the church that came out on top in this, and ensured that future rulers would think twice (or more) before tackling its spiritual power. It will also come as no surprise that when Henry VIII broke with Rome in 1534, one of the first things he did was dismantle Becket's shrine, which would otherwise have been a reminder of previous failed attempts to bring the church under state control, and a focal point for opposition to Henry VIII's religious policy. Even today the incident is still remembered, as T. S. Eliot's play *Murder in the Cathedral* (1935) reminds us, and we can probably be sure that if serious church–state disputes should ever arise again, the ghost of Thomas will return to haunt those unlucky enough to be caught up in them.

Becket is remembered for his political opposition to the king, but his deepest influence on the church lies somewhere else. He had a serious interest in theology and kept abreast of the revival of interest in the subject, and especially in the doctrine of the Trinity that characterized twelfth-century Paris.[12] He was consecrated archbishop on the Sunday after Pentecost (3 June) 1162 and his first act was to decree that that day should henceforth be commemorated by the English church as Trinity Sunday. It still is.

The universities and sacramental theology

By a somewhat different turn of events, England, and in particular Oxford, was now set to become one of the most energetic and productive centres of Christian thought. We do not know for sure when scholars first began congregating in Oxford, but it was probably sometime late in the twelfth century. Most had migrated there from Paris, which already had a flourishing body of schools and

---

12 The outstanding work on this subject was written by the Anglo-Scottish theologian Richard of St-Victor, sometime around 1150. For an English translation, see B. T. Coolman and D. M. Coulter (eds.), *Trinity and Creation* (Hyde Park, N.Y.: New City Press, 2011), 195–382.

scholars. The loss of Normandy by the English Crown in 1204 might have accelerated the growth of Oxford's schools, as Englishmen might have felt less welcome in France after that date, but that is speculation, much of which centres on the figure of Robert Grosseteste (1168–1253), an Anglo-Norman who became the leading light of Oxford in the early thirteenth century.[13] We cannot be certain whether Grosseteste studied in Paris or not, but we know that he was familiar with the teaching methods used there in his youth because he adopted them himself. It also seems likely that he never taught outside England and that his career was spent almost entirely at Oxford. It is claimed that he was the first chancellor of the university chartered there in 1214, but we cannot be certain of that. What we do know is that in 1235 he became Bishop of Lincoln (the see in which Oxford was situated) and that his teaching career came to an end at that point, although he remained affiliated to the new university for the rest of his life.

Grosseteste was by all measures an exceptional scholar and teacher. He was thoroughly grounded in the Bible and used it as the basis for all his theological writing. His teaching methods were traditional, and he resisted the innovations creeping in towards the end of his life, but in some respects he was a pioneer. For example, he was one of the very few people in western Europe who managed to acquire a working knowledge of Greek, which he employed as a translator of sacred texts in his years at Lincoln. He was also active in wider church affairs after he became a bishop, and used his influence to press for a more pastoral approach to the ordained ministry. In particular, he was outspoken in his protests against the tendency to intrude well-connected (as opposed to well-qualified) candidates for ecclesiastical office, and even went to Rome towards the end of his life in order to lodge his objections with the pope in person.

Yet in spite of his activities in the early years of Oxford University, Grosseteste was in many respects the last representative of the old order in theological training, which had been based on monastic values and a mastery of Holy Scripture. During the course of his life the schools of Paris were moving towards a more systematic presentation of theology, codified for posterity in the *Sentences* of Peter Lombard (*c.*1095–1160).[14] Within a generation of Peter's death his great compilation of ancient authorities, together with a running commentary on them, had established itself as the primary textbook for theological education in Paris, and from there it spread across Europe.

---

[13] R. W. Southern, *Robert Grosseteste: The Growth of an English Mind in Medieval Europe*, 2nd edn (Oxford: Clarendon Press, 1992); J. McEvoy, *Robert Grosseteste* (Oxford: Oxford University Press, 2000).

[14] Peter Lombard, *The Sentences*, tr. G. Silano, 4 vols. (Toronto: Pontifical Institute of Mediaeval Studies, 2007–10).

Grosseteste resisted adopting it at Oxford, but after his consecration as bishop he could no longer keep it out. By 1250 it had been accepted by the upcoming generation of university teachers and was to remain the chief theological textbook there (and across Europe) for the next 300 years.

It was Peter Lombard, more than anyone else, who laid the groundwork for the sacramental theology that was to emerge and dominate the western church for the next three and a half centuries.[15] Peter came up with the idea that there are seven sacraments – the perfect number, chosen apparently because it was easy to remember. The various ordinances and rites that he included under this heading had already been in existence for a very long time, but he brought them together and gave them a common label. Later theologians then developed a system out of this raw material, and that system came to be central to the medieval church's understanding of its mission and ministry.

The first of the sacraments was baptism, the point of entry into the church. Baptism was not merely the sign but the means of regeneration. Every human being had to be baptized in order for his or her original sin to be cleansed. Since everyone comes into the world tainted by sin, and given that infant mortality was very high, the sooner a baby could be baptized the better. Once the sacrament had been administered to it, the baby was born again as a child of God and guaranteed entry into heaven as long as it did not commit actual sin. Some people understood that the child would eventually have to take on the obligations of baptism for himself, and so the sacrament was effectively split into two parts. When he was old enough to make the vows his parents and godparents had made on his behalf, he would do so in the presence of the bishop – this was 'confirmation'. After that, he would be admitted into the full, adult life of the church.

The confirmed individual would then be expected to confess his sins to a priest on a regular basis. The priest would determine what penalty to impose, in order to ensure that the confession was meant sincerely. After completing the requirements, the penitent sinner would return to the priest and seek absolution – this was the sacrament of penance. Having been absolved from sin, the penitent would be admitted to Holy Communion, the sacrament of the body and blood of Christ that would sustain him spiritually until he sinned again, when the process of penance would be repeated. As death approached, he would be offered extreme unction, an anointing with oil that was originally intended for healing but that had come to be a preparation for passing from

---

[15] R. Van Nieuwenhove, *An Introduction to Medieval Theology* (Cambridge: Cambridge University Press, 2012), 157–158; W. Rosemann, *Peter Lombard* (Oxford: Oxford University Press, 2004), 145–178.

this life to the next. Someone who received this unction could then die in a 'state of grace' and hope for less time in Purgatory or even (in exceptional cases) immediate entry into heaven as a 'saint'.[16]

In addition to these five sacraments there were two others, which were not compulsory and after 1123 were generally regarded as mutually exclusive. The first of these was the sacrament of holy orders – ordination to the diaconate, priesthood and/or episcopate. Those who received the orders of priest and bishop were sworn to celibacy because it was their calling to live the consecrated life of the angels in heaven here on earth, as a sign to the rest of the church of what was promised to them in eternity.[17] The alternative was matrimony, raised to the level of a sacrament in its own right and regarded, as were holy orders, as 'indelible'. Just as a man who had been ordained could not lose his ordination, so a married person could not be divorced. The grace of God these sacraments conferred was eternal and could not be undone by human sin, however grave it might be. Here there was a contradiction between theory and practice that was never satisfactorily resolved. Some clergymen were defrocked, either because of gross moral turpitude or because of heresy. There were also some marriages that were annulled because they had been contracted under false premises or against the laws of the church, which forbade carnal unions within certain well-defined bounds of consanguinity and affinity. How the notion of indelible grace could be reconciled with these unfortunate realities was never clearly worked out, and in later times it was to prove contentious, especially with regard to matrimony.

Underpinning the sacramental system was the notion of grace. This was interpreted as a gift of God to undeserving humans. Grace was often thought of as a thing in its own right, a kind of medicine stored up in the body and blood of the risen, ascended and glorified Christ. It was the privilege of the church to be allowed to dispense this grace to those in need of it – the entire human race. But what the church was authorized to give it could also withhold, and those who fell foul of its requirements were duly excommunicated – cut off from access to the grace of God and thus effectively condemned to eternal damnation unless they repented.

By far the most important of the sacraments in practical terms was Holy Communion, because it was there that Christians received the body and blood of Christ himself, the ultimate manifestation of divine grace. Using categories of thought traced back to the ancient Greek philosopher Aristotle, medieval

---

[16] See J. Le Goff, *The Birth of Purgatory* (Chicago, Ill.: University of Chicago Press, 1984).

[17] Deacons were exempted from the celibacy rule, but as the diaconate was seldom more than a stepping stone to the priesthood, celibacy made little difference in practice.

theologians came up with the notion of 'transubstantiation'. This was based on the belief that material objects are substances that appear in different accidental forms. Thus, for example, bread can be heavy or light, white or brown, thick or thin, but it is still 'bread'. What happened in the so-called 'miracle of the altar' was that when the priest consecrated this bread, its accidents remained the same but its underlying substance was changed into the body of Christ. In other words it looked like bread, felt like bread, tasted like bread, but in fact was something else. Thanks to the spiritual power given to the priest in his ordination, it had become a supernatural reality. In the formula of the time, grace had taken nature (the material substance) and perfected it for a spiritual purpose.[18]

What happened to the bread also happened to the wine, but here there was a complication. For reasons that are not fully understood, the 'cup' (of wine) was gradually withdrawn from ordinary Christians (the 'laity') and reserved for the priest, who consumed it on behalf of the people. This was justified by saying that since a body contains blood, the consecrated bread contained both the body and blood of Christ, making access to the cup redundant. While this interpretation was clever, it was by no means universally accepted, and in Bohemia there emerged a rebellion against it known as 'Utraquism', from the Latin phrase *sub utraque specie* (under each kind). The Utraquists claimed that the church had gone against the plain teaching of the Bible by promoting Communion in one kind only. Not surprisingly, the Bohemians could not resist the overwhelming power of the universal church and were defeated, but the practice of Communion in one kind threw up a latent conflict between the teaching of Scripture, which everyone regarded as divinely ordained, and the traditions of the church, which had produced interpretations of God's will that contradicted the Word he had revealed to the prophets and apostles.

This unresolved tension would eventually become a major cause of the Protestant Reformation, when the entire sacramental system would be challenged and the practice of the church radically altered. That, however, was for the future. At the time, everyone was expected to conform to what the church decreed without asking questions. The few dissenting voices were silenced and people were reassured that the clergy, and in particular the hierarchy of bishops with the pope at their head, knew what was right and had the authority to impose their teaching on the church as a whole. Church buildings were

---

[18] See M. Rubin, *Corpus Christi: The Eucharist in Late Medieval Culture* (Cambridge: Cambridge University Press, 1991).

constructed to reflect this sacramental system, with a high altar at the east end of the building, which everyone faced. Often this 'east end', or chancel as it was officially called, was screened off from the main body of the church, so that the distinction between clergy and laity was reinforced and the miracle of the altar retained its mystery. The priest faced eastwards, with his back to the people, supposedly representing them in the presence of God, but also concealing from them what he was doing on their behalf.

Elaborate liturgies were constructed in order to highlight transubstantiation and inspire awe in the worshippers, and new forms of devotion were introduced. The consecrated elements were reserved in a corner of the church, supposedly for ministering to the sick but in practice becoming objects of worship in their own right. Belief in the supernatural power of the bread thus conserved even led some people to steal it and indulge in occult practices, which was the ultimate perversion of what the church intended. That was rare, to be sure, but it might not be as far from the perceptions of ordinary people as we would like to think. When the priest took the bread and proclaimed *Hoc est corpus meum* ('This is my body'), it was heard by many as 'hocus pocus', meaningless jargon that suggested a magic trick more than a divine action. Similarly, the service itself came to be called the 'mass', from a misunderstanding of its closing words, when the priest said to the congregation, *Ite, ecclesia missa est* ('Go, the church is dismissed'). What was meant to inspire reverence ended up causing confusion. People who were supposed to be drawing closer to God found themselves further away from him than ever, relegated to second-class status in a church whose beliefs and practices they only partially understood. It was yet another contradiction thrown up by the sacramental system that would explode when the forces of reformation were eventually unleashed.

The friars

Meanwhile a new generation of theologians was emerging. Shortly after 1200 there was a fresh movement of asceticism, led by men like Francis of Assisi (1181?–1226) and Dominic de Guzmán (1170–1221), which criticized the monasteries for having become too worldly and having ignored the most basic precepts of the gospel of Christ. In order to recover those, both men, and others of like mind, advocated a new kind of spirituality, one not tied to institutions but reliant on the generosity of the public. These 'brothers', as they were called, were pledged to beg for their living, from which they came to be known as the 'mendicant orders'. The Latin word for 'brothers' is *fratres*, and so these men came to be called 'friars', who were identified by the habits they wore.[19] The Franciscans were the grey friars and the Dominicans were the black friars, names that still recur in places where they established houses of their own.[20] The Dominicans were also known as the 'order of preachers', because Dominic saw them as an elite band of apologists for the Christian faith, whereas the Franciscans preferred to emphasize their humility and came to be known as the 'friars minor'. Dominicans arrived in England in 1221 and soon made their way to Oxford, where they began teaching in the schools there. The Franciscans turned up in 1224 and were welcomed by the Dominicans, but initially they were more reluctant to get involved in teaching. This was because Francis had stressed poverty above all else, and to teach one had to have books, which were expensive. It also struck a number of Franciscans as compromise with the Establishment, which they were determined to prevent.

Things started to change in 1229, when rioting in Paris forced a number of Franciscans, including quite a few Englishmen who had joined the order there, to migrate to Oxford, where Robert Grosseteste welcomed them. By that time Francis was dead, and the conflict between those who wanted to be allowed to teach and those who objected to what they saw as surrender to the world very nearly split the order in two. In the event it was the Englishman Haymo of Faversham (d. 1244) who led the charge in favour of allowing the Franciscans to teach, claiming that at Oxford they had already demonstrated how learning and poverty could go together. The matter was finally decided by the pope, who sided with Haymo. As a result, Haymo became Minister-General of the order in 1240 and the way was clear for the Franciscans, along with the Dominicans, to play their part in the newly formed universities.

It was not long before the friars dominated the teaching of theology at Oxford, although there was still some residual opposition to them from traditionalists. It seems that among the secular (non-monastic) clergy were those who regarded the mendicants as hypocrites because although they effected poverty they amassed considerable wealth and the influence that went with that. But recent research has shown that there was no real conflict between the mendicants and the seculars, who mostly worked together and in the course of the thirteenth century raised the standards of the parish clergy to a level not

---

[19] C. H. Lawrence, *The Friars: The Impact of the Early Mendicant Movement on Western Society* (London: Longman, 1994); J. R. H. Moorman, *A History of the Franciscan Order* (Oxford: Clarendon Press, 1968); W. A. Hinnebusch, *A History of the Dominican Order*, 2 vols. (New York, N.Y.: Alba House, 1966–72); B. Jarrett, *The English Dominicans* (London: Burns, Oates & Washbourne, 1921).

[20] There were also the Carmelites, named after Mt Carmel in Palestine, who were the 'white friars', the Augustinian (Austin) friars whose habits had no distinguishing colour, and the Friars of the Sack, so called because their habits were made of coarse cloth. Martin Luther was an Augustinian friar.

seen since the fall of the Roman Empire.[21] The key to this was the introduction of Peter Lombard's *Sentences* as the standard theological textbook in the universities. Following a precedent already set in Paris, the Dominican Richard Fishacre (1200?–48) lectured on them in Oxford, and between 1240 and 1245 wrote a commentary on them that survives in several manuscripts.[22] A few years later the Franciscan Richard Rufus (d. *c.*1260) of Cornwall did the same.[23]

Over the following century the friars established themselves both in the universities and in London, attracting some of the brightest and best young minds in the country. One of these was John Duns Scotus (1266–1308), who became a Franciscan and dared to go against the teaching of Thomas Aquinas (*c.*1225–74), a leading Dominican who taught in Paris.[24] As his name suggests, John was born in Duns (Berwickshire) and so was a 'Scot', whatever that meant in the thirteenth century. In practice he trained for the priesthood in England and was educated at Oxford, where he remained until shortly after 1300. He then went to teach in Paris, but did not last long there because his radical views came under suspicion. In 1307 he was suddenly forced to leave the city and went to Cologne, where he died shortly afterwards, but his legacy lived on, not least at Oxford.

Aquinas believed that there were two different kinds of truth, one that applied to this world and another that had to be used of God. The reason for this, he claimed, was that God is a different kind of being from anything we see in the created order, and so the language we use to describe him can only be approximate. For example, I can use the word 'father' of the man who conceived me, but if I call God my 'Father', as Holy Scripture directs me to do, I am using the word in a different sense. Aquinas justified this by pointing out that Aristotle, who did not know God, was nevertheless able to examine the material world, because as a human being he was endowed with the power of reason. His conclusions could be accepted by Christians because we share this power with unbelievers, but the grace of divine revelation allows us to go higher and to integrate the knowledge we gain from such study into a higher synthesis that gives us a complete picture of the universe. The two types of knowledge are in principle incompatible, but as they deal with different aspects of reality they can be harmonized in a comprehensive theology of being.

---

[21] See A. Reeves, *Religious Education in Thirteenth-Century England* (Leiden: Brill, 2015); W. H. Campbell, *The Landscape of Pastoral Care in Thirteenth-Century England* (Cambridge: Cambridge University Press, 2018).

[22] See R. J. Long and M. O'Carroll, *The Life and Works of Richard Fishacre, OP: Prolegomena to the Edition of His Commentary on the Sentences* (Munich: Verlag der Bayerischen Akademie der Wissenschaften, 1999).

[23] See P. Raedts, *Richard Rufus of Cornwall and the Tradition of Oxford Theology* (Oxford: Clarendon Press, 1987).

[24] R. Cross, *Duns Scotus* (Oxford: Oxford University Press, 1999).

In reaction to this, Scotus accepted that there was a material order distinct from the spiritual one, but he challenged the view that the two were incompatible. In his opinion what exists in the created order corresponds to what is present in the mind of God, so that it is possible to use human language to describe both the Creator and the world he has made. Scotus also argued that if it is possible to conceive of an infinite being, then that being must exist, and for him that was the main proof for the existence of God. He also thought that if it was possible for God to do something, and that a particular action befitted his nature and/or plan, then God did it. He used this line of reasoning to defend the immaculate conception of Mary, who (in his opinion) was preserved from the stain of original sin because it was the right thing for God to have done. This was in direct contradiction to Aquinas, who rejected the idea that Mary was born without sin, but it was to prove popular in later times and was made the official teaching of the Roman Catholic Church in 1854.

Scotus also believed that a distinction could be made between the 'absolute' and 'ordained' power of God. This idea went back to Peter Damian (d. 1072), but it was more theoretical than real. What it claimed was that God has ordained everything that comes to pass in the world, which he governs by his sovereign power as revealed in creation (*potentia ordinata*). However, God supposedly has a reserve power that transcends his plan (*potentia absoluta*), which he can use to override it, even though he normally chooses not to do so. Scotus was content to argue on this basis that God could save a person apart from the divinely ordained plan revealed in the sacraments of the church, but his followers went much further. In particular they argued that the pope, as God's representative on earth, could also overrule the law of the church, which in principle represented the divine order of salvation. This happened in 1290, when Pope Nicholas IV rescinded the privileges granted to the friars by his predecessor, Martin IV, relying on the *potentia absoluta* argument, and it was not long before trouble erupted. By 1300 both the church and the university world were in ferment, and the relative calm of the thirteenth century came to seem like a golden age that had been lost beyond recall.

The tithe regime

The parish system was not merely an exercise in pastoral care. It was also the basis for taxation, which in church terms meant the tithe.[25] In principle every

---

[25] For a comprehensive study of the tithe, see R. H. Helmholz, *The Oxford History of the Laws of England*, vol. 1: *The Canon Law and Ecclesiastical Jurisdiction from 597 to the 1640s* (Oxford: Oxford University Press, 2004), 433–473.

Christian was expected to give a tenth of his income to the church, and once parishes were in place it was possible to turn that theory into reality. Most people lived in a barter, rather than in a cash, economy, and so tithes were usually paid in kind. The produce thus collected was stored in barns (French: *granges*), which sometimes still exist or at least have left their mark in street names – Grange Road was the one on which the tithe barn was originally situated. Tithes were divided into 'greater' and 'lesser'. The greater tithes were those levied on wheat, hay and wool, while lesser tithes covered the rest. The choice was not accidental. Wheat was the staple food of man, hay the staple food of domestic animals (just as important in an agricultural society) and wool was the chief cash crop that England produced.

Tithes were payable to the rector of the parish, who in theory was the local priest, or 'incumbent' as he was (and still is) called. But anyone could be a rector, just as anyone could hold the advowson, and as time went on, many rectories fell into the hands of monasteries, which 'appropriated' them, to use the official legal term. Their abbots then became the rectors of the parishes in question but, because they could not perform the parochial duties required of the priest, they were obliged to appoint substitutes, or vicars, to take their place. Other rectors could (and sometimes did) do the same. When that happened, the standard practice was for the rectors to claim the greater tithes and assign the lesser ones to their vicars. This pattern was codified by the Fourth Lateran Council, held at Rome in 1215, where it was decreed that every parish had to constitute a 'benefice' (or 'living' as it is known in English). A benefice was defined as a revenue-generating area sufficient to maintain a clergyman. Some benefices were very wealthy while others were quite poor, but none was supposed to fall below what we would now call the minimum wage.

What happened to people who refused to pay their tithes? Tax avoidance, or evasion, is as old as taxes themselves, and medieval England was no exception to that rule. The wool tithe, for example, was particularly susceptible to abuse because the sheep that provided the wool often moved from one parish to another, and it was not always clear which one ought to receive the tithe revenue. Obviously, pastoral relations between a priest and his flock would not be too good if the priest had to go around inspecting the peasantry, whose deep knowledge of their terrain allowed them to get away with all kinds of undetected chicanery. Besides that, priests had other things to do and could not afford the time and effort needed to procure the revenue to which they were entitled.

This problem was solved by appointing tithe collectors, professionals who would take a cut of the revenue in return for their services. Land would be apportioned to collectors, who would then sign a document giving them the right to chase up the tithes in their allotment. The Latin word for signature is *firma*, and so the document (and then the allotment) came to be called by that name, which has come into English as 'farm'. The 'farmer' was the tithe collector, not the man who tilled the soil (who was the peasant, or the 'boor' as he was then known). In modern usage the words 'farm' and 'farmer' have become standard agricultural terms and their origins in tithing have been forgotten, but the pattern of landholding still reflects the origin of 'tithing' to some extent and ought to be understood by anyone who has dealings with the rural economy even today.

Over time, many benefices were not able to maintain their financial standing, with the result that they could not sustain a functioning ministry. In those cases they either had to be combined with larger livings or suppressed altogether, but many clergy supplemented their income by holding more than one benefice at a time. This practice, known as 'pluralism', began of necessity but soon became abused, as some clergy acquired more and more benefices, often hiring less fortunate priests to do the parish work that was beyond the ability of the official incumbent. This was a chronic problem that was not properly addressed until 1838, when the Pluralities Act finally put a stop to the practice by insisting that no incumbent could hold more than one benefice at a time and that he had to be resident on it. Even so, some exceptions remained, particularly in the case of small and non-viable parishes, which had to be merged with larger ones in order to survive.

Ecclesiastical courts and canon law

The establishment of a universal tithe regime naturally produced difficulties when disputes arose or when people refused to pay what they owed. To deal with such questions it was necessary to set up a system of ecclesiastical courts, which also had jurisdiction over other matters reserved for the church. By the eleventh century it had become customary for the church to perform marriages, although this was never codified in law. It was also increasingly common for the church to prepare (and for priests to witness) last wills and testaments, which would then be subject to probate by an ecclesiastical authority. Other subjects, like defamation, also came into the sphere of the church, because slander was regarded as an offence against a person's soul. Ecclesiastical courts began to appear shortly after the Norman Conquest, but their precise status and jurisdiction remained uncertain for quite a long time. An attempt to sort this out was made in the reign of Henry II, although with limited success. It was not until 1316 that a precise demarcation of responsibilities was finally fixed in what were known as the *Articuli Cleri*. By then the church courts were well established and had become a regular feature of English life, a status they would retain until most of their jurisdiction was secularized in 1858.[26]

Because church courts dealt with what we would now call 'family law', they affected far more people than the king's courts did. They operated not according to common law but according to the canon law of the western church, supplemented by local legislation that had been produced by the provincial synods of Canterbury and York. The universal canon law, known as the *ius commune*, was codified by an Italian monk called Gratian, who was teaching at Bologna around 1140. His great work, officially called the *Concordantia Discordantium Canonum*, but usually known simply as the *Decretum*, was supplemented by collections of papal decretals published at various times up until 1500. The *Decretum* was a mixed bag of synodal canons enacted over many centuries, along with opinions of various theologians and papal bulls. Many of these were presented in the form of case studies, in which Gratian demonstrated how general principles could be applied to particular circumstances. One section was devoted to a series of canons relating to penance, and another to the consecration of churches.[27]

By contrast, the decretal collections were systematically organized into five distinct books, treating respectively jurisdiction (*iudex*), procedure (*iudicium*), the clergy (*clerus*), matrimony (*connubium*) and offences (*crimen*). Pope Gregory IX issued the first collection in 1234, known as the *Liber Extra*, because it supplemented the *Decretum*, although it was official in a way that Gratian's compilation was not. This in turn was joined by the *Liber Sextus*, issued by Pope Boniface VIII in 1298, by the *Constitutiones Clementinae* of Pope Clement V (1317), the *Extravagantes Iohannis XXII*, which were additions made by Pope John XXII (1336), and finally by the *Extravagantes Communes*, further additions made up to 1484 that were arranged by Pierre Chapuis in the first printed edition of what became known as the *Corpus Iuris Canonici* (1500). This *Corpus* remained the basis of Roman canon law until 1917 and should have been abolished in England at the time of the Reformation, but the various

[26] Ibid. 67–309; R. N. Swanson, *Church and Society in Late Medieval England* (Oxford: Basil Blackwell, 1989), 140–190; *The Ecclesiastical Courts: Principles of Reconstruction, Being the Report of the Commission on Ecclesiastical Courts Set up by the Archbishops of Canterbury and York in 1951 at the Request of the Convocations* (London: SPCK, 1954); R. B. Outhwaite, *The Rise and Fall of the English Ecclesiastical Courts, 1500–1860* (Cambridge: Cambridge University Press, 2006).

[27] J. A. Brundage, *Medieval Canon Law* (London: Longman, 1995); R. H. Helmholz, *The Spirit of Classical Canon Law* (Athens, Ga.: University of Georgia Press, 1996); *The ius Commune in England: Four Studies* (Oxford: Oxford University Press, 2001).

commissions set up by King Henry VIII and his successors were unable to reach a definitive agreement as to what should replace it. The curious result is that it is still authoritative in the Church of England, at least to the extent that it has not been superseded by subsequent legislation.[28]

One important point to notice about the ordering of the decretals is the clear distinction between the clergy and matrimony, from which ordained men were henceforth excluded. Clerical celibacy had been advocated for a long time, but became compulsory only after the First Lateran Council in 1123, and even then it took some years for it to be fully implemented. But equally important was the control that the church now claimed over matrimony. In earlier times marriage had been a secular affair with little church involvement. In the New Testament, believers were told not to marry outside the faith and not to desert an unbelieving spouse, although if the unbelieving partner wished to depart of his/her own accord, that was to be accepted.[29] Only much later did the church begin to perform marriage ceremonies, and it was not easy to reconcile the traditional tribal customs of the Anglo-Saxons with the demands of the church. But by the time the canon law was codified, the church had taken control of matrimony and was legislating for it. One of its demands was that marriage had to be by consent. In other words, a woman could not be forced to marry a man against her will, nor could child betrothals (very common) be regarded as legally binding. How many women defied custom and refused to marry a man chosen for them by their parents is impossible to say, but at least they could do so in law – a step forward for women's rights.

A marriage once contracted was for life, because the church did not recognize divorce, even in the case of the famous 'Matthean exception' for adultery that Jesus allowed.[30] In the absence of divorce there were only two options. One of these was separation 'from bed and board' (*a thoro et mensa*), which kept the marriage in existence but dispensed the couple from cohabitation. The other was annulment, a declaration that the marriage had never existed, which had the inconvenience that any children born of it were declared illegitimate. Both these options were open to abuse. Separation often encouraged concubinage, which was in effect a second marriage but was not recognized as such. This could cause serious problems when the man died, because his concubine and her children had no right of inheritance, which went to the legitimate spouse, even though by then she might have been long gone.

---

[28] E. Friedberg (ed.), *Corpus Iuris Canonici*, 2 vols. (Graz: Akademische Druck- und Verlagsanstalt, 1955).
[29] 1 Cor. 7:1–16.
[30] Matt. 19:9.

Annulment was facilitated by being allowed within seven degrees of consanguinity (later reduced to four), which in practice meant that virtually everyone in a village could claim it if necessary. But once again, inheritance was a problem, since in this case the children had no right to their parents' property.

The Fourth Lateran Council in 1215 tried to regulate marriage still further by instituting a system of control that involved a public declaration of intent to marry. The so-called 'banns of marriage' had to be read in church three times before the actual wedding, and potential objectors were given the opportunity to intervene if they thought there was something illicit going on. The banns survive in the Church of England, although they were abolished in Scotland – in 1997! We have no way of knowing how effective they were in the Middle Ages, but after the Marriage Act of 1753 they had to be officially recorded, and it is clear that they were taken seriously. The Protestant churches no longer grant decrees of separation or annulment (unlike the Roman Catholic Church), but the Church of England has never officially recognized divorce and is still reluctant to remarry divorced people whose former spouse is still living. Other churches are more lenient, but the link between the church and marriage has never been entirely broken.

Complementing these canons were sets of local legislation that applied to England only. Many of these were enacted by diocesan synods, which often copied one another, albeit with modifications to suit their particular circumstances.[31] They were supplemented by canons issued by the provincial synods of Canterbury and York, which were intended to cover the entire province. A compilation of the Canterbury decrees was made in 1430 by William Lyndwood (1375–1446), who was then the Archbishop of Canterbury's 'official', or chief legal, officer, and later became Bishop of St David's. This collection, which Lyndwood annotated and published in 1433, is known as the *Provinciale* and was reproduced in successive editions until 1679.[32]

The papacy was involved in operating this legislative process through the appointment of judges delegate, whose duty it was to decide cases as they arose. As a rule these judges delegate were English bishops, but by about 1180 the volume of business was such that they had to appoint subdelegates specially trained in canon law to act on their behalf. Over time the delegation of papal authority was fixed in the offices of the archbishops of Canterbury and York,

---

[31] Powicke and Cheney, *Councils and Synods II*.

[32] W. Lyndwood, *Provinciale seu Constitutiones Angliae cui adiiciuntur Constitutiones Legatinae D. Othonis et D. Othoboni Cardinalium* (Oxford: Oxford University Press, 1679; repr. Farnborough: Gregg International Publishers, 1968).

who were recognized as *legati nati* (born legates) because their jurisdiction was inherent in their office.[33]

This did not prevent the papacy from sending special legates from Rome, known as *legati a latere* (legates from the side [of the pope]), who also had the power to summon provincial synods and legislate for the local church. Among them were cardinals Otho (1237–41) and Othobon (1265–8), who both issued a series of synodical decrees or 'constitutions'. Like the *Corpus Iuris Canonici*, both the *Provinciale* and the legatine constitutions of Otho (1237) and Othobon (1268) remain a source of English ecclesiastical law in so far as it has not been made redundant in the centuries since. The authority of Lyndwood's texts was extended to the province of York in 1462. The church courts thus possessed a body of law, complete with commentaries written by a number of eminent jurists, which surpassed anything of which the state could boast until at least the seventeenth century, when a comparable corpus of English common law and commentary emerged and effectively superseded it.

In principle the same system existed in Scotland and Ireland, but for various reasons was much less developed there. Although both countries produced synodical statutes, these were never collected or applied in the systematic way they were in England. The Irish courts functioned only in the parts of the country subject to the king's lordship, while the Scottish ones were irregular at best, at least until a much later period. In practice the courts of the province of Canterbury were by far the most active and it was in them that the canon law of the western church was most thoroughly studied and regularly applied. The church courts could not condemn anyone to death, and their gravest sanction was excommunication. In theological terms that could be seen as worse than physical death, because it cut the victim off from the ministry of the church and therefore from the means of salvation.

There were two forms of excommunication, applied according to the severity of the offence. The lesser excommunication barred the victim from receiving the sacrament but otherwise did not interfere with his (or more rarely her) daily life. The greater excommunication went beyond this to include public shunning – nobody was supposed to have any dealings with someone who had been subjected to it. In practice the lesser excommunication for tithe offences was by far the most common censure the church courts applied, and it

---

[33] On the establishment and early working of this system, see J. E. Sayers, *Papal Judges Delegate in the Province of Canterbury 1198–1254* (Oxford: Oxford University Press, 1971). The archbishops continue to claim the rights of *legati nati*, centuries after the Church of England broke with Rome, though nowadays their authority is delegated to their chief legal officer, who is called the Dean of the Arches in Canterbury and the Auditor in York.

remained a reality until it was finally abolished in 1813. How effective it was is very hard to say. A prominent person might be exposed by it and be forced to put matters right with the church, but many lesser folk seem to have ignored it and not suffered any serious consequences. In reality the church had very little control over laypeople and when attempts were made to impose its authority, they were often resisted. The result seems to have been that many people saw the church courts as a form of oppression and were alienated by them, a resentment that would come to the surface after the Reformation, when pressure for their abolition became increasingly hard to ignore.[34]

The institutional church

The consolidation of the church as an institution was largely complete by the end of the twelfth century.[35] In England the dioceses and their cathedrals had assumed the classic shape that would endure intact until the mid-sixteenth century and be modified in only secondary ways after that. Many of the great cathedrals that now grace our landscape were begun during that time, and most were essentially completed before 1300. Cathedral building was a long and expensive process, and few people lived to see one constructed from beginning to end. In the course of time new architectural techniques came into use, giving the later cathedrals a grace that the earlier ones lack. This can be seen, for example, by contrasting a cathedral like Durham, where the circumference of the pillars is equal to their height, with the slender columns on which the later cathedrals were erected and which were to form the blueprint for the so-called 'Gothic' style. With the notable exception of London, where the old St Paul's was lost in the great fire of 1666, these cathedrals still survive more or less intact and remain the country's greatest monuments to medieval Christianity.

What happened on a grand (if somewhat limited) scale in cathedrals also occurred at the level of the local parish. Very few Anglo-Saxon church buildings were left standing and almost all were replaced by structures in a distinctively Norman style. Many of these have been modified in different ways over the centuries, but their basic outline is still recognizable as 'typically' English. They usually have a square tower or a spire and their interiors are designed to accommodate the sacramental theology developing in the church

---

34 See M. G. Smith, *The Church Courts 1680–1840: From Canon to Ecclesiastical Law* (Lewiston, N.Y.: Edwin Mellen Press, 2006).

35 See C. R. Cheney, *From Becket to Langton: English Church Government 1170–1213* (Manchester: Manchester University Press, 1956).

at that time. The buildings generally face east, with ample space at the chancel end for the high altar on which the priest would celebrate the Eucharist. Choir stalls would then be placed in the chancel on either side and a rood screen would set it apart from the nave, or main body, of the church building. The nave would be designed to allow the parishioners to stand and, in principle at least, hear what was going on in the chancel. In fact the service was in Latin, much of it sung or chanted, and the priest's words were often barely audible to anyone but himself. Unfortunately, if hearing was a problem for many, seeing was even less satisfactory. This was because the priest would celebrate facing eastwards, with his back to the congregation, and it would only be at the moment when he lifted up the consecrated bread and wine (the so-called 'elevation of the host') that others would catch a glimpse of what he was doing. At this point a bell might be rung in order to attract the worshippers' attention and reinforce the sense that a miracle had occurred – the bread and wine the priest offered had been transubstantiated into the body and blood of Christ. In theory anyone could then approach the altar rail and receive Communion, although in practice few seem to have done so, apart from the special seasons of Christmas, Easter and Pentecost (Whitsun). Worship was basically theatre, with the clergy as actors and the people as spectators, and the new church buildings were designed to reflect this. Pulpits were rare, and were introduced in large numbers only in the fifteenth century, when there was a growing demand for sermons. As for seating, there was virtually none, except for that of the bishop, for whom a chair was provided as a sign of his status.

These developments could not leave the secular state indifferent. The church was the only social organization in existence, since even the king's armies were called into being only in wartime. Gifts and purchases over time produced a situation in which the church (including the monasteries) was by far the largest landowner in the country, but one that claimed exemption from the secular taxation needed to pay for the upkeep of the king's court and the defence of the realm. The church was often prepared to help the king out when necessary, but consistently argued that its possessions belonged to God and not to Caesar (as Jesus would have expressed it), so that whatever concessions it made to the state could be understood only as free gifts or, in the language of the time, 'benevolences'. As the king's government grew more sophisticated, and as the aristocracy went on crusade at the behest of the church and not because of any pressing secular need to do so, conflict over policy and resources was bound to occur sooner or later. That was to be the great drama of the thirteenth century.

Clerical taxation

The consolidation of royal power in England took a great leap forward in the reign of Henry II. By 1188 he had established a regular system of taxation that has continued ever since. The date of his son Richard I's coronation (3 September 1189) became, and still remains, the limit of legal memory, which means that, in the law courts, precedent can be cited going back to that date but no further. Richard I (1189–99), known as the Lionheart, has gone down in English history as a legendary crusader king but this reputation is exaggerated. The British Isles had played only a minor role in the early Crusades because local conditions made sending (and financing) large armies to be deployed in the eastern Mediterranean difficult. Some intrepid knights did go, and when they returned left their mark on the English landscape by building churches to replicate the Church of the Holy Sepulchre in Jerusalem, the best-known of which are the Temple Church in London and the so-called 'Round Church' in Cambridge. Richard I became famous because he was the first English monarch to go on crusade, which gave him special prestige in the eyes of Christendom. The crusade was a failure, and on his return Richard was detained in Austria until his subjects back home could ransom him, but these awkward facts have not been allowed to intrude on a good story and Richard has retained his popular, if largely undeserved, reputation to the present day.

Towards the end of his reign Richard I came under great pressure from the King of France, who was determined to assert himself against the hegemony Henry II had established for himself in that country. By inheritance, marriage and conquest, Henry II had assembled a great Continental empire that his successors would find impossible to hold. In 1204 the Duchy of Normandy was conquered by the French and the link established in 1066 was broken. The reign of John (1199–1216) was to suffer grievously from this defeat, and the church was deeply implicated in the result. Angered by the king's refusal to accept Stephen Langton as Archbishop of Canterbury, the church went on strike, refusing to offer its services to the public until the king mended his ways. This 'interdict', as it was called, lasted from 1208 to 1214 and forced the king's hand, which revealed his underlying weakness. A few years later a similar lesson was administered by the nobility, which forced John to grant them a charter of liberties, the famous Magna Carta that is still held up as the beginning of English democracy.[36]

---

[36] See J. C. Holt, *Magna Carta*, 2nd edn (Cambridge: Cambridge University Press, 1992).

One of the few clauses of Magna Carta that remains in effect is the one that guarantees the 'liberties of the church', but that was not enough to satisfy the ecclesiastical authorities. They denounced John for having granted the charter and did their best to oppose it. Under Henry III (1216–72) the church reordered its affairs, but the king was eventually forced by his barons to create a new consultative body, which we now know as Parliament. The clergy, represented in it, were expected to participate as the landowning power they were. The bishops and a number of abbots were summoned to sit in the Upper House (now the House of Lords), not because of their ecclesiastical status but because they were regarded as barons with taxable property.[37] The cathedral chapters and the remaining clergy were invited to elect delegates to attend the lower house (now the House of Commons).[38] The main purpose was to pass legislation in the king's name and vote taxation that everyone, clergy and laity alike, was expected to pay.

The church was not happy with this, partly because the basis for taxing the laity was different from the concept of a benevolence freely offered by the church, and partly because laypeople were involved in church affairs as long as the rate of payment was decided by both. In 1340 the lower clergy retreated from Parliament and formed their own assembly, claiming the right to grant subsidies to the king uninfluenced by the secular arm. They continued to be summoned to Parliament until 1529, but seldom attended.[39]

The result was that a different procedure for clerical taxation was established. This involved the issuing of a royal writ to the archbishops to summon their respective provincial synods and consider voting a subsidy to the Crown, the amount of which was 'suggested' in the royal writ. It was a compromise of sorts, preserving the appearance of ecclesiastical liberty while at the same time ensuring that the clergy would pay their share of tax. Called 'tax convocations', these synods in the late fourteenth century became so frequent that the regular provincial synods were effectively eclipsed. The result was that the word 'convocation' came to be used as a synonym for 'provincial synod', a habit that has persisted to the present time. The separate clerical taxation was to continue until 1664, when it was voluntarily relinquished by the then Archbishop of

---

[37] This status was first defined in the eleventh constitution of Clarendon, 1164. See Whitelock et al., *Councils and Synods*, 2:881–882.

[38] The deans of the secular cathedrals, the priors of the monastic ones and the archdeacons were also summoned to the Lower House.

[39] For the evidence, see P. Bradford and A. K. McHardy (eds.), *Proctors for Parliament: Clergy, Community and Politics c. 1248–1539 (The National Archives, Series SC 10)*, 2 vols. (Woodbridge: Canterbury and York Society and the Boydell Press, 2017–18). The bishops continued to sit in the House of Lords, as twenty-six of them still do today.

Canterbury, in return for granting the clergy the right to vote in parliamentary elections.[40]

Wales and Scotland

What happened to the church in thirteenth-century Wales and Scotland is unclear. At the beginning of the century there was some hope that St David's might become an archbishopric, heading up an independent Welsh church, but it was not to be. By 1283 the last native princes had been defeated and Wales was firmly tied to the English Crown, with the monarch's son and heir proclaimed as its 'prince'. The church itself remained unaffected. The four Welsh dioceses continued to be part of the province of Canterbury and were treated accordingly, but were too poor and remote to have much impact on it. As far as we can tell, the Welsh church simply merged into that of England and little was heard from it until the abandonment of Latin at the time of the Reformation made translation into the Welsh vernacular a priority.

Scotland is only marginally less of a blank. After being constituted as a special jurisdiction directly subject to the see of Rome, the Scottish church established a provincial synod (1225) but there is no record of its activities. For all anyone knows, it might have met every year or almost not at all.[41] Some time later it did produce a collection of fifty-five canons, which are now known as the general statutes of the medieval Scottish church. Since some of them copy the legatine constitutions of Otho, promulgated for Canterbury in 1237, they must be later than that, but most scholars date them to the thirteenth century.[42] They cover a number of subjects, ranging from the conduct of public worship to the maintenance of the clergy, the revenues of the church, tithes and excommunication. Along the way they take in such subjects as wills and testaments, sanctuary offered on church property and the immunity of the clergy from prosecution in a secular court. The general statutes were complemented by a detailed set of canons for the administration of the sacraments, which were composed at Aberdeen and appear to have

[40] G. L. Bray (ed.), *Records of Convocation*, 20 vols. (Woodbridge: Boydell & Brewer, 2005–6), contains the complete record from 1313 to the revival of the convocations in the nineteenth century. In particular see *Records of Convocation*, 3–12, *Canterbury* 1313–1852; 13–15, *York* 1313–1861. A complete list of the lay and clerical subsidies from 1272 to 1663, with comparisons between them, is in Bray, *Records of Convocation*, 19:363–370.

[41] For the forms used to summon it, see D. Patrick, *Statutes of the Scottish Church 1225–1559* (Edinburgh: Edinburgh University Press, 1907), 1–3.

[42] Ibid. 8–29.

been taken mainly from English sources, in particular from Richard Poore's canons for Durham (1228x1236), themselves derived in part from canons issued by the same bishop for his previous diocese of Salisbury (1217x1219).[43] One feature of these that appears to be of purely Scottish origin is the warning 'the mistresses and concubines of priests or beneficed clergy shall not be admitted into the church'.[44] Was that not just as much of a problem in England?

Similar canons dealing with, among other things, the sexual misconduct of the clergy have also survived from the thirteenth century, as have the diocesan constitutions of David Bernham, Bishop of St Andrews (1239–53), which can be dated to 1242.[45] After that the Scottish church seems to have settled down with its new legislation, much of it adapted from English models, to guide its administration and pastoral practice.

Clerical taxation was a particular problem in Scotland, especially when it came to exactions made by the papacy in order to support projects like the Crusades. The Scots had managed to secure an undertaking from the pope that none of his legates would enter the kingdom without special accreditation, a manoeuvre that seems to have prevented the papal legate Othobon from visiting the country during his stay in England, even though his mandate extended to the whole of the British Isles. The chief difficulty for the Scots was that money raised in this way was usually turned over to the King of England on the excuse that he would go on crusade (which the Scots generally did not do). Needless to say, the Scots were unhappy at seeing their revenues being creamed off by the English, especially as they knew that the crusading zeal of the latter had been considerably exaggerated. It was an unhappy situation all round and greatly complicated Scottish relations with the papacy. This was especially important because the popes wanted the Scots to hold regular synods and reform their church, which had apparently become so lax that in several places unordained men were celebrating the sacraments. But lacking an archbishop of their own, the Scottish bishops had to rely on papal legates to convene such synods, and naturally there was a price tag attached to this apparent 'privilege'. It was a vicious circle that would not be resolved until the very end of the Middle Ages, when a standard provincial system was finally established in Scotland.

---

[43] Ibid. 30–45. For the Salisbury and Durham statutes, see Powicke and Cheney, *Councils and Synods II*, 57–96, 201.

[44] Patrick, *Statutes*, 44.

[45] For the former, see ibid. 51–56, and for the latter, 57–67.

Post-invasion Ireland

The Irish situation is much better documented than the Welsh and the Scottish ones, but the evidence is often difficult to interpret. The Anglo-Norman domination that began in 1171 was soon consolidated, at least in the east and south-east of the island, and in 1186 a synod was held in Dublin that enacted a series of canons designed to bring the Irish church into conformity with the rest of western Christendom.[46] Its decisions were ratified by the papacy, which gave them additional weight, although as always implementation of the results was a continual problem. Unfortunately the synod is remembered mainly because it provides the first clear sign of a conflict between the native Irish and the invading Anglo-Norman clergy, each of whom denounced the other as barbarous and immoral. It is not necessary to investigate these claims, which were common enough when churchmen of different nationalities were forced to come to terms with one another, but it is a reminder that cultural integration of the two peoples was still a long way off.

As the Normans had done in England after the conquest, the Anglo-Norman invaders of Ireland sought to impose bishops of their own nationality on the Irish dioceses, hoping thereby to anglicize them. Had they been able to conquer the whole island such a policy might have worked, but because their fortunes ebbed and flowed over time, it was only partially successful. In many cases an 'English' bishop would be appointed for a time, perhaps in alternation with an Irish one, and definitive anglicization was deferred. What mattered as much as anything else was the degree to which the English Crown was involved in the appointments. In some cases the king was persuaded to nominate native Irishmen to a vacant see and so the diocese remained officially 'anglicized', even though the incumbent was not English. Table 4.1 indicates how this worked across the country.

From this we can see that although there were no more than three dioceses that never had an English bishop, only eighteen were 'anglicized' at the time of the Reformation. Furthermore, in four of those the process had only recently taken place and could not really be considered definitive. Of the provinces, only Dublin was effectively won over in the thirteenth century, the subsequent appointments of Irishmen to Leighlin and Ossory being rare, late and of short duration. Further afield, we can say the same for Meath,

---

[46] Bray, *Records of Convocation*, 16:96–105. The synod is especially notable for the way in which it incorporated many of the decisions of the Third Lateran Council (1179) into Irish legislation within a decade of their original promulgation. The speed with which this was accomplished must have impressed the papacy, which remained a firm supporter of English rule in Ireland.

Table 4.1 Diocesan periods of anglicization from AD 1181 to 1533

Diocese	Periods of anglicization	Definitive from
Province of Armagh (5 of 11)		
Ardagh	1373–95; 1400–16	—
Armagh	1217–27; 1238–56; 1306–33	1346
Clogher	1475–1500	—
Clonmacnois	1369–80; 1397–1423; 1487–1508	—
Connor	1245–1324	1431
Derry	1391–4; 1467–84	—
Down	1258	1258
Dromore	1369–1455; 1457–99	—
Kilmore	1388–9	1530
Meath	1192–1224; 1227–1320	1327
Raphoe		—
Province of Cashel (6 of 10)		
Ardfert	1217–88; 1348–72; 1380–1452	1458
Cashel	1317–26; 1329–31	1373
Cloyne	1247–74	1284
Cork	1225–76	1321
Emly	1286–1444	—
Kilfenora		—
Killaloe		—
Limerick	1215–1399	1426
Lismore	1218–46	1253
Ross	1420–26; 1431–48; 1494–1517	—
Province of Dublin (all 5)		
Dublin	1181	1181
Ferns	1223	1223
Kildare	1223	1223
Leighlin	1217–1419; 1432–1523	1527
Ossory	1202–1421; 1427–78	1487
Province of Tuam (2 of 7)		
Achonry	1373–80; 1424–36; 1442–53; 1470–1504	—
Annaghdown	1325–8	—
Clonfert	1320–23	—
Elphin	1372–1404; 1418–21	1508
Killala	1306–1425; 1500–05	—
Kilmacduagh	1533	1533
Tuam	1286–1312; 1408–37	—

Down, Limerick and Lismore, but elsewhere the English presence was insecure.

The Anglo-Normans appear to have introduced the parish system in Ireland, just as the Normans had done in England, and this proved to be successful. Churches were built all over the country in the first century after the invasion and the system settled down quite quickly. In the conquered areas the church was also able to impose a tithe regime similar to the English one, thereby stabilizing a source of income that had long existed in theory but had frequently been impossible to administer in practice. An Irish Parliament also came into existence in the reign of Henry III and the clergy were summoned to it along the same lines as they were in England.[47] The original intention was to get the archbishops to organize tax collection by turning their provincial synods into tax convocations, as was done in England, but the incomplete conquest of the island made this impossible. Instead bishops and the major abbots, along with proctors from cathedral chapters and the lower clergy, were summoned to Parliament, where they participated in deliberations alongside their secular colleagues. Unlike the lower clergy in England, their Irish counterparts did not secede to form their own tax-granting body but continued to be Members of Parliament until they were forcibly ejected in 1537.

In theory every bishop and diocese were liable to be summoned, but in practice only those directly subject to the king attended Parliament on a regular basis. This meant that the archbishops of Dublin and Cashel were usually present, along with most of their suffragans. The Archbishop of Tuam, on the other hand, hardly ever went and his province, which lay almost entirely outside the king's immediate jurisdiction, generally escaped taxation. Armagh was somewhere in the middle. Most of the province lay outside royal control, although such control was consistently exercised in Meath and occasionally in Down and Connor also. The diocese of Armagh itself was divided between the north (modern County Armagh), which lay in the Gaelic area (*inter Hibernicos*), and the south (modern County Louth), which was 'among the English' (*inter Anglicos*). The archbishop, who after 1346 was always an Anglo-Norman, resided at Termonfeckin, near Drogheda (Louth), and seldom ventured into the Irish north. The English part of the diocese played a role in Parliament, although the archbishop himself refused to attend any assembly that was held in Dublin for fear that his primacy over the Irish church as a

---

[47] On the workings of the parliament, see H. G. Richardson and G. O. Sayles, *The Irish Parliament in the Middle Ages*, 2nd edn (Philadelphia, Pa.: University of Pennsylvania Press, 1962). For a general history of the period, see J. Lydon, *The Lordship of Ireland in the Middle Ages*, 2nd edn (Dublin: Four Courts Press, 2003); and for specifically ecclesiastical affairs, see Bray, *Records of Convocation*, 16–18.

whole would be compromised if he did. We are well informed about Armagh because the archbishop's registers from 1361 to 1559 have survived and we can follow developments there, as well as in the wider church, on a year-by-year basis. What we find is that early attempts to keep the Gaelic and English worlds together under the aegis of a common episcopate were gradually abandoned, and by the end of the fifteenth century the two parts of the Armagh diocese, and by extension the two different cultures of Ireland, were being administered separately and had less and less to do with each other.

As part of its growing anglicization, the Irish church was being brought into increasing conformity with English norms, as had been the expressed desire of the Synod of Cashel in 1172. Cathedrals were established in each of the dioceses, complete with a chapter that was charged with the election of the bishop when the see fell vacant. All of these cathedrals were secular, apart from one. The exception was Holy Trinity (Christ Church) Dublin, which in 1163 was established as a monastic cathedral with a corps of Augustinian canons, rather like Carlisle in England. This was felt to be an anomaly however, and in 1192 Dublin acquired a second cathedral (St Patrick's), which was constituted with a secular chapter modelled on that of Salisbury and using the Sarum Rite in its worship. The curious existence of two cathedrals in one city was to cause trouble later on, because the archbishop was elected by the chapters of both and they did not always agree. But in spite of this the arrangement continued and the two cathedrals remain active to this day.[48]

Developments in the monastic world were more complex. There was a considerable expansion of Cistercian foundations in the thirteenth century, and many existing monasteries adopted the Augustinian pattern, which seems to have suited traditional Irish ways. There was a concerted attempt to ensure that the monasteries were not divided along ethnic lines, but some conflict was inevitable. As in England, the abbots of the larger monastic houses were summoned to Parliament, and a number of them sent proctors to represent them, at least in the early days. The practice seems to have become less frequent as time went on but, as with the lower clergy, they were not ejected until just after the start of the Reformation (1537).

The same pattern was visible with the mendicant orders, which proved to be very popular, perhaps because of their emphasis on poverty in a country that was far from wealthy. Once again, there were periodic attempts on the part of the English to exclude the Irish from becoming friars, but those

---

[48] In recent years Christ Church has been designated as the diocesan cathedral and St Patrick's as the 'national' cathedral for the whole of Ireland, an arrangement that resolves the anomaly by giving each cathedral a different function.

attempts were short-lived and thus unsuccessful. Despite many tensions at local level, the two nations met and mingled rather well, at least as long as the English colony was self-confident in its domination of Ireland and the Gaelic population was resigned to the English presence.

The reign of King Edward I

By the late thirteenth century people were beginning to think seriously of uniting the British Isles under a single monarch and coordinating, if not uniting, the churches within it. The reign of Edward I (1272–1307) was full of promise in this respect. Edward laid claim to the Crown of Scotland and for a time appeared to be successful. He pursued the conquest of Ireland, and domination of the entire island seemed to be within his grasp. Perhaps if he had lived longer, or had had a more competent successor, the unification project might have been realized and the subsequent history of the islands changed accordingly. As it was, the greatest achievement of his reign was a census authorized by Pope Nicholas IV in 1291 and completed over the next fifteen years or so.[49] It is the first evidence we have of the comprehensive economic state of England and Ireland and, despite a number of inaccuracies, it was used as the basis for clerical taxation until the sixteenth century. The *Nova Taxatio*, as the census is called, shows that south-east England and east-central Ireland were the richest parts of their respective countries and expected to yield the greater part of the revenue the king hoped to raise. Its coverage of Ireland is especially fascinating, because it lists a number of places that are not otherwise known and assesses their ratable value. Suspicions are inevitably raised by the fact that these remote parishes all seem to have yielded the same amount of income. That strongly suggests that the tax assessor sat in Galway and just guessed at what might be expected from places that were unlikely to pay anything, because they were effectively beyond the king's control. But leaving things like that aside, the *Taxatio* is often very detailed about the value of places it did know about and that could be expected to pay what was asked of them.

This is about as close as we can get to assessing the vitality of local church life in Edward I's reign. Another important indication of this can be discerned in the ninth canon of the so-called Lambeth Constitutions, entitled *Ignorantia Sacerdotum*, issued by Archbishop John Peckham (1230?–92) in 1281 and ratified by a synod held in that year. *Ignorantia Sacerdotum* laid down the

---

[49] The English and Welsh parts were published by the Record Commission in 1802 (and again in 1834), and this edition is now available online. The Irish part has been published in Bray, *Records of Convocation*, 18:255–370.

qualifications needed for ordination to the priesthood and determined how candidates were to proceed towards it. Seeking to implement reforms already introduced by the Fourth Lateran Council in 1215, but only fitfully applied in England until then, Peckham decreed that everyone seeking holy orders had to be conversant with the Apostles' Creed (doctrine), the Ten Commandments (discipline) and basic devotional practice. By 'conversant' was meant the ability to expound and apply the teaching of these key texts to the lives of the parishioners to whom they were expected to minister. They would have to be able to preach effectively and explain how the principles of theology contained in these classic texts were the necessary foundation of the Christian life that ordinary people were expected to live. In the words of the canon:

> we order that four times during the year, that is once in every quarter on one or several solemn days, each priest in charge of a parish should personally explain or have someone else explain to the people in their mother tongue, without any fancifully woven subtleties, the fourteen articles of faith [the Apostles' Creed], the Ten Commandments of the Decalogue, the two precepts of the Gospel (namely the twin laws of charity), the seven works of mercy, the seven capital sins and their fruits, the seven principal virtues, and the seven grace-giving sacraments.[50]

Peckham was careful to spell out exactly what he meant and how he understood the various items that he wanted priests to expound. His approach clearly reflected the impact of Peter Lombard's *Sentences*, which had already become the principal theological textbook in the universities, and it was such a useful summary that it was adopted, often without acknowledgment, by almost all the dioceses in the British Isles. It may even have some residual authority in the Church of England today (apart from the section on the sacraments, which was clearly repealed at the time of the Reformation). It would certainly do nobody any harm if it were enforced in the modern church!

The seven works of mercy listed by Peckham were taken from the Bible. Six of them are listed in Matthew 25:35–36: feed the hungry, give drink to the thirsty, give shelter to strangers, clothe the naked, visit the sick and comfort those in prison. The seventh came from the apocryphal book Tobit (1:21), which was to bury the dead. The seven principal virtues were faith, hope and charity (theological virtues ordained by God), along with prudence, justice,

---

[50] Powicke and Cheney, *Councils and Synods II*, 900–901, tr. John Shinners, in J. Shinners and William J. Dohar (eds.), *Pastors and the Care of Souls in Medieval England* (Notre Dame, Ind.: University of Notre Dame Press, 1998), 127–128.

temperance and fortitude (human virtues designed for neighbourly relations). Peckham also introduced the seven sacraments for the first time in English canon law: baptism, confirmation, penance, the Eucharist and extreme unction, which are for all Christians, and then holy orders and matrimony, which were incompatible and intended only for some. Peckham's commentary here is interesting, in that he insisted extreme unction should be administered only to those who are dying as long as they are still of sound mind. Holy orders he believed were appropriate for those seeking perfection, with matrimony reserved to those who are imperfect (and who presumably intend to remain that way).

How effective *Ignorantia Sacerdotum* was is hard to say. Ordinary laypeople were silent and are therefore beyond the reach of the modern researcher, and although we know that monastic life was expanding and was apparently healthy, there is no evidence for the quality of the monks' spirituality. We may assume that things were ticking over more or less as they should have been but we cannot penetrate any deeper than that. What we do know is that the reign of Edward II (1307–27) was punctured by a series of crises that undid the work of his father, particularly in Scotland and Ireland. Scottish noblemen, themselves often of Norman descent, rebelled against English rule and spread their rebellion to Ireland, where Edward Bruce, younger brother of the more famous Robert, wreaked havoc for several years and did much to weaken the Crown's hold on the country. The church inevitably suffered from these unsettled conditions and was unable to make the sort of progress that might have been expected if earlier gains had been consolidated.

The reign of Edward I was the high-water mark of the Norman conquest of the British Isles. The Church of England was established along lines that have remained recognizable ever since and many of its characteristic features took on their classical shape at that time. In particular the great cathedrals were rising across the landscape, parish boundaries were becoming fixed and bishops started keeping registers of their activities, which are now a major source of our knowledge of the later Middle Ages. The fourteenth century was to be a disappointment in many ways, but the foundations of the church were secure and have stood the test of time. The Celtic lands were less highly developed, but in different ways England was a model for them to imitate, and over time they came to resemble it more and more. A sense of Britain, rooted in England but embracing more than just a single country, was slowly taking shape and in later years was to become the basis for the island society and civilization we know today.

5

The crisis of Christendom (1307–84)

Crown and mitre

By 1300 the British churches were firmly integrated into western Christendom, recognizing the Roman pope as their head and generally acquiescing in the centralization of the church's administration that the papacy had pursued for more than two centuries. For much of that time the need to raise funds for the Crusades was paramount, and papal taxation, which was meant to support them, had become a standard feature of European finance. Along with that there had been a corresponding growth in the church's bureaucracy, which the popes had to pay for out of whatever resources they could muster. At the same time, the monarchies of western Europe were also expanding their reach, often drawing on ecclesiastics for their own emerging civil services. Church and state thus became rivals for the same revenue and often for the same personnel, and this inevitably led to conflict. In 1296 the pope issued a bull called *Clericis Laicos*, in which he tried to prevent the kings from taxing church property on the ground that it belonged to God and was therefore inalienable. This led to a dispute with the king of France, who decided to solve the problem by seizing control of the papacy. His opportunity came in 1305 when the cardinals elected the Archbishop of Bordeaux, a subject of the English king (who ruled the city as Duke of Aquitaine), as Pope Clement V. The King of France, Philip IV (1285–1314), would not allow him to cross French territory on his way to Rome, and instead took him captive. Eventually the Pope was forced to settle in Avignon, which was established as an autonomous papal enclave entirely surrounded by France. There was not much that anyone could do about this and it was not long before the consequences were felt. Philip IV had fallen out with the knightly order of the Templars, which had been formed during the Crusades in order to protect pilgrims to Jerusalem. The failure of the Crusades made them (and other similar orders) redundant, but they endeavoured to continue their charitable work elsewhere. Unfortunately for them, the Templars had become extremely wealthy and the French king had his eye on their resources. He trumped up charges of heresy (and worse) against them, forced the Pope to dissolve the order and proceeded to persecute any Templars he could lay his hands on. England escaped the worst effects of this, but the Templars were nevertheless suppressed, leaving little but their round churches to remind the country of their existence.[1]

The French domination of the papacy became more of a problem for the English in 1328, when the male line of the French monarchy died out and it was disputed who should become the next king. Edward III (1327–77) claimed the French Crown through his mother, who was the only surviving descendant of the last French kings. It was not clear at that time whether a man could succeed to the French throne through the female line, although it had happened in England, when Henry II claimed the Crown by virtue of inheritance through his mother. The French nobility resisted this precedent however, not least because they did not want to be governed by someone they saw as 'foreign', and appointed a distant male relative of the late king instead. When this relative of the king died, Edward III renewed his claim and inaugurated what was to become the Hundred Years' War with France.

The effect of the war on the English church was to be profound, if indirect. Wars cost money, and the newly established system of clerical taxation would soon be put to good use. This development was made easier by changes in the English church during the fourteenth century.[2] One of the most important of these was the subtle shift in the character of the episcopate. Before 1300 many of the most prominent bishops had been theologians and scholars, fully conscious of the church's dignity and determined to defend it against all comers. There was also a sizable group of monastic bishops who thought along similar lines. But as time went on, the numbers of these declined. Monks were still occasionally appointed, particularly to sees that had monastic cathedrals, although there was no guarantee that such a see would have a monk as its bishop. Scholar bishops were still appointed, but in smaller numbers and to less important bishoprics. The plum posts went increasingly to men in the king's service, whose first loyalty was to him and not to the pope or to the interests of the church.

This tendency was matched by an adroit use of the benefice system, which the king was often able to manipulate to his own advantage. There were two different kinds of benefice – those with the 'cure of souls' (*cura animarum*) and those without (*sine cura*). Broadly speaking, the first of these was what we would now recognize as parish ministry, whereas the second consisted mainly

---

[1] M. Haag, *The Templars: History and Myth* (London: Profile Books, 2008); M. Barber, *The Trial of the Templars* (Cambridge: Cambridge University Press, 1978).

[2] See W. A. Pantin, *The English Church in the Fourteenth Century* (Cambridge: Cambridge University Press, 1955).

of offices in cathedrals (like canonries, for example) that did not involve pastoral work. Thanks to the revenues the cathedrals could draw on, these 'sinecures' were sometimes well endowed but demanded very little from those who held them. Many of the parish benefices were small and had to be combined in order to provide the priest with a decent stipend, but for this to happen, a papal dispensation was required. That was not the case however with the sinecure benefices, which could be held in plurality, virtually without limit. It was very tempting for the king to place his civil servants in these sinecures, multiplying them as required to keep his bureaucrats in the style to which the court was accustomed. It was also possible for a beneficed priest with cure of souls to hold one or more sinecures without needing special permission, and that also became common.

To our minds this system has more than the whiff of corruption about it, but the situation was more complicated than many of us realize. Many beneficed clergy were granted indefinite study leave in the universities, which enabled them to pay for their education and thus serve the church better. If they had access to a sinecure, the revenue they gained from that could be used to pay a substitute (vicar) to do the work of the parish priest, and so parishes would not be deprived of a regular ministry. There was a large number of unbeneficed clergy, often known as 'stipendiary chaplains', who were available for such duties, and so the system functioned fairly smoothly. But there is no denying that it was fundamentally unjust, in the sense that the man who did the work was in every respect inferior to the one who held the position responsible for it, who might have little or no connection to the sources of his revenue.

As the fourteenth century wore on, the civil service bishops became less numerous, but their places were taken by scions of the aristocracy, many of whom had just as high a sense of their dignity as the scholar bishops of the thirteenth century had had, but who lacked their learning and (often) their piety too. Some did not hesitate to stand up to the king, but they did so as politicians rather than as 'saints'. They might suffer demotion and even exile if the king could manage it, but there were no martyrs among them!

One way that the king was able to work the system in his favour was to claim his so-called 'regalian rights' during vacancies. When a bishop died, his revenues would technically revert to the pope until a new man was appointed, but in practice the king was often able to seize what were called the 'temporalities' of the see, if only for a limited time. He was also able to make recommendations about who the next bishop should be, although he was not always successful in this. Even so, very few servants of the king went un-rewarded, even if they did not always get what they wanted or were initially promised. Lower down the scale, the king was often able to appoint his men to cathedral offices and even to parishes, many of which were already in his gift because the church in question had been a royal foundation.

It would be wrong to suggest that the king was able to seize control of the church in the way that he was to do at the time of the Reformation, because despite the many avenues of influence open to him, he was still forced to respect the vested interests of monasteries, bishops, noblemen and even the pope. But at the same time, the separation of church and state implied by the establishment of the tax convocations was more fiction than fact, and nobody could have a distinguished ecclesiastical career without coming to terms with the king at some point.

The kings were powerful and usually got what they wanted, but royal authority was always subordinate in church affairs to that of the pope. As far back as 1265 the pope had claimed the right, as head of the church, to present his candidates to every benefice in Europe. In practice he often failed to exercise this right or delegated it to local bishops, but the theory remained and, if he chose, he could intervene anywhere at any time. One effect of this was that numerous petitioners went to Rome, and later to Avignon, asking for the pope to grant them a particular benefice. Anyone could do this and there was a wide range of applicants, but the surprising thing is that the most frequent English petitioners were the king and members of his family. Table 5.1 illustrates what happened between 1342 and 1366. Column A lists the number of prebends and cathedral dignities that were sought, column B gives the number of lesser benefices and column C is the number (of the total) destined for men who served as clerks to the petitioners.

Table 5.1 Petitioners between 1342 and 1366

Petitioner	A	B	C
Edward II	49	20	41
Edward, Prince of Wales	67	38	42
Henry, Duke of Lancaster	66	32	80
Total	182	90	163

From this it will be seen that at least two-thirds of the benefices petitioned for were sinecures and that about 60% of them were destined for servants of the king or the royal court. Even if not all the petitions were granted, the general pattern is unmistakable and explains why conflict between Crown and papacy was almost inevitable. For the only real reason why the pope would claim the right to provide benefices in England, Wales or Ireland was to reward his own faithful servants and assure them of a sufficient income.[3] English critics of the papal claims to provision were fierce in denouncing what they saw as the alienation of English revenues to foreigners, but their complaints were exaggerated. There were times when aliens occupied anywhere from a quarter to a third of the cathedral dignities in some places, but this was not a universal pattern and the monastic cathedrals (nearly half the total) did not have dignities to be provided. Foreigners were relatively few and far between, but they were highly visible and tended to occupy the more lucrative benefices. They were therefore targets for Englishmen who disliked foreigners, especially during the wars with France, and for those who felt that they or their relatives had lost out to someone who was unknown to them and unlikely even to visit the cathedral where he had been provided with a dignity.

Another problem, related to this, was that the papacy refused to recognize English customary law. In England, advowsons (the right of presentation to a benefice) were regarded as secular property and disputes concerning them were justiciable in the king's courts. The papacy, on the other hand, claimed that all church property lay under its jurisdiction and felt free to reject men who had been nominated to a benefice by a lay patron, or indeed by anyone other than the pope himself. This difference of perception led some people to believe that they could overturn a presentation by appealing their case to the pope, who might well grant their request, not on its merits but in order to assert his authority. It was for these reasons that in 1351 Edward III had Parliament enact a statute against papal provisors, and two years later another statute forbidding appeals to Rome without his permission, a practice known by its Latin name as *praemunire* (to forearm). Here there was a conflict between English common law, which demanded that a case should be heard in a lower court first and only later be appealed higher if permission to do so was granted, and Roman civil law, which allowed a defendant to skip the lower courts entirely and go straight to the top.[4] It remained a living possibility in canon law, which was based on ancient Roman tradition, but could easily be seen as a way of escaping justice by forcing the litigants into a lengthy and expensive process in a foreign court, whose outcome was far from certain.[5]

---

[3] Scotland was not part of Edward III's dominions, but the papacy had full control of the church there – more so, indeed, than in the other countries of the British Isles.

[4] That is effectively what the apostle Paul did when he appealed his case to Caesar and was sent to Rome for trial. See Acts 25:10–12.

[5] The statutes concerning provisors and *praemunire* are printed (in English translation) in G. L. Bray, *Documents of the English Reformation*, 3rd edn (Cambridge: James Clarke, 2019), 535–545.

The statutes against papal provisions and *praemunire* were to enjoy a curious afterlife, particularly in the run-up to the Reformation in the sixteenth century, but at the time they were not enforced. It seems that Edward III was merely making a point and keeping legislation in reserve in case he did not get his way. In practice, all appointments to bishoprics after 1344 were by papal provision, although almost always with the king's consent, which had not been the case earlier.

The clergy

The exact number of benefices and ordained clergymen at any given point in the Middle Ages is difficult to determine, but a total figure of 12,500 parishes for the British Isles is probably not too wide of the mark. Of these, fewer than 2,500 were in Ireland and about 1,100 in Scotland, with the rest in England and Wales combined. A rough guess suggests that there were probably about three times as many ordained clergy, although this figure went up and down, sometimes quite dramatically, and priests were not evenly distributed across the country. What we can say with some certainty is that overall numbers dropped considerably as a result of the plague in the years around 1350, and they did not recover their earlier strength until about 1500, by which time expectations of the clergy had changed considerably. No longer were they needed to fill the king's civil service, and a growing body of educated laypeople wanted them to perform their pastoral duties and provide spiritual nourishment to their parishioners instead. There was a sense among the more educated laity that too many clergymen were enjoying privileges they had done nothing to earn, and that many laypeople were both better educated and more devout than their pastors. Sooner or later something would have to give, as it finally did in the mid-sixteenth century.

Historians have shown great interest in the social composition of the clergy, but it is impossible to generalize about this. We know that men from all walks of life took holy orders, and that it was theoretically possible for the low-born to rise to high office in the church. Serfs and illegitimate children were barred from seeking ordination, but it was possible for them to obtain a dispensation from the pope or one of his delegates, and the surviving records suggest that this happened fairly often. It also seems that the bulk of the clergy were drawn from the wealthier peasantry or the prosperous artisan classes springing up in the towns. We surmise this because these were the people who had the money needed to educate their sons and buy the sort of influence required for obtaining a good benefice. It may also help to explain why overall numbers fell in the fifteenth century, as other opportunities for advancement became available and seemed more attractive than the celibate life of a priest. However, this is a guess based on patchy and inadequate evidence that makes it impossible to generalize, although the upturn in numbers at the end of the fifteenth century might well have been connected with the general increase in prosperity at the same time.

A further complication often ignored is that foreigners were not excluded from English benefices. Quite apart from the papal provision of Italians and others to English bishoprics and cathedral dignities, many French monasteries had daughter houses in England and exercised patronage through them. That was stopped by the Crown in 1410, but even after that it was still possible for a foreigner to obtain an English benefice if he had the right connections. Of course, the same principle applied in reverse – Englishmen could, and occasionally did, obtain posts in other countries. At the top end of the scale, ten Englishmen were created cardinals, beginning with Simon Langham in 1368 and Adam Easton in 1382. Easton was particularly 'international' in his sources of income, being archdeacon of Shetland (then still part of the Norwegian church), precentor of Lisbon Cathedral and prior of the Monastery of St Agnes in Ferrara, in addition to being Provost of Beverley Minster (York), rector of Wearmouth (Durham) and prebendary of Aylesbury in Lincoln Cathedral. Englishmen complained about foreigners occupying sinecures in England but, as far as we know, nobody said a word about Easton!

There were four more creations in the fifteenth century, Henry Beaufort (1426), John Kemp (1439), Thomas Bouchier (1467) and John Morton (1493); and four more in the sixteenth, Christopher Bainbridge (1511), Thomas Wolsey (1515), John Fisher (1535) and Reginald Pole (1536). It is these sixteenth-century creations that were most effective and are best known. Bainbridge lived at the papal court, where he acted as a kind of ambassador for the English, and the other three played an important part in the ups and downs of the English Reformation. By way of comparison, Scotland had only one cardinal, David Beaton, who was not appointed until 1538, and Ireland had none at all in the medieval period.[6]

Returning to the supply of English parishes, what we can say is that there were always more clergymen than the number of benefices available, and that the higher offices were severely restricted in number. There were never more than twenty-one bishops for example, which made episcopal oversight very

---

6 See D. A. Bellinger and S. Fletcher, *Princes of the Church: A History of the English Cardinals* (Stroud: Sutton Publishing, 2001).

difficult in the larger English dioceses. That is why many of them employed suffragans to assist them. Some of these were drawn from Wales and many more from Ireland,[7] but others were specially consecrated for the purpose. The medieval church did not have recognized suffragan sees, so a number of these men were given titles of bishoprics that had long since disappeared. The majority of them were in countries that had fallen to the forces of Islam, so that English bishops would be assigned to exotic places like Selymbria and Sebastopol.[8] In some cases the titular sees cannot now be identified and the suspicion must be that they were invented as the need arose.[9]

Some of the secular cathedrals had large staffs, but the total was never more than about 300, a number reduced by widespread pluralism. The vast majority had to compete for what was available in the parishes, and it was by no means guaranteed that the best-qualified men would get the most desirable livings. Furthermore, posts usually became available only on the death of the incumbent, which was unpredictable. At the time of the plague, rapid advancement was possible and standards were lowered – many parishes had to take what they could get. But later on it became increasingly common for incumbents to try to keep their benefices in the family by a device known as 'resignation in favour' (*resignatio in favorem*), whereby they would hand over their rights to a designated successor, often a nephew or cousin. In this way the number of livings available on the open market decreased over time, making it harder for those without connections to break into the charmed circle of the beneficed clergy.

It may seem logical that a beneficed clergyman had to be a priest, but this was not necessarily so. It was not unusual for well-placed men to acquire a benefice in order to pay for their education, or to maintain them when they were in royal service, and it was unnecessary to be in priest's orders for that. Someone with a benefice could always hire a 'stipendiary chaplain' to perform parish duties, and this was common. The result was a system in which there developed an unbeneficed 'clerical proletariat' that did the actual work, and that in hierarchical terms was more qualified than some incumbents, because their vicars (substitutes) had to be priests. As so often happens, a system that began with good intentions ended up with unforeseen problems that the church's enemies were only too ready to exploit. To make matters worse, it was

---

[7] See Bray, *Records of Convocation*, 20 vols. (Woodbridge: Boydell & Brewer, 2005–6), 16:553–555, for a list of the Irish bishops concerned.

[8] Selymbria is now Silivri in Turkey, and Sebastopol (Sevastopol) is in the Crimea.

[9] This system was suppressed in the sixteenth century, though it is interesting to note that a version of it has been revived among the Eastern Orthodox communities that have settled in Britain. The head of the Russian Orthodox Church in London is the Bishop of Sourozh, which no longer exists, in Russia, and his Greek counterpart is the Archbishop of Thyatira and Great Britain!

not impossible for non-resident clergy to exchange their benefices with colleagues without ever having visited them. In extreme cases it seems that benefices were even gambled away by students and clerks in royal service, although that abuse was more widely publicized in anticlerical literature than the evidence for it would warrant.

More commonly, beneficed clergy might resign their livings but ensure a pension for themselves for the rest of their lives, which their successor(s) would have to pay out of their income. In some cases the pensions amounted to more than half the total revenue of the benefice, making the pensioners wealthier than the incumbents. Abuses of this kind could mean that a benefice was heavily encumbered with debts and not worth anything like its nominal value. This and other factors, like reduced tithe income due to changing agricultural practices, flooding or whatever, could prompt the desire for exchange. Patrons might also be tempted to sell their advowsons, possibly to pay off debts of their own. The result was that there developed a considerable market in churches for sale, which was brokered by merchants known as 'chop-churches' from the old English word 'chop' (buy, trade). That this was a scandal was often recognized, but because the church lacked any internal mechanism for dealing with such problems, it is hard to see that there was any alternative. Outright corruption was rare, but dubious practices abounded and became targets for would-be reformers. But whatever problems there were with the parish system, there can be no doubt that it left an indelible mark on Britain, and in particular on the Church of England, where it is still alive and well in ways that clearly reflect its medieval origins.

Scholastic theology

One consequence of the Hundred Years' War was a growing distrust of the papacy, which many Englishmen believed was in the pocket of the French king. There were other grievances against the popes as well, many of them articulated across Europe. Pope John XXII was so disliked in some quarters that he was referred to as the Antichrist, a label that would be pinned on his successors as time went on. Marsilius of Padua (c.1275 – c.1342) wrote an influential book called *Defensor Pacis*, in which he challenged papal claims to jurisdiction over secular rulers. In England criticism was usually more muted than that, but it was not unknown and was closely connected to the changing fashion in philosophical theology associated with the name of Duns Scotus.

Scotism, as his philosophical system came to be known, was not immediately popular and met with considerable opposition at first, but by about 1315 it was dominant at Oxford, largely thanks to the enthusiasm of the Franciscan John of Reading (d. 1346), who was the leading theological voice in the university until his departure for Avignon in 1322. By the time he left however, Scotism was coming under attack from the young scholar William of Ockham, and John found himself on the defensive against him.

William of Ockham (c.1287–1347), a philosophical theologian of the stature of Duns Scotus, did not go to Oxford until 1304, too late to have met Scotus in person, but at a time when Scotus was still alive and the memory of him there was fresh. Thomas Aquinas was still being read and taken seriously, even though interest in him was declining. William was quick to challenge both of these acknowledged masters. For a start, he rejected their belief that universal concepts manifest themselves to differing degrees in particular objects. To give an example, in Ockham's eyes there was no such thing as 'whiteness' in the abstract, although there are many things that we perceive to be different shades of 'white' and that we group together in our minds. Similarly, he did not accept that there was such a thing as 'humanity' distinct from actual human beings. To put it simply, what we call 'humanity' is a collection of characteristics common to all people everywhere. It is not a real thing in itself, of which actual people are more or less faithful representatives.

William also objected to the large number of pseudoscientific categories that had been inherited from the philosophical tradition associated with the name of Aristotle, and he argued that they should be reduced to the bare minimum needed to explain the existence of an object. Of Aristotle's ten categories – substance, quality, quantity, relation, place, time, position, state, action and passion – William rejected all but substance and quality.[10] This desire to pare down arguments to the essentials has come to be known as 'Ockham's razor', and he is most commonly remembered for that. What he was saying was not new, since nobody wanted to multiply explanatory categories beyond what was necessary, but Ockham differed from his contemporaries in believing that fewer categories were needed than most of them imagined.

William's views might have gone unremarked upon, except that they posed considerable problems for theology. He himself recognized that Christian doctrines like the Trinity, the incarnation of Christ and the transubstantiation of the consecrated elements in the Lord's Supper (Eucharist) demanded more categories of analysis than strict philosophical logic would have found

---

[10] It is not clear why he allowed 'quality' to survive, but the word may have had theological connotations he wanted to preserve. See below.

necessary, and it was here that his thinking came into conflict with the teaching of the church. On the questions of the Trinity and incarnation, William had little choice but to give way to tradition, since they were ancient doctrines that reflected the teaching of the New Testament. It might not have been clear how the Father could be the essence of God, the Son the essence of God and the Holy Spirit the essence of God if there is only one divine essence and the three persons are genuinely distinct, but this had always been acknowledged as a mystery and was accepted as such. Transubstantiation, however, was a relatively new idea that was more obviously dependent on Aristotelian logic, and therefore it was easier to call into question. It was probably because he had to allow for it that William retained the category of 'quality' as something genuinely distinct from 'substance', but this was not very logical and later generations would distance themselves from it, with devastating results for the church's official doctrine.

Transubstantiation was the belief that when the priest consecrated the bread and wine in the Lord's Supper, they were changed into the body and blood of Christ. The doctrine rested on a belief in the relationship between substance and accidents that came from ancient Greek philosophy rather than from the Bible. Ockham rejected that way of thinking in favour of what we now call 'nominalism'; that is to say, that things are what we call them and do not have an underlying substance distinct from their properties in the way many of the ancient Greeks had imagined. Ockham's analysis was closer to the biblical view of reality, and as it caught on, the gulf between what the Bible taught and what the church had based its teaching on was exposed. With respect to transubstantiation, an important Christian doctrine had been elaborated by the church and imposed on the Christian world against what appeared to be the plain teaching of Scripture. Because of that a new controversy opened up. Did spiritual authority rest on the papacy and church hierarchy, or was it derived from the Bible? Nobody knew it at the time, but in this debate lay the seeds of the Protestant Reformation, which would change British Christianity for ever.

What got William into trouble was his attempt to explain the difference between the theoretical *potentia absoluta* and the actual *potentia ordinata* in God. He accepted Scotus's assertion that by virtue of his *potentia absoluta*, God could save an unbaptized person, even though baptism was the ordained means of salvation administered by and through the church, but he argued that God would not do that because it went against his revealed will (*potentia ordinata*). To Pope John XXII this seemed nonsensical, because God's eternal knowledge cannot be altered, and so whatever can happen because of his *potentia absoluta* must happen according to his declared will (*potentia ordinata*) and not go against it. In this case the correct theological conclusion was that only by baptism was salvation possible, because that is what God has revealed in Scripture. In other words the *potentia ordinata* is the only real one, and there is no hidden *potentia absoluta* that can override it. Ockham was furious at what he saw as the Pope's theological imbecility, but of course that only ensured that he would be condemned. He was in Avignon at the time and was denounced by someone there, possibly John of Reading, but he managed to flee to Munich. There he cast himself on the mercy of Duke Ludwig IV of Bavaria, who protected him for the rest of his life.

Meanwhile, back in Oxford, William's views were roundly condemned by Walter Chatton (d. 1343), a fellow Franciscan, who argued that theological tradition and scriptural revelation were to be preferred over abstract philosophical arguments. In Chatton's view that position justified natural theology, because he believed (with Scotus) that the same logical processes could be used to describe both created and divine realities. This was contested by William's friend and supporter Adam Wodeham (d. 1358), who claimed, along with Ockham, that theology was not a science like other sciences because God is not like other beings. In effect both Ockham and Wodeham rejected the notion that theology was the 'queen of the sciences' and put philosophy in its place, a move that would eventually destroy theology's claim to be a science at all. Of course, neither Ockham nor Wodeham saw things that way – to them theology was as superior to philosophy as the Creator was superior to his creation, and arguments drawn from the latter that were designed to prove the existence of God did no more than construct a reduced and ultimately incredible divinity who could not stand comparison to the God of the Bible. Yet the triumph of the sceptics is hardly surprising, as they drew the logical conclusion from what Ockham and Wodeham had said.

The struggle against Ockhamist ideas was carried on by Thomas Bradwardine (1300?–49), who became chaplain to King Edward III in 1339 and ended up as Archbishop of Canterbury, although he died only thirty-eight days after taking office. Bradwardine was a secular philosopher who was (and to those in the know, still is) greatly honoured for the progress he made in the study of mathematics. This may seem to be a long way from theology, but in fact it is not. Mathematics is an abstract but completely logical discipline that can be used to support the view that God is (and must be) in control of everything that happens. Not only can he not go against his own nature but his human creatures cannot go against his will either. We may appear to be free in our decision-making but in fact God is in control of everything, and what we call 'predestination' is the logical outcome of that. Bradwardine suspected (wrongly, as it happens) that William of Ockham denied this and that he was in fact a Pelagian.

The reason for this suspicion was that Ockham had said that God allows us to imagine things that do not exist. Since that is the case, human reason is unreliable and we must be suspicious of it. The only realistic approach to our perception of reality is to be sceptical of it, and therefore to doubt even the existence of substances. This is a form of mind over matter, and therefore of the power of the human will over a supposedly objective reality. Of course, if the will is free to shape its own existence, it follows that it must be free to choose its own salvation, although Ockham did not go that far. Bradwardine drew a logical conclusion from Ockham's principles and simply assumed that Ockham had done the same, which he had not.

The crunch point came with the doctrine of transubstantiation, because the human eye cannot perceive any change in the bread and wine of the Eucharist. But the church said that the substances did change into the body and blood of Christ, so we are called to believe something we cannot perceive or verify by natural reason. The only necessary being is God, and the only way we can know anything is by divine illumination. Ockham held that our understanding of reality is dependent on our perception of things, but in the case of the transubstantiated body and blood of Christ, such perception is impossible. Ockham was therefore putting his faith in something that cannot be proved. As far as Bradwardine was concerned, that meant that it is logically impossible for us to choose salvation, because we have no guarantee that our choice bears any relation to reality. Salvation depends entirely on God, who will convict us of its truth, and not on any 'proof' that we can supposedly demonstrate by our own efforts. God's plan is of course eternal, and therefore unchanging, which gives predestination the edge over changeable free will in any debate about the cause of our salvation.

Bradwardine's defence of predestination, or of the absolute character of the divine *potentia ordinata*, was taken to its logical conclusion by his Oxford contemporary Robert Holcot (d. 1349). Unlike Ockham, Holcot was a Dominican who combined a fine logical mind with a pastoral heart and dedication to preaching. He rejected the use of Aristotelian logic in theology because the two things were incompatible. To Holcot's mind, Aristotelianism was fine for examining the created order, but incapable of dealing with what he believed was the higher logic of supernatural reality. To put it another way, scientific study of this world did not require faith, whereas theology is entirely dependent on it. Theology might be called a science in the sense that it is a pursuit of truth, but it does not proceed along normal rational lines. To understand it requires acceptance of revelation, and that rests on the authority of the church. Holcot therefore concluded that those who try to reason their way into a knowledge of God will end up in heresy, because they have applied the wrong method in their search for the truth.

Holcot was not a sceptic however. He believed that anyone who sincerely sought to know God and was prepared to submit himself to supernatural authority would have the truth revealed to him in due course. In his own words:

> So far it has not been proved by any kind of reason that God exists, or that he is the Creator of the world. But to everyone who behaves innocently in God's eyes and who uses their natural reason to inquire, raising no barriers to the operation of divine grace, God will communicate enough knowledge of himself for their salvation ... whoever uses natural reason without fault will never lack real knowledge of God.[11]

These debates took place in the rarefied atmosphere of the universities, and at the time nobody could predict what impact they would have later on. But from the vantage point of hindsight we can see that seeds were being sown that would bring forth fruit generations later and contribute to the great upheaval we know as the Reformation.

The Black Death

It is possible that the problems the church was facing in the fourteenth century might have disappeared or been resolved fairly easily had not something unforeseen occurred in the meantime. In 1346, rats carrying bubonic plague arrived in Europe from Central Asia, and within a couple of years virtually the entire continent was affected. The plague carried off anywhere from a third to a half of the population, although it did not strike equally everywhere. Some places escaped almost unharmed whereas others were entirely wiped out. In Britain whole villages disappeared, often leaving nothing but the parish church still standing. When a new village was eventually built it was usually some distance away from the old one, so as to prevent contagion, but of course the churches could not be moved. To this day it is not uncommon in parts of East Anglia (in particular) to come across large medieval churches that now appear

---

[11] Robert Holcot, *Super Libros Sapientiae* (Haguenau, 1494; repr. Frankfurt, 1974), lect. 155. The translation given here is adapted from Beryl Smalley, *English Friars and Antiquity in the Early Fourteenth Century* (Oxford: Oxford University Press, 1960), 185.

to be in the middle of nowhere, but that were at the centre of a vibrant community when they were built. These are the remains of the plague villages. Perhaps the best known of them is Little Gidding, where Nicholas Ferrar (1592–1637) set up a religious community in 1626 that T. S. Eliot celebrated in his *Four Quartets*. The medieval church still sits on top of a hill but there is nothing around it, a monument to the devastation caused more than 650 years ago.

The plague carried off people who could not escape it, which meant that it hit the poor disproportionately hard. But, more seriously still, it decimated the clergy, who were called to minister to the sick and dying, and in the course of performing their ministerial duties often caught the disease themselves. Both Thomas Bradwardine and Robert Holcot were carried away by it, as were scores of lesser clergy. This devastation had a knock-on effect in the monasteries, not so much because the monks perished disproportionately, although that was often true, as because there were not enough recruits to keep them going in the next generation. Monasteries had always relied on excess population for their maintenance, as people put younger sons and unmarriageable daughters in them as a way of providing for them. But with nearly half the population gone almost overnight, there was a shortage of labour that had to be made up, and people no longer had the same number of children to spare. Monasteries could not replenish their numbers at the necessary rate, and new foundations were virtually ruled out. Houses that had once held 200 or more monks were often dramatically reduced, sometimes to fewer than 10 active inhabitants. We can see the effects of this when we look at the records they kept. Around 1350 the neat handwriting of professionally trained scribes often gives way to a semi-educated scrawl, because the monasteries had to make do with unskilled scribes, who were pressed into service without adequate preparation.

One effect of the plague was that large tracts of cultivated land were abandoned and went back to bush or scrub because there were not enough people to till the soil. If the land was in private hands it could be sold to such able-bodied peasants as still survived, but if it belonged to the church (and therefore to God), that solution was not available. As a result, much of the countryside was abandoned. Initially that did not make too much difference, but as the population started to grow again the demand for good farmland increased, and it was soon realized that much of it was unavailable. A case for dissolving non-viable monastic houses and releasing their assets started to be made, and although not much happened at first, in the long term some kind of crisis over landholding seemed to be inevitable.

The prospect of this was increased because of the way most people thought about disease and death. If the clergy, whose job was to pray for the peace, health and salvation of the people, were being struck down in disproportionate numbers, did this not mean that there was something fundamentally wrong in the church? The plague was divine punishment for the people's sins and it seemed logical to assume that if the priests were dying at a greater rate, they must be more culpable than others. Somehow God had not heard their prayers for the protection of his people, and that could mean only that they had gone astray. What was wrong? That was a much harder question to answer, but it was not long before influential voices were raised to suggest that the church was corrupt. Not only was it not doing its job properly, but it had fallen into theological error and was being punished for it, just as God had punished ancient Israel for its periodic bouts of idolatry. It was not easy for ordinary people to make a case for this, but university lecturers were in a more privileged position. One who would take advantage of this was John Wyclif or Wycliffe (c.1328–84) of Oxford, and with him began a whole new chapter in the history of the English church.

John Wyclif

John Wyclif came from a noble, if not especially wealthy, family in Yorkshire and seems to have been a younger son destined for the church from an early age. If that is so, then the untimely death of an older brother made him the heir to the family estate, although it did not take him away from his clerical vocation. Wyclif entered Oxford just as the plague was reaching the city. He was too young to have known William of Ockham, who had long since gone into Continental exile, but Ockham's pupils and (more importantly) his ideas had come to dominate the university. Up until that time the universities had played a somewhat peripheral role in English life, and as yet there were none in Scotland or Ireland. By the mid-fourteenth century the universities were attracting the patronage of the bishops, who founded colleges in Oxford and Cambridge to provide shelter and instruction for young men from their own dioceses. Cambridge, founded at almost the same time as Oxford, remained much smaller than its rival and by the end of the thirteenth century it had little to show except Peterhouse, the oldest college in the university and directly dependent on the Bishop of Ely, who is still its official visitor.

Oxford was, and throughout the Middle Ages remained, a much bigger institution. Many colleges there still bear the traces of their diocesan origins – Worcester, Exeter and Lincoln Colleges are obvious reminders of this. At one time there was a Canterbury College, now merged with Christ Church, and a Durham College, which was later dissolved and integrated with both St John's and Trinity. New College was founded by the Bishop of Winchester, and Jesus College was home to students from the Welsh dioceses, giving us an idea of just how widespread this influence was. Wyclif himself started at Queen's College and later became a Fellow of Merton, a college founded by a Lord Chancellor of that name who happened to be Bishop of Rochester as well, although it was not a diocesan establishment. From there Wyclif went on to Balliol, another more secular foundation. He was therefore often under royal rather than episcopal patronage, a fact that gave him greater independence and that might have protected him to some extent once his dissident views became controversial.

Wyclif had a distinguished academic career alongside his progress through the ranks of the church. He was ordained deacon and priest in 1351 but did not receive a living until ten years later. He left Oxford for the parish of Fillingham (Lincolnshire), to which he soon added another one at Westbury on Trym (Bristol), although he could not have spent much time in either place, because by 1363 he had received permission to return to Oxford, where he began an arduous course of theological training. During that time he became Warden of Canterbury College (1365), which turned out to be a poisoned chalice because of disputes between the monks and friars on the one hand, and the secular scholars on the other. As a secular priest himself, Wyclif was a marked man, and it was not long before the monks and friars were trying to get rid of him. Even so, it took them five years to succeed in this, because Wyclif appealed to the pope over the head of John Langham, the new Archbishop of Canterbury, who was only too willing to accede to his critics' demands.

Before this sorry episode ended, Wyclif had managed to exchange his living of Fillingham for Ludgershall in Buckinghamshire (1368), to which he later added Lutterworth (1374), the parish to which he would eventually retire and where he died. Such pluralism was by no means unusual in the fourteenth century, and for a man like Wyclif it provided a steady income that allowed him to do other things, like teach in the university and work in the king's service. The only problem was that Wyclif was a declared opponent of pluralism, which he decried as a corrupt practice! His lofty ideals did not always work out in practice, and this inconsistency is a reminder that Wyclif was not the great reformer that later generations would make him out to be.

Wyclif's modern reputation as 'the morning star of the Reformation' dates from the mid-nineteenth century, when his works were edited and printed by enthusiasts who realized that some of the things he advocated reappeared in the demands of the sixteenth-century Protestants. Today a more balanced view prevails, and it is generally agreed that while Wyclif did indeed hold positions similar to some of the later Reformers, he can only be turned into a proto-Protestant by a selective use of the evidence.[12] He is better understood as the last flowering of the remarkable theological renaissance in fourteenth-century Oxford, where many of the ideas that would be aired 200 years later were already being expressed and debated. Wyclif is remembered in a way that his contemporaries and predecessors are not because he was the right man in the right place, saying the right things at the right time. He can neither be credited with, nor blamed for, what happened 150 years after his death but, in several important respects, once he began to express and circulate his views, England would never be the same again.

Like many of his predecessors, Wyclif lived in relative obscurity until fairly late in his career. The earliest of his writings that can be securely dated is a treatise on logic (*De Logica*), which appeared in 1360 as the first in a series of books on the same subject that were designed to introduce students to what had become an increasingly complex area of study. Wyclif's interest in logic was to last for the rest of his life and put him in the mainstream of theological thought. But he was a logician with a difference. As he wrote in *De Logica* 1, 1:

> Some people who love God's law have persuaded me to compose a reliable treatise in order to make the logic of Holy Scripture clear . . . I intend to sharpen the minds of believers by introducing analyses and proofs drawn from the Scriptures.[13]

This emphasis on the Bible would not have surprised Wyclif's contemporaries, but it stood out as being more explicit in its aim than most of what was appearing at the time. Wyclif is known to have revised his works in later life, when his biblical focus was more pronounced, but it is unlikely that he added this explanation of his purpose long after the original treatise was written. It seems that here we have an expression of his intentions from the start. It is also clear from an analysis of his writings that his main concern was always with the nature of being (ontology). Whatever else he might have been discussing, he kept coming back to this, and it was that more than anything else that led him to reject the 'nominalist' ideas of Ockham and return to the belief in the existence of universals that characterized the thought of Robert Grosseteste.

---

[12] See e.g. G. R. Evans, *John Wyclif: Myth and Reality* (Oxford: Lion Hudson, 2005); S. E. Lahey, *John Wyclif* (Oxford: Oxford University Press, 2009).
[13] Lahey, *John Wyclif*, 9.

In other words, far from being radical in his theology, Wyclif was a traditionalist who was determined to recover something that many thought had been lost in the previous century.

None of this might have mattered very much in the longer term, but in 1372 Wyclif was pressed into the service of John of Gaunt, younger son of King Edward III and the effective guardian of his nephew and the king's eventual successor Richard II (1377–99). He was soon deeply involved in church–state relations and working in the interests of the Crown against the papacy. This was a long-running battle over money and power, which Edward III had pursued with some vigour. Richard II would eventually renew and strengthen the statutes against papal provisors and *praemunire* (in 1390 and 1393 respectively), evidently because the problems persisted, but Wyclif was long dead by then.[14]

To these complaints were added the familiar ones regarding clerical exemptions from royal justice and taxation, as well as the newer charge that clergy who acted in ways unbecoming to their office ought to be defrocked instead of being protected by their special status. Wyclif heartily endorsed these ideas in a treatise on civil government (*De Civili Dominio*), which he published in 1376. In it he argued that all church property should be surrendered to the king, on the ground that property ownership was an effect of Adam's fall and therefore had no place in the church of Christ. The result was uproar. On 13 February 1377, Wyclif was summoned to appear before the Archbishop of Canterbury and the Bishop of London, among many other dignitaries, to answer to a charge of heresy. Pope John XXII had long before (in 1323) defended the right of the church to own property against the objections of the more radical Franciscans, and so the bishops could claim to have had right on their side, although 'heresy' was a rather strong accusation to make. In the event, John of Gaunt stood by Wyclif and frustrated the attempts of the church hierarchy to punish him, but the unforeseen result of that was a popular riot in favour of the bishops in which a mob went so far as to ransack John of Gaunt's London house.

That incident was a turning point. Wyclif seems to have felt that he had been misunderstood and went on to expand his treatise with numerous defences drawn from canon law, the Fathers of the church and (above all) the Bible. Here we see for the first time the topics that were to dominate the last years of his life – the need for thoroughgoing pastoral reform of the church, the problems inherent in taking monastic or fraternal vows of poverty, chastity and

---

[14] Bray, *Documents*, 535–545.

obedience, the whole question of what constituted heresy and, most import-antly, the role of Scripture in the devotional life of both the individual believer and the church.

The English church authorities lost no time in forwarding their accusations to the pope, who had recently left Avignon and gone back to Rome. On 22 May Pope Gregory XI formally condemned Wyclif and wrote to Edward III, demanding that the king take action against him. At about the same time, he also sent Arnald Garnier, one of his agents, to collect money the papacy believed the English Crown owed it. At this point events began to overtake Wyclif. Edward III died on 22 June 1377, leaving the boy king Richard II in the hands of the royal council, presided over by John of Gaunt. The council asked Wyclif for his opinion about the legality of the papal demands for money, and Wyclif repeated what he had said in his earlier treatise about the church owning property. However, this time the council refused to back him. It paid the money that the Pope wanted and allowed the bishops to summon Wyclif to a heresy trial at Lambeth Palace on 27 March 1378. John of Gaunt felt unable to protect Wyclif in the way that he had done before, but Joan, the king's mother, intervened on his behalf, claiming that Wyclif could not be prosecuted by the church for what he had said and done while in the king's service. For his part, Wyclif remained stubbornly loyal to John of Gaunt, even to the point of supporting him in a notorious case of breach of sanctuary in Westminster Abbey, where two knights who had resisted John were tracked down and butchered in cold blood. Unfortunately, that ill-judged support merely embarrassed John and obliged him to cut his remaining ties to Wyclif.

Meanwhile, on the very day of Wyclif's trial at Lambeth, Pope Gregory XI died in Rome. His successor, Urban VI, had been known to support ideas of apostolic poverty, and Wyclif wrote to him, thinking that Urban VI would see that his approach to church property was essentially the same. Wyclif con-tinued to hope for support from Urban VI until the Pope's death six years later, but none was forthcoming. Instead Urban VI so antagonized his cardinals that they deposed him and elected a rival pope (Clement VII), who promptly returned to Avignon and set up an alternative papacy that would endure for a generation. In a way that nobody could have foreseen, this played into Wyclif's hands, and for the next few years a string of pungent treatises poured from his pen, dealing with such subjects as the truth of Holy Scripture (1378), the church (1379), the office of the king (1379), the pastoral duties of the clergy (1379) and the power of the pope (1379). He also found time to produce a number of biblical commentaries and to preach hundreds of sermons. Wyclif was no armchair, ivory-tower theologian. All the time that he was battling the papacy and the English hierarchy he was preaching, teaching and pastoring congregations, some of whom must have been bewildered by what he was saying and doing, but none of whom could have been left indifferent to the issues at stake.

The papal schism of 1378 destroyed the unity of western Christendom, as each country took sides in the dispute. Needless to say, the French supported Avignon. England, which was then at war with France, equally naturally supported Rome. Scotland, seizing its chance to become fully independent of England, also sided with Avignon, creating what would later be known as the 'auld alliance' between Scotland, and in particular the royal House of Stewart (Stuart), and the French. In practice the papacy could no longer intervene effectively in British affairs, and any action against Wyclif would have to come from the local hierarchy. That it did, and in the process a new division opened up in the English church. Wyclif's supporters at Oxford were mainly younger, better-educated and essentially secular clergy,[15] whereas his opponents were largely monks and friars. Wyclif, who had previously been sympathetic to them, now went the other way and issued a blistering attack on monastic vows, which he claimed promoted a form of salvation by works that was contrary to the teaching of the Bible.

To make matters worse, Wyclif also changed his views on the Lord's Supper (Eucharist) at that time. Having defended transubstantiation as recently as 1376, he now denounced it as a logical impossibility and brought down the wrath of the hierarchy on a matter even more central to their interests than the sacredness of church property. He was summoned to trial once more, but this time John of Gaunt stepped in to shield him – on condition that he henceforth keep quiet. Needless to say, Wyclif was incapable of that, and by May 1381 serious dissension had broken out in Oxford. Wyclif left the university shortly afterwards, never to return. He retired to Lutterworth, where he continued to write voluminously as well as to edit the works he had already published.

That might have been the end of the matter, since few people read academic theology then any more than they do today, but coincidentally there was a peasants' revolt in the summer of 1381 that at one point threatened to overthrow the boy king Richard II. Somewhat miraculously, Richard was able to quell the rebellion merely by appearing in front to the rebels, and the whole

---

15 The secular clergy were those who lived 'in the world' (*saeculum*) as ordinary parish priests, as opposed to the monastics, who were called 'regulars' because they lived under a rule of life imposed by their monastic order.

thing fizzled out. But the notion that there was a connection between Wyclif's theological attacks on the established order and the peasants' rebellion against the secular arm of that same order took hold and proved impossible to dislodge, even if there was little substance to it.

One reason for this was that Wyclif had connections with ordinary people that were unusual for someone of his type. The most important of these was his desire to translate the Bible into English so that non-academics could read it for themselves. We know that he began to write in English towards the end of his life, but although a few English treatises have been attributed to him, it is not certain that he wrote any of them. Nor is it likely that he did any Bible translation himself, despite the reputation he has gained for that in modern times. There are in fact two translations that circulated under his name, but both were almost certainly produced by his followers. One of them is a literalistic rendering of the Latin Vulgate, which is hard to understand, and the other is a more colloquial version that became very popular. Taking the two together, about 250 manuscripts survive, of which 21 contain the entire Bible. Compare this with Geoffrey Chaucer's *Canterbury Tales*, written at about the same time, of which there are only 63 surviving manuscripts, none of which is complete. Given that the Wycliffite Bibles were proscribed texts for most of the fifteenth century and were not printed at all until more than 400 years later, this is astonishing. No other medieval English text comes close to the number of surviving Wycliffite Bibles, which proves how popular they must have been.

Popular devotion

What can we say about the spiritual life of individual people in medieval times? Almost all the evidence we have deals with the church as an institution and with the clergy, whose job it was to represent it to the people. What the latter thought about it is often not recorded because it was of little or no interest to the scribes and chroniclers of the time, almost all of whom were clerics themselves. Hardly anybody kept a diary or wrote private letters in which they unburdened their souls, although a few memoirs have survived and allow us a glimpse at life beyond the official dealings of the rulers. How typical are such chance survivals? That is impossible to say, and without a viable sample it is unwise to try to generalize about the population as a whole. We can chart the rise and fall of numbers entering monastic orders or the priesthood, but the reasons for entering the 'religious' life were so varied that we cannot draw any conclusions about the personal piety of those involved. For that, the continued existence and survival of the Lollards is a more reliable guide, but the secretive nature of their activities hinders our ability to assess their impact. The Lollards were followers of John Wyclif, so called by their opponents because they were accusing of 'lolling' (mumbling), presumably in order to prevent attracting attention. When the Reformation came in the sixteenth century, there were still some Lollards around but the Reformers were barely aware of them. One of the people known to have possessed a Lollard Bible was Bishop Edmund Bonner of London, a leading opponent of the Reformers, who tried to use it in order to combat them![16]

The rise and spread of Lollardy was both the cause and the effect of something new in English church life. In the fourteenth century we first come across a wide range of laypeople who were interested in theology and whose religious convictions were strong enough for them to be willing to face persecution. There had always been some religious or spiritually minded people of course, but on the whole they either joined a religious order or kept their piety to themselves. Now, for the first time, such people emerged as an element to be reckoned with in church life. In this respect Wyclif and his followers appeared at just the right time, because there were similar yearnings elsewhere in Europe as well. In the Low Countries for example, men like Gerhard Groote (1340–84) were expounding a new kind of religious life, in which communities of men, women and children sought to emulate aspects of monastic discipline as they went about their daily lives.

The spirituality of these believers had a decidedly mystical streak, and this too was typical of the age. The most popular of the English mystics was Richard Rolle (1290–1349), who flourished in the years immediately before the Black Death but whose work did not become widely known until much later. Rolle was educated at Oxford but he left without taking a degree and retreated to his native Yorkshire. It is not known whether he subsequently went to Paris to study or whether he stayed in his native county until his death at Hampole (near Doncaster), but it is certain that he wrote a large number of works, including several biblical commentaries. His most popular book was the *Emendatio Vitae* (*Emendation of Life*), which survives in 110 manuscripts and was translated at least seven different times from Latin into English. Towards the end of his life he began writing in English himself, producing *The Form of Living*, which is now extant in thirty manuscripts and was intended particularly for the edification of nuns.

---

[16] Bonner quoted the second of the Ten Commandments in the 1388 Lollard version. See G. L. Bray (ed.), *The Institution of a Christian Man* (Cambridge: James Clarke, 2018), 388.

In the next generation there was Walter Hilton (1340–96), who might have studied at Cambridge and who later joined the Augustinian canons. Hilton was familiar with Rolle's work but not uncritical of it. He also wrote in both Latin and English, with his most popular work, *The Scale of Perfection*, appearing in the vernacular and surviving in forty-eight manuscripts. It was also the first English book to be translated into Latin and disseminated internationally – fourteen Latin manuscripts of it are known to exist. These figures may seem small to us, but given the expense of copying and the depredations of time, they indicate that these books were bestsellers. Also from this period is *The Cloud of Unknowing*, an anonymous work that urges its readers to go beyond the disputations of academic theology and seek a personal experience of God. Only seventeen manuscripts survive, but the author is known to have written at least six other treatises as well, and collections of them are still extant.

On a less exalted plane were the growing number of manuals being produced, mainly to aid priests in their pastoral work. These were the fruit of efforts that had been made, ever since the Fourth Lateran Council in 1215, to improve the level of education and devotion, not only among the ordained clergy but also among their flocks. Initially most of these manuals were in Latin and therefore restricted to a small group of readers, most of whom would have been priests or monks. One of the most popular of these was the *Oculus Sacerdotis* (*Eye of the Priest*), attributed to William of Pagula (d. *c.*1332), who wrote a number of treatises on canon law subjects and seems to have had a degree in the discipline from Oxford. William was a most unusual figure, in that he was both highly educated and (apparently) an ordinary parish priest, who had to practise what he preached. The *Oculus* contains all kinds of useful advice for parish ministry, including such things as how to question those coming for penance and what to say to pregnant women. William stands out for the way in which he applied canon law to practical situations, including what to do in cases of financial dishonesty, the refusal of a lord to pay his servants' wages, and the many trials associated with matrimony. Like many medieval people, William was ambivalent about marriage, but he recommended that those who embarked on it should choose ugly wives if possible, because such were less likely to be seduced by others!

William was writing for priests engaged in pastoral ministry, but it is at this time that we begin to find books in the vernacular, which in England meant either French (for the upper classes) or English, that were intended to reach a wider audience. One interesting feature of these is that they were often in verse, no doubt because it was easier for people to memorize them that way. Some scholars believe that they were meant to be sung to popular tunes, giving a moral uplift to what might otherwise be distinctly unedifying songs, but we cannot be certain of that.

What we do know is that they concentrated on certain subjects people were expected to know by heart. These were the Ten Commandments, the seven deadly sins, the seven sacraments and the twelve articles of the Apostles' Creed – one for each of the disciples of Jesus. There was a particular liking for the number seven, and many authors strained to make their subjects fit that paradigm. The result is that we find seven Beatitudes, seven cardinal virtues, seven gifts of the Holy Spirit, seven petitions in the Lord's Prayer, and so on. The really ingenious would then try to match them up, contrasting the seven deadly sins with the seven cardinal virtues for example, as if the virtues had been especially designed to counteract each of the sins in turn. The method was obviously artificial to some degree but, in a world in which people had to commit things to memory because books were scarce and few people could read, it was remarkably effective.

Similar efforts were being made across Europe, and quite a few treatises written in French were translated into English. One of the most popular of these was *Somme le roi*, a French compilation of the late thirteenth century that was translated by Michael of Northgate, a monk of St Augustine's monastery in Canterbury. We know this because he signed and dated the translation himself – as he tells us, he finished it on 27 October 1340! The problem for us is that his 'English' is incomprehensible. Michael wrote in his own Kentish dialect, deliberately in order to reach the local people, but his creative use of the language escapes most modern readers. The title of his translation was *The Agenbite of Inwit*, which we must admit is English of a kind, but what does it mean? The only way to find out is to translate the elements of the words into French or Latin, and then anglicize them. When we do that, we find that 'agen' (again) is 're-' and 'bite' is 'morse(l)', giving us 'remorse'. As for 'inwit', the 'wit' is knowledge or science, and from that we may perhaps deduce that it means 'conscience', the inbuilt knowledge that we all possess. Of course, had Michael titled his work *The Remorse of Conscience*, we would all understand what he was getting at, but to him that would probably have sounded like a kind of French, not English!

One man who definitely wrote for laypeople was John Thorseby, Archbishop of York from 1352 to 1373. Thoresby took his cue from John Peckham's *Ignorantia Sacerdotum* and got one of his monks, John Gaytrick, to turn it into English verse. In that way all the basic texts of spiritual instruction were covered, and as a sweetener Thoresby added that anyone who memorized the entire text would get a forty-day indulgence. In other words hard graft in this life would be rewarded by time off in Purgatory, although whether it was worth it for a mere forty days' relief is open to question. Nevertheless, it is through studying works like these, including the way they were marketed and the number of manuscripts that survive, that we can take the pulse of lay devotion, at least to some extent. Perhaps the best indicator of their popularity is the fact that by the end of the fourteenth century a number of these manuals were apparently being written by Lollards, who used them to inculcate their own doctrines. As a result they came to be regarded with some suspicion by the hierarchy, who wanted to censor them before allowing them to circulate freely, but the demand was great, and at a time when all books had to be copied by hand, censorship was not particularly effective. Then, as now, laypeople read what they liked, and paid only lip service to their pastors. We may be grateful that so much of what they chose to pass on was worth the effort involved in doing so.

The Celtic fringe

Turning from England to the Celtic nations of the British Isles, we are struck primarily by the retrenchment of English influence there during the fourteenth century. Edward I had been on the brink of uniting the whole of Britain and Ireland under his rule, but although he succeeded in Wales, elsewhere his successors were unable to carry his vision through. The last indigenous prince of Wales had been defeated in 1283, and after that the country was ruled by the kings of England. The Welsh dioceses had long been part of the province of Canterbury however, although they and their clergy were much poorer than their English counterparts.[17] They operated on the margins of church life and some of their bishops doubled as suffragans in English sees in order to relieve their endemic poverty, from which there appeared to be no escape.

In Ireland there had been a concerted effort by the English Crown to appoint Anglo-Normans to bishoprics, in the hope of gradually anglicizing the church. But although these efforts never entirely ceased, a resurgence of native Gaelic power and the relative decline of English Ireland made the policy difficult to enforce. The result was a dramatic growth in the number of papal provisions, which became almost universal outside the few dioceses that were still under effective royal control. In other countries, papal provisions were often a means

---

[17] See G. Williams, *Wales and the Reformation* (Cardiff: University of Wales Press, 1999), 21.

of extracting wealth from the local churches and diverting it to the papal court, but the Irish situation was somewhat different. As K. W. Nicholls put it:

> the poverty of Ireland secured its immunity from one abuse of papal provision, the appointment of absentees. The indiscriminate granting of provisions did, however, lead in Ireland to another abuse which was to have serious consequences for the Irish Church. During the second half of the fifteenth century it became the practice to grant provisions to members of great and influential families who were barely in minor orders or were even still laymen but had declared their intention to take orders. In the sixteenth century this practice became more and more widespread.[18]

This trend naturally alarmed the king's government, which sought to ensure that only English-speaking bishops would be appointed, and that they would use the English language in preference to the native Irish, but the growing links between the episcopate and the Gaelic aristocracy made this difficult. A further complicating factor was that English Ireland suffered disproportionately from disease, economic crises and warfare during the fourteenth century, leaving a vacuum that was increasingly filled by Gaelic clergy, whether they could speak English or not. Large tracts of Ireland that had been subject to English rule in 1300 slipped out of the king's hands, and many erstwhile Anglo-Normans were Gaelicized. It was a two-way street, to be sure, and Gaeldom was also transformed by contact with the English, but the long-term trend was unmistakable.

The national question acquired special importance after the papal schism in 1378, because while the English bishops naturally followed the English church's submission to the Roman pope, some in the Gaelic areas were attracted to his rival at Avignon. The prospect of an Ireland permanently divided along linguistic, political and ecclesiastical lines suddenly became very real – a harbinger of developments that would be a recurring feature of the Irish situation in succeeding centuries. Having said that, the Irish church was not without leadership, and there is evidence of serious attempts being made to introduce a discipline among both clergy and laity that more closely resembled the universal norms of the western church. Alexander Bicknor, Archbishop of Dublin (1317–49), was an accomplished scholar and administrator who attempted to establish a university in the capital, and his

---

[18] K. W. Nicholls, *Gaelic and Gaelicized Ireland in the Middle Ages*, 2nd edn (Dublin: Lilliput Press, 2003), 120.

younger contemporary, Richard FitzRalph, Archbishop of Armagh (1346–60), was equally distinguished. His unconventional theological views are said to have influenced the followers of John Wyclif, and he was Chancellor of Oxford University (1332–46) before going to Armagh, although he never had a chance to exercise his academic talents in his native country.[19]

At the level of popular piety, fourteenth-century Ireland saw a rapid growth in devotion to the relics of saints and other superstitious practices that were common in western Europe at that time. A pilgrimage site known as St Patrick's Purgatory on Lough Derg (Donegal) was especially popular – and notorious. The modern mind has no difficulty in dismissing it as fake, but that was less clear in medieval times. Nevertheless, suspicions were aroused and in 1497 the site was temporarily closed down by the pope.[20] More pernicious was the growing belief that the country was infested with witches. Richard Ledrede, Bishop of Ossory from 1317 until 1360, was a notorious heresy hunter, having been sensitized to the danger from his training in Avignon, and spent his pontificate persecuting his own flock, at least one of whom, Petronilla of Meath, was burnt at the stake in 1324 – almost a century before that practice became legal in England. Ledrede was regarded by at least some of his contemporaries as mad, but nobody attempted to stop him, which is a frightening reminder of the power that an unaccountable prelate could wield over his unfortunate victims.[21]

The institutional church was also faced with a growing challenge from the mendicant orders, in particular from the Franciscans. The friars were accused of fomenting rebellion against the English Crown, a charge that was particularly sensitive in the troubled years of Edward II's reign. They also clashed with the diocesan authorities over their pastoral ministry, which many bishops believed transgressed on the latters' prerogatives. One persistent source of trouble was the interpretation of Canon 21 of the Fourth Lateran Council in 1215. This canon, known as *Omnis Utriusque Sexus*, had mandated obligatory confession to a priest, which the French theologian Jean de Pouilly (d. c.1328) claimed meant only the local parish priest, who had the cure of souls in his parish. But in 1321 Pope John XXII condemned this view and issued another decree, *Vas Electionis*, which allowed others, including itinerant friars, to hear confessions and absolve penitents. This enraged Archbishop FitzRalph, who

---

[19] See K. Walsh, *A Fourteenth-Century Scholar and Primate: Richard FitzRalph in Oxford, Avignon and Armagh* (Oxford: Clarendon Press, 1981).

[20] C. Downham, *Medieval Ireland* (Cambridge: Cambridge University Press, 2018), 304. See also J. Le Goff, *The Birth of Purgatory* (Chicago, Ill.: University of Chicago Press, 1984), 190–201.

[21] Downham, *Medieval Ireland*, 306–308.

virtually declared war on them and stirred up a controversy that lasted well beyond his lifetime. Opposition to the friars continued into the fifteenth century, until it was finally condemned by Pope Alexander V in his decretal *Regnans in Excelsis* (1409). After that the controversy died down, but the bad blood between the friars and the ecclesiastical Establishment was not so easily overcome and would continue to resurface from time to time.

Fourteenth-century Scotland presents a very different picture, but our lack of evidence concerning the church is considerably greater than it is for Ireland and so it is hard to say anything for certain. What we do know is that the Scots sided with Avignon during the papal schism and this reinforced the already growing distance between their church and that of England. There also seems to have been some influence from Wyclif and the Lollards, which was absent from Ireland, but it was contained and left no lasting impression on the country. A few canons have come down to us from the diocese of St Andrews, enjoining the residence and chaste behaviour of parish clergy and formulating rules for the celebration of matrimony and the burial of the dead. Of particular interest is the stipulation that a consistory (assembly) of the clergy was to be held every year, shortly after Easter, both in St Andrews and in Edinburgh, in order to receive instructions as to how to perform their parish duties.[22] In these canons, clergy discipline is once more to the forefront, indicating that the bishops were particularly concerned to eliminate lapses in the performance of the clergy's tasks that were bringing their ministry into disrepute. Beyond that there is very little to say, and it would not be until the upheavals of the sixteenth century that the Scottish church would really come into its own.

One unforeseen consequence of the papal schism was the division of the ancient diocese of Sodor and Man. It had originally been founded as the ecclesiastical arm of a Viking kingdom that embraced the Inner Hebrides of Scotland and the Isle of Man, but over time Viking power declined and the kingdom was absorbed into Scotland in 1265. But in 1290 the Scottish royal house died out and Edward I of England laid claim to the country. The Scots resisted and eventually drove the English out, but they never recovered the Isle of Man, which remained under English lordship, although it was not annexed to England. The diocese, which was based on Iona, continued to function as before, but when Scotland sided with Avignon in the papal schism, that arrangement could not continue. The bishop at the time was John Donkan or Donegan (1374–92), who supported Rome, but as a Scottish bishop he was

---

22 D. Patrick, *Statutes of the Scottish Church 1225–1559* (Edinburgh: Edinburgh University Press, 1907), 68–77.

deposed by the Avignon pope on 15 July 1387, after which time his authority was confined to the Isle of Man.[23] Neither side recognized the other and both bishops claimed to rule over the entire diocese; but when the schism finally ended, the separate arrangements it had produced continued. As a result, the diocese of Sodor and Man was cut adrift from the Hebrides (Sodor) in Scotland and was directly subject to the papacy until the Reformation. It was then integrated into the Church of England, and attached to the province of York in 1542, where it has remained ever since.

---

[23] C. Burns (ed.), *Calendar of Papal Letters to Scotland of Clement VII of Avignon, 1378–1394* (Edinburgh: Scottish History Society, 1976), 130.

6

New wine in old wineskins (1384–1485)

Redefining heresy

When John Wyclif died at the end of 1384, it must have seemed to many that his ideas would die with him, but they did not. Some of his erstwhile friends and disciples abandoned him, but the Lollards carried on their translation work and continued to propagate Wyclif's teachings. Groups met up and down the country to read the Bible for themselves and to discuss the issues raised by Wyclif. The authorities in both church and state were alarmed by this, but there were limits as to what they could do about it because there was no legal means by which the Lollards could be repressed. They might be accused of heresy, but heresy was not a crime in English law, nor could anyone say for sure what it was. Any crackpot could be denounced as a Lollard whether he was one or not, and it seems that some were, making it difficult to separate fact from fiction.[1] What is certain though is that before long there was a large body of Wycliffite tracts in circulation. Not all of these reflect the views of Wyclif himself, but many do, and some were little more than translations of his Latin works.[2]

In 1394 a group of Lollards wrote a manifesto containing twelve articles of their belief and distributed it to Members of Parliament during their session in London. King Richard II had just been widowed and had decided to go to Ireland in order to put down the rebellion of some local chiefs there. Thomas Arundel (1353–1414), then Lord Chancellor, was so alarmed by the manifesto that he went to Ireland to beg the king to return and sort things out. He eventually did so, but not before Roger Dymock, a Dominican friar, was able to write a lengthy refutation of the Lollard manifesto, in which he did not hesitate to

---

[1] See R. Rex, *The Lollards* (Basingstoke: Palgrave, 2002), 54–55; M. Bennett, *Richard II and the Revolution of 1399* (Stroud: Sutton Publishing, 1999).

[2] A. Hudson, *The Premature Reformation: Wycliffite Tracts and Lollard History* (Oxford: Oxford University Press, 1988). See also M. Aston, *Lollards and Reformers: Images and Literacy in Late Medieval Religion* (London: The Hambledon Press, 1984).

condemn the twelve points as 'errors and heresies' in the eyes of the church, and in addition to denounce them as treason against the king.[3] From Rome, Pope Boniface IX added his voice to Dymock's and urged the king to take action. Richard II needed no prompting, and in 1395 he ordered a crackdown on the Lollards. Those that could be identified at Oxford were expelled from the university and some members of the king's court were also apprehended and forced to recant.[4] But that was all they could do. Arundel became Archbishop of Canterbury in 1396, but he soon fell out with the king and was translated to St Andrews, a fictitious appointment that lasted until Richard II was overthrown.[5] The will to fight Lollardy was there but the means to do so effectively were not.

The only way to deal with Lollardy was to make heresy a capital crime in England, but that was easier said than done. For some time the papacy had been alarmed at the growth and spread of dissent in different parts of Europe, and had been urging the secular powers to root it out by putting heretics to death. It was common for peasants to be hanged and noblemen to be beheaded, but heresy cut across social divisions and it was a spiritual, rather than a secular, crime. The church therefore preferred a different form of execution – burning at the stake. This was classless, and in theological terms it had the advantage of (possibly) burning out the sin in the victim's soul, so that if he were to recant he might still go to heaven. In England the kings resisted this, partly because they did not want to allow the church to dictate whom they should put to death and partly because the guild of professional hangmen regarded burning at the stake as beneath their dignity. As a result, heresy had never been declared a crime and men like Wyclif were allowed to die in peace.

This situation however was about to change. In 1399 John of Gaunt's son managed to overthrow Richard II and make himself king as Henry IV (1399–1413). In desperate need of allies, Henry IV turned to the church. Thomas Arundel returned to his see of Canterbury and was prepared to help him, but demanded a concession in return. This was that heresy should be made a capital offence. Unable to defy the archbishop, Henry IV acquiesced, and in 1401 Parliament passed the necessary heresy statute (*De Haeretico Comburendo*), which would remain on the books for over a hundred years. *De Haeretico*

---

[3] H. S. Cronin (ed.), *Rogeri Dymmok Liber contra XII Errores et Haereses Lollardorum* (London: Kegan Paul, Trench & Trübner, 1922).

[4] See Bennett, *Richard II*, 68.

[5] St Andrews, being in Scotland, was outside Richard II's jurisdiction, but (more importantly) Scotland at the time recognized the Avignonese pope and not the Roman one, so Arundel had nowhere to go.

Comburendo was a notorious piece of legislation that altered the traditional relationship between the church and the state. In line with the trial of Jesus in the Gospels, the church, which saw itself as the successor of the Jewish Sanhedrin, could pronounce a man guilty of heresy (or blasphemy) but was obliged to turn him over to the secular authorities, who alone had the power to put him to death. But the English kings had never before accepted the view that a court outside their control could pronounce a sentence that they would then be forced to carry out. Now, for the first time, the church was given the power not only to condemn a man to death but to determine the manner of his execution, and the king would have no option but to carry out its wishes. Moreover, the victims were not necessarily clergymen – anyone could be accused, convicted and put to death by the decision of a church court that operated under its own rules and was not subject to the common law of the state. It is not hard to see how this would in time come to appear as a form of tyranny, although that day was not yet at hand.

Once the heresy statute was in place, Arundel realized that he had to define heresy in such a way as to be able to accuse Lollards of it. They were not guilty of any of the classical heresies of antiquity, so new definitions of heresy had to be found.[6] This was done at a provincial synod that Arundel summoned to meet at Oxford in 1407, and its conclusions were subsequently ratified by the Convocation of Canterbury in 1409.[7] It was decreed that translating the Bible into the vernacular and preaching without a licence could incur a charge of heresy, and since the Lollards were the only ones doing that, they were the obvious targets. From then on, anyone condemned for Lollardy could be burnt at the stake. It was not a customary form of punishment, and the initial persecuting zeal died down over time, but at least one element of the antiheresy laws still survives. To this day no one can preach regularly in the Church of England without a licence, a rule that goes back to Arundel's anti-Lollard crusade. It may be added in passing that another regulation stated that anyone who preached incomprehensibly could also be arraigned for heresy and burnt at the stake. How many later generations have lived to regret that this rule has never been enforced!

---

[6] The classical heresies had been defined by Isidore of Seville in the sixth century and were conveniently summarized in the first canon of the Fourth Lateran Council in 1215 (*Conciliorum Oecumenicorum Decreta* [Bologna: Istituto per le Scienze Religiose, 1973], 230–231). That canon was subsequently included in the so-called *Liber Extra* of Pope Gregory IX (1234) and so is now found in the *Corpus Iuris Canonici*, 10.1.1.

[7] G. L. Bray (ed.), *Records of Convocation*, 20 vols. (Woodbridge: Boydell & Brewer, 2005–6), 4:311–318, 349. Provincial synods and convocations were practically the same thing, but the former was called by the archbishop without a royal writ and was therefore not a 'convocation' in the true sense of the word.

After 1409, Wyclif's followers were sought out, put on trial and burnt at the stake if they refused to recant. The most prominent of the persecutors was Philip Repingdon (1345–1424), initially one of Wyclif's most enthusiastic disciples, who had already caved in to pressure and had been rewarded by being made Bishop of Lincoln, the diocese in which Oxford was located, in 1404. The turncoat Repingdon went along with the new order, but there is some indication that his heart was not in it. When the Council of Constance in 1415 ordered Wyclif's body to be exhumed and burnt, he failed to comply and four years later resigned his see. It was only in 1428, nine years afterwards, that the order was finally carried out by his successor, by which time memories of Wyclif had largely faded from public view.

Even in 1409 however, Wyclif's was a voice from the past of little practical consequence. More important were the men who continued to propagate Lollard ideas. In 1419 John Badby was condemned for denying transubstantiation and burnt at Smithfield in London.[8] More significant still was the fate of Sir John Oldcastle (1378–1417), a childhood companion of the Prince of Wales (the future Henry V), who did his best to protect him. Oldcastle incurred the enmity of Thomas Arundel, who was determined to condemn him, and the Convocation of Canterbury duly did its duty in 1413, shortly before the death of Henry IV.[9] Somewhat surprisingly, Oldcastle managed to escape before he could be executed, and for a few years evaded capture, thanks to the protection offered to him by his Lollard contacts. In the end however, he was seized and burnt at the stake on 14 December 1417. The aftermath of the Oldcastle affair saw a sharp rise in the persecution of the Lollards, who could now be accused of sedition as well as heresy. Trials and burnings continued for the next decade, but after 1428 petered out.[10] Lollardy survived as an underground movement, but although there were prosecutions for it from time to time, the sense that it posed a danger to either the church or the state had passed. When the Reformation came in the 1530s, the few remaining Lollards merged imperceptibly into the Church of England and no more was heard of them.[11]

Was Lollardy in any way influential on the English Reformers of the sixteenth century? Many people have assumed that it was, but the question can be satisfactorily answered only in a roundabout way. When Richard II

---

[8] Ibid. 4:362–367. See P. McNiven, *Heresy and Politics in the Reign of Henry IV: The Burning of John Badby* (Woodbridge: Boydell & Brewer, 1987).

[9] Bray, *Records of Convocation*, 4:398–409.

[10] See ibid. 5:1–267 *passim*.

[11] See A. G. Dickens, *Lollards and Protestants in the Diocese of York* (London: The Hambledon Press, 1982).

married Anne of Bohemia (1366–94) in 1382, England came into contact with that country to a greater degree than it would otherwise have done. One effect of this was that John Wyclif's ideas spread to the Czechs, who were unhappy with the level of German influence among them and were increasingly prone to call papal authority into question.[12] The Utraquist controversy galvanized their opposition, which found its champion in Jan Hus (1369–1415). Hus was not originally a Utraquist but eventually made Utraquism a cornerstone of his theology, and he is remembered for that. He and his followers were influenced by the Wycliffites, and a century after Hus's death, Martin Luther admitted that he had been inspired to some degree by him. Thus it can be said that elements of Wyclif's teaching eventually made their way back to England and contributed to his reputation as an unwitting forerunner of the English Reformation.

The state of the English church

When we look at the general state of the English church in the century between the death of John Wyclif and the accession of Henry VII, we are struck above all by the remarkable continuity it exhibited, both in its structures and in its administration. Whereas the Crown lurched from crisis to crisis, with no fewer than four of the seven kings who reigned during that time being dethroned and one more only narrowly escaping a similar fate, the stability of the church is remarkable. Apart from Richard Scrope, the unlucky Archbishop of York (1398–1405) who was executed for taking part in a rebellion against Henry IV, virtually all the higher church dignitaries survived unscathed, even if they moved from one see to another more frequently than had been the case in the previous two centuries. In 1384 there was a growing tendency for the episcopate to be drawn from aristocratic families, but this bias was mitigated by the continuing appointments of worthy civil servants to high office. Competence, more than birth or good connections, was vital not only for ecclesiastical purposes but also for the needs of the royal government, which relied increasingly on bishops and other highly placed clerics.

Never before (or since) had the government of England been as clericalized as it was in the fifteenth century, but although this gave churchmen an influence they would not otherwise have possessed, it was not necessarily

---

[12] German–Czech rivalry was to remain a feature of Bohemian life until 1945, when the Germans were expelled after the Second World War. Hus was (and is) a Czech national hero, and after 1918 a Hussite church was formed to perpetuate his ideas, although the majority of Czechs have remained nominally (if not profoundly) Roman Catholic.

beneficial to the church itself. Pastoral responsibilities were not compatible with ministerial roles at court, and most bishops were drawn to the latter more than to the former. The result was that diocesan administration often passed into other hands and became more obviously juridical than it had been before. Many bishops appointed suffragans to do their work for them and, fortunately for them, such men were seldom in short supply.[13] The habit of appointing men to non-existent sees *in partibus infidelium* (in heathen lands) increased dramatically after the Crusades, when bishoprics in the Crusader states were abandoned without suppressing the office of their bishop. To these could be added a number of Irish bishops who could not go to their sees, either because they were beyond the reach of the Crown's jurisdiction or because such sees had effectively ceased to exist. As a result, England had a number of wandering prelates looking for something to do, and English diocesans were only too happy to employ them.

In addition to the suffragans thus appointed, dioceses increasingly relied on vicars-general, who were licensed to perform episcopal tasks at the pleasure and discretion of the diocesan bishop. In many cases the vicar-general was the bishop's 'official principal', or chief legal officer, for the simple reason that the official knew how the system worked and could easily extend his jurisdiction to cover episcopal responsibilities beyond those belonging to the ecclesiastical courts. By the early sixteenth century the roles of vicar-general and official principal were almost always combined, a situation that continues to the present time, when the two offices have effectively been merged into one.

In addition to these there were also archdeacons in every diocese, whose duty was to supervise work in the parishes. But in many cases the archdeacons were either non-resident or else had archdeaconries too large for them to manage, so they in turn delegated much of the administration to rural deans, who were genuinely in touch with the grassroots. This pattern of non-residence and delegation became the norm in many places, with the inevitable result that the hierarchy of the church was increasingly remote from the parish clergy, not to mention the laypeople.

This situation was unhealthy from the pastoral point of view, and matters were made worse by the growing demands of the state for subsidies, needed to pursue the wars in France. The kings allowed themselves to believe that these wars would ultimately benefit them as they would seize the French Crown, but the English church had no comparable gain in view. The Archbishop of

---

[13] The word 'suffragan', used for 'assistant' bishops, is ambiguous. The diocesan bishops are suffragans of their archbishop, but also appointed assistants who are given the title of 'suffragan' but are not on the same level as the diocesans.

Canterbury would never enjoy any authority in France, and it became increasingly clear that the king of England would be ejected as well. But, in spite of this the financial exactions continued, and the tax convocations needed to legislate for the clerical subsidies to the king multiplied in frequency, with little to show in return (see Table 6.1[14]).

Table 6.1 Convocations during the reigns of English kings from 1337 to 1461

King	Years of reign	Number of convocations
Edward III	50	20
Richard II	22	17
Henry IV	14	6
Henry V	9	7
Henry VI	39	15

Not surprisingly, the church dragged its feet and its representatives increasingly expressed discontent with royal policies, a discontent that was vindicated when in 1453 the French finally drove the English out.

Clerical taxation fell on the cathedral dignitaries and on the beneficed clergy, although these were a relatively small minority of those ordained overall. According to Robert Swanson, there were about 25,000 secular clergy in England at any one time in the fifteenth century, to which may be added a further 8,000 regulars (monastics). Given that there was a total of only 517 cathedral dignities in England and Wales and fewer than 9,000 parishes, this meant that more than two-thirds of those ordained were unbeneficed. Even if many of the beneficed clergy were non-resident and hired their unbeneficed brethren to perform their parochial duties for them, it remains true that over half the clergy were without what we would now call tenured appointment.[15]

This was not the whole story however. More than a third of benefices were appropriated to monasteries, which would naturally place their own monks in them in preference to anyone else. That meant that up to 40% of the regular clergy were beneficed, whereas less than a quarter of the seculars were. In the course of the fifteenth century the church encouraged more ordinands to

---

14 Bray, *Records of Convocation*, 19:364–367.

15 R. N. Swanson, *Church and Society in Late Medieval England* (Oxford: Basil Blackwell, 1989), 27–88. The number of cathedral dignities is derived from the *Fasti Ecclesiae Anglicanae 1066–1857*, 3 series (London: Institute of Historical Research, 1962–2022). Of the 517, only 65 were in Wales and 22 in monastic cathedrals, leaving 437 in English secular cathedrals (391 in Canterbury and 46 in York).

seek a university education, and graduates were better paid than others, but opportunities for ordinands were relatively few. This became a problem, and there were several occasions when the Convocation of Canterbury tried to encourage bishops to appoint ordinands to livings whenever possible.[16] From the church's point of view, graduate clergy were more likely to maintain high standards of preaching and teaching, which is what they wanted, but we must try to see this from the standpoint of the average parish as well. Over 80% were rural, and the clergy were expected to fit in with the peasant way of life. Their literacy would be useful for legal matters, like preparing wills, but otherwise it was better for them to know how to plough a field or milk cows. Unfortunately, neither Oxford nor Cambridge offered instruction in such practical matters – the gap between a university education and the 'real world' was even greater in the fifteenth century than it is now. For their part, graduates were not likely to want to spend their lives with uneducated people who did not share their interests, and so the temptation to become non-resident was greater for them than for others.

On top of all this there was a definite decline in the number of clergy in the fifteenth century. Using the relatively complete ordination figures for the diocese of Coventry and Lichfield, Professor Swanson calculated roughly as follows for the three orders of subdeacon, deacon and priest:[17]

1300–49	6,000
1350–99	4,000
1400–49	2,700
1450–99	5,000
1500–32	5,300

The dip after 1350 is easily explained by the effects of the Black Death. If we accept that a third of the population died from the plague, the relative numbers of those who sought ordination remained about the same as they had been before, although it seems that there was a falling off as the century progressed. That is confirmed by the clear drop after 1400, the very period that saw the greatest efforts to encourage the ordination of university graduates. After 1450 things started to pick up again, and eventually even reached pre-plague levels. In 1483 the number ordained in Coventry and Lichfield exceeded 100 for the

---

[16] Bray, *Records of Convocation*, 5:64–66, 70–74 (14 December 1417), 101–104 (27 May 1421), 384–393 (17 October 1438), 411–412 (8 January 1440).

[17] Swanson, *Church and Society*, 33.

first time since 1377, and in 1498 no fewer than 218 secular priests were ordained, the highest number since 1336.[18] We know too little about these men to be able to say what their motives in seeking ordination were, but the statistics indicate that towards the end of the fifteenth century a clerical vocation was becoming popular once again, and the trend seems to have continued at least up to the eve of the Reformation.

What happened to the large numbers of clergy who never managed to obtain a benefice? Some were employed as chaplains to various noblemen, although there were obvious limits to the number of such posts available. Many seem to have become chantry priests, attached to chantries in parishes and cathedrals, where they received payment for saying masses for the dead.[19] Chantry priests did not have the cure of souls, and since it was possible to say mass quite quickly, they had a lot of time on their hands. Many of them therefore turned to teaching children in the parish to read and write. In several places schools appeared in connection with the local church and were staffed by men like this. It was just as well, because when the chantries were abolished in 1548, these men could easily step into the role of schoolmasters, which many of them did, continuing a tradition of church schools that remains robust to the present time.[20]

One aspect of church life that never recovered from the Black Death was the monastic. The history of monasticism was one of periodic renewal and decay, so the decline after 1350 was not necessarily permanent. It might have been possible for the Lollards for example to have evolved into a religious order, with John Wyclif playing the part of a Francis of Assisi or a Dominic Guzmán, but that did not happen. Instead the friars, like the monks, went into long-term decline as they became institutionalized and lost their initial zeal, although in some cases they would revive in the late fifteenth century. On the whole, however, religious houses lost novices and there were very few new foundations after the mid-fourteenth century. Most clung on stubbornly, but with greatly reduced numbers, and many found that it was only by appropriating parishes and living off their tithe revenue that they could survive.[21]

Life for the regular clergy became even more difficult after 1410, when the king ordered the suppression of the 'alien priories' in England. These were

---

[18] Ibid. 35.

[19] Chantries were so-called because the mass was chanted in a semi-musical fashion.

[20] A. H. Thompson, *The English Clergy and Their Organization in the Later Middle Ages* (Oxford: Clarendon Press, 1947), 132–160, 247–291. It should be said that while chantry priests could be redeployed, chantry revenues were largely confiscated and were not used for the educational purposes that many reformers had hoped they would be.

[21] Ibid. 161–186.

religious houses or cells dependent on Continental foundations, most of them French. As England was at war with France, there was a feeling that these alien priories were a hostile presence in the country, apt to send their revenues abroad at a time when every penny was needed to support the war effort, and claiming exemption from local ecclesiastical jurisdiction. In some cases these priories were able to attach themselves to English houses and carry on much as before, but many were simply dissolved and their income was assigned to others, notably the university colleges now emerging.

One of the chief beneficiaries of this dissolution was the Carthusian order, a relative latecomer on the English monastic scene and one that was bucking the general trend. The Carthusians owed their origin to Bruno of Cologne (1030?–1101), who established a monastery at the Grande Chartreuse in France. In England the monasteries were known as Charterhouses, and the first was founded by King Henry II at Witham in 1181. But growth was very slow. As late as 1343 there were still only two Charterhouses in England, but after that numbers started to increase. By the time the order was suppressed there were no fewer than ten (nine in England and one in Scotland), most of which were founded in the course of the fifteenth century, often from revenues taken from the disbanded alien priories. The Carthusians maintained their rigorous discipline and relative popularity to the very end. When the Reformation came and the monasteries were dissolved, they were the only order that resisted with any consistency, going to their deaths as martyrs even as their houses were destroyed.[22]

To sum up, the state of the English church in 1485 was healthier than it had been for a century or more, and there was every sign that it would continue to improve. The standards of clerical education were getting better and the numbers of those offering themselves for the priesthood were growing steadily. The institutions of church government had survived two generations of political instability and the prospect of future cooperation between the spiritual and temporal orders looked good. Printing was still in its infancy and its impact was yet to be felt, but as yet no one could see what that would be. Similarly, Renaissance humanism was beginning to percolate through from Italy, but it had not yet disturbed the peace of the English universities to any noticeable degree. The future looked promising and there were hopes that the ascent of Henry VII to the throne might usher in the golden age promised by the Arthurian legends of old, but never as yet realized.

---

[22] G. Coppack and M. Aston, *God's Poor Men: The Carthusians in England* (Stroud: Tempus, 2002).

Scotland and Ireland

The late fourteenth and fifteenth centuries were a time of growth and development for the church in Scotland. The last vestiges of subservience to York were discarded in 1359 and after that the Scottish dioceses were treated as a special jurisdiction subject only to the see of Rome. Scotland was a poor country, and its monarchy was weak. It had a parliament similar to that of England but the church in Scotland had nothing to compare with the English convocations, and it remained in an underdeveloped state. An astonishingly high number of parishes were appropriated to monasteries – 86%, as compared with 37% in England – and 56% of these had their vicarages appropriated as well. This means that over half the parish churches in Scotland were totally dependent on a monastic house, which in many cases was far away from the parish itself.[23]

This undesirable situation was made worse by the exceptionally close connection between Scotland and the papacy, which gave the latter a chance to intervene in Scottish church affairs much more than it did in England. Papal provisions, for example, which in England and Ireland were largely confined to bishoprics, extended in Scotland to the humblest parish level, with the result that many Scottish clergymen petitioned Rome (or Avignon) for promotion to a benefice that was formally in monastic (or even laymen's) hands, a procedure that could sometimes take years. Matters were further complicated because successful candidates were expected to pay the equivalent of a year's income to the papacy, and that could cause hardship for anyone who was not independently wealthy.

In one area though, considerable progress was made. Scotland managed to create not two but three universities – St Andrews (1410, chartered in 1413), Glasgow (1451) and Aberdeen (1495) – which were soon turning out graduates of high quality. Education has long been the strength of the Scottish church, and even in its early days its successes in this area were remarkable, although they were still insufficient for the needs of the country as a whole. The most outstanding Scottish theologian of the time was John Mair (1467?–1550), who was educated at Cambridge and spent many years in Paris before returning to teach at Glasgow (1518–23) and St Andrews (1523–6). He then went back to France but retired to St Andrews in 1533, where he was Provost of St Salvator's College until his death.[24] Of the estimated 1,100 Scottish parishes in existence

---

[23] See R. Oram, *Domination and Lordship: Scotland 1070–1230* (Edinburgh: Edinburgh University Press, 2011), 347–350; G. Donaldson, *The Scottish Reformation* (Cambridge: Cambridge University Press, 1960), 11–19.

[24] J. T. Slotemaker, 'John Mair as Theologian', in D. Fergusson and M. K. Elliott (eds.), *The History of Scottish Theology*, 3 vols. (Oxford: Oxford University Press, 2019), 96–108.

at the time of the Reformation (1560), only about a quarter had incumbents who were university graduates. This made expansion and reform a priority for the Reformers, and led to the establishment of the fourth ancient Scottish university (Edinburgh) in 1583. Given that the much larger and richer kingdom of England did not create a third university until the nineteenth century, this was no mean achievement.

Ireland was a different story. The parts of the country that were under English rule enjoyed a system of government similar to that of England, including a church whose constituent provinces had a constitution analogous to that of Canterbury and York. Provincial synods were held at intervals in Armagh, Cashel and Dublin – evidence for Tuam is lacking – and the surviving registers from Armagh reveal an organization not dissimilar to what existed across the water. The number of parishes was high, being in the order of 2,500, but how many were viable units is hard to determine – probably considerably fewer than the total.[25] The church remained extremely poor, it had far too many bishoprics for its slender resources to support, and in the Gaelic areas of the country it was virtually impossible to establish a secure and disciplined administration. Tension between the English and indigenous Irish prevented the kind of consolidation taking place in England. Trends already evident in the fourteenth century became more explicit, as bishops spent more and more time in England, and even the lower clergy were often non-resident. On the other hand there was a noticeable desire to tighten the church's internal discipline, and this was evident in the Gaelic areas as much as in the English ones. Evidence for the former comes from the records of a synod held in the diocese of Clogher on 6 October 1430, which laid down details regarding the revenues of the church and the responsibilities of the erenachs who administered them.[26] Another synod that apparently covered the entire province of Cashel was held at Limerick on 6 August 1453 and issued an extraordinarily long set of canons covering every aspect of church life.[27] There was nothing in contemporary England to compare with this and we must conclude that, in spite of its many difficulties, the Irish church was doing its best to raise its standards. On the other hand the Armagh registers for this period confirm the growing separation of the two halves of the diocese, which became more

---

[25] See E. FitzPatrick and R. Gillespie, *The Parish in Medieval and Early Modern Ireland: Community, Territory and Building* (Dublin: Four Courts Press, 2006). The Irish Ordnance Survey, carried out in the 1830s, found 2,428 parishes, but when the Church of Ireland was disestablished in 1871 it had only 1,518, which is perhaps a more realistic figure for the Middle Ages as well.

[26] Bray, *Records of Convocation*, 16:241–244.

[27] Ibid. 16:253–266.

or less fixed after 1460 and endured until the final conquest of the island in the early seventeenth century.[28]

Both Ireland and Scotland had a large number of monasteries, but these were but a pale shadow of what they had been in the golden age of Irish monasticism. So attached to ancient tribal ways were they that it was not uncommon for an abbot to pass his monastery on to his son, and dispensations for clerical marriage were routine.[29] In this respect Ireland stood out from the other nations of Europe, but its peculiarities were tolerated because there was nothing anyone could do about them. But if the monasteries were in decline, the mendicant orders underwent a renewal and expansion, especially in the Gaelic areas, where they were relatively free from the prejudice against them that was common among the authorities in English Ireland. Coupled with this were movements for internal reform that sought to recapture the original mendicant vision. The Franciscans were particularly successful in this, and the Observants, as those who promoted a return to the more primitive strictness of the order were known, gradually gained the upper hand. It would not be until 1517 that their victory would finally be acknowledged by the papacy, but they had penetrated Ireland long before then. It could not have been foreseen at the time, but these Observant Franciscans would play an important role in resisting the Protestant Reformation when it finally reached Ireland a few years later.

It should be said that it was mainly outsiders (and those Irishmen who had been exposed to outside influences) who were scandalized by the state of the Irish church; most people seem to have been quite happy with the existing situation and felt closely tied to the clergy by bonds of kinship that minimized the difference between the priesthood and the laity. Whatever its faults might have been, the Irish church was a force for social integration in the later Middle Ages, and there was little appetite for radical change when that was eventually forced upon it by events and decisions that came almost entirely from outside its ranks.

Of the quality of pastoral care and the spiritual life of the parishes we can say almost nothing, since records do not exist and there is no sign of the intellectual life stirring in England at that time. Lollardy never reached the Celtic lands, and even large tracts of northern England were virtually free of it. Like it or not, Chaucer's Canterbury was a world away from Armagh or St Andrews, and the gap would not be closed (or even seriously narrowed) until after the Reformation.

---

[28] Ibid. 16:267–278.
[29] See J. Watt, *The Church in Medieval Ireland* (Dublin: University College Dublin Press, 1998), 185–187, for an outstanding example of a clerical dynasty in the diocese of Clogher.

Baptized paganism?

Trying to gauge the spiritual health of the late medieval church is a difficult exercise. On the one hand public life was totally dominated by religious festivals and events of different kinds. The canonization of local saints proceeded apace, and every village, corporation or university had at least one such patron, and sometimes more. Their feast days were times of celebration, but whether this could be called 'devotion' in the true sense of the word may be doubted. Then there were two sets of quarter days, observed by both church and state. One was based on the seasons of the year, but sanctified as the Annunciation (25 March), the birth of St John the Baptist (24 June), Michaelmas, the feast of St Michael and all Angels (29 September) and finally Christmas (25 December). It is not difficult to see the Christological pattern in this, beginning with the angel Gabriel's appearance to Mary, which also marked the new year on the calendar, and continuing through the birth of John, the cousin and forerunner of Jesus, the witness of the angels and finally the birth of the promised Messiah himself. The other set of quarter days is more elusive. It begins with the feast of St Philip and St James (1 May) and continues through the feast of St Peter *ad Vincula* (1 August), All Saints' Day (1 November) and the feast of the Presentation of Christ in the Temple, or Candlemas (2 February). There is no theological logic behind this cycle, but a little research shows that these feasts were superimposed on ancient Celtic tradition, which celebrated Bealtaine (1 May), Lughnasadh (1 August), Samhain (31 October – 1 November) and Imbolc (1–2 February). The pagan origins of these festivals have survived in popular culture, often displacing the Christian overlay, as we can see from May Day, Hallowe'en and (in the USA) Groundhog Day. Lughnasa(dh) seems to have escaped this tendency, but as recently as 1990 Brian Friel wrote a play about it, *Dancing at Lughnasa*, in which the complex interplay between pagan custom and traditional Catholic piety is a major theme.

These dates and many more were woven into the fabric of everyday medieval life, which in turn was governed by the seasons of the year. Animals went into winter pasture at Martinmas (11 November) and the weather on St Swithun's Day (15 July) was held to forecast the next forty days – in effect, the rest of the summer. Did people really believe this sort of thing? Some probably did. Some still do! But baptized pagan folklore, however quaint it may seem to some, is no substitute for true faith in Christ, and even in medieval times many understood that. Yet try as they might, churchmen could do little against popular tradition and prejudice. The great feast of Christ's resurrection from the dead clung to the name of the pagan goddess of the east, with its close associations with the rising sun, the return of spring and fertility in general. It is probably no exaggeration to say that for many people, Easter is mainly about bunnies and eggs – both fertility symbols – and not much else. Paganism is not easily stamped out, and the modern church has its work cut out every bit as much as its medieval forebear had.

In such a climate nobody will be surprised to learn that superstition was rife. Everywhere were holy wells, sacred trees and other phenomena believed to have special powers that could affect people's lives. For many these were places of healing, but there was a darker side as well. Witchcraft was believed to be ubiquitous, and eccentric old women often had a hard time of it, especially if villagers were convinced that their crops had failed or the plague had appeared because a witch had cast a spell. It was no accident that burning at the stake, the punishment originally reserved for heretics, was soon extended to witches, and as time went on came to be almost exclusively associated with them.

Saints' relics – bones and pieces of clothing – were particularly prized, and people would sometimes pay large sums of money to acquire one or more of them. The relics trade was good business, and many churches sought to have a piece of the True Cross or something similar, in the expectation that it would encourage deeper devotion. Sacred sites attracted pilgrims in large numbers. An intrepid few made their way to Santiago de Compostela in Spain, or even to the Holy Land, but most were content to stay at home. Canterbury was an obvious goal, not least because St Thomas Becket was buried there, but Glastonbury ran a close second and there were several others, including Walsingham.

Sometimes superstition could get in the way of serious social and political events. When John Wyclif was summoned for trial, a rare earthquake struck London on the very day proceedings against him opened – 21 May 1382. Several of the judges set to try him were terrified that God might be on Wyclif's side, and Archbishop William Courtenay had to think on his feet in order to continue with the trial. Courtenay rose to the occasion by declaring that, far from being a sign of God's displeasure, the quake was the earth's way of releasing fetid air and spirits, which is exactly what the church was trying to do in its condemnation of Wyclif.[30] These things need to be recalled because

---

[30] W. W. Shirley (ed.), *Fasciculi Zizianorum Magistri Iohannis Wyclif* (London: Longman, Brown, Green, Longmans, and Roberts, 1858), 272–273. It is sobering to reflect that such beliefs have not entirely disappeared. Many will recall that when the heretical David Jenkins was consecrated bishop of Durham in York Minster on 6 July 1984, the cathedral was struck by lightning a few days later – and not a few observers were convinced that they knew why.

they provide the context in which the ministry of the church and the spiritual life of its members have to be understood. If there was a common belief that demonic forces could (and did) use material objects to deceive the unwary, then it was a relatively simple matter for the church to teach that its ordained ministers also had a spiritual power to use material objects for the benefit of God's people. This power was most visible in the sacraments, the means by which the grace of God was communicated to the members of the church. Baptism was the sacrament of new birth by which a child born in sin was cleansed and born again as a child of God. The Lord's Supper (or Eucharist) was a re-presentation of Christ's atoning sacrifice in which bread and wine were turned into his body and blood. They were then administered to communicants as the 'drug of immortality', the means by which the eternal life of Christ was imparted to those who believed in him. The other sacraments had their place, but apart from penance, which was administered as regularly as the Eucharist, they were (like baptism) one-off events that had little immediate relevance to a Christian's daily life.

Given that almost everyone was baptized at birth, the sacraments that claimed most people's attention were penance and the Eucharist. Penance was necessary because although baptism cleansed babies of their inherited (original) sin, it did not take away their sinfulness. Baptized Christians sinned all the time, and it was essential for them to repent of their wrongdoing before coming to the Lord's Supper. This was institutionalized by encouraging people to confess their sins to a priest, who would then tell them what they had to do in order to demonstrate that they were sincerely repentant. When this penance, as it was called, was complete, the repentant sinner would return to the priest and seek absolution from him. Once that was obtained, the erstwhile sinner was regarded as worthy to stand in the presence of God, who was said to be present in the consecrated elements of the Lord's Supper.

What was true of admission to the Lord's Supper on earth was also true of entry into the kingdom of heaven. Without repentance and cleansing, no one could pass directly from this life to that of the saints gathered around the throne of God. Extreme unction was designed to assist the transition from this life to the next, but it could not always be administered to the dying, and even those who passed away in a 'state of grace' were not assured that their sins had been entirely forgiven. To provide that assurance, the church invented the idea of Purgatory, a place to which departed souls would go in order to work off the remaining debt of sin for which they had not paid in this life. Nobody could say for sure how long a soul would have to spend there, but there were ways of reducing the time, however long it was. It was possible for a person to do more penance than was strictly required, to 'go the extra mile' as it were, and to chalk up the superfluous effort as credit to be used to defray the hidden costs of unconfessed sins. It was also possible for individuals to purchase an 'indulgence', which was like paying a fine instead of spending time in jail or doing community service. Indulgences usually came in the form of certificates given to penitents as receipts that proved they had paid their debt of sin, at least up to a certain amount. Indulgences could also be purchased on behalf of others, so that it was possible to shorten the time a loved one would spend in Purgatory, and many people sought to assist their dead relatives in that way.

The practice of penance was central to the pastoral work of the church, which was always trying to encourage people to get right with God before they died. In an age when death was always near, and especially after the plague took so many away without warning, it was a powerful message. Equally important was the healing power of the Eucharist, or 'mass' as it was generally known. In the 'miracle of the altar', bread and wine had been used to produce the body and blood of Christ, with all their healing powers, and that is what counted.

This belief soon led to all kinds of devotional practices that had never existed before. Consecrated bread and wine were set aside and placed in a box (the 'tabernacle'), which was kept in the church building for a variety of purposes. The 'reserved sacrament' could be used for the Communion of the sick, who were unable to attend the public celebration in church, and could also act as a focus of private devotion for those in need of special prayer. As an extension of this, priests could be asked to celebrate private masses with particular intentions. Individuals would pay for these and tell the priest what they wanted prayer for. Chantries became numerous and some were well endowed by people who wanted masses to be said for them during their time in Purgatory. One of the most famous churches in England, King's College Chapel in Cambridge, began life as a chantry for the soul of King Henry VI (1422–61; 1470–71), who was meant to be commemorated there on a daily basis.

It is hardly necessary to say that a system like this was wide open to abuse. Priests would encourage laypeople to invest in their chantries, and saying mass for them was a way of making money on the side. There was also no way of knowing when a debt was paid off, so that masses of this kind could continue for ever. Who was going to say when the soul being prayed for finally got to heaven? Did this happen when the money ran out, or was the poor soul simply deprived of benefits for the duration of its stay in Purgatory? Questions like these were seldom asked and never answered, because no answer could be given, although what the church could do was impose obligations on people that would leave them with the sense that they were headed in the right direction. For some, an obligation might include going on crusade, but that was rare and confined to the aristocracy. More common were obligations to undertake pilgrimages or engage in ascetic practices like fasting. In this last example the obligation to fast in Advent and (especially) in Lent was laid on all Christians, as was abstaining from eating meat on a Friday, the day the Lord was crucified.

It is easy for people today to look askance at such things and see them as so many invitations to self-righteousness; but although that is true, we must also try to see the bigger picture. Pilgrimages were great adventures for people who seldom left their native villages, and helped to build a sense of belonging to a wider community. Fasting might be of considerable benefit to the body, even if it did little or nothing for the soul. Above all, these things gave ordinary people a sense that they could participate in the life of the church and contribute something towards their own salvation. They were a form of assurance for people who had no idea what the future would bring, or when they would pass from this world to the next. Purgatory may sound awful to us but it was far better than hell, because it was a place of hope. Those who entered it knew that eventually they would get to heaven: it was a kind of spiritual fitness gymnasium whose eventual reward was a place at the heavenly Olympics. We have only to look at ourselves to judge how long it might take to achieve such a transformation, but the goal was positive and gave solace to troubled consciences. Of course people knew that the system could be abused and that there were hypocrites in the church, but that is always the case, and in the eyes of most medieval people it did not compromise the efficacy of rituals performed in good faith. The church was very clear about this, insisting that the validity of a sacrament did not depend on the worthiness of the minister, and by its own lights it was right to say that. After all, if no spiritual benefit could be obtained from the ministry of anyone who is less than perfect, there would be no divine grace available at all.[31] We hold our treasure in jars of clay and, for all its faults, the medieval church put that principle into practice.

Public worship

One of the great developments that took place in the Middle Ages was in the field of public worship, where music and liturgy rose to artistic heights never

---

[31] The Protestant Reformers knew this and retained the principle that the unworthiness of the minister does not compromise the validity of the ministry. See Article 26 of the Thirty-nine Articles of 1571.

before seen and continue to attract a following.[32] The church had always had music of some kind. The Old Testament psalter was its hymn book and Christians were soon adding their own contributions. Luke the Evangelist records the song of Mary, which she intoned after the angel Gabriel announced that she would become the mother of the Messiah.[33] To this he added rhythmic verses attributed to Zacharias, the father of John the Baptist, and to Simeon, who greeted the baby Jesus in the temple shortly after Jesus' birth.[34] Whether they were originally meant to be sung or not, they were quickly turned into canticles and have been a staple of the Christian repertoire ever since. Even after the Last Supper, Jesus and his disciples sang a hymn before going out to the Garden of Gethsemane.[35] Later on, the apostle Paul exhorted the Ephesians to sing 'psalms and hymns and spiritual songs', making a joyful noise to the Lord – as an alternative to the drunken rowdiness that apparently accompanied other social and religious gatherings of the time.[36]

Later on, Augustine of Hippo was deeply moved by Christian music, which played at least some part in his conversion. The missionaries who brought the gospel to Britain and Ireland sang as they went, although what they sounded like is hard to say. The best guess is that their music must have been something like the chanting that can still be heard in Greek Orthodox churches – and even in the Muslim call to prayer, which evolved out of a similar tradition. It is not very attractive to most western ears, but its persistence in the Middle East is a reminder of its hypnotic effect on those who are used to it. When British Christianity deferred to Roman usages after the Synod of Whitby in 664, a new element was introduced, although it probably took some time for it to become the norm. Today we call this 'plainsong', or 'Gregorian chant', named for Pope Gregory II (715–31), in whose time it supposedly emerged. If that is correct, it appeared during the lifetime of Bede, but probably too late to have had much impact on England while he was writing his history. More likely, it came in gradually in the following century, and probably did more than anything else to remind ordinary worshippers that they were now part of the wider Roman world.

Plainsong had a simplicity and distinctive purity of tone that gave it wide appeal, and for the next few centuries it was sung in a single tone and (probably) unaccompanied. The singers were mostly always monks and nuns, who either

---

[32] For the story of English church music, see A. Gant, 'O Sing unto the Lord': A History of English Church Music (London: Profile Books, 2015).

[33] Luke 1:46–55.

[34] Luke 1:67–79; 2:29–32.

[35] Matt. 26:30.

[36] Eph. 5:19–20.

performed solo or in choirs formed of their community brothers and sisters. Most churches were small and unable to accommodate large numbers of singers or musical instruments of the kind that became common later on. We have to assume that in most cases the priest would chant parts of the service as he went along, but none of the congregation would have joined in. Nor could they have done so very easily, since the services were all in Latin. Sometime after 900 the monotone chant was expanded to include other voices singing in unison, producing an effect that must have been as startling then as the change from black-and-white to colour television has been in more recent times. This period also saw the development of early organs, which were designed to reflect the new polyphonous style of singing.

As with so many other things, developments that were already underway received an enormous boost from the Norman Conquest. Not only were ties to the Continent, where worship was more advanced, greatly strengthened, but the standards of what could (and should) be achieved were improved immensely as well. Much bigger church buildings became the order of the day, making it possible to experiment with liturgical practices (like processions) that had been impossible before. New musical styles were imported from France and Italy, and gradually adapted to the English (and later to the wider British and Irish) context. By the thirteenth century, church music was becoming indigenized in England and distinctive forms were emerging. At the same time, dramatic re-presentations of biblical stories were also gaining in popularity, and many of these were regularly performed in the open air, to the accompaniment of musical instruments – and in the spoken language. These plays are the earliest indications we have of how the gospel message was communicated to a largely illiterate populace, and they did much to make the Christian message familiar to a broad section of society. People who could not read or own a Bible for themselves could pick up the storyline of the Old Testament from those who re-enacted it, and the events of Christ's life, death and resurrection were frequently portrayed, especially at the great feasts of the Christian year. The modern nativity play, so beloved of generations of primary-school children, originated in this way and has changed relatively little over the course of time.

At the heart of all this was the great drama of the Eucharist, in which the death and resurrection of Jesus Christ were represented on a weekly basis as the central part of Christian worship. As with everything that had gone before it, the celebration of the Eucharist was the work of the priest, not of the people, who were essentially spectators, even though the priest was technically working on their behalf. Congregations could not participate, partly because the standard of musical ability required was constantly improving and partly because it required knowledge of Latin, which almost none of them had. This did not mean they were not 'involved' in some way, but it was more like a modern theatre audience than like a modern congregation. People can go to a play or an opera and be deeply moved by it without participating in it directly, and this spectator aspect characterized late medieval worship. It facilitated the adoption of liturgical vestments whose shapes and colours contained their own message – white for the purity of saints' days and Easter, red for the fire of Pentecost and the sacrifice of the martyrs, purple for the suffering of Christ in Lent and Advent, and green (the colour of life) for the rest of the year, known simply as 'ordinary time'. People recognized the seasons when they saw the priests robed accordingly, and over time they came to understand what was happening, thanks to the gestures the celebrant employed as he intoned the service. When he held up the consecrated bread and the chalice, the people knew that the 'miracle of the altar' had taken place, and that what they were looking at was now the body and blood of Christ himself.

As time went on, church buildings also took on theatrical aspects. Statues and carvings depicted the lives of great saints and biblical characters, as did paintings on the walls. Most wonderfully of all, techniques of staining glass were developed that have never been equalled or surpassed. The ravages of time and religious reform have destroyed much of this stained glass in the British Isles, but it can still be seen in its glory in places like Chartres Cathedral in France, where the entire biblical narrative is laid out in a systematic-ally arranged sequence of magnificent windows. Medieval England also had cathedrals like this, and nineteenth-century romantics tried to replicate them, although with only moderate success. The stained glass we see in so many churches pales by comparison with its medieval equivalent, and its dis-appearance must be regarded as one of the greatest cultural losses in our history.

The wholesale destruction of glass and of many organs in the sixteenth and seventeenth centuries was a tragedy, but the reasons for it have little to do with the philistine vandalism that so many latter-day medievalists have attributed to the Reformers. The growth of elaborate music and liturgy was never a smooth progress from one achievement to the next, and there were always plenty of people, including some prominent in church life, who deplored what they saw as the inordinate attention paid to ceremonial and the corresponding loss of comprehension it often entailed. Even if the services had been sung in English or Norman French, it would often have been impossible for people to understand them because the polyphonic chants were hard to follow even for those few who knew Latin. Aelred of Rievaulx (1110–67) for example criticized what he saw going on in his own time and declared:

> Sound should not be given precedence over meaning, but sound with meaning should generally be allowed to stimulate greater attachment. Therefore the sound should be so moderate, so marked by gravity that it does not captivate the whole spirit to amusement in itself, but leaves the greater part to the meaning.[37]

It is a complaint – and a warning – that is as relevant today as it was when Aelred wrote it nearly 1,000 years ago. The duel between choir and preacher is still with us, and it is by no means clear that preachers have the upper hand now any more than they did back then.

Aelred's voice was a minority one however, and choral music went from strength to strength, supported as it was by the kings and later by the colleges that various bishops founded, not only at Oxford and Cambridge but at Eton and Winchester too. Interestingly, English choirs were encouraged to improvise harmonies, with the result that by the end of the fourteenth century a distinctively English polyphony was being produced and becoming popular. One of the earliest named composers, John Dunstable or Dunstaple (1390–1453), became famous all over Europe because he wrote this down and thus helped to codify it, a process copied by others for a generation or more after his death. Many of the improvisations were rooted in popular folk tunes, which brought church music closer to the people. It was still entirely in Latin, but by the early sixteenth century English religious songs, known as carols, were also being composed and sung in homes and in the streets. The tradition still survives, especially in connection with Christmas, and has now become a permanent fixture of English-speaking Christianity around the world. Musical instruments, in particular organs, also came into vogue, but they did not directly accompany the singing. Instead they provided interludes between the canticles, which continued to be sung a cappella.

The theological content of these compositions was heavily weighted in favour of praise to the Virgin Mary, whose cult was growing exponentially in the later Middle Ages. It is hard to say why this should have been the case, but it is possible that the idea of a virgin mother appealed to medieval men (and it was men who were driving the rise in choral singing) because it

---

[37] Aelred of Rievaulx, *The Mirror of Charity*, tr. E. Connor; introduction and notes by C. Dumont (Kalamazoo, Mich.: Cistercian Publications, 1990).

combined the idea of female purity that figured so prominently in tales of knightly chivalry with the homeliness and comfort of motherhood, which must have been particularly appealing in a world where young boys were often separated from their families at an early age and sent off to a monastery (or some equivalent form of school) from which they would not emerge until adulthood.

The greatest achievement of the medieval church was not in its choral singing, important though that was, but in its liturgies, which were developed around the daily offices inherited from the monastic tradition and centred mainly on the Lord's Supper, or Eucharist.[38] Liturgies had been produced in the late Roman world, and rites that go back to the fourth century, and are attributed to men like Basil of Caesarea (329–79) and John Chrysostom (c.349–407), are still regularly used in the Eastern Orthodox churches. The Latin world of western Europe was slower to develop a comparable tradition, and by the time it did, the English church was a fully functioning part of Latin Christendom with nothing distinctive about it. There is evidence that by the tenth century the Anglo-Saxons were beginning to create more elaborate forms of worship than had been customary in earlier times but, as with so much else, the Norman Conquest provided the catalyst for the emergence of what were to become the standard rites of the later Middle Ages.

The beginnings of this movement can be traced to the work of Osmund, a nephew of William the Conqueror who, thanks to his uncle, became bishop of the new see of Salisbury in 1078.[39] Osmund died in 1099 and was succeeded by Roger le Poer (1102–39) and Jocelin de Bohun (1142–84), who continued Osmund's work and expanded it. Osmund had a gift for both administration and music. He composed a number of liturgical books for use in his cathedral, combining traditional monastic practice with local English and Norman customs to produce a new blend that came to be identified with his church, which was commonly known by its abbreviated name of Sarum. Salisbury continued to be a centre of liturgical creativity at least until the time of Richard Poore, who was Dean of the cathedral there from 1197 to 1214 and (after a brief spell as Bishop of Chichester) its bishop from 1217 to 1228, when he was finally translated to Durham, where he died in 1237. By then the Sarum Rite had developed considerably, and although there is ongoing scholarly debate as to

---

[38] For a detailed history of this complex subject, see R. W. Pfaff, *The Liturgy in Medieval England: A History* (Cambridge: Cambridge University Press, 2009).

[39] The see had been transferred from Sherborne in 1074, along with its bishop, Hereman (1058–78), so Osmund was technically the second bishop of Salisbury, though the first person to be appointed to it directly.

how much of it was the work of Richard Poore himself, it is generally agreed that he was the motivating force behind it. Poore moved his cathedral to its present site in 1225, by which time the Sarum Rite was beginning to spread across England and Wales.[40] It underwent further development in the fourteenth century, and in its final form became something of a universal standard, at least in the province of Canterbury. By 1394 it had established itself at Exeter and in 1414 was accepted at London as well. Places like Hereford and York resisted this trend, but the invention of printing benefited its spread and the Sarum Rite became familiar even in parts of Scotland and Ireland.[41] It was finally mandated for the whole of England in 1543, although its triumph would be short-lived. Yet when it was replaced by the first Book of Common Prayer in 1549, the desirability of uniformity in public worship had already been acknowledged and in that respect the legacy of Sarum was to endure for centuries.

The Sarum Rite was designed for practical use in the daily life of Salisbury Cathedral, which was secular and not monastic, although the daily office, or cycle of seven services held on a daily basis, reflects the monastic tradition. Each of these services included canticles, psalms, prayers and responses appropriate to the time of day they were sung, and the choir would quickly have learned them by heart. The eucharistic liturgy was divided into two parts – one sung at every service, regardless of the occasion, and the other that varied according to the season or purpose for which the service was being held. In the first group were the Kyrie (eleison), the Gloria (in excelsis), the Credo, the Sanctus, the Benedictus and the Agnus Dei. In the second were the Introit, the Offertory, the Communion and a number of prayers that varied according to circumstances. The various parts of the service were known by the first word(s) of the Latin text that was sung, and when they were eventually translated into English in the sixteenth century, these Latin tags were retained, making them appear as titles in modern usage. The one partial exception to this is the Kyrie (eleison), which is Greek for 'Lord (have mercy)'. It was retained in the Latin liturgy as a reminder that the original language of the church was Greek, rather in the same way that we have retained words like Hallelujah and Amen, which reflect the Hebraic roots of our faith. In both cases hardly anyone today knows what these words mean, but they have become fixtures of our worship that are shared by Christians around the world, and there is no

---

[40] It might have been introduced at St David's as early as 1223.

[41] On Scotland, see S. M. Holmes, 'Liturgical Theology before 1600', in Fergusson and Elliott (eds.), *History of Scottish Theology*, 1:54–68.

question of translating them into English. We just accept them for what they are and move on.

In addition to the Sarum Rite there were others (called 'uses') in places that had their own liturgical traditions.[42] Apart from the ones already mentioned, the 'uses' of Lincoln and Bangor seem to have had some influence outside their local areas, although the evidence for them is sparse and their real distinctiveness is controversial.[43] To modern eyes, and in particular to those with no liturgical knowledge, these different uses look much the same because there was an overall pattern, based on the Roman rite, that they all followed to a greater or lesser degree. But they were not identical and the differences were most apparent to those who were closest to them – the clergy and the choirs who sang them. That mattered because the liturgies, for all their beauty and elegance, were theatrical productions in which the laypeople were spectators, not participants. The sixteenth-century Reformers did not abandon them completely, and incorporated much from them (and especially from Sarum) into their own prayer books, but the continuity that gave was often not appreciated, for the simple reason that the congregations started taking a part in the Reformed services, which was a novelty and a sure sign that a new order had dawned.

Private piety

By 1450 there was a growing body of educated laypeople looking for spiritual nourishment, which they could not find within the traditional structures of the church. It was not that these structures were especially corrupt or uninviting, but they were no longer adequate to contain the needs of the population. Many people wanted to get closer to God without taking the vows imposed on monastics. Similarly, they wanted to read books and hear sermons in English, when the church was still using only Latin.[44] Above all, they were looking for a portable and practical spirituality that could serve them in everyday life. The proliferation of private devotional books owned (and presumably used) by individual people bears eloquent witness to this. The idea that holiness was attainable only by separation from the world and the adoption of a rigorous (and arcane) system of discipline was losing credibility, as friars and even

---

[42] See e.g. W. Smith, *The Use of Hereford: A Medieval Diocesan Rite Reconsidered*, Alcuin Club and The Group for Renewal of Worship Joint Liturgical Studies 89 (Norwich: Hymns Ancient & Modern, 2020).

[43] Pfaff, *Liturgy in Medieval England*, 445–528.

[44] This was true even of preaching. For a selection of Latin sermons translated into English, see S. Wenzel, *Preaching in the Age of Chaucer: Selected Sermons in Translation* (Washington, D.C.: Catholic University of America Press, 2008).

secular clergy were going into the public square and preaching to crowds in the open air. The spiritual treasure that for so long had been sealed up in the cloister was gradually spilling out into the wider world, and many of those who lived in that world were increasingly desirous of sharing in it.

One feature of the fifteenth century was the growing popularity of devotional works, many of them dating from generations before. Richard Rolle, for example, enjoyed his greatest fame a century after he passed away, and his works were widely read right up to the time of the Reformation. There is a definite sense that many people were seeking a closer communion with God in their own lives, and were less reliant on the worship services of the church, although they did not reject them. Thomas à Kempis's *Imitation of Christ*, written sometime between 1418 and 1427 and reflecting the tradition of Gerhard Groote, was translated into English and published thanks to the efforts of Lady Margaret Beaufort (1443–1509), mother of the future King Henry VII (1485–1509) and a leading player in the English Renaissance.

In England mysticism proved to be especially popular among women, who were finding their voice to a degree that had not been known since Anglo-Saxon times. The most famous of these is Julian of Norwich (1342–1416), who came from a family wealthy enough that they gave her an education. But although she could read and write, it would be an exaggeration to say that she was 'learned'. Nor does it appear that she either married or went into a convent, the two acceptable career paths for women in her time. As far as we know, she lived on her own and had visions of God, which she then shared with others. The remarkable thing is that, despite her apparent oddity, she earned and retained the respect of her contemporaries, some of whom sought her out for spiritual guidance. Today she is widely recognized as a mystic saint and is often quoted for her sayings about the unifying presence and purpose of God.[45]

More controversial was Julian's younger contemporary, Margery Kempe (1373–1438). Like Julian, Margery was a laywoman who had visions, but she lived in a different time. The emergence of Lollardy and the career of Joan of Arc in France, who had been put to death by the English as a witch, made it more difficult for Margery to keep out of trouble. She was frequently charged with heresy and her lack of formal learning was held against her. It also seems that she had periodic fits, although what caused them remains unknown. She did, however, manage to commit her spiritual experiences to writing, and her

---

[45] N. Watson and J. Jenkins (eds.),*The Writings of Julian of Norwich* (Turnhout: Brepols and University Park, Pa.: Pennsylvania State University Press, 2006); Julian of Norwich, *Revelations of Divine Love* (London: Folio Press, 2017); D. N. Baker (ed.), *The Showings of Julian of Norwich* (New York, N.Y.: W. W. Norton, 2004); J. Ramirez, *Julian of Norwich: A Very Brief History* (London: SPCK, 2016).

book is still widely read.[46] Whatever we think about the validity of these women's claims, and with all due consideration for the repressive nature of the society in which they lived, there can be no doubt that they led remarkable lives and were able to leave a legacy that has endured to the present time. They are also a reminder to us of the important place women have always held in mystical theology. Medieval England would not have been the same without them, and the growing prominence of individuals and their experience of God was something that affected women as much as men, and sometimes more. The paths open to women were few but, as the above examples demonstrate, they were sometimes taken, and the results are still there for us to see.

Another popular work from this period is *Piers Plowman*, now generally regarded as the work of William Langland (*c.*1330–86?). It tells the dream of a certain Will, who makes a pilgrimage through the church of his time, recording all its many faults, before he comes across Piers Plowman, a sure guide who leads him to Christ. Piers is the apostle Peter, whose successor on earth was the pope, an allegory that suggests that the papacy would be the key to reforming the abuses in the church of the time. Of course, it must be remembered that Langland was writing towards the end of his life, when the church was divided by the great schism, so his vision might not have been realized, and the poem ends on an ambiguous note. Will equates Piers with Christ and sees him riding to his crucifixion, whereupon he wakes up from his dream and urges his family to go to mass. During mass he falls asleep again. He hears Conscience recounting the passion of Christ and how Piers/ Peter was given his calling by divine grace. He also finds out about the Holy Spirit and sees how Pride is attacking the church. He then wakes up again and realizes his need for salvation, whereupon he falls asleep once more. But this time he has visions of Antichrist, is attacked by plague and old age, and witnesses Conscience as it goes on pilgrimage in search of Piers, calling on grace for assistance. At that point he wakes up again and the poem comes to an end.[47]

Piers Plowman reveals the tension many must have felt between their own search for God and the evident corruption of the institutional church that was

---

[46] T. D. Trigg, *The Book of Margery Kempe* (Leominster: Gracewing, 2018); S. J. McEntire, *Margery Kempe: A Book of Essays* (London: Routledge, 2019); L. Bavin and R. Rees, *Margery Kempe of Lynn* (Peterborough: Upfront Publishing, 2019).

[47] D. Pearsall, *Piers Plowman* (Liverpool: Liverpool University Press, 2014); A. Cole and A. Galloway, *The Cambridge Companion to Piers Plowman* (Cambridge: Cambridge University Press, 2014); W. Scase, *Piers Plowman and the New Anticlericalism* (Cambridge: Cambridge University Press, 1989); M. Gradon, *The Making of Piers Plowman* (London: Longman, 1990); C. A. Gruenter, *Piers Plowman and the Poetics of Enigma* (Notre Dame, Ind.: University of Notre Dame Press, 2017); A. Thomas, *Piers Plowman and the Reinvention of Church Law in the Late Middle Ages* (Toronto: University of Toronto Press, 2019).

the gateway to finding him. Piers does not reject the Roman church or the papacy, but sees that it is under attack from forces hard to resist, leaving the ordinary Christian in something of a quandary. The truth can be known in and through the church, and especially in the Eucharist, but can it be retained, or is it liable to slip through our hands and leave our consciences wandering in search of it? The poem does not answer this question, but leaves the reader wondering whether the desired goal will ever – or can ever – be attained.

Piers Plowman is remarkable for the way in which it shows the corrupting power of belief in salvation by works. Langland was attracted to the sacrificial lifestyle of the friars, but he understood that it did not – and could not – work in practice. Men who renounced the world and lived by begging would inevitably turn to selling the grace of God in order to survive, and that is what the friars of his day were doing. Good intentions were leading them, and with them the entire church, to hell. The corruption of the church inevitably led to the enfeebling of Conscience, which was formed by the church's teaching, and if Conscience fails to guide believers, they are lost. Somehow Conscience had to break out of this trap and defy the church; but although Langland understood that, he knew that such a move would shatter the world in which he lived, and he recoiled from what he saw as that ultimate horror. It would be more than a century before Martin Luther and his followers would take that step into the unknown, but in *Piers Plowman* we see the prophetic harbinger of what was to come.[48]

Piers Plowman has some affinity with Geoffrey Chaucer's famous *Canterbury Tales*, where the theme of pilgrimage is central to his description of medieval English society in all its complexity. The church and religion inevitably play a major role in the *Tales*, and we meet them in several guises. The Wife of Bath shows us how a typical 'middle class' woman might view piety as a kind of pick and mix, take it or leave it, mixture of various kinds of devotion, to which she is committed only in so far as she can derive some benefit from it. She has travelled the world on pilgrimage and learned a great deal, but she has also had five husbands, an obvious reference to the Samaritan woman in the Fourth Gospel and a clear indication of her moral standards.[49] The Pardoner appears in a very negative light, selling forgiveness for worldly gain, but the poor Parson comes across as a hero of impeccable sanctity, a man who is fulfilling his calling as a servant of God. Of the other religious characters, the women come off much better than the men. The Prioress is respectable and charitable

---

[48] See J. Simpson, 'Religious Forms and Institutions in *Piers Plowman*', in Cole and Galloway, *Cambridge Companion to Piers Plowman*, 97–124.

[49] See John 4:7–30.

in both words and behaviour, while the second nun who appears recounts the life of a saint as her tale, and is supported in this by her priest, who seems to be a reasonably acceptable man. But the Monk, the Friar and the Summoner, whose task it was to summon delinquents to the ecclesiastical courts, all come across as worldly and corrupt, although to varying degrees.

How true to life are these portraits? Undoubtedly Chaucer was stereotyping to a large extent – none of the characters he portrays is 'real' in the way we would now understand that concept. But the stereotypes struck a chord with Chaucer's readers, who must have recognized them in people they knew, and so the overall picture is more accurate than the stylized presentation might initially suggest. Chaucer might have been friendly with some of the Lollards, but as his portrait of the Parson indicates, he was not a rebel against the Establishment. The Parson, who was undoubtedly a beneficed rector of a parish, represented the system as it ought to be, whereas the others were interlopers of various kinds, and not to be trusted. Go for the real thing, Chaucer seems to be saying, and accept no substitutes, however attractive they may appear to be.[50] What is interesting to us is that he shows relatively little interest in the public worship of the church but concentrates on the personal piety of the characters whom he draws, and the picture is far from encouraging.

Pilgrimage was a major feature of late medieval religious practice, and by its nature depended to a large degree on individual spirituality. Of course, for some (as Chaucer shows us) the adventure of travel was in itself an incentive, and where was there to go if not to a religious shrine? Yet for many the search for God was sincere, and pilgrimages testified to their faith that holiness could be found on earth – if not in the pilgrim's home, then somewhere where miracles had been performed and where the bones of great men and women of God had been laid to rest.

The fifteenth century was a time when the cults of various saints mushroomed and when many people adopted patrons from among those whom they believed would intercede for them in heaven. Many of these 'saints' had not been officially canonized by Rome: they were adopted spontaneously by people who believed in their supernatural powers. One of the more remarkable of these cults was the one dedicated to King Henry VI, not a successful monarch by most people's standards, but a pious man whose memory was highly prized, especially during the troubled years that followed

---

[50] G. Chaucer, *The Canterbury Tales* (London: Flame Tree Publishing, 2019); H. Phillips, *Chaucer and Religion* (Woodbridge: Boydell & Brewer, 2010); R. Epskin and W. Robins, *Sacred and Profane in Chaucer and Late Medieval Literature* (Toronto: University of Toronto Press, 2010).

his demise. However, once stability was restored, interest in Henry VI began to wane, and it seems that his cult had virtually disappeared by the time Henry VIII ascended the throne in 1509.[51] Cults like these were widespread for a time but they were never more than private affairs, driven by popular impulses and not sanctioned by any church authority. However, there were other cases where pressures arising from private devotions managed to penetrate into the official teaching of the church, and in the fifteenth century many of these were associated with death and the afterlife.

Life expectancy had never been great in medieval times, but after the Black Death popular awareness of mortality increased dramatically. One result of this was the growing popularity of the doctrine of Purgatory, which first acquired official status at the Second Council of Lyons in 1272–4.[52] As Chaucer's Pardoner reminds us, the practical implications of this were enormous, because the church claimed the authority to remit punishment in Purgatory for those who had performed adequate penance in this life. Initially this was fairly unimportant, and an indulgence, as time off from Purgatory, was given for a maximum of forty days, which was nothing when compared to the thousands (or even millions) of years some people might have to spend there. But after the Black Death there was a massive change. Popular demand for assurance of eventual salvation, coupled with the realization that virtually nobody is good enough to get to heaven when he or she dies, led to what can only be called a vast inflation of indulgences. Oddly enough, from the modern point of view this inflation was accompanied by a corresponding lowering of standards. Whereas initially a penitent might have to work quite hard for a forty-day pardon, by the fifteenth century remissions of thousands of years were being granted for comparatively little – a few prayers said by rote in front of a sacred image was enough to earn 30,000 years of merit.[53] The absurdity of this is clear enough, and it is hard for us to imagine how so many people could have been taken in for so long, but such was the fear that so many had of dying with unforgiven sin. When we understand that, it is no longer so surprising to hear that the Reformation began as an attack on this false

---

[51] Swanson, *Church and Society*, 288–291.

[52] J. Le Goff, *The Birth of Purgatory* (Chicago, Ill.: University of Chicago Press, 1984), 284–286. This was ironic in the circumstances, because the Council was meant to reunite the western and eastern churches. The eastern churches had never heard of Purgatory, but were expected to subscribe to it, even though no church council, even in the west, had proclaimed it before that time. The easterners formally accepted the doctrine at the time but repudiated it immediately afterwards, as they did again when the same demand was made of them at the Council of Florence in 1439. To this day Purgatory remains one of the main barriers to theological understanding between East and West, as it now also does between Roman Catholics and Protestants.

[53] Swanson, *Church and Society*, 293.

teaching, nor that this movement acquired such popularity in a very short space of time.

Much about the fifteenth century is beyond our understanding, but one thing stands out above all else. This is that the institutional church was straining to respond to the increasing demand for assurance that life is worth living, that death is not the end and that imperfect people can still hope for eternal life in heaven. The church responded as best it could but its only answer was to work hard at acts of piety and go on doing more of the same. Gradually it was becoming apparent to a few that something was missing, but nobody quite understood what that was. The old wineskins of ecclesiastical tradition were straining to hold the new wine, but when the breaking point might come nobody at the time could foresee.

7
Tudor church reform (1485–1571)

The crisis of the monarchy

Whatever we think of the religious changes that occurred in the sixteenth century, there can be no doubt that they were definitive for the subsequent history of the British Isles.[1] Similar convulsions were occurring all over western Europe at the same time, but in England and Ireland they were associated with the rise of the Tudor dynasty, which has given its name to the period as a whole. How far the Tudors themselves were responsible for what happened is a matter of controversy, but everyone agrees they played a part in events that would have taken a different course had they not been involved in them.[2] To understand this we must take a look back at the way the English monarchy evolved during the century preceding the accession of Henry VII in 1485, since that history was to have a deep, and not altogether positive, influence on church–state relations under his son and grandchildren.

The deposition of Richard II by his cousin Henry IV in 1399 destabilized the institution of monarchy in England.[3] Henry IV was never entirely secure on his throne, and therefore leaned on the church for support more than another monarch might have done.[4] His son, Henry V (1413–22), was an accomplished warrior king who gained the loyalty of his subjects, but died young, leaving a nine-month-old son as his heir. Henry VI (1422–61; 1470–71) was born in France and was proclaimed king there before he ever set foot in

---

[1] The literature on this subject is vast. The classic modern study is A. G. Dickens, *The English Reformation*, 2nd edn (London: B. T. Batsford, 1989). The best recent study of the English Reformation is P. Marshall, *Heretics and Believers* (New Haven, Conn.: Yale University Press, 2017). For a British Isles perspective, see F. Heal, *Reformation in Britain and Ireland* (Oxford: Oxford University Press, 2003). Also valuable is A. Ryrie, *The Age of Reformation: The Tudor and Stewart Realms 1495–1603*, 2nd edn (London: Routledge, 2017).

[2] G. W. Bernard, *The King's Reformation* (New Haven, Conn.: Yale University Press, 2005), argues that King Henry VIII was entirely in control of the process from the beginning and got exactly what he wanted from it, though most other scholars think that this is an extreme position to hold.

[3] On this history, see Ryrie, *Age of Reformation*, 28–51.

[4] See I. Mortimer, *The Fears of Henry IV: The Life of England's Self-Made King* (London: Jonathan Cape, 2007); P. McNiven, *Heresy and Politics in the Reign of Henry IV: The Burning of John Badby* (Woodbridge: Boydell Press, 1987).

England. But during his reign the vast empire his father had acquired was lost, except for the port city of Calais. Henry VI was a pious monarch and very favourable to the institutional church, but was not a warrior, and the loss of France discredited his rule. In 1461 he was deposed by one of his cousins, the son of the Duke of York, who made himself King as Edward IV (1461–70; 1471–83).

Edward IV, although a competent ruler, was young and brash, making more enemies than friends among the nobility. After nearly a decade, some revolted and reinstated Henry VI, who had managed to escape capture after his deposition. For a few strange months Henry VI occupied the throne once again, a disastrous episode that merely reminded everyone why he had been deposed in the first place. Edward IV was able to rally his troops, and in 1471 defeated and killed Henry VI's only son. This time he left nothing to chance. He captured Henry VI and put him to death, making any further restoration impossible. For the next decade and more he ruled reasonably well, but died young, leaving a 12-year-old son and his younger brother as his heirs. In theory Edward V became king and Edward IV's brother Richard, who had shown his ability as Governor in Ireland, was to be the regent until he came of age. But when it came time for Edward V to be crowned, Richard presented himself instead, and became king as Richard III (1483–5). Edward V and his younger brother (another Richard) disappeared into the Tower of London and were never seen again.

What happened to the 'princes in the Tower' is one of the great mysteries of English history, and to this day debate rages over Richard III – was he the wicked uncle who killed the legitimate heir, or did the boys die a natural death, for which Richard should not be held responsible? Whatever the truth may be, people at the time suspected foul play and looked to another member of the royal family who might step in and depose a man whom they regarded as a usurper. The most viable candidate was the young Henry Tudor, son of a Welsh nobleman and his wife, Lady Margaret Beaufort, through whom Henry had a claim to the throne by descent from Edward III. Henry escaped to Brittany, raised an army and invaded England. On 22 August 1485 he met Richard III at Bosworth Field, near Leicester, and killed him in battle.[5] He then marched on London, where he was proclaimed king as Henry VII (1485–1509).

The legitimacy of Henry VII's accession may be questioned, but the fact of the matter is that he brought stability back to the country and has a fair claim

---

[5] His long-lost body was discovered and reburied in Leicester Cathedral on 26 March 2015. See J. Arens, A. Buckle, G. Campbell and T. Stratford, *The Richard III Reinterment Liturgies*, Alcuin Club and The Group for Renewal of Worship Joint Liturgical Studies 81 (Norwich: Hymns Ancient & Modern, 2016).

to be regarded as the best king England has ever had.[6] He restored the public finances, saw off rebellions that sought to place young men claiming to be Edward V or his brother on the throne, and cemented his title by marrying their surviving sister, Elizabeth. Henry VII's children were therefore direct descendants of Edward IV, and rival claimants to the Crown were effectively eliminated.

Henry VII was not especially 'religious' but he was conventionally pious and maintained good relations with the church, and not least with the papacy. One of the fruits of this was the transfer of the Channel Islands from the French diocese of Coutances to Salisbury in 1496. Three years later they were attached to Winchester, where they were to remain for more than five centuries.[7] In return Henry allowed the pope to appoint his courtiers to the see of Worcester, something the fourteenth-century legislation against provisors had tried to outlaw. Between 1497 and 1535 there were four of them, all Italians, in a succession that was interrupted only by the Reformation.

Henry did everything he could to shore up his position and keep the peace both at home and abroad. Marriage alliances were among his greatest diplomatic weapons. He gave his older daughter, Mary, to Louis XII of France and his younger daughter, Margaret, to James IV of Scotland. The former marriage was childless and Mary returned to England, where she married into the nobility, but the latter was to prove fruitful, and it is through the descendants of James IV and Margaret that the current queen traces her ancestry.[8]

Henry VII also had two sons. He managed to betroth the older one, Arthur, to Catherine, the daughter of Ferdinand of Aragón and Isabella of Castile, who between them created the modern kingdom of Spain. Henry did not know it at the time, but by this marriage he was linking himself to what would soon become the richest and most powerful monarchy in Europe. For it was during his reign that Ferdinand and Isabella not only drove the last Muslim rulers out of Spain but also commissioned Christopher Columbus's expedition to 'India', which he thought he could reach by sailing west. Instead, as we know, Columbus discovered a new world, and Spain became fabulously wealthy as a result.

Unfortunately, Henry VII's stroke of diplomatic luck hit an unforeseen snag. Prince Arthur was a sickly youth and he was already dying when he married

---

[6] See S. B. Chrimes, *Henry VII* (New Haven, Conn.: Yale University Press, 1972).

[7] Sadly, the link was broken in 2014 because of a falling out between the Bishop of Winchester and the Dean of Jersey. The Islands were temporarily assigned to the Canterbury diocese and from 2020 they have been reattached to Salisbury.

[8] Mary's second marriage was more successful and she eventually became the grandmother of Lady Jane Grey, of whom we shall have more to say in due course.

Catherine. Whether they ever consummated their marriage is uncertain, but Catherine always claimed that they did not and she was probably right. When Arthur died, Henry VII decided that rather than send his daughter-in-law back to Spain, he would betroth her to his second son, another Henry. That was against the canon law of the church, but Henry was able to secure a papal dispensation and the betrothal went ahead. Henry and Catherine were not married immediately because Henry was still too young, and the wedding did not take place until shortly after Henry VII's death in 1509. Catherine thus became the queen consort of Henry VIII, the first of six women who would eventually hold that title.

At first everything went well and the future seemed bright. Henry and Catherine were in love, which was rare in the arranged royal marriages of the time, and it was assumed that children would soon follow. Alas, although Catherine got pregnant several times, she either miscarried or gave birth to babies who did not survive. Only one of her daughters, Mary, who was born in 1516, escaped what appeared to be a curse on the royal household, and for many years she was the king's only heiress. Had Mary been a boy this would not have been a problem, but nobody knew whether a woman could rule England in her own right. The last one who had tried that was Matilda, the daughter of Henry I, but she was soon deposed by the nobility and never really established her claim to rule.[9] Would that happen again? Nobody in England wanted to return to the instability of the years before 1485, so the need to produce a credible (male) heir was urgent. It was not only Henry VIII but the entire nation that wanted the king to have a son who could succeed him without question, but as time went on and Catherine grew older, that possibility became increasingly remote.

The crisis came in 1526, when Catherine turned 40. According to the medical lore of the time, her child-bearing days were now over, and Henry appeared to be stuck. The only solution he could see was to find a new wife who could bear him a son, but how could his existing marriage be dissolved? The church did not recognize divorce, so the only way out was to seek an annulment, which Henry VIII thought would work if he appealed his case to the pope. Unfortunately, for reasons that had little to do with him, that would prove to be impossible and he would have to take matters into his own hands. He and many others believed that unless and until he did so, his throne would be in jeopardy and the stability of the nation would be threatened.[10]

---

[9] On the other hand her son succeeded as Henry II.

[10] For a detailed account of Henry's attempt to secure an annulment and an analysis of the questions involved, see J. J. Scarisbrick, *Henry VIII* (New Haven, Conn.: Yale University Press, 1997), esp. 163–240.

Martin Luther

If England had been a completely independent country with its own national church, the problem of Henry VIII's annulment might never have arisen. But the nation was part of western Christendom and was thus obliged to fit into a wider political and ecclesiastical network. In 1519 the Holy Roman Empire had elected the king of Spain, Catherine of Aragón's nephew, as its emperor. Charles V, as we know him, suddenly became the most powerful monarch in the world, when he was still only 19 years old. He might not have realized it at the time, but his newly acquired empire was rapidly becoming a poisoned theological chalice. Less than two years before Charles's election, an obscure professor of New Testament at the newly created University of Wittenberg had challenged the sale of indulgences in Germany. The sale was a political gambit engineered by the Archbishop of Mainz, who was using it to raise money from territories not under his spiritual jurisdiction. That naturally caused resentment among the many secular rulers who were affected by it, and they were ready to pounce on any excuse to escape from this unwelcome imposition.

Martin Luther (1483–1546) was not concerned with the economic or political aspects of the question but concentrated on the theological principles on which the sale of indulgences was based. By what right was the church trying to sell the grace of God? How could the pope reduce the sentences of those who were in Purgatory when his jurisdiction did not extend to the afterlife? What was going on? As he thought the problem through, he composed ninety-five theses, or propositions, that he published for debate. His aim was to discredit the whole enterprise and to persuade the church authorities to desist from activities that could not be justified on theological grounds. His theses, published on 31 October 1517, within weeks were being circulated all over Germany and then more widely in Europe. Without realizing it, Luther had lit a fuse that would cause an explosion tearing the western church apart.[11]

The next few years were taken up with debating Luther's theses and their ramifications. Luther soon discovered that the church Establishment was against him and would do all in its power to silence him. He appealed to the emperor and went to stand before him at Worms in 1521. Charles V hardly knew what to do with him and let him go, but by then Luther was facing excommunication and possible death if he were caught. The pope appealed to the rulers of Europe for support but none was forthcoming, with one exception.

---

[11] There is an almost infinite number of books on Luther and the Reformation. See e.g. H. A. Oberman, *Luther: Man Between God and the Devil* (London: Fontana, 1993); L. Roper, *Martin Luther: Renegade and Prophet* (London: The Bodley Head, 2016).

At the urging of Cuthbert Tunstall, his ambassador to the Holy Roman Empire and soon to be Bishop of London, Henry VIII wrote a treatise against Luther's *Babylonian Captivity of the Church* that he called the *Assertion of the Seven Sacraments*, which he hoped would earn him a title from the papacy.[12] The Spanish monarchs had been recognized as 'Catholic Kings' and the French sovereign called himself the 'Most Christian King', without any objection from Rome, and Henry VIII wanted to be in their league. Faced with a crisis, the pope (who did not want to give Henry anything) finally agreed to make him 'Defender of the Faith', a title the present queen still bears. The irony of course is that the faith she is expected to defend is the one Henry VIII was attacking!

Henry VIII and Martin Luther never hit it off, and had other factors not intervened, it is most unlikely that England would have adopted the Protestant Reformation, at least not in its Lutheran form. But other factors were present, and the history of the time cannot be understood without reference to them. Henry VIII wanted (he would have said 'needed') an annulment of his marriage, and an appeal to the pope was the quickest and simplest way of obtaining one. Having done the papacy a favour by attacking Luther, Henry felt that he was owed something in return, and apparently did not think that he would have any trouble getting what he wanted. Unfortunately for him, the Holy Roman Emperor, Charles V, was his wife's nephew, and she appealed to the emperor in the name of family honour. Charles V also had to deal directly with the Lutherans, and he knew that the popes were to a large extent the authors of their own misfortunes. Determined to force the church to make serious reforms, Charles invaded Rome and made the pope his prisoner. That was the situation when Henry's request for an annulment arrived. Charles made it clear to the pope that he would not agree to Henry's wishes and the pope was in no position to object. There was also the fact that Henry had received a dispensation to marry Catherine from one of the pope's predecessors, and Henry's argument that that dispensation should never have been granted was one that the papacy could not easily accept. There was no doctrine of papal infallibility at that time, but no pope wanted to admit that a previous occupant of the see might have been mistaken, so there were religious reasons, as well as political ones, for denying the king's request.

Needless to say, Henry was not happy with this and took out his frustration on those whom he regarded as responsible for failing to deliver what in his eyes

---

[12] Scarisbrick, *Henry VIII*, 110–115. For the text, see R. Rex (ed.), *Henry VIII Fid. Def., His Defence of the Faith and Its Seven Sacraments* (Sevenoaks: Fisher Press; London: Ducketts Booksellers, 2008). There is also a critical edition by P. Fraenkel (ed.), *Assertio Septem Sacramentorum Adversus Martinum Lutherum/ Heinrich VIII* (Munich: Aschendorff, 1992).

should have been an easy result. Martin Luther played no part in any of this, but later on, when the matter became public knowledge, he sided with Catherine against Henry, because he recognized that the king's case was weak and dishonest.[13] As long as Luther and Henry were alive there would be no real meeting of minds between the Lutherans and the English government, in spite of their common interest in forging an alliance against the papacy.

Henry VIII might have thought that his personal interests, and his antipathy to Luther, would be shared by all his loyal subjects, but the times when the common people would automatically follow their sovereign were no more. Thanks to the Renaissance and the presence of Erasmus in England from 1511 to 1514, there was a significant and growing academic interest in theological matters, and particularly in the convulsions rocking the church in Germany. English intellectuals wanted to know what was going on and to examine Luther's beliefs for themselves. As early as 1520 Luther's writings were making their way into England and on 12 May 1521 there was a public burning of them outside St Paul's in London.[14] In Cambridge a group of academics was meeting in the White Horse Inn to discuss the latest developments in Germany, and the list of attendees reads like a roll call of English Reformers. Initially it seems that these intellectuals were merely curious about Luther's views, but as they studied them more closely they came to sympathize with many of his positions. They could not say so publicly, but gradually most of them came to agree that sinners are justified by faith alone, without the need to perform good works, and that the papacy had exceeded whatever claim a human authority had to govern the church. In particular they realized that the sale of indulgences, and the theology on which it was based, was a perversion of the gospel and was alien to the teaching of the New Testament.

Luther's assertion that Holy Scripture is the final court of appeal in matters of faith struck a chord and raised a question that had lain dormant in England for more than a century. Thanks to the reaction against the Lollards, England was the only country in Europe where translating the Bible into the vernacular was officially forbidden. Luther translated the Scriptures into German, but he was not the first to do so and his efforts were not illegal. Could something similar be attempted in England? One man who thought so was William Tyndale (1494–1536), who wanted to produce an English Bible but

---

[13] Martin Luther, *D. Martin Luthers Werke: Kritische Ausgabe. Briefwechsel*, 18 vols. (Weimar: Hermann Böhlaus Nachfolger, 1930–85), 7:349. The English translation is in J. Pelikan and H. T. Lehmann (eds.), *Luther's Works*, 55 vols. (St. Louis, Mo.: Concordia Publishing House; Philadelphia, Pa.: Fortress Press, 1955–86), 50:126–127.

[14] Dickens, *English Reformation*, 91.

who found himself blocked by the prohibition that went back to the provincial Synod of Oxford in 1407.[15] Aware that he was in danger merely for suggesting what he wanted to do, Tyndale left England and headed to Wittenberg, where he enrolled as a student at the university. Without any doubt, he was the first Englishman to sit at the feet of Luther and his colleagues, and their meeting was to provide a positive contrast to the difficult relations between the Germans and Henry VIII.

Tyndale became a disciple of Luther, and regarded his German Bible as a model for his own translation work. Luther had prefaced each biblical book with a theological introduction and Tyndale did the same in his version, sometimes copying Luther almost word for word. Within a couple of years he had completed the New Testament, which he was able to have printed and which was soon being smuggled into England. He then embarked on the Old Testament, managing to complete the Pentateuch, Joshua and Jonah before he was arrested and forced to suspend his translating activities. He also found time to revise his New Testament, which, despite the censorship, was already achieving a bestseller level of popularity in England.[16] Tyndale was virtually unknown at that time and even today relatively few people have heard of him, yet his contribution to modern British Christianity is arguably greater than that of any other single individual. This is because his felicity for the English language allowed him to produce translations that have stood the test of time and have provided any number of phrases that have entered the language without acknowledgment. Henry VIII might have the rather undeserved reputation of having introduced the Protestant Reformation into England, but it was Tyndale who gave it the vehicle it needed to spread and thrive – a vernacular version of Christianity's sacred texts that was to become the foundation of a distinctive national tradition.

The confused nature of the decade of the 1520s can be seen in the careers and ultimate fate of two men who would later be hailed as Protestant martyrs, even though neither of them really fits the bill.[17] The first of these was Thomas Bilney (1495?–1531), who was ordained in 1519 and six years later received a general licence to preach throughout the diocese of Ely, in which Cambridge

---

[15] On Tyndale, see D. Daniell, *William Tyndale: A Biography* (New Haven, Conn.: Yale University Press, 1994). Daniell also produced critical editions of Tyndale's translations, published by the same press. On the English Bible more generally, see D. Daniell, *The Bible in English* (New Haven, Conn.: Yale University Press, 2003); K. Killeen, H. Smith and R. Willie (eds.), *The Oxford Handbook of the Bible in Early Modern England, c. 1530–1700* (Oxford: Oxford University Press, 2015).

[16] Only three copies of this New Testament are now extant. Two of them are in the British Library and the third was located in Stuttgart as recently as 1996, raising hopes that further copies may eventually turn up somewhere else.

[17] Dickens, *English Reformation*, 101–104.

is situated. At some point Bilney had a personal experience of conversion, apparently after studying Erasmus's New Testament, and was soon preaching justification by faith alone and denouncing the church's teaching about Purgatory and the intercessory power of the saints. He was suspected of heresy, arrested and tried by Bishop Tunstall of London. During his trial, Bilney denounced Luther as 'a wicked and detestable heretic' but was still convicted. Tunstall did not order his immediate burning, but threw him in jail, hoping he would recant. That Bilney eventually did, and was released, only to reoffend by returning to his itinerant preaching ministry. He was then arrested again and condemned by the Bishop of Norwich, who ensured that he was burnt at the stake, in 1531. Bilney proclaimed a key Lutheran doctrine, but on many other points remained firmly Catholic, accepting such things as papal supremacy and transubstantiation, for example. Bilney suffered the worst punishment that the church could inflict, but he can hardly be called a Protestant, or even a heretic in the true sense of the word.

Another man of similar leanings was John Frith (1503–33), whose crime was that he questioned the necessity of believing in Purgatory and in transubstantiation, rather than in any overt denial of them. To Frith these things were *adiaphora*, matters 'indifferent', which a Christian was free to believe or not, as he chose. But to a man like Sir Thomas More (1478–1535), who read Frith's writings and was shocked by their cavalier attitude to doctrinal matters, Frith was a heretic even worse than Luther and well deserving of the death he suffered in 1533. There is no sign that Frith was a Lutheran, or that Luther would have shared his estimation of the doctrines in question. Frith thought for himself and went his own way, and that seems to have been his real 'heresy'. Independent thought was not approved of by anyone in the early sixteenth century, and to show signs of it was to court disaster, whatever official label might be attached to the beliefs in question. It was the duty of loyal Christians and the king's subjects to preach and teach only officially sanctioned doctrine, and those who failed to do so could expect no mercy from either church or state.

The English church on the brink?

The church that Henry VIII inherited was in good shape on the whole.[18] It was financially solvent, it had retreated from direct involvement in political affairs,

---

[18] See E. Duffy, *The Stripping of the Altars* (New Haven, Conn.: Yale University Press, 1992); G. W. Bernard, *The Late Medieval English Church: Vitality and Vulnerability Before the Break with Rome* (New Haven, Conn.: Yale University Press, 2012).

and as the evidence of wills and bequests suggests, it was increasingly popular with a broad segment of society. There were forces of reform at work, but for the most part they were content to operate within the system. Lollardy still existed but had declined into insignificance, and the number of candidates offering for the priesthood was on the rise after a long period of decline.[19] The Dutch humanist Erasmus of Rotterdam (1466–1536) spent three years in Cambridge (1511–14), during which time he enthused a generation of students for the new learning we call the Renaissance. He was even then preparing his edition of the New Testament, which would be based on the original Greek text and offer a new interpretation of the Latin translation. Erasmus was particularly friendly with John Colet (1467–1519), Dean of St Paul's, who was deeply concerned with the low standard of clerical education and was determined to correct it. Colet was critical of the church but worked within it and believed that with enough loyalty and dedication to the existing system, what was wrong could be put right.

The administration of the church was another area that some people thought needed to be overhauled. It could be slow, inefficient and inclined to sweep awkward subjects under the carpet, as bureaucracies everywhere tend to do, but it was not particularly corrupt. Later on, much would be made of the unfortunate case of Richard Hunne, a London merchant who fell foul of the ecclesiastical Establishment because he refused to pay the mortuary fee demanded by his parish priest for the burial of his infant daughter, but Hunne's case was an exception.[20] Whether this fee was legal or not was a matter of dispute but, rather than overlook Hunne's protest, the church authorities had him arrested and thrown into prison, where he was soon found dead. We shall never know what happened, but the suspicion that Hunne had been murdered by the church was hard to refute, and the case became something of a cause célèbre. Perhaps the fairest thing to say about it is that Hunne should never have been treated in the way he was, but that the incident was not typical. To use it, as later polemicists would do, as evidence that the church courts were irredeemably corrupt is going too far, as the bishops pointed out when they were challenged on the subject many years later.[21]

More complicated was the provincial structure of the Church of England, which stood in the way of the administrative centralization favoured by the

---

[19] There was a rise in prosecutions of Lollards for a few years after 1510 and some were burnt at the stake, but on the whole they kept their heads down and were left alone. See Marshall, *Heretics and Believers*, 98–119, for the details.

[20] See Bernard, *Late Medieval English Church*, 1–16. The most detailed treatment of the case is in Marshall, *Heretics and Believers*, 88–95.

[21] In the 'Reply of the Ordinaries, 1532'. See G. L. Bray, *Documents of the English Reformation*, 3rd edn (Cambridge: James Clarke, 2019), 53.

Tudors. The Convocation of Canterbury, containing eighteen of the twenty-one English and Welsh dioceses, was clearly dominant, but the northern Convocation of York could not be ignored, especially since two of its dioceses, York and Durham, were large and important. Ideally the two convocations should have been combined and coordinated with Parliament, which served the entire country, but that was easier said than done. Thomas Wolsey (c.1473–1530), whom Henry VIII appointed as his chief minister and who became Archbishop of York in 1514, wanted to streamline the church's administration, but William Warham, the Archbishop of Canterbury from 1503 until his death in 1532, stood in the way, as did a host of lesser ecclesiastics.[22] He compiled a digest of canon law for the northern province comparable to what William Lyndwood had done for Canterbury, and wanted the York provincial synod to adopt it, but his attempt was frustrated and the project lapsed.[23] Wolsey managed to get himself made a cardinal and papal legate *a latere*, which gave him a status superior to that of Warham, and he used this to convene a national synod of the English church in 1522. To gain support and overcome potential opposition, Wolsey placed his men in as many positions as he could, a form of patronage that could easily be regarded as corrupt but was probably the only way he could effect the reforms he thought were necessary.

Wolsey also realized that many of the monasteries were no longer viable or performing any useful function, and set about closing as many of them as he could. The revenues this generated he ploughed into creating schools and colleges, most notably his own Cardinal College (now Christ Church) at Oxford. Once again, it is easy to see this as vanity and corruption, which is a half-truth, but Wolsey was trying to resolve a problem that was becoming increasingly acute. Monasteries were sitting on vast reserves of underused wealth, measured to a large extent in land holdings, just at the time when the rising middle class of traders was looking for ways to secure the fortunes they were making in commerce.[24] Land was the best investment, but there was not enough of it available and overseas expansion was not yet possible. Pressure

---

[22] On Wolsey, see P. Gwyn, *The King's Cardinal: The Rise and Fall of Thomas Wolsey* (London: Barrie & Jenkins, 1990).

[23] The York *Provinciale*, as this document is called, survives in a single manuscript in the Bodleian Library (Oxford). See G. L. Bray (ed.), *Records of Convocation*, 20 vols. (Woodbridge: Boydell & Brewer, 2005–6), 14:493–499. An English translation has been published; see R. M. Woolley, *The York* Provinciale, *Put Forth by Thomas Wolsey, Archbishop of York, in the year 1518* (London: Faith Press, 1931). In fact it seems that Wolsey composed it in 1514 and intended that it should be published at a synod summoned for 22 January 1515 but never held.

[24] For a study of monasticism in the early sixteenth century, see A. G. Dickens, *Late Monasticism and the Reformation* (London: Hambledon Press, 1994), which contains the register of Butley Abbey from 1510 to 1535, with a commentary, 1–81.

on the church was growing but it needed a catalyst if it were to have any effect. Wolsey was doing his best to defuse the situation before it became too serious, but events were to overtake him.

It was Wolsey's misfortune that Henry VIII expected him to obtain the annulment of his marriage. Wolsey did what he could, but failure was almost inevitable and it rebounded on him. He was deprived of his offices and forced to retreat to his see of York, which he had never previously visited. He died there in 1530, shortly after the convening of a parliament that would take reform of the church to an entirely new level.

The 1529 Parliament

Frustrated by the papacy and still determined to get his way, Henry VIII decided to summon a parliament that he thought he could manipulate to his own advantage.[25] He was right about that, but did not (and could not) foresee the long-term consequences of his action. As a largely lay body (despite the presence of the bishops in the House of Lords), Parliament had never before been directly involved in church affairs, which had traditionally been regarded as outside its competence. But now the king was appealing to it to do what he thought the church should have done, and in the process was creating a precedent that would not be forgotten. The links between church and state we are familiar with owe their origin to this development. Parliamentary control over the church was to grow as its political power increased, and it is only in recent times that the church has been allowed a significant degree of self-government, determined not so much by its own wishes as by the willingness of the state to relinquish some of its powers. To this day the Church of England is as independent of the state as Parliament wishes it to be – no more and no less.

None of that could have been foreseen in 1529, when the king encouraged the House of Commons to find sticks with which to beat the church. It was in their report in 1532 that the Hunne case resurfaced, along with a number of other complaints that are common to bureaucracies the world over.[26] The bishops issued a lengthy and dignified response in the hope of getting things in perspective, but that was not the king's intention and their intervention was ignored.[27] This was soon followed by an order given to the convocations to submit to the laws of the land: in future they would be unable to pass legislation

---

[25] The standard account is S. Lehmberg, *The Reformation Parliament 1529–1536* (Cambridge: Cambridge University Press, 1970).

[26] 'The Supplication of the Commons', in Bray, *Documents*, 38–43.

[27] 'The Reply of the Ordinaries', in ibid. 44–56.

that did not receive royal assent.[28] This submission of the clergy was too much for Thomas More, who had succeeded Wolsey as Lord Chancellor, and he resigned his offices. More has been hailed as a martyr in recent times, and even been canonized as a Roman Catholic saint, but his career and reputation remain controversial.[29] He was a learned humanist and friend of Erasmus, who titled his critique of the church *Encomium Mori* (in praise of folly), a play on More's name. But although he saw the weaknesses of the church of his day, he was a traditionalist in his approach to the church and unsympathetic to serious reform. For example, although in theory he welcomed the prospect of a vernacular Bible, he was fiercely critical of William Tyndale's translation of the New Testament. More was allowed to retire from office but his dissatisfaction with the king's policies was too obvious for him to be able to rest in peace for long.

Having subordinated the English church to his will, Henry VIII next directed Parliament to abolish all forms of subsidy to the papacy, which it did, and to block appeals to Rome. Parliament duly revived the fourteenth-century statues against *praemunire* and against provisors that had been largely ignored until then.[30] If this policy was meant to sway the pope in the king's favour, it was spectacularly unsuccessful. In 1534 Henry finally ordered the convocations to break their ties to Rome and declare that he was the Church of England's 'supreme head' on earth. Canterbury did so on 31 March and York followed suit on 15 May. Parliament ratified their decision on 17 November, and England cut loose from the papacy.[31] Thomas More and John Fisher (1469–1535), the Bishop of Rochester, both refused to recognize the king's newly assumed title and were condemned to death, but the rest of the ecclesiastical hierarchy and the secular officers of state acquiesced.[32] Lower down the social scale few people seem to have taken much notice at the time, although it would not be long before serious opposition would rear its head.

Within a matter of months a new regime was put in place, headed by Thomas Wolsey's protégé and More's nemesis, Thomas Cromwell (1485–1540).[33] By the

---

[28] 'The Submission of the Clergy', in ibid. 58.

[29] J. Guy, *Thomas More: A Very Brief History* (London: SPCK, 2017). See 70–80 for a detailed account of More's canonization process, which began in 1555 but was not concluded until 1935, in circumstances far from edifying.

[30] For the relevant legislation, see Bray, *Documents*, 59–93.

[31] Ibid. 92–98.

[32] Fisher was executed on 22 June 1535 and More on 6 July. Fisher was canonized at the same time as More, in equally dubious proceedings. On Fisher's theology, see R. Rex, *The Theology of John Fisher* (Cambridge: Cambridge University Press, 1991).

[33] For the definitive modern biography of Cromwell, see D. MacCulloch, *Thomas Cromwell: A Life* (London: Allen Lane, 2018).

time the 1529 Parliament ended, Cromwell was the most powerful man in England after the king, and was in charge of making reform of the church a reality. As it turned out, Cromwell would become a convinced Protestant in a way Henry VIII never was, with the result that as long as he was in charge, reform would be pursued even beyond the limits envisaged by the king. Another important move was the appointment, ratified by the pope, of Thomas Cranmer (1489–1556) as Archbishop of Canterbury.[34] Cranmer had been an early supporter of the king's desire to annul his marriage to Catherine of Aragón and would remain loyal to Henry VIII as long as the king lived. His theological outlook would move gradually in a more Protestant direction, which would put him at odds with Henry VIII, but neither man allowed that to break their relationship, and when the king died Cranmer found himself in a position to implement the Reformation he had been planning for more than a decade.

One of Henry's first moves was to order a census of church property to replace the one made by Pope Nicholas IV in 1291. This was called the *Valor Ecclesiasticus*, and it gives us a good idea of how much benefices and other church offices were worth.[35] The *Valor* was to be the basis of clerical taxation for the next three centuries, but large parts of it were soon inoperative because Henry decided to confiscate the monastic lands and close the monasteries. He did this in two phases. The smaller monasteries were dissolved in 1536 and the larger ones after 1538, so that by the end of the decade they were all gone. The monks were pensioned off or became parish priests. Nuns were also pensioned, although the younger ones were encouraged to break their vows of chastity and marry. The dissolution of the monasteries provoked a violent reaction in Lincolnshire and Yorkshire, where a series of rebellions in 1536–7 have been remembered as the 'pilgrimage of grace'.[36] The 'pilgrims' attracted a lot of popular support and at one point came close to bringing down the government, although ultimately they failed and their rebellion petered out. As so often in the English Reformation, the defence of the status quo was traditionalist and reactionary, with little sense that an outmoded system needed rejuvenation, and so in the end it proved unable to resist the forces of change.

At the same time Henry established a commission to overhaul the canon law, which had been the major obstacle to his quest for an annulment of his

---

[34] The best biography of Cranmer is D. MacCulloch, *Thomas Cranmer*, rev. edn (New Haven, Conn.: Yale University Press, 2016).

[35] Printed in six volumes by the Commissioners on the Public Records (London, 1834). There was also an Irish *Valor*, printed in Bray, *Records of Convocation*, 18:371–437.

[36] For a recent assessment, see MacCulloch, *Thomas Cromwell*, 372–421.

marriage. The commission was initially active but its mission was aborted and no more was heard of it for the rest of Henry's reign.[37] The faculties of canon law at Oxford and Cambridge were dissolved and their activities transferred to the recently established Doctors' Commons, an institution based in London that trained men in canon and civil law procedures. The members of Doctors' Commons were almost all laymen, which meant that the administration of the ecclesiastical courts was effectively secularized.[38]

Henry VIII's break with Rome created a new situation internationally. Countries that remained in communion with the papacy would inevitably come under pressure to attack England in the hope of winning it back, although neither France nor Spain – the two most likely candidates for this role – did much immediately. On the other hand it was virtually inevitable that the English and Continental Protestants would be drawn to each other, although it was far from clear what form an alliance between them might take. The German princes who were allied against the emperor Charles V wanted Henry VIII to join the League of Schmalkalden, which they had set up in order to defend their interests. The English, for their part, could use a few allies, although their need for them was less pressing. The main difficulty the two sides faced was not military or political but theological. The Schmalkaldic League was an association of the like-minded, of princes who had adopted Lutheran beliefs as enshrined in the confession of faith presented to the emperor at the Diet of Augsburg in 1530. Could Henry VIII sign on to that?[39]

The challenge this presented was fundamentally new. For the first time in the history of English Christianity, the nation and its church were being asked to take a theological decision that would put them on one side of the growing divide in the western church. Before 1534 only a tiny minority would have sided with Luther and even they had only a limited understanding of what was at stake. A few theologians in Cambridge had been reading Lutheran books, but not even they had had any personal contact with their authors or knew what Protestantism involved in terms of worship or church polity. They were just about coming around to accepting an English-language Bible, but that was not yet authorized, church services were still in Latin and clerical celibacy remained compulsory. Deeper theological matters had not yet been raised, but if there was to be an alliance with the Lutherans there would have to be an

---

[37] For the surviving evidence, see G. L. Bray, *Tudor Church Reform* (Woodbridge: Boydell & Brewer, 2000), 2–143.

[38] See G. D. Squibb, *Doctors' Commons: A History of the College of Advocates and Doctors of Law* (Oxford: Clarendon Press, 1977).

[39] For the history, see R. McEntegart, *Henry VIII, the League of Schmalkalden, and the English Reformation* (London: Royal Historical Society, 2002).

accommodation with their theology. So at the end of 1535 a delegation of Englishmen set out for Wittenberg to see what could be done. It was led by Edward Foxe, recently consecrated as Bishop of Hereford, and included Nicholas Heath (1501?–78), Christopher Mont (1496–1572), a German who had been granted English residence in 1531, and Robert Barnes (1495?–1540), all of whom were sympathetic to Protestantism in so far as they understood it.[40] Reconciling Henry VIII and Martin Luther would not be easy, but these men felt that it had to be tried because one way or another, they knew that the fate of England and its church rested on the outcome of their deliberations.

England's Lutheran moment?

In 1890 the American Lutheran scholar Henry Eyster Jacobs (1844–1932) published a seminal study of the English Reformation that highlighted what he called the 'Lutheran movement', which characterized its early phases.[41] The book has frequently been reissued and its thesis has entered the common mind of those who study the period. According to Jacobs, England went through a Lutheran phase in which it came close to adopting a form of Protestantism similar to that of northern Germany and Scandinavia, but the moment passed and within a few years it had been all but forgotten. How accurate is this assessment?

There can be no doubt that the English delegation that went to Germany in 1535 was charged with the task of discussing theology with the Lutherans, and it was understood on all sides that agreement on that was the condition for any alliance between the Germans and England. The question of Henry's annulment was the first item on the agenda, but here there was no meeting of minds. The Germans were prepared to accept bigamy as a way out of Henry's dilemma, but not the annulment of a legally contracted marriage. The two sides never agreed on this, but Catherine's death, followed a few months later by the execution of Anne Boleyn, made any discussion redundant and the matter was never raised again. More important was the degree to which the English might accept the Augsburg Confession, and here there was some limited progress.

[40] See ibid. 26–76 for a full account of their mission. On Robert Barnes, see K. D. Maas, *The Reformation and Robert Barnes* (Woodbridge: Boydell & Brewer, 2010).

[41] H. E. Jacobs, *The Lutheran Movement in England During the Reigns of Henry VIII and Edward VI and Its Literary Monuments* (Philadelphia, Pa.: Frederick, 1890). On the impact of Luther in England, see C. R. Trueman, *Luther's Legacy: Salvation and the English Reformers, 1525–1556* (Oxford: Oxford University Press, 1994); M. S. Whiting, *Luther in English: The Influence of His Theology of Law and Gospel on Early English Evangelicals* (1525–35) (Eugene, Oreg.: Pickwick Press, 2010); K. Gunther, *Reformation Unbound: Protestant Visions of Reform in England, 1525–1590* (Cambridge: Cambridge University Press, 2014). See also E. Hughes, *Theology of the English Reformers*, 3rd edn (Abington, Pa.: Horseradish, 1997).

Henry VIII had made it clear to his ambassadors that he would never sign a Lutheran confessional document, so that straightforward approach, which the Germans would have preferred, was ruled out from the beginning. What the discussions concentrated on was a point-by-point examination of what the Augsburg Confession taught, to see how much of it could be recycled for English consumption. The surviving notes of their deliberations very helpfully detail which articles they discussed and how they linked several of them together to form a more coherent whole.[42] This is especially obvious in the section devoted to penitence and justification, where no fewer than five articles of the Augsburg Confession were rolled into one. Given the centrality of this theme for the Lutherans, their flexibility on this point is quite remarkable and shows how far they were willing to go in order to meet English concerns. What appears to have happened during these discussions is that the English delegates came face to face with detailed Lutheranism for the first time and were converted to it. They must have realized that Henry VIII would not share their opinions and made no attempt to persuade him. Instead, when they returned to England they devised ten articles of their own, which they subdivided into two equal parts. The first half touched on the principal sources of the church's traditional doctrines, all of which were reaffirmed, followed by more specific treatments of baptism, penance, the Eucharist and justification by faith. The second half was devoted to ceremonies, including the use of images, the honour given to saints, including the propriety of praying to them and the rituals associated with their feast days, and finally Purgatory.[43] In general they uphold traditional practices but advise against superstitions that had sometimes been linked to them, including the erroneous belief that papal pardons were efficacious for the souls of the departed.

The Ten Articles touch on only three of the traditional seven sacraments (baptism, penance and the Eucharist), which happen to be the three Luther was then still prepared to accept as legitimate. The article on justification does not quite say that we are justified by faith in the work of Christ for our salvation, and not through any works of our own, but it points in that direction. Its precise words are that

---

[42] These notes are collectively known as the Wittenberg Articles. See Bray, *Documents*, 102–140, for the original texts and an English translation. Apart from articles 6 and 12–15, which V. L. von Seckendorf copied into his *Historia Lutheranismi* in 1692, these articles were unknown until 1904, when a complete copy was rediscovered in Leipzig. None has ever turned up in England, though there is some indication that Archbishop Cranmer had one that he used when elaborating his own doctrine of the sacraments in his Thirteen Articles of 1538. See Bray, *Documents*, 105–106, 119, 122.

[43] Bray, *Documents*, 141–152.

to the attaining of the same justification, God requireth to be in us not only inward contrition, perfect faith and charity, certain hope and confidence, with all other spiritual graces and motions, which . . . must necessarily concur in remission of our sins, that is to say, our justification; but also he requireth and commandeth us, that after we be justified we must also have good works of charity and obedience towards God . . . for although acceptation to everlasting life to be conjoined with justification, yet our good works be necessarily required to the attaining of everlasting life . . .[44]

Subsequent theological reflection would go further than this, taking out the requirement of charity for example, while retaining the emphasis on good works that follows the above: 'after we be justified we must also have good works of charity and obedience towards God, in the observing and fulfilling outwardly of his laws and commandments'.[45] The reason for this change was that 'charity' (love) is not a work contributing to our justification before God but the fruit of a justification already obtained, which must then be manifested in charity and good works if it is to be a genuine witness to the grace of God. The Ten Articles had not quite reached that point but they were heading in that direction, as subsequent developments would show.

The Ten Articles were phrased in the way they were in order to get past the eagle eye of Henry VIII and to be acceptable to the Convocation of Canterbury, to which they were presented by Bishop Foxe on 11 July 1536, shortly after his return from Germany. They then formed the basis for an extended theological commentary published the following year as *The Institution of a Christian Man*, which is popularly known as the Bishops' Book because it was signed (although not composed) by the entire house of bishops.[46] The Bishops' Book was much more explicit than the Ten Articles had been, and that fact did not escape the king's notice. He is known to have annotated at least two copies of the book, correcting points of grammar as well as making adverse comments on more important matters of theology. Archbishop Cranmer replied to the king in detail, so we have a clear idea of where the two men differed in 1537, and it is evident that the archbishop was even then moving closer to Luther than Henry VIII ever would.[47] To get an idea of this, consider what the Bishops' Book says about the first article of the Apostles' Creed: 'And I believe also and

---

[44] Ibid. 148–149.
[45] Ibid. 148.
[46] G. L. Bray (ed.), *The Institution of a Christian Man* (Cambridge: James Clarke, 2018).
[47] Ibid. 215–237.

profess, that he is my very God, my Lord and my Father, and that I am his own son, by adoption and grace, and the right inheritor of his kingdom.'[48]

Henry VIII altered the words 'the right inheritor' to 'as long as I persevere in his precepts and laws, one of the right inheritors'.[49] Cranmer responded to this alteration at great length, saying among other things:

> there is a general faith, which all that be Christian, as well good as evil, have: as to believe that God is, that he is the Maker and Creator of all things, and that Christ is the Saviour and Redeemer of the world, and for his sake all penitent sinners have remission of their sins . . . And all these things even the devils also believe, and tremble for fear of God's indignations and torments, which they endure and ever shall do. But they have not the right Christian faith, that their own sins by Christ's redemption be pardoned and forgiven, that themselves by Christ be delivered from God's wrath, and be made his beloved children and heirs of his kingdom to come.[50]

Here we see how the archbishop was moving from understanding 'faith' as an intellectual acceptance of God's existence towards a personal relationship with him expressed by the concept of adoption, which was the key to understanding the Reformation experience of God. Adoption is not earned by good works but proceeds from the will of the adopter, who chooses whomever he wants to and establishes a relationship with that person. Those who are adopted not only believe in an objective sense but they experience the forgiving presence of God in their lives. Justification by faith is not merely an intellectual assent to the power and love of God, important though that is. It is also a new life in Christ, made possible by the indwelling presence of the Holy Spirit. Cranmer was too politic to say so, but his lengthy exposition of this theme suggests that he doubted whether the king had had that experience. In effect Cranmer was using his theological responses to the king's 'corrections' of the Bishops' Book as a means of preaching the gospel to him without saying so.

Another remarkable feature of Cranmer's replies to Henry VIII's criticisms of the Bishops' Book is the strong emphasis on predestination that comes across. It had not always been so. In his early interactions with Luther's theology, Cranmer had come down in favour of Erasmus's doctrine of free will, and might be said to have been almost as opposed to Luther as the king

---

[48] Ibid. 38.
[49] Ibid. n. 4.
[50] Ibid. 216–217.

was.[51] But by 1537 all that had changed, and predestination had come to occupy a central place in his thought. This was entirely logical. Anyone who believes that Christians are adopted by God, and that he has chosen them for reasons that have nothing to do with any merit of theirs, is bound to believe in predestination, whether he states it expressly or not. The doctrine was by no means new to Luther or Cranmer – it is found in the New Testament and was memorably developed by Augustine of Hippo in his arguments against Pelagius.[52] What Cranmer perhaps did not realize is the revolutionary potential of such a doctrine in a society in which heredity counted for everything. God's choice is a sovereign act of his, not a human entitlement, and when that realization sank in, the old order in both church and state would be overturned.[53]

That, however, was for the future. The immediate result of Henry's editing was the setting up of a new commission to revise the text of the Bishops' Book in a more traditionalist direction, which it duly did. Almost all of Henry's objections were accepted, either by incorporating them into the Book or by dropping the original text and replacing it with something else.[54] The result was the so-called King's Book of 1543, which became the official interpretation of the Ten Articles, at least until Henry's death four years later.[55]

The bishops played an important part in determining the church's doctrine, but ultimate control of ecclesiastical affairs lay with the king's chief minister, Thomas Cromwell, who was increasingly sympathetic to the cause of reform. In 1536 Cromwell drove home the meaning of royal supremacy by seizing the chair at the meeting of the Canterbury Convocation, a rather crass move and one that was not repeated, although it made the point that real power now lay with the Crown. In the same year Cromwell issued a set of 'injunctions', as they were called, ordering the clergy to fall into line with the king's break with Rome and the Ten Articles.[56] For good measure he added that the clergy should 'in no wise, at any unlawful time, nor for any other cause than for their honest necessity, haunt or resort to any taverns or alehouses'. Instead 'they shall read

---

[51] MacCulloch, *Thomas Cranmer*, 34–35.

[52] See Gal. 1:15; Eph. 1:3–10.

[53] On the wider social impact of this idea, see A. Walsham, *Providence in Early Modern England* (Oxford: Oxford University Press, 1999).

[54] The passages quoted above were deleted altogether, perhaps because they hit too close to home for comfort.

[55] See Bray, *Institution of a Christian Man*, where the two texts are collated and compared. The King's Book was never withdrawn but it faded out of use. However, it was revived by T. A. Lacey in the early twentieth century, who claimed that it was still official Anglican doctrine. See *The King's Book or a Necessary Doctrine and Erudition for any Christian Man, 1543* (London: SPCK, 1932).

[56] 'The First Henrician Injunctions, 1536', in Bray, *Documents*, 153–156.

somewhat of Holy Scripture, or shall occupy themselves with some other honest exercise'.[57] The Reformation was starting to bite!

One problem that had to be resolved was the status of the English Bible, which was still unlawful. In 1535 Miles Coverdale had completed the translation begun by William Tyndale and, after the break with Rome, banning it was not practically possible. Instead of that, Cromwell and the king decided not only to legalize the translations that had been made but to authorize the printing of enough copies in folio format for one to be set up in every church. It is a sign of how unprepared the country was that there was no printer capable of doing that, and the work had to be sent to Paris, where the typeface was initially impounded on the ground that England had fallen into heresy. That difficulty was overcome by diplomacy, and in 1538 a second set of injunctions ordered every parish to obtain a copy and install it in a place where the congregation could have ready access to it. These injunctions also ordered parishes to keep a systematic record of baptisms, marriages and burials, which remained a church monopoly for the next three centuries. Generations of genealogists have reason to be grateful to Cromwell for this, since these records make it possible for many ordinary people to trace their ancestry back to the early days of the Reformation.[58]

The second Henrician injunctions turned out to be the high-water mark of the Protestant wave sweeping over England. Particular attention was paid to the need for good preachers who would be loyal to the recent changes, and who would suppress devotional exercises like pilgrimages and the veneration of relics. As the injunctions put it:

> If you have heretofore declared to your parishioners anything to the extolling or setting forth of pilgrimages, feigned relics or images, or any such superstition, you shall now openly, afore the same, recant and reprove the same, showing them, as the truth is, that you did the same upon no ground of Scripture . . .[59]

It would soon become apparent that the state was undermining the authority of the church and its official representatives, the parish clergy, who were being ordered to admit their past errors and to correct them in the light of Scripture. If the Bible was being made public and the traditional teaching authority of the clergy was being undermined at the same time, it could hardly be long

---

[57] 'First Henrician Injunctions', 7. See ibid. 155.
[58] 'The Second Henrician Injunctions, 1538', in ibid. 157–160.
[59] 'Second Henrician Injunctions', 10. See ibid. 159.

before a new type of Christianity would emerge, one that laid much greater emphasis on a direct personal encounter with divine revelation and encouraged those who had had such an encounter to question and even deny the ability of the official church pastors to interpret God's will for them.

These were also the years when the dissolution of the monasteries was in full swing. The smaller houses had been wound up from 1536 onwards but the larger ones had initially been spared. No longer. Now they would all have to go. Many were simply abandoned but some became parish churches. Their revenues and properties were seized by the Crown and then sold off to those who could afford to buy them, thereby creating a large gentry class that had a vested interest in making sure that the Reformation would not be reversed. Meanwhile Archbishop Cranmer was privately working on a new statement of faith, using the Augsburg Confession as his model and sticking as closely to it as he could.[60] As far as anyone could tell, the Reformation was now unstoppable, and before long England would accept the Lutheranism of the northern German states, whether or not it officially adopted the Augsburg Confession.

It was all too good to be true. Not all the bishops were as keen on reformation as Cromwell and Cranmer were, and Henry VIII took care to ensure that traditionalist voices were heard alongside more radical ones.[61] Some of these were now seriously alarmed and began to intrigue behind Cromwell's back, hoping that they could play on the king's conservative instincts in order to halt, and even reverse, the progress of change.

The crunch came in 1539. Worried that the pace of reform was speeding out of control, Henry VIII got Parliament to enact a law that would put a stop to further attempts to alter the traditional faith of the church.[62] Of course, there could be no going back on what had already been done, and the king had no intention of submitting to the papacy. But on matters of doctrine and worship, particularly those touching the sacraments, he thought it was time to reassert the Catholic position before it was swept away. Six items in particular were singled out:

1 Transubstantiation was to be affirmed.
2 Communion in one kind only was to be encouraged.

---

[60] Sixteen articles of what would have become a new confession of faith survive among Cranmer's papers. See ibid. 161–194.

[61] See A. A. Chibi, *Henry VIII's Bishops: Diplomats, Administrators, Scholars and Shepherds* (Cambridge: James Clarke, 2003).

[62] 'The Act of the Six Articles, 1539', in Bray, *Documents*, 195–204.

3 Priestly celibacy was to be maintained.
4 Vows of chastity and widowhood were to be respected.
5 Private masses were to be allowed.
6 Confession to a priest was to be retained.

These six 'articles' as they were called were clearly designed to resist the spread of Lutheranism, which traditionalist bishops and others believed (correctly) was making great strides among their reform-minded colleagues. The Act of the Six Articles (1539) was too much for Hugh Latimer (1487–1555), a gifted preacher and by now a convinced Protestant, who had been made Bishop of Worcester in 1535. Objecting to it, he was forced to resign his see and was imprisoned in the Tower of London, although he escaped with his life. Later on he was set free and allowed to continue preaching, but he never again served on the bench of bishops. Thomas Cranmer kept his opinions to himself and survived, preferring to concentrate on what was allowed and to wait for better times. In 1540 he wrote a stirring preface to the Great Bible that was then being placed in churches, and it is evident that he regarded the dissemination of the Scriptures as the key to a deep and lasting reformation. As he put it:

> every man that cometh to the reading of this holy book ought to bring with him first and foremost this fear of Almighty God, and then next a firm and stable purpose to reform his own self according thereunto; and so to continue, proceed and prosper from time to time, showing himself to be a sober and fruitful hearer and learner. Which if he do, he shall prove at the length well able to teach, though not with his mouth, yet with his living and good example, which is sure the most lively and most effectuous form and manner of teaching.[63]

If that advice were followed, thought Cranmer, a body of believers would be created that could withstand whatever opposition they might have to face. Cranmer was in for the long haul, and in the end his strategy would prove to be more effective than the brave, if short-lived, protests of his more forthright colleagues.

Even as Cranmer was writing, the skies were darkening for the cause of reform.[64] Thomas Cromwell was executed and even Robert Barnes was burnt

---

[63] 'Cranmer's Preface to the Great Bible', in ibid. 205–214. This extract is from para. 15 on 214.
[64] On the difficulties faced by the reformers in the last years of Henry VIII, see A. Ryrie, *The Gospel and Henry VIII: Evangelicals in the Early English Reformation* (Cambridge: Cambridge University Press, 2003).

at the stake, a reminder that Henry VIII was just as willing and able to get rid of proto-Protestants as he was to despatch traditionalist Catholics who refused to go along with his policies.[65] The king's last years were difficult for almost everybody, but especially for those who wanted to pursue a reforming agenda. Alec Ryrie has catalogued no fewer than thirty-three people who were burnt for heresy during that time, along with three more who were executed for treason, three who died in custody and thirty-seven who were forced into exile. By 1546 most reformist writing was being printed abroad, and traditionalist tracts were on the increase, making the future direction of the church seem very uncertain.[66]

But although reform was slowed it did not stop altogether. Between 1539 and 1541 the monastic cathedrals were secularized and five new dioceses created. Lincoln was partially dismembered when the archdeaconries of Northampton and Oxford were elevated to bishoprics, with Peterborough Abbey and King Henry VIII College (formerly Cardinal College and now Christ Church) as their respective cathedrals. Gloucester and Bristol appeared at the same time, carved out of Worcester, Bath and Wells and Salisbury. In the north a new diocese of Chester was formed out of the archdeaconries of Chester (Coventry and Lichfield diocese) and Richmond (York diocese) and, just as importantly, was attached to the northern province, which in 1542 acquired the diocese of Sodor and Man as well. Westminster Abbey was also elevated to cathedral status as the seat of a new bishopric of Westminster, but proved to be ephemeral. Ten years later the diocese was suppressed, although the Abbey retained, and in some respects still retains, a semi-cathedral status.

The convocations of Canterbury and York continued to meet, and in 1542 the former commissioned a series of sermons, or homilies, intended to be used by parish clergy to teach their flocks the basics of the faith. The project involved traditionalist as well as reforming clergy, and the sermons were composed quite quickly, being presented to the Convocation on 16 February 1543.[67] They were not printed at the time, but Archbishop Cranmer kept them on file for use at a later date, and they duly appeared six months after Henry VIII's death.[68]

---

[65] Robert Barnes was one of three proto-Protestants to be burnt at the stake, the other two being the less-well-known Thomas Garrett and William Jerome. See S. Brigden, *London and the Reformation*, rev. edn (Oxford: Clarendon Press, 1991), 316–324. In a gesture of even-handedness, Henry VIII also executed three Catholics for 'treason'; i.e. continuing loyalty to the pope. Henry was nothing if not an equal-opportunities executioner.

[66] Ryrie, *Gospel and Henry VIII*, 261–271.

[67] Bray, *Records of Convocation*, 7:270–271.

[68] They are now known as the First Book of Homilies. See G. L. Bray, *The Books of Homilies: A Critical Edition* (Cambridge: James Clarke, 2015), 7–119.

In 1544 an English-language litany was published, the first sign of public worship in the vernacular that again would have to wait until after the king passed away.

Unremarked at the time, but of great long-term significance, from 1545 the convocations were coordinated with sittings of Parliament, an arrangement that would last until 1966. Thus, in various ways, the foundations for the later Reformed Church of England were being laid during Henry VIII's declining years, and there are signs that the king himself knew that change was on the way. On 24 December 1545 he gave a remarkable address to Parliament in which he explained his life's work as a constant desire to work for the glory of God and the betterment of the state (or 'commonwealth' as he called it), even quoting St Paul's great paean of praise to the virtue of love in 1 Corinthians 13 as the basis for his (and their) policies. By then he had married Catherine Parr, his sixth and last wife, who was sympathetic to the Reformation and ensured that Henry's younger children, Elizabeth and Edward, were brought up by those of like mind to hers.

Martin Luther died on 18 February 1546 and Henry VIII followed him to the grave eleven months later, on 28 January 1547. There had never been a meeting of minds between the two men, and their departure left matters hanging both in Germany and in England. In Germany the emperor Charles V and a number of Catholic princes saw their opportunity to suppress Protestantism once and for all, and in this they were aided by the papacy, which had finally managed to call a council of the church into being. Meeting in the northern Italian city of Trent (Trento) from 13 December 1545 onwards, the council lost no time in preparing decrees designed to counter Protestant claims and reinforce the opposition of Rome to what it saw as Lutheran innovations. At its fourth session on 8 April 1546 it approved a decree stating for the first time what the canonical books of Scripture were (including the so-called Apocrypha of the Old Testament) and another one stating that only the Latin Vulgate translation was to be used for determining the church's doctrine. These were followed in the fifth session (17 June 1546) by two further decrees, one on original sin and the other on reading and preaching in the church. Next came a lengthy decree on justification, approved at the sixth session on 13 January 1547, which was accompanied by a further decree enjoining clerical and episcopal residence in their appointed charges. Finally, on 3 March 1547, the council issued a decree on the sacraments, focusing on baptism and confirmation, which was accompanied by a general call for the reformation of the church's discipline. Taken together, these decrees would form the basis of the Roman church's pushback against Protestantism, and also determine how the Protestants, including the theologians of the Church of England, would respond to them.[69]

Can it then be said that the Church of England became a Lutheran body under Henry VIII, in spite of his well-known antipathy to Luther himself? There is no doubt that Lutheran ideas powerfully influenced the early English Reformers, and had Thomas Cranmer had his way in 1538, the church probably would have become Lutheran in practice, if not explicitly so. But it must be remembered that at every step of the way there was opposition to the Reformers' plans, which had not progressed very far on matters of substance by the time Luther and Henry VIII both died. In the new climate of Catholic resurgence, Lutheranism would suffer heavy reverses, although it would survive and regroup its forces in the second generation. By then however, the attention of the English had been drawn more towards Switzerland, and in particular to the Reformation in Zurich.

Contact between Heinrich Bullinger (1504–75), the leading Zurich Reformer after the untimely death of Huldrych Zwingli in 1531, and the English dated from the mid-1530s, when Bullinger put out feelers to the newly independent Church of England. An exchange of students followed that continued off and on for a decade. Bullinger did not attract the ire of Henry VIII in the way Luther had done, and so these contacts seem to have escaped his notice. In fact the Swiss were more radical than Luther in their sacramental theology, and had already fallen out with him before there was any contact with England. At first Cranmer sided with the Lutherans against the Swiss, but as time went on he became more sympathetic to the latter, just as the returning students were beginning to create a kind of Swiss lobby in England.

At the heart of the debate between the two types of Protestantism was the nature of the consecrated elements in the Eucharist. Both sides denied transubstantiation, but the Lutherans continued to insist that there was an objective (real) presence of Christ 'in, with and under' the elements of bread and wine, whereas the Swiss denied that. For them, sacramental communion with Christ was entirely spiritual. The difference between the two sides was most apparent when the question of 'unworthy reception' was raised. Both agreed that an unbeliever might receive the consecrated elements, but was such a person partaking of the body and blood of Christ? The Lutherans said that he was,

---

[69] For the decrees, see *Conciliorum Oecumenicorum Decreta* (Bologna: Istituto per le Scienze Religiose, 1973), 660–689. An English translation, keeping the same pagination, was published by N. Tanner, *Decrees of the Ecumenical Councils* (London: Sheed & Ward; Washington, D.C.: Georgetown University Press, 1990). The council itself adjourned after the tenth session on 2 June 1547, and resumed on 1 May 1551. It adjourned again after session 16 on 28 April 1552 and reconvened on 18 January 1562. It was concluded after session 25 on 4 December 1563. All its decrees are published in *Conciliorum*, 657–799.

but the Swiss denied it, saying only that while the unbeliever was certainly profaning the sacrament, he was in no sense communing with Christ, who was not objectively present in the bread and wine. The Reformers of the Church of England wanted to maintain a 'middle way' (*via media*) between Wittenberg and the Swiss, but on this point there could be no compromise. After much hesitation and debate, the English church would emerge as a member of the (Swiss) Reformed family of Protestants, not the Lutheran one, and there it has remained ever since.[70]

Thomas Cranmer's reformation

When Henry VIII died and left the throne to his 9-year-old son Edward VI (1547–53), something unprecedented in English history happened. A regency council was formed and Thomas Cranmer, as Archbishop of Canterbury, was given effective control of church affairs. He could not act entirely on his own, but had more latitude than any individual before or since to shape the half-reformed church in the way he preferred.[71] Every church has to have a set policy on its doctrine, its discipline and its form of devotion, and Cranmer tackled all three. First on the list was doctrine, which was contained in the sermons (homilies) he already had to hand. Like the Ten Articles, the twelve homilies he published were divided into two parts. The first half dealt with theological questions and the second with pastoral matters. Among the first six were sermons on Holy Scripture (largely a repeat of what he had already written in the preface to the Great Bible of 1540), the fall of man, salvation in Christ, faith, good works and Christian love. We know that the second and sixth of these were written by conservative opponents of Cranmer's policies, and most people think that he himself wrote the others, although they are all officially anonymous. The second group consists of warnings against swearing and perjury, the danger of falling away from God, an exhortation against the fear of death and another enjoining obedience to the civil authorities, a sermon against fornication and another against brawling, which was evidently a major problem in sixteenth-century England.

---

[70] It should be said that this debate is much less significant today than it was in the sixteenth century. The modern Church of England has established intercommunion with several Lutheran churches, though not with Reformed ones, not because of a shared eucharistic doctrine but because the Lutherans have bishops whereas most of the Reformed do not. It has been a triumph of form over substance, which is characteristic of the modern ecumenical movement.

[71] For the details, see D. MacCulloch, *Tudor Church Militant: Edward VI and the Protestant Reformation* (London: Penguin Books, 1999).

Next, Cranmer set about composing an English-language liturgy that would replace the Sarum Rite. It was printed in March 1549 and came into force at Whitsun (9 June). Much of it was taken over from Sarum, but there was significant input from some of the more conservative Lutheran liturgies, in particular the one used in Brandenburg and Nürnberg.[72] It was more than just a compilation of other sources though, and Cranmer felt free to adapt his borrowings in ways that would eliminate any suggestion that the church was offering a sacrifice to God in the hope of meriting his approval. Above all, he was concerned to convey the message of justification by faith alone, but without offending traditionalists, who were still wedded to the medieval doctrine of transubstantiation and the ritual practices that derived from it. The result can be seen in the words of administration in the service of Holy Communion: 'The body of our Lord Jesus Christ which was given for thee preserve thy body and soul unto everlasting life.' Here we see a clear affirmation that salvation is the work of Christ, to which the believer makes no contribution, but it is not clear what the celebrant is saying about the status of the bread being given to the communicant. Is it still just bread, or has it been transformed into the body of Christ? Either interpretation is possible, and we should not be surprised to find that both were claimed – the former by the more Protestant-minded and the latter by the more traditionalist.[73] Such ambiguity could not continue, and Cranmer had no intention that it should. The 1549 book was a dry run for a further revision, which he set about producing almost immediately and which was in use from All Saints' Day (1 November) 1552. This second book was much more clearly Protestant than the first had been, as the words of administration indicate: 'Take and eat this in remembrance that Christ died for thee, and feed on him in your hearts by faith, with thanksgiving.' Here there is no doubt that the communicant was eating bread that remained what it had always been, and that his communion with Christ was a spiritual experience in the heart, not a physical one in the stomach.[74]

The 1552 Prayer Book is the direct ancestor of the 1662 Book of Common Prayer, which is still the official liturgy of the Church of England. It reflects a theology that has moved on from a concentration on the status of the elements of bread and wine to a consideration of the spiritual condition of the believer.

---

[72] See MacCulloch, *Thomas Cranmer*, 414–422, for the details.

[73] For the text, see *The Book of Common Prayer: The Texts of 1549, 1559 and 1662* (Oxford: Oxford University Press, 2013).

[74] *The Second Prayer Book of King Edward VI, 1552* (London: Church of England, 2015); repr. from a copy in the British Museum. See also G. Jeanes, *Signs of God's Promise: Thomas Cranmer's Sacramental Theology and the Book of Common Prayer* (London: T&T Clark, 2008); A. Null, *Thomas Cranmer's Doctrine of Repentance* (Oxford: Oxford University Press, 2000).

The same approach, *mutatis mutandis*, is found in the liturgy of baptism and the other worship services this Prayer Book contains. The basic principle is that, while outward signs and gestures are aids to faith, they are not a substitute for it. The sacraments of the church demonstrate what the gospel can and does do to transform the lives of those who receive them rightly, but they cannot supply a faith that is not there or transform the life of a person who is not in tune with their message. To put it another way, the sacraments are the ministry of the Word of God by other means – they bring home the truth of salvation that a believer has heard and received from the preaching of the gospel of Christ.

While Cranmer was preparing his Reformed liturgies, wider events at home and abroad were affecting the course the Church of England was taking. On the Continent, the resurgence of Catholicism was driving many Protestants into exile, and England was a promising place of refuge. Cranmer understood this and issued invitations to well-known Protestant theologians, whom he would attempt to put into prominent positions in Oxford, Cambridge or elsewhere. Several took him up on this, most notably the Italian Pietro Martire Vermigli (1499–1562), the Pole Jan Łaski (1499–1560) and the Alsatian Martin Bucer (1491–1551), the man who more than anyone else incarnated the *via media* between Wittenberg and the Swiss, and whose influence would help to shift the English even further in the direction of the latter. Another man who appeared in England at that time was the Scot John Knox (1514–72), who had been sent to France as a prisoner and had been set free at the instigation of the English government, which recognized him as one of its chief supporters in Scotland.[75] Knox was despatched to Berwick-upon-Tweed, where he could minister to refugee Scots but, after serving for a time there and in Newcastle-upon-Tyne, went south to London, where he would play a significant part in Cranmer's ongoing Reformation.

At home Cranmer faced increasing opposition from conservative bishops who had supported Henry VIII through thick and thin, but who refused to go along with Cranmer once Henry was out of the way. The first to raise his head in opposition was Stephen Gardiner (1497–1555), Bishop of Winchester from 1531, who refused to participate in the publication of the homilies in 1547. His dogged resistance soon landed him in prison, but he was not deprived of his see until 14 February 1551.[76] Long before that, Edmund Bonner (1500–69),

---

[75] See J. E. A. Dawson, *John Knox* (New Haven, Conn.: Yale University Press, 2015); R. K. Marshall, *John Knox* (Edinburgh: Birlinn, 2000).

[76] See G. Redworth, *In Defence of the Church Catholic: The Life of Stephen Gardiner* (Oxford: Basil Blackwell, 1990).

Bishop of London from 1540, who had grudgingly gone along with Cranmer until the publication of the 1549 Prayer Book, had been arrested and deprived on 1 October 1549. Another prominent opponent of Cranmer was Cuthbert Tunstall (1474–1559), Bishop of London (1522–30) and then of Durham, who somehow managed to escape the fate of his colleagues despite sympathizing with their views. In addition to them, several lesser figures shared their outlook and formed a significant counterweight to Cranmer's more radical supporters.[77]

The political situation in 1549 was difficult for the church. The government had been headed by the Duke of Somerset, the king's uncle, but his perceived incompetence led to his overthrow on 10 October.[78] He was not formally replaced, but John Dudley, then Earl of Warwick and soon to become Duke of Northumberland, took effective control of state affairs. Cranmer had worked well with Somerset, but although he accepted Dudley and was allowed to continue his reformation, the relationship was never as warm and in the end it would turn out badly. One of the features of Edward VI's reign was the increasing use of Parliament as an instrument of reform, even concerning matters that should have been entirely within the church's own competence. Thus we find that in 1549, and again in 1552, the use of the Prayer Book was authorized by an Act of Uniformity, a practice that would be repeated in later reigns and become standard. The notion that a largely secular body could and should determine the pattern of the church's worship would have sounded strange in earlier times, but it was to set a precedent that would have echoes into the twentieth century.[79] Another matter that really belonged to the canon law and not to the state was the authorization of the marriage of priests, which was also passed by Parliament in 1549.[80] About a third of the clergy took up the chance to get married, only to find themselves forced to choose between their wives and their ministry when the Act was repealed four years later.

Before long, action was underway to compose a comprehensive confession of faith for the reformed church, a project that had been contemplated since the Ten Articles of 1536. There was now no intention of producing a revised version of the Augsburg Confession, and Cranmer set about composing what was essentially a new, and considerably more systematic, document. It initially comprised forty-five articles, but four of these were subsequently combined into one on the sacraments, giving a total of forty-two when they were finally

---

[77] See E. A. Macek, *The Loyal Opposition: Tudor Traditionalist Polemics, 1535–1558* (New York, N.Y.: Peter Lang, 1996).

[78] He was the brother of Jane Seymour, Henry VIII's third wife and the mother of Edward VI.

[79] Bray, *Documents*, 235–240 (1549) and 250–252 (1552). Parliament last debated the Prayer Book in 1928, when it rejected proposals put forward for its revision.

[80] Ibid. 248–249.

promulgated on 19 June 1553, only seventeen days before King Edward VI died.[81] It is often claimed that the Articles of Religion were not a systematic confession of faith, but that is the view from hindsight that makes seventeenth-century Confessions the benchmark for evaluating what was produced earlier. In their own time the Forty-two Articles were one of the most systematic and comprehensive statements of faith that Protestants had yet produced. To understand their overall structure, they can be analysed as follows.

1–7: The 'Catholic' articles, restating doctrines common to all Christians, although with certain Protestant emphases. The first four touch on the Trinity, the incarnation of Christ, his descent into hell and his resurrection, beliefs that everyone could affirm without hesitation. Then came the doctrine of Scripture, and in particular the continuing authority of the Old Testament, followed by a reaffirmation of the three ancient Creeds – the Apostles', the Nicene and the Athanasian. The only innovation here was the insistence that no one could be compelled to believe any doctrine that is not contained in the Bible, an obvious point of contention between the Reformers and the papacy.

8–33: The 'Protestant' articles, which deal with the controversies of the sixteenth century. They can be broken down further into subsections, as follows.

8–19: The way of salvation. These articles deal with original sin, the nature of free will, grace, justification, good works, sin, predestination, the unique-ness of salvation in Christ and the continuing relevance of the moral law of the Old Testament for Christians. Of particular interest is Article 16, on the blasphemy against the Holy Spirit, which is defined as 'when a man of malice and stubbornness of mind doth rail upon the truth of God's Word manifestly perceived, and being enemy thereunto, persecuteth the same'.[82] It was a good attempt to define something that has always been regarded as a mystery, but was not very convincing and so was dropped from the later revisions.

20–33: Church (20–23), ministry (24–25) and sacraments (26–32), together with tradition (33). Here we come to the most obviously controversial subjects, and the differences between Protestants and Catholics are made perfectly clear. The infallibility of the church is denied and the doctrine of Purgatory rejected. Worship must be conducted in the spoken language. The sacraments, of which there are only two (baptism and the Lord's Supper), must be properly admin-istered and are not to become objects of superstitious reverence. Compulsory

---

[81] Ibid. 253–278, where they are collated with the subsequent revisions of 1563 (1562) and 1571.
[82] Ibid. 261.

clerical celibacy is rejected as being contrary to God's law. On the other hand excommunication is retained and is to be rigorously enforced as part of regular church discipline, not least against those who refuse the right of the local church to determine its own practices and traditions, provided they do not go against anything taught in Scripture.

34–36: The 'Anglican' articles, applicable only in England (and perhaps in Ireland). These cover the homilies, the Prayer Book and obedience to the civil authorities ('the civil magistrate').

37–38: These articles affirm the right of Christians to own their own property and the propriety of swearing lawful oaths before a magistrate, beliefs that had been contested by the monastic tradition and were rejected by the more extreme Anabaptists.[83]

39–42: The eschatological articles. These covered the final resurrection and the fate of souls after death, concluding with condemnations of millenarianism and universalism. These were all matters that had engendered sectarian controversy, sometimes going back well before the Reformation, where Cranmer thought that the church's official position ought to be clarified.

The Forty-two Articles had no immediate effect because of the king's death, but provided a benchmark against which acceptable and unacceptable beliefs could be measured. They would be revised a decade later, but their basic structure would remain the same and would continue to provide the framework for the reformed church's confession of its faith.

Less successful was Cranmer's attempt to reform the church's disciplinary structures and procedures. The Henrician Canons of 1535 were not revived, but a new attempt to codify the canon law was made, drawing on a number of traditional sources and modifying them to suit the main tenets of the Reformation, especially regarding matrimony and divorce. Cranmer worked on this project himself, with considerable help from Pietro Martire Vermigli and canon lawyers who provided assistance on specialized subjects like last wills and testaments. The final text was cobbled together early in 1553 and presented to Parliament, but Northumberland's opposition seems to have killed it. Whether it was ever submitted to the Convocation of Canterbury is not known; but what is certain is that when Edward VI died, it had not been ratified by either church or state, and therefore lacked any formal authority.[84]

---

[83] Anabaptists, so called because they rejected infant baptism and insisted that believers must be 'rebaptized' on profession of faith, were virtually unknown in England, though some had taken refuge in the country and been persecuted for their beliefs. A native form of Anabaptism did not appear until the early seventeenth century.

[84] For the text, a translation and commentary, see Bray, *Tudor Church Reform*, 150–743.

Edward VI died on 6 July 1553 and Cranmer's freedom to reform the church more or less as he chose came to an end. The immediate future looked unpromising, but from the vantage point of hindsight we can see that the years 1547–53 were seminal for the development of a reformed Church of England. Its liturgy had been revised twice, and settled into a pattern that would survive, with only minor changes. Its doctrine had been clarified and would remain substantially the same in subsequent revisions. Its discipline, sadly, had not been confirmed, a failure that would have grave consequences in the next generation and beyond. It was not a perfect situation, to be sure, but much had been achieved in the space of only six years, and for that Thomas Cranmer must be given the lion's share of the credit.

The revival of Catholicism

The death of the young Edward VI provoked a constitutional crisis. The legitimate heiress was Mary, the daughter of Henry VIII and of Catherine of Aragón, a fervent Catholic whose determination to reimpose her faith on the English nation grew as her chances of ever being able to do so appeared to diminish. Many in the government were unhappy at the prospect of a return to Rome, the Duke of Northumberland among them. In order to forestall that, and to cling on to power, he promoted Lady Jane Grey, granddaughter of Henry VIII's sister Mary and Northumberland's recently acquired daughter-in-law, as queen instead. Jane had the advantage of being a Protestant and she would no doubt have ratified the changes made under Edward VI, but she was distant in the line of succession and she was another woman. Had she been male she might have succeeded in retaining the throne, as King Stephen had done in the twelfth century when faced with the rival (but more legitimate) claims of Henry I's daughter Matilda, but for those who wanted a strong and effective monarch there was little to choose between two women. Mary's title was far stronger and before long the nobility rallied to her banner, allowing her to assume the crown on 19 July, only thirteen days after her half-brother's death.[85] Jane, her husband and father-in-law were arrested and put to death, and in the wake of their fall several prominent churchmen also found themselves in trouble. Within months no fewer than nine diocesan bishops had been deprived of their sees – Thomas Cranmer (Canterbury), George Day (Chichester), Miles Coverdale (Exeter), John Hooper (Gloucester and Worcester), John Harley (Hereford), John Taylor

---

[85] On Mary I, see J. Edwards, *Mary I: England's Catholic Queen* (New Haven, Conn.: Yale University Press, 2011).

(Lincoln), Nicholas Ridley (London), John Ponet (Winchester) and Robert Holgate (York). Cranmer, Hooper and Ridley were arrested and tried for treason, supposedly because they had supported Lady Jane Grey, but in reality for their Protestantism, and those who had been deprived under Edward VI – Stephen Gardiner of Winchester and Edmund Bonner of London – returned in triumph to their dioceses. Unsurprisingly, these men and their followers were out for revenge and, with a queen determined to put right her mother's disgrace, those who had made them suffer for their obstinate traditionalism had little hope of obtaining mercy from the new regime.

Queen Mary I demanded that Parliament should return the country to the Roman obedience and it agreed to do so, as long as she assured them that those who had acquired monastic lands at the dissolution would not be obliged to surrender them. The restoration of Catholicism would not be a simple return to the past. Even so, there were some ways in which the queen was able to turn the clock back, notably on the question of clerical marriage. Those who had taken advantage of the 1549 legislation on that subject were put out of the ministry, even though the church could ill afford such a huge loss of its personnel. For twenty years no one had trained as a Catholic priest in England and most of the clergy had conformed to the changes the Reformation had introduced. Even going back to the Latin mass was not straightforward because service books were in short supply. The English Bible could not simply be wished away, but as yet there was no acceptably Catholic translation and few people wanted to return to the Latin Vulgate. The universities in particular, with their Erasmian and Renaissance heritage, could not repudiate their newly discovered scientific approach to ancient texts, nor was there any desire to revive scholastic theology or restore the faculties of canon law that had been abolished in 1535.

The traditionalists who welcomed the return to Catholicism were aware of this and for the most part they tried to adapt to the new situation. Edmund Bonner, for example, issued his own book of homilies, recycling two of the ones that had been printed in 1547 with only minor alterations.[86] He did the same with the King's Book, which he revised and expanded in order to accommodate traditionalist thinking.[87] Much of the material was new, but the overall pattern of presentation reflected the declining years of Henry VIII more than anything else. In these and other ways the Catholic restoration was more of a continuation of Henry VIII's post-Reformation policies than anyone cared to admit.

---

[86] See Bray, *Homilies*, 123–201.
[87] See Bray, *Institution of a Christian Man*, 239–478.

Mary I even retained the title 'supreme head of the Church of England', despite the fact that she officially deferred to the pope.

One of the difficulties Catholic restoration faced was that the Roman church had also changed in the years since England had broken with the papacy. A new and militantly papist religious order had emerged – the Society of Jesus, which was dedicated to world mission and to taking a hard line against the Protestants. There had been cardinals in Rome who had sought dialogue with the Lutherans, and considerable progress had been made, even on the central issue of justification by faith alone. But these moderates were gradually pushed aside by the Jesuits, so that when the Council of Trent opened in 1545, any hope that Protestants might attend and seek reunion with a reformed Rome was soon dashed. Rome would indeed reform itself, but in a way that would set it apart from the Lutherans and declare war on all who refused to submit to papal authority.

One of the men caught up in this was Cardinal Reginald Pole (1500–58), a distant relative of the English royal family whom some had hoped might claim the Crown.[88] Pole had escaped from England just as Henry VIII was breaking his ties with Rome, and his mother had been executed as a warning to anyone who might have been plotting to put her or her son on the throne. He had gone to Rome and later had spent considerable time in Germany, where he encouraged dialogue with Luther and his colleagues in the hope of reaching a genuine theological agreement. When Mary I came to the throne, he was despatched to England as a papal legate, charged with overseeing the reimplantation of Catholicism. He brought with him the latest decrees of the Council of Trent, which had just gone into recess for the second time, along with plans for establishing seminaries for the training of priests in a much more rigorous way than had ever been the case before. Despite his English origins, Pole was a stranger to the ways of the English church and had little time for its hierarchy or its convocations. As papal legate he appealed to the example of his thirteenth-century predecessors, Otho and Othobon, and summoned a legatine synod at which he simply dictated the constitutions that he wanted the church to adopt.[89] There were twelve of these, and they give us a clear idea of what he had in mind:

1 The date of England's reconciliation with Rome (30 November 1553) was to become an annual celebration.

---

[88] See T. F. Mayer, *Reginald Pole: Prince and Prophet* (Cambridge: Cambridge University Press, 2000).
[89] See G. L. Bray (ed.), *The Anglican Canons, 1529–1947* (Woodbridge: Boydell & Brewer, 1998), 68–161, for the Latin texts and English translations.

2 The canon law was to be restored in its entirety, with additional emphasis on the supremacy of the pope and the centrality of the sacraments.

3 All church officials of whatever rank were to reside in their appointed places and perform the tasks allotted to them.

4 The bishops themselves were to preach and also appoint preachers to represent them. Clergy who could not preach were to read the appointed homilies.[90]

5 The clergy were to lead holy, respectable and celibate lives.

6 Candidates for ordination were to be thoroughly examined in the basic tenets of the Catholic faith.

7 Benefices were to be filled as soon as possible when there was a vacancy and sinecures were to be abolished.

8 No one was to attempt to assure the succession to a benefice by appointing a successor before it became vacant (the practice of *resignatio in favorem*).

9 No one was to buy a benefice or demand payment for institution to one.

10 Church property was not to be alienated or leased to outsiders.

11 A seminary for training young men was to be established in every cathedral church.

12 Bishops were to conduct a visitation of their dioceses at least once in every three years.

It will be seen from this list that Pole was much more concerned with administrative abuses than with theology or patterns of worship, which he assumed would simply be handed down from Rome. The variety of rites (or 'uses') that had characterized the medieval scene would no longer be tolerated – those who were nostalgic for the Sarum Rite would have better luck with the reformed Prayer Book than with anything Pole might provide. His was a church that would be more highly centralized, more closely controlled from the top down, and more uniform than anything England had known before 1549.

Unfortunately there was a snag. A church centralized around the pope has to have good relations with him, and it was here that Pole came unstuck. He had been sent to England by Pope Julius III (1550–55), a man whom he trusted and who trusted him. Julius III was succeeded by Marcellus II, but he died after only twenty-three days in office. His successor was Paul IV (1555–9), an Italian who was consumed with hatred for Spain and the Habsburg dynasty.

---

90 It is not clear what homilies Pole had in mind, but they were probably Bishop Bonner's.

Unfortunately Mary I was half-Spanish, and on 25 July 1554 had married her Spanish cousin, the future Philip II of Spain. England had effectively become a Habsburg client state, and Pole was part of it. Paul IV did the only thing he could – he revoked Pole's legatine commission on 9 April 1557. So horrified was Mary when she heard this that she refused to allow the revocation to be published in England. The result was that for the last eighteen months of his life, Pole was trying to establish a church that would be loyal to a pope who had repudiated him and his mission – not the best situation to have been in.

Nor was that all. The Spanish marriage had been designed to make it possible for Mary, who was already in her late thirties, to give birth to a credible heir who would maintain the Catholic succession. Philip, who was much younger than she was, came to England and attempted to do his duty in this respect, but failed and eventually went back to Spain, leaving her behind – and childless. Worse still, the Spanish alliance encouraged Mary to adopt Spanish methods for dealing with heretics. She hunted them down and burned them at the stake, usually in full public view. On 16 October 1555, Nicholas Ridley and Hugh Latimer perished this way in Oxford, with Latimer apparently telling Ridley to 'take courage and play the man' because on that day they would light a fire in England that would never be extinguished. Cranmer was forced to watch this gruesome spectacle, knowing that he would be next. For a few months he was tortured and obliged to recant his 'heresies', but nothing could save him and on 21 March 1556 he followed Ridley and Latimer to the stake. As the flames enveloped him he stuck out the hand that had signed the recantations as the ultimate sign of defiance.

Not only great men like these but also dozens of smaller fry were caught up in the dragnet – 282 souls in all.[91] Nearly 40% of these were in London, giving the residents of the capital a ringside seat as they watched what the restoration of Catholicism might mean for them. The fact that many of the victims were ordinary people who were no threat to anyone increased popular revulsion at their undeserved fate, and it may be true to say that by her actions Bloody Mary, as the queen came to be known, did more to secure Protestantism in England than any monarch more favourable to reform could ever have done.

---

[91] See D. M. Loades, *The Oxford Martyrs* (London: B. T. Batsford, 1970). The burnings were not evenly spread across the country. There was only 1 in the northern province (in Chester), and only 3 in Wales – 2 in St David's and 1 in Llandaff. The dioceses of Carlisle, Durham, York, Sodor and Man, Bangor, St Asaph, Hereford, Worcester and Bath/Wells recorded none at all. Oxford had only the 3 already mentioned. By contrast, London had 112, Canterbury 49, Chichester 41 and Norwich 31. The rest were spread more thinly – 7 in both Winchester and Coventry/Lichfield, 6 in Salisbury, 5 in both Gloucester and Rochester, 4 in Bristol, 3 in Ely, 2 in both Lincoln and Peterborough, and 1 in Exeter.

Of course, England was not a tyranny in the modern sense, and escape from persecution was possible for many. The foreign refugees who had flocked there under Edward VI went away again, and many Englishmen followed them. They set up exile churches in places like Frankfurt, where they were welcomed with open arms, and vowed to carry on the struggle. John Knox took a lead in this, and for a while became the main preacher in the Frankfurt congregation. Knox, a fiery character who had been on the more radical end of the Reformation in England, had left his mark on the 1552 Prayer Book. He had objected to the practice of kneeling to receive Holy Communion because he thought the gesture would be mistaken for worship of the consecrated elements, and to allay this fear Cranmer had agreed to insert an extra rubric making it clear that kneeling was not to be interpreted in that sense. It was a last-minute addition to the Book, which meant that it had to be added in black ink, instead of the customary red. Thus it became known as the 'black rubric', the nickname it still bears.[92]

The English church in Frankfurt was one of a number of 'stranger churches' that Protestant states permitted in their territories for the use of foreigners. In Edward VI's reign they had been established in London and various Continental cities had English churches in exchange.[93] They were permitted to worship according to their own rules, which reflected the relative indifference of Protestants to matters of church polity and discipline. At Frankfurt, Knox began by using the 1552 Prayer Book but saw nothing wrong in modifying it in an even more Protestant direction. He got away with that until the arrival of Richard Cox (1500–81), a prominent refugee from Oxford, who insisted that an English exile church did not have the right to alter what Parliament had approved. Cox was not necessarily against further reform, but he believed that it ought to wait until the Protestant church was re-established in England and could legislate changes for the whole country.

The result of this conflict was a division in which Knox and his supporters were branded as troublemakers and forced to leave Frankfurt. They went to Geneva, where they were welcomed by John Calvin and his colleagues, and there they set about establishing the kind of church they preferred. Knox was deeply impressed by the discipline he found in Geneva and regarded the city as 'the most perfect school of Christ' he had ever seen. He might not have been

---

[92] The black rubric was omitted from the 1559 Prayer Book but was restored in 1662 as a concession to Puritan sentiment, and remains in the Prayer Book to the present day.

[93] On the stranger churches in London, see A. Pettegree, *Foreign Protestant Communities in Sixteenth-Century London* (Oxford: Oxford University Press, 1986). The French and Dutch Protestant churches still exist.

fully aware of the problems that Calvin had with the city council, who were often very reluctant to implement his plans for reform and especially for discipline, but from an outsider's perspective that hardly mattered. Calvin's chief assistant and eventual successor was Théodore de Bèze (1519–1605), or Beza as he is usually known in English, who was the leading biblical scholar of his time and the true heir of Erasmus. It was Beza who introduced verses into printed Bibles and encouraged the practice of placing notes in the margins in order to explain difficult words and passages. The English exiles were greatly taken with this, and soon began preparing a new English translation based on the latest scientific principles.

It would not be until 1560 that this Geneva Bible was published, but it marked a turning point in English Bible translation. William Tyndale, Miles Coverdale and the Great Bible had all used the standard Erasmian edition of the Greek New Testament, along with the traditional Hebrew text of the Old. The Hebrew remained much the same but as new manuscripts of the Greek New Testament came to light, revisions to the Erasmian edition became inevitable. The Geneva Bible was therefore the first 'scientific' translation into English, basing itself on the best manuscripts available rather than on any received tradition. It also added notes in the margin, the most notorious of which was its anachronistic statement that the word 'antichrist' in 1 John referred to the pope on the ground that he falsely claimed to be the 'Vicar of Christ' on earth![94] The publishers of the Geneva Bible were also clever entrepreneurs. Instead of producing large and expensive folio editions, they printed ones that were small enough to fit into a saddlebag and cheap enough to be afforded by most ordinary people. As a result, the Geneva Bible became the translation of choice for most Englishmen in the later sixteenth century. It was the version that William Shakespeare (1564–1616) knew and that the Pilgrim Fathers took to America in 1620.[95] It also became the official Bible of the Church of Scotland, helping to spread the use of standard English in that country. Mary I would not have known it, but without her persecution of the Protestants, the Geneva Bible might never have come into existence.[96]

---

[94] The word occurs in 1 John 2:18, 2:22, 4:3 and in 2 John 1:7. The identification of the pope with the Antichrist was a common theme of radical antipapal polemic even before the Reformation, and was picked up by Martin Luther in his *Babylonian Captivity of the Church* (1520), so it was not as surprising to the translators of the Geneva Bible as it seems to most people today.

[95] Shakespeare's relationship to the religious culture of his time was subtle and has been surprisingly little studied. See however H. Hamlin (ed.), *The Cambridge Companion to Shakespeare and Religion* (Cambridge: Cambridge University Press, 2019).

[96] See Daniell, *Bible in English*, 275–357, 369–426.

By 1558 the Marian regime was in crisis. War between Spain and France had dragged England into a conflict that it did not want, and the only result was that the country lost Calais, its last remaining bridgehead on the European continent. Mary's days were numbered but her persecuting zeal continued unabated, turning public opinion against her and against the Catholic Counter-Reformation that she and Cardinal Pole were sponsoring.[97] In what was becoming an increasingly tense and unstable situation, John Knox decided to intervene by writing a stinging tract against Mary's rule. Never temperate at the best of times, Knox went overboard in condemning female rule of any kind, which he regarded as contrary to nature and the chief cause of England's troubles. *The First Blast of the Trumpet Against the Monstrous Regiment of Women* tells us all we need to know about the contents of this diatribe, and its publication was one of the greatest mistakes Knox ever made.[98] John Calvin rejected its thesis and tried to distance himself from it, and even Knox came to regret his intemperance when Mary was succeeded on the throne by her half-sister Elizabeth. By then it was too late. In the eyes of Elizabeth and her supporters, Knox was an enemy who could not be allowed back into England, and anything coming from Geneva was suspect. The queen undoubtedly over-reacted, but in the difficult and uncertain circumstances of the time she could take no chances. The result, unfortunately, was to be a division in English Protestantism between the radicals (who came to be known as 'puritans') and the moderates who supported Elizabeth. One way or another it is a division that has continued to the present time and still colours debates about church polity among Reformed Protestants who otherwise share much the same theological inheritance.

The Elizabethan Settlement

Mary I and Cardinal Pole died on 17 November 1558, within twelve hours of each other. That cleared the way for a change of direction under the new regime, which now devolved on the last remaining child of Henry VIII, his daughter Elizabeth, whose mother had been Anne Boleyn. Given that her parents'

---

[97] See Edwards, *Mary I*, 325–326, who writes of the burning of heretics, 'The peaks were in June and July 1558, with seven fatalities in each month, and a final effort, as things turned out, took place in November, with five being burnt in Canterbury just a week before Mary's death. There has been some debate over the direct role of Pole in heresy trials, but there is no doubt that he was supervising things closely in 1558, not least in his own diocese of Canterbury.'

[98] 'The First Blast of the Trumpet Against the Monstrous Regiment of Women', in D. Laing (ed.), *The Works of John Knox*, 6 vols. (Edinburgh: Woodrow Society 1846–64; repr. Edinburgh: Banner of Truth Trust, 2014), 4:349–422.

marriage was not recognized by Rome, Elizabeth could not easily have continued her half-sister's policies, even if she had wanted to. Accepting the pope's authority would logically have entailed her abdication, which was rather too much to ask of her. There was some suggestion that the papacy might be prepared to compromise on that point, but Elizabeth had no desire to explore the possibility. From her point of view her priority was to survive long enough to establish herself as the rightful monarch and then to produce a credible heir. She succeeded in the first of these quite brilliantly, but not in the second, at least not during her lifetime. From the Protestant point of view, she had to survive because her most likely successor would have been her cousin Mary, Queen of Scots, who was then married to the French Dauphin. Had Mary produced a son by that marriage, he would have become heir to the thrones of Scotland, England, Ireland and France, a combination that was enough to strike fear into the hearts of many who had grown weary of the Spanish alliance foisted on England by Mary I. There were of course others who relished that prospect, and there was no lack of potential conspirators who would do their best to realize their dream by dispatching Elizabeth as quickly as possible.

It was in this atmosphere, and against this backdrop, that her settlement of religion in 1559 must be understood. Compromise of some kind was inevitable, but what form it would take (and how long it would last) nobody at the time could have known or foreseen. As soon as word reached the exiles that Mary I had died, they began streaming back into England, looking to take up positions that had been vacated by martyrs or by Catholics who refused to recognize the new queen. Prominent among them was Richard Cox, who became Bishop of Ely and was a pillar of the Elizabethan regime until his death. Even more important in the long run was John Jewel (1522–71), who became Bishop of Salisbury and was one of the major architects and defenders of the Elizabethan Settlement. His *Apologia Ecclesiae Anglicanae* became the classic defence of the reformed Church of England in the face of its Catholic opponents, and remained a standard source for Anglican thought for hundreds of years.[99] Less exalted but ultimately better known was John Foxe (1516–83), whose famous *Actes and Monuments* was made required reading for the clergy in 1571 and is still in print, usually in popular abridgements.[100] Foxe wrote about martyrs from the beginning of church history to his own day, but concentrated on

---

[99] J. Jewel, *Apologia Ecclesiae Anglicanae* (London: Reginald Wolfe, 1562). Published later in the same year by the same publisher as *An Apologie, or Answer in Defence of the Church of England*. A modern edition of that translation has appeared as *An Apology or Defence of the Church of England* (Cambridge: Modern Humanities Research Association, 2016). For a critical study of the work, see G. W. Jenkins, *John Jewel and the English National Church: The Dilemmas of an Erastian Reformer* (Aldershot: Ashgate, 2006).

[100] J. Foxe, *Actes and Monuments of These Latter and Perillous Dayes* (London: J. Day, 1563).

those who had suffered for their Protestantism under both Henry VIII and Mary I. He was bitterly attacked by his Catholic opponents, and until quite recently his work was regarded as propaganda more than as genuine history. But in the past generation it has been demonstrated that Foxe, although not perfect, was largely accurate in his portrayal of the martyrs of his own time, and his work is now treated as serious source material for the period. It contains a wealth of information, like lists of books seized in the homes of prominent Protestant sympathizers, that tell us what was then circulating in England, and for which there is no other source.

As her Archbishop of Canterbury, Elizabeth I chose Matthew Parker (1504–75), a renowned scholar and supporter of Lady Jane Grey who had managed to survive the Marian era without leaving the country. Parker published little himself but was largely responsible for revising the Forty-two Articles of Religion and is known for the vast collection of medieval and sixteenth-century manuscripts he bequeathed to Corpus Christi College Cambridge, where they are now housed in the Parker Library, which is one of the major repositories of archival material from that period and earlier.[101]

First on Elizabeth's agenda was a major overhaul of the House of Bishops. Most of the incumbent prelates were Marian appointees, and almost to a man were unwilling to support the new regime. They were accordingly deprived of their sees and placed under house arrest, although there was to be no return to the violent persecution of Mary I's reign. Eventually four bishops were found who would consecrate Parker as archbishop, and the reconstruction of the Protestant church could begin in earnest. It was Elizabeth I's policy to return to the status quo that had obtained at the death of her half-brother in 1553. All Marian legislation was duly repealed, and forms of doctrine and worship that had been in effect in 1553 were revived, although with some modifications. On 24 June 1559 a new Prayer Book was introduced, which was basically that of 1552, with some material from 1549 incorporated in order to give it a more traditionalist feel. The most important change was that the 1549 words of administration at Holy Communion were combined with those of 1552, as they have remained ever since. Apart from a few minor modifications and additions made in 1604, it remained the standard liturgy of the Church of England until it was abolished in 1646 and then replaced in 1662.[102] At the

---

[101] He also lent his name to the series of fifty-five volumes published by the Parker Society in the nineteenth century. This was a comprehensive collection of writings, including Prayer Books and other liturgical material, from the Reformation period that was designed to give the public a better understanding of what had happened in the sixteenth century.

[102] See J. Booty, *The Book of Common Prayer, 1559* (Washington, D.C.: Folger Books, 1976), for a text and commentary.

same time, Elizabeth dropped the title 'supreme head' of the church and replaced it with 'supreme governor', in order to placate those who insisted that Christ alone is head of the church. Whether it made any difference in practice may be doubted, but it was a recognition that the monarch was subject to a higher authority, a principle that would be recalled two generations later when the king tried to intervene in church affairs in ways that many people regarded as contrary to the will of God as revealed in Holy Scripture.

The Forty-two Articles of Religion were also revised and reduced to thirty-nine, one of which (Article 29) was struck out by the queen for fear that it might offend the Lutherans by its rejection of the 'ubiquity' of the body of Christ. The basic pattern of the Articles was retained, with the Catholic (1–8), Protestant (9–34), Anglican (35–37) and miscellaneous (38–39) ones following in the same sequence as before. There were however some important additions, such as Article 5 on the Holy Spirit, who had unaccountably been overlooked ten years earlier, and a complete list of the canonical books of the Bible in Article 6. This was in response to the Council of Trent's decree on the canon, which accepted the longer Augustinian view of the Old Testament as opposed to that of his contemporary, the biblical scholar Jerome. The underlying argument was typical of the sixteenth century, since it was essentially between tradition and 'science'. Augustine had argued that the longer (Greek) Old Testament had been the Bible of the apostles and of the early church, whereas Jerome claimed that the shorter (Hebrew) canon had been that of the Jewish people, who were the Old Testament children of God and therefore the proper heirs and custodians of the divine text. Protestants generally sided with Jerome (Hierome) in this controversy, as Article 6 explicitly states and, as a result, it is the Hebrew canon that is now printed in most Bibles as the Old Testament.[103]

Elsewhere there were significant modifications to Article 11 on justification, and the addition of a new Article 12 on good works. The old Article 16 on blasphemy against the Holy Spirit was dropped. The Articles on the sacraments underwent some important changes, including the addition of Article 29, already mentioned, and Article 30, which enjoined Communion in both kinds. The so-called 'Anglican' articles (35–37) were also substantially modified.

---

[103] An interesting omission from the list in Article 6 is the book of Lamentations, which was apparently considered to be part of Jeremiah. Today this argument has been largely superseded by modern research, which takes place on an ecumenical basis. All sides now accept the Hebrew canon as primary, but they also recognize that the Greek translations often contain evidence of an earlier textual tradition that was lost until the discovery of the Dead Sea Scrolls in 1947. The rejected books, once known as the Apocrypha, are now commonly called 'deuterocanonical' or 'intertestamental', at least in scholarly circles, and are valued as witnesses for the development of Judaism between the end of the Old Testament period and the time of Jesus.

Article 35 now included a complete list of the homilies contained in the Second Book that was issued simultaneously with the Articles themselves, Article 36 was devoted to the Ordinal (the form of consecration used for bishops, priests and deacons) but omitted all reference to the Prayer Book, and Article 37 gave a much fuller account of the civil magistrate. The final Articles dealing with eschatological matters were left out, either because they were thought to be superfluous or because they were unnecessarily controversial.[104]

The Second Book of Homilies was a mixture of items originally promised at the end of the First Book but apparently never composed, plus a number of sermons tied to the main events of the Christian year – Christmas, Easter and Pentecost in particular. Many of them, like the ones against idolatry and against rebellion, were extraordinarily long and were subdivided, because they could not all be read at a single service. On the whole it must be said that the Second Book reads more like a series of lectures than like a collection of sermons, which (to the modern mind at least) are less appealing than the simpler ones in the First Book, some of which can be preached today with little or no alteration.

By 1563 the Elizabethan Settlement, as the sum total of revisions and accompanying injunctions are collectively known, was in place and would determine the queen's religious policy for the rest of her reign. It was initially accepted by the more radical Protestants as the best they could hope for in the circumstances, and the papacy did nothing in response. Even so, it was clear to many convinced Catholics that the wind was blowing in the opposite direction, and some of them began to leave the country, imitating their Protestant fellow countrymen of the previous decade and migrating to places like Louvain (Leuven) and Douai. There they either joined or established seminaries for the training of priests who, they hoped, would be deployed for the re-Catholicization of England as soon as the opportunity arose.

Their dream turned into a nightmare when Pope Pius V excommunicated Queen Elizabeth I and absolved her subjects from their allegiance to her. In an extraordinary bull, known as *Regnans in Excelsis* and published on 27 April 1570, the Pope said the following:

we do out of the fullness of our apostolic power declare the aforesaid Elizabeth to be a heretic and favourer of heretics, and her adherents in the matters aforesaid to have incurred the sentence of excommunication

---

[104] As a result, the Church of England has no clearly defined eschatology and various views can be held with equal conviction.

and to be cut off from the unity of the body of Christ. And moreover, [we declare] her to be deprived of her pretended title to the aforesaid crown and of all lordship, dignity and privilege whatsoever. And also [declare] the nobles, subjects and people of the said realm, and all others who have in any way sworn oaths to her, to be forever absolved from such an oath and from any duty arising from lordship, fealty and obedience ... We charge and command all and singular the nobles, subjects, peoples and others aforesaid that they do not dare obey her orders, mandates and laws. Those who shall act to the contrary we include in the like sentence of excommunication.[105]

It was a declaration of war against the queen and the English state, and her response was inevitable. Those who obeyed the Pope were traitors to her and would suffer the consequences. She had no desire to persecute anyone on religious grounds and had done what she could to forestall that, but she was left with no choice. After 1570 many Catholic priests, trained at Douai and other places, would be smuggled back into England in order to propagate their faith in secret. They were hidden by a network of Catholic 'recusants', as those who rejected the Elizabethan Settlement were called, and their exploits became the stuff of legend. Most of them were eventually caught and paid a heavy price for their loyalty to Rome. They protested, probably rightly, that they had no interest in politics and were concerned only with matters of belief, but the queen's government did not see matters that way and could not afford to take chances. There were plots against her life and, in the secret world in which the recusants lived, who could be sure what was really going on? Sir Geoffrey Elton's measured judgment seems right:

Elizabeth always maintained that she was hunting out priests because they represented a political danger, and though undeniably many of her subjects joined in the chase with religious passion in their hearts, the persecution cannot be described as religious in the real sense. The queen did not want to save souls or make converts; she wanted to protect the safety of her realm.[106]

Protestant discontent with the Settlement was somewhat slower to emerge, and when it did it took a different course. In order to enforce its provisions

---

[105] The original Latin text and an English translation are in G. R. Elton, *The Tudor Constitution*, 2nd edn (Cambridge: Cambridge University Press, 1982), no. 197, 423–428.
[106] Ibid. 423.

Elizabeth I had established a series of High Commission courts charged with implementing them, and these soon discovered that a number of Protestant ministers were quietly disregarding such things as the wearing of the prescribed liturgical vestments.[107] This was a controversy that went back to the time of Edward VI, when John Hooper had refused to wear the episcopal robes that he was expected to put on as Bishop of Gloucester, and was imprisoned for his obstinacy. Archbishop Cranmer's reasoning was that vestments had no theological significance and were matters of indifference (*adiaphora*, to use the theological term), so that the church could impose them as a matter of discipline without offending anyone's conscience. Hooper (and others like him) claimed that vestments reminded people of the medieval system and that if the clergy continued to wear them, many would assume that there had been no Reformation at all.

Modern people find this sort of thing hard to understand, but in the sixteenth century it was axiomatic that a person's status could be determined by his or her clothes. Noblemen, gentlemen and peasants were all told what they could (and could not) wear, and clerical vestments were simply the uniforms of the clergy – a means of identifying them in society. Even today, clergymen often wear a clerical collar that sets them apart from others, although nobody would assume that it has any theological or spiritual significance. Hooper believed that the clergyman was first and foremost a preacher and teacher, and so ought to dress the part by wearing a black academic gown instead of the surplice and stole of the medieval priest. This became the substance of the so-called 'vestiarian controversy' in the 1560s, and the official reaction was the same as Cranmer's had been – conformity to the prescribed norm was important, while theories about the possible theological significance of the garments were not.[108]

The outcome of this dispute was paradigmatic for much of what was to follow. The official line on the wearing of vestments was upheld, and some clergymen were disciplined for violating it. They reacted by claiming that the Church of England was not yet fully Reformed and that further change was necessary, which the government resisted. Meanwhile a number of clergymen

---

[107] See R. G. Usher, *The Rise and Fall of the High Commission* (Oxford: Clarendon Press, 1913). See also R. Houlbrooke, *Church Courts and the People During the English Reformation 1520–1570* (Oxford: Oxford University Press, 1979).

[108] See P. Collinson, *The Elizabethan Puritan Movement* (London: Jonathan Cape, 1967; Oxford: Clarendon Press, 1990). See 67–83, 88–89, 93–96 of the Oxford edition for the details. For the official reaction, see 'The Advertisements for Due Order, 1566', 5, in Bray, *Anglican Canons*, 169–170. It should be noted however, that the queen refused to sign the document, leaving it up to the Archbishop of Canterbury to publish the regulations on his own authority.

quietly disregarded orders, since nobody could police every parish to ensure that the regulations were being followed to the letter, and sympathetic bishops turned a blind eye, hoping that the whole problem would die down and eventually go away. The inevitable result of course was that resentment was fuelled on the side of the radicals, who felt that things were not moving fast enough in their direction, and there was increasing frustration in the Establishment at the apparent inability of the bishops and other authorities to keep the lid on. A matter that in itself meant nothing and should never have been allowed to divide the church thus became a badge of identity that divided the radicals from the conservatives. It was a bone of contention that would needlessly exacerbate people's feelings about 'conscience' and lead first to civil disobedience and then, in the longer term, to civil war. It was an absurd situation, but one that would persist in the Church of England and that still rears its head.[109]

The Elizabethan Settlement was not perfect, but in the troubles of the period it proved to be remarkably successful. At a time when France was wracked by a series of religious wars that seemed to have no solution, England remained quiet. Church papists and nascent Puritans grumbled, but on the whole they conformed, and most of the population grew accustomed to the new order. Had Elizabeth died younger it might not have been so, but the fact that she reigned for over forty years – long enough to outlive most of those who could remember the time before she ascended the throne – made her Settlement seem to be the natural order of things. Controversies there would continue to be, but she could claim to have laid the foundations for a church that would be flexible enough to resolve them, as long as there was good will and a willingness to compromise on all sides. It was when those crucial factors were found to be in short supply that her Settlement broke down, but it took a generation for that to happen and she went to her eternal reward believing that she had saved her country from a fate worse than death.

Did Elizabeth I have a faith of her own or was she just a politician who operated within the limits imposed by her circumstances? This question has been asked ever since the sixteenth century, and it is not surprising that those who were most engaged in theological polemics were also the ones who were most doubtful about what the queen believed. On the radical side were those who thought that the fact that she had a silver cross and candlesticks on the

---

[109] This is especially true at ordinations, where bishops are inclined to insist that ordinands wear a stole, and Evangelical candidates often object on grounds of 'conscience'. In their different ways both sides are arguing over something that has no official significance at all, but often neither is willing to give in to the other.

Communion table in her private chapel was a sign that she was a secret papist. She certainly had a prejudice against John Calvin's Geneva, but that was because of John Knox's pamphlet against the 'monstrous regiment of women', which she found personally offensive, even though it was not meant for her. The real difficulty seems to have been that Elizabeth was a vain woman who liked flattery, and the Protestants of Knox's type were decidedly short on charm.

With the Catholics, things were more clear-cut. As Pius V put it in *Regnans in Excelsis*, Elizabeth was

> the pretended queen of England and the servant of crime . . . having seized the crown and monstrously usurped the place of supreme head of the Church [she has] . . . reduced this same kingdom . . . to a miserable ruin.[110]

It was hardly a balanced or accurate assessment of her rule, and we should not be surprised if she dissented from the Pope's conclusions. Elizabeth presided over a golden age of English literature but she wrote relatively little herself, and so it is hard to assess what her personal beliefs were. But we do have some prayers she composed in six languages – English, French, Italian, Spanish, Latin and Greek – and they make it clear where her heart lay. In one of her Italian prayers she wrote:

> God, my Father and Protector, greatly do I feel myself a debtor to Thy mercy for having called me early by the preaching of the Gospel of Jesus Christ to the true worship and sincerity of Thy religion, to the end that with the authority which Thou hast given me and with the zeal for which I am indebted to Thee, I might be made Thy instrument for replanting and establishing in this part of the world, where it hath pleased Thee that I reign in the name of Thy kingdom, Thy worship, and most holy religion. I pray Thee, my God and good Father, that as in part by Thy grace I have served Thee in this according to Thy holy will, so may it please Thee to remove all impediment and resistance of unbelief from my people, and to inspire me from well to better yet, goodwill and ardent zeal; giving me efficacious means, apt and sufficient instruments, so that I may be able to do as I desire, uprooting every wicked seed of impiety, to spread, plant, and root Thy holy Gospel in every heart, increasing throughout this Thy

---

[110] Elton, *Tudor Constitution*, 426.

earthly kingdom, that heavenly one of Jesus Christ, to whom be evermore honour and glory, Amen.[111]

Reform in Ireland

The advent of the Tudor dynasty was not popular in Ireland, where the Anglo-Irish aristocracy had had close links to the Yorkist branch of the royal family and was prepared to offer succour to the Yorkist pretenders Lambert Simnel and Perkin Warbeck.[112] But as he did elsewhere, Henry VII dealt with these and other matters with a firm hand. As early as 1488 he created what came to be known as the 'pale' of settlement around Dublin, consisting of the four 'obedient shires' – Louth, Meath, Dublin and Kildare. To govern this territory he turned to the earls of Kildare, who held it as a virtually hereditary fief. This arrangement was a practical necessity more than anything else.[113] Henry needed stability in Ireland, and although the Geraldines (as the earls of Kildare were known because FitzGerald was their family name) were not always reliable, they were the best option available. Henry also tried to control the Irish Parliament by forcing it to enact a statute that made it illegal for it to assemble or to transact business without the king's express authorization.[114] The Irish church was not singled out for such special treatment, but because it remained closely connected to the parliament its affairs were inevitably affected. A provincial synod held in Dublin in 1496 made a second attempt to found a university in Ireland but, despite a programme that got as far as proposing a salary scale for the prospective lecturers, which was approved at a second synod in 1511, it failed to gain traction and the project was abandoned.[115] Viewed from hindsight this was unfortunate, since the wider world was beginning to feel the impact of the Renaissance, much of which reached northern Europe through the universities. At a time when Oxford and Cambridge, as well as the three Scottish universities, were beginning to stir with new ideas, Ireland found itself somewhat out of the loop, and when the new learning arrived there was no obvious constituency to which it could appeal.

---

[111] L. S. Marcus, J. Mueller and M. B. Rose (eds.), *Elizabeth I: Collected Works* (Chicago, Ill.: University of Chicago Press, 2000), 153–154. The prayer is taken from the original collection, *Christian Prayers and Meditations in English, French, Italian, Spanish, Greek and Latin* (London: J. Day, 1569). That collection was anonymous, but it is clear from the contents who the author was.

[112] See A. Crawford, *The Yorkists: The History of a Dynasty* (London: Continuum, 2007), 158–162.

[113] See S. G. Ellis, *Ireland in the Age of the Tudors, 1447–1603* (London: Longman, 1998); S. J. Connolly, *Contested Island: Ireland 1460–1630* (Oxford: Oxford University Press, 2007).

[114] This statute was known as Poynings' Law, because it was brought to the parliament by Sir Edward Poynings, the king's special envoy to Ireland in 1494–5.

[115] Bray, *Records of Convocation*, 16:313.

In other respects however, the Irish church appeared to be in good health. Provincial synods were a regular feature and some passed canons to regulate the behaviour of both clergy and laity. One of the more interesting of these was the stipulation, made in the provincial Synod of Dublin in 1518, that clergy caught playing football would be fined eighty pence, to be divided equally between the archbishop and the parish where the offending game had been played.[116] As far as we know, this was the first, and probably the only, reference to football in the canons of the church anywhere in the British Isles. The Armagh registers allow us to affirm that it was business as usual there, with semi-annual synods meeting on a regular basis to review the diocesan and provincial administrations, but without being obliged to do anything much to reform them.[117] Gaelic Ireland continued to go its own way, different from the English areas but not cut off from them. The two national traditions had reached a modus vivendi that allowed each to flourish independently of the other but did not entail any radical separation between them.

Looking back from a great distance in time, we can see that this was the calm before the storm. The Gaelic areas could hardly have maintained for long their anomalous customs that permitted clerical concubinage and even sanctioned the transmission of church offices from father to (illegitimate) son, and Tudor centralization would eventually have led to attempts to unite the island under the rule of the king. This became apparent when Henry VIII broke with the papacy in 1534 and the Earl of Kildare, who was already suspected of disloyalty, was summoned to London. Kildare left his son and heir, 'Silken Thomas' Lord Offaly (1513–37), to hold the fort in Ireland, but before long 'Silken Thomas' was in open rebellion against the king, citing the latter's break with Rome as an excuse for throwing off his allegiance. In Thomas's view, Henry VIII was lord of Ireland because Pope Hadrian IV had granted the country to Henry II in 1155, and if the link with Rome was broken, then the papal grant ceased to have any validity. Needless to say, this argument did not appeal to Henry VIII, who was forced to suppress the rebellion and do what he could to make the Irish Parliament fall into line with the policies he was implementing in England. To remove any doubt about his title to the lordship, Henry VIII simply abolished it by getting the Irish Parliament to proclaim him King of Ireland (1542). From then on the papacy was a

---

[116] Ibid. 16:328. See canon 8 for the details. There is obviously some doubt as to what 'football' was at that time, but that is a secondary matter we can afford to ignore for our purposes.

[117] See H. A. Jefferies, *Priests and Prelates of Armagh in the Age of Reformations 1518–1558* (Dublin: Four Courts Press, 1997).

constitutional irrelevance, although, as we know, Ireland would not be won so easily for the Reformation.[118]

The Irish Parliament dutifully passed the legislation needed to bring Ireland into conformity with England, including the suppression of the monasteries, but its writ ran only in the areas under English control. Elsewhere the old order continued, and many of those who had been dispossessed in the pale found it relatively easy to escape to the unaffected parts of the country. It soon became apparent that religious change in Ireland would be partial and insecure as long as most of the island remained outside royal control. But to conquer it would require a massive military campaign for which Henry VIII had neither the time nor the money, nor even the inclination, to pursue. As a result, things carried on much as before, with little apparent impact on the ground. The most noticeable effect was that the lands of the dissolved monasteries passed into the hands of the leading residents of the pale, many of whom were unsympathetic to the religious change that had made this windfall possible. Later on they would happily confess their Catholicism, but one thing was clear – as in England, they had no intention of giving the monastic lands back to the church, and so the dissolution of the monasteries remained permanent, regardless of any changes in ecclesiastical allegiance.

The reign of Edward VI saw a sharp acceleration in the Reformation in England, but not much of this extended across the Irish Sea. No Irish Parliament was called during his reign, so no legislation could be passed. About all that happened was that the 1552 Book of Common Prayer was published in Dublin, the first book to be printed in Ireland, and a couple of Protestant bishops were appointed. One of them was John Bale, who was consecrated to the see of Ossory in 1553. Bale was by all accounts received with enthusiasm in Kilkenny, but was there only a few months before the king died and religious policy changed dramatically. Another was Hugh Goodacre, who was consecrated Archbishop of Armagh on 2 February 1553 but died only three months later, on 1 May. He was succeeded by George Dowdall, the man whom he had dispossessed and who now became a leading light in the restoration of traditional Catholicism in Ireland.

Mary I took the country back to Rome but, unlike England, it did not have far to go, since almost nothing had changed since 1537. Nobody was put on trial for Protestant heresy or burnt at the stake either, although in one respect Mary was to be remembered as the unwitting progenitor of Protestant

---

[118] See C. Brady, *The Chief Governors: The Rise and Fall of Reform Government in Tudor Ireland, 1536–1588* (Cambridge: Cambridge University Press, 1994).

expansionism in Ireland. There had already been plans to plant the country with English settlers who would supposedly civilize the native Irish around them and secure the country for the Crown. It was left to Mary and her husband Philip to implement this policy by creating two new counties, named King's and Queen's after them, with their capitals at Philipstown and Maryborough respectively.[119]

Elsewhere in the country the Armagh synods resumed under Mary and continued until 1559, when the last of them was held. By then Archbishop Dowdall had died and the see was vacant, not to be filled until Queen Elizabeth I felt secure enough to do so, although imposing her settlement of religion on Ireland was to prove even more challenging than the situation faced by her father a generation before.[120] By 1571, when the ecclesiastical situation in England was finally starting to settle down, Ireland was about to erupt in a prolonged period of warfare and religious confusion that would not end for at least 120 years, and in some respects has not ended yet.[121]

Pre-Reformation Scotland

The Tudors never ruled Scotland, and so to some extent that country escaped the religious turmoil that they introduced in England and Ireland.[122] But Scotland was not immune to upheavals south of the border. Henry VII had married his daughter Margaret to James IV, uniting the royal houses in a way that they had never been united before and opening the possibility that at some point they would merge into one. We know that eventually they did so, but even before James VI succeeded Elizabeth I in 1603 there were attempts to bring the two crowns together. After the death of James V in 1542, Henry VIII tried to arrange for his son Edward to be betrothed to James's infant daughter Mary, and even made his point by invading the country in what is known as the 'rough wooing'. It did not work, and the young Mary was sent away to France, where she grew up to marry the Dauphin and become his queen in

---

[119] The plantation failed in its purpose and of course the ultra-Catholic Mary and Philip had no intention of spreading Protestantism (as later plantations were expected to do), but that did not spare them from the wrath of modern Irish nationalism. After the Irish Free State came into being in 1922, their counties were renamed Offaly and Laois (Leix) respectively, and the county seats became Dangan and Portlaoise, their founders' conspicuously devout Catholicism evidently being no protection against the more visceral Anglophobia of the new regime.

[120] See Jefferies, *Priests and Prelates*.

[121] For an overview of this, see M. Tanner, *Ireland's Holy Wars: The Struggle for a Nation's Soul 1500–2000* (New Haven, Conn.: Yale University Press, 2001).

[122] On the history of this period, see J. E. A. Dawson, *Scotland Re-formed 1488–1587* (Edinburgh: Edinburgh University Press, 2007).

1559, when Scotland was still in communion with Rome. But we are getting ahead of ourselves.

The Scottish church was not properly integrated into western Christendom until the end of the fifteenth century, when the provinces of St Andrews (1472) and Glasgow (1492) were finally created. This inevitably lessened the role of the papacy in Scottish affairs, but that was not necessarily an improvement because it led to a great increase in royal influence, especially over the appointment of bishops. The elevation of St Andrews to the status of an archbishopric enraged King James III, who immediately exempted Glasgow, Aberdeen and Moray from its jurisdiction. Furthermore, from 1497 to 1513 the see was held by two young princes who were styled 'administrators', and the revenue was creamed off by the royal treasury. The coming of the Reformation in England made this situation worse because it gave the Scottish king greater leverage in church appointments. Fearful that James V might go the way of his English cousin, the pope allowed him to grant not only the priory of St Andrews but also the abbeys of Holyrood, Kelso and Melrose to his illegitimate children, who held them as 'lay commendators'. Scotland was still obedient to Rome in things spiritual, but the king despoiled the church to a degree that had never been known before.

Scotland had been only marginally affected by Lollardy in the fifteenth century and heresy was rare, if not completely unknown. Yet when Martin Luther's ideas began to circulate, the Scottish Parliament felt obliged to ban them.[123] The first statute against Lutheran literature was passed in 1525, but it was repeated and extended several times – in 1527, 1535 and 1541, on which last occasion Parliament chose to affirm the seven sacraments, the veneration of the Virgin Mary and the authority of the pope. How much Protestant literature was making its way into the country at that time is unknown, but the suspicion is that Tyndale's New Testament was the main target of the legislation. Scotland even acquired a Protestant martyr before England did, when the young Patrick Hamilton (1504–28) was burnt for having espoused Lutheranism. Hamilton had come across it as a student in Paris and had taken it back to Scotland in 1523, when he was still a teenager. He was therefore the first known Protestant in Britain, having reached his convictions almost before anyone in England knew what Protestantism was.

Patrick Hamilton was precocious but he was also unique. Nobody followed him to the stake, although there must have been a good deal of discussion

---

[123] On the pre-history of the Scottish Reformation, see A. Ryrie, *The Origins of the Scottish Reformation* (Manchester: Manchester University Press, 2006).

about Lutheran ideas in the universities and among the better-educated laity. After the English Bible was made legal in the southern kingdom, Scotland felt obliged to follow suit, and an act of Parliament in 1543 made it available in Scotland as well. This was significant, not only because it authorized the reading of the Scriptures but because it also authorized the use of the English language. Like Ireland, Scotland was linguistically divided, but it was between Gaelic in the west and north, and 'Scots' in the south and east. Scots was an Anglo-Saxon dialect that might have developed into a separate language as different from English as Portuguese is from Spanish. But it did not. Protestantism brought the English language with it, which effectively displaced Scots as the normal means of public communication.[124]

It is at this time, in the dying days of James V, that we first come across John Knox, who was then still a young and aspiring Catholic priest. Knox was drawn to the currents of reform circulating among young men of his type, but his interest was not confined to church politics as it was in so many other cases. Sometime in the early 1540s, Knox came to accept the Lutheran doctrine of justification by faith alone, which seemed to be making headway among Roman Catholics as well. But after the failure of the Colloquy of Regensburg in 1541, when it seemed that agreement had been reached on this crucial subject, he began to realize that his days as a priest were numbered. Yet it was dangerous for him to stick his head above the parapet, because religious policy in Scotland was dictated by the ultra-conservative Cardinal David Beaton (1494–1546), who was determined to do everything he could to stamp out heresy. It was only when reading the Bible in English became legal that Knox began to speak out, and in the next few years he engaged in intensive Bible study of his own. In John 17 he found the key that linked justification and sanctification to predestination – three fundamental pillars of what would become established Protestant doctrine.

On 13 December 1545, when attending a sermon by the Protestant preacher George Wishart (1513–46), Knox finally committed himself to the Reformation. Wishart had spent time in Switzerland and had been converted to its form of Protestantism. He even translated the First Helvetic Confession of 1536, thereby introducing Swiss Reformed thinking into Scotland some years before it reached England. Knox learned many things from Wishart, but perhaps the most important was that the true church is not a worldwide institution of

---

[124] In the eighteenth century Robert Burns wrote an English larded with Scottish expressions, but this was not Scots in the true sense. Modern Scottish nationalists also claim to speak it (as do some Ulster Protestants), but this is nonsense. Scottish English has local words and regional expressions, but it is English nevertheless.

government but a persecuted minority of faithful believers who resurface in every generation and suffer the consequences of their faithfulness. Wishart was soon arrested by Cardinal Beaton's agents, tried for heresy and executed on 1 March 1546, making him the second great martyr for the Protestant cause in Scotland. Knox naturally feared that Wishart's death would be the beginning of persecution, but it was not. Beaton was cautious about creating martyrs, not least because he knew that he was only making enemies by doing so, and he had enough of them already – so many in fact that he was murdered only a few months later (on 29 May 1546) by a group of eighteen men who seized the castle of St Andrews and defended it against the inevitable wrath of the government. Scotland was thus divided between an 'English party', that favoured reformation of the church along English lines, and a 'French party', that was theologically conservative and aligned with the Establishment running the country in the name of the young Queen Mary, who was still a child and growing up at the French court.

During this time Knox was lecturing in St Andrews, and was challenged by his fellow Protestants to accept the calling of a preacher – something that, as George Wishart had discovered, was tantamount to a death sentence. In later years Knox tended to exaggerate his part in bringing Protestantism to Scotland, but of his involvement with the rebels of St Andrews there can be no doubt. When the French took the city on 7 August 1547, Knox was among those of the 'English party' who were arrested and taken captive to France, where he was indentured as a galley slave. It was an experience that put steel into his soul and reinforced his already strong belief that he belonged to the persecuted remnant who were Christ's true church on earth. It was a faith that would sustain him through his years of exile and determine much of his conduct when he finally set foot in his native land again.

The events of 1546–7 made it clear to the Scottish hierarchy that serious reform of the church was necessary, and the next decade saw a flurry of activity previously unknown in Scotland. The initiative for this came from John Hamilton (1512–71), archbishop of St Andrews from 1547 until his death. At a synod held in 1549, clergy discipline was top of the legislative agenda, with canons regulating celibacy, dress, behaviour and ministry. Special effort was to be made to search for runaway monks and nuns, who would be compelled to return to their monasteries and convents. Particular attention was paid to the need to teach theology and preach sound doctrine. Every cathedral and monastery was obliged to employ a resident theologian and all candidates for ordination were to be taught properly and examined before receiving their orders. Incumbents were to be resident on their benefices and pluralism was to be stamped out. The synod recognized that the reforming Catholic Council of Trent had met from 1545 to 1547 and, although it had been adjourned, it had not been dissolved. Care would therefore be taken to implement the canons of that Council that had already been promulgated and to ensure that when it resumed, the decisions taken would also be received in Scotland. The procedures of the ecclesiastical courts were overhauled and provisions made for the pursuit and punishment of heretics. All in all, the synod aimed to apply the strategy of the Catholic Counter-Reformation (as we now call it) to a still obedient Scotland, although with what success remained to be seen.[125]

Further synods were meant to be held on an annual basis, but whether they were or not is unclear. One was definitely held on 26 January 1552, which repeated the need for good preaching and filled in a number of gaps that had been omitted in 1549, including the probate of wills, regulations governing matrimony, and the procedures to be followed in cases of excommunication.[126] Finally we have the canons of a synod held in March and April 1559, which repeated many of the same themes, putting particular emphasis on the suppression of clerical concubinage and the need to preach sound doctrine.[127] The intentions were good, but it could not have escaped anyone's notice that the president of the synod was himself the father of several illegitimate children and was thus anything but a shining example to his flock.

With the benefit of hindsight it is easy to conclude that these reforming synods were cases of 'too little too late', and that is undoubtedly true, but the real problem was that they failed to carry conviction at the time. Too many of those involved were guilty of the misdemeanours that the synods censured. John Lesley, who later became Bishop of Ross (1566–76), characterized them as follows:

> They made many sharp statutes, and commanded all the bishops, abbots, priors, deans, archdeacons, and all the rest there presently assembled, and others throughout all the parts of the realm, to make themselves able, and use their own offices according to their foundations and callings, within the space of six months, under the pain of deprivation; which was the principal cause that a great number of young abbots, priors, deans and beneficed men assisted to the enterprise and practice devised for the

---

[125] D. Patrick, *Statutes of the Scottish Church 1225–1559* (Edinburgh: Edinburgh University Press, 1907), 84–134.

[126] Ibid. 135–148.

[127] Ibid. 149–191.

overthrow of the Catholic religion . . . fearing themselves to be put out according to the laws and statutes.[128]

The 1559 synod continued to respect the decrees of the Council of Trent, which had resumed its sessions; although by the time the Council ended in 1563, Scotland had broken with the Roman see. It was already clear that the Catholic restoration under Mary Tudor had failed in England, but what that might portend for Scotland was not yet known. The French king Henry II died on 10 July 1559 of a wound incurred while jousting and, as a result, Mary, Queen of Scots became Queen Consort of France. The prospect of a Catholic Franco-Scottish alliance against England persuaded Elizabeth I and her ministers to intervene in the northern kingdom. The result was that Scotland acquired a Protestant church and parliament, controlled by Scots to be sure, but backed up by an English army – just in case.

The Scottish Reformation

When the prisoners of St Andrews were exiled to France in 1547, most people assumed that their cause was lost for good and that no more would be heard of them. Things did not turn out that way. Unnoticed by many in power, the courage of the Protestants was widely reported across Scotland and sympathy for their position grew. We do not know how the word spread, but when John Knox returned to the country on a reconnaissance trip in 1555–6, he was astonished by the changed atmosphere. Everywhere he went he was asked to preach, and even some of the nobility were prepared to listen to him. Here and there small groups of convinced Protestants were meeting for worship and Bible study. Before long, these groups were appointing elders to supervise their activities and impose a moral and spiritual discipline on their membership. It was all informal and grassroots activity, but it soon came to the notice of the authorities, who were duly alarmed by it. Marie de Guise, the regent acting for her daughter the queen, summoned the known ringleaders to meet with her at Stirling on 10 May 1559, but she got more than she had bargained for.

John Knox had just returned to Scotland for the second time, and he decided to join those who were going to see the regent. On the way they gathered a large number of supporters from Dundee and the north-east who also wanted to show their solidarity with those who had been summoned. Fearing that their

---

[128] Quoted in J. H. S. Burleigh, *A Church History of Scotland* (London: Oxford University Press, 1960), 141. The spelling has been modernized for ease of comprehension.

numbers might frighten the government, the marchers sent John Erskine ahead of them to explain the situation and to ask for a postponement of the meeting. But instead of granting his request, the regent outlawed the preachers on the ground that they had failed to obey the summons! At that point they were in Perth, and on 11 May, Knox went into the parish church there and preached a stirring sermon against 'idolatry', which was code for the Catholic Church. He might not have expected it, but the reaction was immediate and violent. Before long, a mob had wrecked the church and turned its wrath on the friaries that lay just outside the town. The civic authorities, who were sympathetic to the preachers, failed to intervene and instead outlawed the celebration of the Catholic mass in the town, a move they apparently thought would calm the situation.

The whole affair was bad publicity for the Protestants, who lost the support of many leading nobles and others who turned to the regent as a bastion of law and order. But Marie de Guise proved unable to capitalize on her good fortune, and many of those who had initially supported her went back to their Protestant friends when they saw that she had lost control of the situation. These men included the Earl of Argyll, the most powerful nobleman in the west, and James Stewart, an illegitimate son of James V who might become a candidate for the throne if it should become vacant. These men assumed control of the Protestant forces and branded themselves 'Lords of the Congregation', a political pressure group that would henceforth campaign for the introduction of a Protestant Reformation into Scotland. They marched on St Andrews, where they had a lot of latent support, and before long had taken over the city. From then on, St Andrews and Fife would be the main base of the Protestants as they engaged in civil war against their Catholic opponents.

The Lords of the Congregation quickly seized much of central Scotland but they were unable to capture Edinburgh, and their struggle was stalemated. In these circumstances they needed English help, which Knox strongly favoured even though he was *persona non grata* with Queen Elizabeth. The queen was extremely reluctant to intervene in Scottish affairs but pressure from her council was increasing and at the end of 1559 she finally gave way. An English fleet set sail for Leith in midwinter, and its appearance turned the tide of war in the Protestants' favour. In April 1560 an English army joined them, only to discover when they arrived outside Edinburgh that the regent was on her deathbed. With Marie de Guise no longer at the helm, the 'French party' collapsed and the French troops who had been guarding them were sent home. Scotland was not worth a drop of French blood and most people across Europe were relieved that a potentially damaging conflict had been prevented.

By mid-1559 parts of Scotland were in a revolutionary state and few could predict what the eventual outcome would be. John Knox found it impossible to moderate his condemnation of Catholic practices and of those who continued to support them, and there was a constant danger that popular reaction would lead to violence and destruction. In the event, more irenic voices prevailed, at least most of the time, and the Scottish Reformation was both more peaceful and more consensual than reformation was in many other places.[129] A number of Catholic leaders, including a few bishops, were won over to the Protestant cause and accepted by the Reformers without serious reservations. Particularly interesting was the case of John Winram (1492–1582), subprior of St Andrews, who had privately supported Knox in 1547 and who by 1559 was thoroughly disillusioned with the half-hearted attempts at 'reform' that the ecclesiastical hierarchy was proposing. He went over to the Reformation, along with several others of like mind, and his conversion was welcomed, not least by the often-censorious Knox.[130] St Andrews was in the forefront of the Reformation, and to those who were based there it seemed that this success portended well for the rest of the country, but this was an illusion. Fife, Angus and Ayrshire were fertile ground for the Reformers, but the rest of Scotland proved to be more challenging, and not least the capital city of Edinburgh itself.

In May 1560 Knox was appointed minister of St Giles Cathedral in Edinburgh, a post he would retain (off and on) for the rest of his life. Edinburgh was not as favourable to the Reformers as St Andrews, and Knox found it prudent to flee the city on more than one occasion, but used the opportunity the pulpit of St Giles provided to ram home the implications of 'godly reformation' not only to the people but to the government located in the city. In August 1560 a parliament was called and concrete proposals for reformation were put to it. The parliament had been sanctioned by the absent Queen Mary but its decisions never received royal assent, calling their legality into question later on, although at the time there was no doubt. On 17 August 1560 the Scots voted for a full-blown reform of the church, overturning the heritage of centuries in a single day and laying the groundwork for a Reformation that would embrace the three pillars of ecclesiastical polity – doctrine, discipline and devotion. On doctrine, Parliament sanctioned the First Scottish Confession, a document that shows signs of somewhat hasty composition but clearly reflects Reformed theology as that was currently understood in Calvin's

---

[129] See G. Donaldson, *The Scottish Reformation* (Cambridge: Cambridge University Press, 1960), 53–75.

[130] See Dawson, *John Knox*, 196–197.

Geneva.[131] It also adopted a metrical psalter for use in public worship as a prelude to the Book of Common Order, modelled on the practice of Geneva, which appeared in 1562.[132] Finally there was the Book of Discipline, which seems to have been composed before the summoning of the parliament but was not received by it, at least not in full.[133] As in England, vested interests proved to be too strong to resist and it was only gradually that the main programme envisaged by Knox was adopted by the church as a whole.

The 1560 Parliament abolished Catholic worship but did not substantially affect the structures of the medieval church. The bishops were allowed to remain in place, although their roles were greatly circumscribed and supplemented by the appointment of 'superintendents', who would oversee the church at parish level. The monasteries were not dissolved either, although the situation there was complex. For at least a generation the Scottish Crown had taxed the monastic establishments extremely heavily, with the result that many had become indebted to lay 'commendators', who had the money needed to bail out the abbots. When the Reformation came, many of these commendators simply assumed control of the religious houses already heavily mortgaged to them. The monks and nuns were allowed to leave but if they chose to stay they were not molested. Over time they simply died out. It was not until 1587 that the Crown formally annexed monastic establishments and gradually transformed them into lay estates, which were then often sold or granted to private individuals. It was a slow process however, and was not fully completed until the early decades of the seventeenth century.

The Scottish Confession contains twenty-five articles or chapters, of which the first twelve are little more than a restatement of ancient creedal theology, although with certain emphases that were to distinguish the Reformed tradition later on. It begins, as was customary at the time, with a statement on the unity and Trinity of God, followed by the creation of man, original sin, the revelation of God's promise of redemption in the Old Testament and the establishment of the church as God's people from Israel to the present. After that comes the incarnation of Christ, an explanation of why the Mediator had to be both God and man, the free election of those who were to be saved, Christ's

---

[131] For the text of this Confession, see P. Schaff, *The Creeds of Christendom*, 3 vols. (New York, N.Y.: Harper & Row, 1931), 3:437–479, where the original Scots and Latin versions are printed in parallel columns. For a modern critical edition of the Scots text, see I. Hazlett, 'Confessio Scotica 1560', in A. Mühling and P. Opitz (eds.), *Reformierte Bekenntnisschriften*, 3 vols. in 8 (Neukirchen-Vluyn: Neukirchener Verlag, 2002–16), 2/1, 209–299. For the text in modernized spelling, see J. T. Dennison Jr (ed.), *Reformed Confessions of the Sixteenth and Seventeenth Centuries in English Translation*, 4 vols. (Grand Rapids, Mich.: Reformation Heritage Books, 2008–14), 2:186–206.

[132] Laing, *Works of John Knox*, 6:275–380.

[133] Ibid. 2:183–260.

passion, death and burial, his resurrection and ascension. Here it is to be noted that election is placed after the incarnation but before Christ's death, making it clear that he died only for the elect – a doctrine that would later come to be known as 'limited' or 'definite' atonement and would become one of the great controversies of classical Reformed theology.[134] The twelfth article is devoted to the Holy Spirit, and is noticeably fuller than what would later appear in the Thirty-nine Articles of the Church of England.[135] Articles 13–25 deal more specifically with matters that were controversial in the sixteenth century. Chief among them was the question of good works, which can be performed only under the influence of the Holy Spirit and are defined by God's commandments as revealed in the Bible. This is followed by a reassertion that God's law is perfect and that no human being is able to keep it, making any confidence in one's own works 'damnable idolatry'. Articles 16–20 deal with different aspects of the church and spiritual authority. The church is defined as the invisible body of the elect that cannot be equated with any earthly institution, and a clear distinction is made between these elect, who are eternally saved, and the reprobate, who are eternally damned – there is no room for Purgatory or for a 'second chance' after death.

Following that, the Confession outlines the criteria by which the true church can be distinguished from the false. This has to do with the preaching of the true Word of God, and the right administration of the sacraments. The Bible is the final court of appeal in such matters, but general councils of the church may also be referred to as interpreters of what these things mean in instances of controversy. Only baptism and the Lord's Supper are recognized as sacraments, with the former being applicable to infants but not the latter. Finally Article 24 expounds the role of the civil magistrate, one of whose duties is the defence of true religion, and Article 25 concludes with the promise of future judgment and the ultimate vindication of God's elect. Perhaps the most remarkable thing about the Confession, from the perspective of what would come later, is the almost complete absence of the doctrine of predestination. This is not because it was not controversial. Knox wrote a lengthy treatise in defence of it against an unnamed Anabaptist opponent, whom the historian John Strype later identified as Robert Cooke.[136] But Anabaptism was not a

---

[134] It still is, but there is no doubt that the earliest Reformed theologians taught that Christ died for the elect and not for all people indiscriminately.

[135] The Holy Spirit was not mentioned at all in the earlier Forty-two Articles, which Knox was familiar with.

[136] Laing, *Works of John Knox*, 5:21–468. Originally published at Geneva in 1560. See also J. Strype, *Ecclesiastical Memorials, Relating Chiefly to Religion, and the Reformation of It, and the Emergencies of the Church of England, Under King Henry VIII, King Edward VI, and Queen Mary I*, 3 vols. (Oxford: Clarendon Press, 1822), 2:70.

major threat in Scotland and the time had not yet come when theologians claiming to be Reformed would show equal displeasure with the doctrine. So it was left aside – at least for the moment.

The metrical psalter that the Parliament of 1560 approved is equally remarkable and its approach was to survive the test of time better than many might have imagined. The psalter had already been translated into English by Miles Coverdale, and incorporated into the English Book of Common Prayer, where it still remains. But it was a more or less literal translation that was meant to be chanted by choirs and others who were trained to do so. Then, as now, ordinary people found that difficult and few joined in. John Knox wanted full participation from the congregation, and setting the words to singable music was an obvious way to ensure that. The snag of course is that adapting the Psalms to English rhyme and metre meant changing the words, and that risked altering the sense as well. For people who believed that God spoke Hebrew, that could seem to be a step too far. What confronted the Scots was the dilemma that faces many translators – should a rendering be 'faithful' to the original, even if that sounds odd, or should it be 'contextualized', adapted to the rhythms and habits of the recipients while trying to stay as close to the original as possible?

In spite of the difficulties involved, metrical psalms proved to be very popular and some have endured to the present. Getting the right 'feel' was not always easy, nor did it come immediately, but once a satisfactory version was found it had a way of staying in people's memory. Consider for example Coverdale's translation of Psalm 23 (A) with three metrical versions, one produced by William Whittingham (c.1524–79), a close colleague of John Knox (B), one by Thomas Sternhold (1500–49) (C) and finally one by Francis Rous (c.1579–1659) (D), which was not published until 1650 but has remained in the repertoire to the present day. As it happens, all three versifiers were Englishmen, but it was in Scotland that their efforts would be most appreciated:

A: The Lord is my shepherd: therefore can I lack nothing.
He shall feed me in a green pasture: and lead me forth beside the waters of comfort.

B: The Lord is only my support
And he that doth me feed
How can I then lack anything
Whereof I stand in need?

C: My shepherd is the living Lord
Nothing therefore I need
In pastures fair, near pleasant streams
He setteth me to feed.

D: The Lord's my shepherd, I'll not want
He makes me down to lie
In pastures green he feedeth me
The quiet waters by.

A: He shall convert my soul: and bring me forth in the paths of righteousness, for his Name's sake.

B: He doth me fold in cotes most safe
The tender grass fast by
And after driveth me to the streams
Which run most pleasantly

C: He shall convert and glad my soul
And bring my mind in frame
To walk in paths of righteousness
For his most holy name.

D: My soul he doth restore again
And me to walk doth make
Within the paths of righteousness
Even for his own Name's sake.

A: Yea, though I walk through the valley of the shadow of death, I will
fear no evil: for thou art with me; they rod and staff comfort me.

B: And when I feel myself near lost
Then doth he me home take
Conducting me in his right paths
Even for his own name's sake.

And though I were even at death's door
Yet would I fear none ill
For by thy rod and shepherd's crook
I am comforted still.

C: Yea, though I walk in vale of death
Yet will I fear no ill
Thy rod and staff do comfort me
And thou art with me still.

D: Yea, though I walk through death's dark vale
Yet will I fear no ill
For thou art with me and thy rod
And staff me comfort still.

A: Thou shalt prepare a table before me against them that trouble me:
thou hast anointed my head with oil, and my cup shall be full.

B: Thou hast my table richly decked
In despite of my foe
Thou hast mine head with balm refreshed
My cup doth overflow.

C: And in the presence of my foes
My table thou shalt spread
Thou wilt fill full my cup, and thou
Anointed hast my head.

D: My table thou hast furnished
In presence of my foes
My head thou dost with oil anoint
And my cup overflows.

A: But thy loving-kindness and mercy shall follow me all the days of my
life: and I will dwell in the house of the Lord for ever.

B: And finally while breath doth last
Thy grace shall me defend
And in the house of God will I
My life for ever spend.

C: Through all my life thy favour is
So frankly showed to me
That in thy house for evermore
My dwelling place shall be.

D: Goodness and mercy all my days
Shall surely follow me
And in God's house for evermore
My dwelling place shall be.

Here we can follow how medieval chant and plainsong turned into popular hymnody. Coverdale's translation is not especially poetic but it is meant to be chanted, as it still is, mostly in 'choirs and places where they sing', as the Book of Common Prayer puts it. The early metrical versions are often somewhat awkward but they could be learned by ordinary people and sung to easily memorized tunes. In no time at all Scots were singing the psalms in many different circumstances, including demonstrations against Catholic worship. They were known by heart, and even if they were not as accurate as the formal translations that would be used in expository sermons, they became part of the spiritual furniture of generations, as Rous's translation is to this day.

The (First) Book of Discipline set out a comprehensive and somewhat idealized vision of what a Reformed church and society ought to look like.[137] Its most important provisions concerned the need for universal education. Knox believed that there should be a school in every parish and that literacy should become the norm rather than the exception. In particular he set very high standards for ministerial candidates, and tried to insist that the clergy should be properly supported from the revenues of the church. Unfortunately for him, many of the traditional sources of clerical income had been seized by lay magnates, who were unwilling to surrender them; and since their support was needed if the Reformation was to succeed, Knox was unable to press the point. Nevertheless the ideal was stated publicly and remained as a standard to aim for, even if it could not be achieved in the short term.[138]

Knox expected a great deal and we should not be surprised that he was unable to realize his vision in its entirety, but the fact that he got as far as he did was remarkable, as a comparison with England makes plain. It was not for nothing that English radicals came increasingly to look north for inspiration, and to hope that if the king of the Scots were to succeed their own queen, he would bring Scottish standards and ideals to bear on the Church of England.

---

[137] J. K. Cameron (ed.), *The First Book of Discipline* (Edinburgh: St Andrew Press, 1972); J. C. Whytock, *Continental Calvinian Influences on the Scottish Reformation: The First Book of Discipline (1560)* (Lewiston, N.Y.: Edwin Mellen Press, 2009).

[138] See Burleigh, *Church History of Scotland*, 163–177, and Donaldson, *Scottish Reformation*, 76–129. For the development of ministerial education in Scotland, see J. C. Whytock, *'An Educated Clergy': Scottish Theological Education and Training in the Kirk and Secession, 1560-1850* (Milton Keynes: Paternoster Press, 2007).

But that is to look ahead. In 1560 the Protestants were able to get away with their radical proposals because the monarchy was weak to the point of non-existence. As long as Queen Mary was in France they had little to fear, but that was about to change. King Francis II, Queen Mary's husband, died of an ear infection on 5 December 1560, and suddenly Knox's worst fears sprang to life. Mary could hardly stay in France, but the only place she could go was Scotland. So a few months later she turned up, a stranger in her native land, with no knowledge of the country and no friends she could trust to guide her through an extremely difficult political situation. Knox had seen it all before. Only eight years previously he had witnessed how Mary's cousin, another Mary as it happened, had come to the throne in England and had taken the country back to Rome. Would this dire scenario now be repeated? Mary, Queen of Scots might have been a foreigner for all practical purposes, but she was also the legitimate queen, and many in the country respected her for that reason. Even the Reformed church preached obedience to the rightful rulers, whether they were Protestants or not, so there was nothing to hope for from that quarter either.

Knox understood how high the stakes were and how easily the Reformation could have been crushed by a resurgence of traditionalism supported by a popular monarch. Mary was a devout Catholic, and did nothing to hide the fact. She demanded and was allowed to keep her own private chaplain, who celebrated Catholic mass for her and her retinue. In 1563 she even wrote to the Council of Trent, apologizing for her inability to send Scottish representatives to it and holding out the hope that she would be able to do so in the future.[139] If that was indiscreet, her personal life was a disaster. In July 1565 she married her cousin Lord Darnley, who gave her a son before the marriage broke down. Darnley blamed Mary's secretary, the Italian David Rizzio, whom he then had murdered. Not long afterwards Darnley was blown up, most likely with the connivance (or worse) of James Hepburn, the fourth Earl of Bothwell, whom Mary then married. This was one scandal too far, and before long Mary was imprisoned by her own subjects. On 23 July 1567 she abdicated in favour of her infant son and left the kingdom, casting herself on the mercy of her cousin, Queen Elizabeth of England. For the next two decades she would be at the centre of a number of intrigues designed to put her not only back on the throne of Scotland but on that of England as well. In the end Elizabeth reluctantly agreed to put her on trial and she was condemned to death, but by then Scotland was well and truly Protestant.

---

[139] See Patrick, *Statutes of the Scottish Church*, 220–221.

Mary's exile was not the end of Catholic resistance in Scotland, which was tolerated to a degree almost unheard of elsewhere. But in 1571 the Archbishop of St Andrews, who had never really accepted the Reformation, was involved in the murder of James Stewart, the king's uncle and regent. The archbishop was arrested and hanged for treason. Peace was not finally secured for a further two years, but serious resistance to the Reformation in Scotland was over. When Knox died on 24 November 1572, he knew that it had come to stay.

8

The calm before the storm (1571–1625)

The rise of Puritanism

By 1571 it seemed as though the Reformation in the British Isles was virtually over and that Protestantism had triumphed. In Scotland, John Knox was putting the finishing touches on his ecclesiastical programme, although lack of funds and lingering resistance made progress slower than he had hoped. The infant King James VI (1566–1625) was being brought up in the Reformed faith, and the Church of Scotland would do all it could to ensure that he would become a model Christian ruler when he came of age. In England, Queen Elizabeth's fence-sitting between Catholicism and Protestantism was over, thanks to papal intervention as much as anything else, and to many the time seemed ripe for the implementation of a thoroughgoing Reformation on the Scottish model. Not much was happening in Wales, which officially followed England, although there were stirrings among the gentry that would lead to the translation of the Bible into Welsh and so secure the country for Protestantism.

Ireland, as usual, was a different story. Most of the English population, the descendants of medieval settlers whom we may now call the 'Old English', were 'church papists' rather than outright recusants, and there was a chance that over time they could be won round, as many of their English counterparts would be.[1] Parts of the country were being planted with 'New English' settlers who could be relied on to be loyal to the Crown, and whose impact might eventually anglicize the native Gaelic population. There was even hope that the latter could be brought under royal control by a system of 'surrender and regrant', by which the Irish lords would abandon their Gaelic titles and customs

---

[1] A 'church papist' was someone who attended the parish church after the Reformation but who privately remained loyal to the Roman pope. On the effects of this in Ireland, see A. Ford and J. McCafferty (eds.), *The Origins of Sectarianism in Early Modern Ireland* (Cambridge: Cambridge University Press, 2005); N. Canny, *Making Ireland British 1580–1650* (Oxford: Oxford University Press, 2001). On English church papists, see A. Walsham, *Church Papists: Catholicism, Conformity and Confessional Polemic in Early Modern England* (Woodbridge: Boydell & Brewer, 1993).

and accept English ones in their stead. If they did so, they would have security of tenure, which appealed to many of them, but the English practice of primogeniture excluded younger sons and others from the same inheritance, and would create a class of resentful nobles who might easily be persuaded to rebel. There was also the unsolved question of language – would the new faith and customs be conveyed to the people in English, or would an effort be made to translate them into Irish and thus indigenize them? The future was still unclear, and it would be a generation or more before answers would be given to questions like these.

The history of the English church in the decades after 1571 is largely one of the struggle of the so-called 'Puritans' to impose their vision of Reformation on the church and extend it to the 'dark corners of the land', where traditionalism and superstition still held sway. Those who know England will not be surprised to discover that the 'dark corners' covered most of the north, a good deal of the west and south-west, and (of course) Wales and Ireland too. Then, as now, London and the south-east set the tone for the rest of the country.

What exactly was Puritanism? Differences of opinion about this have plagued accounts of the subject, and it sometimes seems as if everyone has his or her own definition of the term. As far as we can tell, the word originated as a pejorative description of those who instigated the vestiarian controversy. Their opponents thought that they were going too far in their opposition to the Elizabethan Settlement and called them idealists – or 'Puritans' as they put it. These 'Puritans' were unhappy with any compromise that smacked of the old regime and wanted what they saw as a consistently Reformed church. As the conflict over vestments demonstrates, it was not so much a question of doctrine as of appearances. To the Puritans, if a minister of the gospel looked like a pre-Reformation priest then he was a pre-Reformation priest, whatever anyone might say to the contrary. The 'Puritans' were by no means anti-intellectual, but they understood how the common people might think and wanted to make sure that the outward trappings of religion matched the faith within.[2]

Having said that, the Puritans were loyal members of the Church of England. They wanted to take the Elizabethan Settlement further and pressed the queen and government to be more consistent in their application of Reformation principles. They were not separatists or sectarians, although in later years those who were either or both of those were often labelled 'Puritans' by people who could not (or would not) distinguish them from those in the mainstream.[3] The

---

[2] See C. Hill, *Society and Puritanism in Pre-Revolutionary England* (London: Secker & Warburg, 1964).

[3] R. Martin, *A Guide to the Puritans* (Edinburgh: Banner of Truth Trust, 1997), is an excellent resource for the study of Puritanism.

Puritans, although serious, were not the killjoys of later legend. They came down heavily against swearing, brawling and other forms of antisocial behaviour, but then so did the official homilies of the church. Rural England was a peasant society full of people with crude manners, and the Puritans wanted to make them what we would now call 'middle class' or 'bourgeois' – sober, industrious and productive members of society who would prosper by hard work and dedication to the service of the common good. It was an ideal, certainly, but one they believed was achievable, and they set out to achieve it.[4]

Puritanism was above all a movement in favour of stricter church discipline. The Puritans had no quarrel with the Thirty-nine Articles of Religion or even with most of the Prayer Book, although they wanted greater flexibility in public worship and the removal of certain traditionalist features that had been retained in order to placate the conservatives. What they most objected to was the Reformation's failure to change people's lives. To put it crudely, they wanted the ancient monastic ideals of spirituality to be applied to every Christian. They believed that regular prayer and Bible reading, which had been at the centre of the monastic life, ought to become the mainstays of every Protestant. The spiritual comfort that had been derived from the sacraments and ancillary devotions was henceforth to be supplied by the faithful preaching of God's Word. In their eyes, performing rituals was relatively easy and required little education, but preaching demanded high standards of teaching and preparation. The church had to become a school of practical spirituality in which every thought and deed would be held captive to Christ and assessed by the degree to which they conformed to his Word and his will.

To those with this aim in view, vernacular liturgies and ready-made homilies were useful tools but they could only be stepping stones to what they desired. Real prayer could only come from the heart, not from a book. True preaching had to carry conviction and be applied to the hearers in a way that a prepared text was unable to do. Only a man who had had a personal experience of conversion and who possessed the spiritual gift of preaching could rise to these lofty heights, and that was the problem. Such men existed, but were few and far between. England needed at least 10,000 qualified preachers to fill its pulpits and, with the universities turning out no more than a few hundred a year (by no means all of whom were fit for the task in hand), there was a considerable mountain to climb.

---

[4] See P. Collinson, *The Elizabethan Puritan Movement* (London: Jonathan Cape, 1967; Oxford: Clarendon Press, 1990); *The Religion of Protestants: The Church in English Society 1559–1625* (Oxford: Oxford University Press, 1982).

Matters were made worse by the failure to reform the appointments system. The dissolution of the monasteries had resulted in the transfer of the advowsons of many churches to lay patrons, who 'impropriated' the tithe revenue of the parish that had formerly gone to a monastery and were expected to fund a clergyman out of it. There was no way of ensuring that this would be done properly, and the provision of adequate clerical stipends became a serious problem, especially as clergy married and had children. The Reformed ministry was a good deal more expensive than the pre-Reformation priesthood had been, but the alienation of so much church property made it hard to find the necessary funds.[5] There was also the difficulty that lay patrons of a benefice could nominate anyone they chose to fill a vacancy, and all too often their choice fell on a younger son, a family friend or someone who could pay for the privilege, with little or no regard for their academic qualifications or spiritual suitability. The result was that far too many parishes had incumbents who were not up to the job and who had no real sense of their vocation. To the Puritans this was scandalous, but little could be done about it without a root-and-branch reform of the system, and vested interests stood in the way of that.

It is often thought that Puritan feeling grew out of frustration at the limitations of the Elizabethan Settlement after 1559, but this is misleading. While it is true that Puritanism first manifested itself at that time, its roots go back to the Edwardian Reformation, and in particular to the *Reformatio Legum Ecclesiasticarum*, the reform of the canon law proposed by Thomas Cranmer but rejected by the House of Lords in 1553. In 1571, John Foxe, one of the most articulate spokesmen for the reforming party, published the *Reformatio*, bringing its disciplinary proposals to public attention for the first time. Many of them were similar and even identical to what the Puritans were proposing, which is proof that the latter were closer to the mind of Cranmer and his colleagues than they are often given credit for.[6]

When the Canterbury Convocation met in 1571, it touched up the Thirty-nine Articles, most notably by restoring Article 29 (on the unworthy reception of Holy Communion), which ten years earlier the queen had struck out because she thought it might have offended the Lutherans. That was no longer a problem in 1571, partly because the Lutherans were then divided among themselves and partly because relations between them and the Church of England had all but ceased. The Convocation also enacted a series of canons

---

[5] See C. Hill, *Economic Problems of the Church from Archbishop Whitgift to the Long Parliament* (Oxford: Clarendon Press, 1956).

[6] For the evidence, see G. L. Bray (ed.), *Tudor Church Reform* (Woodbridge: Boydell & Brewer, 2000), 150–743.

regulating the various offices of the church, starting with bishops and working down to laymen like churchwardens and patrons of livings. Of particular importance was the demand that preachers should surrender their licences and ask for new ones. This was a means of ensuring that only the right people would be allowed in the pulpit. Non-preaching ministers (of whom there were many) would have to use the homilies instead of composing their own sermons – a way of ensuring that congregations would be taught solid Reformed doctrine.[7] It was an attempt to get to grips with the problem of church discipline highlighted by the publication of the *Reformatio*, but stopping well short of the comprehensive reform of the canon law that many felt was needed.

Shortly afterwards, in 1572, an anonymous tract appeared, called *An Admonition to the Parliament*, which was composed of two parts. The first part, written by Thomas Wilcox (1549?–1608), outlined the failure of the church to carry through a thorough reform of its discipline. The second part, written by John Field (1545–88), objected to what he claimed were lingering elements of 'popery' in the Prayer Book. This *Admonition* was soon followed by a second one, which advocated the abolition of episcopacy and installation of a presbyterian form of church government. It took the Puritan message to a whole new level. It was one thing to advocate greater freedom in worship and even the appointment of elders to oversee discipline in the parish, but quite another to propose the abolition of the church's structure and its replacement by an untried system. There were many who favoured the former but recoiled from the latter and so, almost from the very beginning, a division was sown in the Puritan ranks that would never be overcome.[8]

The *Admonitions* were resisted by the church authorities but attracted some sympathy in the House of Commons, which would become the main forum for the promotion of Puritan ideas in the years ahead. The need to do something about supplying preachers was particularly acute, and in some parts of the country local clergymen took it upon themselves to organize small groups where they could preach to one another and improve their sermons. Edmund Grindal (1519–83), who succeeded Matthew Parker as Archbishop of Canterbury in 1575, was particularly supportive of them, but the queen was not. To her, any group of people meeting independently for any purpose was

---

[7] For the canons, see G. L. Bray (ed.), *The Anglican Canons, 1529–1947* (Woodbridge: Boydell & Brewer, 1998), 172–207.

[8] For the texts of the *Admonitions*, see W. H. Frere and C. E. Douglas, *Puritan Manifestoes: A Study of the Origin of the Puritan Revolt* (London: SPCK, 1907), 5–39, 81–133. The commentary to this edition is hostile to Puritanism and highly misleading at many points. For a more recent edition of the first part of the first *Admonition* in modernized spelling, see I. H. Murray, *The Reformation of the Church: A Collection of Reformed and Puritan Documents on Church Issues* (London: Banner of Truth Trust, 1965), 8–19.

a potential threat, and she ordered them to disband. Grindal protested, and in response the queen stripped him of his authority. For the rest of his life he remained archbishop but was unable to carry out his functions. The clergy interceded on his behalf but Elizabeth refused to listen, a clear sign that she was not prepared to relinquish her control of church affairs, even on a matter that appeared to be primarily about religion and not politics.[9]

Elizabeth's high-handedness with the bishops showed itself in other ways as well. When a see fell vacant, its revenues reverted to the Crown, and this became a valuable source of royal income. The see of Oxford was kept vacant for ten years (1557–67) and that of Ely for nineteen (1581–1600). Bristol was also vacant for ten years (1593–1603), and several others for two or three years between appointments.[10] The episcopate was not cut back as much as it had been in Scotland but was seriously weakened, and many cathedrals and collegiate churches fell into disrepair. Elizabeth wanted bishops in her church, but saw them as servants of the Crown, not as shepherds of the flock of Christ, an attitude that in the long run would incline more Puritans to favour presbyterianism as a way of ensuring that discipline was properly applied in the parishes.

The seeds of the presbyterian controversy were sown in the early years of the Elizabethan Settlement. It can be traced in the contrasting careers of Thomas Cartwright (c.1535–1603), England's leading advocate of a presbyterian form of church government, and his contemporary John Whitgift (1530–1604), his determined opponent who became Elizabeth I's third Archbishop of Canterbury (1583–1604) and the chief enforcer of her religious policy.[11] Both men studied at Cambridge, Cartwright at Clare and St John's Colleges, Whitgift at Queens' (briefly), and then at Pembroke and Peterhouse. Cartwright's mentor was Thomas Lever (1521–77), Master of St John's (1551–3), who left for Zurich when Mary I came to the throne. He became a prominent figure in the English Protestant diaspora, so much so that he was asked to mediate between John Knox and Richard Cox in Frankfurt, where after Knox's departure he became the congregation's chief minister. Cartwright did not leave Cambridge immediately but before long followed Lever into exile, where he was able to

---

[9] On Grindal, see P. Collinson, *Archbishop Grindal 1519–83: The Struggle for a Reformed Church* (London: Jonathan Cape, 1979).

[10] Bath and Wells (1581–4; 1590–93), Chester (1577–9), Chichester (1582–5), Salisbury (1589–91; 1596–8), Worcester (1591–3) and York (1568–70).

[11] See M. Dawley, *John Whitgift and the English Reformation* (New York, N.Y.: Charles Scribner's Sons, 1954); A. F. S. Pearson, *Thomas Cartwright and Elizabethan Puritanism 1535–1603* (Cambridge: Cambridge University Press, 1966). Also, P. Lake, chapter 'Thomas Cartwright: The Search for the Centre and the Threat of Separation', in his *Moderate Puritans and the Elizabethan Church* (Cambridge: Cambridge University Press, 1982), 77–92.

study the workings of the Swiss Reformed churches at first hand. After returning to England he became a Fellow of Trinity College, Cambridge (1562), and Lady Margaret Professor of Divinity (1569). When Elizabeth I visited Cambridge in 1564, Cartwright was enlisted to oppose a motion in a staged debate – with John Whitgift. The motion was 'monarchy is the best form of government', and it took all Cartwright's skill to oppose it without offending the queen.

Whitgift was then Lady Margaret Professor, having sat out the Marian years in Cambridge and been ordained by Richard Cox soon after the latter's appointment to the see of Ely (1559). He was the archetypal Establishment man, a stickler for law and order and a determined upholder of the Elizabethan Settlement, not so much because he agreed with it as because it was official policy. Cartwright was not bound by such scruples and in 1569 gave a lecture in which he outlined the government of the earliest churches, which he thought was presbyterian. He had derived that view from his Swiss colleagues and tried to persuade the Fellows of Cambridge of its merits. His remarks produced an uproar. Some supported him but others saw him as a troublemaker who was out to overturn the established order. Whitgift, who by this time had become Master of Trinity College, naturally sided with the latter and by the end of 1570 Cartwright had been ejected from his professorship. A couple of years later he was deprived of his college Fellowship as well, although by then he had left the country.

It is not known what role (if any) Cartwright played in the production of the *Second Admonition to the Parliament*, but when Whitgift attacked it, it was Cartwright who replied in its defence. From then on the battle lines were drawn. Cartwright did not return to England until 1585, but when he did he was arrested and imprisoned, although he was soon released thanks to the influence of sympathetic friends. By then he had become closely associated with Walter Travers (1548?–1635), who was also a Fellow of Trinity College, Cambridge, and had been driven out by John Whitgift at about the same time and for the same reasons. Travers made his way to Geneva and then travelled around the Continent until he found a post in the Netherlands, where he was ordained in the Dutch Reformed Church. Shortly after that he returned to England and became a lecturer at the Temple Church in London (1581–6). Things went fairly smoothly until Richard Hooker (1554–1600) was appointed Master of the Temple in 1585 and the two men fell out with each other, mainly over their different views of the church of Rome. Travers regarded Rome as apostate and totally unchristian, whereas Hooker thought it was a true church that had fallen into error. This difference of opinion was later interpreted as a quarrel between Puritans and so-called 'Anglicans', but that is a misperception. On most points of theology, Hooker and Travers were agreed. Their dispute was essentially about secondary matters, but it was unedifying and in 1586 Archbishop Whitgift forced Travers to resign.

By then however, the presbyterian movement was gathering steam, and in 1587 Travers wrote (or perhaps merely compiled) a Book of Discipline, which set out how a presbyterian order could function in the Church of England.[12] Needless to say, that led to another round of repression in which Travers, like Cartwright, was imprisoned for a time. But neither Travers nor Cartwright, or indeed any of their fellow Presbyterians, was trying to overthrow the established Church of England. When they realized that the church faced greater threats from a revived Catholicism on the one hand, and an increasingly militant radical separatism on the other, they willingly conformed to the episcopal order of things and caused no further trouble.[13]

One of the factors behind the rise of presbyterianism was the growing influence of Genevan Protestantism in England. This went back to John Calvin (1509–64) and the welcome he gave John Knox and his friends when they were forced to leave Frankfurt. Queen Elizabeth I never warmed to either man and remained suspicious of Geneva for the rest of her life, but that did not prevent the spread of Calvinist thought in England. One reason for this was that many English people spoke (or at least read) French, and could follow what was going on in Geneva at the popular level, as well as among the academics.[14] Calvinism was also the dominant form of Protestantism in France, which was close to England and familiar to many. But there was more to it than that. Calvin was a brilliant teacher and organizer, who had deliberately set out to provide manuals of instruction for the education of pastors. He wrote commentaries on the Bible in order to expound its meaning. He produced successive versions of a systematic theology, known to us as the *Institutes of the Christian Religion*, the structure of which resembled Peter Lombard's *Sentences*, which it replaced as a basic theological textbook. He also preached expository sermons on biblical texts, something that the first generation of English Reformers had not done.[15]

There was no theologian in England of the stature of Calvin, and his many writings filled a vacuum. Before long they were being translated into English

---

[12] For the text, see Murray, *Reformation of the Church*, 178–191.

[13] Travers became Provost and President of Trinity College, Dublin (1594–8), but after that went into semi-retirement and little more was heard of him. Cartwright too ended his days in honourable retirement.

[14] The Genevans used Latin for serious theology, as did everyone else. But the English could communicate with them in a way that they could not with the Lutherans, since at that time hardly anyone in England spoke or read German.

[15] The homilies were thematic in their presentation, not systematically expository.

on a massive scale – in fact there were more sixteenth-century translations of Calvin's Latin works into English than into any other language, including his native French. It was from Calvin that the English learned to preach the message of the Bible systematically, and it was through his *Institutes* that their minds were formed theologically. Calvin had not been a convinced presbyterian – like Luther before him, he was fairly indifferent to the structures of church government and was prepared to live with bishops, as long as they did not interfere with him. Geneva's non-episcopal system of church government predated his arrival in the city, and had come about because before the Reformation the local bishop had also been its secular ruler. The Reformation could not have happened without deposing him, but as there was no one to appoint a successor, Geneva did without one and Calvin did not bother about it one way or the other.

In this respect Calvin's successor, Theodore Beza, was different. Beza studied the scriptural evidence and could find nothing that would support the traditional threefold order of bishops, priests (presbyters) and deacons. In particular he could see no justification for an episcopal order that was set above the parish clergy and that was effectively a branch of the nobility. He did not object to having a teaching elder who would preside over a congregation and in that sense act like a bishop, but such a man should be chosen by the people and work as part of a team of elders, not rule over them in the way that the bishops of his time did. Beza developed his ideas soon after Calvin's death and communicated them in person and by correspondence with various people in England and Scotland. He later wrote a book on this subject that was translated into English by John Field, who naturally agreed with his position.[16]

Beza's opinions were very influential. His reputation was high in England, and the admiration was mutual. In 1581 he even gave the University of Cambridge an ancient Greek manuscript of the Gospels, the so-called Codex Bezae, which is still cited as an important source for establishing the original text of the New Testament. The fact that the codex had been looted from a French monastery in 1562 by a marauding band of Protestants, who had then deposited it with Beza in Geneva, was conveniently forgotten, and the Codex Bezae remains one of the treasures of the Cambridge University Library.

Beza's views might not have taken hold had it not been for other factors at work closer to home. One of the most ardent supporters of the new regime was Edward Dering (*c*.1540–76), who wrote such a stirring defence of it that the

---

[16] T. Beza, *The Judgement of a Most Reverend and Learned Man from Beyond the Seas, Concerning a Threefold Order of Bishops* (London, 1585?).

queen invited him to preach at court on 25 February 1570.[17] After praising the queen for her efforts to reform the Church of England, Dering got to the point – there was still much that was unreformed, but the queen was not doing enough to put the principles she embraced into practice. Elizabeth was reportedly so enraged that she tried to silence Dering by forbidding him to preach any more, but failed. His offending sermon – ironically dedicated to her – went through sixteen editions before his early death six years later, and was the most widely read work of its kind in sixteenth-century England. Another man who did not mince his words was Laurence Chaderton (c.1536–1640), who in 1584 became the first Master of the newly founded Emmanuel College, Cambridge. Emmanuel was to become a major centre of Puritan thought, and Chaderton set the tone by preaching a detailed and well-argued sermon on Romans 12:3–8 in which he outlined a programme for reforming the ministry of the church.[18] The sermon was printed by Robert Waldegrave (c.1554–1603), a strong supporter of Puritan reform, of whom we shall hear more.

It had long been the policy of men like Cartwright and Travers to wait until after the death of the monarch before campaigning for change in the church, a policy that was known at the time as 'tarrying for the magistrate'; that is to say, waiting for the civil government to catch up with the latest theological developments. But by the late 1580s some younger men were getting restless and decided to act on their own. They obtained a printing press, and with the help of Robert Waldegrave began to produce a number of seditious tracts, which they attributed to a fictitious 'Martin Marprelate'.[19] Despite a concerted manhunt, the government was unable to find either the printing press or the printers, and panic set in. Eventually the press was found and destroyed, but the ringleaders were never identified.

One likely culprit was Job Throckmorton (1545–1601), a Warwickshire gentleman who had strong Puritan connections, who was also a Member of Parliament in 1572 and again in 1586–7, when he made his name by advocating, among other things, the death penalty for Mary, Queen of Scots. His intemperate outbursts got him into trouble with the government, but he

---

[17] E. Dering, *A Sermon Preached Before the Queens Maiestie by Maister Edward Dering* (London: John Awdely, 1569 [1570]).

[18] L. Chaderton, *A Fruitfull Sermon upon the 3.4.5.6.7. & 8. Verses of the 12 Chapter of the Epistle of S. Paule to the Romans* (London: Robert Waldegrave, 1584).

[19] 'Martin' for Martin Luther and 'Marprelate', meaning 'bishop-slanderer' from 'mar' and 'prelate', another term for 'bishop'. For the texts, see J. L. Black, *The Martin Marprelate Tracts: A Modernized and Annotated Edition* (Cambridge: Cambridge University Press, 2008). See also W. Pierce, *An Historical Introduction to the Marprelate Tracts: A Chapter in the Evolution of Religious and Civil Liberty in England* (New York, N.Y.: E. Dutton, 1909).

escaped by leaving London before he could be arrested. He was eventually implicated in the Marprelate affair, but managed to avoid imprisonment and spent the remainder of his life in comfortable retirement. Another Puritan who moved in the same circles was the Welshman John Penry (1559–93). He escaped to Scotland when the Marprelate affair burst out into the open, but later returned to England, where he was caught, put on trial and executed. It will come as no surprise to discover that the first person to sign his death warrant was none other than John Whitgift, the ever-vigilant Archbishop of Canterbury.[20] Robert Waldegrave also escaped to Scotland but had the good sense to remain there, where he was protected by James VI until it was possible for him to return to London following the queen's death.[21]

With Penry's execution, Elizabethan Puritanism reached a turning point. Those who believed in tarrying for the magistrate kept their counsel, knowing that the queen could not live much longer, and those who could not wait tended to leave the country, finding refuge in the nearby Netherlands. These were the 'Separatists', so called because they deliberately separated themselves from the Church of England, which they regarded as irredeemably corrupt. Separatism had already been brewing for some time, and seems to have originated in the preaching ministry of Richard Greenham (1535?–94), Rector of Dry Drayton, Cambridgeshire (1570–91). Greenham, a moderate in his views who opposed the Marprelate Tracts when they appeared, attracted and influenced a number of more radical followers, including Robert Browne (1550–1633) and Robert Harrison (1550–85), who in 1582 set up an independent congregation in Norwich. They were soon being harassed by the local authorities and decided to emigrate to the Netherlands, where they established an English church in Middelburg.

They were both highly articulate and lost no time in explaining their views to a wider public. Browne published a programme for spiritual reformation and Harrison soon followed it with a resounding address to his fellow ministers in England. He challenged them to justify their practices by an appeal to Scripture, and if they could not find any warrant for them in the Bible, to change their behaviour accordingly.[22] The radicalism of the Middelburg congregation soon led to divisions within it, and Browne returned to England (by way of

---

[20] For a recent assessment of the evidence, see Black, *Martin Marprelate*, xxxiv–xlvi.

[21] Waldegrave intended to resume his publishing ministry in London but was struck down by the plague soon after his arrival and died on 22 October 1603.

[22] R. Browne, *A Booke Which Sheweth the Life and Manners of All True Christians* (Middelburg: Richard Painter [R. Schilders], 1582); R. Harrison, *A Little Treatise upon the Firste Verse of the 122.Psalm, Stirring up unto Carefull Desiring a Dutifull Labouring for True Church Governement* (Middelburg: R. Schilders, 1583).

Scotland), where he eventually conformed to the established Church, although not before giving his name to Separatism, which his contemporaries regularly referred to as 'Brownism'. Harrison stayed on in the Netherlands but died soon afterwards, leaving the Middelburgers to cope as best they could. Traffic to and from the Netherlands was not all in one direction however. A Dutch sect apparently begun by Hendrik Niclaes (c.1501–80) and supported by Christopher Vittel (fl. 1543–79), a Dutchman resident in Southwark, managed to establish itself in England, and especially in the fertile soil of Cambridgeshire, where it seems to have been centred around the village of Balsham. It was called the Family of Love and was more of a fellowship than a church in the usual sense of the term. The Familists were wise enough not to separate openly from the established Church, even though they seem to have adopted the Anabaptist practice of rejecting infant baptism. They managed to attract sympathy in high places, including at court. In fact it seems that Queen Elizabeth I knew about them and was tolerant of their activities to an astonishing degree. Apparently it was their willingness to conform to the Church of England in outward appearances that won her over, and they thrived under her protection, if not her patronage.[23]

Meanwhile other Separatist voices were starting to be heard in England. John Greenwood (1556–93) and Henry Barrow (1550–93) both began to preach a radical form of separation from the church and suffered for it even before the appearance of the Marprelate Tracts, with which they were (probably wrongly) associated.[24] Caught up in the post-Marprelate crackdown, both men were executed as 'recusants', thereby demonstrating that a law originally designed to repress Roman Catholics could equally well be used to suppress radical Protestants. Somewhat surprisingly, Robert Browne turned against them because they were less radical than he was – all three believed in independent church government, but Browne held out for direct democracy, in which every member of the congregation would have an equal voice, whereas Greenwood and Barrow preferred a system of elders. A difference of this kind would hardly be worth mentioning, except that it was exactly the sort of thing that would continue to divide independent churches and give ammunition to their opponents, who wanted law and order, however much they might have agreed theologically with the principles the independents were trying to uphold. It was a problem that would resurface throughout the seventeenth

---

[23] C. W. Marsh, *The Family of Love in English Society, 1550–1630* (Cambridge: Cambridge University Press, 1994).

[24] L. H. Carlson, *The Writings of John Greenwood and Henry Barrow, 1591–1593* (London: Allen & Unwin, 1970).

century and do great damage to the Puritan cause, and (it must be said) continues to afflict that kind of church.

Greenwood was briefly released from prison in 1592, at which time he and Francis Johnson (1562–1618) were elected as teacher and pastor respectively of the Separatist congregation in London. Renewed persecution followed however, and those who were not put in jail took ship for Amsterdam, where they regrouped in 1595 and chose Henry Ainsworth (1571–1622) as their pastor. A year later they produced a confession of faith, almost certainly written by Ainsworth, which came to be regarded as the founding document of a new type of church, known at the time as 'independent' and nowadays as 'congregational'.[25] Johnson was soon set free and joined them in the Netherlands, but eventually he and Ainsworth fell out over the question of elders. Johnson shared Greenwood's belief that every congregation should have elders, but Ainsworth sided with Browne. On 16 December 1610, Ainsworth withdrew from Johnson's group, taking a significant number of people with him, and established what became the first Independent or Congregational Church in the English-speaking world.

The Marprelate affair turned out to have more consequences than anyone could have imagined. It was the first time in England that theological discourse was conducted by widespread popular pamphlets read by large numbers of people and known by many more. The furious and prolonged reaction of the authorities suggested to many that Marprelate had something to complain about, and the suspicion grew that all was not well with the church. That feeling was only strengthened by the nature of the attacks made against the offending tracts. From the queen downwards, the biggest objection to them was that they questioned the legitimacy of the social hierarchy, which was naturally reflected in the church. It was feared that if Marprelate ideas spread, there would be a breakdown of law and order, leading to a concept of universal equality that would destroy existing society. The codeword for that was 'Anabaptism', a term taken from radical movements that appeared in Switzerland and in Germany in the 1520s and was associated in the popular mind with social revolution.[26] This analysis was flawed in the sense that the

---

[25] For the confession, see W. L. Lumpkin and B. J. Leonard, *Baptist Confessions of Faith*, 2nd edn (Valley Forge, Pa.: Judson Press, 2011), 75–91.

[26] Popular perception of the Anabaptists was often inaccurate, as modern scholars point out, but that is irrelevant to the fear 'Anabaptism' inspired, especially in England, where real Anabaptists were virtually unknown. A few refugees had arrived in England in the time of Henry VIII, who in 1535 executed fourteen of them as dangerous revolutionaries but, as they were all foreigners, they had almost no impact on English society. Anabaptists occasionally surfaced later on, but they were isolated cases. See I. B. Horst, *Radical Brethren: Anabaptists and the English Revolution to 1558* (Nieuwkoop: B. De Graaf, 1972).

English Presbyterians had no desire to level class differences, but perhaps the authorities sensed that there was something latent in their theology that had not yet been articulated properly.

That was the doctrine of predestination, which came back into prominence in the late sixteenth century and was held by many people who opposed the presbyterians, including Archbishop Whitgift. On 20 November 1595, after the Presbyterian menace had been disposed of, Whitgift issued the so-called Lambeth Articles, which were short but very much to the point when it came to predestination:[27]

1 From eternity God has predestined some humans to life and condemned others to death.

2 The moving or efficient cause of predestination to life is not the foresight of faith or of perseverance, or of good works, or of anything inherent in the persons predestined, but only the will of God's good pleasure.

3 There is a predetermined and fixed number of the predestinate which cannot be increased or diminished.

4 Those not predestined to salvation will necessarily be condemned because of their sins.

5 A true, living and justifying faith, which the Holy Spirit sanctifies, cannot be extinguished, nor can it fall away or disappear in the elect, either finally or totally.

6 The true believer, that is, one who possesses justifying faith, is certain, by the full assurance of faith, of the forgiveness of a person's sins and of eternal salvation through Christ.

7 Saving grace is not granted, communicated or given to all humans, so that they might be saved by it if they wish to be.

8 No one can come to Christ unless it is given to him [or her] [to come], and unless the Father draws him [or her], and not all humans are drawn by the Father to come to the Son.

9 It is not placed in the will or power of any and every person to be saved.

It would be difficult to find a more uncompromising statement of predestination than this one, and it is all the more remarkable in that it came from the leading anti-Puritan of the time. The key is the connection in Article 6 between predestination and assurance. Predestination is not just a fact hidden

---

[27] The Articles were issued in Latin and English. See G. L. Bray (ed.), *Documents of the English Reformation*, 3rd edn (Cambridge: James Clarke, 2019), 359–360.

in the mind of God but something that true believers know in their own experience. Armed with that assurance, anything is possible, and this was the true power of so-called 'Calvinism'. The electing grace of God is no respecter of persons, and his sovereign choice cannot be thwarted by merely human criteria like social hierarchy. It does not matter whether you are a nobleman or a peasant: if God has chosen you, then you are free to serve him as he pleases and nobody will be able to stand in your way. Whitgift would doubtless have been horrified if he had been told that a penniless tinker from Bedford would one day be called by God to rise up and challenge bishops and kings alike, but that is what John Bunyan (1628–88) would do only a generation after Whitgift's death. When that happened, the result would change Britain, and indeed the world, at least as much, and perhaps more, than the original Reformation had done.

The Catholic opposition

If it took some time for Protestant opposition to the Elizabethan Settlement to crystallize, the Catholic reaction to it was much swifter. At Elizabeth's accession almost all the bishops and a large number of Fellows in Oxford and Cambridge colleges were loyal to the Roman church, and in particular to the reforming policies of the Council of Trent. Elizabeth deprived them of their posts and some ended up in prison, but none was put to death and most were soon released. The deposed bishops went into retirement but a number of the academics left the country, mainly for what was then still the Spanish Netherlands. There they regrouped and made plans for the reconquest of England for what they regarded as the true faith. One of them was Thomas Harding (1516–72) of Oxford. Harding had originally accepted the Reformation, but when Mary I came to the throne he declared himself a Catholic and subsequently became an articulate opponent of John Jewel and his defence of the Church of England. He wrote no fewer than six books against Jewel, of which the best known is his attack on the *Apologia*.[28] Harding often scored on points, picking Jewel up for sloppy or inaccurate references to his source material, and Jewel had little choice but to correct his errors in subsequent editions of his work. But on Jewel's main argument, Harding failed to make an impression, and that was typical of the Catholic scholars' approach. Thomas Stapleton (1535–98) was another Catholic refugee who supported Harding in print, and even translated Bede's *Ecclesiastical History* as a reminder to Elizabeth I of the

---

[28] T. Harding, *An Answer to Maister Juelles Chalenge* (Louvain: John Bogard, 1564).

ancient tradition that the Church of England was supposedly abandoning, but the results were similar. These men were traditionalists who took refuge in the past, not visionaries with a viable plan for the future.

One of the most prominent Catholic exiles was William Allen (1532–94), a Lancashire man educated at Oriel College, Oxford. After some hesitation, he went to Louvain but was soon back in his native Lancashire, where he imagined that the local population was so discontented with the change of religion that it was ready to rise in revolt against the new queen. He did his best to organize such opposition but was soon detected and forced to leave the country again in 1565. He went to Douai, where he founded an English College in 1568 and then on to Rome, where he did the same thing.

Allen believed that the campaign to re-Catholicize England had to be both intellectual and political at the same time. He was an enthusiastic supporter of the papal bull *Regnans in Excelsis* and lost no time in training priests to send into England, knowing full well that they were courting death for treason. For Allen and his colleagues of course, these men were martyrs, and some of them were canonized as such as recently as 1970, much to the displeasure of many English Protestants, who claimed that they were executed for political, not religious, reasons. Opinions are bound to differ on such a delicate subject, but there can be no doubt that Allen knew what he was doing. Along with most of his colleagues, he was eagerly anticipating the death of the queen and the expected succession of the Catholic Mary, Queen of Scots. Allen was not directly involved in the many plots against Elizabeth I's life but his sympathies were clear, and when a Spanish invasion of England became a strong possibility he was openly supportive of it.

Before then however, he was active on another front. This was in the translation of the Bible, which the exiles undertook. The New Testament was published at Reims (Rheims) in 1582, but it would be another twenty-seven years before the entire Bible appeared at Douai (Douay), by which time Allen was dead. The Catholic translation of the Bible was a disaster. There were already several English versions available, although of course they were Protestant and therefore unacceptable to people like Allen. But with the appearance of the Geneva Bible and its subsequent revisions, a text based on the most recent scientific principles was readily available, and the standard of English used was high. Translation was not a simple matter, not least because English had never been used for theological discourse and was lacking in appropriate vocabulary. Sometimes the translators simply adapted Latin words, like 'circumcision', because there did not seem to be a readily available English equivalent. But other times they made an effort to create or adapt existing English words to convey the desired meaning. Some of these were very successful, like 'gospel' for the Greek *euangelion*. How many English people were aware that 'gospel' was an abbreviation of 'good spell' or that 'spell' meant good 'message' is hard to say, but the word caught on and is universally used today. Another word like that is 'atonement' (at-one-ment), used to mean 'reconciliation'.

Perhaps the best of these coinages was 'Passover'. Faced with the Hebrew *pēsaḥ* and the Greek *pascha*, which was just an adaptation of the Hebrew and not a translation, William Tyndale was faced with a dilemma. Could he have said 'pasch', or perhaps 'pascha'? Rather than do that, he looked for an English word that does not translate the Hebrew but rather sounds reasonably like it and conveys a similar meaning. That was how he came up with 'Passover', which is a marvellous description of the Jewish feast that celebrates the night when the angel of death 'passed over' the houses of the Hebrews in Egypt. The snag is that it cannot be used for the Christian *pascha*, which is not a passing over in that sense. Unfortunately we are stuck with 'Easter', a pagan name for the goddess of the east (the rising sun), which has no Christian associations at all. Almost nobody notices this now, but for those who are theologically sensitive it can be something of an embarrassment, particularly when a Greek word like Pentecost has been taken over without difficulty.[29]

The Catholic translators of the New Testament rejected all this. They were mainly concerned to translate the Latin Vulgate, not the original Greek, because that is what the Council of Trent had decreed, but they were prepared to appeal to the Greek when it seemed to support Catholic doctrine better than the Latin translation did.[30] They also wanted their English to be as Latinate as possible, especially when the words involved had doctrinal implications:

> we say, *The advent of our Lord* and *imposing of hands*, because one is a solemn time, the other a solemn action in the Catholic Church; to signify to the people that these and suchlike names come out of the very Latin text of the Scripture. So did *penance, doing penance, chalice, priest, deacon, traditions, altar, host* and the like (which we exactly keep as Catholic terms) proceed even from the very words of Scripture.[31]

---

[29] 'Pentecost' means 'fiftieth' in Greek because it is the fiftieth day after Easter. In popular English it is also called 'Whitsun' (white Sunday) because of the liturgical colour traditionally worn on that day. The Catholic translators were well aware of this. See Bray, *Documents*, 352–353.

[30] Ibid. 342–343, 349–350.

[31] Ibid. 353.

It is clear from this that sixteenth-century Catholic doctrine was used as the criterion for determining what the most acceptable translation of a first-century text would be, an unhistorical approach that no modern scholar would ever consider. In some places the desire to stay as close to the Latin as possible produced phrases virtually incomprehensible in English. For example, Ephesians 6:12, which in the King James (Authorized) version of 1611 reads, 'against spiritual wickedness in high places', the men of Reims translated as: 'against the spiritual of wickedness in the celestials', whatever that is supposed to mean. The reality is that the Reims New Testament is almost unreadable, and we should not be surprised to discover that very few people ever tried to read it.[32] David Daniell, the acknowledged authority on English translations of the Bible, summed up the preface, in which Gregory Martin (c.1542–82), the chief translator, explained his motives and methods as follows:

> this is one of the most extraordinary documents in the history of Bible translating. There is nothing like it anywhere else. Large parts of the twenty-six pages are written in bile. To find a way through the maze of Latinate clauses is hard enough, without the way being made so unpleasant. As well as playing the deafening music of a whole brass band of self-righteousness in his constant assertion of the correctness of the Church and the Fathers, Martin harps on one string, of his detestation of Reformation scholars, particularly Beza, until the eyes and ears protest.[33]

The failure of the Catholic translation of the New Testament was matched by the fate of the Spanish Armada six years later. King Philip II of Spain, Elizabeth I's one-time brother-in-law, was convinced that she was aiding the Dutch rebels who were trying to free the Netherlands from his rule. Her execution of Mary, Queen of Scots in 1587 provided an excellent excuse for him to intervene in English affairs and eliminate that source of hostility to his and the Catholic cause. William Allen was right behind the project, and would probably have secured high office in the Church of England had the Armada succeeded, but it was not to be. The Armada struck bad weather in the English Channel, its galleys could not be easily manoeuvred in the narrow straits, and the fleet scattered. Elizabeth was saved by the 'Protestant wind', as it came to be known, and a cult grew up around her as the Virgin Queen, a secular counterpart to the suppressed devotion once offered to the Virgin Mary, queen

---

[32] See D. Daniell, *The Bible in English* (New Haven, Conn.: Yale University Press, 2003), 358–368.
[33] Ibid. 367. For the complete text, see Bray, *Documents*, 327–356.

of heaven. So strong was this that when English settlers in the new world named their colony after her they called it Virginia, a name it still retains.

It was both a spiritual and a political defeat for the Catholic cause, but they did not give up just yet. In 1605 a Catholic conspirator by the name of Guy Fawkes tried to blow up Parliament, but the plot was detected just in time, and ever since then Fawkes's failure has been an integral part of English folklore – Bonfire Night, the fifth of November, which is the anniversary of that great event. There was also the final completion of the English Old Testament in 1609, named after the English College at Douai.[34] It was the last gasp of a dying movement. English Catholicism did not disappear, but it became a marginal force and ceased to have any serious impact on English society. When the Civil War broke out in the 1640s and innumerable sects appeared to contest the religious battleground, the English Catholics were nowhere to be seen. Those who survived lay low, aware that they were no longer part of the national conversation (if it can be called that) on religion, and that while they might attract some sympathy from the Catholic powers abroad, it was unlikely to translate into anything like a new Armada. Not until the middle of the nineteenth century would Roman Catholicism reappear as a serious force in English society, and by then the conditions in which it would assert its presence were very different from what they had been 250 years earlier.

The Church of England: a fragile consensus (1571–1603)

The declining years of Queen Elizabeth I appeared to be a time of relative peace and quiet. The Presbyterian and Catholic threats had been seen off, the queen was secure on her throne, it was becoming daily more apparent that James VI of Scotland, a clear and well-educated Protestant, would succeed her, and the government of the Church of England was in safe hands. A rising star was Richard Bancroft (1544–1610), who on 9 February 1589 preached a rousing sermon at Paul's Cross in London in which he denounced the Puritans in almost violent terms and laid out the first detailed case for the 'divine right' of episcopacy.[35]

---

[34] For the preface, see ibid. 360–371. It was just as bad as the Reims New Testament, and for the same reasons. In the eighteenth century, Bishop Richard Challoner (1691–1781), a convert to Rome from the Church of England, revised the text of both translations to make it read more like the King James (Authorized) Version of 1611, and that revision constitutes the Douai (or Douay) version read today.

[35] Paul's Cross was an outdoor pulpit in the courtyard of the cathedral, where prominent preachers were accustomed to proclaim the official interpretation of God's Word to the passers-by. The evidence for the surviving sermons is found in M. MacLure, P. Pauls and J. C. Boswell (eds.), *Register of Sermons Preached at Paul's Cross 1534–1642* (Ottawa: Dovehouse Editions, 1989).

It was so extreme that it alarmed the government, who thought it was an attack on the royal supremacy, but Bancroft was able to reassure them that it was not, and after that went from strength to strength. In 1597 he was made Bishop of London and succeeded John Whitgift as archbishop when the latter died in 1604.

This was also the time when Richard Hooker published the first four (of eight) volumes of his *Laws of Ecclesiastical Polity*, an extensive argument in favour of the Elizabethan Settlement that some have regarded as the constitution of the Church of England and even as the basic theological justification for Anglicanism.[36] That view, promoted in recent times mainly by American Episcopalian scholars, is now widely rejected, but has led to a distorted understanding of the period, contributing in particular to a false estimation of the Puritans as anti-Anglican.[37] Where Hooker differed from the Puritans was in his commitment to the Elizabethan Settlement of 1559, which he defended because it was the law of the land. From that perspective, Catholics and Puritans were both 'Dissenters', although for very different reasons. Hooker opposed the Catholics on both doctrine and practice, but opposed the Puritans on practice only – their doctrine was to all intents and purposes identical with his.

Richard Hooker's place in the history of English Christianity is controversial and difficult to assess objectively. Bradford Littlejohn has navigated these treacherous waters better than most and has shown that Hooker must be seen basically as a Reformed writer who wanted to insist that civil government was just as subject to the rule of Christ as that of the church was, and that if Puritan ideas were allowed to go unchecked, the freedom of the Christian would be imperilled. Either the church would become a tyranny, imposing what it saw as 'biblical' norms on society and claiming that, because those norms were the will of God, no change or development of them was possible, or church and state would move apart from each other, and Christian values

---

[36] W. S. Hill (ed.), *The Folger Library Edition of the Works of Richard Hooker*, 7 vols., vols. 1–5 (Cambridge, Mass.: Belknap Press of Harvard University); vol. 6 (Binghamton, N.Y.: Medieval Texts and Renaissance Texts and Studies); vol. 7 (Tempe, Ariz.: Medieval Texts and Renaissance Studies, 1977–98). There is an extensive secondary literature on Hooker. See esp. R. K. Faulkner, *Richard Hooker and the Politics of a Christian England* (Berkeley, Calif.: University of California Press, 1981); N. Atkinson, *Richard Hooker and the Authority of Scripture, Tradition and Reason* (Carlisle: Paternoster Press, 1997); B. Secor, *Richard Hooker, Prophet of Anglicanism* (London: Burns & Oates, 1999); N. Voak, *Richard Hooker and Reformed Theology: A Study of Reason, Will and Grace* (Oxford: Oxford University Press, 2003); W. B. Littlejohn and S. N. Kindred-Barnes, *Richard Hooker and Reformed Orthodoxy* (Göttingen: Vandenhoeck & Ruprecht, 2017); A. Dominiak, *Richard Hooker: The Architecture of Participation* (London: T&T Clark, 2020).

[37] For the origin of that view of Hooker, see M. Brydon, *The Evolving Reputation of Richard Hooker: An Examination of Responses 1600–1714* (Oxford: Oxford University Press, 2006). The inadequacy of this approach was demonstrated by P. Lake, *Anglicans and Puritans? Presbyterianism and English Conformist Thought from Whitgift to Hooker* (London: Allen & Unwin, 1988).

would cease to govern wider society.[38] Hooker believed that human reason was guided and corrected by biblical revelation, and that in submission to Christ it was capable of devising a legal order in which the conscience of individuals could be reconciled with obedience to state authority for the advancement of the common good.

Within the church, public rites and ceremonies ought to reflect the spiritual principles of the gospel. This did not mean that the sacraments (for example) confer divine grace, as Roman Catholics taught, but that they bear witness to it and teach us what the gifts of the Holy Spirit will do in the lives of those who receive them. It was the duty of the civil magistrate to further this purpose by establishing an ecclesiastical order conducive to it. In this respect Hooker could justly claim to be following the principles laid down by the first English Reformers a generation before.

The problem for Hooker was that the state and church authorities of his time were enjoining conformity to rules and regulations that did not obviously further this stated aim. In the eyes of men like John Whitgift and Richard Bancroft, conformity to the established order was right because it had been imposed by authority, not because of its intrinsic merits. Hooker could advance the principle that the outward forms of worship ought to reflect inward principles of the gospel, but in the situation that he found himself in he was forced to justify the existing system, whether it reflected that principle or not. His Puritan opponents knew that in some respects it did not, because the Elizabethan Settlement was an attempt to comprehend both Catholic and Reformed sensibilities and was therefore offensive to those who believed that all traces of Catholicism ought to be abolished.

It is probable that if the 'remnants of popery', as these Catholic elements were termed, had been done away with by lawful state authority, Hooker would have been quite happy to go along with the decision, but the queen would not deviate from her Settlement, and so that resolution of the difficulty was not adopted. Hooker's theoretical constitution of church–state relations was not practical politics, nor did it ever become a realistic option. Later admirers, who looked back to him for their inspiration, were fighting against the tide and, try as they did, they could not resurrect the ideal they imagined lay at the heart of 'Anglicanism'.

In 1597 the Convocation of Canterbury authorized a new set of canons for the church, and for the first time in her reign the queen agreed to sign them,

---

[38] W. B. Littlejohn, *The Peril and Promise of Christian Liberty: Richard Hooker, the Puritans, and Protestant Political Theology* (Grand Rapids, Mich.: Eerdmans, 2017).

giving them the force of law. It was an indication that she felt that the church was secure enough for her to allow some modifications to her Settlement – quite an achievement after nearly forty years of resistance to any change at all. The canons were essentially an upgraded version of others that had been issued in 1584, so in effect the queen was approving them retrospectively.[39] As usual, they dealt with the reform of particular abuses. Careful attention was paid to the institution of clergy in benefices where the scope for corruption was great. Nobody was to be instituted unless he was properly qualified – and the benefice was vacant – nor was anyone to hold more than one benefice at a time without special dispensation. Incumbents were expected to reside on their livings and perform their duties. Marriages were not normally to be solemnized without the publication of banns, nor were sentences of annulment or separation to be granted without careful investigation of the circumstances. Excommunication was to be pronounced only by a bishop or commissary in holy orders acting at his direction, and due penitence was to be exacted, not commuted to a fine. This was a demand of the Puritans, who wanted to see discipline exercised and resented the way in which those who could afford it often escaped their punishment by making a cash payment in lieu. The canons also show concern for the keeping of parish registers, which by now were common everywhere, and for sending transcripts of them to the diocesan office. This last provision has had the effect of preserving records of baptisms, marriages and burials in cases where the parish registers are defective and so has been of particular usefulness to modern genealogists in search of their ancestors.[40]

Why Elizabeth decided to sign these canons is not clear. She knew her end was approaching, and perhaps she wanted to insure her legacy against what might happen when her successor took the throne. If so, she need not have worried. When she died on 24 March 1603, the Crown passed to James VI of Scotland, now James I of England and Ireland as well, and the British Isles were finally united under a single ruler, one who was determined to protect his inheritance and integrate his three kingdoms as much as he could.[41] Elizabeth would have been pleased.

An important feature of the late Elizabethan period was the growing interest in preaching and the considerable improvement in its quality. There were still a number of parish priests who were unable to preach or who could not do it

---

[39] The royal seal of approval also extended them to the province of York, although the northern convocation never approved them directly. The inclusion of York without its consent would be challenged a few years later, and it did not become a habit.

[40] For the text of the canons, see Bray, *Anglican Canons*, 232–257.

[41] For a general introduction to religious policy under the Stuarts, see J. Spurr, *The Post-Reformation 1603–1714* (Harlow: Pearson, 2006).

satisfactorily, and many laypeople were unhappy with that. There was also a growing number of university graduates who were unable to find a suitable living but who needed something to do. A solution was found in the development of lectureships. What happened was that laypeople in a parish were allowed to invite a 'lecturer', that is to say a preacher, who would offer sermons in addition to the worship services of the church. Normally these lectures would take place after the morning service, and attendance at them was encouraged. However, there was a problem. For generations it had been the custom of parishioners to socialize with one another on Sundays after church, the only time in the week when most of them had the leisure and opportunity to do so. Traders would turn up with their wares to sell, and the men would be encouraged to buy beer from the church. The money earned from these 'church ales', as they were called, was intended to go to the repair of the church building, so the parish had a direct interest in keeping the ale on tap.

When the men were sufficiently merry, they would pick up a ball and either kick or bat it around in improvised games that are the direct ancestors of several modern sports. Unfortunately these activities ate into the time reserved for the lecturers, and a tug of war developed at parish level. The lecturers, virtually all of whom were Puritans, discovered that respecting the Sabbath was not merely a question of 'rest', which might include recreation, but of holy living, which meant devoting time to study. Sunday trading and Sunday sports were ungodly activities that had to be suppressed so that true religion could be taught. This was the origin of Sabbatarianism, a peculiarly British phenomenon that remained characteristic until the late twentieth century and has only disappeared (more or less) under the pressures of modern life in the past generation.

One of the best-known lecturers was William Perkins (1558–1602), a Fellow of Christ's College, Cambridge, who in 1594 was appointed to the church of St Andrew the Great, just across the street. Perkins was a highly gifted theological teacher and biblical expositor. His sermons on Galatians are among the earliest (and best) examples of systematic preaching in English, and they were widely circulated. Perkins died after reaching the first verse of the last chapter, but the series was completed by Ralph Cudworth (1617–88) and the sermons are now once more available as part of his complete works.[42] The achievement of Perkins inspired a whole generation and took English preaching to a new

---

[42] William Perkins, *The Works of William Perkins*, 10 vols. (Grand Rapids, Mich.: Reformation Heritage Books, 2014–20). On Perkins, see W. B. Patterson, *William Perkins and the Making of a Protestant England* (Oxford: Oxford University Press, 2014); R. A. Muller, *Grace and Freedom: William Perkins and the Early Modern Reformed Understanding of Free Choice and Divine Grace* (Oxford: Oxford University Press, 2020).

level. His example was copied everywhere and the result was a golden age of the English pulpit that would not be seen again until the nineteenth century.

Perkins was a great preacher but he was also a considerable theologian and philosopher, more distinguished in many ways than his contemporary Richard Hooker and unjustly neglected by posterity. Perkins defended the Elizabethan Settlement against the Separatists, but he was also a moderate Puritan, hoping that the necessary reforms more radical colleagues proposed would be enacted in due course. Above all, Perkins was a doctor of the soul, concerned with questions of conscience and of social justice to a degree rare in his time. That would appeal to many people today, if only they were aware of his interest in such questions.[43] This is a man whose rediscovery is long overdue.

Another great preacher of a slightly later time was Richard Sibbes (1577–1635), whose sermons are full of warm-hearted exhortations to Christian fellowship and concentrate on the mystical experience of union with Christ to a degree that was unusual in his time. Like Perkins, Sibbes remained loyal to the Church of England throughout his career, although he lived long enough to see the storm clouds gathering on the horizon.[44]

To seventeenth-century observers who looked back on late Elizabethan England, the church at that time appeared to have enjoyed a harmonious unity. Troublemakers were few and for the most part they were effectively marginalized. Ordinary English people adjusted to the Reformation, and what had gone before it was largely forgotten. Catholicism was the religion of persecutors, either under Mary I, her husband Philip II of Spain (who lived until 1598) or successive rulers of France, which was consumed by a seemingly endless series of civil wars rooted in religion. Foreign Protestants were admired and supported in their struggles, but while England adopted the theology of Geneva it reserved the right to go its own way on matters of church government, and nobody much minded. Yet barely a generation later the apparent calm of those years had been shattered and the country was at war with itself. How had that happened? Was the Elizabethan Settlement a model for all time, or had it been no more than a transitional phase, given an artificial air of permanence by the queen's long life and determination not to change anything of significance in the religious compromise that she had brokered at the beginning of her reign?

---

[43] Patterson, *William Perkins*, 90–113, 135–167.
[44] R. Sibbes, *Complete Works of Richard Sibbes*, ed. A. B. Grosart, 7 vols. (Edinburgh: J. Nicol, 1862–4; repr. Edinburgh: Banner of Truth Trust, 1983); M. Dever, *Richard Sibbes: Puritanism and Calvinism in Late Elizabethan and Early Stuart England* (Macon, Ga.: Mercer University Press, 2000).

The Reformation in Wales

When Henry VIII broke with the papacy in 1534, Wales was still a patch-work of different jurisdictions, some directly under the Crown and others belonging to what were called the 'marcher lordships', semi-independent fiefdoms granted to noble families who were supposed to guarantee law and order. The church however was part of the province of Canterbury and therefore intimately connected to England. The problem was that it was not entirely clear whether legislation passed by an English Parliament that affected the church would have legal force in Wales, which was not represented in that body. This difficulty was resolved by annexing Wales to England in 1536, after which it would be a full participant in English affairs. Of course, annexation did not change anything on the ground. Wales was still very poor and very conservative. Most of the population spoke Welsh but not English, making translations into the 'vernacular' somewhat problematic. When the Bible and liturgy were produced in English, the Welsh dioceses had to accept them, but for most of the people they were just as foreign and incomprehensible as their Latin predecessors had been.

As far as the broad lines of the Reformation went, the situation in Wales was virtually indistinguishable from that in England.[45] The monasteries were dissolved and the churches reordered according to the injunctions that emanated from the king, although there were many parishes where the latter were not fully implemented. The Tudors were of Welsh descent, after all, and loyalty to them was strong – in sharp contrast to Ireland. When Catholicism was restored under Mary I, the Welsh went along with it and there has been some suggestion that if Mary had lived longer, Catholicism might have taken hold in the country. But she did not, and when Elizabeth I came to the throne, Wales conformed once again, despite considerable opposition from the bishops and some of the more influential nobility. The path towards acceptance of the new state of affairs was smoothed by the practice of appointing Welshmen to Welsh bishoprics. This had begun under Mary, but of the sixteen men Elizabeth nominated for Welsh sees, no fewer than thirteen were indigenous to the country.[46]

The Church undertook a visitation of the four Welsh dioceses in order to sound out what was going on in them, but the results were inconclusive. It appears that most laypeople had no opinions at all or, if they did, were too

---

[45] See G. Williams, *Wales and the Reformation* (Cardiff: University of Wales Press, 1999); G. Williams, *Renewal and Reformation Wales c. 1415–1642* (Oxford: Oxford University Press, 1993).
[46] Williams, *Wales and the Reformation*, 224.

cautious to express them, and the same was probably true of the clergy also. A few diehard opponents of the Reformation were expelled, but otherwise not much changed and some clergy survived in spite of everything. Dr Ellis Price was the rector of three parishes in St Asaph from 1538 to 1594, but his longevity was matched, and even exceeded, by Hugh Puleston, Vicar of Wrexham from 1520 to 1566, and John Griffith, who served at Llysfaen from 1524 to 1587. William Leveson, the Archdeacon of Carmarthen, was classed as a Catholic in 1559 but survived in his parish until his death in 1583, although everyone knew where his sympathies lay and he was even publicly denounced for his church papistry.[47]

One of the explanations for this situation was that there were very few clergy in Wales at all, and the Church could not afford to lose them. In particular there was a great shortage of preachers, which was not helped by the lack of a Bible or Prayer Book in the native language. This defect was quickly noted and a small group of Welsh Protestants, led by Richard Davies (c.1505–81) and William Salesbury (c.1520 – c.1584), were soon on to the case. Salesbury began to translate a few texts, and on 12 November 1561 Thomas Davies, the new Bishop of St Asaph, ordered that the Epistle and Gospel were to be read in Welsh as well as in English, along with the Litany and Catechism.[48] Momentum was gathering apace, and in 1563 Parliament passed an act demanding that the Bible and Prayer Book should be made available in Welsh by 1 March 1565 at the latest.

The deadline proved to be too ambitious, but the intention that lay behind it was not forgotten or neglected. As Glanmor Williams has remarked:

> The Act was one of tremendous importance for Wales. For the first time it gave official sanction and a specific mandate for a Welsh Bible. That represented a major reversal of policy on the part of the government in relation to the language of public worship in Wales, and it promised to overcome what had hitherto been the biggest hindrance to the progress of the Reformation there. Its prime concern was to help convert the Welsh more speedily to the Protestant faith, and thereby to achieve greater political cohesion, not to save the Welsh language, though in due course it would accomplish that as well.[49]

There then followed a comedy of errors of a kind that serves to remind us that the will of God cannot be thwarted by human folly. The Welsh bishops

---

[47] Ibid. 225–228.
[48] Ibid. 236.
[49] Ibid. 239.

were unenthusiastic about the project and only Edmund Grindal, then Bishop of London, really supported it. Wales had no printing press, so the texts had to be printed in London, typeset by men who had no knowledge of the language. The Act made no provision for financial assistance with the cost, which was higher than it would have been had the books been printed locally, and the work was held up because of that. Most importantly of all, the translators had to have an excellent command not only of the original languages of the Scriptures but also of their own Welsh tongue, which was rich in oral poetry but rather deficient in prose works, which were in any case difficult to obtain. In a country of only 250,000 people, this was a tall order and the few men who could be found to dedicate themselves to the task were run off their feet. But the miracle occurred. Against all the odds, Wales managed to produce translators of high calibre who cooperated with one another (by no means a given in the sixteenth century) and produced a New Testament and Prayer Book ready for use in 1567, only two years later than the official deadline.[50] The quality of the language was uneven, ranging from a high literary style, which few ordinary people could understand, to local dialect, which was virtually incomprehensible outside its native area. But even so, texts in Welsh were now available, and the only way forward was up.

Catholic recusancy was not unknown in Wales, and after the papal excommunication of the queen it raised its head more boldly, as it did in England, but to little effect.[51] To the Catholic world, Wales was a sideshow and the Welsh were unpopular among the English exiles in the Spanish Netherlands. Perhaps most seriously of all, the Welsh recusants generally misread their compatriots' conservatism. Welsh people were traditionalists but not necessarily attached to the papacy, and they were generally resistant to the post-Tridentine reforms being pushed in Rome. On the other hand they were loyal to the queen and trusted her to keep the peace, which she did throughout her reign. They might not have been particularly enthusiastic about Protestantism, but they wanted a quiet life, and in the late sixteenth century it was the Elizabethan Settlement that provided it.

However, the real triumph of the late Elizabethan period was the completion of the Welsh Bible. Davies and Salesbury had embarked on the Old Testament but they had fallen out with each other, and the work on it ground to a halt. We do not know what the cause of their quarrel was, but it might have had something to do with Salesbury's quirky use of the Welsh language, which

---

50 Ibid. 239–244.
51 Ibid. 259–279.

often made it incomprehensible.[52] A new departure was required, and it came from William Morgan (1545–1604). Morgan was a bilingual scholar who went to St John's College, Cambridge, in 1565. At that time St John's was in the forefront of both English Protestantism and classical learning, and Morgan imbibed both. He was also fortunate enough to make lifelong friends in Cambridge, many of them fellow Welshmen, who would be his most loyal supporters in later life.[53] Morgan was ordained at Ely in 1568 but soon returned to Wales, where he served in a number of parishes in different parts of the country before taking up residence at Llanrhaeadr-ym-Mochnant in 1578. It was there that his most important life's work was done, but it was not without opposition from the locals. One in particular, a choleric barrister by the name of Ifan Maredudd, was to be a thorn in Morgan's side throughout his ministry in Llanrhaeadr. But Morgan was determined not to let that deflect him from his declared aim to translate the Bible, and there are indications that the enmity he faced was in fact a spur to further labours to that end.

It seems to have been in 1579, when Morgan was engaged in litigation with his parishioners, that he met John Whitgift, who was then Bishop of Worcester and president of the Council of the Marches, the body before which Morgan was pleading his case. Whitgift took to Morgan immediately and gave him every encouragement to carry on with his work. Not only did he have to render the Old Testament into Welsh from scratch, but he had to undertake a thorough revision of the New Testament and of the Prayer Book as well. The latter proved to be too much in the short time available, and it would not be until 1599 that he was finally able to publish a satisfactory Welsh Prayer Book, but the priority he gave to the Bible paid off. With the help of friends who knew the original languages better than he did, and the advice on Welsh style he received from local bards and others, Morgan achieved the impossible. On 22 September 1588 the Privy Council wrote to the four Welsh bishops to tell them that the Welsh Bible was now in print and they were to ensure that copies were placed in their parish churches as soon as possible. As always, that took longer than expected, but the desired result was eventually achieved and Morgan's Bible became the Welsh equivalent of the King James Version in English. In literary terms, Morgan was Wales's Tyndale, the man who exploited the hidden resources of his native tongue for the glory of God. When his translation appeared, all opposition to him melted away and he was hailed as a literary genius, a status that the passage of time has confirmed. Morgan was not perfect

---

[52] Ibid. 339–340.
[53] Ibid. 342–360.

and his Welsh is now outdated, but his reputation lives on and the survival and vigour of the Welsh language is one of his greatest legacies to his people.

The 1588 Bible was soon being revised. The appearance of the King James Version in 1611 allowed the Welsh to make comparisons with their own translation and improve it accordingly. This was done mainly by Richard Parry (1560–1623) and his brother-in-law, John Davies of Mallwyd (1567–1644), and their version was published in 1620, to be followed the next year by a revised Prayer Book. The Prayer Book was subsequently altered slightly, following the changes made in 1662, but the Bible remained unchanged until it was replaced as recently as 1988.[54] After 1620 the Welsh dioceses settled down as an integral part of the Church of England. In the troubles of the next generation, Wales mostly sided with the king and Puritanism had little impact. The country went back to being a backwater, and so it would largely remain for the next century or more.

Scotland between England and Geneva (1572–1603)

To understand what happened in Scotland in the late sixteenth century, and the impact that events there would later have on England, we must go back to the fundamental outlook of the first Scottish Reformers. When John Knox and his colleagues brought the Reformation to Scotland, their main aim was to reshape its church in the image of the Church of England as Knox had known it under Edward VI. They believed that a godly king should govern it, along with bishops appointed by him and clergy ordained by them. This view was based on the belief that church and state were two aspects of a single body politic in which everyone was called to worship the same God in the same way. Unfortunately for them, the Scottish situation differed in certain fundamental respects from the English one, which made this plan difficult (if not impossible) to put into practice. One big difference between England and Scotland was that whereas the English Reformation had been initiated by the king and was to a large extent controlled by him, the Scottish one was more like a rebellion against the Crown. Scotland found itself in the position of having a monarch who was fundamentally at odds with the church, which forced its Reformers to adopt a different strategy from the one pursued in England. In order to counter the opposition that it was bound to face, the church established a General Assembly,

---

54 For the history of the Welsh Bible and its reception, see E. White, *The Welsh Bible* (Stroud: Tempus, 2007).

which in many respects acted like a shadow parliament. It seems that this was initially envisaged as a temporary expedient, until such time as the Crown would firmly be in Protestant hands, but in 1560 that day was still some way off.

In 1560 the Scottish Parliament had agreed to adopt the Reformation in principle but it did not authorize any major changes to the structures of the church. The bishops and monasteries continued to exist and to claim their accustomed revenues, even though in many cases the monasteries were so highly mortgaged that the intended recipients had to live on a fraction of their theoretical income. This meant that there was little left to pay the preaching ministers that the Reformers wanted to introduce. The Reformers concocted a grand scheme for redrawing the ecclesiastical map of Scotland by turning the thirteen dioceses, whose boundaries often made little sense, into ten districts, each of which would be governed by a 'superintendent', who would perform the duties that most of the bishops had neglected. Where a bishop accepted the Reformation and was prepared to preach and exercise discipline as he should, he was allowed to do so, and in those (rare) cases the office of superintendent and that of bishop virtually coincided. There was still a problem in that the district boundaries did not correspond to the dioceses, but that was a relatively minor difficulty that would have resolved itself as the old bishops died out.

The lords of the regency council, who were responsible for the appointment of bishops as long as the throne was vacant, went along with this scheme and in the course of a year they managed to appoint five superintendents, who were meant to supplement the three bishops who had accepted the Reformation. The arrival of Mary, Queen of Scots, in August 1561 put a stop to this, because she would not appoint superintendents, nor would the church willingly have accepted her candidates. But Mary did continue to nominate bishops and to seek papal confirmation for them, which of course meant that the episcopate became even more hostile to the Reformation than it had been before. That ceased when she fled the country, but the lords of the council were reluctant to appoint any more superintendents. It is not clear why, but various factors might have played a role. The episcopate could not simply be abolished, because too much of the bishops' income was tied up in grants and pensions that went to other people, and they would suffer as much as, if not more than, the bishops if their revenues were suddenly confiscated. Superintendents were also expensive. They were in effect parallel bishops, appointed for life, unattached to a parish, and doing the administrative work that the official episcopate should have been doing, apart from such formalities as the ordination of clergy and their induction to benefices. To get around this, the General Assembly appointed commissioners as short-term administrators, and for the most part they were parish ministers on secondment.

The result of this was that by 1571 Scotland had three different forms of church government operating simultaneously. There were bishops appointed by the Crown, commissioners appointed by the General Assembly and super-intendents appointed by the Crown but answerable to the General Assembly, or so the Assembly thought. A compromise was worked out according to which the Crown would continue to nominate bishops, but they would be subject to confirmation by the General Assembly, who would expect them to act like superintendents. Now that the king was officially Protestant, there was some talk of disbanding the Assembly and relying on Parliament instead. But as James VI was still a child, the royal prerogative would continue to be exercised by a regent, who could not necessarily be trusted to do the church's bidding, and bishops (although not superintendents or commissioners) had the right to sit in Parliament. So the General Assembly was not abolished, and a parallel church government continued to function. Instead of working itself into redundancy, as the original Reformers might have intended, the General Assembly increasingly saw itself as the church's parliament and sought to wrest control of ecclesiastical affairs from the state as much as possible.

By 1573 it could be said that, as far as outward appointments and theoretical duties were concerned, Scottish bishops resembled their English counter-parts and the two national churches were operating almost identically.[55] But the underlying reality was rather different. England had no equivalent to the Scottish General Assembly and its bishops were responsible to no one but the queen, who appointed them. The convocations of Canterbury and York played a role in formulating the worship and doctrine of the church, but every-thing had to be submitted to the queen for her approval, which might or might not take the form of an act of Parliament. Whether the English monarch could govern the church without consulting Parliament was an unanswered question that would come to haunt the country in the seventeenth century, but in Scotland things were much clearer. From 1572 onwards, bishops were nomin-ated by the Crown, which promised to secure their revenues (temporalities), but were answerable to the Assembly for the conduct of their spiritual duties as superintendents. The sticking point concerned the status of these bishops with respect to the rest of the clergy. Were they supposed to be parish minis-ters with additional responsibilities or were they a distinct order, detached

---

[55] G. Donaldson, *The Scottish Reformation* (Cambridge: Cambridge University Press, 1960), 149–182. See also 228–233, where the forms for the consecration of bishops and the administration of discipline in the two churches as used in 1573 are compared and shown to be virtually the same.

from parish ministry (and therefore from regular preaching, which was one of the main responsibilities of a Reformed bishop) and entitled to sit in Parliament as peers of the realm? To many of the clergy, any compromise on this score smacked of the unreformed episcopate that had dominated the country before 1560 and, given that a few members of the old order were still exercising episcopal functions, it was not hard to see why they might think so.

It was in this context that presbyterian ideas made their way into Scotland. They were already circulating in England and elsewhere, and it was probably only a matter of time before their influence would have been felt in Scotland in any case. Andrew Melville (1545–1622) was a Scot who had spent a decade in France and Geneva before returning home in 1574, when he was appointed Principal of the University of Glasgow. He was ordained in 1577 and held a number of important posts in the Church of Scotland over the next twenty years. He was elected Moderator of the General Assembly on four occasions (1578, 1582, 1587, 1594), became Principal of St Mary's College in St Andrews in 1580 and was appointed rector of the university in 1590. Melville used his privileged position to press for further reformation of the church, and in 1578 the General Assembly approved the Second Book of Discipline. It detailed how a comprehensive reform of the church's structures could be achieved, and introduced, for the first time, the notion that all ministers were equal.[56] For the sake of order, some of them might be given special administrative responsibilities and titles like 'superintendent' or 'bishop', but they did not constitute a distinct or superior class of clergy. Unfortunately for Melville and his supporters, the Second Book of Discipline did not appeal to the civil authorities, who refused to endorse it, although it remained on the table as a series of recommendations to which reference could be made if desired.

Three years later, following rumours that Roman Catholics were plotting to restore Catholicism, the king and his council were persuaded to issue a stinging denunciation of all things papist. This has come to be known as the Second Scottish Confession, although in fact it was more like an appendix to the first.[57]

Frustrated by what looked like the compromising tendencies of the government, a group of Protestant rebels captured the king in August 1582 and held him for the next ten months. That was a step too far, and even the General Assembly condemned it. However, concessions were made to the rebels and

---

[56] J. Kirk, *The Second Book of Discipline* (Edinburgh: St Andrew Press, 1980).

[57] P. Schaff, *The Creeds of Christendom*, 3 vols. (New York, N.Y.: Harper & Row, 1931), 3:480–485. It was not forgotten, and in 1638 was resurrected to form the first part of the National Covenant, when the Church of Scotland made a decisive break with the anglicizing policies of the king (see below).

elements of the Second Book of Discipline were accepted, but after the king's release in June 1583 there was a strongly conservative reaction, as a result of which Melville was arrested in 1584 and imprisoned for alleged treason. He was released a year later, but James VI did not forget where Melville's sympathies lay, and when he visited St Andrews in 1597, Melville was ejected from his rectorship. After the king went to England, Melville continued to campaign in favour of granting the church full freedom to order its own affairs, and for that he was summoned to London and imprisoned in the Tower. Upon his release in 1611 he left for France, and was given a chair at the Protestant academy in Sedan, where he stayed for the rest of his life.

Melville fell out of favour with the king because he advocated the adoption of a fully presbyterian system of church government. Unlike John Knox, who had regarded church and state as different aspects of the same society, Melville thought of them as two separate realms, each with its own principles and system of government. In the state the king was supreme, but in the church he was just an ordinary member like anyone else. Melville got as far as he did because he wanted to abolish both the episcopate and the benefice system. If those funds could be released, he argued, they could be distributed more equally to the ministers, whose posts could then be adequately funded.

In 1587 Melville and his supporters had some success, when the secular revenues of the bishops and surviving monasteries were annexed to the Crown and made available for ministerial stipends.[58] Increasingly the parish clergy were grouped together into presbyteries, and the functions thitherto exercised by the bishops gradually devolved on these clergy. The bishops were not formally dispossessed, and in some places continued to function much as they had always done, but elsewhere they became little more than the chief ministers of their local presbyteries. They were still represented in Parliament, which set them apart from other ministers, but although they continued to perform their traditional functions of ordination and institution to parishes, they did so only by the leave of the presbyteries, which were answerable to the General Assembly. The Crown continued to appoint them, and also to summon the General Assembly, which thus appeared to convene under royal authority. Whether the king could suppress the Assembly by refusing to convene it (and thus take full control of the church) was the great unanswered question, but it would be two generations before it had to be faced and for the time being everything seemed to operate smoothly.

---

[58] This confiscation did not extend to the tithes (teinds), which were left in the hands of the church because they were regarded as spiritual, not temporal, revenue.

This mixed presbyterian-episcopal polity was established by law in 1592, after which time it can truly be said that the government of the Church of Scotland was no longer anything like that of its sister church to the south. In many ways it was an admirable blending of two quite different systems, and had the church been free to order its own affairs it might have worked. But of course bishops were still theoretically appointed by the Crown, and the king came to see that any diminution in their authority was also a diminution in his. This was particularly problematic because James VI came to believe that he ruled by 'divine right' (*ius divinum*), a claim that was also being made both for episcopacy and presbyterianism, especially in England. 'Divine right' did not give the king (or the bishops) the power to act without regard for the interests of their people, as many modern observers mistakenly think. On the contrary, in the hierarchically ordered society of the late sixteenth century, it placed a burden on those who were so privileged to act responsibly in the eyes of God, who saw far more than any human being ever could, and whose judgment would correspondingly be more severe – and eternal. Faced with having to decide whether to obey God or man (in the form of a parliament or general assembly), James VI understandably put God first, as he would have expected his subjects to do in certain circumstances.[59] Furthermore, James VI made no secret of his views. He published them in a book called *Basilikon Doron* (*Royal Gift*), which was printed by none other than Robert Waldegrave, and was widely read in both Scotland and England.[60] However, as we might expect, it did not impress Andrew Melville, who felt free to attack much of what it said and did so without hesitation.

James VI did not have the power to silence Melville, but the two men were clearly on different wavelengths, and the king naturally came to see presbyterianism as inimical to his own authority. 'No bishop, no king' became his watchword, and it made him wary of the English Puritans, whom he suspected of sympathizing with Melville. There is no reason to think that he was right about that, at least not at the beginning, but as often happens with these things, the king's hostile attitude would eventually help to produce the result he most feared, and after his death his son would suffer the consequences.

---

[59] Theoretically this might even involve disobeying the king, particularly if he were not a (Reformed) Christian, but as James VI himself was in a covenant relationship with God, he claimed that this option did not apply to his subjects.

[60] James VI, *Basilikon Doron* (Edinburgh: Robert Waldegrave, 1599). It is available in a modern edition, J. Sommerville (ed.), *James VI and I: Political Writings* (Cambridge: Cambridge University Press, 1994), 1–61.

The union of the Crowns – and churches? (1603–25)

The death of Queen Elizabeth was the moment the Puritans had long been waiting for, and they lost no time in making their views known to the new king. At some point during his progress from Edinburgh to London in April–May 1603, a group of Cambridge divines presented him with a petition in which they outlined the reforms they wanted him to implement. They were inspired by his Scottish background, believed that he would be sympathetic to their outlook and claimed to represent a thousand ministers, whence the name by which the Millenary Petition is commonly known.[61] The authors of the petition outlined four areas of concern. First, they wanted what they saw as the remains of pre-Reformation superstition that had survived in public worship to be removed. This included such things as the signing with the cross in baptism, the use of the word 'priest' and the imposition of particular vestments. Second, they wanted only ministers who could preach, and suggested that those who could not ought to be removed from office, although treated in a humane way by being pensioned off, not burnt at the stake! Third, they attacked pluralism in the holding of benefices, particularly by bishops and other dignitaries, and wanted the practice stopped. Lastly, they wanted church discipline, including excommunication, to be restored, but at the same time reserved for serious offences, and urged that proceedings in the ecclesiastical courts should be speeded up and be more equitably administered.

The king did not immediately respond to their requests, but referred the matter to a conference he summoned to meet at Hampton Court early in 1604.[62] There, for the first time, there was a public confrontation between Archbishop John Whitgift and his Puritan opponents. Whitgift died not long afterwards, but he was succeeded by the equally intransigent Richard Bancroft, who was determined to resist Puritanism in any way he could.[63] A commission was established to sort out the church's canons and its report was a clear victory for the Establishment. On almost all the contentious matters raised by the Millenary Petition, the canons came down on Bancroft's side, and the king duly ratified them after they had been approved by the Convocation of

---

[61] For the text, see J. Kenyon, *The Stuart Constitution*, 2nd edn (Cambridge: Cambridge University Press, 1986), 117–119. On seventeenth-century Puritanism in general, see J. Spurr, *English Puritanism 1603–1689* (Basingstoke: Macmillan, 1998).

[62] See C. Buchanan, *The Hampton Court Conference and the 1604 Book of Common Prayer*, Alcuin Club and The Group for Renewal of Worship Joint Liturgical Studies 68 (Norwich: Hymns Ancient & Modern, 2009).

[63] See S. B. Babbage, *Puritanism and Richard Bancroft* (London: SPCK, 1962).

Canterbury. But this time the York Convocation did not go along with the decision, and demanded the right to vote for the canons independently, which it did, but only two years later.[64] Parliament refused to acknowledge them; but although that did not prevent the canons from becoming law, it did raise the question of whether they could be applied to the laity as well as the clergy, since the laity (Parliament) had not approved them.[65]

The canons of 1604 were to have a long life, surviving with only a few alterations until they were finally superseded in 1969.[66] By then of course most were dead letters, but they were not seen that way in the early seventeenth century. On the contrary, in order to make sure that they were obeyed, the king revived the courts of High Commission that had originally been established in 1559, and for the next generation their activities would become one of the main sources of the Puritan grievances that gradually accumulated against the regime.[67] James's position as a foreigner in England made things difficult for him, and it is clear that there were those in high places who were only too glad to flatter his anti-Puritan prejudices. One of these was John Overall (1559–1619), Dean of St Paul's in 1604 and later to become a bishop. Overall had dissented from Whitgift's Lambeth Articles in 1595, but that had not prevented him from climbing the ecclesiastical ladder, and James I was pleased by his explanation of predestination at the Hampton Court conference. But there can be no doubt that Overall's theological position was extreme, to the point of eccentricity. In 1606 he presented a book of canons to the Canterbury Convocation in which he made some extraordinary claims, as for example:

> If any man shall affirm that the Son of God, having from the beginning a church upon earth, did leave them till the flood without priests, and priestly authority to govern and instruct them in those ways of their salvation, and in the right manner of the worship and service of God; or that they might teach them any other doctrine in that behalf than that which they had received from God himself, he doth greatly err.[68]

---

[64] See Bray, *Anglican Canons*, 258–453.

[65] The debate went on for a long time and was resolved only by the decision in Middleton vs Crofts (1736), which exempted the laity from any duty of canonical obedience. The church never accepted this, and as long as the canons were in force, some argued that they ought to apply to clergy and laity alike.

[66] The church officially calls them the canons of 1603, because the royal writ authorizing their composition was issued before 25 March 1604, and therefore in what was then still technically 1603.

[67] See R. G. Usher, *The Rise and Fall of the High Commission* (Oxford: Clarendon Press, 1913), 236–334; R. A. Marchant, *The Church Under the Law: Justice, Administration and Discipline in the Diocese of York 1560–1640* (Cambridge: Cambridge University Press, 1969; R. B. Outhwaite, *The Rise and Fall of the English Ecclesiastical Courts, 1500–1860* (Cambridge: Cambridge University Press, 2006).

[68] Canon 1.4. For the complete text, see Bray, *Anglican Canons*, 454–484.

From there Overall went on to interpret the whole of the Old Testament as a prototype of seventeenth-century England, where priests and kings ruled by divine right. Earlier spokesmen for the church had referred to King Edward VI as the new Josiah, and Queen Elizabeth I as a latter-day Deborah, but nobody had ever extended the typology as far as Overall did. It was too much even for James I, who refused to ratify the canons, but they did not disappear. In the later seventeenth century they were resurrected and adopted, by what had by then become a 'High Church' party in the Church of England, as their ideological foundation.

In the short term, Overall's project failed, but he was soon involved in another that would have extraordinary success. Since the appearance of the Geneva Bible in 1560, there had been controversy in England over which version should be used by the church. The bishops were authorized to revise the Great Bible of 1538, which they duly did. Their translation, known as the Bishops' Bible, appeared in 1568 and was authorized as the 'official' text for use in churches. But the Bishops' Bible was expensive and of poorer quality than the Geneva one, and few people used it.[69] The Puritans wanted a new translation that would replace both existing ones, and the Hampton Court conference agreed. A series of committees was appointed to undertake the work, which King James insisted should be based on the Bishops' Bible and not contain any marginal notes, which was one of the main features of the Geneva Bible.

Once again, the king's anti-Puritan bias can be seen at work, but the translators ignored what he had to say about preferring the Bishops' Bible and set about trying to produce a more scientifically reliable translation based on the best Hebrew and Greek manuscripts. The fruit of their labours appeared in 1611, and has become known to posterity as the King James Bible or the Authorized Version, even though it was never officially authorized by anyone. The King James Version was not immediately dominant, but within a generation it had ousted all its rivals to become, as it has remained, the English Bible par excellence. It was lightly edited and modified at periodic intervals as words changed their meaning and better manuscripts became available, so that the text we read today dates from 1761, when this process of gradual revision came to a halt.[70] By about 1640 it had displaced earlier translations and, with rare

---

[69] It might be compared to the New English Bible, which was launched with great fanfare in 1970 and again (in a revised form) in 1989, but has never caught on with the general public. The author of this book was presented with a copy at his priesting in 1979, but it has stood unopened on the shelf ever since. One suspects that the Bishops' Bible suffered a similar fate.

[70] D. Norton, *A Textual History of the King James Version* (Cambridge: Cambridge University Press, 2005).

exceptions, it was used by all Protestant Christians in the English-speaking world for more than three hundred years. It is now outdated, both in its language and in its translations, which are based on Hebrew and Greek texts that have since been superseded, but its peculiar cadences make it clear to anyone who hears them that this is the Bible, and it remains the version most frequently cited by people who do not normally attend church.

The King James Version is more traditional than many people realize, in that approximately 90% of its New Testament is taken over from William Tyndale, but it was also based on what were then the latest scientific principles and evidence, offering in that respect a model for future translators. It was also generally free of theological bias, although not entirely so, as words like 'church' and 'bishop' are often used when modern scholars would be more cautious and attempt to prevent the anachronistic connotations that such terms can have. Words that are not in the original text but have to be supplied in order to make sense in English are indicated by the use of italics, a useful concession to scholarly accuracy, although one that is often misunderstood by people who mistakenly think that the italicized words are meant to be stressed! Whether (or to what extent) the King James Version is still usable is a matter of controversy, pitting traditionalists against others, but one thing at least is clear – it is and will always remain the classical English Bible, unrivalled by any competitors and destined to endure as long as the language itself.

The King James Version was a remarkable success story as far as English Protestantism was concerned, and although James I himself took no part in the translation, his genuine desire for Christian unity entitles him to claim at least some credit for that. But James's desire to bring Christians together went further than this. There were essentially three levels at which he sought to reunite a sundered Christendom. The first of these was the (apparently) relatively simple matter of uniting the Church of England with that of Scotland. The second was achieving pan-Protestant unity. And the third was preparing the ground for the wider unity of all Christian churches, including Rome and the Eastern Orthodox. James must have known that he would not live to see the last of these come to fruition, but his ecumenical vision was real and is of great interest today, when his original quest is once more in vogue around the world.[71]

The English Puritans shared James's desire to unite the churches of England and Scotland, but they tended to assume that the Scottish model, of which they approved, would also be applied to England. Had James been a fan of that he

---

[71] See W. B. Patterson, *King James VI and I and the Reunion of Christendom* (Cambridge: Cambridge University Press, 1997).

might have had his way, but he was not and the project never got off the ground. As far as he was concerned, the union of the two great churches of Britain would come about, if at all, by anglicizing the Scottish church, not the other way round. James I could argue that his intentions were much the same as those of John Knox and his colleagues, and in a way they were, but things had moved on since then, not least in Scotland. The Scottish church was not democratic in the modern sense, but power within it was much more evenly dispersed than it was in England, and the king could not hope to control it to the same extent. James I, sensible enough to realize that, proceeded slowly. He did what he could to distribute the revenues of the annexed benefices to loyal supporters (mostly laymen), and restored the bishops to the functions they were supposed to perform. He did not abolish the presbyteries, but did much to reduce their influence by reforming the episcopate. He was more cautious about interfering with public worship, which was a good deal less formal than it was in England, but on 21 October 1618 ratified a decision taken at the General Assembly, held at Perth in the preceding August, to adopt a five-point programme of 'restoration'.[72] The five points were as follows:

1 The Christian year was to be observed, and in particular the great feasts of Christmas, Good Friday, Easter, Ascension and Pentecost. On those days preachers were to teach the true meaning of the events being commemorated and suppress any superstitious practices that had grown up around them.
2 Baptism in private houses was to be allowed when necessary.
3 Eight-year-old children were to be catechized and presented to the bishop for confirmation.
4 Holy Communion was to be administered to sick people privately at home.
5 Communicants were to receive the Holy Communion kneeling.

None of these demands sounds particularly threatening to us and no doctrine was affected by them. Items two and four could be presented as common sense, and the first and fourth might have had genuinely positive effects. Only the last was obviously contentious, having already attracted the ire of John Knox as far back as 1552, when it inspired the black rubric in the English Prayer Book of that year.

---

[72] See G. Donaldson, *Scottish Historical Documents*, corrected edn (Glasgow: Neil Wilson Publishing, 1974), 184–185.

Unfortunately for James, his Scottish subjects did not see things in the same way. To many of them the Five Articles of Perth were the edge of a very thin wedge that would eventually expand and lead the church back to Rome. Even before the Five Articles of Perth, the Church of Scotland was prevailed upon to compose another confession of faith. This was approved by the General Assembly in 1616 and for more than twenty years was accepted as the official statement of the church's doctrine, but it is now so obscure that there is no modern edition of it and it is almost never printed, even in collections of historical documents.[73] Its theology is thoroughly Calvinist and it could easily have been written by any leading English theologian of the time, but it is not clear whether it was intended to be a stepping stone towards church union with England or not. Its closing paragraph however is revealing:

> We believe and constantly affirm that the Kirk of Scotland, through the abundant grace of our Lord, is one of the most pure Kirks under heaven this day, both in respect of truth in doctrine and purity in worship, and therefore with all our hearts we adjoin ourselves thereto, and to the religion publicly professed therein by the King's Majesty, and all his true subjects, and authorized by His Majesty's laws, promising by the grace of God to continue therein to the end of our life, according to all the Articles which are here set down, which as we believe with our hearts, so we confess with our mouths and subscribe with our hands, understanding them plainly as they are here conceived, without equivocation or mental reservation whatsoever. So may God help us in the great day of judgment.

Whatever else the Scots were expected to confess, royal supremacy lay at the heart of it, and in this respect at least, James VI and I insisted that the churches of Scotland and England were one.

---

[73] It seems that there are only two editions of it in print. One is D. Calderwood, *The History of the Church of Scotland from the Beginning of the Reformation, unto the end of the Reign of King James VI* (n.p., 1678), 668–673. A facsimile edition was published by the Scolar Press, Menston, Yorkshire, in 1971. The other is *Acts and Proceedings of the General Assemblies of the Kirk of Scotland from the Year 1560 Collected from the Most Authentic Manuscripts, Part Third* (1593–1618) (Edinburgh: Church of Scotland, 1845), 1132–1139. This edition contains the proceedings of the General Assembly held at Aberdeen, 13–18 August 1616, where the confession was adopted on 17 August. The proceedings of this Assembly were rescinded in 1638, along with those of all the assemblies held after the restoration of episcopacy in 1606. (The last legally recognized Assembly before 1638 was the one held in 1604.)

Britain on the European stage

On the wider European scene, James I was active in the pursuit of pan-Protestant unity in a way that had never been the case previously. His daughter Elizabeth (1596–1662) was married to Frederick V, elector of the Palatinate in the Holy Roman Empire and a staunch Protestant in the Swiss mould. When the largely Protestant nobility of Bohemia rebelled against their Austrian Habsburg rulers in 1618, they invited Frederick to become their king, an offer he unwisely accepted. He managed to reign in Prague for just over a year (1619–20), but the Habsburgs would not let Bohemia go. They defeated him and drove him not only out of Bohemia but out of the Palatinate as well. He was forced to take refuge in the Dutch Republic, which was still fighting for its independence against the Spanish Habsburgs, and it was there that Elizabeth gave birth to a daughter, Sophia (1630–1714). In 1658 Sophia married Ernst Augustus of Braunschweig [Brunswick]-Lüneburg, who ruled the small German state of Hanover. In 1692 Hanover was elevated to the status of an electorate, by which time Sophia was in line for the British throne.[74] She almost inherited it, but died less than two months before Queen Anne, with the result that the British Crown passed to her son, who became King George I (1714–27), the ancestor of the dynasty that still sits on the throne. James's Continental involvement was thus to have long-lasting effects, which in a sense are still with us.

James I did not approve of his son-in-law's rashness, but could hardly dissociate himself completely from the Protestant cause. In the same year, 1618, the States-General (parliament) of the Dutch Republic summoned a pan-Protestant synod to meet in the city of Dordrecht (Dort) in order to sort out a theological controversy that had been dividing the country for a decade. It had arisen over the claims made by Jacob Arminius (1560–1609) to be the true heir of John Calvin at a time when most of Calvin's followers were moving in quite a different direction. In opposition to them Arminius claimed that Calvin's views on such sensitive subjects as predestination were considerably more flexible than his supposed heirs would allow, and that naturally stirred up opposition. Arminius died before significant hostility broke out, but it was not long before his supporters penned a Remonstrance to the States-General in which they advocated acceptance of Arminius's views. This action by the Remonstrants forced their opponents to strike back, and it was that which led to the Synod of Dort. The Dutch understood that the questions at stake were

---

[74] The Holy Roman Empire was an elective monarchy, in which the leading princes were the electors. In practice they always picked a member of the House of Habsburg, but it was still a matter of honour to be included among the electorate.

of theological importance for the whole Protestant world and decided to open the synod to representatives of all the Reformed churches.

The Lutherans refused to attend, and the French Protestants were not allowed to send delegates, but the British turned up in force and played a major role in the deliberations. It was the first – and so far only – time that all the national churches of the British Isles got together to form a united delegation, and the first time that British theologians made a serious impression on their European colleagues. Before Dort, England and Scotland had taken their theology from various Continental sources without giving anything back, but from 1618 and for the rest of the seventeenth century this pattern was to be reversed. British theology came to enjoy a reputation in Continental Europe greater than any it had known before – and indeed, greater than any it has known since. From having been marginal bit-players on the international scene, the British suddenly found themselves at centre stage.[75]

The delegates to Dort encountered a local church that was deeply divided, with the opponents of the Remonstrants inclined to go to extremes of their own that, if left unchecked, would alienate many of their Reformed brethren who disliked the Remonstrants' positions but who were less personally involved in the debates than the Dutch were. The British therefore inclined towards a moderating stance, supporting the anti-Remonstrant cause in principle but steering it in a balanced direction that would command general support. This they succeeded in doing, and the result was a triumph for British theologians just as much as it was for orthodox Dutch theology. What they determined was as follows.[76]

1. *Unconditional election* is the eternal purpose of God for salvation. He chose Israel not because of its merits but in spite of them, and the same is true of Christians. As we have already remarked, this was the most radical doctrine of predestination because it undercut every kind of human pretension and highlighted the sovereignty of God in all things.

2. *Limited atonement* is the true meaning of Christ's death on the cross. His sacrifice is sufficient to cover every kind of sin, but it was not destined to be applied to every sinner. Just as the high priest in Israel had offered sacrifice for the sins of the people, so Christ offered sacrifice for the sins of his people – the elect.

---

[75] See A. Milton, *The British Delegation and the Synod of Dort (1618–1619)* (Woodbridge: Boydell & Brewer, 2005). Also Patterson, *James VI and I*, 260–292.

[76] For the text of the canons, see Bray, *Documents*, 408–430. In popular usage they are often abbreviated as TULIP, from their initial letters, but although that is helpful as a mnemonic device, it obscures the order, which is properly ULTIP.

3. *Total depravity* is the condition of humankind after the fall of Adam. No human being can contribute anything towards his or her salvation, and those who are chosen for that blessing owe everything to God and nothing to their own efforts. Depravity is not to be confused with 'corruption', because it means 'twisted', not 'destroyed'. Sinful people are still capable of many good acts, but because there is nothing in them that has escaped the taint of sinfulness, they have no healthy spiritual cells that can fight back against the cancer of sin.

4. *Irresistible grace* is the gift of God to his chosen people. If God has determined to save someone, that person cannot resist him indefinitely. Saul of Tarsus is the classic case of a man who had no desire to become a Christian but who was overpowered by the sovereign grace of God. The same is true of every believer. Just as we cannot choose to be saved, so we cannot refuse to be either.

5. *Perseverance of the saints* is the promise God makes to his chosen ones. Once we are saved from sin, we cannot fall away again, even if we wander for a time. Those who do fall away were never truly chosen to begin with, while those who are chosen will be tempted, as Jesus himself was tempted, but by the grace of God they will be given the power to resist and overcome every obstacle on their path towards the kingdom of heaven.

The canons of Dort were never formally adopted by the churches of England, Scotland or Ireland, but they set out a definition of Reformed theology that would come to be known as 'Calvinism' and still characterizes British Protestantism. There are many who do not swallow the entire package, calling themselves 'four-point Calvinists' or whatever, and others who embrace the designation of 'Arminian' in opposition to it, but whatever the case, they are not indifferent to the decisions taken at Dort, which remain fundamental for the different Reformed churches even now.[77] In their own time the canons of Dort became the defining benchmark of the Puritans, who saw in them not only the truth of the biblical gospel but also the basis on which they were united with Protestants in other countries.

Looking further afield, James was bound to have meagre results in his attempts to reach out to Roman Catholics. Theological polemics were at their height in his time, and it was too much to expect them to diminish, let alone disappear, overnight. But it was to be a different story with the Eastern

---

[77] For the Calvinists, limited atonement is usually the article that provokes the greatest dissent, both because it is seen as a discouragement to evangelization and because it can be interpreted as inherently 'racist', or at least biased in favour of a particular group of the 'saved'. Arminianism is characteristic of Methodism and is widespread today among Evangelicals, though many of them are not sufficiently literate in theology to be able to recognize it.

Orthodox churches. Britain had had almost nothing to do with them since the time of Theodore of Tarsus, the third Archbishop of Canterbury, but after the Reformation there was a renewal of contact. This was partly the result of curiosity in the West as to how an ancient church had survived since New Testament times without submitting to the papacy, and partly it was the result of pressures from the East, as Greeks in the Ottoman Empire chafed under a Muslim yoke that at times could be quite onerous. They looked to the West for protection and support, and were naturally drawn to those who would respect their ancient customs and not demand submission to western norms, as the papacy was wont to do. The Church of England, as an episcopal body with a number of surviving traditions from pre-Reformation times, was particularly congenial to the Eastern Orthodox, and before long good relations between them were established.[78]

The first Greek student to arrive in England was Christopher Angelos, who turned up in 1608 and went initially to Trinity College, Cambridge, and then in 1610 to Balliol College, Oxford, where he remained until he died in 1638. He might have been the one who encouraged George Abbot, Archbishop of Canterbury from 1611 to 1633, to write to Cyril Lukaris (1572–1638), then the Greek Orthodox Patriarch of Alexandria, asking him to send four Greek students to England. Cyril sent Metrophanes Kritopoulos, who went to Balliol College, where he stayed for several years before returning to the east. He left a mixed impression on his hosts but relations between the two churches continued to develop. After he moved to become Patriarch of Constantinople in 1620, Lukaris sent to England a codex of the Bible that he had brought with him from Alexandria. It is now housed in the British Library as the Codex Alexandrinus, one of the most famous manuscripts of the Bible in existence. Cyril Lukaris was attracted to Calvinism, which drew him even closer to the English, and he kept sending students to Oxford for the rest of his life.[79] Undoubtedly the most memorable of these was Nathanael Konopios, who was in Oxford from 1637 to 1648 and is recorded as having been the first person to have brewed coffee in England.[80] He is not known for any theological achievement, but generations of students and others have him to thank for helping them get through their studies. Ecumenical cooperation has seldom been as productive as that.

---

[78] See S. Runciman, *The Great Church in Captivity* (Cambridge: Cambridge University Press, 1968), 289–319; Patterson, *James VI and I*, 196–219.

[79] On Lukaris, see Runciman, *Great Church in Captivity*, 259–288; G. A. Hadjiantoniou, *Protestant Patriarch* (Richmond, Va.: John Knox Press, 1961).

[80] Runciman, *Great Church in Captivity*, 295–296.

James VI and I did what he could to bring people together, but in many ways he was ahead of his time. He wanted to be known as King of Great Britain, but although the union of the Crowns of England and Scotland was to endure, political unity was not achieved until 1707, more than a century after he first went to London. He managed to bring the national churches closer together than they had ever been before, but this show of unity was ephemeral and broke down once it became apparent that it would have resulted in the absorption of a largely presbyterian Church of Scotland into a doggedly episcopalian Church of England. As for international ecumenism, the Synod of Dort turned out to be a high-water mark from which the British churches receded in the following decades, even as political relations with the Netherlands grew deeper and more extensive over time. Finally, overtures to the Eastern Orthodox world were hampered by the fact that Christians there were subject to Muslim rule and there was not much anyone could do about it. But if many of James's projects were ahead of their time and/or doomed to failure, it remains the case that his efforts opened up new horizons and bore fruit in ways he could not have envisaged. British Christianity was now a player on the world scene and so it would remain, whether it was successful in its endeavours or not.

Developments in the Church of England

One of the changes James I brought to the Church of England was greater concern for bishops. In Elizabeth I's time hardly any of them appeared at court and many sees were vacant for long periods of time. James changed all that. He wanted bishops who were active pastors in their dioceses and who would also wait on him as required. He gave money to repair dilapidated cathedrals and collegiate churches and saw to it that they were properly staffed. He took a personal interest in the men whom he appointed to the episcopate, and wanted them to be good theologians and competent administrators.[81] He did not expect them all to share the same theological viewpoint and he relished academic debate on the great questions of the day. To some extent he resembled Henry VIII in encouraging variety among the prelates and a balance on the episcopal bench. He did not hesitate to disagree with a man like John Overall for example, but as long as Overall was loyal to him he did not hold him back. That said, the majority of James's bishops were preaching pastors in the Calvinist mode. They were worried about creeping Catholicism and possible Separatism,

---

[81] K. Fincham, *Prelate as Pastor: The Episcopate of James I* (Oxford: Clarendon Press, 1990).

but on the whole got along well with the Puritan clergy, whose evangelistic zeal they appreciated and often shared. Occasionally they would crack down on Nonconformity in matters such as vestments, and they were often more tolerant in theological matters than many of the Puritans were, especially in their estimation of the church of Rome, but this was a matter of degree and did not usually cause any problems. George Abbot, Archbishop of Canterbury from 1611 to 1633, a solid Calvinist in his theology, approved of the Synod of Dort and was generally respected by the Puritans. Some bishops, like Miles Smith of Gloucester (1612–24) and Lewis Bayly of Bangor (1616–31), were less satisfactory, but they were exceptions.[82] As Kenneth Fincham puts it, 'The propagation of the gospel, the defence of correct doctrine and the provision of a learned ministry were issues around which many Puritan clergy could unite with the hierarchy.'[83]

But there was another side to the episcopate that did not share the goals or spirituality of the majority. In a sermon preached on 3 December 1626 at the consecration of Francis White as Bishop of Carlisle, John Cosin (1594–1672), chaplain to Richard Neile, Bishop of Durham (1617–28), criticized the Evangelical bishops for putting so much emphasis on preaching that they neglected the due order of the church:

> They now which preach us all gospel and put no law among it, *bishops* and priests that will tell the people all is well if they can but say their Catechism and hear sermons, make them believe that there is nothing to be done more but to believe and so be saved, these men, they preach by some other pattern sure, for Christ, He is sent not to preach down the old law so much as to preach up a new. Now to make men observe and do what the Church teaches is, or should be, in the bishop's hands.[84]

It would not be until 1660, after the Restoration, that Cosin was elevated to Neile's see of Durham, but he was already showing himself the worthy disciple of his anti-Calvinist master. Neile was not alone however. Among those who shared his views were Lancelot Andrewes (1555–1626),[85] William Barlow

---

[82] Ibid. 273–274.

[83] Ibid. 275.

[84] J. Cosin, *Works*, 5 vols., ed. J. Sansom (Oxford: John Henry Parker, 1843–55), 1:96–97.

[85] Bishop of Chichester (1605–9), Ely (1609–19) and Winchester (1619–26). He has a considerable reputation as a preacher with mystical tendencies. See N. Lossky, *Lancelot Andrewes the Preacher (1555–1626): The Origins of the Mystical Theology of the Church of England* (Oxford: Clarendon Press, 1991).

(d. 1613),[86] Samuel Harsnett (1561–1631)[87] and the soon to be notorious William Laud (1573–1645).[88] They were relatively few in number but they occupied prominent sees and spent much of their time in or near London, giving them easy access to the king. That enabled them to exercise an influence disproportionate to their true weight in the Church, and when James I was succeeded by his son Charles I (1625–49), who favoured their anti-Calvinist opinions, they were well placed to take advantage of the opportunity to advance their views both at court and in the country.[89] What this might entail is described by Kenneth Fincham, who points out that Samuel Harsnett was the only Bishop of Chichester between 1606 and 1636 to bother surveying the fabric and furnishings of the parish churches in his diocese, even though that was formally stipulated by Canon 86 of 1604. In 1619 he moved on to Norwich, where

> he apparently encouraged the adornment of city churches, and insisted that women be churched wearing a white veil, an interpretation of the Prayer Book rubric which the High Commission upheld as an ancient ceremony of the Church. Such an interest in ceremonial, and the revival of pre-Reformation practices, was entirely characteristic of these churchmen.[90]

When we consider that after Harsnett's visit to St Andrew's, Norwich, in 1620 the churchwardens were prosecuted for presenting women to be churched without wearing a veil, we can understand how such pernicketiness could become a major irritation to those who did not share it.[91]

Lancelot Andrewes believed that the Puritans were out to change the polity of the church from episcopalianism to presbyterianism, and regarded the defeat of the latter as more apparent than real. To his mind, every instance of ceremonial Nonconformity was indicative of an underlying Puritan plot in that direction, whether there was any evidence for that or not. In 1618 he heard that John Preston (1587–1628) had preached in Cambridge against the use of set prayers in the Church, and warned the king that unless Preston were

---

86 Bishop of Rochester (1605–8) and Lincoln (1608–13).

87 Bishop of Chichester (1609–19), Norwich (1619–28) and Archbishop of York (1629–31).

88 Bishop of St David's (1621–6), Bath and Wells (1626–8), London (1628–33) and Archbishop of Canterbury (1633–45). On Laud, see H. Trevor-Roper, *Archbishop Laud 1573–1645*, 3rd edn (Basingstoke: Macmillan, 1988).

89 N. Tyacke, *Anti-Calvinists: The Rise of English Arminianism c. 1590–1640* (Oxford: Clarendon Press, 1987).

90 Fincham, *Prelate as Pastor*, 281–282.

91 Norfolk and Norwich Record Office, VIS/5/1 (unfol: 10/6/20). Cited by Fincham, *Prelate as Pastor*, 282, n. 163.

expelled from the university, episcopacy's days were numbered. In the back of his mind was the constant fear that England would go the way of Scotland, a fate he regarded with horror.[92] More serious was the covert support Andrewes and others gave to the Remonstrant cause at the Synod of Dort, although neither he nor they attended it in person. Unable (or unwilling) to attack the doctrinal positions of the Synod directly, they fell back on the excuse that the Dutch church was not episcopalian and therefore its decisions were not legitimate. The British delegates to the Synod naturally denounced this opinion as a red herring at best and almost heretical at worst, but it became one of the major arguments against the Synod and over time helped to ensure that all British participation at Dort was erased from memory.[93] As part of the struggle between the 'High Church' elements within the Church of England and the Puritans, this is a prime example of how the former consistently emphasized form over substance, thereby ensuring that the Church would eventually fall apart.

By the first decade of the seventeenth century the patience of some Puritans was beginning to run out. A Puritan lecturer in Lincoln called John Smyth (1570–1612) grew disenchanted with the Church of England and around 1607 he organized a Separatist congregation in Gainsborough. Around the same time, Richard Clifton (d. 1616) was organizing a similar group at nearby Scrooby. Faced with persecution the two congregations joined forces and left for the Netherlands, where they arrived early in 1608. They met up with the existing congregation of Francis Johnson but they soon fell out among themselves. It seems that Clifton's followers initially decided to join Johnson's church but many of them were not happy with it. Under the leadership of John Robinson (1576–1625) they struck out on their own and petitioned the Dutch authorities for permission to settle in Leiden from 1 May 1609. The permission was granted and for the next decade they remained there. Over time however, many of them became disenchanted with the Netherlands and wanted to leave, either for England or for somewhere else where they would be able to practise their religion in an English-speaking environment.

In 1616 a group of them returned to England under the leadership of Henry Jacob (1563–1624), who established an informal congregation in Southwark that was not part of the Church of England but was not clearly separate from it either.[94] Their theology was strictly Calvinist and there was little to distinguish

---

[92] Ibid. 285.

[93] Milton, *British Delegation*, xxviii–xxxvi.

[94] See J. F. McGregor, 'The Baptists: Fount of all Heresy', in J. F. McGregor and B. Reay (eds.), *Radical Religion in the English Revolution* (Oxford: Oxford University Press, 1984), 23–63, esp. 27.

them from the Puritans in the established Church. Three years later, John Robinson followed Jacob back to England, but not for long. In 1618 James I had issued a Book of Sports in which he upheld the right of parishioners to enjoy their recreation after church on Sunday instead of attending the Puritan lectures scheduled at the same time. This so incensed some of the erstwhile Separatists that they concluded England was unreformable. They collected others of the same mind and decided to leave the country for the new world. English colonization of North America was still in its infancy, and the region north of Virginia was largely unclaimed, apart from the St Lawrence Valley, where the French had founded settlements of their own. The Separatists were able to occupy some land in what is now Massachusetts, and in 1620 they established their own colony of Plymouth – the beginning of what was to become New England.

At the time, Robinson's adventure was little noticed and the few who knew about it did not give it much hope of survival. But Robinson's colonists were hand-picked and they were determined to build a Christian Commonwealth on virgin soil. Difficulties and discouragements there certainly were, but to true believers and visionaries that is the price they have to pay for faithfulness, and eventual success. The Pilgrim Fathers, as they came to be known, have gone down in legend as the founders of the United States of America, but this analysis is at best a half-truth. It comes as a surprise to modern Americans to discover that their original founders were doing their best to escape from having to tolerate games like football, which they regarded as diabolical, and few people mention that their desire for 'freedom of religion' was intended only for themselves, not for others. They would have abhorred the secular constitution adopted in 1787 and would have denounced modern America in the same way they denounced contemporary England, but such facts are seldom allowed to interfere with convenient myths. Americans now celebrate what they see as the quintessential Puritan feast of Thanksgiving – although who is being thanked (if anyone) is left to the determination of each individual, something the Puritans would never have imagined possible, let alone countenanced.

Before long, the Plymouth Separatists were overshadowed by a large migration of mainstream Puritans, driven out of England by the repressive policies adopted by the government after 1629. By then however, New England was starting to feel the strain of trying to hold together different views of what constituted a true biblical church. Before too long, discontented colonists were moving out to start other colonies of their own – Connecticut for example, and Rhode Island. Rhode Island became especially notorious because it refused to establish any church and invited free spirits of every kind to settle there.

The result was that outcasts, disreputable people and even criminals made their way to the colony, giving it a reputation for ungodliness that it would take a generation or more to shake off. Religious toleration and social order were incompatible in the early seventeenth century, and it would be some time before an alternative basis for civil life could be found and imposed on the population as a whole.

Meanwhile the Separatists under John Smyth, who had originally gone to Amsterdam with Richard Clifton, also decided not to join the Johnson congregation. But unlike the Clifton group, they soon found another reason for staying apart from them. Sometime in 1608 Smyth came into contact with local Anabaptists, in this case followers of the Dutch preacher Menno Simons (1496–1561), who lived in Waterland. He was convinced, either by the Waterlanders or through contact with them, that infant baptism was unscriptural. He initially sought Mennonite baptism but decided that the Mennonites were heretical because of their anti-Calvinist views of such things as free will. Unable to find anyone to baptize him, Smyth decided to baptize himself, and then baptized a number of his followers as well. Before long however, he began to have doubts about this and decided that he had been too quick to condemn the Mennonites. So he sought to join the Waterlanders, only to meet with opposition from many in his congregation, who did not share his doubts about the validity of his own baptism. This opposition was led by Thomas Helwys (c.1550 – c.1616), who broke with Smyth over it and started a small congregation of his own. There were others who dissented from Smyth as well, apparently because they were not convinced of the Mennonites' theological orthodoxy.

There followed a period of confusion as the Helwys group tried to persuade the Mennonites not to accept Smyth and his followers, and as some of the Waterlanders grew uneasy about admitting a congregation to their fellowship without consulting Mennonites elsewhere. Smyth died in 1612 but three years later his group finally joined the Mennonites and ceased to have an independent existence. By then Helwys and his followers had decided to return to England, where they founded what they called the General Baptist Church. It retained certain Mennonite features, notably an insistence on believers' baptism, but it was less anti-Calvinistic than the Mennonites were and it quietly abandoned or disregarded such Mennonite doctrines as pacifism and the refusal to take oaths.[95] By 1626 the General Baptists had established

---

[95] For the various statements and confessions of faith these groups drew up, see Lumpkin and Leonard, *Baptist Confessions of Faith*, 91–129.

five congregations in England, but little is known about them and they did not resurface as a group until the 1640s. By then some of the members of Jacob's Southwark congregation had come to accept the doctrine of believers' baptism that Helwys's followers advocated, but they were more consistently Calvinistic in their theology. They obviously could not join the General Baptists and instead set up their own network of congregations, calling themselves Particular Baptists and producing a confession of their own in 1644.[96]

What strikes the modern observer of these developments is the extreme fissiparousness of the different groups involved. All of them were dissatisfied with what they saw as the Catholicizing drift of the Church of England, but they could not agree on how best to respond to it. Once they decided to leave the church, they found it impossible to cooperate, and in some extreme cases even worked against one another. For those who believed religious practice was a private matter that individuals could decide for themselves – very few in number in the early seventeenth century – that might not matter very much, but for anyone who thought that Christianity had to be manifested in a fellowship of believers and that there could be only one church, however flawed it might be in certain respects, the Separatist option was unappealing, and complete religious toleration seemed to be irresponsible at best and criminal at worst. It is hardly surprising that the authorities sought to crack down on what they saw as an intolerable danger, even if the methods they resorted to seem to us to have been unchristian and counterproductive.

The religious scene in England in the first decades of the seventeenth century was extremely rich and varied, and there were many people who cannot easily be classified as either 'High Church' or Puritans. Among them was Nicholas Ferrar, who founded a community at Little Gidding, Cambridgeshire, that consisted mainly of his extended family, along with some friends. Ferrar wanted to develop what we would now call a commune, a kind of secular monastery where a regular pattern of daily devotions would be combined with all manner of daily work. For a few years its fame spread and several people were attracted to it, although most spent only a few days there before moving on. One of them was King Charles I, who welcomed the chance to get away from his troubles, if only for a short time. One of Ferrar's friends was George Herbert (1593–1633), whom he had met when they were both undergraduates at Cambridge. Herbert never went to Little Gidding but on his deathbed he bequeathed a book of his poetry to Ferrar. The latter was so impressed by it

---

[96] This was the First London Confession. For the text, see ibid. 130–160.

that he published it as *The Temple*, a series of poems and hymns on the Christian life that remains a classic of English literature. Even more famous was John Donne (1572?–1631), who, after a somewhat wasted youth, turned to Christ and dedicated his life to writing deeply meditative poetry that expresses the Christian experience of God in an intense and compelling way. None of these men formed a school of thought – they were all individuals, if not individualists, whose legacy has come to us in their writings. What we find in them is a spirituality fully in tune with the Puritan vision, even though it did not wear that label. Consider for example the words of George Herbert:

Teach me, my God and king
In all things Thee to see,
And what I do in anything
To do it as for Thee.

A man that looks on glass
On it may stay his eye;
Or if he pleaseth, through it pass
And then the heaven espy.

All may of Thee partake;
Nothing can be so mean,
Which with this tincture 'for Thy sake'
Will not grow bright and clean.

A servant with this clause
Makes drudgery divine:
Who sweeps a room, as for Thy laws,
Makes that and the action fine.

This is the famous stone
That turneth all to gold;
For that which God doth touch and own
Cannot for less be told.

No one is too unimportant, nothing is too mean for God to be glorified in and through them – the Puritan vision of what it means to have a calling from him could hardly be stated any better than this.

Ireland at the crossroads (1571–1625)

The ecclesiastical situation in Ireland after 1571 can only be described as confused.[97] The papal excommunication of Queen Elizabeth I was designed to make people choose between loyalty to the Crown and loyalty to the papacy, but things were not that simple. Eugene O'Harte for example was Bishop of Achonry from 1562 to 1603, apparently recognized by both the queen and the pope. The same seems to have been true of Richard de Burgo or Bourke, who was Bishop of Clonfert from 1534 to 1580. Then there was Redmond O'Gallagher, Bishop of Killala from 1545 to 1569 and subsequently of Derry, until his death in 1601. Like de Burgo, he seems to have been appointed by the pope but recognized by the Crown, whatever that meant in a part of the country where royal control was weak to non-existent. Finally there is the case of Miler Magrath, who served as Catholic Bishop of Down and Connor from 1565 to 1580 but as Protestant Archbishop of Cashel from 1572 to his death in 1622. He presumably left Down and Connor in 1572, but did the papacy continue to recognize him as Bishop there or not? That is not clear, and most likely Magrath himself was in no hurry to explain to Rome what was going on.

One result of the papal excommunication of the queen was that for the first time in Ireland people were executed because of their religion. The difficulty, then as now, is knowing whether these deaths were spiritual or political in character. Catholics naturally claim the former, whereas Protestants generally prefer the latter explanation. It is hard to decide, because political and religious allegiances were so intertwined. Things were complicated still further when it was realized by English recusants that Ireland had not been properly Protestantized and they would be welcomed there. A number made their way to Ireland and some were arrested and put to death, as they would have been in England. Were they martyrs and, if so, were they Irish or English ones?

The papal excommunication also made the conquest of the whole of Ireland a matter of urgency for the government. If the Catholic powers of Europe, Spain most notably but later France as well, were to get wind of the fact that Ireland was potentially rebellious against the Crown, they might be tempted to invade the country and strike England in the rear if they could. As early as 1579 a series of religiously based rebellions broke out, mainly in the south-west (Munster) and led by local noblemen, but with token support from Spain as well. The 'Old English' families of the pale around Dublin had been sending their sons to the Continent for their education, since there was no university

---

[97] Ford and McCafferty, *Origins of Sectarianism in Early Modern Ireland*.

in Ireland, and many of them were returning with anti-Protestant beliefs inculcated by the Counter-Reformation. As a result, and for the first time, there were solidly English palesmen who were supporting the mostly Gaelic or Gaelicized rebels. Retribution was swift and harsh. Many officials in the government had come to believe that none of the Irish would be persuaded to change their religion voluntarily and they would have to be coerced. It was even claimed by some that Catholics would have to be killed or driven out if the Reformation was ever to succeed. By 1583, when the rebellions were finally put down, large tracts of Munster had effectively been depopulated, and were therefore open to plantation from England. Settlers were sought, but most of those attracted to Ireland were the kinds of people England was only too glad to be rid of. These 'New English' were disproportionately misfits, ne'er-do-wells and renegades, who were technically 'Protestant' but who would never have converted anyone to Protestantism.[98] If anything, their presence was counterproductive and made the existing population, both Gaelic and 'Old English', even more determinedly Catholic than they had been before.

The Spanish Armada was a failure, but many people believed that Spain was now seriously interested in restoring Catholicism in the British Isles and would soon return for another attempt. The Gaelic lords of Ulster were tempted to rebel against the queen in the hope of getting support from abroad, and church papistry, which had been widespread in the more English parts of the island, declined dramatically after 1588. People voted with their feet and no longer attended the parish churches, evidently hoping that they would obtain relief following a successful foreign invasion.

Things were made worse by the hesitant approach of the English government, which never allocated enough men and resources to subduing Gaelic Ireland and never settled on a consistent policy.[99] The queen was parsimonious, resources – human and otherwise – were insufficient and London's attention span was short. There were some determined Protestant clergy, notably Adam Loftus (c.1533–1605), a Yorkshireman who became Archbishop of Armagh at the uncanonical age of 28 and four years later was translated to Dublin – technically a demotion! He toured England, desperately looking for young men who would devote themselves to ministry in Ireland, but it was hard to

---

[98] See M. MacCarthy-Morrogh, *The Munster Plantation: English Migration to Southern Ireland 1583–1641* (Oxford: Oxford University Press, 1986).

[99] See C. Brady, *The Chief Governors: The Rise and Fall of Reform Government in Tudor Ireland, 1538–1588* (Cambridge: Cambridge University Press, 1994); Canny, *Making Ireland British*; J. G. Crawford, *Anglicizing the Government of Ireland: The Irish Privy Council and the Expansion of Tudor Rule, 1556–1578* (Dublin: Irish Academic Press, 1993); *A Star Chamber Court in Ireland: The Court of Castle Chamber, 1571–1641* (Dublin: Four Courts Press, 2005).

persuade them to give their lives in the service of a poor country that was in continual turmoil. Loftus did not give up easily however, and in 1593 was appointed the first provost of the newly opened Trinity College, Dublin. Trinity was intended to be the first college of the new University of Dublin, and so it was, but what nobody could have foreseen at the time was that it became, and has remained, the *only* college of that university. It was set up for the training of Irishmen who would evangelize their own country and, initially at least, it was not the vehicle of anglicization so many have thought. There was provision for an Irish-language chair and a project for translating the Bible and Prayer Book into the native language. Work on these was entrusted to a small group of Irish-speakers, but soon fell almost exclusively to William Daniel, or Uilliam Ó Domhnuill (1570–1628), who completed the New Testament in 1602 and the Irish Book of Common Prayer in 1608. The project was beset with financial and other difficulties, many of them caused by the strange belief that Irish had to be written in a special script for which no typeface was available. Queen Elizabeth I provided the funds for creating one and the work went ahead, although not without interruptions.[100]

Progress in subduing the Gaelic tribes was slow, but after their defeat at Kinsale in 1601 it was clear that the end was nigh. The last Gaelic chiefs surrendered to Queen Elizabeth I six days after she died, although the news had not yet reached them. When it did, they surrendered again, and so James VI and I became the first man to reign over the entire British Isles. The Gaels were at first optimistic about James because he was a Scot and therefore presumed to be sympathetic to them, but they were soon disabused of that notion. Fearful of renewed persecution, in 1607 many of their leading earls fled to the Continent, the beginnings of an Irish diaspora that was to prove of great importance in the country's subsequent history. With their leaders gone, the Gaels were demoralized and their lands in Ulster were open to plantation. Commercial land companies were granted concessions and invited to find suitable tenants to till the soil. The best-known of these was the London Company. They obtained much of the country around Derry, which they promptly renamed after themselves – Londonderry.[101] Unfortunately for them,

---

[100] See A. Ford, *The Protestant Reformation in Ireland 1590–1641* (Dublin: Four Courts Press, 1997), 107–109; M. Caball, 'The Bible in Early Modern Gaelic Ireland: Tradition, Collaboration and Alienation', in K. Killeen, H. Smith and R. Willie (eds.), *The Oxford History of the Bible in Early Modern England, c. 1530–1700* (Oxford: Oxford University Press, 2015), 332–349, esp. 332–342. When the Bible was adapted for use in Scotland, it had to be reset in Roman type, which was the norm for Gaelic books published there.

[101] To this day it is a mark of religious allegiance as to how one refers to the city. It is Derry to the Catholics and Londonderry to the Protestants, although in everyday parlance 'Derry' is common to both sides and in certain contexts it must be used. For example, the Protestant bishop presides over the see of Derry and Raphoe, for the simple reason that his title long antedates the plantation.

they could not find enough colonists to occupy all the land allotted to them, and so they invited Catholic tenants to take up the slack, giving the country a more Catholic appearance than it would otherwise have had. It was all rather like Israel's piecemeal colonization of Canaan as recorded in the book of Joshua, where God's people defeated the indigenous people without being able to displace them entirely. The imagery is not fanciful – even today it is sometimes employed as a means of explaining how Catholics and Protestants relate to each other and why reconciliation between them has proved so difficult to achieve.

The plantation of Ulster was also open to Scotsmen, who were now subjects of the same monarch as the English and the Irish. To many of them, Ireland appeared to be a land of milk and honey, much more promising than their barren and infertile homeland, and within a few years they had established substantial settlements in the north-east. They were Protestants, but of the Scottish type, and followed developments in that country rather than in England. As a result, Ulster came to have three distinct communities – native Irish Catholics, conformist English Protestants and potentially Nonconformist Scottish ones, a mixture still evident that gives Northern Ireland its distinctive character.

By the time James VI of Scotland became James I of England and Ireland, Counter-Reformation Catholicism was starting to have a serious impact on the Irish church. In the previously unconquered Gaelic areas were monasteries that had maintained their existence, and sea travel made it relatively easy to infiltrate Catholic priests among a largely sympathetic population. By 1606 they were strong enough to be able to hold a provincial synod at Carrick-on-Suir (Cashel), the first of nine that would be convened in the king's reign.[102] The re-establishment of a Catholic hierarchy proceeded apace, and by 1630 there were no fewer than seventeen resident Catholic bishops in Ireland.[103] Their priority was to reconstruct a Catholic Church along the lines laid down by the Council of Trent, whose decrees formed a template for their directives. As far as relations with the secular government were concerned, Catholics were determined to profess their loyalty to the king while at the same time staying out of politics as much as possible. This was not always easy. In January 1624 there was a real likelihood of war with Spain, and the government ordered all

---

[102] Four would be held in the province of Cashel, three in Armagh, one in Dublin and one jointly in Cashel and Dublin, though it met at Kilkenny (Cashel). There were none in Tuam before 1631, even though it was the most Catholic province in the country. See A. Forrestal, *Catholic Synods in Ireland, 1600–1690* (Dublin: Four Courts Press, 1998).

[103] Ibid. 33.

Catholic clergy to leave the country because of their presumed links with the enemy. In response the Synod of Kilkenny held that year enjoined prayers for the king and queen, for reasons summed up by Alison Forrestal:

> the synod of Kilkenny proved anxious to demonstrate the loyal and unsubversive nature of the Catholic Church in Ireland, the precepts urging the recitation of prayers being deemed the best method of achieving this. Outward manifestations of tranquillity and allegiance by the Catholic laity and their clergy aimed to alleviate the threat posed by repressive religious policies on the part of the state, and thus to permit the Catholic Church to continue its work in relative security.[104]

These synods were also preoccupied with promoting the celebration of the sacraments and the instruction of church members, especially the young. Given the lack of schools and the general illiteracy of much of the population, this teaching had to be conveyed through rituals as much as anything else, which naturally gave them added significance in the devotional life of the laity and incidentally helped to convince Protestants that most Catholics were ignorant peasants wedded to superstition. The boundaries between genuine piety and magic were certainly permeable, and the church did not always find it easy to separate one from the other, despite its efforts to do so. The clergy remained a breed apart, endowed with special powers that set them above their flocks, and that perception, based as it was on doctrines like transubstantiation, would continue to dominate Catholic religious life until the late twentieth century. In some ways Irish Catholicism might have been more superstitiously devout than Catholicism elsewhere, but if so, it was a matter of degree rather than of kind. It was a picture Protestants could not relate to, and continued to shape their hostility to 'priestcraft', as they called it, into modern times.

As Catholicism revived, the established Church of Ireland became more clearly Protestant and organized itself accordingly. It had been slow to adopt a confession of faith or canons of its own and, in so far as it had any, it relied on English precedent and example. But from 1615 onwards a new independence can be discerned. In that year a convocation of the clergy was held in Dublin, and a set of Articles was adopted, based to some extent on the Thirty-nine Articles of the Church of England but going much further – even incorporating the Lambeth Articles of 1595 that had never received official sanction in

---

[104] Ibid. 45.

England.[105] The convocation was meant to reflect English practice, but the resemblance was not exact. In England the convocations were provincial, but in Ireland there was only one national body, tied to the Irish Parliament and meeting in tandem with it. The four archbishops took turns presiding over the sessions, which voted subsidies to the king as their English counterparts did. The 1615 convocation adopted the Irish Articles as its confession of faith, but left the canon law undefined, at least for the time being, a delay that would prove to be very costly to the church when it finally got round to sorting the canons out.

The 1615 convocation is notable also because it is the first time we meet with James Ussher (1581–1656), regarded by some as the most learned man of his time.[106] Ussher was born into one of the few Old English families that accepted the Reformation and was among the first class to enter Trinity College, Dublin, when it opened. There he imbibed Puritan theology and developed antiquarian interests that were to make him one of the leading defenders of the Church of Ireland's claim to be the ancient church of the country. He became a Fellow of Trinity in 1600 and later made several book-buying trips to England, establishing contacts there that would stand him in good stead later. It is not clear what role he played in composing the Irish Articles, but whether he wrote them or not, he subscribed to them wholeheartedly and defended them throughout his career. He then spent two years in London before being appointed Bishop of Meath in 1621 and Archbishop of Armagh in 1625. From then on he was the chief voice of the Church of Ireland and used his position to further the Reformed theology to which he had been committed since his student days.

Ussher did not attend the Synod of Dort but he made a valuable contribution to its deliberations by publishing an essay on the extent of Christ's atonement shortly before the Synod began.[107] In it he sought to reconcile the New Testament statements that Christ had died for the sins of 'all men' with the Calvinist view that only the chosen ones (the 'elect') were saved. Ussher did this by drawing a distinction between sins and sinners. Christ had died for the sins of the whole world, in the sense that nobody can commit a sin that his sacrifice is insufficient to atone for. But at the same time, Christ also died for people,

---

[105] For the Irish Articles, see Bray, *Documents*, 394–407. For the proceedings of the convocation, see G. L. Bray (ed.), *Records of Convocation*, 20 vols. (Woodbridge: Boydell & Brewer, 2005–6), 16:375–396.

[106] R. B. Knox, *James Ussher Archbishop of Armagh* (Cardiff: University of Wales Press, 1967); A. Ford, *James Ussher: Theology, History and Politics in Early Modern Ireland and England* (Oxford: Oxford University Press, 2007). See also R. Snoddy, *The Soteriology of James Ussher: The Act and Object of Saving Faith* (Oxford: Oxford University Press, 2014).

[107] Ford, *James Ussher*, 108. His essay was entitled, 'The True Intent and Extent of Christ's Death and Satisfaction'.

not for things, and those people were the sinners chosen for salvation from before the foundation of the world. Some modern theologians and historians call this 'hypothetical universalism' and regard Ussher's position as unorthodox from a Calvinist point of view, but this is mistaken.[108] His purpose was to do justice to each side of the argument. He was 'inclusivist' when talking about things (sins) but 'exclusivist' when talking about people (sinners). In so far as anyone has come close to resolving this apparent paradox, Ussher must be given credit for producing the most satisfactory resolution to a problem that in the final analysis remains a mystery hidden in the mind of God.

Ussher did not convince everyone of his position but he managed to persuade many of those who mattered, including Samuel Ward (1572–1643), John Preston and John Davenant (1572–1641), all of whom went to Dort and argued there for his understanding of the matter. It was admittedly a subtle position and open to misunderstanding, as became clear in the teaching of Moïse Amyraut (1596–1664), a French Protestant who picked up Ussher's ideas, or something very similar to them, from the Scot John Cameron (c.1579–1625), who became Professor of Divinity in the Protestant academy of Saumur in 1618. Amyraut would later teach a doctrine of universal atonement, meaning that Christ had died for all people, although not all were chosen for salvation. This view, known as Amyraldianism, makes no sense because it assumes that God has done something (provided for the salvation of everyone) that has not taken effect, a failure that implies some limitation on his sovereignty. That is certainly not what Ussher believed or taught![109]

Somewhat unfortunately, Ussher is now remembered mainly for his work on biblical chronology. By calculating the periods of years given in the genealogies of the Old Testament, he worked out that the world was created on 23 October 4004 BC, and his prestige was so great that his theory came to be accepted by many people as accurate. The date was even printed in Bibles into the nineteenth century; but of course it is rejected today, even by those who take a literalist view of the creation narrative in Genesis. Ussher was wrong, but before we ridicule his efforts we should acknowledge that he was working according to scientific principles as they were generally understood and accepted in his day, and learn from his mistake that no human

---

[108] Ussher would have understood 'hypothetical universalism' as a contradiction in terms, because there can be nothing hypothetical about the mind of God, who knows all things. It was obvious to him, of course, that God is not a universalist.

[109] See J. D. Moore, *English Hypothetical Universalism: John Preston and the Softening of Reformed Theology* (Grand Rapids, Mich.: Eerdmans, 2007), who has popularized this misunderstanding. This is an area of English/Irish Reformed theology that remains underexplored and therefore open to misinterpretation by those who do not understand what Ussher was trying to say.

theory, however soundly based it may appear to be, can be regarded as definitive.

Ussher combined in his person all that his native land could and should have been if only reason, balance and moderation had been held together. He was episcopalian, but in a way that could accommodate presbyterians and congregationalists.[110] He was catholic and reformed in the best sense, rather than Catholic and Reformed in an antagonistic one. He was extremely learned but did not live in an ivory tower, isolated from the problems of his time. Above all, he was respected by everyone he met, not least Oliver Cromwell, who allowed him to be buried in Westminster Abbey according to the liturgy of the 1604 Book of Common Prayer – a banned book at the time. It is hard not to think that if the times had been kinder and there had been more men like him, Ireland's history would have been considerably happier than it in fact turned out to be.

---

[110] See R. Snoddy (ed.), *James Ussher and a Reformed Episcopal Church: Sermons and Treatises on Ecclesiology* (Leesburg, Va.: Davenant Institute, 2018).

9
Sowing the wind (1625–53)

The world is turned upside down (1625–40)

An observer of the British scene around 1620 would probably have concluded that all was peaceful and well. Compared with France, where religious strife was still not over, despite the limited toleration granted to Protestants by the Edict of Nantes (1598), or the Holy Roman Empire, where what would become a thirty-year war of religion had recently broken out, Britain and Ireland must have seemed like an oasis of calm. The Church of England was functioning reasonably well, and the king was doing what he could to repair the damage caused by the financial losses of the previous century. Scotland appeared to have settled into a mixed presbyterian and episcopal system that kept most people happy. In Ireland both Catholics and Protestants were organizing themselves, but they tended to keep their distance from each other, and the Catholics, in particular, appeared to want no more than the kind of toleration given to the Protestants in France. Differences of opinion there certainly were, and fringe groups that would never be happy with existing conditions could be found here and there, but they were marginal and could always go off to America if life at home became too intolerable. Yet within twenty years the British Isles would be aflame with religious discord and the system carefully constructed over the previous century would come crashing down. How and why did that happen?

Many explanations for the catastrophe can be (and have been) offered, but at the heart of them all lies one person – King Charles I (1625–49).[1] Charles was the second son of James I and was not originally due to inherit the throne. He was born in Scotland in 1600 but left before he turned 4, and returned only briefly during his reign. He never visited Ireland, or even most of England. He became heir to the throne when his elder brother died unexpectedly in 1612, and he was not truly prepared to succeed. He was quite different from his

---

[1] Several good studies of Charles I exist. See, among others, C. Carlton, *Charles I: The Personal Monarch* (London: Routledge & Kegan Paul, 1983); M. B. Young, *Charles I* (Basingstoke: Macmillan, 1997); R. Cust, *Charles I: A Political Life* (London: Pearson Longman, 2005); D. Cressy, *Charles I and the People of England* (Oxford: Oxford University Press, 2015).

father. James I was an intellectual but he was also very crude in his mannerisms. Charles was the opposite – not very interested in theology but fastidious in his appearance and a discerning collector of art. He was also faithful to his wife, a rare trait in a seventeenth-century monarch. Unfortunately he was a true believer in the divine right of kings and saw no reason why he should explain himself to anyone, least of all his subjects. He regarded his ministers and bishops as tools of his policies, and when they were no longer useful he discarded them without pity or regret. He had no idea that promises ought to be kept and was completely untrustworthy because he believed that whatever he did was justified by his status before God. In the end he was tried and put to death by his own people, but never showed any sign that he understood why, and regarded their actions as illegal. Most astonishingly of all, after his death he was widely hailed as a saint and became the only modern British monarch to have churches dedicated to his memory – King Charles the Martyr.[2] Even today there are a few people who commemorate his death on 30 January every year, which makes him unique in the annals of British kingship. Yet to anyone who examines his career at all closely, he was the most foolish king who ever ruled the British Isles, and his downfall comes as no surprise to anyone. For better or for worse – and in this case, usually for worse – his shadow looms large over the events of his reign, and everything that happened in it leads inexorably back to him as its ultimate author.[3]

Charles I's troubles began with his marriage to Henrietta Maria, daughter of Henry IV of France. Henry IV had been a Protestant who inherited the French throne by dynastic accident. The Catholic Establishment refused to accept him, and after a four-year stalemate Henry IV gave in and converted, famously saying that 'Paris is worth a mass.' He then granted a measure of toleration to the Protestants in the famous Edict of Nantes (1598), which lasted for the rest of his life. But religious feelings ran high and in 1610 Henry was assassinated by a Catholic fanatic. His children were brought up as Catholics and were considerably more dedicated to their faith than their father had been. Louis XIII (1610–43) did what he could to whittle down the privileges granted to Protestants by the Edict of Nantes, and England was naturally expected to intervene on their behalf, which it did. But Charles I was married to Louis XIII's sister and, as part of the marriage agreement, she was allowed to retain her religious practice in a special chapel in Whitehall. This chapel was not entirely private, and both Henrietta Maria and her priests saw it as their duty to

---

[2] In Potters Bar, Falmouth and Peak Forest, Derbyshire.
[3] See J. Davies, *The Caroline Captivity of the Church: Charles I and the Remoulding of Anglicanism* (Oxford: Clarendon Press, 1992).

proselytize for Catholicism as much as they could. They were not dramatically successful, but a few courtiers did convert, leaving the impression that the king was sympathetic to Rome and merely waiting for the right moment to reveal his hand. When we remember that Queen Elizabeth I had been criticized merely for having a silver crucifix on the Communion table in her private chapel, we can understand why the reaction to this was so severe.

Suspicions that Charles I was heading in a Catholic direction were only increased by his attempts to placate the Old English element in Ireland, who petitioned him to allow them to retain their property and serve in their traditional offices, even though they were Catholics. Charles I looked favourably on this and in 1628 he granted most of their requests in what are known as the 'graces'. Putting toleration of this kind into effect was not always straightforward, but on the whole it seems that the 'graces' were initially observed and that, for a time, Catholic relief from civil disabilities was real, if not entirely satisfactory.[4] Unfortunately, although hardly surprisingly, the 'graces' provoked a negative reaction from Protestants, both in Ireland and in England, even as they left Catholics asking for more. It was a moderate solution that in the end pleased nobody and sowed the seeds of future trouble.

In England, Charles I abandoned the cautious policy of his father with regard to the church and sided openly with the anti-Calvinists, or so-called 'Arminians'. It is unclear to what extent the king sympathized with their theology, or even understood it, but that was not his main interest. Charles was what we would now call a Prayer Book fundamentalist, attached to every letter of the rubrics the Puritans were famous for disregarding. What he wanted above all was beautiful and dignified worship, as laid down in the Prayer Book and in the 1604 canons; and as we have seen, that was also a major concern of the Arminian bishops. There was thus a natural alliance between them that was to have theological implications when Charles sought to impose his ritualistic ideas on the church as a whole. Matters were further complicated by genuine theological controversy, which focused on Richard Montagu (1577–1641). Montagu had been educated in the strict Calvinism of John Whitgift, but whether that turned him against it later on is unclear. He was certainly opposed to Rome, and in 1624 answered a tract that had been written at Douai by John Heigham, a Catholic exile there.

Heigham had called his tract *The Gagge of the Reformed Gospel*, and in it cited forty-three points on which the Church of England had deviated from the true faith of Rome. Montagu replied to this with *A New Gagg for an Old*

---

[4] On this, see A. Clarke, *The Old English in Ireland, 1625–42* (Dublin: Four Courts Press, 2000), 44–59.

Goose, in which he countered Heigham by saying that in fact there were only eight points on which Rome and the Church of England were in disagreement. This was interpreted by the Puritans, including Members of Parliament, as the thin wedge of creeping Catholicism, and Montagu appealed to James I in his defence. James read the tract and apparently agreed with its main argument, although he died soon afterwards and nothing came of that. Instead criticism of Montagu grew louder, and in 1625 he wrote a second book, *Appello Caesarem*, in which he tried to defend himself against attacks that now included the charge of Arminianism.[5] In fact Montagu had only recently started reading Arminius directly, although his sympathies undoubtedly lay in that direction.[6] Whatever the rights and wrongs of the case might have been, Montagu was censured by the House of Commons, where Calvinism, if not necessarily Puritanism, was widespread, and Charles I sided with him against the parliamentarians. In 1628 he even appointed Montagu Bishop of Chichester, a mark of favour that went well beyond mere sympathy with Montagu's opinions.[7]

Charles I was bored with theological debate and regarded those who engaged in it as troublemakers. On 24 December 1628 he issued a Declaration in which he insisted that the Thirty-nine Articles of 1571 were the true and sufficient doctrine of the Church of England, and forbade all theological discussion that went beyond them. Considering that further discussion had been going on at least since the publication of the Lambeth Articles in 1595, and that revision of the Articles had been accomplished in Ireland (in 1615), this was bolting the stable door after the horses had escaped. But that did not deter Charles, who concluded his Declaration with the following warning:

> if any public reader in either of our universities, or any head or master of a college, or any other person respectively in either of them, shall affix any new sense to any Article, or shall publicly read, determine or hold any public disputation, or suffer any such to be held either way, in either the universities or colleges respectively, or if any divine in the universities shall preach or print any thing either way, other than is already established in Convocation with our royal assent, he, or they the offenders, shall be liable to our displeasure, and the Church's censure in our

---

[5] The Latin title of the book means 'I appeal to Caesar', the words of St Paul when he was tried before the Roman authorities in Palestine. See Acts 25:11.

[6] See N. Tyacke, *Anti-Calvinists: The Rise of English Arminianism c. 1590–1640* (Oxford: Clarendon Press, 1987), 125–163.

[7] Montagu served in Chichester for ten years and was then translated to Norwich in 1638, where he died three years later.

commission ecclesiastical, as well as any other; and we will see there shall be due execution upon them.[8]

This was soon followed by a reaction in the House of Commons, where on 24 February 1629 a subcommittee complained about the king's policies in the following terms:

Here in England we observe an extraordinary growth of popery, insomuch that in some counties, where in Queen Elizabeth's time there were few or none known recusants, now there are above 2000, and all the rest generally apt to revolt. A bold and open allowance of their religion, by frequent and public resort to mass, in multitudes, without control, and that even to the queen's court, to the great scandal of his majesty's government ... The subtle and pernicious spreading of the Arminian faction; whereby they have kindled such a fire of division in the very bowels of the state, as if not speedily extinguished, is of itself sufficient to ruin our religion, by dividing us from the Reformed Churches abroad and separating amongst ourselves at home . . .[9]

Charles I's response was swift and brutal. A month later he shut down both the parliament and the convocations that met in tandem with it, and embarked upon a 'personal rule' that would last until 1640. During that time he demonstrated that his determination to suppress theological discussion was no idle threat, and the High Commission courts that had originally been set up to enforce the Elizabethan Settlement embarked on the most active (and notorious) phase of their somewhat chequered existence.

One immediate consequence of Charles I's crackdown was that a number of prominent Puritans began to think seriously about abandoning the country. One of these was John Cotton (1585–1652), who in 1612 became rector of St Botolph's Church in Boston, Lincolnshire.[10] Cotton was an eminent and much sought-after preacher, and before long had acquired a considerable following. After 1629, life became gradually more difficult for him because of his pronounced Puritan views, and in 1633 he finally decided that he had to leave for New England, where he was warmly welcomed. He settled in Boston,

---

[8] The Declaration is still printed in the 1662 Book of Common Prayer, just before the Articles. It can also be found in G. L. Bray (ed.), *Documents of the English Reformation*, 3rd edn (Cambridge: James Clarke, 2019), 433–434.

[9] J. Kenyon, *The Stuart Constitution*, 2nd edn (Cambridge: Cambridge University Press, 1986), 141.

[10] The name 'Boston' is a corruption of 'Botolph's Town'.

Massachusetts (naturally), and became the most influential pastor and religious statesman in the colony. Cotton was a congregationalist in terms of ecclesiastical polity, and persuaded the Massachusetts churches to accept that form of government. Later on he tried to encourage the parliamentary party back home to do the same, but he lost out to the Presbyterians, and New England went its own way. In this we see for the first time how transplanted British Christianity would come to differ from that of the mother country. The basic beliefs were the same, but the form of church organization and the priorities in teaching and evangelism would work out differently over time. Nobody in England tried to impose an order on the colonial churches, although the Church of England managed to retain some control over its transplants by not appointing bishops in the colonies. That meant that intending clergymen had to go to England for their education and ordination, a situation that continued until the American Revolution but which was detrimental to the attempts occasionally made (or mooted) to establish the Church of England in America.

The Puritans solved the problem of educating their clergy by establishing a college just outside Boston in 1636. The place was named Cambridge, because so many Puritan ministers had been educated there, and in 1638 the college was named after John Harvard (1607–38), a young minister who had recently emigrated to the colony and had left a sizeable bequest to the new foundation. A few years later similar efforts were made in Connecticut, but it would not be until 1701 that the foundation of what is now Yale University would be properly laid. The New England colleges were the first in the English-speaking world that were independent of the state church and offered a theological education that would keep the Puritan tradition alive even when attempts were being made to suppress it in England. Thus we see how the personal rule of Charles I had unintended consequences.

The evidence of the High Commission courts during this time is fascinating and particularly instructive because it sheds rare light on what was happening at parish level. The reports must be read with some caution, because only the most egregious cases came to the Commission's attention. One of these was Anthony Lapthorne, Rector of Tretire with Michaelchurch in Herefordshire from 1631 to 1634. On 9 October 1634 he was charged with not having read divine service according to the Prayer Book and for interrupting the reading of Scripture with impromptu expository sermons on the text. The accusations against him went on:

> In expounding he inveighed at some of his parishioners with whom he was offended. He never observed any holy days or fasting days except at

Christmas, Easter and Whitsuntide. At baptism he refused to take the child into his arms, or to sign it with the cross. In holy communion, after having said the words of benediction to one or two, to the rest he said: 'Take and eat', or 'Take and drink.' He reviled some of the parishioners who bowed at the name of Jesus . . . He had also taught that Christ did not descend into hell . . .[11]

Reading between the lines we can detect that Lapthorne's real crime was that he had offended some of the congregation, probably by a failed exorcism he had tried to perform, and that they were getting their revenge by reporting his misdemeanours to the High Commission.[12] His infractions were neither serious nor uncommon, and many others would have done the same. The only doctrinal point mentioned is that he apparently denied Christ's descent into hell, but this seems to have been added to the charges against him as an afterthought that was probably intended to reinforce the gravity of the accusations made against him. The court duly found him guilty and he was deprived of his living, although what happened to him afterwards is unknown.[13]

In another case a layman called John Elkins, of Isham in Northamptonshire, was arraigned on 16 October 1634:

Charged with irreverent behaviour in wearing his hat during divine service, in causing 100*l*. to be told over the communion table, and tendered to the use of John Pickering in performance of a bargain for house and lands, and in saying in the streets of Isham in scorn that a ploughman is as good as a priest. Fined 100*l*., ordered to make a public submission in the church of Isham, and condemned in costs.[14]

Was Elkins a deliberate troublemaker? Churches were often used for secular purposes when divine service was not in progress, and there does not seem to have been anything unusual in his conduct. In any case he was charged with only a single offence, which seems excessive. Once again, reading between the lines, it is not difficult to discern what his real crime was – he was saying publicly that the clergy were no better than the laity, and the humble, illiterate

---

[11] Kenyon, *Stuart Constitution*, 164–165.

[12] The attempted exorcism is reported in *Calendar of State Papers, Domestic 1634–5* (London: Her Majesty's Stationery Office, 1864), 263.

[13] He had been a Fellow of Exeter College, Oxford (1593–1600), and a chaplain to King James I. The claim made in the *Alumni Oxonienses* that the Westminster Assembly appointed him as Rector of Sedgefield, Durham, in May 1647, is not supported by the surviving minutes of that Assembly.

[14] Kenyon, *Stuart Constitution*, 165.

laity at that. Such behaviour could not be tolerated, and so he was fined for exercising an unwelcome freedom of speech that brought the established social order into question.

The High Commission courts were an obvious irritant in the lives of many people, who could be denounced by their neighbours for trivial reasons. Real persecution of the Puritans was more commonly reserved for the court of Star Chamber set up under Henry VII in order to provide justice in cases involving prominent people, whom the ordinary courts might hesitate to deal with. Over time it came to exercise extraordinary judicial powers that went beyond the usual framework of the courts. In the 1630s, anti-Calvinist bishops like William Laud and Richard Neile sat on it and used their influence to convict people who were guilty of nothing more than the usual Puritan disregard for liturgical and canonical niceties. The elevation of Laud to the archbishopric of Canterbury on 6 August 1633 gave the king a reliable weapon for the prosecution of his campaign against Puritan disorders, and Laud proved to be equal to the task.[15]

On 18 October, following enquiries, the king reissued the Book of Sports and insisted that it should be read and applied with much greater rigour than had been the case in 1618.[16] Soon afterwards Laud followed up with orders to place the 'holy table' at the east end of every church and to fence it off with railings, at which communicants were expected to kneel. Laud even added insult to injury by freely referring to the table as an 'altar', a word that inevitably recalled the idea of eucharistic sacrifice that had been rejected by the Reformers and was anathema not only to the Puritans but to much mainstream church opinion as well.[17] Both measures stirred up a hornet's nest of opposition, but Charles I and Laud carried on, believing that they were bringing order and decorum back to a church that had apparently forgotten what to them was the beauty of holiness, and quite heedless of the negative reaction they were causing.

Matters came to a head in 1637 when three men, Henry Burton (1578–1648), John Bastwick (1593–1654) and William Prynne (1600–69) were summoned before the Star Chamber, charged with having defamed both the king and the church.[18] All three had been in trouble before, all were vociferous critics of royal policy and all were openly contemptuous of the court proceedings. Very

---

[15] See Davies, *Caroline Captivity*, 46–86.
[16] For a careful analysis of this, see K. Sharpe, *The Personal Rule of Charles I* (New Haven, Conn.: Yale University Press, 1992), 351–363.
[17] K. Fincham, 'The Restoration of the Altars in the 1630s', *Historical Journal* 44.4 (2001), 919–940.
[18] Sharpe, *Personal Rule*, 758–765.

few people had any sympathy for them, and even their Puritan allies were shocked by their ungodly behaviour. Had they been quietly fined and sent away, probably nothing more would have been heard of them. But the judges of Star Chamber wanted to make examples of them so as to deter others, and decreed that they should all have their ears cut off. Mutilation was obviously preferable to execution and in that sense the men were treated leniently, but there was another problem. Burton was a respected theologian, Bastwick a trained physician and Prynne a notable lawyer.

Cropping ears was the sort of punishment meted out to peasants, not to respectable gentlemen like them. In punishing them like this the court was refusing to honour their social status, and it was this that swayed public opinion in their favour, because other educated people realized that they too could be disrespected in this way. Even Establishment figures who had no sympathy with them felt uneasy at this breach of custom. It was one thing for street preachers to rail against class divisions, but for the upholders of law and order to ignore them was to undermine something even deeper than the state. As word of their fate spread, the men became heroes and martyrs to the cause of freedom, something that they did not deserve and was certainly never intended. But as so often in the life of Charles I, the realization that his official policy had backfired came too late. The reputation of the Star Chamber, and with it the authority of the bishops who sat in it and ultimately of the king who sanctioned it, was deeply compromised. It was the beginning of the end for his personal rule.

If Charles I had done nothing but try to impose stricter discipline on the Church of England he might have got away with it. But his ambition went much further than that. He was determined to sort out the religion of Ireland and Scotland as well, which was a very different proposition. Ireland came first. With the English Parliament out of the way, the king felt free to disregard the 'graces' by which he had previously offered toleration to Catholics, and he renewed plans to plant Protestants on lands seized from them. The Old English, who stood to lose most from this change of policy, naturally reacted against it but, instead of rebelling, they rather cleverly decided to work on Sir Thomas Wentworth, from 1640 Earl of Strafford (1593–1641), when he was appointed Lord Deputy in 1632.[19] Their aim was to persuade him that the king's interests lay in supporting them by confirming the 'graces', and for a time they seemed to have succeeded. But an alliance between Old English Catholics and the Lord

---

[19] See H. Kearney, *Strafford in Ireland 1633–41: A Study in Absolutism* (Cambridge: Cambridge University Press, 1959).

Deputy would inevitably be anti-Protestant, and such a position was untenable for Wentworth. In the end he repudiated the 'graces' and sought to neutralize the Old English by summoning a parliament that he hoped would vote a subsidy to the king and confirm his policies. Somewhat surprisingly, his manoeuvre succeeded and the Old English found themselves isolated and deceived by a parliament only too willing to do whatever Wentworth asked. Buoyed by this success, Wentworth decided that he could go on and reform the Protestant Church of Ireland as well.

In theory, the king and Church of Ireland were on the same side, but in fact they had very different ideas about what Protestantism ought to mean. The Church of Ireland was a minority in the country but it was more united around Calvinistic Puritanism than the Church of England was. James Ussher was its primate and he was personally committed to the Irish Articles of 1615, which were the most advanced confession of faith in the Reformed church up to that time. In a sense the Church of Ireland did not have Puritans because it did not need them – everyone (more or less) was on the same wavelength.[20] There was nobody to promote the king's vision of what the church should be, and so it fell to John Bramhall (1594–1663), a Yorkshireman with no Irish connections, to accompany Wentworth to Ireland and undertake the reforms the king desired. Bramhall began as Archdeacon of Meath, but in 1634 was consecrated as Bishop of Derry, which gave him standing in the parliament and convocation that met in the same year.[21] The aims of Wentworth and Bramhall were basically two – to replace the Irish Articles with the Thirty-nine Articles of 1571, and to adopt the 1604 canons, both in the name of achieving conformity with the Church of England.[22]

Bramhall's chief opponent was James Ussher, who had virtually the entire church behind him. Ussher did not reject the Thirty-nine Articles of course, but objected to the sidelining of the Irish Articles, and ensured that they remained authoritative in Ireland.[23] But when it came to adopting the canons of 1604, Ussher put his foot down. He knew how those canons were being used in England to attack the Puritans, and was determined not to allow anything like that to happen in Ireland. Many of the 1604 canons were inoffensive, and

---

[20] See C. Gribben, *The Irish Puritans: James Ussher and the Reformation of the Church* (Auburn, Mass.: Evangelical Press USA, 2003).

[21] For the proceedings of the convocation, see G. L. Bray (ed.), *Records of Convocation*, 20 vols. (Woodbridge: Boydell & Brewer, 2005–6), 16:402–458.

[22] See J. McCafferty, *The Reconstruction of the Church of Ireland: Bishop Bramhall and the Laudian Reforms, 1633–1641* (Cambridge: Cambridge University Press, 2007).

[23] They were effectively set aside at the Restoration in 1660 but have never been repudiated by the Church of Ireland, and it can be argued that they are still part of its doctrine today.

he was happy to see them adopted. But a controversial subject like the signing with the cross in baptism, which had been enjoined by Canon 30 of 1604, was a step too far and was omitted from the Irish Canons.[24] In addition to that, the Irish Canons added certain provisions designed to reinforce Puritan principles. For example, Canon 12 says:

> The ministers . . . shall teach the people to place their whole trust and confidence in God and not in creatures, neither in the habit or scapular of any friar, nor in hallowed beads, medals, relics or such like trumperies. They shall do their endeavour likewise to root out all ungodly, superstitious and barbarous customs, as using of charms, sorcery, enchantments, witchcraft or soothsaying, and generally to reform the manners of the people committed to their charge, unto a Christian, sober and civil conversation.[25]

Neither Wentworth nor Bramhall could object to that, but it was not the sort of thing they would have thought to include either. Ussher also ensured that there would be a place for the Irish language in public worship, something Bramhall opposed.[26] This was a particularly sensitive subject because William Bedell (1571–1642), Provost of Trinity College from 1627 and Bishop of Kilmore and Ardagh from 1629, insisted on promoting the use of Irish in all situations, and made sure the whole Bible was finally translated into that language.[27] Unfortunately it was not published until 1685, when the political situation was very different and, although it was used in Scotland, where the local Gaelic language was still close enough to classical Irish to make it a viable option, it fared badly in Ireland. Almost incomprehensibly to the modern mind, Bedell's efforts were hampered by his colleagues in the Church of Ireland, even by Archbishop Ussher, who deplored Bedell's evangelistic efforts on the ground that Parliament had made it illegal to preach the gospel in Irish.[28] Thus the anti-Irish prejudices of the Old English clashed with the evangelistic zeal of an English Puritan who felt no inhibition in crossing

---

[24] For the Irish Canons, see G. L. Bray (ed.), *The Anglican Canons, 1529–1947* (Woodbridge: Boydell & Brewer, 1998), 485–531.

[25] Ibid. 493–494.

[26] See Canon 8 in ibid. 491–492.

[27] See M. Caball, 'The Bible in Early Modern Gaelic Ireland: Tradition, Collaboration and Alienation', in K. Killeen, H. Smith and R. Willie (eds.), *Oxford History of the Bible in Early Modern England, c. 1530–1700* (Oxford: Oxford University Press, 2015), 332–349, esp. 342–349.

[28] The ban on the use of Irish was held to date from the legislation passed in the 1537 Irish parliament that recognized the king's supremacy in ecclesiastical affairs. The Irish Act of Uniformity (1560) had provided that Latin, not Irish, should be used in places where English was not understood.

the cultural divide and did all he could to bring godly reformation to the Irish church.[29]

This difference of approach was a great pity, not least because it did nothing to further the cause to which both Ussher and Bedell were committed. In the words of Crawford Gribben:

> Despite their differences, Ussher's scholarship and Bedell's management skills and missionary interests had demonstrated the authenticity of the Irish Church. Nevertheless, their efforts to reach the minds and hearts of Catholic Ireland lacked spectacular success. The Protestant apologetics of the Irish Puritans contributed a great deal to establishing the Irish credentials of the Protestant faith, but they saw little in the way of true revival.[30]

The Scottish crisis

Ireland was difficult and its confessional mix intractable, but it was to be in Scotland that the religious policies of Charles I and Archbishop Laud were to come unstuck. Like his grandmother Mary, Charles was a stranger to Scotland, but unlike her he did not go there and misgovern it directly. Instead he directed its affairs from a distance, in so far as he was able to do so and had the time to spare. Soon after his accession he revoked all the grants of church revenue that had been made by the Crown since 1542 – well before the Reformation. The intention was to rationalize the income of the church and provide adequate stipends for its ministers, but the fact that Charles acted without consulting any of those affected meant that it alienated the lords and others who had benefited from the ecclesiastical lands and revenues that had been assigned to them. In the end, a fair settlement was worked out, so that the lay impropriators of the benefices were given adequate compensation and the ministers were provided for out of the tithe (teind) income to which they had always been theoretically entitled. It was a solution that would endure for 300 years, and so must be regarded as a success, but it left the governing classes wondering what the king, without bothering to tell them about it, might do next.[31]

---

[29] See Bray, *Records of Convocation*, 16:458–459, for the reforming canons of the diocese of Kildare, 1638.

[30] Gribben, *Irish Puritans*, 37.

[31] See G. Donaldson, *Scottish Historical Documents*, corrected edn (Glasgow: Neil Wilson Publishing, 1974), 185–188. In the 1630s, Archbishop Laud of Canterbury would try to achieve the same result in England, but without success. See Davies, *Caroline Captivity*, 83–86.

In 1633, Charles I finally managed to get to Scotland for his coronation, and he was well received. But unfortunately he brought with him William Laud, then still Bishop of London but soon to become Archbishop of Canterbury. Worse still, he ignored the local clergy and entrusted the coronation arrangements to Laud, who made sure that everything was done according to English norms. Thinking to impress the locals, Charles announced that Edinburgh would become the seat of a new diocese, but then he appointed William Forbes, a cleric of Laudian principles, as its first bishop. Forbes died a few months later, which was perhaps just as well but, as so often with Charles I, the effects were devastating. Those who disagreed with Laud – the vast majority of the Scottish clergy – were offended by the appointment of Forbes, while those few who supported him were soon left without a champion. It was the worst of both worlds.

The next thing the king did was to hold a parliament that he managed to pack with his own supporters. Among its business was a bill that restated and reinforced the king's right to determine the vestments the clergy ought to wear. Needless to say, Charles dictated that these should be the same as those worn in England, despite the fact that many in the southern kingdom resented them.[32] A number of parliamentarians voted against the bill, and the king made a note of who they were. When they later expressed their disquiet by submitting a modest petition to him, he took offence and had the petition's chief author, Lord Balmerino, arrested and tried – for treason![33] After a trial lasting more than six months, Balmerino was eventually pardoned, but the damage had been done. To make matters even worse, the Archbishop of St Andrews was promptly appointed as Lord Chancellor, an office no cleric had held since the Reformation and which was purely secular. By that time Charles I and Laud had gone back to England, leaving a trail of bitterness behind them and fear for what might still be to come.

Those who were in doubt about that did not have long to wait. The Church of Scotland had no canons, a defect that the king and Laud were determined to remedy as soon as possible. In 1636 they produced a book of *Canons and Constitutions Ecclesiastical*, which was approved by royal authority and put into effect without so much as a nod in the direction of the General Assembly of the Church of Scotland, which had not met since the fiasco of the Five Articles of Perth in 1618.[34] In case anyone should question the king's right to impose such legislation on the church, Canon 2 made it clear:

---

[32] See Donaldson, *Scottish Historical Documents*, 188–190.
[33] See ibid. 191–194.
[34] See Bray, *Anglican Canons*, 532–552.

Whosoever shall hereafter affirm that the king's majesty hath not the same authority in causes ecclesiastical that the godly kings had amongst the Jews, and Christian emperors in the primitive Church, or impeach in any part his royal supremacy in causes ecclesiastical, let him be excommunicated and not restored, but only by the archbishop of the province after his repentance and public revocation of these his wicked errors.[35]

It was everything a Laudian could wish for – the divine right of the king to legislate for the church and the prerogative of the archbishop to decide the fate of the accused without consultation. It comes as no surprise that along with these canons was a new Prayer Book, supposedly based on the English one but in fact somewhat different. The Scottish bishops had suggested to Laud that a genuinely Scottish Book might have a better chance of being accepted in Scotland than the English one would have had, and Laud was only too happy to comply. But what he produced was a Book that had virtually nothing distinctively 'Scottish' about it. Instead it harked back to the 1549 English Prayer Book, a halfway house between Catholicism and Protestantism that by then had largely been forgotten in England. Different it certainly was, but in all the wrong ways – the king and Laud had scored yet another own goal. Charles I nevertheless ordered it to be used in the Church of Scotland, although the implementation of his proclamation was delayed for several months. Finally, on 23 July 1637, the fateful day for its inauguration came, and a great crowd of dignitaries gathered in St Giles Cathedral in Edinburgh. But as the dean began to read the service, a humble woman called Jenny Geddes threw her stool at him and a riot broke out.[36] The service was concluded with difficulty, but it was obvious that the Book was unacceptable and its use was suspended.

Charles I naturally refused to accept this and tried to reassure the Scots that their fear that the new Book was an attempt to reintroduce Catholicism was unfounded. They were not persuaded. Over the next few months a group of nobles got together and worked out a plan of opposition. They composed a document in three parts – the first part was simply the so-called Second Scottish Confession of 1581, which repudiated anything to do with the church of Rome. The second part was a rehearsal of all the Reformation legislation passed by the Scottish Parliament since 1560. The third – and ultimately the most important – part was a statement of the obligation of every churchman to resist the innovations recently introduced into the church and to uphold the

---

[35] Ibid. 533.
[36] The story about Jenny Geddes has been embellished by legend, but there is no doubt that there was a riot that day.

true Reformed religion. This document was called the National Covenant and it was signed by the country's leading nobles in Greyfriars Kirk, Edinburgh, on 28 February 1638.[37] It was then circulated around the country and signed – sometimes under compulsion – by virtually every adult male who could write his name. Only Aberdeen and the Highlands were not represented, the former because of local opposition and the latter because it was populated by Gaelic-speakers whom nobody bothered to consult.

The king was at his wits' end. Foolish to the last, he appointed the Marquis of Hamilton as his special envoy to treat with the Covenanters in the hope of bringing them round to his point of view. Hamilton did what he could, but to no avail. The king was forced to withdraw the canons and the Prayer Book, and to allow both a General Assembly of the church and a parliament to meet freely. That, alas, merely provoked another dispute. The bishops wanted the General Assembly to be composed of themselves and representatives of the clergy, along the lines of the English convocations. But the Covenanters, most of whom were laymen, would not accept that. They insisted that lay elders should also be represented in what would be a genuinely presbyterian Assembly. Unable to object, the king gave way and the Assembly duly convened in Glasgow on 21 November 1638. It proved to be a watershed in the history of the Church of Scotland.[38] The smouldering resentments of the past decade now burst into flames and the result was revolution. On 4 December all six of the General Assemblies that had met since the union of the Crowns in 1603 were declared null and void on the ground that their decisions had not been taken freely.[39] The High Commission courts James VI had established in imitation of their English counterparts were abolished on 6 December and, two days later, so was episcopacy. On 19 December the Assembly declared that ministers of the church should not hold civil office, which was deemed incompatible with their calling. Furthermore, it declared that the next General Assembly would convene on 18 July 1639, although it allowed that the king might decide otherwise. Such deference to the king seems surprising, but it must be remembered that the Covenanters were not rebels – at least not in their own eyes. They were loyal subjects of their monarch, whom they believed had been seduced by evil counsellors – the age-old excuse for overlooking bad royal policies. This residual loyalty to the king was not to be trifled with however. Years later, when the English parliamentarians executed Charles I, the Scots

---

[37] For the text, see Donaldson, *Scottish Historical Documents*, 194–201.

[38] See ibid. 202–206 for extracts of the most important proceedings.

[39] They were the assemblies of Lithgow (1606 and 1608), Glasgow (1610), Aberdeen (1616), St Andrews (1617) and Perth (1618).

refused to accept the abolition of the monarchy and promptly hailed his son as King Charles II, a decision that would lead to war and an English invasion. As they saw the matter, ancient Israel had had evil kings but the monarchy was still part of God's covenant with that nation, and Scotland would not be any different.

Reduced to desperation, Charles I decided to invade Scotland and reduce the country to obedience by force of arms.[40] The Marquis of Hamilton supported him, as did some nobles in Aberdeenshire, but they could not prevail against the majority of the country. The king went to Berwick-upon-Tweed in the hope of rallying his troops, who were by then thoroughly demoralized, but there was no military action. On 16 June 1639, Charles agreed to withdraw and Scotland was left in peace – for the time being.

At this point the Earl of Strafford returned to London from Ireland and urged the king to summon a parliament in order to raise money for a proper invasion of Scotland. Thinking he had nothing to lose, the king took this advice and the English Parliament met on 13 April 1640, for the first time in over eleven years. It soon turned out that the House of Commons had no intention of giving the king any money to fight the Scots, especially not in order to re-establish episcopacy there. They had plenty of other grievances as well, and before long it was clear that the king was not going to get anywhere with them. So, on 5 May 1640, he dissolved the 'Short Parliament', as it came to be known, and resorted instead to a different tactic for raising money.

Ever since 1545 the English convocations had met in tandem with Parliament and had voted a clerical subsidy to the Crown that had been distinct from the lay taxation since 1340. Charles I hit on what to him was the brilliant idea of maintaining the Canterbury Convocation in being after the dissolution of Parliament, and asking them to vote him the usual subsidy so that he could prosecute the war with Scotland. Given that the cause at issue was an ecclesiastical one, this must have seemed fair enough to him, and the bishops went along with the plan because it enabled them to do something else as well – enact a new set of canons. The Convocation sat until 29 May, during which time it was exceptionally busy.[41] The subsidy had already been voted on and was confirmed without any difficulty, but it was the new canons that excited the greatest interest. Here at last was the opportunity the king and Archbishop Laud had been waiting for to reshape the Church of England in their own image, and they lost no time in going about it. On 21 May 1640 they enacted

---

[40] See M. C. Fissel, *The Bishops' Wars: Charles I's Campaigns Against Scotland, 1638–1640* (Cambridge: Cambridge University Press, 1994).

[41] For the proceedings, see Bray, *Records of Convocation*, 8:165–231.

seventeen new canons, which they claimed they had every right to do. These put a clearly Laudian stamp on the church.[42]

The first two canons dealt with the royal supremacy and the celebration of the king's accession. Then came the measures to be taken to suppress Catholicism, followed by one against Socinianism,[43] and another against the different sects that had sprung up in recent years. After that came an oath that the clergy were expected to take, promising to resist all innovations in doctrine and church government, followed by another concerning rites and ceremonies, both of them clearly anti-Puritan in intent. Canon 8 obliged the clergy to preach in favour of conformity to the established rules and regulations governing the church, and the remaining nine covered various aspects of ecclesiastical administration, including excommunication and clerical discipline.

The canons of 1640 were never put into effect because the political situation soon deteriorated to the point where it was impossible to do so, and their legality was questioned by Parliament, which claimed that the Convocation could not meet when Parliament was not sitting. Charles had exploited a grey area in the English constitution, and it was never formally decided whether his action in prolonging the Convocation after the dissolution of Parliament was valid or not. In later years the church ignored the canons but it did not officially abandon them until 1969, when canon law revision finally made them redundant. In 1640 this question of legality hardly mattered. Once again, the king and his archbishop were seizing control of the church and trying to persecute its godly members, and at long last the latter were running out of patience.

The final act in the drama was played out a few days later in Scotland, when on 2 June 1640 the parliament in Edinburgh confirmed the abolition of episcopacy by the General Assembly eighteen months earlier. Charles I had acquiesced in that at the time, but with his usual duplicity had promised the bishops, many of whom had fled to England, that he would restore them as soon as he could. Yet when he paid a quick visit to Edinburgh in the following year in the hope of gaining support, he had no choice but to ratify the decision taken by Parliament and abandon all hope of recovering the position he had been trying for the previous three years to impose on an unwilling nation.[44]

---

[42] For the text, see Bray, *Anglican Canons*, 553–578. For a discussion of them, see Davies, *Caroline Captivity*, 251–287.

[43] An antitrinitarian heresy promoted by Faustus Socinus (1539–1604) and disseminated in England through the Racovian Catechism, named after the Polish town of Raków, where the Socinians had established their headquarters.

[44] The date of his surrender was 14 August 1641.

Onward Christian soldiers (1640–49)

Charles I's second attempt to subdue Scotland was even less successful than the first. In the summer of 1640 the Scots invaded England and occupied the counties of Northumberland and Durham after defeating the English army at the Battle of Newburn on 28 August 1640. On 26 October, Charles finally signed a treaty at Ripon, acknowledging the Scottish occupation of the north-east of England and retreating to London to lick his wounds, and incidentally to summon another parliament, which he could no longer dispense with. The 'Long Parliament', as this one came to be called, met on 3 November 1640 and, despite many ups and downs, it was not finally dissolved until 16 March 1660, more than nineteen years later. Quite a lot happened in the meantime.

The Long Parliament was summoned by the king but from the beginning it was antagonistic to him and especially to those in his entourage whom it regarded as chiefly responsible for his failed policies. On 16 March 1640 the Earl of Strafford, who had returned to Ireland, summoned a parliament in order to persuade it to subsidize the king's war against the Scots. Only twelve of its sixty-one members were Catholics, but they were all effusively loyal to Charles I and wanted to participate in the war.[45] They naturally saw this as politically advantageous to them, but it was viewed quite differently in England, where there was no desire to fight the Scots and where the suspicion naturally grew that the king was courting Irish Catholics to wage war on Protestants everywhere. Strafford was seen as the chief agent of this policy, and within days he was arrested and put on trial. But what was he guilty of? All along he had done the king's bidding, nothing else, and how could that be a crime? In the end Parliament overruled the arguments he put forward in his defence and the king abandoned him. He was executed on 12 May 1641, realizing too late that his loyalty to Charles had been misplaced.

Next it would be the turn of Archbishop Laud. On 22 November 1641, Parliament passed what is known as the Grand Remonstrance, which it presented to the king on 1 December. In it they called for Laud's arrest and imprisoned him in the Tower of London. There was considerable reluctance to put him on trial, partly because of his age and partly because, in spite of everything, he was a man of the cloth, and when he was finally put before a court in 1644 it was difficult to accuse him of any specific crime. Like Strafford he had done what he was told. But once again, Parliament would not accept any mitigating

---

[45] Clarke, *Old English in Ireland*, 127–128. For a good overview of seventeenth-century Ireland, see P. Lenihan, *Consolidating Conquest: Ireland 1603–1727* (London: Routledge, 2008).

excuses and sentenced him to death. He was executed on 10 January 1645 and subsequently turned into a martyr by his admirers, chief of whom was Peter Heylyn (1599–1662), one of the bitterest opponents of the Puritans and most determined supporters of the Laudian vision of the church.[46]

The execution of Strafford was a signal to Irish Catholics that they had nothing to hope for from the English Parliament. On 23 October 1641 they rose in rebellion, particularly in Ulster, where the dislocation caused by the plantations was still fresh. Several hundred Protestants were killed and many others fled for their lives, spreading tales of horror that only grew in the telling. Even William Bedell was captured and imprisoned for a time, although his evident love for the native Irish spared him the worst. Even so, the trauma was too great for him and he died from the mistreatment he had received. When word of all this reached England, there was panic. Rumours claimed that not merely hundreds but hundreds of thousands had been put to death by vengeful Catholics. By some reckonings about twice as many Protestants were killed as lived in Ireland, but few people paused to consider the facts and real information was hard to come by. For their part, the Catholic rebels had proclaimed their loyalty to Charles I and insisted that they would be content with the toleration he had promised them, but that had been denied by his lieutenants.

What is certain is that the disturbances in Ireland were religiously motivated to a degree that had not previously been the case. In particular the Old English and the native Irish, who were historic enemies, were moving closer to an alliance based on their shared Catholicism. This movement was greatly encouraged by an Old English priest called Geoffrey Keating (c.1580 – c.1644), who in 1634 wrote a monumental history of Ireland up to the Anglo-Norman invasion. Keating propagated the myth of a special relationship between Ireland and Catholicism that was to be deeply influential in shaping later Irish nationalism. Although he himself was of English stock, Keating's family had been more or less assimilated into the Gaelic-speaking population and he wrote in Irish, which gave him additional credibility among his target audience.[47]

---

[46] See A. Milton, *Laudian and Royalist Polemic in Seventeenth-Century England: The Career and Writings of Peter Heylyn* (Manchester: Manchester University Press, 2007).

[47] G. Keating, *Foras Feasa ar Éirinn: The History of Ireland*, 4 vols., ed. and tr. D. Comyn and S. Dinneen (London: Irish Texts Society, 1902–14). See also B. Cunningham, *The World of Geoffrey Keating: History, Myth and Religion in Seventeenth-Century Ireland* (Dublin: Four Courts Press, 2000). Keating's history was translated into Latin (1674) and into English twice (1688 and 1722). The second translation was widely read by Protestant scholars, who ignored the Catholic bias as much as they could but valued the work for its use of little-known source materials.

Keating was writing at a time when the old bardic culture of Gaelic Ireland was decaying, but it seems that a number of its representatives ended their days as members of Catholic religious orders. Of special importance was the Franciscan house at Louvain (Leuven), which for a time became the chief centre of Gaelic literary culture. One of its friars, Michael O'Cleary (c.1590–1643), returned to Ireland in 1626 and spent the next decade seeking out sources for his own history, which he finally published in 1636. He called it the *Annála Ríoghachta Éireann* (*Annals of the Kingdom of Ireland*) and took the story from earliest times up to 1616.[48] But far from being a work of antiquarianism, O'Cleary's history doctored its sources to make them appear as Catholic as possible. Like Keating, his theme was that to be Irish was to be Catholic, and neither language nor ethnicity mattered. The next generation would see men of purely Gaelic ancestry who would be regarded as foreigners because they had accepted Protestantism, whereas immigrant English people who were (or who became) Catholic were quickly embraced within the Irish nation.

It was the great and lasting achievement of men like Keating and O'Cleary that they managed to forge a new kind of Irishness, one that not only united the previously antagonistic English and Gaelic cultures but also (and ultimately more significantly) divided the English element into 'Old' and 'New' – Old being Catholic and New being Protestant. The English language would eventually displace Irish as the lingua franca of the people, but the New English religion would never become the majority faith, with the result that for many, Irishness and Britishness would come to seem mutually incompatible.

This transformation did not happen overnight of course, and there was still some way to go before the Old English and the native Irish would merge into one. Tensions flared when the former showed that they were more prepared to compromise with the king's government than the latter were, but a precedent for cooperation had been set and it would develop over time. Meanwhile people in England were convinced that an Irish Catholic army was about to invade the country in support of the king against Parliament. It was not true, but in the fevered atmosphere of the time anything seemed possible, and the anger of the parliamentarians was soon turned against the king, who was known for both his duplicity and hostility towards Puritanism.

---

[48] Today his work is usually known as the *Annals of the Four Masters*, because O'Cleary was assisted by three equally scholarly colleagues. For the text, see *Annála Ríoghachta Éireann = Annals of the Kingdom of Ireland, by the Four Masters, from the Earliest Period to the Year 1616*, 2nd edn (Dublin: Hodges, Smith, 1856). For a commentary, see B. Cunningham, *The* Annals of the Four Masters: *Irish History, Kingship and Society in the Early Seventeenth Century* (Dublin: Four Courts Press, 2010).

By 1642 the government in London had broken down. The king fled the city and Parliament took control, effectively declaring war on the Crown. That was easier said than done. To the extent that England had an army, it was mostly in the hands of the nobility, who generally supported the king. Parliament, by contrast, was stuffed with lawyers and merchants who had never been part of the military class and had no experience of warfare. It seemed that it would only be a matter of time before the king would rally his troops, return to the capital and put Parliament in its place.

The parliamentarians were desperate, but they were not entirely without allies. The Scots in particular had an army they were willing to use on behalf of the Puritan cause in England, but there was a price to be paid for their support. Already in August 1641 Parliament had bought them off with a subsidy of £300,000, an enormous sum for its day, and that had been enough to get them to vacate Durham and Northumberland. But if they were to enter into an alliance with the English, they wanted much more than that. The Scottish cause had always been primarily about religion, and they had invaded England in order to secure a presbyterian form of church government back home. It was that government and the theology that lay behind it that they now insisted on as the price for their support. They could not ask the English to sign the National Covenant of course, but they came up with the next best thing. In August 1643 they revised that document and submitted it both to the Scottish Parliament and the newly created Westminster Assembly, which had been called together to sort out the religious situation generally. Both parties approved, although the Westminster Assembly made some minor revisions before sending the text to Parliament. The House of Commons passed it on 25 September 1643 and the House of Lords on 15 October. On 5 February 1644 it was imposed on all adult Englishmen and became the charter for the union of the Protestant forces in England, Scotland and Ireland.[49]

The Solemn League and Covenant, as this charter was called, committed the signatories to a presbyterian system of church government along Scottish lines. The English accepted it out of desperation, but they were not nearly as wedded to it as the Scots were. Irish attitudes were more mixed, but tended to break down along national lines – the Ulster Scots were for it but the New English settlers in the rest of the country shared the hesitations of their brethren in England. The basic problem was that presbyterianism was virtually unknown in England, its last advocates having ceased their campaign half a century before. There was plenty of opposition to episcopalianism, especially

---

[49] See Bray, *Documents*, 435–437; Donaldson, *Scottish Historical Documents*, 208–210.

in its Laudian form, but those who objected to Laud were not necessarily attracted to presbyterianism as the alternative. As they saw it, both episcopalianism and presbyterianism were forms of clericalism. The only difference was that episcopalians believed that some ministers were more important than others, whereas presbyterians considered them all as equals. But both agreed that church discipline should be in the hands of the clergy, however constituted, and that it should be applied to the laity whether the latter consented to it or not. Given that the parliament was a lay body (apart from the bishops who sat in the House of Lords), their exclusion from the disciplinary mechanisms of the church was both unwelcome and troubling. They wanted greater freedom to think and worship as they pleased, and regarded enforced submission to the clergy as a form of tyranny. Independency (congregationalism) was therefore more to their taste than presbyterianism was, but beggars cannot be choosers, and in the circumstances they felt that it would not be too much of a sacrifice of their principles to accept the Scottish proposals.

Reliance on the Scots was important but it was not enough, and the English Parliament was also engaged in forming an army of its own. The member for Cambridge, Oliver Cromwell (1599–1658), dedicated himself to the task. Cromwell was a distant relative of the Thomas Cromwell who had been Henry VIII's chief minister, but his family was rooted in Huntingdonshire, where his father had hosted James I on his progress from Edinburgh to London in 1603. Not much is known about Oliver Cromwell's early life, but he entered Parliament in 1628 (shortly before it was shut down by the king) and a few years later he had an intense religious conversion. For the rest of his life his faith guided everything he did, and that faith was essentially, although not narrowly, Puritan. Cromwell was a man who had been born again of the Spirit of God, and anyone who was similar to him in that way was a brother in Christ, if not always a friend. In the complex ecclesiastical situation of his time, that gave him a wide range of sympathetic contacts that cut across more obvious and more traditional lines. He got along equally well with James Ussher, the Archbishop of Armagh, and the Quaker George Fox (1624–91), with whom he frequently dined and discussed theology. The people he could not abide were Roman Catholics and 'malignants'; that is to say, Protestants who were not born-again Christians. Most of these malignants were episcopalian of course, which put Cromwell at odds with the Laudians as well as the Catholics.

Although Cromwell had almost no military experience when he joined the army, he learned quickly and soon showed himself to be a master strategist. From reading about the ancient Macedonian phalanxes he came up with the idea of regiments, which he would line up in orderly fashion to form a barrier against the king's cavalry. The foot soldiers were dressed in uniform – another novelty – and had their hair cropped for the sake of efficiency, which is why they were called Roundheads. Their plainness and simplicity contrasted with the flair of their Cavalier opponents, who treated war as a kind of tournament in which individual bravery and skill counted for more than disciplined organization. In many ways it was a parable of their different theologies, the Cavaliers being more inclined to High Church flamboyance and the Round-heads to Puritan dullness. As the famous Sellers and Yeatman satire *1066 and All That* put it, the Roundheads were Right but Repulsive whereas the Cavaliers were Wrong but Wromantic. Sadly, as with Mary, Queen of Scots, the posthumous reputation of the Wrong Wromantics has fared better than that of their opponents, with the result that the general public today has an unfairly distorted (and often unduly negative) opinion of their Puritan opponents.

Once the Roundhead army was in place it was invincible, and by 1646 it had won the war against the king. At that stage there was still some hope that Charles I would repent of his earlier ways and do as Parliament wished, and he promised to do so. But as things turned out, his word was untrustworthy and, as soon as he could, he regrouped his forces and started the war again. He was defeated a second time of course, but the patience of Parliament had run out. Instead of negotiating with him they put him on trial, condemned him to death and executed him on 30 January 1649. In the circumstances it is hard to see that they had much choice, but there were many, then as now, who thought that regicide was a crime and who turned against the parliamentary party as a result. England was declared a 'Commonwealth' (republic) and the trappings of hierarchy, like the bishops and House of Lords, were abolished; but they did not go away and in due time they would come back to exact their revenge.

Meanwhile the Civil War in England was playing out in different ways in Scotland and Ireland. In Scotland there had been almost no war at all, but when the king was executed the Scots refused to accept it. They were monarchists and promptly recognized Charles II (1649–85) as the dead king's lawful heir. He was spirited away to Edinburgh and crowned there, having promised to uphold the Covenant and the presbyterian system of church government. The English could hardly allow such a move to go unchallenged, since Charles II claimed to be their lawful king as well, and the result was that Cromwell's army turned on the Scots. On 3 September 1651 he defeated them at Dunbar and took control of Scotland, imposing the English view of Reformed Protestantism on the country and alienating the Presbyterians in the process. The Scots were now exposed to preaching by Independents, Baptists and Quakers, all of whom were at least tacitly encouraged by the government, which wanted to break the grip the Presbyterians had on the people. These preachers were never strong or numerous enough to overturn the established Church, but they were more successful than is often imagined, and denominational pluralism now became a feature of the Scottish scene.[50]

In Ireland things were, as always, much more complicated. When war broke out in England, the Catholics who had rebelled in 1641 organized themselves as the Confederation of Kilkenny and took over the government of most of the southern half of the island.[51] The Confederates were officially Royalists and did not set up an independent or alternative government, even though they acted as one and were seen as such by the Protestants. They were a mixture of Old English and native Irish, with the former more inclined to compromise with the king and eager for a settlement that would protect their position. In fact they were caught between two unenviable alternatives. If they had achieved a peace by submitting to England, they would almost certainly have lost a good deal of their land and prestige, since even the king would have had to keep his parliament happy. On the other hand if they had succeeded in becoming independent, they might have faced retribution from both the Catholic Church and the native Irish, because in the past they had profited from the seizure of both monastic and native lands. They were a people caught in the middle and did not know which way to turn.

The Confederation sought help from Catholics abroad, but neither France nor Spain could come to their aid. The only source of effective help was the papacy, and in 1645 Cardinal Giovanni Battista Rinuccini (1592–1653) arrived in Kilkenny with money to buy troops and weapons and the promise of support from Rome. Unfortunately he turned up just as the Confederates were about to sign a peace treaty with the king's government in Dublin that would guarantee the rights of the Old English and, in a secret protocol attached to the main treaty, promise to restore land taken from the Catholic Church. Rinuccini was unhappy with this, but he had word of another treaty being negotiated between Queen Henrietta Maria and the papacy, which promised freedom of worship to Catholics as well. He demanded the right to share this with the Confederates, who then agreed to wait until 1 May 1646 to see whether anything would come of this papal peace.

---

[50] See R. S. Spurlock, *Cromwell and Scotland: Conquest and Religion 1650–1660* (Edinburgh: John Donald, 2007).

[51] See M. Ó Siochrú, *Confederate Ireland 1642–1649: A Constitutional and Political Analysis* (Dublin: Four Courts Press, 1999).

Before that however, the Confederates broke their promise to Rinuccini and signed a treaty with the lord lieutenant, although they agreed not to publish it until after 1 May. In the meantime the papal peace collapsed and the king recalled the lord lieutenant, making it unlikely that anything would come of his proposals. In the event they were resuscitated, and on 30 July 1646 a treaty between the king and the Confederation was signed and published.

Rinuccini was deeply disturbed by this turn of events, particularly as the Confederation was starting to win military victories at least partly made possible by the funds he had brought from Rome. He summoned a synod to meet at Waterford and, with the help of sympathetic Irish clergy, excommunicated anyone who supported the treaty. He then urged the Confederates to march on Dublin, convinced that if it fell, even more papal assistance would be forthcoming. It was a disastrous decision. Dublin did not fall, the Confederate army was internally divided between its Old English and native Irish elements, and Rinuccini had run out of the money he would have needed to carry on the struggle. He expected help to arrive from Rome but it did not come until March 1648, by which time the lord lieutenant had surrendered Dublin, not to the Confederates but to the English parliamentary army. Rinuccini clung on, hoping that the native Irish commander Owen Roe O'Neill (1585–1649) could save something from the wreckage, but he only succeeded in starting a civil war within the Confederation. In the end the Old English preferred to throw their lot in with the lord lieutenant rather than with O'Neill, and the Confederation effectively collapsed. Rinuccini went back to Rome, convinced that the native Irish were better Catholics than the Old English were, because the former were more extreme in their opposition to Protestant England.

That might have been the end of the story, but it was not. Once Charles I was out of the way, Cromwell was free and felt obliged to turn his attention to Ireland. He knew that he could be facing many years of warfare there with little result, and to forestall that he adopted a radical plan of attack. Rather than try to conquer the entire country, he concentrated on two fortresses where the Royalist armies were still holed up – Drogheda and Wexford. By capturing them and slaughtering their garrisons, most of whom were English, not Irish, he would strike such terror into the hearts of the rest that they would surrender. It was a tactic that the Americans would repeat in Japan in 1945, when they dropped atomic bombs on Hiroshima and Nagasaki, hoping to end the war without too much loss of life. In both cases the strategy worked, although Cromwell's reputation in Ireland has suffered because of it ever since.[52] Warfare is an ugly business and it is hard to see how Cromwell could have come out of it in a positive light, but one thing is certain. After 1649 he and his army were in control of Ireland and were free to do what they liked. It was then that his latent hostility to Catholics and malignants would be given full rein, and Ireland would be impacted in ways that have endured to the present time.[53]

Land belonging to Catholics was seized and redistributed on a scale thitherto unknown, and it would be this mass dispossession that would blacken Cromwell's name in Irish history more than the siege tactics he had employed at Drogheda and Wexford. There was a major attempt to recruit clergy from England and from the American colonies too. Quite a number of men who had fled across the Atlantic were enticed back, although the numbers were never enough to meet the need. Fortunately this effort was chronicled in detail by St John D. Seymour, an Irish clergyman who worked in the Public Record Office in Dublin shortly before its destruction in 1922. Thanks to his thoroughness and dedication, we know far more about this than we otherwise would and can trace clergy names and the places they went to with considerable and detailed accuracy.[54]

The poverty of the Irish church had always been acute and providing for the maintenance of ministers was a Cromwellian priority. It was soon realized that tithe income was insufficient to meet the need, and so a system of state subsidy was devised that lasted from 1651 to 1658. In the latter year it was reformed and tithe revenue was reintroduced as the mainstay of clerical income, although with the proviso that if it fell short of eighty pounds a year the state would make up the difference.[55] So impressed were contemporaries by this solution that many of them wanted it to be introduced into England, but the scheme had hidden weaknesses and collapsed before anything could be done.

As in Scotland, the English army introduced Puritan religious pluralism into Ireland, giving Baptists and Quakers (in particular) a platform that they had not previously had. The result was that Protestants fell into controversy with one another, when their energies might have been better employed in trying to convert Catholics. The debates were lively and often impressive, but

---

[52] See T. Reilly, *Cromwell: An Honourable Enemy. The Untold Story of the Cromwellian Invasion of Ireland* (London: Phoenix Press, 1999); M. Ó Siochrú, *God's Executioner: Oliver Cromwell and the Conquest of Ireland* (London: Faber & Faber, 2008).

[53] On the consequences, see S. J. Connolly, *Divided Kingdom* (Oxford: Oxford University Press, 2008).

[54] St J. D. Seymour, *The Puritans in Ireland (1647–1661)* (Oxford: Clarendon Press, 1921).

[55] T. C. Barnard, *Cromwellian Ireland: English Government and Reform in Ireland 1649–1660* (Oxford: Clarendon Press, 1975), 153–160.

they were a luxury Irish Protestants could ill afford.[56] Roman Catholics were less active in the 1650s than they had been before but they were far from crushed, and when conditions allowed them to resume their activities they proved to be stronger than ever.[57] For those in search of undivided truth, the spectacle of warring Protestants was decidedly unattractive and it is probably true to say that any realistic chance of converting Ireland to Protestantism was killed off in the years when the Puritans were in control.

The Westminster Assembly

Religion was not the only cause of the conflict we know as the English Civil War or, more correctly, as the war of the three kingdoms, but it was a major ingredient, and resolving the problems it raised was one of the most urgent priorities facing Parliament in its battle with the king. The importance of this can be seen from the fact that Parliament did not wait until hostilities were terminated, but began the process of ecclesiastical reform and reconstruction shortly after hostilities started, and carried on with it throughout the war and afterwards. The first session met on 1 July 1643 and the last (Session 1163) was wound up on New Year's Day (25 March) 1652. By then the visible face of British Christianity had been altered almost beyond recognition.[58]

The Assembly was overwhelmingly English in composition, although there was one representative from Ireland and after the signing of the Solemn League and Covenant, a Scottish delegation also appeared.[59] Three delegates were also invited from New England, including John Cotton, but they did not attend.[60] The first item of business, not surprisingly, was the revision of the Thirty-nine Articles, something the Irish church had done in 1615. Discussion of this had

---

[56] C. Gribben, *God's Irishmen: Theological Debates in Cromwellian Ireland* (Oxford: Oxford University Press, 2007).

[57] See the list of synods given in A. Forrestal, *Catholic Synods in Ireland, 1600–1690* (Dublin: Four Courts Press, 1998), 195–196.

[58] Minutes survive for Sessions 45–199 and 155–1163. They have been printed in C. Van Dixhoorn (ed.), *The Minutes and Papers of the Westminster Assembly 1643–1652*, 5 vols. (Oxford: Oxford University Press, 2012). An account of Sessions 1–44 is in the *Journal of John Lightfoot*, Cambridge University Library, MS Dd. XIV 28 (4). For a history of the Assembly written before the rediscovery and publication of the minutes, see R. S. Paul, *The Assembly of the Lord* (Edinburgh: T&T Clark, 1985).

[59] The Irish representative was Joshua Hoyle (1588–1654), an Englishman who informally represented Trinity College, Dublin. There were six Scottish clergy and nine lay delegates, who attended from Session 56 (15 September 1643) onwards. See Van Dixhoorn, *Minutes and Papers*, 1:175. They did not stay to the end, and most had gone home by Christmas 1647. For biographical sketches of the members of the Assembly, see W. Barker, *Puritan Profiles: 54 Influential Puritans at the Time When the Westminster Confession of Faith Was Written* (Fearn: Mentor, 1996).

[60] See Van Dixhoorn, *Minutes and Papers*, 1:106–147; Barker, *Puritan Profiles*. In addition to John Cotton, Thomas Hooker (1586–1647) and John Davenport (1597–1670) were also invited but declined to attend. On Hooker, see F. Shuffelton, *Thomas Hooker (1586–1647)* (Princeton, N.J.: Princeton University Press, 1977).

hardly begun when it became apparent that an entirely new confession would be needed. The members of the Assembly were too diverse in their theological opinions to be able to agree how to proceed with this, and at Session 73 (12 October 1643) Parliament curtailed the discussion by ordering them to stop talking about doctrine and go on to something more practical – church discipline and liturgy![61]

One of the most active members of the Assembly was the Scottish theologian Samuel Rutherford (1600–61), who is chiefly remembered for the many pastoral letters he wrote.[62] From the Westminster Assembly he addressed two letters to noble friends back in Scotland, which are precious witnesses to the way in which he perceived what was going on. On 4 March 1644 he wrote to Lady Kenmure as follows:

> There is nothing here [at Westminster] but divisions in the Church and Assembly; for beside Brownists and Independents (who of all that differ from us, come nearest to walkers with God), there are many other sects here of Anabaptists, Libertines, who are for all opinions in religion; fleshly and abominable Antinomians and Seekers, who are for no church ordinances, but expect apostles to come and reform churches; and a world of others, all against the government of presbyteries.[63]

On 25 May 1644 he had this to say to Lady Boyd:

> the truth is, we have many and grieved spirits with the work; and for my part, I often despair of the reformation of this land, which never saw anything but the high places of their fathers, and the remnant of Babylon's pollutions; and except that not by might, nor by power, but by the Spirit of the Lord [Zech. 4:6], I should think God hath not yet thought it time for England's deliverance: for the truth is, the best of them almost have said, 'a half reformation is very fair at the first,' which is no other thing, than 'it is not time yet to build the house of the Lord' [Hag. 1:2] ... As for myself, I know no more if there be a sound Christian (setting aside some, yea not a few learned, some zealous and faithful ministers, whom I have met with) at London (though I doubt not but there are many) than if I were in Spain ...[64]

---

[61] Van Dixhoorn, *Minutes and Papers*, 2:195.

[62] T. Smith (ed.), *Letters of the Reverend Samuel Rutherford* (Edinburgh: Oliphant, Anderson and Ferrier, 1881).

[63] Ibid. III, 52, 541.

[64] Ibid. III, 53, 542–543.

Rutherford's opinions were generally shared by the Scottish delegates, who were not prepared to accept anything less than full and unadulterated presbyterianism. They were not without support in England, as Rutherford admitted to Lady Boyd, but had to compete with many others.[65] In the circumstances it is something of a wonder that the Assembly was able to agree quite quickly on a directory for ordination and to submit it to Parliament for ratification.[66] Worship was a more difficult subject, and led to open disagreements between Presbyterians and Congregationalists that would never be fully overcome. But in spite of everything, a directory for public worship was passed on 30 December 1644 and came into effect almost immediately. The Book of Common Prayer was superseded and replaced by a series of texts considerably more flexible in what they allowed. Ministers were encouraged to follow a certain pattern but a great deal of latitude was permitted, and most of the independent-minded clergy were prepared to accept it. So was the House of Commons, although the spirit of tolerance was less apparent there. In the words of Chad Van Dixhoorn:

When it was able to consider the directory in 1645, the Commons showed its approval of the text by making limited revisions, and by debating the range of possible punishments to be levelled against the directory's critics. Life imprisonment was considered for anyone convicted for a third time of speaking or writing against the directory. Sir Simonds D'Ewes argued that banishment from England was more appropriate. Eventually it was decided that the most appropriate response to subversive opposition to the directory was a fine and imprisonment at the third and every subsequent offence.[67]

Not even Archbishop Laud had dared to go as far as that. By the time this debate was taking place it was clear that the Presbyterians had the upper hand in the Assembly and that whatever it proposed regarding church government would reflect their views. Throughout 1644 and into 1645 there was a determined rearguard action by the minority of Congregationalists, but it had

---

[65] In fairness it should be said that in December 1646 the ministers of Sion College, London, published a book in which they defended presbyterianism along lines that Rutherford approved of. See D. W. Hall (ed.), *Ius Divinum Regiminis Ecclesiastici, or The Divine Right of Church Government* (Dallas, Tex.: Naphtali Press, 1995).

[66] Van Dixhoorn, *Minutes and Papers*, 5:63–86. The first draft was sent to Parliament on 19 April 1644 and the final text was approved by 4 September.

[67] Ibid. 1:28.

no effect,[68] although significant trouble came when the Presbyterians attempted to impose strict discipline on people whom they regarded as 'ignorant and scandalous'. It was the formers' desire to excommunicate the latter, but the House of Commons refused to acquiesce in a system where the definition of those to be disciplined was so vague and potentially arbitrary. Parliament agreed with the Presbyterians in principle, but did not want the clergy to decide who should be punished or how. In practical terms this was a move towards Congregationalism on Parliament's part and that drift was to grow stronger as time went on. In the end both houses of Parliament passed an ordinance on church discipline that the majority in the Assembly regarded as ineffectual, but their protest was rejected. On 19 June 1646 the Presbyterians in the Assembly gave way, but not before objecting to the inadequacy of what Parliament had ordained.[69]

To modern readers these debates seem arcane and tedious and it is hard to understand how such strong feelings could have been aroused over them. But we need to appreciate that behind the questions at issue lay a deep and fundamentally unbridgeable gulf between two different conceptions of what a Christian society should be. The Presbyterians, for all their reforming zeal, represented an older pattern of Christendom, according to which Christian principles should be written into law and punishment meted out to those who refused to abide by them. Naturally they believed that obedience to the law should come from the heart and that, if it did, the law would not be needed; but the most important thing was that order should be preserved, and if punishment was required to make that happen, then so be it. On the other side, was the belief that because heartfelt obedience to the Word of God was a gift given to a minority, it ought not to be imposed on others. In the real world the godly and reprobate had to live together and it was not right to force practices on the latter that only the former could really understand and abide by in the right spirit.

This was not just an abstract debate among theologians. Samuel Rutherford for example was a leading exponent of the rule of law in society, quite apart from the church, and he sincerely believed that godly rule was best for everyone.[70] On the other side, the poet John Milton (1608–74), who started out as a

---

[68] One of these Congregationalists, Thomas Goodwin, wrote an account of how he believed that his colleagues had been manoeuvred into an impossible position, but it took half a century for his work to be published! See T. Goodwin, *Of the Constitution, Right, Order, and Government of the Churches of Christ* (London: Thomas Snowden, 1696).

[69] Van Dixhoorn, *Minutes and Papers*, 5:300–302.

[70] J. Coffey, *Politics, Religion and the British Revolutions: The Mind of Samuel Rutherford* (Cambridge: Cambridge University Press, 1997).

Presbyterian but moved progressively towards Congregationalism and finally to a virtual agnosticism, wanted to see a legal order that allowed for circumstances the godly would not tolerate among themselves. It must be admitted that he was set on that course by his own interest in divorce. He had married a woman who was incompatible with him and wanted to get rid of her, but was hindered from doing so by laws that proclaimed the indissolubility of marriage on the basis of New Testament principles. Milton was able to produce a book written by Martin Bucer during his time in England and dedicated to King Edward VI, in which he advocated a more flexible approach to matrimonial questions.[71] Milton's strategy was obviously to pit a father of the Reformation against the godly divines of his own times, who falsely claimed to be its heirs, but it did not go down well with the latter. The Presbyterians did not give way and English divorce law remained as strict as it had ever been until it was finally relaxed in the nineteenth century. For the time being, and for the foreseeable future, the godly Commonwealth won out against even its most prestigious and articulate critic.

The glory of the Westminster Assembly, and the main reason why it is remembered, is not its directories for ordination, worship or church government, none of which has much currency now. Rather it lies in its Confession of Faith that became and, in many forms both original and modified, remains by far the most widely accepted doctrinal statement in the English-speaking world – and beyond.[72] Presbyterian churches everywhere acknowledge it, and so (in modified forms) do many others, including Baptists in particular.[73] The Anglican Communion does not recognize it but, as almost all its compilers were members of the Church of England, it can reasonably be regarded as an 'Anglican' document also.[74] Its importance goes beyond the use to which it has been put however. The Westminster Confession is the most systematic presentation of what is known as 'covenant theology', a way of reading the Bible

---

[71] F. Wendel (ed.), *Martini Buceri Opera Latina XV: De Regno Christi* (Paris: Presses Universitaires de France; Gütersloh: C. Bertelsmann Verlag, 1955). An English translation appeared in W. Pauck (ed.), *Melanchthon and Bucer* (Philadelphia, Pa.: Westminster Press, 1969), 155–394, but annoyingly, the chapters on divorce were not included in this edition on the ground that they were translated by John Milton and are readily available in any edition of his prose works. See e.g. J. Milton, *The Works of John Milton*, 18 vols. (New York, N.Y.: Columbia University Press, 1931), 4:1–61. For a study of the question, see H. J. Selderhuis, *Marriage and Divorce in the Thought of Martin Bucer*, Sixteenth Century Essays and Studies 48 (Kirksville, Mo.: Thomas Jefferson University Press, 1999).

[72] For the text, see Bray, *Documents*, 438–468. For a theological analysis of the Confession, see R. Letham, *The Westminster Assembly: Reading Its Theology in Context* (Phillipsburg, N.J.: Presbyterian and Reformed Publishing, 2009).

[73] The Baptist Second London Confession of 1689 and the Philadelphia Confession of 1742 are slightly modified versions of it that acknowledge Baptist sacramental and ecclesiological distinctives. See Bray, *Documents*, 521–526, for the details.

[74] On the curious failure to recognize this, see Van Dixhoorn, *Minutes and Papers*, 1:26.

and the Christian message based on the covenant(s) God has made with his people.[75]

Covenant theology is based on the belief that God made a covenant with Abraham, choosing him from among the nations to be the ancestor of a people that would be specially dedicated to him. This covenant was repeated in Abraham's son Isaac and grandson Jacob, who was given the name of Israel because he struggled with God and prevailed.[76] This covenant was renewed in Moses, the giver of the law, and in David, the king of Israel who would be the ancestor of the Messiah. It was fulfilled in Christ, the prophet, priest and king who was at the same time the Word, the sacrifice and the kingdom, the ultimate fulfilment of God's promise to Abraham. Christians have been integrated into Israel by their union with Christ, so that the promises made to the ancient patriarchs are now made to us as well.

It is not clear who first enunciated this covenant theology. There are traces of it in William Tyndale and in the *Reformatio Legum Ecclesiasticarum* but it is not found in Calvin, even though those who developed it did so in the context of Calvin's theology and biblical exegesis. By the seventeenth century it had become the template for interpreting the Bible, and Protestants increasingly identified with ancient Israel. We can see this in the growing habit of naming children after Old Testament characters. Whereas in earlier times it was more common to call boys after saints (Thomas being especially popular in England because of Thomas Becket) or by inherited Anglo-Saxon or Norman names (Edward, Richard, Henry), in the seventeenth century we increasingly come across Abrahams, Isaacs and Jacobs, among others. Girls too, who were traditionally named Mary or Anne, were now often called Ruth, Rebecca, Rachel or Deborah.[77] Readers of the Bible were encouraged to take its characters as types of God's children, with all the positives and negatives that implied. God's chosen people were not perfect – they often sinned and suffered accordingly – but in the end God redeemed them because they belonged to him.

This was the narrative that sustained the Puritans. They might be persecuted in this life. They might fall away from God because of their own disobedience. Their enemies might triumph over them and reduce them to slavery or send

---

[75] It is sometimes called 'federal' theology, from the Latin word *foedus* (covenant), but as this word is now used mainly in a political sense, it is best avoided so as not to cause unnecessary confusion.

[76] Gen. 32:28.

[77] Anne was popular because St Anne was the mother of the Virgin Mary. The name is derived from the Greek form of Hannah, and was probably given to Mary's mother because when Mary heard that she was with child she broke out in Hannah's song, known to us as the *Magnificat*. Compare Luke 1:46–55 with 1 Sam. 2:1–10.

them into exile, as happened to ancient Israel. But these were the trials of the elect. Salvation is a work of divine grace, not of human merit, and true believers know that however bad things may be at any given moment, eternal life awaits them in the end. That hope runs like a thread through Puritan writings. The promise of a final deliverance is what kept them going and gave them confidence to walk through the valley of the shadow of death yet fear no evil.[78] It was the confidence that allowed a man like Samuel Rutherford, put on trial at the end of his life for having supported the revolt against the king, to stand firm and not recant. Rutherford died in his bed before he could be executed, but in his last days he wrote to his fellow prisoner, James Guthrie of Stirling, in the following terms:

Happy are ye if you give testimony to the world of your preferring Jesus Christ to all powers. And the Lord will make innocency and Christian loyalty of his defamed and despised witnesses in this land, to shine to after-generations, and will take the man-child up to God and to his throne, and prepare a hiding place in the wilderness for the mother, and cause the earth to help the woman.[79] Be not terrified; fret not; forgive your enemies. Bless and curse not; for though both you and I should be silent, sad and heavy is the judgment and indignation of the Lord that is abiding the unfaithful watchmen of the Church of Scotland. The souls under the altar are crying for justice, and there is an answer returned already.[80] The Lord's salvation will not tarry. Cast the burden of wife and children on the Lord Christ. He careth for you and them. Your blood is precious in his sight. The everlasting consolations of the Lord bear you up, and give you hope: for your salvation (if not deliverance) is concluded.[81]

This is the spirit in which the Westminster Confession was composed, and that must be understood before it can be read and properly evaluated. Its authors looked forward to the eschatological realization of the promises of God, which many of them were convinced they would live to see.[82] They were not building for the future, but for eternity, because they thought that time

---

[78] Ps. 23:4.

[79] An allusion to Rev. 12:1–17.

[80] Rev. 6:9–10.

[81] Smith, *Letters of the Reverend Samuel Rutherford*, III, 67, 558. The date was 15 February 1661. Rutherford died on 20 March and Guthrie was hanged on 1 June.

[82] See C. Gribben, *The Puritan Millennium: Literature and Theology 1550–1682*, rev. edn (Carlisle: Paternoster Press, 2008).

was running out. Salvation was a matter of urgency that had to be pressed home to people before it was too late. They could not save anyone – only God could do that – but they had a duty to proclaim what his salvation was and to bear witness to that by their own teaching and life. The Westminster Confession was their statement of what the gospel is and how it should be proclaimed.

The Confession is divided into thirty-three chapters, each of which contains multiple subsections. The first chapter is a statement about the inspiration and content of Holy Scripture. Traditional confessions had either not mentioned that or else had begun with the doctrine of God, but from the time of the Second Helvetic Confession in 1566 the Reformed churches adopted a new procedural method. They began with the Bible, because the Bible was the only source of their theology. It might be possible to guess from looking at nature or from reasoning about reality that there must be a Supreme Being, but this 'God of the philosophers', as he would later be called, was not the God who reveals himself in Scripture. It was therefore necessary to make that point by beginning with revelation and going on from there. The second chapter continues with the doctrine of God, following the traditional division between God as one and God as three. Then in chapter 3 we come to the key issue of the eternal decree by which God has chosen some for salvation but not others. The entire work of Christ has to be understood in this context – it is the working out of the plan of salvation for the elect.

Next in logical sequence comes the creation of the world. God chose his elect before he created them, a belief technically known as 'supralapsarianism', the 'lapse' referring to the fall of humankind by the sin of Adam. Salvation is not an emergency rescue operation made necessary by human failure, but the eternal plan of God from the beginning. Sin is not proof of reprobation, so the elect have no cause to despair. God knew Adam would fall away but chose us in spite of that and has redeemed us without reference to any merit we might have.

After creation comes providence, the mechanism by which God continues to govern the world he has made. Salvation is not an intervention into a world that runs autonomously, but the sovereign act of a God who governs it as his own possession. Strictly speaking, there are no 'miracles', because the sovereign Lord is free to do what he pleases with what he has made. Experience tells us he normally operates according to certain principles or 'laws', but these laws are not immutable. They are subject to his divine power and can be suspended or altered at his command.

Next comes the doctrine of the fall and the punishment it deserves. This is important because the covenant God has made with us is intimately bound up with the fall. According to the Westminster divines there are two covenants God has made with humankind:

> The first covenant made with man was a covenant of works wherein life was promised to Adam, and in him to his posterity, upon condition of perfect and personal obedience. Man by his fall, having made himself incapable of life by that covenant, the Lord was pleased to make a second, commonly called the covenant of grace, wherein he freely offereth unto sinners life and salvation by Jesus Christ, requiring of them faith in him that they might be saved, and promising to give unto all those that are ordained unto eternal life his Holy Spirit, to make them willing and able to believe.[83]

Chapter 8 follows on naturally with Christ the Mediator, showing how it was necessary for him to be both God and man in order to be able to take our place on the cross and pay the price God's justice demands for our redemption. Next comes a short chapter on free will, which may be summarized as follows. Humans before the fall had free will, but lost it by their sin. At conversion humans are transported into a state of grace and enabled to do God's will, but this is only by the power of the Holy Spirit. Only after death, in the state of eternal glory, will human free will be fully restored.

Chapter 10 treats of the effectiveness of God's call. Nobody and nothing can deter God from saving those whom he has chosen. This grace extends to infants and others who cannot be called outwardly to repentance:

> Elect infants, dying in infancy, are regenerated and saved by Christ, through the Spirit, which worketh when, where and how he pleaseth, so also are all other elect persons who are incapable of being outwardly called by the ministry of the Word.[84]

This clause is a subtle rebuke to the Anabaptists, who required profession of faith for salvation. Infant mortality was very high in the seventeenth century, and what would happen to babies who died before they could bear personal witness to their faith? It is interesting to note that the compilers of the Confession also took account of the mentally handicapped, without specifically saying so.

---

[83] Westminster Confession, 7.2–3, in Bray, *Documents*, 444.
[84] Westminster Confession, 10.3, in ibid. 447.

Chapter 11 repeats the standard Reformation emphasis on justification by faith alone, and adds for good measure that 'the justification of believers under the Old Testament was in all . . . respects one and the same with the justification of believers under the New Testament'.[85] Salvation for those who came before Christ is the same as salvation for those who have come afterwards – there is only one covenant people of God.

Chapters 12–18 take us step by step through the pattern of salvation, or *ordo salutis* as it is known. First comes adoption as children of God, followed by sanctification, the implanting of saving faith in the heart of the believer, repentance, good works, perseverance to the end and the assurance of grace and salvation. Each one of these builds on the previous one. Adoption is the natural outworking of election and the necessary precondition for sanctification. Faith and repentance come afterwards, because it is only those who have been chosen and prepared who can receive the grace required for realizing the promises of God. Good works are the fruit of this calling, not a justification for (or proof of) it, and it is when we see the work of the Holy Spirit in our lives that we come to understand that God will keep us safe to the end and grant us eternal life. Believers do not have to worry that they will fall away or be rejected, because the God who has chosen us will fulfil his promises.

Up to this point it can be said that virtually all Reformed Protestants are in agreement. Differences begin to appear however when we come to the second part of the Confession. This begins with a statement about the law of God, given to Adam as a covenant of works and now held out to us as the standard God requires of us, but which can be achieved only by his grace. In the Old Testament the law can be analysed into its component parts – the moral law, which is applicable to everyone everywhere, the ceremonial law, which was given to the Mosaic priesthood and fulfilled in Christ, and the civil law, by which Israel was governed. Christians are also called to live under civil laws, but these laws are not prescribed in detail as the law of Moses was for Israel, and we are free to adapt them according to our circumstances. Here there is room for differences of practice and even for disagreements among true believers, and the church must not impose rules and regulations that are matters of indifference as far as God's plan of salvation is concerned.

This point is driven home in chapter 20, which defines Christian liberty and the place of conscience in the believer's life. The moral law is obligatory for everyone, but in matters of faith and worship there is a freedom granted to the conscience of the individual believer that must be respected. To act in a way

---

[85] Westminster Confession, 11.6, in ibid. 448.

that harms the conscience is sinful, even if the act itself is good or harmless. This extends to patterns of worship, but within certain limitations. No images are to be used in the church and time must be set aside for people to gather together to pray, to read the Bible and to hear the Word of God expounded to them. That time is the Sabbath day, which by the fourth of the Ten Commandments is to be set aside and kept holy, although Christians have transferred it from the seventh to the first day of the week, in honour of the new creation we are in Christ.

After that come chapters on the taking of lawful oaths, obedience to the civil magistrate, marriage and divorce. On the last of these the Westminster divines were prepared to allow not only adultery, but also 'such wilful desertion as can no way be remedied by the church or civil magistrate' as sufficient reasons for allowing divorce, a relatively liberal position at the time, but one that was to be carefully monitored by the disciplinary agents of the church.[86]

Chapter 25 on the church makes a careful distinction between the invisible church, which is the fellowship of all true believers wherever they may be found, and the visible manifestation of Christ's community that exists where the Word of God is faithfully preached. Some visible congregations have departed so far from this that they have become synagogues of Satan, and here Rome is singled out for special mention. The pope is nothing less than 'that man of sin and son of perdition that exalteth himself in the church, against Christ and all that is called God'.[87] Nowadays that clause is downplayed or even omitted in modified versions of the Confession, but there can be no doubt that it represented the feelings of those who compiled it and that they were prepared to act on the consequences. Tolerance of different opinions did not extend to the Antichrist, and it would be centuries before this prejudice would be overcome.[88]

From there the Confession moves on to the communion of saints and develops its sacramental theology. Baptism, which is to be administered to both believers and their children, and Holy Communion, which is to be reserved for those able and willing to make a personal profession of faith, are the two ordinances of the gospel instituted by Christ for its proclamation, and so must be observed correctly in every congregation. Chapters 30 and 31 deal with church censures and the role of synods in establishing church discipline, areas of perennial conflict but regarded as essential for the spiritual health of

---

[86] Westminster Confession, 24.6, in ibid. 456.

[87] Westminster Confession, 25.6, in ibid. 457.

[88] Anti-Catholic prejudice has not completely disappeared from Protestant circles, but it is much weaker than it once was, even in Northern Ireland.

any Christian community. Finally chapters 32 and 33 cover eschatological questions – the state of those who have died, the resurrection of the body and the final judgment. There is nothing unusual or unexpected in them, but their presence is a reminder of the importance for believers of the future hope we have in Christ. These matters were originally included in the Forty-two Articles of 1553 but were dropped from the Thirty-nine Articles in the revision ten years later, and the Westminster divines were determined not to make the same mistake again.

Today when we read the Westminster Confession, we find that each of its statements is backed up by references to Scripture, the so-called 'proof-texts' meant to justify what the Confession asserts. These proof-texts were not part of the original document; but when it was submitted to Parliament, the members requested the divines to add them in justification of their assertions. It was not enough to claim to be biblical: they had to demonstrate that by showing what the sources of their beliefs were.[89] Initially the Assembly resisted the request, and on 19 December 1646 it submitted the Confession to the House of Commons without the proof-texts attached.[90] That was not good enough and, after a further request from Parliament, the Assembly gave in and did as it had been asked.[91] To the uninitiated this may seem like a logical step to take and we may be puzzled that the Westminster divines were so hesitant about it, but those who have studied theology know that it can be dangerous to cite a biblical text out of context, and are reluctant to do so. Today we must admit that not every verse cited proves what the Confession states, and the wisdom of the Assembly's reticent approach is clearer to us than it was to the parliamentarians of the time. But this is a minor point. What the Confession states is broadly faithful to what the Bible teaches, even if other interpretations are possible and have been offered by those who are unhappy with certain aspects of the original text. On the whole the Westminster Confession has stood the test of time and remains an achievement without parallel in the history of British Christianity.

The Confession continued to have a bumpy ride through the English Parliament, especially where the chapters on church discipline were concerned. Various proposals were put forward to have it printed without them, but they failed, and in the end the Presbyterian polity was approved. It was a grudging acquiescence however, and the Presbyterians lost a lot of sympathy because

---

[89] Van Dixhoorn, *Minutes and Papers*, 5:310–311. The House of Commons made its request to the Assembly on 9 October 1646.
[90] Ibid. 314.
[91] Ibid. 322. The date was 26 April 1647.

of their intransigence. When the time came, they would find that support for their position had melted away, and it proved impossible to impose the discipline that the Assembly had voted for. Scotland was a different matter, but the Assembly had always understood that its decisions could be implemented in that country only by its own General Assembly. By 1647 the Scots were falling out with the English, not least over English attitudes to the king. Hard as it is to understand, it would not be long before the Scottish army was invading England in support of Charles I, little though he deserved it. The idea of a covenant monarchy was kept alive in the northern kingdom, and would survive in spite of all the evidence that the king was unworthy of such an exalted position.

After the Confession was produced, there remained one further task for the Assembly to accomplish before its work was done. This was the production of a catechism, which was duly undertaken and completed within a few months. The text was submitted to Parliament on 22 October 1647.[92] Although shorter than other catechisms already in existence, it was still very long, with no fewer than 196 questions. It set out the doctrines of the Confession, complete with scriptural proofs. Following established tradition, there is a long section devoted to the Ten Commandments (questions 91–149) and another, much shorter one, on the Lord's Prayer (questions 186–196), but there is no mention of the Apostles' Creed, probably because it is not part of the Bible and was therefore of lesser authority in the minds of the compilers of the Catechism.

The Larger Catechism, as this text came to be known, was too long for ordinary use and it was soon realized that an abridged version would be necessary. This was quickly produced and submitted to Parliament on 25 November 1647. Parliament accepted it the following day and it was printed immediately.[93] With only 107 questions it was thought to be more manageable and it was soon adopted for use in the churches. There is still a long section on the Ten Commandments (questions 41–81) and a shorter one on the Lord's Prayer (questions 99–107), but the answers are much more concise. The Shorter Catechism has proved its worth and is still widely used in Presbyterian churches as a means of inculcating Reformed theology into the minds of children and of converts to the faith.

---

[92] Ibid. 332–333. For the text, see J. T. Dennison Jr (ed.), *Reformed Confessions of the Sixteenth and Seventeenth Centuries in English Translation*, 4 vols. (Grand Rapids, Mich.: Reformation Heritage, 2008–14), 4:299–352.

[93] Van Dixhoorn, *Minutes and Papers*, 5:336. For the text, see Dennison, *Reformed Confessions*, 4:353–368.

After the Catechisms were produced, the main work of the Assembly was completed and many of the members went home. A small number continued to meet however, and spent most of their time examining ministers for appointments to parishes in different parts of England and Wales. It was a necessary task, but not one that required an Assembly of the Westminster kind, which soon faded into insignificance. Its minutes run out in 1652 but its existence is attested for at least a year after that. It had no formal closure, but we may assume that it expired with the Long Parliament, which was finally dissolved on 12 December 1653.

The sectarian fringe

Any survey of British, and especially English, Christianity in the seventeenth century has to come to terms with the great explosion of sects that occurred in tandem with the Civil War of the 1640s. At the time of the Reformation there was an outburst of radical sectarianism in Germany that was violently repressed by the secular authorities, but England (and even more the rest of the British Isles) was scarcely affected by that. A few Anabaptists turned up now and again and some were duly executed, but they never made much of an impression on the locals. On the contrary, English people who did not like what was going on in England usually emigrated to more favourable climes, especially the relatively tolerant Netherlands. It was from there that Thomas Helwys returned to England with his tiny band of Baptists, intending to plant a church in his homeland. He had little success, and the fact that he is occasionally remembered owes more to the survival of Baptists in later times than it does to anything Helwys achieved.

The Baptists did not come to public attention until 1640 or so, when the breakdown of ecclesiastical order allowed independent groups like theirs to flourish. By then their movement had two wings that did not have much in common with each other, apart from the rejection of infant baptism. There were the General Baptists, followers of Helwys, who preached universal atonement and believed that individuals could choose whether to be saved or not, and the Particular Baptists, who were Calvinists that had accepted believers' baptism as the norm. Because of this fundamental difference in theology, they did not cooperate with each other, and outsiders who lumped them together usually did so on the assumption that their movement was essentially anarchic.[94] The

---

[94] J. F. McGregor and B. Reay (eds.), *Radical Religion in the English Revolution* (Oxford: Oxford University Press, 1984), 29–30.

things that they did have in common were largely accidental – a tendency to hold revivalist meetings, to engage in debates with ministers of the Church of England and to disseminate Baptist propaganda. In one particular they were not Anabaptists at all – they rejected pacifism, and were quite happy to join Cromwell's New Model Army, which they saw as God's instrument for cleansing the land of popery and tyranny.

This link with the army was a godsend to the Baptists, as it was to other radicals. Parliament had created a standing force of men, most of them fairly young and free to travel, who were grouped together and were away from home for large portions of the year. They had chaplains to serve them and so were exposed to serious preaching, but they also had a lot of time on their hands to discuss the issues involved and to contemplate the possibility of a more radical approach to political and religious affairs. They had little to lose and nothing to gain from a parliamentary victory, which would probably see them disbanded and sent home to lead the kind of humdrum lives that were the lot of most people in those days. Someone who came along and challenged them to seek a better life by thumbing their noses at established authority was almost bound to attract a hearing, and that seems to be what happened. There were army commanders who tried to maintain law and order among their troops, but many of them were attracted to independency (Congregationalism) and were disinclined to submit to the discipline the Presbyterians wanted to impose.

The Baptists took full advantage of this situation. Both General and Particular varieties were active all over England, although there is some evidence to suggest that the former were stronger in the south and east and the latter in the north and west.[95] Nobody seems to know why, but the Particular Baptists were better organized in regional fellowships, whereas the General Baptists are harder to pin down. All we can say with some confidence is that they operated independently of each other, at least most of the time.

The basic principle of Baptist ecclesiology was that every congregation was a voluntary association of equals who were united in their hostility to what they saw as the laxity and ungodliness of the established Church. They wanted to return to what they regarded as the 'pure' church of the apostles, a gathered fellowship of those whom God had called and sanctified by his grace. Their problem was that while God called individuals, he wanted them to live together in community, and that required agreement. It seems that the first Baptists were naive enough to imagine that all true believers would think alike. It was

---

95 Ibid. 32–39.

accepted that there were some people who had tender consciences, but they were basically immature believers who had to grow in the faith. What this meant in practice was that Dissenters who persisted in their opposition to the majority were expelled from their ranks as unbelievers. It also meant, if only by implication, that those who did not join them were unbelievers, something that the latter not unreasonably found offensive. They tended to respond to such treatment by inventing lurid tales about the Baptists, claiming for example that their pastors liked to dip women naked, so that they could satisfy their lusts even as they won them for the Lord. This association between radical religion and sexual immorality is something that has long been common, although the truth, then as now, is much harder to discern. Perhaps there were some unscrupulous pastors like that, but that can hardly have been true of the majority and we must conclude that in this matter at least, the Baptists were more sinned against than sinning.[96]

On the other hand it is legitimate to ask why they felt obliged to separate themselves from others, especially when there were many who agreed with them on most things other than the practice of baptism. The Baptists made no claim to be better than other people, but their exclusiveness was an invitation to outsiders to regard them as 'holier-than-thou' and to find fault with them accordingly. It did not help matters that Baptists tended to separate from one another because of some deviation from the true path. An example of this was the tendency of General Baptists to lay hands on new converts after their baptism, a practice that might have derived from confirmation in the Church of England. Disagreement over the propriety of this split their movement, to no apparent advantage. Particular Baptists, as one might expect, usually opposed this innovation and so were less affected by division, but it is hard to think of a quarrel like this as anything other than trivial. In the words of J. F. McGregor:

> The Baptists' preoccupation with building the true Church on the firm foundations of Scriptural ordinances easily lapsed into narrow intolerant legalism. The apparent obsession with formal observance to the detriment of spiritual experience alienated fellow Puritans and pushed many dissatisfied Baptists into enthusiastic movements ... which denied all external ordinances. For the majority, however, the security of elite fellowship according to the true law of Christ was the principal attraction of the sect.[97]

---

[96] Ibid. 41–42.
[97] Ibid. 43.

Baptists also liked to emphasize their distinctiveness by insisting on high moral standards. Playing musical instruments was suspect, dancing was dangerously erotic and modest dress (especially for women) was essential. Obviously, maintaining these principles required constant policing, and members were implicitly encouraged to spy on one another – in love, of course. On a more positive note, Baptists took charitable giving seriously and did their best to ensure that none of their members suffered destitution. Needless to say, that too was open to abuse – how many people joined them because they wanted what we would now call social security? Such interlopers might have been few, but the possibility that they existed at all was enough to arouse suspicion and lead to yet more policing of true godliness.

The Baptists also faced a conflict between the right of individual choice in matters of faith, and social obligations that were generally accepted by everyone, including them. This hit women particularly hard. Baptists were very conservative in their approach to women, and believed that they must be subject to their husbands within the family, but at the same time they insisted that a woman must be free to make her own decision for Christ. It was just as common then as it is now for women to be more spiritually committed than their husbands were, but whom were they to obey when the demands of the church and home came into conflict? Inevitably Baptists were accused of trying to break up families, a charge that horrified most people but was not without its attraction to some who were stuck in unhappy marriages. If spiritual experience could be used to solve that problem, then claiming it as an excuse to separate from others would certainly appeal to anyone who felt trapped by the social expectations of the age.

To sum up, the Baptists appeared to their contemporaries as people whose ideas were full of contradictions. On the one hand they believed that the established Church was unchristian, but on the other hand they agreed with other Puritans that it could be reformed and turned into a godly institution. They preached obedience to the civil magistrate but voted with their feet when the latter tried to impose a common discipline on the churches. They wanted religious toleration, but not when it meant putting up with people whose behaviour they found offensive. In their view freedom was a gift of grace, not a right of nature, and was therefore the privilege of the godly alone. To put it a different way, freedom of religion was right for them, but not for anyone else. They welcomed the execution of the king and the establishment of the Commonwealth because it gave them freedom from compulsory church attendance and held out the expectation that tithes would be abolished, but they broke with the Levellers, another radical sect, when the latter advocated freedom for all, including the reprobate. In the end the Baptists wanted to have their cake and eat it too, something even some of them admitted was a logical impossibility.

The Baptists were to survive the chaos of the civil-war era and establish themselves as one of the very few groups that eventually assimilated into the mainstream of British Protestant life, even though they kept their distinctive position on believers' baptism. General and Particular varieties tended to merge over time, with the movement's official doctrine leaning towards the Particulars but their evangelistic practice looking more like the Generals. Broadly speaking, that is still the case, although Strict and Particular Baptists continue to exist on a small scale. The only other sixteenth-century sect of which the same might be said is that of the Quakers, whose origins and beliefs were very different from those of the Baptists, with whom they clashed on more than one occasion. Unlike the Baptists, who derived their inspiration from abroad, the Quakers were a purely homegrown English movement. Their founder and chief theologian, if that is the word for him, was George Fox.

Fox was a charismatic figure with a genius for attracting people who felt left out of the Puritan revolution.[98] His first followers were agricultural labourers in the north of England and only later did his movement spread to the rest of the country. There it was able to build on the work of other sectarian groups that have long since disappeared, like the Seekers and the Fifth Monarchists. The Seekers believed that they should sit still and wait for the Lord to come and reveal himself to them, a belief that subsequently became central to Quakerism. They were convinced that the true church had disappeared in the course of time, and that the rituals of the Church of England were invalid. Only a fresh wind of the Holy Spirit could revive this defunct body, and it was that that the Seekers believed they had experienced. The Spirit blows where he wills of course, and so it is pointless to look for any fixed doctrine or organization among the Seekers. They were a group of like-minded but essentially independent people who would join anyone who shared, or who appeared to share, their basic quest for religious experience.[99]

The impact of the Seekers, and subsequently of the Quakers, was rooted in an aspect of the Reformation that is frequently ignored or misunderstood. At its heart, the divide between Protestantism and Catholicism was a theological division over the question of the work of the Holy Spirit. Did the Spirit work through institutions, sacraments and rituals, or did he come into the hearts and minds of chosen believers and give them new life in Christ? Catholics

---

[98] Ibid. 141–164.
[99] Ibid. 122–129.

opted for the former and Protestants for the latter. In the sixteenth century, bodies like the Church of England preserved as much of the traditional structure of religion as they could, partly in order to keep traditionalists on board but partly also because they realized that such a neat division was impossible. The official rituals of the visible church were outward and visible signs of an inward and spiritual grace, and therefore they had a place in the preaching and teaching ministry of the church. The problem was that Catholics believed the visible signs conferred the spiritual grace, whereas mainstream Protestants insisted that although sacraments bore witness to grace and were promises of it, they could not convey it. There would always be people who received the signs but not the substance they represented. Whether it was possible to receive the substance without bothering with the signs was a question they did not confront, and it was here that the sectarians of the seventeenth century made their impact.

The Baptists had begun the movement towards a more spiritually based Christianity by insisting that unless and until there was evidence that the Holy Spirit had worked in a person's life, it was inappropriate to administer the sacrament of baptism to that person. Baptism could not convey the grace of salvation; it could only bear witness to it. The difference between Baptists and other Puritans was simply that whereas the majority believed that the rite was an extension of their preaching ministry, a sign of what ought to happen to the individual who received it, the Baptists waited until there was evidence that the grace had been received before sealing it with the sign. Of course, it was but a short step from there to claiming that the sign was not necessary at all, and this is where the Seekers, and after them the Quakers, ended up. Quite a number of Baptists followed them in this, and it is easy to see why. In a world in which everyone was baptized in infancy but few could be said to be living a recognizably Christian life, the attraction of belief in the primacy of spiritual experience is obvious. The sectarians wanted reality, not hypocrisy, which they (often rightly) saw in the official church. To then seal that reality by having recourse to the practices of the hypocrites seemed to them to be not only unnecessary but sinful. After all, what need did a person who was filled with the Spirit have of outward signs and symbols?

The result of all this was a rather amorphous group of people who were nevertheless open and susceptible to the attraction of charismatic 'prophets' and leaders. In the words of J. F. McGregor:

There was no sect of Seekers in revolutionary England. There were, however, alienated individuals in plenty for whom we have no better category than the heresiographer's definition of the Seeker as a lost, wandering soul, finding no solace in the discipline of Church or sect, anticipating wondrous events in the last days, vulnerable to the charisma of a crackpot messiah or the solipsism of the divine inner light.[100]

It is too simple to say that the Seekers morphed over time into Quakers, although the latter have often been portrayed in that way. But the Quakers undoubtedly appealed to the same kind of people and met a need for spiritual satisfaction that nobody else seemed to recognize or cater for in the way that Quakers did. It is probably best to say that Quakerism gave form to a longing that had already expressed itself in the Seekers, and that that made the latter redundant. As a result, Quakers survive to this day, whereas the Seekers have disappeared into the history books.

One of the main reasons why the Seekers and later the Quakers attracted such opposition from the mainstream Puritans is that they sat light to questions of doctrine and were prepared to accept the testimony of many people who claimed to have had an experience of the Spirit, even if their ideas about other things were far from orthodox. In particular, personal testimony was more important than the teaching of the Scriptures. The Bible remained an important part of their religious expression of course, and it could hardly have been otherwise in the seventeenth century. But Scripture was not supreme or determinative. George Fox himself declared that it was 'not the letter, nor the writing of the Scripture, but the ingrafted Word [that] is able to save your souls'.[101] Once the Bible was relegated to a secondary level, the rest of traditional Christian doctrine scarcely stood a chance. The Trinity was quickly sidelined, and even the historical work of Christ was subordinated to the living experience of his presence in the heart of the believer. As for the hope of resurrection and final judgment:

> The [Quaker] tendency was to internalise, with the emphasis once again upon the present. They did not actually deny that there would be a final judgment and resurrection, but the stress was on the resurrection and judgment within each Quaker ... There was a tendency to talk of heaven and hell as internal states. Heaven was in the hearts of God's people; hell was to be found in the conscience of every malefactor.[102]

---

[100] Ibid. 129.
[101] London, The National Archives, Assi 44/6, quoted in ibid. 146.
[102] Ibid. 147. The words are those of Barry Reay.

It is surprising how few people today stop to think that the name Quaker derives from 'quake', a reminder that the first ones were an ecstatic group that habitually shook when filled with the Spirit. They believed that they had been made perfect by the indwelling presence of the divine, and this often led to extreme and bizarre behaviour. George Fox kept a diary of the miracle cures he had performed, and others did the same, although they were seldom as successful as he claimed to have been.[103] He is also said to have run naked through the streets when filled with the Spirit, something that in the English climate is hard to imagine without supernatural assistance. Fasting was a particular challenge, because it was meant to prove that they could survive without food. Many did, but some people died as a result and the practice eventually declined in significance. Despite such antisocial behaviour, Quakers took a keen interest in the world around them. They were opposed to hierarchy in the church, and eventually that opposition extended to the state as well. They wanted freedom and prosperity for all, although how that was to be achieved was less clear.

During the Commonwealth period the Quakers were generally supportive of the regime, but their independent-mindedness meant that they were often perceived as subversive. That did not matter too much in England, but in Scotland and Ireland, where Commonwealth rule was less secure, their presence in the army was regarded as dangerous and they were purged.[104] They did not welcome the return of the king in 1660, and when they realized that they had no hope of achieving their social aims they took refuge in pacifism, which then became one of their hallmarks. Over time, Quaker eccentricities were increasingly regarded as intolerable, and even in England they were persecuted for stepping out of line. The most extreme case occurred in Bristol in October 1656, when James Nayler (1618–60) entered the city on a donkey and proclaimed himself to be the second coming of Christ. By any standard this was blasphemy, and George Fox was quick to dissociate himself from it. Nayler was arrested and put on trial, but demands for the death penalty were thwarted. Instead he was branded, mutilated and sentenced to hard labour for the rest of what turned out to be a rather short life.

Legislation directed against the Quakers soon followed, although the intended victims were seldom named. For example, in 1657 Parliament renewed the Elizabethan Vagrancy Act, giving local magistrates the power to arrest idle persons who appeared to have no business to keep them occupied. This statute

---

103 H. J. Cadbury (ed.), *George Fox's 'Book of Miracles'* (Cambridge: Cambridge University Press, 2012).
104 McGregor and Reay, *Radical Religion*, 154–155.

was used to imprison Quakers, although there was no mention of them. At the same time, Parliament also enacted a statute enjoining compulsory attendance at a meeting place of Christians, and Quakers were prosecuted under that statute because the definition of 'Christians' was framed in such a way as to exclude them. Paradoxically, popular hostility to the Quakers contributed to the restoration of the monarchy, as people recoiled from what they saw as the anarchy so-called 'freedom' was bringing.

On the fringe of the Seekers and Quakers were the Ranters, who appealed to similar types of people but took their practices to extremes. Those who supported them regarded them as honest folk who did not try to cover up their extremism with a veneer of respectability, as the Quakers supposedly did, but such favourable voices were few. The more common view was that they were mentally deranged and blasphemous, living openly immoral lives and claiming that the Spirit gave them the freedom to do so. It is difficult to know what to say about the Ranters because so much of our information about them comes from their enemies, but the fact that even the generally tolerant Oliver Cromwell persecuted them suggests there was not much to be said in their favour. In any case they soon died out and no more was heard of them.[105]

Another important ingredient of Puritan sectarianism was the strong belief that they were living at the end of time and the last judgment would not be long delayed. Millenarian movements based on the prophecies in the biblical book of Revelation had long been present on the fringes of the church and can be traced back to the Montanists of the second century, if not earlier. They resurfaced with a vengeance at the time of the Reformation but the leading Reformers either opposed or ignored them. John Calvin never wrote a commentary on Revelation and the Church of England dropped eschatology from its Articles of Religion when they were revised in 1563. Even the Westminster Confession had little to say about it. It may well be that silence on this matter was ultimately counterproductive, because it left a gap that more radical thinkers could fill without necessarily incurring the wrath of the authorities, at least not on theological grounds. The history of millennial apocalypticism is one of false dawns, but that does not necessarily discredit the phenomenon. After all, there were many false messiahs in Israel before the true one appeared, and the same may well be true of the Millennium. The New Testament tells us in several places that the end will come as a thief in the night, but not that it will not come at all.[106] Those who think that they can

---

[105] Ibid. 129–139.
[106] See Matt. 24:43; 1 Thess. 5:2, 4; 2 Peter 3:10; Rev. 16:15.

predict it precisely are wrong, but the doctrine itself is embedded in the most orthodox Christianity and cannot be willed away by the failures of deluded people. This is why it is always ready to spring up anew, and why in times of trouble and social unrest it has a particular appeal to Christians, who know that their ultimate hope does not lie in this world.

The Bible is clear that the end of time will be preceded and accompanied by spiritual warfare in which the Antichrist will arise and seek to persecute the people of God. In Protestant eyes that Antichrist was Rome and in particular the pope. From 1618 to 1648, Catholic forces loyal to him were battling Protestants in Germany, and it was by no means certain that the Protestants would survive the contest. Germany was ruined in the process, and although Protestantism was not wiped out it was largely confined to its strongholds in the north (and in Switzerland). The British Isles had escaped this conflict to a large extent, but had their own mini-versions of it – the struggle between Catholics and Protestants in Ireland for example, and the disputes over Laudianism within the Church of England. It was clear to the Puritans, and not only to the extremists among them, that the Antichrist was on the prowl, a fact that merely heightened tensions and encouraged people to think that the end was at hand.

Ironically, the tolerance Oliver Cromwell showed to dissenting religious opinion increased the fears of the godly that apocalyptic chaos was on the horizon. Even presbyterianism was denounced by some extremists as a manifestation of the Antichrist, something that must have shocked the authors of the Westminster Confession.[107] The overthrow of the king recalled the prophecy of Daniel that there would be four great monarchies in the world before they were all swept away by the everlasting kingdom that would descend from heaven.[108] This was the fifth monarchy, and those who saw it as their duty to usher it in were called Fifth Monarchists.[109] They were implacably opposed to the Commonwealth because they saw it as a compromise that was holding back the introduction of the Millennium. When Oliver Cromwell finally staged a military coup in April 1653 and sent Parliament packing, the Fifth Monarchists were ecstatic. Cromwell appointed an assembly of his own, known to history as the 'Barebone's Parliament' because of the unusual name of one of its members, and for a time it seemed as though it would implement the Fifth

---

[107] McGregor and Reay, *Radical Religion*, 165–189.

[108] Dan. 7:1–28.

[109] B. S. Capp, *The Fifth Monarchy Men: A Study in Seventeenth-Century English Millenarianism* (London: Faber, 1972); T. Liu, *Discord in Zion: The Puritan Divines and the Puritan Revolution 1640–1660* (Den Haag: Nijhoff, 1973).

Monarchist programme. But attempts to abolish tithes and overturn the existing order frightened the propertied classes, who were soon in revolt against the radicals. In the end Cromwell was forced to accept the assembly's enforced 'resignation' and to rule as a dictator, or Lord Protector as he was called. The idealism of the Fifth Monarchy men was shattered and they turned against their erstwhile saviour, but there was nowhere for them to go. As the Commonwealth imploded and the king returned to claim his throne, they retreated into irrelevance and then disappeared, yet more victims of a false millenarian hope.

Millenarians were united in proclaiming a future in which evil would be routed, justice would be done and eternal peace, order and prosperity would reign. The New Jerusalem foretold in Revelation 21 was frequently cited as their model, and many of them thought that they would live to see it, if not descending from heaven, then built by their own efforts. Their vision was captured by the mystical poet William Blake (1757–1827), writing more than a century after their failure but still moved by their heroic spirit. Blake's words have entered the folklore of England, so close to the heartbeat of the nation did he appear to be:

And did those feet in ancient time
Walk upon England's mountains green?
And was the holy Lamb of God
On England's pleasant pastures seen?
And did the countenance divine
Shine forth among these clouded hills?
And was Jerusalem builded here
Among these dark satanic mills?

Bring me my bow of burning gold
Bring me my arrows of desire
Bring me my spear, O clouds unfold
Bring me my chariot of fire!
I will not rest from mental fight
Nor shall my sword sleep in my hand
Till we have built Jerusalem
In England's green and pleasant land.

Blake's New Jerusalem will always be a work in progress, and will never be realized in this life. But the desire to build it is one that has echoed down the centuries, in both religious and secular forms. It is the greatest legacy that sectarian millenarianism has bequeathed to us. Yet even at the time there were differences of opinion as to how the work would be accomplished. One of the more surprising features of the age was that as it became increasingly clear that the Commonwealth was not the paradise its promoters had originally hoped for, more and more 'prophets' began to claim that the age of gold would be ushered in only when the king was restored. When that happened, the Jews would be converted to Christianity, Irish Catholics would become Protestants, the English class system would be abolished – there was no end to the miracles that would occur, although what is surprising is that this dream, which started as a form of rebellion against the Crown, often ended up as a desire to bring the Crown back. The wheel had turned full circle.[110]

Many examples of bizarre sectarians could be produced, but one above all deserves a mention. This is the sect named after Lodowicke Muggleton (1609–98).[111] It began with a message given to John Reeve (1608–58), repeated on three successive days in February 1652, that he and his cousin Lodowicke were the two witnesses foretold in Revelation 11:3–12. He went to Muggleton immediately and persuaded him to accept this as a calling from God to either bless or curse those whom they met. Reeve had been a Ranter and the two men were soon in trouble with the authorities; but after Reeve died, Muggleton took their followers in a markedly different direction. He taught that it was godly to be 'quiet and still', not to rant or quake. He held some unorthodox views, such as that hell was just a state of mind and that public worship should be forbidden. He was a Unitarian in theology, curiously reviving the so-called 'economic Trinity' of the early church, according to which the Father was God in the Old Testament, the Son was God in the life of Jesus and the Holy Spirit is God in the experience of the church. This is the heresy of modalism, which states that the Persons of the Godhead are not real in themselves but only manifestations or roles played by the one God at different times in history. Whether Muggleton knew that he was resurrecting an ancient heresy may be doubted, but that is what he ended up with.

Muggleton was a charismatic figure who seems to have had a special appeal to women, with whom he corresponded. This is fortunate for us because we have a record of his beliefs and pastoral practice that otherwise would not exist. Unlike George Fox, Muggleton did not travel up and down the country seeking converts, and his sect never numbered more than a few hundred. When he

---

[110] See the examples given in McGregor and Reay, *Radical Religion*, 183–189.

[111] See esp. W. Lamont, *Puritanism and Historical Controversy* (London: University College London Press, 1996); *Last Witnesses: The Muggletonian History 1652–1979* (London: Routledge, 2006).

died in 1698, there were 248 mourners at his funeral, and that seems to have been the sum total of the sect's membership. It was all downhill from there. In 1850 there were only 46 people present at a Muggletonian meeting in Clerkenwell, in 1906 only 17, and in 1927 as few as 8. The amazing thing, from our perspective, is that there were any at all. The Muggletonians did not proselytize and it was only through their families that they passed on their beliefs from one generation to the next. Over time those beliefs gradually lost their distinctiveness and by the early twentieth century it was hard to say what they were. The Muggletonians did not think that they alone were saved, but apparently were convinced they had an assurance of their salvation that others lacked. They sometimes went to meetings held by other groups, not to proselytize directly but to make themselves available to anyone who might want to seek them out. They were convinced that a large number of people would be saved, including all children who died in infancy, but also believed in damnation – for those who learned about their doctrines and then rejected them.

In 1974 Christopher Hill (1912–2003) wrote an article in *The Times Literary Supplement* in which he told the world he was surprised to discover that, of all the sects John Milton engaged with, the Muggletonians were the ones who came closest to Milton's beliefs.[112] That sparked off a lively correspondence, out of which contact was made by the 'last of the Muggletonians', Philip Noakes, a farmer in Kent who had rescued the Muggletonian archive from the London Blitz during the Second World War. He made it available to interested researchers and, after his death on 26 February 1979, it was donated to the British Library, where it is now housed in eighty-nine volumes. This extraordinary find has made it possible for modern researchers to study the Muggletonians on their own terms, and not just through reports prepared (in most cases) by their enemies, and we can see how harmless they really were. Members of the Muggleton family still exist and there may be further archive material to be found – a reminder that even so apparently small and obscure a group can leave important traces, some perhaps still undiscovered, that can help us to understand the past better than we otherwise would.

Faith versus reason?

At the heart of the theological debates of the seventeenth century was the question of the right relationship between faith and reason. In the medieval

---

[112] He later published this in a book. See C. Hill, B. Reay and W. M. Lamont, *The World of the Muggletonians* (London: Temple Smith, 1983).

church it had eventually been agreed that matters of faith were known by revelation, which was contained in the Bible and interpreted by the church, whereas secular truths could be known by unaided human reason. In practice this was an accommodation with ancient Greek philosophy and science, collectively known as 'Aristotle' and transmitted to western Europe principally through the Arab world, where ancient Greek knowledge had been translated and developed for centuries.

It was that kind of 'science' that allowed the church to define such things as transubstantiation, a doctrine that depends on the Aristotelian distinction between 'substance' and 'accidents'. Normally a substance like bread cannot change but its accidents (colour, weight, taste, etc.) are variables. In transubstantiation this pattern is reversed. The substance of bread becomes the body of Christ but the accidents remain those of bread, so the communicant consumes something that looks like bread, feels like bread and tastes like bread, even though it is no longer bread.

In the sixteenth and seventeenth centuries this Aristotelian way of looking at the world was abandoned by most scientists, but the Catholic Church could not adjust to this. The result was that progressive scientists like Galileo were condemned for heresy because they rejected a doctrine based on indefensible pseudoscientific premises. Protestants were not constrained by this, but they did not always find it easy to break with age-old traditions either. The development of modern science was a slow process, but it was unstoppable and Protestants were committed to it.[113] The rejection of beliefs like transubstantiation led to a reappraisal of the way in which the spiritual and material worlds interacted. Protestants came to view as 'superstition' the idea that there could be sacred trees or wells, which had proliferated in pre-Reformation times.[114] There was also a corresponding decline of belief in magic, including things like witchcraft and demon possession. In a world ordered by the providence of the Creator God and in a country where almost everyone officially professed belief in him (and was therefore entitled to receive his protection), the persistence of such ideas seemed out of place. The last person in England to be condemned to death for witchcraft was burnt in 1612, although the statute outlawing witchcraft was not revoked until 1677.[115]

---

[113] See R. Hooykaas, *Religion and the Rise of Modern Science* (Edinburgh: Scottish Academic Press, 1973); J. Morgan, *Godly Learning: Puritan Attitudes Towards Reason, Learning and Education, 1560–1640* (Cambridge: Cambridge University Press, 1986).

[114] See A. Walsham, *The Reformation of the Landscape: Religion, Identity and Memory in Early Modern Britain and Ireland* (Oxford: Oxford University Press, 2011).

[115] See K. Thomas, *Religion and the Decline of Magic* (London: Weidenfeld & Nicolson, 1971).

When it came to the interpretation of Scripture, the Puritans were committed to respecting its divine inspiration, which meant accepting that demon possession was possible, as were miracles and so on, but they did not believe that this contradicted the validity of scientific inquiry. There were 'laws' in nature, implanted there by the Creator and generally maintained in force by him, but the Creator was sovereign over his creatures and could suspend the normal 'rules' as and when he chose to do so. This flexibility was explained by the doctrine of providence, according to which the Creator continues to govern and uphold what he has made. There was therefore no distinction between what was 'natural' and what was 'supernatural', as there had been in medieval thinking, because the material world was not autonomous in the eyes of God.

To put this another way, it was theology that determined the Protestant approach to the 'natural' sciences and not the other way around. Miracles were not dismissed because they broke the 'laws' of nature; rather it was the laws of nature that had to be accommodated to the revealed will of God. The implications of this for practical living were enormous. On the one hand Protestants could study the natural world, hopeful of discovering its inner structure, but they could also pray for divine 'intervention' in the normal processes without fear of contradiction. For this to work properly, it was first necessary to get the theology revealed in the Bible right, so that believers would start with the right principles and not find themselves defending scientific impossibilities like transubstantiation on the spurious ground that they were 'revealed truth'. This required skill in the original languages of Scripture and the ability to determine what the correct text was. Protestants were in the forefront of such research and British scholars, many of whom were trained in Geneva or according to the methods established there by Theodore Beza and his disciples, were second to none in their ability to read and interpret the sacred texts. They made it their business to pass this knowledge along, and to ensure that British schools kept abreast of the latest discoveries in this field. This gave them both the right and the ability to take part in the most sophisticated theological debates in the Reformed world, most notably at the Synod of Dort and later at the Westminster Assembly.

To those who accepted these principles, Reformed theology seemed to be logical and true in a scientific sense as well as any other. Pastors were doctors of the soul, called to apply biblical principles to the practical questions of life in much the same way as a medical doctor would apply his knowledge to the healing of the body. In the seventeenth century the main difference between the medical doctor and the pastor was that medical science was still in its infancy and was prone to error, whereas theological science was clear and relatively easy to apply once one had the requisite training. This is what Puritan pastors tried to do, and why so many of them believed that presbyterianism, or something like it, was necessary to ensure quality control. Charlatans could not be allowed to practise independently, because they would bring the entire profession into disrepute. Just as there are still people who prefer quack remedies and popular treatments to officially sanctioned medicine, so there were people in the seventeenth century who rejected the official ministers of the church in favour of charismatic prophets, but then as now such people were pursued by the authorities, who did their best to stamp them out.

This situation might have continued indefinitely, but it was challenged by those who rejected the theological principles on which it was based. In Italy Lelio Sozzini (1525–62) and his nephew Fausto (1539–1604) rebelled against the Catholic Church and claimed that there was no connection between the metaphysical, or spiritual, world and the material one. As far as they were concerned, the spiritual world was fictitious, an invention of the priests who wanted to delude the people and control them. This teaching had a great appeal to many Protestants, but only a minority accepted their theological conclusions. The Sozzinis naturally rejected the idea of a divine incarnation, which led them to deny the Trinity and the atoning work of Christ on the cross. To them Jesus was a human example to follow, not God in human flesh who had given his life for the salvation of the world.

Socinianism, as their doctrine came to be called, struck at the heart of Christianity, because without the incarnation and the atonement, Jesus of Nazareth was no more than a prophet like any other great religious teacher. The Sozzinis were persecuted and had to flee with their followers, ending up in Poland, where they managed to establish themselves in Raków. There Fausto Sozzini composed a catechism of their beliefs that was soon translated into many languages and circulated across Europe. It is not known how many people in Britain were affected by this teaching, and the probability is that Socinianism was a bogeyman in polemical literature more than a force to be reckoned with on the ground. But even if that was true, the fact that it was widely denounced spread awareness of it and excited the curiosity of those who wanted to know more.[116]

Socinianism had two things going for it in the early seventeenth century. The first was its emphasis on the supremacy of reason. The Socinians refused

---

[116] S. Mortimer, *Reason and Religion in the English Revolution: The Challenge of Socinianism* (Cambridge: Cambridge University Press, 2010). For an appraisal of the importance of Socinianism for Enlightenment thought, see J. I. Israel, *The Enlightenment That Failed: Ideas, Revolution and Democratic Defeat, 1748–1830* (Oxford: Oxford University Press, 2019), 97–105.

to accept as true anything that could not be demonstrated by rational means, and that meant the bulk of traditional theology. This was in line with developing scientific thought and it was easy to portray their doctrine as a purified, rational form of Christian belief that concentrated heavily on moral behaviour and disregarded anything supernatural. This kind of Socinianism had a certain appeal to intellectuals, who wanted to think that they were capable of passing judgment on spiritual matters and resented the discipline the church authorities were trying to impose on them.

The other thing that worked in the Socinians' favour was the growing tendency to rely on personal experience rather than on official church teaching. We have already noted how prevalent this emphasis was among many sectarians, who were easily persuaded to abandon the teaching of the Bible or of the church, especially if they could claim to have had spiritual experiences of their own. This appeared to be quite different from scientific rationalism, but in reality it was not. Experience was 'real' and had to be accounted for. A man would know that he had fallen into a trance and seen visions of heaven, but he could not prove that he would be saved by faith in Jesus Christ, even though the church assured him that was the case. Once the basis for belief started to shift in this way, Socinianism found itself on fertile ground and it progressed accordingly.

In England, Socinianism entered the world of respectable discourse largely thanks to the work of Lucius Cary, Viscount Falkland (1610–43), whose estate at Great Tew, Oxfordshire, became a centre for independent spirits who wanted to discuss religious questions away from the polemics dividing the country at that time. The Great Tew circle, as this group came to be called, sought for common ground on which all Christians could agree, and aimed to distinguish that as primary from second-order issues causing disagreement. They were not themselves fully united, it must be said, but they all opposed Catholicism, which they saw as a form of tyranny, and they tended to suspect something similar in official Protestantism as well, although they remained loyal members of the Church of England. The common ground they sought was inevitably based on what was reasonable, and it was because of that that they began to take an interest in Socinianism.

Critics of Great Tew accused its members of heresy because of this, but that is going too far. Most were prepared to use Socinian ideas when that suited them, but none was committed to the sect and there were some things about it that they rejected, notably the Socinians' indifference to social and political life. But having said that, the Great Tew circle showed an openness to rationalism that was rare in their time and was to be influential later on. The best-known member of this circle was William Chillingworth (1602–44), Archbishop Laud's godson. In 1637 he published *The Religion of Protestants a Safe Way to Salvation* in which he stated quite clearly that Protestants (unlike Catholics) believed the Bible and nothing more, and that they read the sacred text with their eyes and minds open. They were not committed to a particular dogmatic scheme of interpretation but were free to come to their own conclusions about what a particular text meant, or might mean. The fact that these conclusions were different from one another did not worry them, because in their opinion freedom of thought was what really counted, not subscription to a dogma that would inevitably have been composed by someone else and imposed on them as being uniquely true. The Great Tew circle did not survive the Civil War, in which Lord Falkland was killed on the side of the Royalists, but it sowed seeds that would bear fruit in the next generation and lead to the first flowering of the movement we now call the Enlightenment. For the time being, the Puritans were triumphant, but little though they knew it, the seeds of destruction that would eventually overturn them were already germinating under their noses.

10
Reaping the whirlwind (1653–1717)

Puritanism triumphant

The civil wars of the 1640s ended with the victory of the Puritans, but as the dust of battle began to clear, the problem of what would happen next loomed ever larger. The Long Parliament that had sat from November 1640 was a diverse body, many of whose members were prepared to come to terms with Charles I, even after he had demonstrated his untrustworthiness as monarch. Among the victors, frustration with this willingness to compromise began to grow, especially in parts of the army. On 6 December 1648 Colonel Thomas Pride (d. 1658) marched his troops into the House of Commons and arrested as many of the moderate reconcilers as he could find. By the time his round-up was finished, about a week later, only a remnant of about 200 radical members was left sitting. It was this so-called 'Rump Parliament' that sentenced the king to death and then tried to rule the country. The Rump had no electoral mandate and did not seek one. When members died or resigned they were replaced internally, in the hope that the Rump's reforming zeal would not be diluted.

Popular expectations were high. There was a feeling abroad that an epoch-making revolution had taken place and that a new world order was about to be inaugurated. Colonel Pride was a Fifth Monarchist, but they were a coterie of zealots who could not dominate the Rump Parliament. In the spring of 1653 the Rump was dissolved, and Oliver Cromwell, along with his chief advisers, began to look for something to replace it. With the help of the Fifth Monarchists (still a minority) they came up with the idea of a nominated assembly that would seek to refashion the British Isles along what they saw as 'godly' lines.

This assembly, which was soon called a parliament, consisted of 150 members, of whom five were Scottish, six Irish and the rest English. It is not entirely clear how the members were nominated. Apparently there was a desire to seek candidates from churches across the country, but although some names were certainly submitted by particular congregations, we have no way of knowing how typical that was. All we can say for sure is that the members of this parliament were all Puritans and that they represented a cross-section of society, contrary to the common criticism that most of them were socially inferior and unqualified to be lawmakers. However, we do know that one of the London members was a leather worker named Praise-God Barebone (c.1598–1679), in mockery of whom the assembly came to be called Barebone's Parliament. It was a gathering of the 'godly' in which the Fifth Monarchists exercised disproportionate influence, and it was intoxicated with apocalyptic visions of the new order.

Needless to say, fantasy cannot rule a country, and before long Barebone's Parliament had to get down to what it saw as its major task – the reform of the church. In the view of most of its members, tithes ought to be abolished and clergy left to depend on the generosity of their congregations, which they believed would be forthcoming as long as they preached the gospel. Formal church structures could be dispensed with, because the godly knew who they were and would ensure that the true church of the saints would prevail, unhindered by human constraints on the Spirit's activity. The traditional debates over episcopacy, presbyterianism and/or congregationalism were swept aside. The result was that those who advocated one or other of those systems were now ranged in an uncomfortable alliance against the radicals, who were still a minority but were gaining in confidence and strength. On 6 December 1653 a committee on tithes reported back, recommending the institution of a board of 'Triers' for the examination of new ministers, and the retention of the tithe system as the chief means of paying them. This report was narrowly rejected by the house, which prompted the moderate members to ask Cromwell to intervene. Two days later Barebone's Parliament dissolved itself, and the way was open for the proclamation on 16 December of Cromwell as Lord Protector of the Commonwealth.

Cromwell was now dictator for life. After a delay of nearly nine months he finally appointed another parliament (on 3 September 1654), whose members were hand-picked by him, and in that way he governed the country until his death. Cromwell faced strong pressure to replace the tithe system with some other means of financing the clergy – either by state subsidy or by voluntary contributions. Opponents of the traditional tithe believed it insulated the clergy from their people by giving them an independent source of income, making quality control of the ministry more difficult. Pastors who were directly dependent on the state (or on the goodwill of their congregations) would be easier to supervise, it was asserted, and tithe reform went hand in hand with the new system of 'Triers' for examining and appointing ministers. Alongside them was also to be a series of committees of 'ejectors', who would have the power to depose clergy who did not meet the required standard. These duties were taken seriously. The surviving records show that the Triers appointed men all over England and it is estimated that up to 2,300 clergymen might have been ejected for being unsuitable. Although we know much less about the activities of these bodies in Wales, Scotland and Ireland, it seems likely that the system never took root there in the way it did in England.

The central government could hardly extend its control beyond the appointment of ministers to parishes, something that in the circumstances of the time was already a very demanding task. But the work of the Triers was only the tip of a very large iceberg of church discipline. The men appointed to parishes were expected to undertake a thorough visitation of their parishioners, catechizing them in their homes and doing their best to ensure high standards of moral and spiritual accomplishment. In the nature of things it is impossible to judge how successful they were at this, but we have two indications to help us evaluate the process. The first is the large supply of notes made by the clergy themselves, in which they were not slow to criticize the ungodliness of their flocks. The second is the existence of manuals of pastoral care, most notably *The Reformed Pastor* of Richard Baxter (1615–91), which is a classic of spiritual devotion and so good that it is still in print.

Baxter is an important figure in seventeenth-century Puritanism, not least because he was a moderate who genuinely desired reconciliation among the different factions that had arisen in the wake of the Civil War. Fundamentally presbyterian in outlook, he nevertheless saw virtues in independency and was even prepared to accept the kind of reduced episcopacy advocated by Archbishop Ussher. He met Ussher in 1656, shortly before the latter's death, and the two men came to agreement on the subject in less than an hour, which shows just how close their views were. Shortly before that, Baxter gave the series of lectures that later became his *Reformed Pastor*.[1] He was the incumbent of Kidderminster at the time, and had been invited to address a local meeting of ministers on the subject of pastoral care and oversight. Baxter tackled the subject with a degree of methodical exposition that has seldom been equalled and has been a challenge to pastors ever since.

To what extent was Baxter's programme for pastoral care put into practice? Evidence from Kidderminster suggests that he was remarkably successful, but that might have been due to his personality and dedication as much as anything else. Could it be replicated across the country, and if so, to what extent? There were certainly many places and large numbers of people who were influenced

---

[1] R. Baxter, *The Reformed Pastor* (London: Banner of Truth Trust, 1974).

by the Puritans, and godly standards of honesty and hard work were instilled in the population to a degree that had never previously been seen. Even today the legacy of that can be felt, as the British public expects high standards of behaviour, not only from its clergy but from its elected representatives and from people in general. Even when the religious background and motivation are missing, or have been obscured, the Puritan work ethic continues to operate in many spheres of life, to the undoubted benefit of society as a whole.

Having said that, there is an inherent contradiction in the Puritan programme that doomed it to failure in the longer term. Puritan belief was that the godly were a divinely chosen minority, predestined to eternal salvation and called to work that out on earth as they made their pilgrim way to the celestial city. But the majority of the population were not so blessed. They were reprobates, condemned to eternal damnation and unable to save themselves by their own efforts. If the godly were in control of the government, as they were in the 1650s, the reprobates could be constrained by legal sanctions against them, which is the policy the state adopted. But compelling people to be 'good' in that way was bound to provoke resentment and prove unworkable. The Puritan gospel, which was a source of great joy and liberation for those who embraced it wholeheartedly, became an odious moralizing tyranny for the many who were not in tune with it. Conversion could not be forced on anyone by law, making compulsory conformity to godly rule an open invitation to hypocrisy.

Things were not made easier by the growing Puritan emphasis on individual revelations and the role of conscience in the Christian life. It is no accident that the inauguration of Cromwell's Protectorate coincided with a great increase in visionary prophecies and eccentric behaviour. Not everyone went as far as the unfortunate James Nayler, who imagined himself as a reincarnation of Jesus Christ, but the Quakers and others like them claimed to have mystical visions and hear divine voices guiding them, and if the results were extreme, then so be it. In fact eccentricity was almost required in a mindset that pitted the evil world against the godliness of the elect. When George Fox was filled with the Spirit and ran naked through the streets, who could say that this was not the will of God? Even Oliver Cromwell, being a man who would never knowingly quench the Spirit, tolerated him. Such behaviour did nothing to commend Puritanism though, and provided ammunition to its opponents, who saw it as socially destructive. Unfortunately it was these excesses that people tended to remember, so that when the steam finally ran out of the Puritan revolution its enemies had more popular support than a balanced view of the facts would have warranted.

In other spheres Puritanism had a galvanizing effect that would prove to be long lasting. Academic life at Oxford and Cambridge was transformed. This was the golden age of English theology, represented above all by the remarkable figure of John Owen (1616–83), a man who stands head and shoulders above his non-Puritan contemporaries. Owen has a good claim to being regarded as the greatest English divine who ever lived, and his prodigious output still impresses modern observers, although few go to the trouble of reading him.[2] His massive multivolume commentary on Hebrews remains unsurpassed and is perhaps the greatest single monument of Puritan biblical scholarship. As Dean of Christ Church Cathedral, Oxford (1651–60), and Vice-Chancellor of the university (1652–7), Owen was well placed to influence the quality and direction of theological education, and the years of his tenure were a golden age of divinity at Oxford.

Another well-known Puritan was Owen's contemporary John Milton, Latin secretary to the Commonwealth government and universally acknowledged as an outstanding poet in the English language, as well as one of the greatest political thinkers England has produced.[3] Although Milton was a Puritan, he was a strong advocate of religious and intellectual freedom, something that made him willing to tolerate heterodox views to a degree that most Puritans would never have countenanced. His own theology has been the subject of much debate, although it seems that his personal faith remained orthodox, despite his alienation from both the Church of England and the dissenting sects that emerged in his lifetime. His most famous work is his epic *Paradise Lost*, in which he recounts the story of the fall of humankind, linking it to the political events of his own time. It has often been remarked that his portrait of Satan is more convincing than his portrayal of God, but that is not surprising, since evil is a more varied and intriguing phenomenon than perfect goodness. Among his prose works, *Areopagitica* remains the most widely read,

---

[2] W. H. Goold (ed.), *The Works of John Owen*, 23 vols. (London: Johnstone and Hunter, 1850–55; repr. London: Banner of Truth Trust, 1966). Some of his works have been published separately in recent years; e.g. K. M. Kapic and J. Taylor (eds.), *Overcoming Sin and Temptation* (Wheaton, Ill.: Crossway, 2006); *Communion with the Triune God* (Wheaton, Ill.: Crossway, 2007). For studies of Owen, see P. Toon, *God's Statesman: The Life and Work of John Owen* (Exeter: Paternoster Press, 1971); C. R. Trueman, *The Claims of Truth: John Owen's Trinitarian Theology* (Carlisle: Paternoster Press, 1998); B. Kay, *Trinitarian Spirituality: John Owen and the Doctrine of God in Western Devotion* (Milton Keynes: Paternoster Press, 2007); C. Gribben, *John Owen and English Puritanism: Experiences of Defeat* (Oxford: Oxford University Press, 2016); *An Introduction to John Owen: A Christian Vision for Every Stage of Life* (Wheaton, Ill.: Crossway, 2020).

[3] H. Darbishire (ed.), *The Poetical Works of John Milton* (London: Oxford University Press, 1958); D. M. Wolfe (ed.), *Complete Prose Works of John Milton*, 8 vols. in 10 (New Haven, Conn.: Yale University Press, 1953–82). See also C. Hill, *Milton and the English Revolution* (London: Faber & Faber, 1977); *The Experience of Defeat: Milton and Some Contemporaries* (London: Faber & Faber, 1984).

probably because it is a defence of intellectual freedom that is still quoted in support of that cause.

Owen and Milton were intellectual giants in an age rich in theological talent. They were well educated and prominent in academic and civil affairs throughout the Puritan Commonwealth. But the power of Puritanism went deeper than that. For the first time in British history, it became possible for men of humble birth to rise to prominence as preachers and teachers of the Word of God. The most famous of these was John Bunyan, born to a poor family near Bedford and lacking any formal education that would qualify him for ordination. Bunyan believed that he was called by God to preach and did so without a licence – an offence that landed him in jail.[4] Today most people would deplore such a fate, but in Bunyan's case it was truly providential, because prison gave him the leisure (and motivation) to produce some of the most compelling works of English spirituality ever to have been written. His *Pilgrim's Progress* became and has remained a classic account of the Christian life, on a par with Augustine of Hippo's famous *Confessions* but completely different in its approach. Bunyan tells the story of how his hero, Christian, battled the trials and temptations of this life before entering into his heavenly reward. Then, remarkably for a seventeenth-century writer, he repeats the exercise with Christiana, Christian's wife. Both tales are allegories, but the fact that Bunyan thought female spirituality was just as important as male spirituality, and that he (as a man) was prepared to write about it, shows how much English life was being transformed by the doctrine of predestination. In Bunyan's world anyone could be a pilgrim, and many quite ordinary people were. Remarkably, Bunyan had poetical gifts as well, and his accounts are peppered with verse. Among the best known is the 'Pilgrim's Song', which is still regularly sung in churches and captures the spirit of the average Puritan better than a thousand learned treatises could do:

Who would true valour see
Let him come hither
One here will constant be
Come wind, come weather.
There's no discouragement
Shall make him once relent
His first avowed intent
To be a pilgrim.

---

[4] See C. Hill, *A Turbulent, Seditious and Factious People: John Bunyan and His Church* (Oxford: Clarendon Press, 1988).

Whoso beset him round
With dismal stories
Do but themselves confound
His strength the more is.
No lion can him fright
He'll with a giant fight
But he will have a right
To be a pilgrim.

Hobgoblin nor foul fiend
Can daunt his spirit
He knows he at the end
Shall life inherit
Then fancies fly away
He'll fear not what men say
He'll labour night and day
To be a pilgrim.

The intensity of Puritan devotion comes across clearly in hymns like this, and it changed the face of British Christianity. Before this time Christian faith had been defined mainly in collective terms – membership of the universal church, adherence to an orthodox creed or confession of faith, participation in common worship. Contrary to popular belief, the Puritans did not belittle or discard those things, but to them true Christianity was something different. It was a walk with God, in which each individual was expected to demonstrate that he or she had been called by him. It was a transformation of life that would be seen in changed behaviour, and the goal of that transformation was entry into the celestial city of which the believer was already a citizen. There might be differences of opinion as to when and how that goal would be reached. Most, like Bunyan himself, thought that it would come at the point of death, but there were some who expected it to come down to earth in a millennial apocalypse they eagerly awaited. In the nature of things, the millennial hope was liable to be disappointed, and (so far at least) that has proved to be the case; but it is still there, and it periodically resurfaces as new generations are inspired to hope for the final realization of Christ's promises and the establishment of his eternal kingdom in heaven and on earth.

The Puritan age was a time of spiritual exaltation and its greatest exponents have left us an enduring legacy. And yet the Commonwealth they established lasted barely more than a decade. After Oliver Cromwell's death it fell apart with remarkable speed and nobody ever tried to revive it. On the contrary, although many Puritan ideas were gradually absorbed into the social and political system, and the old order was never restored to the extent that its proponents wished, Puritanism came to be regarded as an unfortunate interlude, an aberration in the history of England that should never be repeated. Why was that?

One reason for the failure of Puritanism was its latent idealism. As the name suggests, Puritans wanted purity, and in a fallen world purity does not exist. What happens instead is that flawed individuals conceive their own notions of what purity ought to be and then seek to impose them as the norm, whether others agree with them or not. All Puritans agreed that the Bible is the Word of God and that a Christian society ought to be based on its teaching. But what did that mean? Were the laws of Old Testament Israel meant to be applied in a Christian Commonwealth? The sixteenth-century Reformers had rejected that idea, but many of the Puritans disagreed. Their covenant theology allowed them to identify themselves with ancient Israel and read its laws as normative for them. The most obvious example of that was observance of the Sabbath. This had never featured very prominently in Christian thinking before about 1600, nor did it affect Continental European Protestantism in the way it affected Britain, where Sabbath observance almost became an article of faith.

More seriously, the Puritans could not agree on a form of church government that would include everyone. Different groups pressed for presbyterianism, congregationalism and even episcopacy, but although they could all make a case based on the New Testament, none was able to do so in a way that effectively justified its position to the exclusion of the others. The result was not merely stalemate but division. Presbyterians and Independents (congregationalists) in particular were often at each other's throats, even though their theological differences were virtually non-existent. Baptists insisted on rejecting infant baptism, which set them apart from others, although John Bunyan, himself a Baptist of sorts, refused to follow them in this. Bunyan accepted that two different views on this subject were possible, and in his chapel in Bedford he insisted that both of them should be accommodated.[5] To this day, Bunyan Meeting, as it is called, has two membership rolls – one for Baptists and the other for non-Baptists, an almost unique example of a tolerance that was in short supply during Bunyan's lifetime.

---

[5] See J. Bunyan, 'Differences in Judgment About Water-Baptism no Bar to Communion', in T. L. Underwood (ed.), *The Miscellaneous Works of John Bunyan*, vol. 4 (Oxford: Clarendon Press, 1989), 189–264.

Sadly Britain was not ready for such tolerance, and it proved impossible to find a consensus that would endure. When Oliver Cromwell toyed with the idea of making himself king, John Owen fell out with him and the two men went their separate ways, despite their common faith and high regard for each other. Lower down the scale were similar dissensions and a good deal of intransigence, especially from the Presbyterians and their Scottish allies. If there were ever to have been a united Puritan church, it would have had to be essentially presbyterian, and something of that kind was proposed when the time came to restore the monarchy. Unfortunately other forces, deeply hostile to the Puritans, were also in play, and they conspired to make the project unworkable. The expected demise of the Commonwealth emboldened some Royalists to action, and in 1658 an anonymous book called *The Whole Duty of Man* appeared, which is generally thought to have been the work of Richard Allestree (1622?–81). It was a devotional work that appealed to a generation tired of the spiritual excesses of the Protectorate, and it became very popular after the Restoration. Its main message, derived from Ecclesiastes 12:13, was 'Fear God and keep his commandments', an exhortation to good behaviour (if not exactly 'good works').

Another person who encapsulated the spirit of this age was Jeremy Taylor (1613–67), an Englishman who went to Ireland in 1658 and became Bishop of Down and Connor in 1661. He had already written the two works by which he continues to be known – *The Rule and Exercises of Holy Living* (1650) and *The Rule and Exercises of Holy Dying* (1651). Taylor showed himself to be an exponent of a regulated spirituality, quite at variance with the 'Spirit-inspired' tendencies of the Puritans under the Commonwealth. In his earlier years he had been an advocate of religious tolerance, but after being made a bishop he became a rather authoritarian disciplinarian, driving many clergy of presbyterian sympathies out of the church. He also compelled Irish-speaking Catholics to attend Protestant worship conducted in English, a counterproductive policy that was incompatible with the practice of William Bedell a generation earlier and did nothing to commend the restored Church of Ireland to the majority of the population.

Future historians would describe the late seventeenth and early eighteenth centuries as an age of 'moralism', as opposed to authentic Christianity, a judgment that may be unfair but one that reflects the changed atmosphere soon to dominate church affairs.[6] As a result, instead of a moderately Puritan

---

[6] See C. F. Allison, *The Rise of Moralism: The Proclamation of the Gospel from Hooker to Baxter* (London: SPCK, 1966).

settlement at the end of the Commonwealth period, there was an openly anti-Puritan reaction that would permanently divide the British churches and produce both the Establishment and dissenting traditions with which we are familiar today.

The Great Schism

Oliver Cromwell died on 3 September 1658 and before long the Commonwealth of which he had been Lord Protector started to unravel. Cromwell's son, Richard, succeeded him but was unequal to the task, and within a year he was gone. The Rump Parliament, to the extent that it still existed, was recalled, but it was soon dissolved by the army. In its place the full Long Parliament of 1640 was restored and met from 21 February to 16 March 1660, when it dissolved itself. In that short period it revived the presbyterian system of church government and made the Westminster Confession the official doctrine of the state. For a while it looked as though a moderate form of presbyterianism would prevail and those who advocated it took pains to reach out to others as far as they could. In particular they wanted to heal the breach with the Independents by allowing greater freedom to individual congregations than strict presbyterianism would have countenanced, but feelings between the two groups were inflamed and they had limited success. The moderates approached Charles II in exile, hoping that he would support them, and to some extent he did, although he made it clear that he would expect a restoration of both the Prayer Book and the episcopate.[7] It soon became apparent that the best that could be hoped for was a 'reduced' form of episcopacy, similar to that advocated by the late Archbishop Ussher. Parish ministers would have considerable freedom in matters of worship, dress and (crucially) discipline, retaining the right to excommunicate parishioners who in their view were unworthy to partake of the sacrament.

A settlement of that kind seemed possible for about six months after the restoration of the king on 29 May 1660, but there was trouble ahead. The presbyterians fell out with one another over the degree of latitude they were prepared to tolerate, and they failed to present a united front in the negotiations that began in 1661. By then it was also clear that there was a vocal group of Puritans who would not accept any compromise, and who rejected the kind of quality control of the ministry that was implicit in a presbyterian system. On the other side, the pre-Civil-War clergy and bishops who had remained

---

[7] For Charles's declaration of religious liberty, see G. L. Bray (ed.), *Documents of the English Reformation*, 3rd edn (Cambridge: James Clarke, 2019), 490–491.

loyal to the king returned to claim what they believed was rightfully theirs, and they were determined not to grant any serious concessions to the presbyterians. Matters were complicated still further by the existence of a small group of Catholics at court who wanted toleration for themselves and their co-religionists. There was some sympathy for them in circles close to the king, but the majority of both presbyterians and episcopalians were united against them. The idea that religious toleration might extend to Catholics – who, it must be remembered, would not have given it to others if they had been in power – was anathema, and fear that it might be granted to them played into the hands of those who wanted to restore the old order.[8]

Discussions among the various parties went on for a year or so, but the result was to harden attitudes on both sides.[9] The episcopalians were convinced that only a wholesale restoration of the old order would bring lasting peace and stability to the country, and some held up the memory of Charles I and Archbishop Laud as martyrs to their cause. Puritanism in all its forms was interpreted as rebellion against the established order and was condemned in that light. Even Charles II thought this was going too far, but he could not afford to alienate his most avid supporters and in the end allowed them to have their way. A slightly revised Prayer Book was composed and passed by the Convocation of Canterbury early in 1662, and it was sent from there to Parliament for its approval. In the subsequent Act of Uniformity, Parliament established the rites and system of the Church of England as the state religion and outlawed any dissent from it. Those clergy who did not conform to this settlement would be expelled from the church on St Bartholomew's Day, 24 August 1662, in what came to be known as the 'Great Ejection', which is considered to be the birthday of the dissenting tradition in English Protestantism.[10]

How significant was the Great Ejection? This has long been a matter of controversy among historians, many of whom have been influenced by partisans of one side or the other. According to many Dissenters (also known as 'Nonconformists' and nowadays usually described as 'Free Churchmen'), as many as 2,000 clergymen left their posts in protest against the settlement. This

---

[8] See R. S. Bosher, *The Making of the Restoration Settlement: The Influence of the Laudians 1649–1662* (London: Dacre Press; Adam & Charles Black, 1951); J. Spurr, *The Restoration Church of England 1646–1689* (New Haven, Conn.: Yale University Press, 1991); P. Seaward, *The Cavalier Parliament and the Reconstruction of the Old Regime, 1661–1667* (Cambridge: Cambridge University Press, 1989), 162–195; G. Tapsell (ed.), *The Later Stuart Church 1660–1714* (Manchester: Manchester University Press, 2012).

[9] See C. Buchanan, *The Savoy Conference Revisited*, Alcuin Club and The Group for Renewal of Worship Joint Liturgical Studies 54 (Cambridge: Grove Books, 2002).

[10] The text of the Act of Uniformity, parts of which are still in force, can be found in Bray, *Documents*, 492–504.

must be compared with the estimated 2,300 clergymen who had been deposed or who had abandoned their livings during the Civil War and under the Commonwealth, many of whom returned in 1660 to reclaim them. How should such figures be interpreted? The ejection of traditional clergymen from 1643 onwards was not the result of a single act and had a number of different causes. Some of these clergy were loyal to the king and simply abandoned their posts, going into exile with him in the hope that he would win the Civil War and they could return home. Many men were deprived of livings that they had never really occupied – they had been absentees and their deposition was more of a formality than anything else. In other cases clergymen were sent packing because, in the eyes of the Puritan commissioners who investigated them, they were not doing their job properly. Admittedly the criteria used were open to question. For example, a clergyman who could be shown to have read Charles I's Book of Sports would be deprived of his benefice for that cause alone, something that to modern minds seems excessive. But the overall pattern was one of enforcing church discipline, and hardly any of those who suffered have left us any indication that their departure was a serious loss to the church.

The ejections of 1660–65 were quite different. In some cases parishes had been taken over by extremists who were merely filling a vacuum and had no authority from anyone. They obviously had to go, but there were not very many of them – perhaps 200 at the most. More numerous were legally ordained men who had been appointed by the Commonwealth Triers to vacant livings, and who now found themselves confronted with their expelled predecessors. They too were forced to vacate their posts, although whether they could properly be called 'Dissenters' is doubtful. Quite a number of them had sought episcopal ordination from bishops who had gone into retirement (or hiding), and virtually none could be accused of having neglected their duty.[11] Many were soon to be found occupying other benefices that were vacant because the previous incumbents had died or did not wish to reclaim them, and so their ejection was only temporary. A few others left in the heat of the moment but then repented at leisure, and were allowed back into the church, always provided that they had received, or were willing to accept, episcopal ordination, which was now made compulsory. Others went into retirement and often continued to attend their parish churches, where they might even be asked to preach on occasion. When these different circumstances are taken into

---

[11] See K. Fincham and S. Taylor, 'Vital Statistics: Episcopal Ordination and Ordinands in England, 1646–60', *English Historical Review* 126.519 (April 2011), 319–344, for a detailed analysis of this phenomenon.

account, it seems that the true figure for dissenting ministers is something less than 1,000, or about half the number often claimed.

How many laypeople followed their clergy is impossible to determine with any accuracy. Some obviously did, and dissenting congregations appeared up and down the country, but how many of their members really 'left the church' is hard to say. Many kept a foot in the door, continuing to use the parish church for baptisms, weddings and funerals but preferring to worship on a regular basis with a dissenting congregation. This phenomenon, known as 'occasional conformity', became an accepted feature of English life and has still not entirely died out, although it is much less significant now than it once was. There are prominent examples of people, the late Margaret Thatcher (1925–2013) being one of them, who were brought up in Nonconformity but became Anglicans in the course of their careers, often because it seemed like the 'natural' thing to do as they rose up the social scale. In the late seventeenth century, pressure to conform was much greater than it has been since then, and so we are not surprised to discover that denominational ambiguity was more prevalent then too. Overall it is probably true to say that dissenting clergy were somewhere between 5 and 10% of the total, whereas dissenting laity were much fewer, probably no more than 1 or 2% of the population.

Of course, statistics like these can be highly misleading. Dissenters might have been few in number but were highly committed to their cause and were quite possibly more numerous than those who were supportive of the episcopal Establishment. Ten or twenty dedicated believers are worth more than one or two hundred nominal ones, as the Church of England would soon find out. Nobody went to a dissenting congregation in the hope of securing social advancement or of staying out of trouble – there was often a sense of martyrdom to their cause and, for a few years at least, discrimination against them was a reality they had to endure. It was also true that the leaders of dissent were on the whole more learned and more pious than those who took the posts such leaders were forced to vacate. Who in the Establishment was the equal of John Owen or Richard Baxter? Or John Bunyan, for that matter? There was also the fact that Puritanism could not be expelled from the church entirely. The bishops and higher clergy might rail against it, but lower down the scale were many parish priests who quietly maintained their theological convictions and continued to preach them, preserving a tradition that two generations later would contribute to a widespread revival of religion.

The Restoration Settlement would not have gone as smoothly as it did had there not been a significant body of men who had been brought up under the Commonwealth but who were nonetheless prepared to come to terms with the king. These men were disapproved of by the dissenting Puritans and reviled by the High Churchmen who had always been king's men, but the fact that they had a foot in both camps allowed them to act as a bridge between them and to go some way towards healing the divisions of the Civil War era. They came to be called 'Latitudinarians' because of their moderate theological views, but this pejorative title does not do justice to them. For the most part they were orthodox in their beliefs, although their openness to new ideas could be disconcerting to those who were determined to revive the lost certainties of the pre-1640 era.

Among the Latitudinarians, pride of place belongs to Edward Stillingfleet (1635–99), who began as an advocate of a church in which episcopalian, presbyterian and congregational elements would all find a place, but who ended as a staunch defender of the 1662 settlement. He was particularly critical of mystical theology, which was enjoying something of a revival in his time, and censured those who claimed to have extraordinary visions and spiritual experiences, on the ground that they were expressions of irrational emotionalism. No doubt many of his strictures were justified, but after his death they were used to condemn the revivalism that broke out in the 1740s and this misuse of his writings has had a negative effect on his longer-term reputation. Simon Patrick (1625–1707) was another man in the same mould, as was John Tillotson (1630–94), both of whom played a major part in the events surrounding the deposition of James II in 1688, when they stood up for the Reformed doctrine of the Church of England and resisted what they saw as the spurious claims of loyalty to the king that were being advanced by some of the High Church bishops and clergy. Another of their number who deserves special mention is Thomas Tenison (1636–1715), who became Vicar of St Martin-in-the-Fields, then the most fashionable London church, whose sermons were legendary and who became one of the chief promoters of the charity-school movement, a philanthropic effort intended to give the London poor a sound and Christian education. In this he was followed by William Wake (1657–1737), who went even further and instituted evening-worship services for the convenience of servants and others who could not attend in the morning. Wake also reached out to Continental Protestants and was sincerely interested in a union of all the Reformed churches, although his conviction that the Church of England, complete with its episcopate and Prayer Book, should serve as the model for the reunited church did not find as much favour with those whom he was seeking to embrace as he thought it should. It is a measure of the calibre of the church hierarchy at the time that Tillotson, Tenison and Wake succeeded one another as archbishops of

Canterbury, lending a distinction to that office reminiscent of the Reformation era that has not been matched since their time.

Somewhat of an outlier among the Latitudinarians was Gilbert Burnet (1643–1715), a Scotsman who avoided the travails of episcopalianism in his native land by emigrating to England. There he became a champion of the Reformation and wrote an influential exposition of the Thirty-nine Articles that earned him the odium of the High Church Tories because of his willingness to embrace a breadth of theological views that they found unpalatable. Burnet was a Latitudinarian more by accident than by design, but his work became the standard textbook for aspiring ordinands in the Church of England and is still occasionally read and referenced.

On the legal and political front the supporters of the Restoration Establishment lost no time in consolidating their position. Even before the Act of Uniformity in 1662, Parliament had passed a Corporation Act (1661), which forced office holders to disavow the Solemn League and Covenant of 1643, thus excluding Dissenters from public office. Then came the Conventicle Act of 1664, which forbade the gathering of more than five people for purposes of worship outside a parish church or similarly licensed premises. Finally there was the Five-Mile Act of 1665, which barred Nonconformist ministers from coming within five miles of an incorporated town, and also banned them from teaching in schools. Taken together these acts constituted the 'Clarendon Code', named after Edward Hyde (1609–74), the first Earl of Clarendon, who was Charles II's Lord Chancellor. Ironically, Clarendon was charged with the enforcement of the code, even though he did not agree with much of it in practice – a telling sign of the half-heartedness that characterized so much of the Restoration Settlement and eventually led to its undoing. The Clarendon Code was further supplemented by the Test Act of 1673, which reinforced the Corporation Act of 1661 and remained on the statute books until 1828.[12]

The intention of this legislation was to enforce religious conformity, and if possible to eliminate dissent altogether. But its effect was to leave the impression that the church lacked confidence in its own beliefs and practices, and had to resort to persecution in order to persuade people to accept what in theory was a religion of love. The differences between the Establishment and moderate Presbyterians were not great, and many people believed that with goodwill on both sides they could have been overcome. Failure to achieve this was to have long-lasting consequences, not only for the church but also for Christianity itself. In 1662 all sides recognized one another as Christians, but were

---

12 For the Test Act, see Bray, *Documents*, 508–513.

seemingly unable to show the charity towards one another that is required of disciples of Christ. As Robert Bosher expressed it:

> Many within the Church of England today would agree that an oppor-
> tunity was tragically lost of retaining the more moderate dissenters in the
> national Church, and that the sacrifice was made for an ideal of little value.
> The final refusal in 1662 to come to terms with the Continental Reforma-
> tion was ... a major blunder, and productive of many future ills.[13]

Students of this period focus so heavily on England that they tend to forget that similar legislation was also passed in Scotland and Ireland, although with markedly different results. Scotland had never warmed to episcopacy, which was weak there even before the Reformation, but that did not deter Charles II from restoring it in 1660. Many Scots justifiably felt aggrieved by this, since they had supported the king after his father's execution and had led the way to his restoration, which they thought would benefit presbyterianism. The restored episcopate was considerably weaker and less popular than its English counterpart, and before long there was open rebellion in parts of the country. These rebels, known as Covenanters, were remarkably successful in opposing the restored king's government. For a time they dominated the south-west of Scotland, but in the end they were beaten back. However, the government could keep order only by instituting what amounted to a reign of terror, creating martyrs for the Presbyterian cause. It soon became clear that Scotland would not be held for long in an episcopalian restoration, although how and when that would be overturned remained unknown.

In Ireland the restored Church of Ireland was imposed on a country where only a small minority of the population – never more than 15% – conformed to it.[14] Another 10% or more were Protestant 'Dissenters', although since most of them were Presbyterians of Scottish origin, the term 'Dissenter' is ques-tionable when used to describe them. The remaining 75% of the population was Catholic, unreconciled and probably unreconcilable to the regime. This Catholic population comprised both Old English and native Irish (Gaelic) elements, which for centuries had been at loggerheads with each other but were now drawn together by a common sense of purpose and identity.[15] Race and

---

[13] Bosher, *Making of the Restoration Settlement*, 276.

[14] T. Barnard, *A New Anatomy of Ireland: The Irish Protestants, 1649–1770* (New Haven, Conn.: Yale University Press, 2003).

[15] See J. G. Simms, *Jacobite Ireland* (London: Routledge & Kegan Paul, 1969; reissued Dublin: Four Courts Press, 2000); W. Burke, *The Irish Priests in the Penal Times (1660–1760)* (Shannon: Irish University Press, 1969).

religion have gone together in Ireland in ways that have not been the case in Great Britain, although, as this example demonstrates, the link between the two has not always been clear-cut. In the Catholic case it is arguable that religion created a single 'race' out of two thitherto disparate peoples. It would be a 'race' in which the English language would predominate but also one in which Roman Catholicism would become the chief badge of national identity, something that was not challenged until the twentieth century and has still not been displaced in the popular mind.

Throne and altar

In the German Reformation of the sixteenth century one of the guiding principles in the search for peace was that the various states should conform to the religion of their secular ruler – *cuius regio eius religio*, as the Latin tag has it. This principle was perforce adopted in Britain as well, where it was generally assumed that subjects would loyally follow the religion of the king. But there was no check on the monarch himself. Could Charles II have converted to Catholicism and taken the country with him? Many feared that he could – and would – and that there was no way he could be stopped. But would England follow him? What about Scotland? Ireland could perhaps be relied on to support him, but the Protestant minority there would surely have fought back and urged their British co-religionists to do the same.

Charles II had a Catholic mother and a Catholic wife. He himself was indifferent to religion, and someone whose morals were closer to those of his Protestant-persecuting cousin Louis XIV of France than to any Puritan. Who could tell what he might do? Catholics were thin on the ground in Britain, but the major European powers were Catholic, and two of them – Spain and France – were plausible invaders who might try to restore the Roman church to its pre-Reformation status. If they could do that by using a puppet king, then so much the better. Mary I had almost made England a vassal state of Spain, and so there seemed to be no reason why the same thing might not be achieved a century or more later by using the monarchy and its international connections to achieve that essentially religious aim. Charles II had a number of children by different women, but none by his wife, making his younger brother James the lawful heir to the throne. James had married Anne Hyde, daughter of the Earl of Clarendon, by whom he had two daughters, who were also in the line of succession and would eventually reign as queens. But Anne died and James subsequently married an Italian noblewoman, Mary of Modena. More importantly, he also converted to Catholicism around 1673, more or less ensuring that the next king would be Catholic. For a long time the second marriage was childless, so Protestants could argue that time would bring a Protestant back to the throne after James's death, but this left everything to chance and few people were satisfied.

James's conversion to Catholicism produced a constitutional crisis. How could a Catholic king be the head of a Protestant state and supreme governor of its church? Would he not be obliged, if not by his conscience then by the papacy to which he professed allegiance, to attempt to overturn the Reformation settlement? On the other hand did anyone have the right to interrupt the legitimate succession? The customs of the monarchy and the established religion of the state were coming into conflict, and it was not clear which would prevail. Charles II supported his brother, but large sections of the public, including Members of Parliament, did not. They wanted to bar James from the throne on account of his religion and did their best to pass a law to that effect. The king fought back and in the end he got his way, but the long-term result of this so-called 'exclusion crisis' was a permanent division in the English Parliament between those who supported the king and the established Church and those who argued for a more moderate and tolerant Protestant state. The former were nicknamed Tories (Irish bandits) and the latter Whigs, an abbreviation of the Scottish 'Whiggamores', who were Presbyterian Covenanters opposed to any reconciliation with Charles I in 1648 – a subtle reminder that English affairs were now inextricably bound up with the other kingdoms of the British Isles.[16] Both the Tories and the Whigs were perforce members of the Church of England, since they could not have been in Parliament otherwise, but it was not long before they came to be associated with 'High' and 'Low' Church respectively, the former wishing to retain the monopoly of the Church of England (sometimes mocked as 'the Tory party at prayer') and the latter wanting an accommodation with Dissenters, although not (at this stage) with Catholics or non-Christians.

The England of Charles II lived in fear of a potential Catholic plot that might use elements close to the throne, along with the disaffected Irish, to undo the Reformation, and in the process subordinate the British Isles to a Continental European empire. It was this fear that explains the extraordinary career of Titus Oates (1649–1705).[17] Oates, who was the son of a clergyman, became a

---

[16] The Tories still exist as the Conservative Party in both the United Kingdom and Canada. The Whigs transmuted in the mid-nineteenth century, becoming the Liberal Party (in the United Kingdom and Canada) and the Republican Party (in the United States). In that form they survive to this day in all three countries.

[17] J. Lane (E. Dakers), *Titus Oates* (London: A. Dakers, 1949; repr. London: Greenwood Press, 1971); J. Kenyon, *The Popish Plot* (London: William Heinemann, 1972; repr. London: Phoenix Press, 2000).

Baptist under the Commonwealth but eventually reverted to the established Church. He was sent to Cambridge as a young man but failed to take a degree. He lied about that to the Bishop of London, who ordained him in 1670, before he had reached the canonical age. Oates was several times accused of both perjury and homosexual practice, but each time he either fled or was let go because of his clerical status. In 1677 he converted to Roman Catholicism, went to the Continent and enrolled in the Jesuit order. That did not last long, and within a year he was back in England, claiming that his experiences abroad had given him extensive knowledge of a Catholic plot to assassinate Charles II. Charles did not take this seriously but some of his courtiers did, and before long Oates had drawn up a list of several hundred 'traitors', some of whom were tried and executed on the basis of letters forged by him.

Such was the febrile state of public opinion that Oates got away with this for two or three years, before suspicions began to grow. His last and in some ways most prominent victim was Oliver Plunkett (1625–81), the Roman Catholic Archbishop of Armagh, who was executed in London on 1 July 1681, to general dismay. After that, public opinion turned against him and his influence waned. He was severely punished for his perjury during the reign of James II (1685–8), but eventually he was pardoned and even given a pension for the rest of his life, which he passed in obscurity. The shocking thing about this is not so much the initial success of Oates's forgeries, bad though that was, but the leniency with which he was treated in later life. That a known liar could receive a state pension merely for his anti-Catholicism is a disgrace, but it speaks volumes about the atmosphere in Britain at that time and helps us to understand why events unfolded in the way they did.

One factor that has to be taken into account was the growing persecution of Protestants (Huguenots) in France. Louis XIV (1643–1715) was determined to rid his kingdom of them. The toleration that had been granted to them by the Edict of Nantes in 1598 was gradually stripped away, and in 1685 they were given the stark choice – convert, be killed or emigrate. Most converted to Catholicism, but large numbers chose exile and fled to Germany, the Netherlands and Britain, where they were welcomed with open arms as victims of religious persecution. Unfortunately there were Tories in England who admired Louis XIV for his policies, not because they were secret Catholics but because, like the French king, they believed in *un roi, une loi, une foi* (one king, one law, one faith). They also liked the fact that Louis XIV permitted the continued existence of the General Assembly of the French Clergy, a tax convocation similar to the ones that had existed in England since the Middle Ages.

This was a sore point with the Tories, because shortly after the Act of Uniformity was passed in 1662, the Archbishop of Canterbury had done a deal with the government, surrendering the clerical privilege of self-taxation in return for the right to vote in parliamentary elections. This meant that although the convocations of Canterbury and York continued to exist on paper, they had nothing to do and were effectively suspended. The Tories wanted the church to recover its powers of self-government, including the traditional taxation, and they did not hesitate to point to France as their model. The fact that Louis XIV was an absolute monarch in a way that Charles II could never be was irrelevant to them, but it was noted by their Whig opponents, who saw the expulsion of the Huguenots as evidence of what Catholic rule might entail.

It was an unfortunate coincidence that the revocation of the Edict of Nantes came just as Charles II died and his brother ascended the English and Irish thrones as James II and the Scottish one as James VII.[18] James was intelligent enough to know that he could not copy his French cousin's policies, but everything he did was interpreted as a move in that direction, and so his reign was ill-fated from the start. Rebellions broke out but they were crushed, not least with the assistance of the Church of England. The Tory bishops hoped that this would work to their advantage and tried to turn a blind eye to the king's Catholicism, but to no avail. James II claimed the right to dispense with statute laws when he thought it was expedient to do so, and on 21 June 1686 a hand-picked group of judges upheld his view. Soon the king was dispensing with the Test Act and the penal laws of the 1660s, granting toleration not only to his fellow Catholics but to Baptists and Quakers as well. It soon became apparent that his strategy was to win toleration for Catholics, for which there was little popular sympathy, by linking it to toleration for Dissenters, for which there was significant support in the country. The Dissenters themselves were thrown into disarray. They obviously wanted the concessions they were being given, but they also knew these were being used as a means of reintroducing Catholicism, which they did not want any more than the Tories did.

There was also the problem that the king could not control the preaching of the Church of England's clergy, most of whom were fiercely anti-Catholic and were prepared to say so. The king regarded this as 'seditious preaching', which had been outlawed in 1662, but the church disagreed. On 14 July 1686, in response to the bishops' refusal to discipline their clergy, the king created a new Ecclesiastical Commission, which strongly resembled the High

---

[18] Studies of James II/VII are few and far between. One of the best is J. Miller, *James II* (New Haven, Conn.: Yale University Press, 2000). On the Scottish aspect of his rule, see A. J. Mann, *James VII: Duke and King of Scots, 1633–1701* (Edinburgh: John Donald, 2014).

Commission courts that had been so instrumental in starting the Civil War and had been abolished in 1641. The new Commission promptly summoned Bishop Henry Compton (1632–1713) of London to appear before it, accused him of disobeying the king by continuing to enforce the penal laws against Catholics and Dissenters, and suspended him from office. Archbishop William Sancroft (1617–93) of Canterbury, who had refused to join the Commission when it was set up, was punished by being dropped from the Privy Council, and he withdrew from the court.

James's apparent success in muzzling opposition persuaded him to come clean and issue a Declaration of Indulgence on 4 April 1687, which effectively abolished the penal laws altogether. There followed an intense propaganda campaign, the aim of which was to get the bishops to support the Declaration. On 4 May 1688, James II ordered that it should be read in the churches on 20/27 May in London and on 3/10 June in the rest of England. The bishops and concerned clergy hastily met to devise a strategy to counter this, and on 18 May they presented a petition to the king, asking to be excused from reading the Declaration in their pulpits. It is estimated that about 400 clergy complied with the king's request but that the rest refused. The Archbishop of Canterbury and six of his suffragans were then arrested and put on trial for having defied the monarch's wishes.[19] While waiting for proceedings to begin, the bishops were kept in the Tower of London, where a delegation of Dissenters went to see them. United in adversity, the two sides agreed to reopen negotiations for a revision of the 1662 Prayer Book, which they hoped would lead to a liturgy of comprehension that would bring most of the Dissenters back into the established Church.[20]

Meanwhile something nobody had expected occurred. On 10 June 1688 Queen Mary gave birth to a son, making him the heir to the throne in place of James's daughter Mary, who by that time was married to William III of Orange, the *stadhouder* (governor) of the Dutch Republic, who was himself a Stuart through his mother and a possible claimant to the British thrones. On 30 June the bishops were acquitted and greeted as heroes by the people of London. After that, the balance of power slowly began to shift in favour of Parliament and against the king, although he did not seem to notice what was happening.

The Ecclesiastical Commission continued to search out those clergy who had refused to read the Declaration of Indulgence, but cooperation was not

---

[19] They were the bishops of Bath and Wells, Bristol, Chichester, Ely, Peterborough and St Asaph. See W. Gibson, *James II and the Trial of the Seven Bishops* (Basingstoke: Palgrave Macmillan, 2009).

[20] T. J. Fawcett, *The Liturgy of Comprehension 1689: An Abortive Attempt to Revise the Book of Common Prayer* (Southend-on-Sea: Mayhew-McCrimmon, 1973).

forthcoming and on 5 October the king, bowing to pressure from the church, abolished the Commission altogether. There immediately followed a torrent of demands, including a suggestion that the king should return to the Church of England. He paid no attention, but instead pressed on as if nothing had happened. On 15 October he had his son baptized in the Catholic Church and went on appointing his own placemen to vacant episcopal sees, including the archbishopric of York. The rest of the bishops and people in general were growing increasingly disillusioned and desperate, and rumours of an impending Dutch invasion began to circulate. That invasion occurred on 5 November (the anniversary of the Gunpowder plot in 1605), when William III landed at Torbay. James was pressured into summoning a parliament that would guarantee the Protestant character of the state, but his time was fast running out. Moving at a steady pace across the country, William reached London in mid-December, causing James to withdraw to Rochester and finally flee to France. The House of Lords then invited William to form a government, pending a final solution to the crisis, which he agreed to do.

At this point the church's residual loyalty to the Stuart dynasty suddenly resurfaced. Despite all that they had been through, the clergy rallied to James and demanded his recall. Preaching to Parliament on 30 January 1689, John Sharp (1645–1714), who in 1691 would be consecrated Archbishop of York, urged the assembly not to depose James, and led prayers for him as their sovereign. Parliament was divided down the middle, with some applauding Sharp and others calling for his arrest. It soon became apparent that James would not be restored to his throne, his escape to France being viewed as a cowardly act of abdication that effectively deprived him of it. On 13 February William III and his wife, Mary II, were proclaimed joint sovereigns of England, and Scotland followed suit on 4 April.[21]

The result was that Archbishop Sancroft, who had only recently been imprisoned by James II, refused to swear allegiance to William and Mary, as did eight other English bishops, four of whom had been with Sancroft in the Tower of London.[22] They were joined by about 400 clergy, far fewer than the number that had left in the Great Ejection of 1662. These so-called 'Nonjurors' soon split into those who wanted to consecrate further bishops and maintain an independent church, and those who felt that when James II died in 1701 they could in good conscience return to the established Church. In fact internal schism became the hallmark of the Nonjurors, and was repeated from one

[21] In Scotland William was known as William II.
[22] They were the bishops of Bath and Wells, Chichester, Ely and Peterborough, joined now by those of Chester, Gloucester, Norwich and Worcester.

generation to the next, even as their ranks were occasionally strengthened by the adherence of a few clergy and laity who refused to come to terms with the Hanoverian succession. Inevitably they were drawn to antiquarian studies in an effort to support their views about the right relationship between church and state, and this led them down some strange paths. Lacking the historical scepticism of a later time, they were inclined to take texts like the *Apostolic Constitutions*, a late Roman set of canons, as the work of the Apostles themselves, and thus to interpret New Testament Christianity in terms more suited to the early Middle Ages than to the biblical period.

One of their oddities, which was to have a long future, was the belief that the Prayer Book was corrupt because it omitted the 'four usages' that they believed went back to apostolic times.[23] These were as follows:

1 The offering up of the elements of bread and wine in the Lord's Supper.
2 The invocation of the Holy Spirit on these elements (the epiclesis).
3 The absence of a distinction between the 'Church militant' here on earth and the 'Church triumphant' in heaven, which allowed them to abolish the distinction between the living and the dead, and thus to pray for the latter as well as the former.
4 The mixing of water with wine in the eucharistic chalice.

Not all of the Nonjurors accepted these 'usages', and so the result was further division among them, but these spurious liturgical studies were to be influential in later times, when High Churchmen among the Scottish Episcopalians and later in the Oxford Movement wanted to introduce them into Anglican worship on the grounds of their supposedly primitive origin. The Nonjurors limped on through the eighteenth century but soon declined into insignificance and disappeared after their last bishop died in 1818.[24]

In Ireland only the Bishop of Kildare and Ardagh took the same path, along with a small number of clergy, and the schism soon died out there. Scotland was a different story. There the bishops and their few supporters were removed entirely and a presbyterian church established instead. As a result, the Scottish Episcopal Church was formed as a dissenting body and had a chequered existence for a century or more. It was naturally suspected of owing allegiance to

---

[23] See J. D. Smith, *The Eucharistic Doctrine of the Later Non-Jurors: A Revisionist View of the Eighteenth-Century Usages Controversy*, Alcuin Club and The Group for Renewal of Worship Joint Liturgical Studies 46 (Cambridge: Grove Books, 2000).

[24] For a detailed and balanced assessment of the Nonjurors, see E. G. Rupp, *Religion in England 1688–1791* (Oxford: Clarendon Press, 1986), 5–28.

the deposed Stuarts, and its freedom was therefore restricted. After the rebellion of 1745 in which Charles Stuart, the grandson of James VII, came dangerously close to overthrowing the Hanoverian monarchy, it was outlawed altogether. Not until 1792 was it permitted to function freely again, but by that time the Nonjuring schism was effectively over and the Stuart pretender was a Roman cardinal who had no hope of recovering his ancestral crown.

It is difficult for a neutral observer to have much sympathy for the Nonjurors. One or two of them – like Thomas Ken (1637–1711), the deprived Bishop of Bath and Wells, and William Law (1686–1761), author of *A Serious Call to a Devout and Holy Life* (1729), which was to have a profound effect on the Wesleys – rose above the limitations of their fellows, but that very fact makes them atypical. For the most part the position of the Nonjurors was determined by a supposed alliance of interest between the throne and the altar that could not be realized, because the king refused to belong to the church and campaigned against it as much as he could. In the end they found themselves professing allegiance to a monarch who did not want them, which is a rather absurd position to be in. To make matters worse, many of the Nonjuring bishops and clergy were men of considerable personal piety, something that was decidedly not true of the Stuarts, whose right to rule the Nonjurors so tenaciously upheld. From every point of view they were barking up the wrong tree and the only wonder is that they kept at it for so long.

The last act in the drama of what came to be known as the 'Glorious Revolution' of 1688–9 took place, as we might expect, in Ireland. The advent of James II and the Declaration of Indulgence came as a godsend to the majority Catholic population there, which saw the change of policy as giving them not only freedom but control of the country's destiny. Catholics were appointed to high office and even given military commands. Protestants were not immediately discriminated against, but they were understandably fearful of what might be coming, and the arrival of refugee French Huguenots did nothing to allay their fears. When James II fled to France, the Irish remained loyal to him; William III was not proclaimed king in Dublin. That naturally encouraged James to turn to Ireland for support in regaining his multiple crowns and, before long, he was in the Emerald Isle – the first sovereign since Henry II to have spent much time there.

William III obviously could not tolerate James II's presence in Ireland, and James, for his part, was using the island only as a stepping stone to the greater prize of England (and Scotland). So in 1690 William gathered an army together and went to Ireland, where on 1 July 1690 he met James in battle on the River

Boyne and defeated him.[25] The Battle of the Boyne was not the end of Catholic resistance in Ireland but it was the turning point, and has gone down in history as a great Protestant victory. Within a year Catholic rule had been brought to an end, much of the land still remaining in Catholic hands had been confiscated, and the penal laws had been tightened and enforced to a degree not previously known. There were several ironies to this. Pope Innocent XI was wary of the growing power of Louis XIV and was delighted when his client James II was defeated – so delighted, in fact, that he ordered the church bells of Rome to be rung in celebration. The fact that his own Catholic subjects were the ones to suffer from the defeat did not seem to bother him too much. On the other side, William III was not the Protestant champion his devotees expected. He was personally more tolerant than they were, and wanted a settlement in Ireland that would give maximum freedom to all. Unfortunately he could not restrain his followers and thus found himself being commemorated as their great champion and deliverer. To this day the Protestant Orange Order, named after William III, keeps the memory of these events alive, and distorts them to its own political advantage. That Protestant–Catholic rivalry and enmity continue in that country is at least partly the legacy of the Battle of the Boyne, which neither side has forgotten – or forgiven.

William III was a Protestant, but he was a member of the Dutch Reformed Church, not the Church of England. His accession was supported by the philosopher John Locke (1632–1704), whose timely *A Letter Concerning Toleration* appeared in 1689 and advocated a de facto separation of church and state on the ground that the two entities were quite different and should not be interfering with each other. Locke's views would not come into their own until a century later, but it was in the aftermath of the Glorious Revolution that they were first put forward as practical policy.[26] The Huguenot pastors who had taken refuge in Britain and Ireland were admitted to the established Church's ministry without reordination, and nobody seriously suggested that William III could not receive Communion in the English or Irish church. But in order to prevent any possible controversy, William III reserved ecclesiastical affairs to his English wife, Mary II. Had the couple produced children, it is possible that Britain and the Netherlands would have been united, but that did

---

[25] The date is that of the Old Calendar. When the Gregorian Calendar was adopted in 1752, 1 July became 12 July, and it is on that date that the victory is now commemorated.

[26] Locke was however associated with the religious tolerance granted to the colony of Carolina (subsequently divided into North and South) in 1669, although the extent of his involvement and the nature of the toleration granted are both controversial. On his thought in general, see J. Waldron, *God, Locke, and Equality: Christian Foundations in Locke's Political Thought* (Cambridge: Cambridge University Press, 2002).

not happen. Mary II died at the end of 1694 and William III did not remarry. His heiress was Mary's sister Anne, married to prince George of Denmark (a Lutheran), and mother to a large number of children, all of whom unfortunately died in infancy. Meanwhile the young James III was growing up in France and might one day seek to reclaim his father's thrones, so the question of the succession became urgent.

What the events of 1688–9 did was establish the sovereignty of Parliament, at least in English affairs. That included the power to dispose of the monarchy, a right Charles II had contested but that could no longer be claimed by the reigning sovereign. After some deliberation, the English Parliament passed an act of succession in 1701, establishing that the throne was to be inherited in the Protestant line and that whoever was to occupy it must be or become a communicant member of the Church of England.[27] That meant that the heiress to the throne (after Anne) would be Princess Sophia of Hanover, a granddaughter of James I, through his daughter Elizabeth. The snag was that although the act could be held to cover Ireland, which was a dependency of the English Crown, it did not apply to Scotland. Could the Scots decide to choose their own sovereign on the death of Anne, and could that be James VIII? Forestalling that unwelcome possibility was one of the factors that persuaded the ruling classes in both countries to press for full legislative union. That was not popular in Scotland, which feared that it would lose its national identity, but after concessions were made, allowing the Scots to keep their own systems of education, law and presbyterian religion, the Scottish Parliament was eventually persuaded to dissolve itself. On 1 May 1707 the United Kingdom of Great Britain was born.

The new UK was an anomaly in contemporary Europe. Although it had two state churches, one for England and the other for Scotland, they were not in communion with each other. In England the monarch was the supreme governor of the national, episcopal church, but in Scotland he was a mere member of a presbyterian congregation, with no special privileges at all. The united parliament consisted of members drawn from the established churches only, which made it impossible for English Dissenters or Scottish episcopalians to sit in it. It even happened that extraterritorial congregations were established in both countries to cater for itinerant Englishmen and Scots. The Church of England congregations in Scotland gradually merged into the Scottish Episcopal Church, the last of them as recently as 1987, but there are still Church of Scotland churches in England, a living reminder of that bygone era. The

---

[27] For the text of the act, see Bray, *Documents*, 527–531. It is still in force today.

union of 1707 excluded Ireland however. In theory Ireland should have been part of it, since its legal, educational and ecclesiastical systems were identical to those of England. Had the country been mainly Protestant, it is likely that it would have been integrated into the union along with the other two countries, but of course it was not. One of the hidden effects of the revolution of 1688–9 was that henceforth the consent of the governed would be the ultimate measure of legitimacy, and that consent was not given (or at least was not obvious) in Ireland. Whether a Catholic country could ever have been absorbed into a Protestant state is doubtful and, as we know, in Ireland it was not to be. The future of that country was still not clear in 1689 however. There was a lingering hope that it could be Protestantized in some way, and efforts to achieve that would be made periodically for the next 150 years, although without success.

Liturgies of non-comprehension

When the episcopal government of the Church of England was re-established in 1660, it was understood that some effort would have to be made to accommodate those who had been alienated from it by the activities of Archbishop Laud and his followers that had contributed so much to the outbreak of civil war. Concessions to them were suggested but in the end most were rejected, and from 1662 onwards the old regime was restored in something like its original form. This was particularly noticeable in the Book of Common Prayer, the canons regulating the conduct of public worship and the powers of the ecclesiastical courts. Moderate people in the Church of England recognized that there was room for flexibility, even for improvement, in these areas, but they were inhibited from acting by the uncertain political climate of the time and the fear that if too many concessions were made to Dissenters, the unity of the church would collapse.

The assault on Protestantism under James II allowed for a rethink. Protestant unity suddenly seemed more important than divisions over secondary issues, and many of the passions aroused by the Civil War period had died down. Did it really matter whether a minister wore a surplice when officiating at public worship? Could the signing with the cross at baptism be omitted without damaging the efficacy of the sacrament? There was a growing sense that on details like these compromise was possible, and a number of people began to look for ways of achieving it. Basically there were two options – toleration and comprehension. Toleration meant accepting that some Protestants could not be included within the structures of the established Church because their doctrines would not allow that, even though they shared the same faith. The most prominent examples were the Baptists, who refused to accept the validity of infant baptism, and the Quakers, who rejected all forms of organized worship. For them toleration was the only viable option. In the case of the Presbyterians however, there were no doctrinal barriers to union, and it seemed that a few minor concessions on matters of ritual would be enough to satisfy most of them. With a little sensitivity, they could be comprehended within a single church structure. The Independents fell somewhere between these two options. Doctrinally they were like the Presbyterians and therefore could be comprehended by the Establishment, but structurally they were more like the Baptists, with a congregational church order. Still, it was thought that they too could be brought into the church, perhaps with some guarantees of greater local autonomy. As far as church discipline was concerned, the Presbyterians (in particular) wanted it to be stricter, not more lax, and that too was far from disagreeable to the bishops.

In 1688 considerable progress towards a liturgy of comprehension was made when the bishops were in the Tower of London, and efforts to achieve even more were continued in 1689, when both sides were free to meet and discuss their differences openly. A broad-based commission was set up and proceeded to deliberate a number of subjects. There was general agreement as to the desirability of comprehension, both for the internal harmony of society and for the face the country presented to the outside world. Most people did not really care very much about the issues being debated and would have been content with whatever solution was adopted. It was therefore incumbent on the commissioners, so the argument ran, to balance the approach adopted by giving something to both sides. Most of the commissioners were themselves moderates willing to compromise in this way, but they reckoned without the extremists who did not take part in the debates.

Foremost among these were the Tories, who did not want any change at all to the established forms of liturgy and government. They pointed to the way in which episcopacy was being overturned in Scotland, and argued that the same thing would happen in England if Dissenters were allowed to have their way. They further argued that most of the points under discussion were secondary matters that no reasonable person ought to raise theological objections to. The Dissenters were therefore cast as being unreasonable troublemakers. There was also the problem that the Archbishop of Canterbury and eight of his suffragans were under suspension as Nonjurors, and in those circumstances it was doubtful whether the Church of England could decide any serious matter. Only a convocation of the clergy had the power to act on the questions being discussed, and the Dissenters would have to put their case to it, not to the commission.[28]

Personal rivalries were also at work. Bishop Henry Compton of London was theoretically in favour of comprehension but he knew that he was being side-lined as a candidate for the see of Canterbury, which was more likely to go to John Tillotson, and so out of pique he gravitated to the Tories, represented by William Jane, the Dean of Gloucester. When the Canterbury Convocation was finally summoned on 25 November 1689, a prolocutor (speaker) for the Lower House had to be elected, and the choice was between Jane or Tillotson. Tillotson, who like Compton was in favour of comprehension, was the logical choice, but Compton threw his weight behind Jane, who opposed any sort of revision. Largely thanks to that, Jane was elected and any prospect that the Convocation would vote for comprehension was lost. Instead the clergy spent their time discussing what to do about the Nonjurors and ignored the Dissenters almost completely. It was a hopeless situation, and the king finally prorogued the Convocation on 25 June 1690, realizing that it could achieve nothing. Comprehension went by the board and the proposed liturgy disappeared into the archives, not to emerge until 1854, when it was finally published. The Tories won by default, and the damage was done. In the words of John Spurr:

> In 1689 the Church of England was denied a valuable transfusion of talent and enthusiasm, which went instead to strengthen rival Protestant denominations. But far more importantly, the Glorious Revolution's religious settlement reduced the Church of England from the *national* to merely the *established* Church.[29]

It was a demotion few people understood at the time but was to have long-term consequences for the future of Christianity in the British Isles. A faith that embraced the nation was one thing, but a church propped up by the government was quite another. One of the effects of this was that the established Church found it increasingly difficult to impose its discipline on the laity. Those who were supposed to attend church, receive Communion three times a year and generally conform to the clergy's expectations could still be presented by churchwardens and subjected to fines or other forms of punishment, but this became harder when the accused could legitimately claim to be Dissenters. It took some time for this new reality to sink in, but the evidence

---

[28] There were of course two convocations, but the northern one was conveniently overlooked.
[29] Spurr, *Restoration Church of England*, 103–104.

suggests that by 1720 church discipline had virtually become a dead letter, at least as far as the laity were concerned. Periodic attempts to revive it were unsuccessful, leaving more conscientious clergy frustrated at their inability to enforce what they believed was a godly order and convincing many others that the church was trying to impose a social tyranny in the name of Christian morality.[30]

Most serious of all, in the debates over the details of liturgy and worship, the fundamental truths of the gospel had been laid to one side. Of course, it can be argued that that was because all the main protagonists agreed about them, so there was nothing to discuss. But true although that might have been, it raises the question of why the essentials of the faith did not occupy a more prominent place in the preaching and teaching ministry of the churches supposed to be proclaiming it. This is not merely a view from hindsight – there were people at the time who were just as disturbed by this. On 30 August 1694 Robert Meeke, who was curate of Slaithwaite chapel in the parish of Huddersfield from 1684 to 1724, confided to his diary:

> There are since the Toleration many chapels builded. Lord, grant it may be for the good of souls. We all preach the same doctrine, pray for the same things; all the difference consists in garments, gestures and words; and yet that difference breedeth heats, dissensions, divisions, prejudice, jealousies, suspicions, censorious judgings, strangeness and coldness of charity and Christian affection amongst friends. I am afraid that this is the effect of such separate meetings, and different modes of worship.[31]

The failures of 1689 show how Christians can easily get distracted by secondary matters that divide the church and do nothing to commend the Christian message. That is what happened in the seventeenth century, not only in Britain but across Europe, and the judgment was not long in coming – from a quarter few could have suspected at the time.

The light of reason?

Doubts about the truth of the Christian faith surfaced from time to time in the sixteenth and seventeenth centuries, but for the most part they remained

---

[30] For the details, see N. Patterson, *Ecclesiastical Law, Clergy and Laity: A History of Legal Discipline and the Anglican Church* (Abingdon: Routledge, 2019), 1–37.

[31] H. J. Morehouse (ed.), *Extracts from the Diary of the Rev. Robert Meeke* (London: H. G. Bohn, 1874), 86–87. By 'Toleration' Meeke meant the Act of Toleration (1689).

marginal to society as a whole. There was considerable agitation over the prevalence of antitrinitarianism, mostly in the form of Socinianism, but it was generally suppressed and made relatively little impact. The Protestant emphasis on reason as opposed to superstition led to a sharp decline in magical practices and belief in such things as holy wells and so on, but reason was for the most part contained within the bounds of revelation and few people had any significant doubts about the latter. It was almost universally accepted that the world had been created in six twenty-four-hour days, that the first five books of the Old Testament (the Pentateuch) had been written by Moses, the great lawgiver of Israel, that the miracles and extraordinary events recounted in both Testaments had occurred in the way they were recorded, and so on. Nobody thought to go to the lands of the Bible to dig up the places mentioned in it – archaeology as a science did not exist. The only criteria for judging the accuracy of the Scriptural accounts were faith and reason, which all Christians, Catholics as well as Protestants, believed were mutually confirming. A doctrine like the Trinity might not be biblical in the strict sense of the term, but it was the logical outworking of New Testament teaching and had been proclaimed as such by the councils of the early church. Catholics believed that these councils were divinely inspired, whereas Protestants thought that they were fallible human testimonies to divine revelation, but either way their conclusions were the same – on fundamental matters of Christian doctrine the councils, and the creeds they had composed or authorized, had got it right.

This universal conviction began to dissolve in the later seventeenth century. The end of the many wars of religion had seen the imposition of doctrinal orthodoxy in every country of Christian Europe. The problem was that the content of this orthodoxy varied from place to place, according to the wishes of the local rulers. There was a broad consensus on the most essential matters, to be sure, but a number of questions remained in dispute, particularly with regard to the sacraments. There was also the important issue of eternal salvation – was it possible to go to heaven without being in communion with the pope? What did a man or woman have to believe in order to be saved, and who decided what that was? Why did Protestants fall out with one another when they all professed to believe in the same thing – the supreme authority of Holy Scripture for the faith of individual believers and the life of the church? Was there such a thing as objective truth and, if so, how could it be found?

In an attempt to answer these questions intellectuals across Europe began to emphasize the importance of human reason. They believed that this was shared by all normally sane people, and that if something could be demonstrated by means of it then it would have to be accepted by all as objective fact.

A doctrine like transubstantiation was based on the belief that there are material substances like bread and wine that may come in many different forms but that remain essentially unchanged. In the miracle of the altar, as it was called, the priest could change those substances into the body and blood of Christ without affecting the outward forms, or 'accidents'. This way of analysing reality, which could be traced back to Aristotle, was abandoned in the seventeenth century in favour of what we now call the empirical scientific method. As a result, transubstantiation became irrational and therefore unbelievable. That suited Protestants very well of course, but the method could be extended to cover other things where more fundamental convictions were involved. Men do not return from the dead, so is it possible to believe in the resurrection of Jesus? Deuteronomy 34 recounts the death of Moses – could he have written that himself? And how could the universe have been created in six twenty-four-hour days when the sun and moon did not appear until the fourth of them? Looked at rationally, many key biblical passages made no sense, at least not if they were supposed to be compatible with scientific laws.

The process by which the European mind moved from being theistic in a Christian guise to atheistic (or at least agnostic) has been documented and analysed by a number of scholars, who have come to essentially the same conclusion – between 1650 and 1750 a revolution in human thought occurred that shook the foundations of Christianity to their root.[32] Proponents and defenders of this new way of thinking have dubbed it the 'Enlightenment', and the 'age of Reason', although whether this is truth or propaganda is a more difficult question to resolve. One of the odder features of modern times is that Enlightenment thinking continues to expand and assert its claims over the intellectual world, where its pieties are almost unquestioned (and unquestionable), even as empirical evidence to support them is far from persuasive and there is much to point in the opposite direction. That was certainly the view taken in the century of its development and the thought of the radicals was vigorously contested, often with success. Nevertheless, and despite the often stupendous attempts to counter it, anti-Christian thought established a foothold in European culture in the late seventeenth century and it has never successfully, still less definitively, been dislodged.

---

32 P. Hazard, *The European Mind 1680–1715* (London: Hollis & Carter, 1953), a translation of *La crise de la conscience européenne* (Paris: Fayard, 1935); P. Gay, *The Enlightenment: An Interpretation*, 2 vols. (New York, N.Y.: Norton, 1966); J. I. Israel, *Radical Enlightenment: Philosophy and the Making of Modernity 1650–1750* (Oxford: Oxford University Press, 2001); M. J. Buckley, *At the Origins of Modern Atheism* (New Haven, Conn.: Yale University Press, 1987); E. Shagan, *The Birth of Modern Belief: Faith and Judgment from the Middle Ages to the Enlightenment* (Princeton, N.J.: Princeton University Press, 2019).

Relatively few people realize it, but English thinkers were major contributors to the Enlightenment in its early stages. They were not atheists but men who wanted to find rational solutions to the denominationalism that had emerged after the Civil War and the failure to reconcile different parties within the national church. Was it not possible to have a religion based on belief in God, without demanding too much in terms of doctrine? It seemed reasonable to posit a kind of natural theology in which there was a Supreme Being who governed the universe, but was it equally necessary to decree that this Being was a Trinity of three persons, or that it was restricted to the God of the Old Testament? As explorers travelled around the world they discovered that virtually every tribe and nation had a deity or deities of its own, and were these not just different names for the same thing? This was not atheism, not least because many of these deists expressly repudiated that, but it was not Christianity either. The deists believed that a Supreme Being was needed in order to underpin morality, and therefore to bolster the social order, but they saw no need to go into specific details and thought it wrong to insist on what they saw as an overly narrow orthodoxy.[33]

As far back as 1660 a group of scientists in London founded The Royal Society, a body dedicated to the pursuit of rational knowledge from which discussions of politics and religion were to be excluded. The effects of this did not become fully apparent until 1695, when the government of William III abolished the censorship of printed books. Almost overnight there was a flood of what would previously have been banned publications, some quite deliberately attacking the church and religious beliefs. The most notorious of these was a book called *Christianity not Mysterious*, written by John Toland (1670–1722) and published in 1696. Toland took aim at the supernatural claims of the Christian faith, debunking everything he could with an air of intellectual superiority that was notoriously light on factual evidence. The resulting scandal forced Parliament to enact a blasphemy law that remained on the statute books until 1967. No prosecutions were ever brought under the act, but its existence served as a reminder of the potential danger that faced anyone who made outrageous comments about the Christian faith.[34]

One beneficial result of the commotion was that a number of churchmen became convinced of the need to provide instructional material on the basics of the Christian faith and to take religious education seriously. It could no

---

[33] See J. I. Israel, *The Enlightenment that Failed: Ideas, Revolution and Democratic Defeat, 1748–1830* (Oxford: Oxford University Press, 2019), 126–158.

[34] Even after the act was repealed, blasphemy remained a common-law offence until 2008 in England and until 2016 in the Republic of Ireland.

longer be left to preachers and heads of families, many of whom scarcely knew where to begin. Within a few years Thomas Bray (1656/1658–1730), a clergyman in the diocese of London, was inspired to found the Society for the Promotion of Christian Knowledge (1698) and the Society for the Propagation of the Gospel in Foreign Parts (1701). Both survive to the present day, the second having gone through several changes of name and become more Anglo-Catholic in orientation than was originally the case. Thomas Bray also instituted parish libraries that he stocked with the books he published and made available to a broad swathe of the population who would otherwise have had no access to Christian literature. Bray took a special interest in the colony of Maryland, where he is credited with having established the first public libraries in North America.

The impact of these labours was considerable. Bray was an unapologetic advocate of the Church of England and did much to make its presence felt among the population at large. He was even prepared to publish and distribute books in Welsh and Manx, so that those who knew no English would not be unduly disadvantaged. For the established Church, this missionary effort was an altogether new departure, and its long-term effects became apparent a generation later, when John Wesley (1703–91) began to preach up and down the country. It seems that by then, the work of the SPCK and the Bray libraries had created a hunger for Christian instruction that Wesley and his fellow evangelists were able to build on, and the result was widespread religious revival. Certainly there was no question of allowing the deists to have their way, and Bray did a great deal to counter their impact.

The activities of Thomas Bray coincided with a revival in the Church of England's fortunes that promised to have significant consequences. Initially William III had been disillusioned by the Convocation of Canterbury because it failed to effect a reunion with the leading Dissenters, and so he prorogued it for more than a decade. But the growing threat from unbelief, and the pressure put on him from the church itself, produced a change of heart. In 1701 he allowed the Canterbury Convocation to transact business again, and it would continue in active session for the next sixteen years.[35]

As had been the case in 1689, the Lower House was dominated by High Church Tories, who would ideally have liked to restore the Church's tax-granting powers and who would have been sympathetic to the succession of 'James III' (1688–1766), provided he renounce his Catholicism and enter into

---

[35] For the proceedings, see G. L. Bray (ed.), *Records of Convocation*, 20 vols. (Woodbridge: Boydell & Brewer, 2005–6), 9–11.

communion with the Church of England. That ambition could not be voiced openly of course, but its existence was widely suspected and cast a certain pall over the proceedings, since nobody really knew how loyal the clergy were to William's regime. The bishops in the Upper House were more firmly on the government's side and saw it as their duty to keep the lower clergy in check. The result was years of procedural wrangling between the two houses that distracted them from the real business of the Church and eventually led to widespread disillusionment with the whole proceeding.

That, however, is the view from hindsight. At the time things seemed quite different, especially at the beginning. William III died not long after the Convocation opened and so it fell to Queen Anne (1702–14), herself a devoted supporter of the Church, to preside over its affairs as best she could. One of the most important things she did was to release the ecclesiastical income that had been seized by the Crown in the time of Henry VIII and whose loss had seriously compromised the Church's ability to pay its way. The return of this revenue, known as Queen Anne's Bounty, laid the foundation for the financial independence of the Church of England, from which it still benefits.[36] Needless to say, this made her very popular in the Church and it is no accident that a statue of Anne stands outside St Paul's Cathedral in London, an enduring symbol of the Church's gratitude to her.

The reign of Queen Anne was a time of war for the UK, which was engaged in a major conflict with France over the question of the succession to the Spanish Crown. The Habsburg dynasty that had ruled the country since the late fifteenth century died out in 1700, and Louis XIV seized the opportunity to put his grandson on the throne, hoping thereby to 'abolish the Pyrenees' and establish a Bourbon alliance that would dominate Europe. The Protestant states of the north were deeply opposed to that, and embarked on the War of the Spanish Succession, which would not end until 1713, just a year before Anne died. By then Britain had conquered Gibraltar and had become a great European power for the first time in its history. Patriotic feeling ran high in the country, which chimed in very well with Tory views of church–state relations. As victory drew nearer, so Tory ambitions for the Church grew more assertive. For a few years after 1708 it seemed as though the old order swept away in 1640, and not properly revived twenty years later, might finally be restored.

In this atmosphere of hope and expectation the clergy commissioned a report on the state of religion in England that they intended to present to the

---

[36] Queen Anne's Bounty was merged with other sources of income in 1947 and the whole is now administered by the Ecclesiastical Commissioners, who are responsible, among other things, for ensuring that the clergy are adequately paid.

queen as a blueprint for action to secure the position of the Church in a rapidly changing society. A number of people were involved in producing this document, but the main editor was Samuel Wesley, rector of Epworth in Lincolnshire and father of John and Charles, who would subsequently revolutionize the religious landscape of England. The older Wesley, who was the son of a Puritan, had conformed to the Establishment in 1662 and become a man of solidly High Church views, although he retained much of the zeal of the Puritans as well. This combination meant he was deeply unhappy with the state of popular religion in the country, and he was determined to do something about it. On 21 March 1711, he presented a draft report to the Lower House of the Canterbury Convocation, which was then sent to the bishops.[37] They revised and abridged it, and on 16 May 1711 authorized the archbishop to lay it before the queen.[38]

The *Representation of Religion* is unfortunately little known today but is very revealing, not only of the state of the church in the early eighteenth century but of the mentality of those who were in charge of it. If we look at the final text, we find that the clergy were deeply disturbed by a combination of 'heresy and irreligion', which they saw as rampant in the country. Furthermore, they were in no doubt that this lamentable state of affairs was the direct result of the freedom of religion that had been granted during the Civil War and under the Commonwealth:

> The hypocrisy, enthusiasm and variety of wild and monstrous errors which abounded during those confusions, begat in the minds of many men too easily carried into extremes, a disregard for the very forms of religion, and proved the occasion of great libertinism and profaneness, which hath ever since too much prevailed among us; the seeds of infidelity and heresy which were then sown did soon after appear, and the tares have sprung up in great abundance.[39]

The *Representation* then goes on to specify what these heresies were. The first and most important of them was the rejection of the divine inspiration of Holy Scripture, on which the doctrines of the church rested. This was particularly evident in the doubt cast upon the biblical miracles, which were compared with similar accounts in pagan writers and dismissed accordingly. Similar treatment had been meted out to any sort of mystery that might be found in the church, like the efficacy of the sacraments for example. Denial of the

---

[37] Bray, *Records of Convocation*, 10:280–291.
[38] Ibid. 10:119–125.
[39] Ibid. 10:120.

Trinity, from both neo-Arians and Socinians, was another cause for alarm. Other beliefs that had been called into question were the immortality of the soul, the claim of the church that it had been instituted by Christ with clergy ordained to administer the Word and sacraments, and the false assimilation of Protestant ministers to pagan and Catholic priests, with the effect that the frauds perpetrated by the latter were assumed to be attributable to the former as well.

The intellectual disarray these complaints reveal was matched by a moral decay no less severe and potentially even more dangerous, because it was rampant among the mass of the population. Censured were stage plays, which presented immoral behaviour as somehow acceptable and were turning the minds of young people away from godly living. There was also the considerable licence given to those who resented the building of new churches, which were needed to meet the requirements of an expanding population but which these critics openly derided as monuments of superstition and ignorance. There was insufficient revenue, especially in country districts, to provide a full-time resident ministry, with the result that in many places there were few if any services on a Sunday and almost no attempts to catechize the young. In the countryside, where (it must be remembered) the great majority of the population still lived, a number of people were taking advantage of the relief granted to Dissenters and not attending any place of worship at all. Sunday was often not a quiet day of rest and spiritual reflection in the worship of God, but an occasion for drinking and playing games – wholly unsuitable activities for the Lord's Day.

Worst of all, the dreadful spiritual condition of England was allowing Roman Catholic missionaries to enter the country and preach that such licentiousness was the inevitable result of Protestantism. The effects of this were not hard to see:

> They have swarmed in our streets of late years, as they do more particularly at this time, and are very busy in making converts, nor do we doubt but that divers of your majesty's subjects, either from the scandal taken at the infidelity, heresy and profaneness they see, or from sharing the contagion of it, have by their arts been perverted.[40]

Modern readers find it hard to know how to react to complaints of this kind. On the one hand the licentiousness condemned in the early eighteenth century

---

[40] Ibid. 10:123.

is far more widespread now, where everything the *Representation* complains about has become the norm and it is the church that is on the defensive, if indeed it dares to say anything at all. On the other hand there is a strong sense today, which there was not in 1711, that legislation and coercion will not produce the desired results. We now believe that apostasy and general ungodliness are spiritual problems that must be resolved by spiritual means, which can come into play only by a change of heart brought about by the Spirit of God and not by acts of Parliament.

In fairness to the *Representation*, the picture it paints is not entirely bleak. It notes that there have been a number of rebuttals to the books advocating heresy and infidelity, and in particular that Robert Boyle (1627–91), the Anglo-Irish son of the first Earl of Cork who was both a devout churchman and an accomplished scientist, had endowed a series of lectures that were designed to demonstrate the underlying harmony between faith and science and that had enjoyed considerable success since they were launched in 1692.[41] Mention was made too of the many societies for the reformation of manners that had sprung into existence, with fulsome praise for the work of Thomas Bray, although he was not named. The *Representation* then goes on to give credit where credit is due:

> the infidelity of some hath been attended with this good consequence in others, that the zeal of devout persons hath thereby been excited to do everything that in them lay towards resisting and stemming the increase of this great evil, nor have their endeavours been altogether fruitless. Our eyes daily see the happy effects of them, divine service and sacraments have of late been oftener celebrated and better frequented than formerly, the catechizing of youth hath been more generally practised and with greater success, vast sums have been furnished by private contributions to sustain the charge of educating poor children in the pious manner above-mentioned, and many other new and noble institutions of charity have been set on foot.[42]

In addition to all this the repair of churches had not been neglected, with the expense largely borne by the parishioners, and new churches were being

---

[41] The Boyle Lectures continued on a regular basis until the late nineteenth century but only sporadically after that. They were revived in 2004 and are now given on an annual basis. See R. R. Manning and M. Byrne (eds.), *Science and Religion in the Twenty-first Century: The Boyle Lectures 2004–2013* (London: SCM Press, 2013).

[42] Bray, *Records of Convocation*, 10:123–124.

built, many with public funds. A recent act of Parliament had authorized the building of fifty new churches, and although the target was never met, a number of new buildings did in fact make their appearance. The most note-worthy of them were designed by Nicholas Hawksmoor (1661–1736) and are still standing, among them Christ Church, Spitalfields, St Anne's, Limehouse, and St Mary Woolnoth, the last of which was the rebuilding of an earlier foundation.

Almost as an afterthought, the *Representation* brought up what it called the 'pernicious custom' of duelling, which they hoped the queen would use her influence to ban. The church had attacked the custom as far back as the Fourth Lateran Council in 1215 and there had been periodic attempts to outlaw it, but without success. Unfortunately the *Representation* failed to achieve its object and duelling continued until the mid-nineteenth century, when it finally went out of fashion. From this it can be seen that the *Representation* had little prac-tical effect when it came to inducing the government to take action. What it recommended was either taking place already (like the building of new churches) or failed to gain enough support to become law, but is a valuable witness to the state of affairs late in Queen Anne's reign and shows that, despite the gloom brought on by the abolition of censorship and other liberal meas-ures, there was still an active body of people determined to resist the spirit of the age and to fight for the Christian values they believed ought to underpin society. It was not immediately apparent how far they would succeed in this, but by the end of the eighteenth century it had become clear that their efforts had laid the foundations for a genuine revival of faith and godly living across the country as a whole.

Meanwhile, as the *Representation* itself indicates, the Canterbury Con-vocation had tried to suppress heresy among the clergy, and particularly in the universities. One of the most egregious offenders was Matthew Tindal (1657–1733), who had been a Fellow of All Souls College, Oxford, since 1678. In 1706 he published a book entitled *The Rights of the Christian Church Asserted*, which was more or less the opposite of what its title might suggest. Tindal launched a broadside attack on the established churches of both England and Scotland, and was particularly critical of what he saw as a privil-eged clerical caste who were intent on deceiving superstitious, ignorant and gullible people with their trumped-up doctrines. The Church of England demanded that Parliament suppress the book, and in 1710 it was burnt by the public hangman.[43]

---

[43] See Israel, *Enlightenment that Failed*, 43–51, for the details.

Another dangerous free thinker was Anthony Ashley Cooper, third Earl of Shaftesbury (1671–1713), whose *A Letter Concerning Enthusiasm* (1708), ostensibly an attack on fanaticism, was really an all-out denunciation of contemporary Christian moral teaching, including that of John Locke. Shaftesbury escaped punishment, partly because of his exalted social status and partly because poor health compelled him to leave the country for Italy in 1711, but the fact that so prominent a person was openly attacking the church could not go unchallenged.[44]

On 16 April 1711 the Upper House of the Canterbury Convocation entered the fray by addressing the queen, asking her whether it had the authority to pass judgment on William Whiston (1667–1752), a Cambridge mathematician who had lost his Fellowship in 1710 because of his unorthodox theological views.[45] Whiston was by no means an extreme deist, and as recently as 1707 had delivered the Boyle Lectures, which were intended to refute their claims. But he did have a rationalist approach to the Bible, and insisted that it nowhere taught a doctrine of hell, or of the Trinity. It was the second of these that caused the greater disquiet, and he was soon branded an 'Arian'. After leaving Cambridge he was able to continue his scientific work in London, where he was greatly respected for it, but never renounced his unorthodox theological opinions. The queen apparently did not know what to do with the Convocation's request, and 'lost' it on two occasions. When she died, there was still no reply to it, and the matter was allowed to drop, but it was clear which way the wind was blowing. Despite her personal piety and orthodoxy, Anne was unwilling to let the Convocation exercise the disciplinary authority to which it believed it was entitled, and if she was reluctant, it can only be imagined what others must have thought. The failure of the Whiston case was the harbinger of what was to come and, to those with eyes to see, it revealed the true limitations of the establishment of religion in England after the Glorious Revolution.

William Whiston was not the only target singled out for censure by the Lower House of the Canterbury Convocation. Another was Samuel Clarke (1675–1729), who like Whiston had been a Boyle Lecturer (in 1704 and 1705), when he had defended a natural theology based on scientific reasoning. That was acceptable to contemporaries, but in 1712 he published *The Scripture Doctrine of the Trinity*, a long discourse in which he tried to show that the Bible did not support the orthodox doctrine proclaimed by the first Council of Nicaea in 325 and held by the church ever since. Instead Clarke asserted that

---

[44] See ibid. 140–147.
[45] Bray, *Records of Convocation*, 10:97–98.

the arch-heretic Arius was closer to the biblical text, and that his views had been widely held before the Nicene declaration made them heretical. This was too much for the Tories in the Lower House, and on 28 May 1714 they demanded that the bishops should take notice of his work and condemn it.

The bishops received the protest on 2 June and registered it in their act book, but took no action.[46] Incensed by that, the Lower House repeated its accusation and request, this time backing it up with substantial quotations from the book itself. The Upper House considered the matter again on 23 June but, despite the evidence, still refused to act.[47] Instead it asked Dr Clarke to explain himself, which he did, in a letter sent to the Bishop of London that was read in the Upper House on 5 July.[48] In it he promised not to say anything further on the subject and the bishops agreed to drop the matter, much to the chagrin of the Lower House, which felt that the bishops were in effect countenancing heresy by their laxity and unwillingness to prosecute a man who had so openly denied the teaching of Scripture and the confession of the Thirty-nine Articles of Religion.

But the final blow to the claims of the Convocation to be able to discipline members of the church who stepped out of line fell three years later, and on a different subject altogether. Queen Anne died on 1 August 1714 and was succeeded by George of Hanover, who had inherited the succession from his mother, Princess Sophia, who had died only a few weeks before. George was a complete stranger to the British Isles and spoke little or no English. He was a Lutheran, but agreed to conform to the Church of England and so was accepted as king on that basis, but the somewhat unsatisfactory nature of his qualifications left ample room for others to propose alternative candidates for the throne, most notably the so-called 'Old Pretender' or 'James III', the son of the late James II.

The chief advocate of the Jacobite cause was Francis Atterbury (1663–1732), who served in the Lower House of the Canterbury Convocation from 1701 onwards, was elected its prolocutor (speaker) in 1710 and was finally raised to the episcopate as Bishop of Rochester in 1713.[49] For over a decade Atterbury campaigned to get the Convocation recognized as the clerical equivalent of Parliament, and in particular the Lower House as the counterpart to the House of Commons, with all its attendant rights and privileges. He wrote

---

[46] Ibid. 11:62–63.
[47] Ibid. 11:70–72.
[48] Ibid. 11:78–79.
[49] See G. W. Bennett, *The Tory Crisis in Church and State 1688–1730: The Career of Francis Atterbury, Bishop of Rochester* (Oxford: Clarendon Press, 1975).

voluminously, if not very accurately, on the history of convocation, which prompted the church authorities to reply in kind. The result was a series of weighty tomes by William Wake, White Kennett (1660–1728) and most effectively Edmund Gibson (1669–1748) that delved into the history of church synods and convocations and exposed the weaknesses of Atterbury's case. The Canterbury Convocation was not a national synod of the Church of England, because the northern province of York was not represented in it, nor was its membership truly representative, even of the beneficed clergy who alone could vote for it. It had been designed for tax purposes, but there was no chance that the separate clerical taxation abolished in 1664 would be restored, let alone left to the clergy to determine. There was also no lay voice in Convocation, a major defect that would resurface in the nineteenth century when serious reform of the synods was proposed once more.

None of this deterred Atterbury however, who became even more active in the High Church cause. He supported Henry Sacheverell (1674–1724), a fierce and vocal critic of Low Churchmen and Latitudinarians who was unwise enough to preach his vitriol at St Paul's Cathedral in London on 5 November 1709. He was supposed to commemorate the unmasking of the gunpowder plot in 1605 along with the landing of William III at Torbay in 1688, but substituted the execution of Charles I on 30 January 1649 for the latter. By doing that he was able to blame all the ills of state and church on the Commonwealth, the Puritan Dissenters and their Whig allies. The last of these were so outraged that they had Sacheverell put on trial, and he was formally condemned by the House of Lords on 20 March 1710. But clever manoeuvring by Atterbury and his friends turned this defeat into a popular triumph and Sacheverell became the improbable martyr of the High Church cause. For a brief moment the Tories gained the upper hand, and it was this that enabled them to proceed with the *Representation of Religion*.

The High Churchmen's triumph was brief and did not survive the Hanoverian succession in 1714, when some of them joined the Nonjurors and others were suspected of latent Jacobitism. Atterbury had no choice but to accept George I as king, but he distanced himself as much as he could from the welcome given to him on his arrival in England and retreated into a silent opposition.[50] That might have continued for some time, but the new government moved quickly to appoint bishops of a Low Church persuasion, especially after the aborted uprising in favour of 'James III' in 1715. One of those appointed was Benjamin

---

[50] His covert Jacobitism was eventually unmasked however, and in 1723 he was deprived of his bishopric. He was exiled to France and died at the court of 'James III' but his body was returned to England and buried in Westminster Abbey, of all places.

Hoadly (1676–1761), a prominent Whig who was anti-Puritan as well as anti-Jacobite. His adherence to confessional orthodoxy was sometimes questioned, but he always professed it and was wise enough not to publish anything that might be construed as opposed to it, even if his zeal for the standards of church doctrine was not particularly obvious.

In 1716 Hoadly was made Bishop of Bangor and a few months later he published a pamphlet entitled *A Preservative Against the Principles and Practices of the Non-Jurors, both in Church and State*. This was an obviously anti-Jacobite document and the High Churchmen who dominated the Canterbury Convocation were alarmed by it, even though it did not directly involve them. On 31 March 1717, Hoadly went further and preached a sermon, which he then published as *The Nature of the Kingdom, or Church, of Christ*, in which he openly attacked High Church positions more broadly. Francis Atterbury and his friends were incensed, and the Lower House of Convocation commissioned a report on both publications, which they received on 10 May.[51] It was a broadside attack on Hoadly, accusing him of subverting the order and government of the Church of England in a manner worthier of a Dissenter than of a bishop.[52] Alarmed by this development, the government immediately prorogued the Convocation and, apart from formal sessions in conjunction with Parliament, it did not meet again to transact business until 1852.[53] The state had effectively muzzled the church, or at least the lower clergy, since the bishops continued to sit in the House of Lords. Never again would the clergy be allowed to meddle in politics, and church affairs would henceforth be kept as far as possible out of the political arena. Christianity in various forms would continue to be the religion of the people and would undergo massive changes, but none would ever again be able to overturn the secular government. It was truly the end of an era and the beginning of something quite new in the history of the British Isles.

Atterbury did not long survive the suspension of the Canterbury Convocation. Before long he was embroiled in Jacobite intrigues to re-establish the Stuart dynasty, with the result that he was arrested in 1722 and exiled to France, where he joined the court of the Old Pretender. For a time it seemed as though the High Church element in the church was in permanent eclipse because of its political leanings, but things changed somewhat as the eighteenth

---

[51] Bray, *Records of Convocation*, 11:255–263.

[52] See A. Starkie, *The Church of England and the Bangorian Controversy, 1716–1721* (Woodbridge: Boydell & Brewer, 2007).

[53] There was a brief exception in 1742, but it was of no real significance. Hoadly suffered nothing from the incident but went on to a successful ecclesiastical career as Bishop of Hereford (1721), Salisbury (1723) and finally Winchester (1734).

century wore on. One person who influenced a High Church revival was John Hutchinson (1674–1737), an Oxford polymath with an eccentric belief that Hebrew was the original speech of humankind and that studying it would unlock the secrets of all human knowledge. That bizarre idea failed to catch on, but Hutchinson was propelled by an intense devotional spirit that attracted a number of followers, who modified and adapted his views. The Hutchinsonians came to be known for their dedication to personal holiness of life, and belief that only the established Church (and not dissent) could provide an adequate base for the spread of the gospel.

More influential was the position adopted by Samuel Horsley (1733–1806), who not only advocated traditional orthodoxy in the face of the rationalistic critics of the so-called 'Enlightenment' but also claimed that it included a high doctrine of the Church's ministry, in particular the apostolic succession of the episcopate. That belief led him to advocate toleration for Roman Catholics, which earlier High Churchmen had routinely rejected, but also opposition to non-episcopal forms of dissent, which those same High Churchmen had usually accepted as valid, even if they were undesirable in certain ways. This shift towards Rome extended to his view of the Lord's Supper, where he was drawn to pre-Reformation ideas of eucharistic sacrifice and the 'real presence' of Christ. He never embraced the Roman doctrines in their fulness, but his move in that direction opened a way forward for the next generation and was to contribute to a revival of traditional Catholicism in the Church of England in the mid-nineteenth century. He died before that happened, but later observers looked back to him for inspiration and saw him as one of those who had maintained the Catholic tradition within the established Church at a time when the fortunes of that tradition were at a particularly low ebb.

The Dissenters

The pluralism of religious practice that emerged during the Civil War and Commonwealth made it inevitable that remnants of it would survive the reimposition of religious uniformity in 1662. It would also be the case that the Dissenters, as those who refused to conform were usually called, would differ among themselves and be vulnerable to fissiparousness. There is only one way to conform, but there are many kinds of dissent, and when Nonconformity entailed deprivation and sacrifice, those who chose that path were more likely than most to have strong feelings about the reasons why they did not go along with the majority. So it proved in the later seventeenth century.

At first the leading group of Dissenters were presbyterians, who were poised to take over the Church in 1660 and might have done so if they had been more united and flexible. As it was, they were forced into opposition and after that tended to fragment. Fifty years after the Great Ejection they were a spent force, and shortly after that most of them gave up orthodox Christianity altogether and became Unitarians. This remarkably rapid decline and fall has been the subject of much wonderment and no entirely satisfactory explanation of it has ever been given. One factor was that a man like Richard Baxter, who was a prominent leader of the Puritan Dissenters, hesitated to call himself a presbyterian, even if he more or less was one. The basic problem seems to have been that presbyterianism is a form of collective church discipline that requires a degree of organization and authority that a nonconforming body could not hope to have. As a result, people who might have accepted a state-sponsored presbyterianism of the kind later established in Scotland found themselves drifting into congregationalism because only in the context of particular congregations could the discipline they desired be implemented.

By 1675, Presbyterians and Congregationalists were meeting together for worship and the differences between them, which had once been so serious, tended to fade into the background. This process went hand in hand with a laxer attitude towards doctrinal orthodoxy that came to a head in 1719, when the remaining Presbyterians voted to ordain ministers who did not subscribe *ex animo* to the Westminster Confession. Before long what had begun as a charitable attempt to accommodate tender consciences became an open door to heterodoxy, and Unitarianism was the result. Orthodox trinitarian Presbyterianism virtually disappeared and was revived only later in the eighteenth century by an influx of Scottish immigrants, who brought it with them.

Congregationalism meanwhile went from strength to strength. Its inherent flexibility made it easier for Congregationalists to adapt to whatever situation they found themselves in, and they managed to straddle what had previously been a divide between the so-called 'gathered church' and the Establishment concept. Congregationalists saw themselves as a voluntary association of true believers but they were prepared to work with the civil authorities and did not cut themselves off from society. In New England they even constituted a church Establishment of their own, which survived the American Revolution, and in the case of Massachusetts lasted until 1833. In theory they put the emphasis on the essentials of the faith and left other matters to the discretion of individual congregations, although it must be said that where they were able to act as the Establishment (as in New England) this kind of toleration was not much in evidence. Even so, they were able to accommodate different views of baptism in a way other churches were not, so that their protestations of tolerance were not all hypocritical. What mattered to them above all was spiritual commitment – a heartfelt faith that stressed conversion and separation from the mindset of the world without going to semi-monastic extremes. Outwardly, Congregationalists continued to live like ordinary members of society, but inwardly they had a spiritual commitment that set them apart. In that sense they were the forerunners of the Evangelicals of the next generation, who were often more congregationalist in mentality than anything else.

More distinctive than either the Presbyterians or the Congregationalists were the Baptists, who were subdivided into Arminians (General Baptists) and Calvinists (Particular Baptists). The General Baptists were closer to their Mennonite cousins and had a strong sense of being connected to one another by a common profession of faith. They were clearly a 'gathered church' and in that way similar to the Congregationalists, but their insistence on believer's baptism set them apart. Within their churches they made a clear distinction between elders, who pastored the local congregations (often on a part-time or non-stipendiary basis), and deacons, who were responsible for taking care of the material needs of church members. The Baptists looked after one another to a degree that was unusual at the time, and that too bonded them together. The Particular Baptists were more strictly Calvinistic in outlook, which in some cases led to a closed mentality that eschewed evangelism. But in one important respect they were pioneers. Odd though it may seem to us, it was the Strict and Particular Baptists who first popularized the singing of hymns, as opposed to metrical psalms. Their initial compositions were rather simple and unattractive to outsiders, but the principle caught on and within a generation their apparent innovation had spread to embrace a far wider spectrum of Protestant belief. It should also be noted that in the eighteenth century there were many more Particular Baptists than there were General ones. The best estimates suggest that the ratio was about two to one in favour of the former, which seems strange until we remember that in groups that suffer discrimination a high level of commitment is to be expected. It was harder to be Strict and Particular, and so it is not surprising that those who knew they would face discrimination opted for what to them was the genuine.

Even more distinctive than the Baptists were the Quakers, the only other radical Puritan sect to have survived to the present day. The Quakers began as an ecstatic movement, but they soon settled down to a life of quiet introspection. They eschewed the formalities of institutional church life and conducted their affairs with neither clergy nor liturgy. Instead they waited for outpourings of the Spirit in line with the 'inner light' that guided all those who were in true communion with God. For the most part the Quakers continued to revere the Scriptures as the divine Word, and saw their prophecies as being in continuity with Scripture, but it is easy to see how error could creep in and why so many observers found their practices distasteful. But if their theology was open to question, there could be no doubt about the Quaker dedication to good works and philanthropy that set them apart from other Dissenters and still characterizes them. Under the leadership of William Penn (1644–1718) they established a colony in the New World that was devoted to their principles, including pacifism and tolerance of different theological opinions. Of course, modern Pennsylvania is a far cry from the Quaker paradise envisaged by its founders, but elements of their idealism remain embedded in the collective consciousness there and still surface from time to time in outpourings of social reform. In Britain a number of Quaker families rose to prominence as bankers and industrialists and their names are still familiar – Barclay, Fry and Cadbury among them. Never a large group, they have punched well above their weight and the English-speaking world would not be what it is without their distinctive, if somewhat eccentric, witness.

Given the legal situation of Dissenters, being outside the established Church was more important than belonging to a specific group or denomination. Even many prominent people are hard to classify in such terms – was Richard Baxter a Presbyterian? Or John Bunyan a Baptist? Others have claimed them as such, but they themselves were more flexible – Bunyan even had his children baptized in the parish church. This freedom from denominational labels was especially evident among laypeople, who circulated freely from one congregation to another. Among them was the hymn writer Isaac Watts (1674–1748), born into a dissenting family and loyal to that inheritance, but something of a rebel and innovator, who did more than any other single individual to change the character of English worship, both among Dissenters and (eventually) in the Church of England as well.

Before Watts's time, music had played only a secondary role in the churches, and much of it was of poor quality. Dissenting services were generally dull, often being little more than a sermon with prayers and perhaps a metrical psalm attached. Watts set out to change that. He did not neglect the psalter, and one of his best hymns is 'O God Our Help in Ages Past', which is an almost literal rendering of Psalm 90. But he soon branched out and left a body of hymnody greater than anyone before him. Of the nearly 700 hymns he composed, about 40 are still frequently sung and regular churchgoers will be familiar with many of them. They are full of sound Reformed theology enhanced by a sensitive personal touch that never fails to move the hearts of worshippers. Watts knew that the cross of Christ, the symbol of his atoning sacrifice, is the very centre of Christianity, and he expressed this in lines that will never be forgotten:

When I survey the wondrous cross
On which the Prince of Glory died
My richest gain I count but loss
And pour contempt on all my pride.

Forbid it Lord that I should boast
Save in the death of Christ my God
All the vain things that charm me most
I sacrifice them to his blood.

See from his head, his hands, his feet
Sorrow and love flow mingled down
Did e'er such love and sorrow meet?
Or thorns compose so rich a crown?

His dying crimson like a robe
Hangs o'er his body on the tree
Then I am dead to all the globe
And all the globe is dead to me.

Were the whole realm of nature mine
That were a present far too small
Love so amazing, so divine
Demands my soul, my life, my all.

A group apart from the normal run of Dissenters was the community that remained attached to the 'old religion'. Not everybody accepted the Reformation, but although these 'recusants', as they were called, were few, many of them came from ancient and noble families with deep roots in the country. Unable to organize openly anywhere in the king's dominions, they nevertheless managed to set up a network of colleges on the European continent where priests could be trained and sent back to Britain and Ireland on 'mission'. The Irish ones were well received by a majority of the population, but their English and Scottish brethren had a harder time of it. They were largely dependent on the loyalty of gentry families who were able to conceal them from the authorities and give them room to celebrate mass in private. The situation was complicated by the fact that many foreign powers were Catholic and potential enemies of the British state. Priests trained abroad might protest that they were interested only in religion, but nobody knew that for sure and so penalties were imposed both on them and on those who succoured them in any way.

The brief reign of James II saw a measure of relief for the Catholics, but they suffered for that in the aftermath of the Glorious Revolution. Oaths were imposed on office holders that no Catholic could take, and financial penalties were exacted from landed families that had the resources needed to support the Catholic 'mission'. It is true that the various laws and restrictions against Catholics were often unenforced but they were there in case of need, and every once in a while some unfortunate person would suffer the consequences. Above all, there was a deep-seated animosity towards Catholicism in England and Scotland, as well as among the Protestant settlers in Ireland, and the state could not guarantee the safety of Catholics threatened by periodic mob violence. Roman Catholicism survived, but its adherents were if anything worse off after the grant of toleration to Dissenters than they had been before, and it would be another century before attitudes – and the law – would start to change in their favour. After 1689, Protestantism and loyalty to the state went hand in hand – those who rejected the former were automatically assumed to be in rebellion against the latter, and they were treated accordingly.

Presbyterian Scotland

It is a curious fact that the Glorious Revolution of 1688–9, which took place mainly in England, had its greatest impact in Ireland and also in Scotland, although for completely different reasons. In Ireland it spelled the end of any sort of toleration for Catholics and the beginning of the most serious persecution that country was ever to see.[54] For a few years Catholic priests were hunted down and expelled from the country, and all the gains they thought they had won after 1660 were lost. This persecution did not last however, both because Catholics were too numerous and the Protestants were divided. The established Church was episcopal in structure and closely tied to the Church of England, whose fortunes it followed. But there were also large numbers of Protestant Dissenters, most of them Presbyterians of Scottish descent, who were especially prominent in the north-east.[55] Unable to integrate them into the Establishment,

---

[54] S. J. Connolly, *Religion, Law and Power: The Making of Protestant Ireland 1660–1760* (Oxford: Clarendon Press, 1992).

[55] See F. Holmes, *The Presbyterian Church in Ireland: A Popular History* (Dublin: Columba Press, 2000).

but equally unwilling to outlaw them in the way it outlawed Catholics, the government compromised by granting them a subsidy, known as the *regium donum* (royal gift), for the support of their ministers. The *regium donum*, accepted by those most directly concerned, did not prevent many lay Dissenters from siding with Catholics in a long struggle against the Establishment. It also encouraged many of them to emigrate, and in the course of the next century a steady stream of Protestants moved across the Atlantic, where they were known as the 'Scots-Irish' and played a considerable role in the formation of the United States of America.

Scotland was something else again. Presbyterianism had struggled for supremacy before the Civil War, and it was not until 1638 that the Church of Scotland legislated for it to the exclusion of any other form of church government. But the newly presbyterian church was soon engulfed in war and, despite its support for the king, suffered the consequences of defeat when episcopacy was re-established in 1662. For the next twenty-seven years, Presbyterians suffered persecution for their convictions, an experience that caused some to compromise but also steeled the resolve of others. When the opportunity came to redress the wrongs they believed they had suffered, they were not slow to take it, and before long presbyterianism was once more established as the Church of Scotland's form of government.

There is no doubt that that was the will of the majority at the time, but it was not carried through without opposition. There were some extreme Presbyterians, mainly Covenanters originally led by Richard Cameron (1648–80), who refused any form of state Establishment, even one that conformed to their own principles of church government, and who ended up creating what they called the Reformed Presbyterian Church.[56] The Cameronians were the first in what would become a steady stream of dissenting Presbyterians in Scotland. To this day the largest and most influential of the Free Churches in that country are just as presbyterian as the established Church or (as they would see it) even more so, which makes the Scottish church scene quite different from that of England, where hardly any of the Free Churches are episcopalian in polity.

The Church of Scotland's General Assembly did what it could to pacify the Cameronians, and some were successfully reintegrated into it, but matters were more complicated with the surviving episcopalians. Because of the 1662 settlement, every Scottish incumbent in 1689 was theoretically episcopalian,

---

[56] It was not formally constituted until 1743 and in 1876 joined the Free Church of Scotland, but the Cameronians were in existence from the late seventeenth century and a remnant survives to this day, with significant connections in both Ireland and the USA.

although many were quite happy to accept a presbyterian system. Others however were more resistant, and in the Highlands and north-east were particularly numerous and influential. When the Scottish Parliament abolished episcopacy, it also abolished the system of patronage that had been a running sore since the Reformation. That made it much easier to appoint presbyterian ministers, but alienated the landowning classes, whose patronage rights had been summarily removed. Many of them were not only episcopalian by preference but also Jacobite, and the two causes tended to go together to an unhealthy degree.

Faced with opposition of this kind, the General Assembly reacted with determination. King William II (as he was known in Scotland) wanted all ministers who were prepared to swear allegiance to him to be included in the Establishment, whether they were convinced Presbyterians or not. But the General Assembly regarded such royal intervention as compromise and was reluctant to agree. The Scottish Parliament had to intervene and assure all incumbent ministers that they could retain their posts as long as they swore allegiance to the new regime. They would not be compelled to accept the Presbyterian Settlement but they would be excluded from the church courts and denied any say in church government. As late as 1707 perhaps as many as 165 parish ministers (out of a total of about 1,000) were in this position, but after the failed attempt at a Jacobite restoration in 1715, numbers declined rapidly and in a few years hardly any were left.[57] The compromise with episcopalianism was largely the work of William Carstares (1649–1715), himself a Presbyterian minister and for many years prior to the Glorious Revolution a confidant of the future King William II in the Netherlands. He accomplished the rare feat of remaining in the good graces of both the king and the General Assembly, and his patient moderation did much to secure the Presbyterian Settlement.

The main problem facing the Presbyterian Establishment was the shortage of suitable ministers. Those who had been ejected in 1662 were reinstated if they were still alive and able to serve, but they were obviously an older generation who would soon die out, and it took time to train successors. Lay eldership could also be a problem, although it had continued to exist under the episcopalian regime in force from 1662 onwards, so it was not as difficult to find suitable people as it might otherwise have been. Even so, Presbyterianism demanded a high level of education and commitment from people who lacked

---

[57] The last of them is said to have been Archibald Lundie, minister of Saltoun in East Lothian from 1696 to 1759, but his name does not appear in D. M. Bertie, *Scottish Episcopal Clergy 1689–2000* (Edinburgh: T&T Clark, 2000).

formal theological training, and it would be many years before its hold on Scotland was really secure.

The union of 1707 brought new dangers to the Scottish church. Fear of integration into England and the restoration of episcopacy led most of the Presbyterian ministers to oppose it, but Carstares was able to secure guarantees that the internal organization of the church would be left undisturbed and his word was trusted. What perhaps nobody could foresee was that the union Parliament would be dominated by English Tories whose dislike of Presbyterianism was matched only by their ignorance and lack of concern for Scotland. Trouble began in 1709, when an episcopalian minister called James Greenshields returned to Scotland from Ireland and discovered that, since the union, there were a large number of Englishmen living in the country who wanted to worship in the English manner. Greenshields obliged, much to the chagrin of the Edinburgh presbytery, which ordered him to desist. The case eventually went to the House of Lords, which ruled in Greenshields' favour, thereby opening the door for other episcopally minded clergy to start using the English Prayer Book.

In order to allow for dissent of this kind the union Parliament proceeded to enact a toleration bill that allowed the use of the English liturgy in the Church of Scotland, as long as the ministers swore allegiance to Queen Anne and abjured the claims of 'James III'. To prevent the obvious charge that this was aimed primarily at the Scottish episcopalians, the act demanded that all Scottish ministers, Presbyterians included, must swear the oath, something that in the case of the latter was unnecessary and regarded by some as offensive, since it called their loyalty into question. The oath was modified after the failure of the 1715 rebellion, when the Presbyterians had demonstrated their complete loyalty to George I, but it had set an unhappy precedent.

Much worse though was what followed. In 1712, Parliament reintroduced patronage into the Church of Scotland. Once again it was the English Tories who lay behind this initiative, and the opposition to it, led by the indefatigable Carstares, was ineffective. It is true that the presbyteries were still to be involved in the appointment of ministers and that many patrons were initially reluctant to insist on their rights, but the freedom of congregations to choose their own ministers had been curtailed, without the consent of the church, and resentment soon spread. It was only a matter of time before abuses would start to creep in, and when they did the result was another secession from the church, although that did not materialize until 1737. Once again, it was a case of one group of Presbyterians breaking with another, a pattern that by then was firmly established in Scottish life.

Yet in spite of all the problems, the establishment of the presbyterian Church of Scotland was maintained, and over time it came to represent the national identity of the Scottish people in a UK where they were a small minority of the total population. Interference from English Members of Parliament was always a possibility, but as church and state settled into their respective spheres, and the church was increasingly left to its own devices, the dangers this posed receded into the background. There was even some cooperation between the Church of England and the Church of Scotland, as for example in the activities of the Society for the Promotion of Christian Knowledge, which served the Scottish Establishment as much as the English one and did not seek to proselytize on behalf of episcopalianism. The potentially awkward position of the monarch, who theoretically belonged to both establishments, was mitigated in practice by the fact that no king ventured into Scotland until George IV (1820–30) paid a visit there in 1822 and attended divine service in the Church of Scotland on 25 August. The precedent had been set, and for the past 200 years worshipping as a presbyterian has remained an integral part of the sovereign's forays into the northern kingdom.

The world of the parish

When John Wesley was criticized for preaching up and down the country, instead of remaining in a particular pulpit, he is said to have replied, 'The world is my parish.' It was a somewhat ironic reply, because for most people the opposite was true – the parish was their world. One of the effects of the Reformation was to increase the parish's importance in people's spiritual lives. The dissolution of monasteries, confraternities, chantries and other extraparochial outlets for popular devotion meant that the parish church became the Reformation's uniquely privileged focus. Parishioners were exhorted, and increasingly compelled by legislation, to attend their church on a weekly basis. The Reformed pattern of worship engaged lay participation to a degree that had previously been unknown, and the regular provision of sermons turned the church into a school for the instruction of the congregation in the basic principles of the Christian faith. The traditional rites of baptism, matrimony and burial continued as before, but now they were officially recorded, and participation in them was virtually compulsory. Not everybody was comfortable with this and not everyone complied, but for the vast majority of the population the so-called 'rites of passage' were centred on the church building and gave local communities a sense of cohesion.

Parish churches might technically 'belong' to the patron who presented the minister or to the minister himself, once he had been instituted, but neither of these could function without the support of the local laypeople. Every adult male resident of a parish was entitled to vote at the annual vestry meeting, which determined who the churchwardens would be and how the money needed for the upkeep of the building and its services would be raised. Over time, these vestries tended to delegate their responsibilities to a committee, known as the 'select vestry', which was elected at the annual general meeting. For the most part, lay roles within the church were performed by a few individuals who remained in office as long as they were able to fulfil their duties, but the principle of annual election was maintained and could occasionally make a difference.

The institution of the vestry was a means by which Nonconformists were able to maintain links with the parish church and in some cases control its activities. They could be elected to parish offices and it was far from uncommon for churchwardens to be Dissenters to one degree or another. This bothered some High Church people, especially clergymen who felt they were being undermined by people who were not fully on board with them. But in the village culture of the time it was a way of keeping the peace and ensuring that religious differences, however strongly felt, did not destroy the local community.

The parish system existed throughout the British Isles but its character differed from one country to another. It was most effective in Scotland, where the pattern of lay eldership established by the first Reformers ensured that everyone in the community was kept in contact (and under surveillance) by the local church. This was especially important at Communion seasons, when every parishioner was expected to receive the sacrament. In Scotland this occurred at least once a year, usually around Easter time, and compliance was all but universal. In England, parishioners were expected to communicate at least three times a year – at Christmas, Easter and Whitsun (Pentecost) – although Easter Communion was by far the most frequently observed. But the absence of a system of lay elders meant that compliance was relatively low. Exact figures are impossible to obtain, but the evidence we have suggests that no more than a quarter of those eligible were regular Easter communicants, and the figures for the other great festivals were much lower.

One of the reasons for this might have been the success of Puritan preaching. The Book of Common Prayer enjoins people to 'try and examine themselves before presuming to eat of that bread and drink of that cup', and it appears that many did so, with the result that they abstained from taking part.[58] Was this a sign of success or of failure on the part of the ministers? It depends on one's point of view. Conviction of sinfulness is not the sum total of the gospel message, but it is a necessary starting point. To those of us who live in an age when sinfulness is often an alien concept and reception of Holy Communion without any kind of preparation is assumed as a matter of course, the scruples of these conscientious abstainers stand as a rebuke to our own laxity and indifference, even if our levels of participation are statistically higher.

In Ireland the scene was greatly complicated by ongoing religious warfare and the fact that parish churches were in the hands of the small Protestant minority. The inevitable result was that parishes there could not function in the way they did elsewhere, even though the fundamental structures (and expectations) were the same. Catholics and Presbyterians could attend vestry meetings for example, and seek to influence parish policies, which forced the Irish Parliament to legislate against their participation, although with mixed results.[59]

Keeping the church buildings in good repair was a major problem and it took time for reasonable solutions to be worked out. It was generally accepted that the laypeople were responsible for the nave (where they sat) and the incumbent for the chancel (where he ministered), but although tithe income would go some way towards paying for the latter there was no fixed provision for the former. Initially much of the revenue for that came from church ales and the like, but the Puritans disapproved of these and they were in any case an irregular and undependable source of income. In the course of the seventeenth century they were therefore replaced by church rates, imposed by the vestry on the entire parish. Every ratepayer had to contribute to these because the parish church belonged to everyone, although Dissenters and Catholics naturally resented the imposition, which was finally abolished in 1868.

How many people played a part in the life of their parish church? The question is fairly easy to answer for Scotland (almost everyone) and Ireland (very few people), but England and Wales are more problematic. There was certainly a great variation between parishes, some of which were well supported and others not, but an overall picture is hard to obtain because reliable evidence is lacking. One person who tried to find out was Richard Baxter, who surveyed

---

58 J. Spurr, *The Post-Reformation 1603–1714* (Harlow: Pearson, 2006), 281–287.

59 E. FitzPatrick and R. Gillespie, *The Parish in Medieval and Early Modern Ireland: Community, Territory and Building* (Dublin: Four Courts Press, 2006). See esp. T. Barnard, 'The Eighteenth-Century Parish', 297–324, and W. Roulston, 'The Role of the Parish in Building and Maintaining Anglican Churches in the North of Ireland, 1660–1740', 325–344.

his congregation in 1658 and came to the conclusion that out of 1,800 potential communicants, about 500 could be described as enthusiastic Puritans and another hundred or so were sincere Christians who went along with the Puritans but lacked their all-consuming zeal.[60] Beyond them were others who were true believers but either weak in their faith or else wedded to the banned services of the traditional Church of England.[61] The rest were 'secret heathens', who displayed some signs of outward conformity but who were either ignorant or contemptuous of the gospel. Among them were a few antinomian sectarians and Roman Catholics, although they seem to have been statistically insignificant.

The result of this analysis would lead us to conclude that Baxter could count on a third of the parishioners to support him more or less unreservedly. Adding in the other sincere believers, we may reach something over half the total, but there can be no escaping the fact that the largest single group remained the unconverted. Baxter was a dedicated and painstaking minister, so it is reasonable to assume that he had more support than would have been normal, which leaves us with a pretty bleak picture overall. When Baxter was forced into dissent in 1662, how many of his parishioners were prepared to follow him? Again we have no way of knowing that for sure, but probably it was a small minority, even of those whom he would have described as his most enthusiastic supporters. The ties of the parish could not so easily be broken. In all the upheavals caused by civil war and revolution, at least two-thirds of the Church of England's clergymen remained in post, conforming outwardly (and with varying degrees of enthusiasm) to the many changes, but remaining at heart loyal to the ministry to which they had been called. The evidence suggests that their parishioners by and large shared their outlook.

---

[60] R. Baxter, *Confirmation and Restoration*, quoted in Spurr, *Post-Reformation*, 227–228.

[61] There were many more of these people than has generally been recognized. See J. Maltby, *Prayer Book and People in Elizabethan and Early Stuart England* (Cambridge: Cambridge University Press, 1998).

11

An age of faith (1717–1832)

A reasonable religion

The suspension of the Canterbury Convocation in 1717 was a political act, but it had important theological implications that would not become apparent for some time. Apart from the sparring between the Upper and Lower House over the rights and authority of the latter, the Convocation had taken the trouble to examine the writings of William Whiston and Samuel Clarke, both of whom it suspected of heresy. For good measure, it had also registered disquiet at the propositions of men like Gilbert Burnet and Benjamin Hoadly, who were themselves orthodox in theological terms but inclined to tolerate a range of opinions the High Church party regarded as dangerous and subversive. By cutting these debates short, the government of George I signalled that it would not tolerate personal attacks, particularly if they were to lead to heresy trials and punishment of the offenders for deviating from the accepted orthodoxy.

This is not to say that the authorities were indifferent to matters of doctrine. They believed, as did virtually everyone in the Church of England, that the Reformers had got it right, that the kind of Protestantism that had emerged out of a century and a half of conflict was the purest form of Christian truth ever devised by man, and that all right-minded people ought to assent to it. But for that very reason they thought that persecution was out of place. Like Gamaliel before the Sanhedrin in the early days of the church, they believed the truth would prevail on its own.[1] Attempts to suppress it would not work and defending it against its detractors was unnecessary. What was required was not judicial repression – the weapon preferred by those in error, like the French Catholics, who persecuted the Huguenots – but reasoned argument, to show that the teaching of the church, drawn from divine revelation in the Bible, accorded with the facts of history and nature. To portray the debates of the time as a conflict between faith and reason is therefore mistaken. Both

---

[1] Acts 5:34–40.

sides believed in reason – the difference was that one of them said that reason agreed with the tenets of faith and the other said it might not.

Some of the attacks on traditional orthodoxy, like John Toland's notorious *Christianity not Mysterious*, were so outrageous that refutation was hardly necessary, but the criticisms of men like Whiston and Clarke were more measured and subtle. It was not immediately obvious that the New Testament taught a doctrine of the Trinity, nor was it easy to account for miracles once it was accepted that the universe obeyed a series of natural laws that could be discovered and analysed by the human mind. Mathematicians like Sir Isaac Newton (1642–1727) were particularly hesitant to accept the notion that natural laws could be overruled, even by the God who had made them, and they were therefore inclined to put 'miracles' down to lack of scientific understanding on the part of those who witnessed them. Something unexplained is not necessarily inexplicable; the trick is to discover what the explanation might be, and the assumption was that it could eventually be found within the parameters of the space–time universe.

The rationalist case against miracles was put most succinctly by David Hume (1711–76) in an essay on the subject that he wrote in 1748. He concluded:

> upon the whole, we may conclude that the Christian religion not only was at first attended with miracles, but even at this day cannot be believed by any reasonable person without one. Mere reason is insufficient to convince us of its veracity: and whoever is moved by faith to assent to it, is conscious of a continued miracle in his own person, which subverts all the principles of his understanding, and gives him a determination to believe what is most contrary to custom and experience.[2]

Hume's scepticism has had a ready audience in modern times, but it had already been answered by Joseph Butler (1692–1752) in his *Analogy of Religion*, first published in 1736:

> Whether this scheme of nature be, in the strictest sense, infinite or not, it is evidently vast, even beyond all possible imagination. And doubtless that part of it which is opened to our view is but as a point, in comparison of the whole plan of Providence, reaching throughout eternity, past and future: in comparison of what is even now going on in the remote parts

---

[2] D. Hume, *Dialogues Concerning Natural Religion*, ed. N. Kemp-Smith (Oxford: Oxford University Press, 1935), 57–58.

of the boundless universe: nay, in comparison of the whole scheme of this world. And therefore, that things lie beyond the natural reach of our faculties, is no sort of presumption against the truth and reality of them; because it is certain there are innumerable things, in the constitution and government of the universe, which are thus beyond the natural reach of our faculties.[3]

From the Christian point of view rationalism is myopic and inadequate, good enough perhaps within its own limited sphere, but unable to comprehend the mystery of things above and beyond it. Times and arguments have changed since Butler's day, but the difference of perspective – and the Christian critique of rationalism – remains essentially the same.

In the eighteenth century the basic dispute was over the nature of divine providence. Almost everyone believed in it in principle, but the argument was over how it worked in practice. Had God created the world with an inbuilt logic that then worked without his periodic intervention, or had he created an 'open' universe in which he was constantly at work? At a time when the natural sciences were finally freeing themselves from superstition and the false assumptions of the ancient Greeks, the appeal of a self-contained rational system was obvious. But for a Christian who wanted to have a direct relationship with a God who can guide and protect him through all the changing scenes of life, a distant, non-interfering God was of no use at all. Could these two different points of view be reconciled or was it necessary to choose between them? Reconciliation was the desired outcome, and it was to that end that the eighteenth-century apologists of the Christian faith directed themselves, with a remarkable degree of success. Today we must admit that their arguments have been critiqued and in many cases superseded, but that is also true of the rationalism of their opponents. In their own day they were doughty and respected defenders of orthodox Christianity, so much so that the deism they combated almost died out in Britain, even as it was making inroads in France, Germany and elsewhere as the so-called 'Enlightenment'.

Butler was perhaps the most active and best known of the intellectual defenders of orthodox Christianity but was by no means alone. In their different ways Richard Bentley (1662–1742), classical scholar and Master of Trinity College, Cambridge, from 1700, George Berkeley (1685–1753), an Irishman who was Bishop of Cloyne from 1734 onwards, Jonathan Swift (1667–1745), another Irishman who became Dean of St Patrick's Cathedral in Dublin

---

[3] J. Butler, *The Analogy of Religion*, pt 2, ch. 2 (London: J. M. Dent, 1906), 136–137.

in 1713, and is still famous as a satirist of his times,[4] and Daniel Waterland (1683–1740), Master of Magdalene College, Cambridge, from 1714 onwards and the greatest theologian of his generation, all contributed their talents to the same cause. A later representative of this school was William Paley (1743–1805), best known for his arguments for a divine creation based on the principle of design. Paley argued that a world as complex as ours could not have emerged by accident, and that it required the intelligent mind of a creator in order to function with the precision it does. Paley's natural theology was to dominate religious thought in Britain for most of the nineteenth century and resurfaces today in various forms of creationism and so-called 'intelligent design'. It can still be persuasive, as the 'conversion' of the atheist philosopher Antony Flew (1923–2010), which he announced in 2007, demonstrates.

The extraordinary success of the defenders of Christian orthodoxy against their atheistic and sceptical opponents is perhaps best measured by comparing what happened in France during the same period, where the church was undermined by the almost universal criticism of its intellectual opponents. Writing of that a century later, the brilliant French observer Alexis de Tocqueville (1805–59) had this to say:

Throughout the eighteenth century infidelity had famous champions in England. Able writers, profound thinkers, embraced its cause. But they won no victories with it, because all who had anything to lose by revolutions hastened to the support of the established faith. Even men who mixed in French society, and did not reject the doctrines of our philosophers, considered them dangerous. Great political parties, such as exist in every free country, found it to be in their interest to espouse the cause of the Church; Bolingbroke was seen to join hands with the bishops. Animated by this example, and encouraged by a consciousness of support, the clergy fought with energy in their own defence. Notwithstanding the vice of its constitution, and the abuses of all sorts which teemed within its organisation, the Church of England withstood the shock unmoved; writers and speakers sprang forth from its ranks, and defended Christianity with ardor. Infidel theories were discussed, refuted, and rejected by society, without the least interference on the part of the government.[5]

---

[4] See C. J. Fauske, *Jonathan Swift and the Church of Ireland 1710–1724* (Dublin: Irish Academic Press, 2002).

[5] A. de Tocqueville, *The Ancien Régime*, tr. J. Bonner (London: J. M. Dent, 1988), 122–123. The original French edition was published in 1856. Henry St John (1678–1751), created Viscount Bolingbroke in 1712, was personally antireligious but nevertheless supported the political claims of the Church of England.

The religious Establishment

The Glorious Revolution of 1688–9 had ensured that eighteenth-century British society would be a Protestant constitutional monarchy in which state churches would live side by side with Dissenters who agreed with them theologically but who, for a variety of reasons, did not want to remain in (or join) the Establishment.[6] Roman Catholics were excluded from this, as were Scottish Episcopalians, although that was mainly for political reasons. As time went on and the Jacobite threat receded, the legislation passed against both these groups was increasingly ignored, but it was not until after the outbreak of the French Revolution, when any threat from the European continent was removed, that formal toleration was granted to them. Roman Catholics in particular remained unpopular and had to wait until 1829 for complete emancipation from their civil disabilities – a year after similar legislation restricting the activities of Dissenters had also been abolished.

The position of the established churches of England and Ireland, as well as that of the Church of Scotland, was unsettled for some time, not least because it was thought that the majority of Anglican clergy were passively Jacobite in sympathy. But this began to change after 1717. The suspension of the Convocation of Canterbury had the effect of removing party politics from the day-to-day life of the Church of England. There was still a major difference of outlook between the government-appointed bishops and the more High Church lower clergy, but as neither group could impose its will on the other, conflict between them was pointless and gradually faded out. Instead of that there was a marked improvement in diocesan administration and parish life generally. There was still a large number of parishes that had no resident incumbent, but closer examination reveals that in many cases the clergymen who served them resided nearby and could minister to them on a regular, even weekly, basis. Parochial libraries were founded in many places, largely thanks to the efforts of Thomas Bray, church schools were better supervised and high standards of clerical discipline were maintained. This was all the more remarkable in that appointments to benefices were mostly in lay hands (and often in private ones too), so that it was difficult for the bishops to insist on a rigorous standard for the clergy. Fortunately for them, they were ably assisted by a number of voluntary societies, many of them organized and staffed by women, who worked tirelessly for what they called 'the reformation of manners'

---

[6] For a detailed study of this, see R. Brown, *Church and State in Modern Britain* (London: Routledge, 1991); N. Yates, *Eighteenth-Century Britain 1714–1815* (Harlow: Pearson Education, 2008).

and who did all they could to improve the godliness of the population in general. The most famous of these women today is Susannah Wesley (1669–1742), wife of Samuel and mother of John and Charles, who held Bible studies and prayer meetings in the vicarage at Epworth and gave her sons a practical example of what could be achieved in the lives of ordinary people if they were taught properly.

The church had no legislative power of its own, but Parliament was on its side and did what it could to strengthen it. In 1753 Parliament passed a Marriage Act, making it compulsory for all marriages in England and Wales to be solemnized in the Church of England, including those of Roman Catholics. Exceptions were made for Jews and Quakers, but that was all. The effect of this was to eliminate the curse of clandestine marriages, which had occurred because of a loophole in earlier legislation that allowed chaplains of the Fleet to marry people quickly and with no questions asked. The original intention had been to make life easier for sailors, but by the early eighteenth-century Fleet ceremonies were notorious for providing services to those who had eloped. There was a similar escape route in Scotland, where the border village of Gretna Green, on the highway between Carlisle and Glasgow, was widely renowned for the same thing. After 1753 these loopholes were closed and every marriage required the reading of banns in the parish church(es) of the bride and groom.[7] Inevitably the Marriage Act had the effect of bringing the general population closer to the established Church, if only for legal purposes, and allowed the church courts to supervise marital irregularities more closely. The Church of England had (and has) no provision for divorce, which until 1837 could be obtained only by a special act of Parliament, so its power to oversee marital questions was far from being purely notional.

The Marriage Act was accepted and worked as well as it did because both dissent and Roman Catholicism were in long-term decline. The pressures to conform to the Church of England were not especially great, but over time had an effect, particularly among non-conforming Protestants, who realized that whatever had persuaded their grandparents to strike out on their own was no longer of great significance and not worth the inconveniences they had to suffer as a result. The Roman Catholic Church was in a different position but, despite its ability to organize its congregations with the appointment of itinerant bishops directly responsible to Rome, lost about a quarter of its members in the first half of the eighteenth century. Its leading representative

---

[7] Banns were established by the Fourth Lateran Council in 1215 and are still required for marriages in the Church of England.

during the latter part of the century was Richard Challoner (1691–1781), whose great achievement was a much-needed revision of the Catholic Douai-Reims Bible. The effect was to bring it much closer to the King James Version, and therefore to the mainstream Protestant tradition, although few people seem to have noticed that at the time.

Roman Catholics also suffered from popular prejudice against them, which could be whipped up in times of trouble. The worst case occurred in 1780, when Britain was at war with France and Spain, both of which were supporting the rebellious American colonies in their quest for independence. The instigator was Lord George Gordon (1751–93), who formed a Protestant Association in order to oppose plans to grant legal relief to Catholics. Gordon did not take part in the riots of which he is generally regarded as the sponsor, although he was tried for treason as a result of them. The Gordon riots effectively put Catholic relief on hold for a number of years and Gordon himself, rather oddly, abandoned Christianity for Judaism in 1787.

What was true of the Church of England was also true of the established churches in Scotland and Ireland. Discipline was tightened in both of them, and standards were raised as a result. Information for Scotland is hard to come by, but the church-court records show that prosecution for marital irregularities of different kinds remained a powerful social deterrent for many. It was relatively easy for Scotsmen to leave the established Church and join one of the breakaway presbyterian groups, but as these tended to be stricter than the national church, their attraction was limited.

In Ireland the established Church became more English than it had ever been before (or than it has been since), with many of the higher clergy being imported from across the water. The Irish Convocation met in tandem with the Canterbury one in Queen Anne's reign, but its internal divisions were less serious and it was able to enact legislation for the improvement of the ministry. If anything, its standards were higher than those of the Church of England in almost every way, a fact that might have owed something to the ever-present Presbyterians in Ulster and Roman Catholics everywhere. Both of those bodies followed a pattern similar to that of their counterparts in Great Britain, although their numbers did not dwindle. Catholics remained about 75–80% of the population, while Presbyterians accounted for another 8%. Statistics are hard to come by, but the Presbyterians declined in numbers as the eighteenth century progressed, largely because so many of them emigrated to America. They were to play a significant role in American life, especially after the Revolution, even as their influence at home began to decline.

The strength of the Church of Ireland lay in the fact that the so-called 'political nation' (those who could vote and take part in civic affairs) all belonged to it. This was of great help in attracting state subsidies, which were given to it on a generous scale through the Board of First Fruits, a body set up to administer church finances. As a result the Church of Ireland was a disproportionately rich body in a poor country, an unjust situation that could not last. As time went on, the government realized that it had to grant relief to both Catholics and Dissenters (mostly Presbyterians) as well, and to some extent did so, although without diminishing the privileged position of the state church. In 1782 the Irish Parliament was prevailed upon to allow Catholics to own land, and ten years later they were permitted to practise law. In 1793 they were even given the right to vote on the same terms as Protestants, something then virtually unique in the British world.[8] The enforced closure of Catholic seminaries in Continental Europe following the French Revolution led the British government to support the founding of an Irish seminary at Maynooth, which was even accorded a grant for its maintenance. As a result, when rebellion against the Crown broke out in 1798, the Catholic Church condemned the rebellion outright.

The rebellion was led by Wolfe Tone, a renegade Protestant, and supported by Presbyterians and some Catholics, who turned it into an anti-Protestant crusade when they got the chance. It failed, and when the British government decided to unite Ireland to Great Britain, the Catholic hierarchy supported the move, believing that they would be better treated by a British than an Irish Protestant Parliament. Ironically, the union was opposed by the Church of Ireland, which feared a serious loss of influence. It was right to be concerned. In the union Parliament, which met for the first time in 1801, Irish episcopal representation was limited to four bishops, who served in rotation for one session at a time, making it virtually impossible for any one of them to gain the parliamentary experience necessary to represent the church's interests adequately. When those interests were threatened, as they would be in the mid-nineteenth century, the Church of Ireland would pay a heavy price for its 'union' with the Church of England. Meanwhile Catholics would also be disappointed, because the emancipation they had hoped the union would bring did not materialize. Many have blamed this on the intransigence of King George III (1760–1820), who refused to compromise the oath he had taken at his coronation to uphold the Protestant faith; but although his attitude was

---

[8] The only other place where Roman Catholic British subjects could vote was Canada, where they had been granted the right in 1791. But unlike the Canadians, Irish Catholics could not sit in the parliament – they could only elect Protestants to represent them there.

certainly unhelpful, it was not the only factor involved. The lingering anti-Catholicism of both England and Scotland also played an important part, and the memory of the Gordon riots, which was still fresh, did at least as much as the king to delay a just resolution of the problem for almost another generation.

The Evangelical Revival

The conservative reaction to Enlightenment deism was important, but like deism itself, it touched only a small number of people – the intellectual elite who discussed such deep questions. The tendency for the established churches to recoup ground lost in the Civil War and afterwards was more widely felt, but it was gradual and hardly noticed by most of those affected by it. Things were very different with what came to be called the 'Evangelical Revival'.[9] This was a spiritual movement among Protestants that transcended existing categories and eventually transformed both the religious landscape and the secular society of the British Isles.[10]

Evangelicalism, as we know it, traces its origins to late seventeenth-century Germany.[11] The religious settlement there had divided the country into Protestant and Catholic states, with the former being further subdivided into Lutheran and Reformed. These groups had their own confessions of faith and little love was lost between them. Many people knew that it was inherently absurd to suppose that the inhabitants of Saxony had the 'truth' whereas those of the Palatinate did not – the Holy Spirit does not work along such territorial lines and some allowance had to be made for the possibility that true believers might be found in other churches, even if they had a different confession of faith and were not in communion with each other. These people were driven back to consider what the fundamentals of Christianity were. It was not so much a matter of doctrine, although they were fully orthodox and insisted on that. It was more a question of experience and practice. How many people in the churches were genuinely filled with the Spirit of Christ? Did their lives bear any relation to the beliefs they officially confessed? Honest observers had to

---

[9] In Germany it was known as Pietism and in the United States as the Great Awakening. For an overview of the Evangelical movement, see K. Hylson-Smith, *Evangelicals in the Church of England 1734–1984* (Edinburgh: T&T Clark, 1988).

[10] See e.g. B. Hilton, *The Age of Atonement: The Influence of Evangelicalism on Social and Economic Thought 1795–1865* (Oxford: Clarendon Press, 1991); W. Gibson and J. Begiato, *Sex and the Church in the Long Eighteenth Century* (London: I. B. Tauris, 2017).

[11] See W. R. Ward, *Early Evangelicalism: A Global Intellectual History, 1670–1789* (Cambridge: Cambridge University Press, 2006); D. B. Hindmarsh, *The Spirit of Early Evangelicalism: True Religion in a Modern World* (Oxford: Oxford University Press, 2018).

admit that German Protestantism was a series of very mixed bags, and they despaired that the state authorities, who were charged with maintaining spiritual standards, were almost invariably more interested in external conformity than in internal transformation into the image and likeness of Christ.

The German situation was further complicated by the existence of groups that were neither Lutheran nor Reformed in the standard sense of those terms. There were still some Mennonites and other Anabaptists around, but few people bothered with them. More important were the Moravians, a Protestant group that traced its origins back to Jan Hus and that had thrown its lot in with the Lutherans without becoming disciples of Luther or of his followers. They were severely persecuted in their native Moravia (now part of the Czech Republic) and many were seeking refuge elsewhere. They practised what we might call 'mere Christianity', a practical faith that stuck to basics and avoided complex theological debates over the sacraments or predestination.

It was to this group that Count Nikolaus von Zinzendorf (1700–60) was drawn, after an education among the Pietists at their newly founded university of Halle. He offered them refuge on his estate, where they built the model village of Herrnhut. But Zinzendorf was not just a philanthropist wanting to help some unfortunate people out. He was deeply committed to the ideals of the group, joined it and transformed its outlook and behaviour. From being a small and isolated community, the Moravians spread out to extend their message of basic Christianity to a much wider world. Before long they had chapels in England and even a few colonies in America. Zinzendorf himself went everywhere and met everyone he could. He even reached out to Roman Catholics and the Eastern Orthodox, and for that reason has a fair claim to be considered the first modern ecumenist.

The Moravians came to exercise an influence on the nascent Evangelicalism out of all proportion to their numbers, but they were not the only ones who longed for spiritual renewal. In England and Wales a faithful remnant of Puritans remained both within and outside the national church. It is generally stated nowadays that the leadership of the Church of England abandoned Puritanism more or less completely after the Restoration, but this is an exaggeration. Even if the anti-Puritan party was in power, there was still a large contingent of Puritans and Puritan sympathizers lower down the scale.[12] As the Restoration turned sour in many people's minds, this semi-underground Puritanism began to seem more attractive and started to gain in strength,

---

[12] On this seriously under-researched subject, see S. Hampton, *Anti-Arminians: The Anglican Reformed Tradition from Charles II to George I* (Oxford: Oxford University Press, 2008).

although imperceptibly at first. It was a situation similar to that encountered by the prophet Elijah in ancient Israel. When Elijah despaired of the nation's apostasy, God reminded him that there were still 7,000 who had not bowed the knee to Baal, and told him that it was his duty to return and minister to them.[13] Likewise, post-Restoration England contained a remnant who had remained faithful to the Puritan gospel, and from among them a new generation of prophets would emerge.[14]

The developments at Herrnhut and the smouldering embers of English Puritanism came together in 1737, when Zinzendorf visited England. Ten years earlier the Moravians had experienced a collective revival, which had spurred them towards mission and evangelism, and it was not long before the results started to show. An initial foray into England faltered, but by 1734 the Moravians were cooperating with Thomas Bray's successors to establish a mission in the new colony of Georgia. They were also attracting the favourable notice of High Churchmen like the redoubtable Thomas Wilson (1663–1755), Bishop of Sodor and Man from 1698 and the longest-serving prelate in the history of the Anglican Communion. Wilson was an outlier in the British world. He had been ordained in Dublin in 1687, when (thanks to James II) the city was under Catholic control, but although he submitted to William III, his political loyalty remained somewhat suspect. He was a man of considerable ability and deserved a bishopric, but his dubious background meant he was sent to the Isle of Man, which was part of the Church of England but not politically tied to the country. Nobody could have foreseen it at the time, but Wilson made the most of his anomalous position and transformed his tiny diocese of seventeen parishes into a model Christian Commonwealth.

Wilson was a friend of Thomas Bray and shared his outlook. He established parish libraries on Man, published the first books in the Manx language and generally did his utmost to train and equip islanders for the task of mission to their own people, something he himself found difficult because he was not conversant in Manx. He even set up a Manx Convocation, which to this day continues to meet in tandem with the island's parliament, the Tynwald.[15] Because of this, the tiny diocese of Sodor and Man is the only one of which

---

[13] 1 Kgs 19:18.

[14] See Hylson-Smith, *Evangelicals*, 17–32. Hylson-Smith points out that a number of clergymen in the early eighteenth century experienced an Evangelical type of conversion without being in contact with one another. It was only later, as a recognizable movement developed and spread, that connections with (and among) them were established.

[15] See G. L. Bray (ed.), *Records of Convocation*, 20 vols. (Woodbridge: Boydell & Brewer, 2005–6), vols. 1 and 2. Since the establishment of synodical government in 1970 the Manx Convocation has had only a residual significance, not unlike that of the English convocations. For a general history of the Manx Church, see J. D. Gelling, *A History of the Manx Church (1698–1911)* (Douglas: Manx Heritage Foundation, 1998).

we have detailed day-to-day knowledge in the eighteenth century, since the records of the Convocation are preserved and tell us a great deal about the church on Man. Wilson did not have an easy time of it. He was opposed by the dukes of Atholl, who governed the Isle under the protection of the English Crown, until the latter reclaimed its rights in the so-called 'revestment' of 1765. Poor Wilson even went to prison for his beliefs, the closest thing to martyrdom that the Church of England has produced since the Civil War period.

Wilson was the kind of man the Moravians attracted, but he was by no means alone in his admiration for them. In 1735 George Whitefield (1714–70) had a conversion experience, as did the Welshman Hywel (Howell) Harris (1714–73). Shortly afterwards they were followed by another Welshman, Daniel Rowland (1711–90). All three men were to have an enormous impact through their preaching and teaching ministry, but in the eyes of posterity they would be eclipsed by the larger-than-life figure of John Wesley, with whose name the Revival will for ever be associated.

At first glance, Wesley was not the sort of person one would expect to find at the heart of a revival movement. His father, Samuel, was a noted High Churchman and decidedly anti-Puritan, when most of the early revivalists were the opposite. Wesley took after his father theologically, and this was to prove a bone of contention – and of division – in the revival movement. He thought of himself as an 'Arminian' and used the word quite freely – at one point he even edited a magazine called *The Arminian*. But the way in which Wesley and his contemporaries used this term had little to do with the Dutch theologian Jacob Arminius, after whom the doctrine was named, or even with Archbishop William Laud, who had (erroneously) been tarred with that label.[16] To Wesley an Arminian was above all someone who rejected the doctrine of double predestination and the belief in limited (definite) atonement that went with it. For him Christ had died for everybody, and it was up to each individual to decide whether to take up the divine offer of salvation or not. When he looked at the orthodox party in the Church of England, Wesley saw people who had so emphasized the work of God in salvation that they refused to evangelize at all. In their distorted view God had chosen whom he wanted to be saved and no human being had any right to interfere in what was exclusively his work.

That was a caricature of the so-called 'Calvinist' view of course, and those whom Wesley criticized scarcely recognized themselves in it. They believed

---

[16] In some ways Wesley was closer to the Calvinism of John Owen than to the classical Arminians. See A. C. Clifford, *Atonement and Justification: English Evangelical Theology 1640–1790 – An Evaluation* (Oxford: Clarendon Press, 1990).

that they were called to preach the gospel, and that God would open the eyes of those who had been chosen for salvation. This might appear in the form of a personal 'decision for Christ', but such a decision was possible only if the Spirit of God was at work in the heart of the hearer. The evangelist was like the sower of Matthew 13:1–9, 18–23. The sower scatters his seed everywhere and it falls on different kinds of ground, but only that which lands on good soil will bear fruit – and the sower does not determine where that good soil is to be found. The evangelist must therefore expect rejection and failure in many cases, but his efforts will be crowned with success if he perseveres – not because he has done anything to deserve it, but because God is in control.

The Moravians were blissfully ignorant of these divisions within the Church of England. They cooperated with High Churchmen and gained their trust, and they worked with men like Whitefield too. In 1735 John Wesley set out for Georgia as part of the Bray mission, and stayed there for the better part of two years. Unfortunately the seed he sowed during that time fell on stony ground, and he returned to England discouraged and depressed. On his journeys across the Atlantic he happened to meet some Moravians, who told him of their mission and experience. What Wesley probably would never have accepted from somebody like Whitefield he was prepared to receive from foreigners who cut across the familiar English dividing lines. When he got back to England, he visited the Moravian chapel in Aldersgate Street in London, and it was there, on the evening of 24 May 1738, that he felt his heart 'strangely warmed' and that he was fully and irrevocably converted to the gospel of Christ.[17] After that he never looked back.

Wesley's experience in Aldersgate Street has become the stuff of legend and is now often regarded as the true beginning of the Evangelical Revival. But as with all such things, the origins can be traced further back. Wesley himself thought that the so-called 'Holy Club', founded by his brother Charles in Oxford in 1729, was the beginning of the new movement, and the spiritual disciplines the Club encouraged became an integral part of his future ministry. It was there that the methodical approach to devotion gave rise to the term 'Methodist' that would later be applied to the revivalists, whether they were followers of Wesley or not. One of the members of this Holy Club was George Whitefield, who joined it in 1732, three years before his conversion. The memory of that ensured that in later years, when the Wesleys and Whitefield fell out over theological questions, their personal relations remained cordial and respectful, because Whitefield never forgot what he owed to Charles

---

[17] J. Wesley, *The Journal of John Wesley*, ed. N. Curnock, 8 vols. (London: Epworth Press, 1931), 1:476.

Wesley. In fact it was Charles who suggested Whitefield ought to go to Georgia to carry on the mission work he and his brother John had attempted. Whitefield did so, beginning an association with the American colonies that was to take him up and down the Atlantic seaboard until his death in Connecticut in 1770.

Whitefield's frequent absences from Britain lessened his influence on the way the Revival developed, but he remained a force to be reckoned with. On a return visit to England in 1739, he preached to a company of miners in Kingswood, near Bristol, and did so in the open air. This was a new departure, and caused a sensation. Hundreds, then thousands, flocked to hear him, but he also attracted opposition from the authorities, who feared public disorder. John Wesley was initially disconcerted by this technique but he was soon won over, and open-air preaching became a hallmark of the Revival. Not everybody was pleased by this, and people in London pelted Whitefield with rotten eggs and fruit when he stood up to preach, but he persevered and his courage soon won the majority over. To the astonishment of many, including such well-known figures as Horace Walpole, the king's First Minister, and Benjamin Franklin, Whitefield was able to hold congregations spellbound for hours, and conversions rivalled the scenes in Jerusalem on the first Christian Pentecost.[18]

At this stage the revivalists were working together and supporting one another, but trouble was not long in coming. Some of the Moravians, who in the initial stages were virtually indistinguishable from the so-called 'Methodists', reacted against the emotionalism they witnessed and advocated a quiet waiting on God in place of what they saw as a riotous explosion of animal spirits among the newly converted. Wesley saw that as unacceptable mysticism and a departure from Luther's teaching about the power of the Word of God to transform its hearers. Relations between him and the Moravians started to cool, particularly when it began to seem that the Moravians would take over the Revival movement. Fitful discussions, involving Zinzendorf himself, failed to resolve their differences. Wesley could not understand Zinzendorf's insistence that the grace of God poured out on the believer did not automatically produce a growth in sanctification, whereas Zinzendorf was appalled by what he saw as Wesley's belief in the possibility of Christian 'perfection'. It is probable that the two sides were not as far apart as they believed they were, but neither was in the mood for compromise and so they drifted apart.

At the same time another controversy, and one that was to prove much more divisive, arose – over predestination. Whitefield and the Welsh Methodists were of Puritan background, whereas Wesley was not. Just as the latter called

---

18 Acts 2:37–41.

himself an 'Arminian', so the former came to label themselves 'Calvinists', perhaps with somewhat more justification. Unfortunately there were some extreme 'Calvinists', known nowadays as 'hyper-Calvinists', who pushed the doctrine of predestination to the point where they eschewed any form of evangelism. Wesley was understandably outraged at such a doctrine and roundly condemned it, although without specifying that the 'Calvinism' he was attacking was an extreme form that Whitefield and his colleagues did not accept. The result was further division, exacerbated by the Calvinists' rejection of Wesley's perfectionist notions. Wesley responded positively to Whitefield's pleas to tone down his criticisms of predestination, but their followers were less accommodating and division over this key theological doctrine did not disappear. After Whitefield's death in 1770 it would resurface with a vengeance and lead to a permanent schism among the Methodists.

But disagreements within the Revival movement were as nothing compared to the opposition the revivalists faced from others. It is no exaggeration to say that revivalism caught the church unawares and nobody really knew what to do about it. There were sober voices, like those of Edmund Gibson and Joseph Butler, who saw the dangers in unfettered enthusiasm and were quick to denounce the excesses they perceived. There is no doubt that the revivalists were riding the crest of a spiritual wave they could not control, and sometimes what started as an orderly meeting turned into a riot. This was especially likely to happen when converts came from socially disadvantaged groups that used their newfound enthusiasm to press for economic and political reforms. Radicalism of that kind would become common in the nineteenth century and lead eventually to the formation of what is now the Labour Party and the trade unions (whose local associations are still sometimes known as 'chapels'), and its beginnings were understandably feared by the landowning Tory Establishment. But plenty of other people were upset too. Ordinary workers did not want to be told that they could not drink, play games or gamble, and the non-enthusiastic clergy were offended when young revivalist preachers denounced them as non-Christians.

For their part, the leaders of the Revival were not slow to repudiate their own pre-conversion lives as a failure, and to emphasize the need for spiritual rebirth, something that inevitably left those who had not had that experience out in the cold. For many, this was the aspect of Evangelicalism that caused the greatest heart-searching – and the greatest offence. To become an Evangelical was to embrace a form of Christianity that had little time for formal religion. People became Christians not by being baptized but by being converted, and it soon became apparent that although many were called (baptized) few were chosen (converted).[19] Even two centuries later, when the impact of the Wesleys, Whitefield and their colleagues could not be denied, there were churchmen who continued to regard John Wesley's conversion as problematic, because it effectively denied the authenticity of his earlier spiritual life.[20]

As the Revival matured, its leaders toned their rhetoric down and became more tolerant of those whose lives had followed a less dramatic path, but the distinction between Evangelicals and others did not go away. The former continued to believe they were the most authentic (if not necessarily the only) Christians, with the result that others were alienated or hostile in varying degrees. Evangelicals found it hard to be ordained and were often discriminated against. Many were forced into a form of dissent because they were refused permission to open places of worship to meet the growing need. Their willingness to train lay leaders and experiment with new forms of worship more suited to the unlearned aroused suspicion, and the inability (or unwillingness) of many bishops and others in authority to distinguish between moderate, orthodox Evangelicalism and the lunacy of some on the radical fringe merely deepened division. Over time, Evangelicals would establish themselves in both the state and dissenting churches but they have always remained outsiders. To this day their spiritual experience is more important to them than their denominational affiliation (if they have one), with the result that they neither fully trust nor are fully trusted by those in the institutional churches who are of a different spiritual outlook.

What did the leaders of the Evangelical Revival believe and teach? They were thoroughly orthodox in their theology, regarding the Bible as the written Word of God and embracing the creeds of the ancient church, along with the Thirty-nine Articles of Religion or (in Scotland) the Westminster Confession of Faith. They might have their disagreements about predestination and occasionally some inadvertently fell into heresy, as did Hywel Harris, when he taught that the Father had suffered along with the Son on the cross. That error cost him the fellowship of men like George Whitefield, but it was a mistake on Harris's part, more than a deliberate deviation from the truth, and it had no lasting impact. What united the revivalists was far greater than what divided them, and it is this core of common belief that makes it possible to characterize them as representatives of a single movement.

---

[19] See Matt. 22:14. In eighteenth-century Britain virtually the entire population was baptized, but only a minority became Evangelicals.

[20] Thus J. R. H. Moorman, *A History of the Church in England*, 3rd edn (London: A&C Black, 1973), 298–302, consistently spoke of Wesley's 'conversion' in inverted commas, as if he could not bring himself to believe it was real.

The first, and in some ways most important, ingredient of their teaching was the total depravity of the human race. Anyone who wanted to enjoy the gift of God in Christ had first to come to a confession of his/her sinfulness and a realization that no amount of human endeavour could do anything to put a man or woman right with God. This was authentic Christian teaching of course, but although there was no trouble finding it in the New Testament, the works of Augustine and of the Protestant Reformers, experiencing total depravity as an overwhelming sense of lostness was another matter. Few people really had that deep conviction of their own sinfulness or desperate desire to 'flee from the wrath to come' that marked the spirit of the true believer. Those who did were not concerned with secondary matters like forms of worship – they were longing to find peace with God and assurance that they were going to heaven.[21]

Those who felt the burden of sin were set free by the gospel of the redeeming Christ, who had paid the penalty demanded by God's justice when Christ died on the cross, and whose Holy Spirit now put the assurance of faith into their hearts. The task was then to work out their salvation in fear and trembling and, in order to do that more effectively, John Wesley grouped newly converted believers together in what were termed 'class meetings', or 'house groups' as we would call them today. In these small groups, consisting of about twelve persons each, members would confess their sins and support one another as they sought God's grace to transform their lives. This was the heart of Methodism. Belief by itself was not enough: there had to be a corresponding amendment of life, which was what made the difference. Evangelicals were admired by some – and often feared or mocked by others – because they were changed people. As they expressed it, they were 'born again' to a new life, 'following the commandments of God and walking from henceforth in his holy ways', a familiar exhortation that preceded Holy Communion in the Book of Common Prayer but was now brought to life in their experience.

Inevitably a movement as spiritually demanding as the Evangelical Revival would have its share of failures. Some respondents were initially caught up in the emotion of it all but fell away when the temptations of this world got the better of them. Others went to extremes, sometimes with the example of their leaders to encourage them. The overpowering compulsion to preach the gospel far and wide led some men to desert their families, and there were failed

---

[21] D. B. Hindmarsh, *The Evangelical Conversion Narrative: Spiritual Autobiography in Early Modern England* (Oxford: Oxford University Press, 2005).

marriages to account for – including John Wesley's own. Zeal had a way of outrunning knowledge, and the fact that so many Methodists were from the lower orders of society did not help. A few rose above the limitations of their lack of education and became learned divines in their own right, but many lapsed into simplistic interpretations of Scripture, especially where moral behaviour was concerned. A form of Pharisaism took hold in some quarters, so that outward conformity to certain rules came to be seen as a proof of godliness, while the weightier matters of the law, like justice and mercy, were lost or banished in the name of discipline and commitment. In extreme cases there were even false prophets who arose to deceive the elect. One of these, a Devon woman called Joanna Southcott (1750–1814), attracted a considerable following that to some extent persisted even when it had become obvious her claims were false.

As the Revival grew larger, differences of approach became more obvious and led to forms of division that might have been prevented if more thought had been given to them at the time. Chief among these was the divide between those who clung to the established Church and its constraints and those who broke the bounds of convention and set out on new paths. It might be thought that the Wesleys would have been among the former group, but they were not. Much as they desired to remain within the Establishment and refused to countenance separation from it, they found themselves propelled by the development of their own movement to appoint men who would be able to supervise their congregations independently of the parish system. One thing led to another, and soon they were licensing such men to take Communion services and behave in ways that until then only the parish clergy would have done. At the same time, the ministry of these men was usually itinerant in ways the Establishment could not countenance. No clergyman could preach freely in another man's parish, but the Wesleyans did so and in the process found themselves in the position of Dissenters, whether they wanted to be or not. Meanwhile other Evangelicals managed to get ordained within the Church of England and stuck to the traditional parish ministry, believing that that was where God had called them to serve.

These two approaches could sometimes be reconciled and there were cases of parish clergymen cooperating with visiting Methodist preachers, as well as of Methodists refraining from preaching in places where there was already an Evangelical clergyman. But these cases became increasingly exceptional, and it was more usual for the two types of minister to rival each other and end up in conflict. After the Wesleys died, this conflict grew sharper, and in the early nineteenth century it led to separation – the parish Evangelicals stayed within the Church of England and the Methodists went their own way as a separate denomination.[22]

Yet when all is said and done, the positive impact of the Evangelical Revival far outweighed the negative consequences that accompanied it. For the first time in British history large numbers of laypeople were touched by the Spirit of God and were determined to take control of their spiritual lives, whatever the church authorities might say. In a sense it was the fulfilment of what had been promised by the Reformation and the rise of Puritanism, but had never been realized. Christianity at last moved out of the cloister, liberated itself from the tutelage of a clerical class all too often unworthy of its high calling, and became accessible to the masses. A church in which all believers were priests, where God did not dwell in temples made with hands and where the Word of God was freely available to everyone, had finally come into being. It was not always welcome and many traditionalists felt threatened by it, but its message would not be dislodged. From that time onwards the state would no longer be able to tell people what to believe, and the institutional church would lose whatever residual power it still had to discipline the laity. It was a new world.

The sound of music

Today when people think of church, one of the first things that comes to mind is the singing. For years *Songs of Praise* has been the most popular religious programme on the BBC and it is not unusual for worshippers to comment on the music they hear during a service. That may vary from classical highbrow compositions at the higher end to choruses and guitars at the lower, but singing there will almost certainly be. A few people may comment on the sermon or the version of the Bible being read, but they are a tiny minority compared to those who choose a church because of its 'worship style', by which they mean its musical offerings. It therefore comes as something of a shock when they discover that until the eighteenth century congregational singing played little part in Christian worship. Hymns and 'spiritual songs' had existed since the beginning of course, and there had always been choirs to sing them, especially in cathedrals and collegiate churches. But ordinary worshippers in a local church were unlikely to have heard more than the psalms, chanted or sung in a metrical version, and usually a cappella. As late as 1662 the Book of Common Prayer made no provision for hymns, and in the early 1700s they were rarely heard outside a few dissenting chapels, most of them Baptist.

---

[22] See Hylson-Smith, *Evangelicals*, 33–37.

All this was to change dramatically in the eighteenth century. After the Restoration there was a growing public interest in secular concerts and this gradually spilled over into the church. In Germany, Lutheran organists, of whom the acknowledged master was Johann Sebastian Bach (1685–1750), began to compose majestic pieces of music, including choir pieces for use during worship. When the house of Hanover ascended the British throne in 1714, elements of that tradition began to appear in Britain. By far the best-known composer of that type was Georg Friedrich Handel or, more properly, Händel (1685–1759), who settled in London as early as 1712 and so was already established there when the Hanoverians arrived two years later. Handel quickly became a leading figure on London's musical scene, and his deep faith, which had been nurtured in German Pietism, was very much in evidence. At the coronation of George II in 1727 his *Zadok the Priest* was performed for the first time and ever since then it has been a staple of coronations. More famous still was his *Messiah*, an oratorio comparable to those of Bach, which became and has remained a perennial favourite with the public. It sets the words of the King James Bible to music, making people who have never read the text familiar with its haunting cadences.

The new thirst for music was quickly seized upon by the Wesleys, and in particular Charles, John's younger brother. They both understood that one of the best ways to inculcate deep theology into the minds of ordinary people was to set it to music, and before long hymn singing, as we now recognize it, was born. Everywhere Methodists went they took their hymns with them, and singing soon became a hallmark of their revival meetings. John and Charles both composed verses and issued collections of them for popular use – fifty-seven to be exact, in the space of fifty-three years. The culmination of their work was the great Methodist Hymn Book of 1780, which soon became for the Methodists what the Book of Common Prayer was for the Church of England. Perhaps inevitably, much of their verse is of low quality, and some of it is pure doggerel. Of the more than 1,000 hymns they wrote, only about 200 are ever sung today, but those that are retain their place among the great glories of the English language, and their Evangelical message comes across loud and clear:

And can it be that I should gain
An interest in the Saviour's blood?
Died he for me who caused his pain,
For me whom him to death pursued?
Amazing love, how can it be!
That thou, my Lord, shouldst die for me.

Long my imprisoned spirit lay
Fast bound in sin and nature's night
Thine eye diffused its quickening ray
I woke, the dungeon flamed with light
My chains fell off, my heart was free
I rose, went forth and followed thee.

No condemnation now I dread
Jesus and all in him is mine
Alive in him, my living head
And clothed in righteousness divine
Bold I approach the eternal throne
And claim the crown of Christ my own.

Hymn writing caught on and even became a medium through which theological debates were conducted. The most bitter of these was the ongoing quarrel between the 'Calvinists' and 'Arminians'. One of the most vocal controversialists on the Calvinist side was Augustus Toplady (1740–78), whose ministry was cut short by an early death but who has left us some stirring hymns of his own:

Rock of Ages, cleft for me
Let me hide myself in thee
Let the water and the blood
From thy riven side which flowed
Be of sin the double cure
Cleanse me from its guilt and power.

Not the labours of my hands
Can fulfil thy law's demands
Could my zeal no respite know
Could my tears for ever flow
All for sin could not atone
Thou must save and thou alone.

Nothing in my hand I bring
Simply to thy cross I cling
Naked come to thee for dress
Helpless look to thee for grace

Foul I to the fountain fly
Wash me Saviour, or I die.

When I draw this fleeting breath
When my eyes shall close in death
When I soar to realms unknown
See thee on thy judgment throne
Rock of Ages cleft for me
Let me hide myself in thee.

The symbolism of the Rock that followed the people of Israel in their forty-year journey through the wilderness of Sinai, which the apostle Paul identified as Christ,[23] is a reminder to us that many of the hymn writers stressed the unity of God's covenant with Israel and the church by writing lyrics that could have come straight out of the Old Testament. Thomas Olivers (1725–99) for example took the Jewish canticle *Yigdal* and turned it into English as 'The God of Abraham praise', which is still sung in churches. This renewed appreciation for the Hebrew Bible and Jewish tradition would help pave the way for Jewish emancipation in the nineteenth century and for the deep sense of belonging to the covenant people of God that is so typical of Evangelicalism, and not only in the English-speaking world.

Even before the Methodist Hymn Book appeared in 1780, there was another collection on the Calvinist side that would become famous as a source of English hymnody. This was the *Olney Hymns*, a collection put together by John Newton (1725–1807) and William Cowper – pronounced 'Cooper' (1731–1800). Newton was a former slave trader who had been converted and become curate of Olney (Buckinghamshire) in 1764.[24] Cowper, a melancholy soul, was eventually driven to suicide by his illness. For a few short years in the 1770s the two men worked together in Olney to produce hymns that could be sung in church, and not just at Revival meetings. Newton's greatest hymn testifies to his own conversion experience and reminds us of what lay at the heart of the Revival:

Amazing grace! How sweet the sound
That saved a wretch like me.
I once was lost but now am found
Was blind, but now I see.

---

[23] 1 Cor. 10:4.
[24] See D. B. Hindmarsh, *John Newton and the English Evangelical Tradition* (Oxford: Clarendon Press, 1996).

'Twas grace that taught my heart to fear
And grace my fears relieved!
How blessed did that grace appear
The hour I first believed.

Through many dangers, toils and snares
I am already come.
'Twas grace that brought me safe thus far
And grace shall lead me home.

Cowper's own testimony is less dramatic but all the more remarkable given his disturbed mental condition:

Oh for a closer walk with God,
A calm and heavenly frame,
A light to shine upon the road
That leads me to the Lamb.

The breadth of range and depth of feeling poured out in the hymns of the Evangelical Revival have never since been equalled. Remarkably perhaps, they have managed to cross the great divide between the Calvinists and the Arminians, so that today the descendants of both sides sing each other's hymns, blissfully unaware of the theological passions that drove their authors. Antagonists in this world, the Wesleys and Toplady have been reconciled in the piety of the church, which preserves the memory of all three men and honours them for their contribution to the spiritual life of their progeny.

The Welsh Revival

Mention of hymnody leads almost inevitably to a consideration of the spiritual state of Wales, which was impacted by the Revival more than any other part of the British Isles. Before the eighteenth century, Wales was not really a nation but a mountainous refuge where the ancient Britons had held out against their Anglo-Saxon conquerors for more than a thousand years. After 1536 it was fully integrated with England and had no identity of its own, apart from its Celtic language, which survived better than Gaelic did in Scotland or Ireland. There had long been a Welsh Bible and clergy who could preach in Welsh, but on the whole the church was seen as an agent of anglicization, and was promoted as such. The Revival could not stop that process, which had been going on for centuries and is now nearly complete, but it did give the Welsh language a new lease of life and Welsh culture acquired a musical tradition for which the country is still famous. Revival had broken out in Wales even before John Wesley's conversion, and was largely 'Calvinist' in orientation. Wesleyan chapels were slow to take root there and the Calvinistic Methodists, who in 1928 would rename themselves the Presbyterian Church in Wales, dominated the field.

The Calvinistic Methodists preached and conducted worship in either English or Welsh, depending on the locality, but it was in the latter language that they excelled. Welsh preachers, filled with that unique Celtic fire known as the *hwyl*, stirred people up all over the country. Their itinerant ministries gave them, and the people to whom they ministered, the sense of belonging to a nation that transcended the valleys in which they lived. As in England, the leadership was mostly drawn from the ranks of the ordained Anglican clergy, and there was no thought of separation from the established Church. But the social structure of Wales was such that it was easy for the anglicized elite, and an episcopate that generally had no knowledge of the local language, to feel threatened, and opposition to the Methodists was strong. In the circumstances the loyalty of these clergymen to their church is remarkable. Thomas Charles (1755–1814) trained under John Newton at Olney and then returned to his native Wales, where he sought employment in the church. He was initially successful but his Evangelical credentials worked against him and before long he was dismissed from his charge near Bala. In 1784 he was forced to join the Calvinistic Methodists in order to make a living, but it would not be until 1811 that he finally agreed to ordain Calvinistic Methodist ministers. Until then he tried to remain a loyal son of the Church of England, even though it rejected his services.

It was in 1800 that Charles was visited at Bala by a 15-year-old girl called Mary Jones, who had gone there in search of a Welsh Bible. She had saved up to buy one, but there were none to be had and Charles, deeply moved by her plight, resolved to do something about it. Gathering friends from both Wales and England, he helped to set up the British and Foreign Bible Society in 1804. It was to become a major element of the missionary endeavours of the nineteenth century, and is still very active, having spawned branch-and-daughter societies in most countries of the world.

Another Welshman who fell foul of the church was William Williams (1717–91), better known by his bardic name of Pantycelyn. Williams was ordained a deacon in 1740 but was never priested, because he soon became an itinerant preacher who could not be tied down to a single parish. Pantycelyn wrote almost exclusively in Welsh and his great hymns are still sung in both his mother tongue and in English translation. One in particular is a perennial favourite, and the English version shows us how deeply the imagery of the Old Testament penetrated his perception of Christ:

Arglwydd, arwain trwy'r anialwch	Guide me O thou great Jehovah
Fi, bererin gwael ei wedd.	Pilgrim through this barren land
Nad oes ynof nerth na bywyd	I am weak but thou art mighty
Fel yn gorwedd yn y bedd	Hold me with thy powerful hand
Hollalluog, hollalluog	Bread of heaven, bread of heaven
Ydyw'r Un a'm cwyd i'r lân.	Feed me till I want no more!
Colofn dân rho'r nôs i'm harwain	Open thou the crystal fountain
A rho'r golofn niwl y dydd;	Whence thy healing stream doth flow
Dal fi pan bwy'n teithio'r manau	Let the fire and cloudy pillar
Geirwon yn y ffordd y sydd;	Lead me all my journey through
Rho i mi fanna, rho i mi fanna	Strong deliverer, strong deliverer
Fel na bwyf yn llwfrhau.	Be thou still my strength and shield!
Pan fwy'n myned trwy'r Iorddonen	When I tread the verge of Jordan
Angeu creulon yn ei rym	Bid my anxious fears subside
Ti est trwyddi gynt dy hunan	Death of death and hell's destruction
P'am yr ofnaf bellach ddim?	Land me safe on Canaan's side
Buddugoliaeth, buddugoliaeth	Songs of praises, songs of praises,
Gwna imi waeddi yn y llif![25]	I will ever give to thee.

Opposition to the Revival from the established Church was only to be expected, but was to have more serious consequences in Wales than in England. The Revival brought a distinctively Welsh form of Christianity into being, which made the Anglican Establishment seem even more alien than it was. Before long, active members of the Church of England were a minority in the country and resentment over its status began to grow. It took a century to mature, but by 1914 Parliament was legislating for the disestablishment of the church in Wales. The outbreak of war postponed it to 31 March 1920, by which time some of the proponents of the measure were starting to regret it, but it was too late to change course. The formal separation of church and state, which nobody could have foreseen in the late eighteenth century and which few at

---

[25] This is the original Welsh text. The version usually sung today differs in the second and third stanzas, which are closer to the English translation.

that time desired, was destined to be one of the most enduring results of the Evangelical Revival in Wales.

Daughters of Zion

The role of women in the history of Christianity has varied over time, but it would be fair to say that, apart from exceptional figures like the queens regnant who took an interest in church affairs, they were not very prominent in the British Isles before the eighteenth century. The Evangelical Revival changed all that. From the beginning, women played a prominent part in it, and not just as behind-the-scenes supporters of male evangelists. Of course, support of that kind was not lacking and it went back a long way, as we have already seen. But the Revival gave women a new opportunity to exercise their spiritual gifts. The creation of class meetings, consisting of only a dozen or so people, allowed them to minister in small-group settings. This may not seem much to those expecting to play more public roles, but the class meetings were an important vehicle for the spread of the gospel message, and they should not be discounted as being of little significance. Being as numerous and widespread as they were made it possible for large numbers of women to be involved, something that had never happened before. Just as many of the male leaders of these meetings rose to prominence from humble origins, so women's voices were given an outlet that would lead to greater things in the future.

Women of higher social standing were of course in a better position to take part in events and influence their outcome. One was Hannah More (1745–1833), who had begun her career as a dramatist in London but was converted to Evangelical faith sometime in the 1780s. She became a friend and associate of men like John Newton, and was active in the establishment of charity schools and in various movements for the 'reformation of manners'. She wrote a large number of tracts on various spiritual matters that were intended for popular distribution, and in 1799 she helped to found the Religious Tract Society, which still exists.

More important still was Selina, Countess of Huntingdon (1707–91), who supported the Methodists from as early as 1739. At first she was drawn to the Wesleys, but her own theology was 'Calvinist' and by 1744 she had moved into the orbit of George Whitefield and Hywel Harris. Faced with difficulties in getting Evangelical incumbents placed in parishes, the Countess set up chapels, targeting places where the wealthy and well connected could be found – Brighton (1761), Bath (1765) and Tunbridge Wells (1769). Before long she had fallen foul of the church authorities, in particular the Bishop of London, and in 1782 she seceded from the Church of England. By then she had a network of chapels across England, some of which are still in existence. The Countess of Huntingdon's Connexion was to prove to be a model for other Evangelicals later on, especially for those who remained within the Church of England but who realized that if they were to survive, they would need to establish a network of parishes where they could place preachers of their own kind. In some ways these chapels were a rebuke to the inflexibility of the Church of England, which all too often seemed to be incapable of retaining the allegiance of some of its most dedicated supporters.

Another woman who had considerable influence in her day was Sarah Trimmer (1741–1810). Although largely forgotten now, Mrs Trimmer was a pioneer in the Sunday-school movement, for which she wrote textbooks and edited magazines. She worked together with Robert Raikes (1735–1811), a layman with a vision similar to hers, and together they launched a movement that would transform the country and lead eventually to the introduction of compulsory public education in 1870. Sunday schools have declined in popularity in recent years, but until the middle of the twentieth century were still significant in almost all the Protestant denominations, and many children learned the basics of the Christian faith in them. They were often a means by which working-class children could learn to read and write, and started many on the path towards successful business careers and middle-class respectability. By no means all Sunday-school children became churchgoers in later life, and it must be admitted that the popularity of Sunday schools contributed to the widespread belief that Christianity is a religion for children that adults would later grow out of. But that was never their intention and we must always remember that those adults who went on to profess faith had received a solid foundation in the Sunday schools of their youth that stood them in good stead later on.[26]

Transforming the nation

No account of the Evangelical Revival would be complete without mentioning the role played by prominent laymen in the social transformation of the British Isles in the late eighteenth and early nineteenth centuries. Until the Revival, laypeople had seldom taken a role in church affairs. The king and Parliament were the voice of the laity, such as it was, but that was more the inevitable result

---

[26] See S. Orchard and J. H. Y. Briggs, *The Sunday School Movement: Studies in the Growth and Decline of Sunday Schools* (Milton Keynes: Paternoster Press, 2007).

of establishment than anything else. What was new in the eighteenth century was widespread lay involvement in social reform. One of the pioneers in this was John Howard (1726?–90), originally from a dissenting family in Bedford, who conformed to the Church of England and became High Sheriff for Bedfordshire. That made him responsible for the local prisons, whose conditions so appalled him that he dedicated his life to prison reform. Howard travelled all over Europe to inspect the condition of prisons in other countries, and died in a Russian forced-labour camp from a disease he caught from one of the inmates. He had to battle apathy and vested interests for most of his life, but inspired a generation of followers to take up the cause, and they were more successful.

One of Howard's admirers was William Wilberforce (1759–1833). He was not a preacher but was very active in political affairs, serving as the Member of Parliament for Kingston-upon-Hull, 1780–84, for Yorkshire, 1784–1812, and for Bramber in Sussex, 1812–25. After his conversion in 1785 he used his position to further social reforms of many kinds, and is best remembered for his long struggle against slavery, which was finally abolished in the British Empire just a few days before his death. But getting rid of slavery was only one of Wilberforce's interests. He was also involved in the establishment of the Church Missionary Society, which is still active, and the Bible Society.

In addition to all that, Wilberforce was a key member of a group of concerned laypeople popularly called the 'Clapham Sect', because most of them lived in Clapham, where John Venn (1759–1813) became the rector in 1792. Venn was the son of Henry Venn (1725–97), a High Churchman who had been converted to Evangelicalism sometime in the early 1750s. The younger Venn shared both his father's passion for saving souls and Wilberforce's social conscience.[27] Together they gathered an impressive group of prominent people – Hannah More, Henry Thornton (1760–1815), James Stephen (1758–1832), Zachary Macaulay (1768–1838) and John Shore, Baron Teignmouth (1751–1834), all of whom shared the same vision and had both the contacts and the financial resources necessary to pursue their reform goals.[28] Today these people are regarded as heroes, but they faced great opposition in their own time. It is hard to believe it now, but the vested interests that defended the practice of slavery were determined not to give in easily, and for years they did everything they

---

[27] John Venn was the grandfather of another John Venn (1834–1923), who invented the Venn diagram. Unfortunately the grandson lost his faith and resigned his orders in 1883. His son, John Archibald Venn (1883–1958), was president of Queens' College, Cambridge, and the last of the line. He and his father together produced the *Alumni Cantabrigienses*, the standard biographical work of Cambridge graduates from the Middle Ages until 1900.

[28] D. M. Lewis, *The Blackwell Dictionary of Evangelical Biography 1730–1860* (Oxford: Basil Blackwell, 1995).

could to block serious reform measures in Parliament. It was only gradually, and over a generation or more, as Evangelical religion seeped into the body politic, that public opinion was sufficiently aroused to make their causes both respectable and viable. The abolition of slavery was resisted because the sugar economy of the West Indies relied on it, and it was feared that it would collapse if cheap labour were suddenly removed. In South Africa the Dutch settlers (Afrikaners) were so incensed by the emancipation of the slaves that many of them set out to trek into the heart of Africa, where they could establish republics independent of British rule. Unfortunately they succeeded, with the result that racial segregation became a feature of South African life until it was finally abandoned in 1994.

The Evangelical abolitionists were not moved by such considerations. Everywhere they went they brought the same high moral standards to bear. In India they forced the East India Company, which had operated under a charter since its founding in 1600, to abolish the cruel custom of burning widows on the pyres of the deceased husbands (*sati*) and agitated for the Company to be taken under government control, which it eventually was. For the rest of the nineteenth century, Evangelical missionary activity reached out to hidden corners of the globe, and missionaries called on British forces to back them up when social and moral problems had to be dealt with. In East Africa for example, it was the missionaries who went inland in pursuit of the Arab slave traders profiting from the relative disorganization of the country. It was largely because of these slave traders that the British found themselves in Zanzibar, Kenya and Uganda, where they stamped out the trade and established forms of civil government that have endured to the present.

As the fight against the slave trade demonstrates, the Evangelical Revival gave rise to the modern missionary movement, which quickly spread across the world. Missionaries from every part of the British Isles and from every denomination were soon to be found in Africa, India and China. Other countries also took part in this, but Britain remained the hub of the effort. This was in spite of the fact that British societies sometimes found it hard to recruit men for their missions. The Church Missionary Society (CMS), founded in 1799, had to send German and Scandinavian Lutherans to India because there were not enough English Anglicans willing to go.

High Churchmen recoiled at this – they were not at all ecumenically minded – but the Evangelicals crossed denominational boundaries with relative ease. It is true that the CMS was founded by Anglican Evangelicals in reaction to the interdenominational London Missionary Society that had been established four years earlier, but too much should not be made of this. The imperatives of foreign mission were such that those involved were often inclined to ignore theological differences that might interfere with their primary task of preaching the gospel. This was the stated policy of John Venn's son Henry (1796–1873), secretary of the CMS from 1841 to 1872, and he did much to promote the establishment of indigenous churches in the Global South that would be free of European influence. Henry Venn did however draw the line at cooperation with High Church missionaries, who insisted that episcopacy was essential to the church and that congregations without bishops were not fully Christian.[29]

On the mission field the contrast between Christians and people of other religions was so great that differences between Episcopalians, Presbyterians, Baptists and so on paled in comparison. It would be an exaggeration to say that there were no rivalries at all, but cooperation was usually paramount and led eventually to a comity agreement. That was fleshed out at the World Missionary Conference held in Edinburgh in 1910, which divided the non-Christian world into zones that would be reserved for the work of particular denominations and missionary societies. As a result, there are now tribes and regions in the Global South where the local Christian population belongs to one denomination or another, not because of any great theological conviction but because the European missionaries assigned them to one group. In the longer term this would encourage what became the Ecumenical Movement of the twentieth century, and it even led to church unions in some places, notably India.

Among the most prominent early missionaries was William Carey (1761–1834), a Baptist who went to India, where he devoted himself to a study of native languages and traditions, translating the Bible into Assamese, Bengali, Hindi, Marathi, Odia (Oriya) and Sanskrit. Another was Henry Martyn (1781–1812), an ordained Anglican who translated the New Testament into Persian and Urdu before dying of disease when he was only 31. These men, and others like them, were the spearhead of a vast movement that led to the founding of Christian churches, based on British models, all across the Global South. They are famously portrayed in Charlotte Brontë's novel *Jane Eyre*, where the dedicated St John Rivers incarnates the otherworldly idealism that animated so many of them. It was all too much for Charlotte, whose heroine chose the morally dubious Edward Rochester as her husband in preference to St John, but she did not mock the latter or claim that his zeal was hypocritical. Like so

---

[29] Thus he distanced the CMS from the Universities' Mission to Central Africa, led by Bishop Charles Frederick Mackenzie (1825–62), a divide that is still clearly visible between the Anglican Churches of East and Central Africa, particularly in Tanzania, where both traditions are represented – in different dioceses.

many others of her time, she admired a man of faith even though she could not emulate him, and believed that both Rochester and Rivers were on the road to redemption, although by very different routes.

Overseas missions were complemented and sustained by equally strenuous efforts on the home front. Gradually more and more clergymen were won over to the Evangelical cause and it became somewhat easier to place them in parishes, although difficulties remained. There is evidence to suggest that from about 1770, High Churchmen began to fear Evangelical influence, and opposition to Evangelicals intensified. A classic example of an Evangelical who suffered in this way is Charles Simeon (1759–1836), an Old Etonian who matriculated at King's College, Cambridge, and found himself forced to take the sacrament in the college chapel. He knew that he was unprepared for such a solemn event, and set about reading *The Whole Duty of Man* and Bishop Thomas Wilson's *A Short and Plain Instruction for the Better Understanding of the Lord's Supper* as he geared himself up for the great day.[30] On Easter Sunday (4 April) 1779 his heart was put at rest and he knew that Christ had died for him. From that moment on he was a changed man. Four years later he was appointed lecturer at Holy Trinity Church in Cambridge, but found his way blocked by the churchwardens, who disliked his theology and did not want him preaching in their church.

Simeon battled against this opposition and eventually won through. In a ministry that lasted until 1836 – more than half a century – he transformed not only the church but the university and the city of Cambridge as well. Scores of young men, including Henry Martyn, entered the ministry, and although some fell away and others were unsuccessful, the impact on the Church of England and beyond was profound. Even today Cambridge has an Evangelical tradition in its parish churches that is to a great extent Simeon's legacy. Simeon secured this by adopting the strategy pioneered by the Countess of Huntingdon and others, which he adapted to the realities of the Church of England. He went around buying up advowsons and securing them in a trust that would ensure that future incumbents of the parishes would be Evangelicals. He was also strategic in his aims – he went to places like Cheltenham, Bath, Leamington Spa and Islington,[31] where the fashionable and influential people of his day

---

[30] Simeon had a lifelong devotion to the Book of Common Prayer. See A. Atherstone, *Charles Simeon on The Excellency of the Liturgy*, Alcuin Club and The Group for Renewal of Worship Joint Liturgical Studies 72 (Norwich: Hymns Ancient & Modern, 2011).

[31] Islington became the home of the Islington Clerical Conference, founded in 1827 by Daniel Wilson (1778–1858), then vicar of the parish and later Bishop of Calcutta. It met annually until 1982. See D. Bebbington, 'The Islington Conference', in A. Atherstone and J. Maiden (eds.), *Evangelicalism and the Church of England in the Twentieth Century: Reform, Resistance and Renewal* (Woodbridge: Boydell Press, 2014), 48–67.

were inclined to spend their leisure time. These places, and others like them, acquired an Evangelical tradition that they still possess, thanks to the Simeon Trust and other similar societies, and it is fair to say that Evangelicalism in the Church of England would be much weaker today had Simeon not acted in the way he did.

Theologically speaking, Simeon cut across the divide between 'Calvinists' and 'Arminians' by saying that each side has a valid point to make and that the truth was to be found in combining them. In other words, God is fully sovereign and in control of his universe, but uses human agents to effect his purposes and enters into a relationship with them that sets them free to do his will out of love for him. Simeon also stuck rigidly to the Bible and refused to engage in speculations or debates that went beyond its witness. In order to ground his principles in a way that could influence future generations of preachers, he wrote sermon outlines for selected passages throughout the entire Bible, which were published as *Horae Homileticae*. Although no longer widely used, these outlines provided a model that has been copied and adapted many times, making Simeon one of the founders of expository biblical preaching in the modern Church of England.[32]

Bible translation work was a major part of overseas missionary expansion, but most people would suppose that there was no need for it in the British Isles. By the late eighteenth century the King James Version had reached its final form (in the 1761 edition) and Bibles were available in Welsh and Gaelic, even if they were sometimes hard to obtain. But one language spoken in Britain had never had a translation of the Scriptures – Manx. Ever since the Reformation, the Manx clergy had been obliged to translate the text as they went along and even the great Bishop Wilson had continued that practice. But his successor, Mark Hildesley (1698–1772), Bishop of Sodor and Man from 1755 until his death, was more ambitious. He assembled his clergy and apportioned parts of the Bible to each of them for translation. The work took many years, but by the time of his death a Manx Bible was ready for publication.[33] When Methodism arrived in the island a few years later, there was a vernacular Bible waiting for it, and before very long a large number of islanders had been converted. Hildesley was not himself an Evangelical, but his determination to translate the Scriptures into the language of the people helped that cause. Unfortunately the Isle of Man was too small to sustain a Manx-language culture and

32 C. Simeon, *Horae Homileticae*, 11 vols. (London: Richard Watts, 1819–20). The complete and definitive edition, containing no fewer than 2,536 sermons, was published in 21 vols. (London: Holdsworth and Ball, 1832–3.)

33 Bray, *Records of Convocation*, 1:267–268, 277, 283, 293–296, 303, 305.

within a generation it was moribund, eventually becoming extinct in the twentieth century.[34] But the Evangelical faith of many Manx people survived and traces of it can still be found, both in the established Church and in the many Nonconformist chapels that dot the island landscape.

Moderates and Evangelicals in Scotland

The union of the Crowns of England and Scotland in 1707 had preserved an independent Scottish church with a presbyterian form of government. Dissenters were few and many of them were also Presbyterians. With an active lay eldership in every parish, the church was firmly rooted in everyday life and when the Evangelical Revival reached the country, it was absorbed more readily into the existing Establishment than was the case in England. But in other respects Evangelicalism had a hard time of it in Scotland, where the presbyterian system allowed non-Evangelical ministers to discipline any who (in their view) stepped out of line. The patronage system also worked against the Revival, because few patrons were sympathetic to it and most simply wanted to keep the peace. Given that there was a significant Episcopalian and even Roman Catholic element in the remoter parts of the country that remained a source of potential rebellion, this desire for a quiet life was understandable, even if those who wanted a more active spirituality were frustrated by it.

From the beginning, Reformed theology had been faced with the need to explain the true relationship between law and grace. The scriptural doctrine that salvation was by divine grace working through faith in the believer was accepted by everyone, but determining the practical implications of that was more difficult. Some believed that 'freedom from the law' amounted to per-mission to do whatever one pleased, an attitude that could all too easily descend into lawlessness (antinomianism). To combat that, some Reformed divines began to insist that true believers must give evidence of their conversion, which would be seen in a transformed lifestyle that we would now characterize as 'middle-class morality'. A few went even further, claiming that a desire to live a respectable life was a precondition for the working of God's grace in a believer's heart. This amounted to a form of legalism, which was held out to the godly as the only real assurance they were saved.

Neither of these options was a true expression of the Reformed position, and as early as 1645 an obscure Englishman by the name of Edward Fisher (d. 1650) had written a book to set matters straight. He called it *The Marrow*

---

[34] The last indigenous speaker died in 1974.

of Modern Divinity and set out the different positions in dialogue form – Nomista (the legalist) argued with Antinomista and Evangelista for the soul of Neophytus (the young Christian).[35] It was left to Evangelista to persuade Neophytus that the other two were wrong. True Christian discipleship was founded on grace alone, with no prior conditions attached, but far from leading to lawlessness, the indwelling presence of the Holy Spirit put the law of God into the heart of believers. This did not make them sinless but showed that what God required of them had been accomplished on their behalf by Christ, whose atoning sacrifice (and not the accomplishments of a transformed life) is the true assurance of the Christian. Fisher's book was popular and went through several editions, but by the end of the seventeenth century had largely faded from view.

In 1700 a young Scottish minister called Thomas Boston (1676–1732) happened to see a copy of it on the shelf of an elderly parishioner, who had taken part in the English Civil War more than fifty years previously. Boston, who was to become the most prolific Scottish theologian of the eighteenth century, asked to borrow the book and it changed his life.[36] He came to see that in their struggle for law and order, many Reformed ministers, and in particular those of the Church of Scotland, had erred on the side of legalism and were preaching morality instead of salvation. His own preaching and teaching changed dramatically, and over time he was able to win over his congregation and influence some of his friends and colleagues to follow his example.

Matters might have rested there, but in 1717 the General Assembly of the Church of Scotland was moved to condemn a proposition put forward by the presbytery of Auchterarder (Perthshire) that it was asking all candidates for ordination to affirm. It read, 'I believe that it is not sound and orthodox to teach that we must forsake sin in order to our coming to Christ, and instating us in covenant with God.' The intention was to counter the legalistic belief that it was necessary to prepare oneself in order to receive the grace of God, but many disagreed with this proposition, which was also adding a requirement for ordination beyond what the Church normally imposed. It was in the course of the debate over this that Thomas Boston recommended *The Marrow* to James Hog (1658?–1734), a fellow minister. Hog found a copy of the book and had it reprinted, with a preface by himself. Unfortunately he was not a good

---

35 E. Fisher, *The Marrow of Modern Divinity* (Fearn: Christian Focus, 2009).

36 S. McMillan (ed.), *The Whole Works of the Late Reverend Thomas Boston*, 12 vols. (Aberdeen: G. and R. King, 1848–52); repr. as *The Complete Works of Thomas Boston*, 12 vols. (Wheaton, Ill.: Richard Owen Roberts, 1980). See also A. T. B. McGowan, *The Federal Theology of Thomas Boston* (Carlisle: Paternoster Press, 1997).

publicist and, despite his enthusiasm for *The Marrow*, was unable to convey its message in a compelling, or even coherent, way. But the ensuing controversy drew attention to the book as nothing else could have done and, despite repeated condemnations by the General Assembly, '*Marrow* theology', as it came to be called, attracted a determined and loyal following.[37]

In 1726 Thomas Boston reprinted it, this time with copious notes of his own designed to show that *The Marrow* was thoroughly orthodox in its theology and that its opponents were in error. Boston was censured but not deposed from the ministry, and two of his colleagues, Ebenezer Erskine (1680–1754) and his brother Ralph (1685–1752), took up the cause. The Erskine brothers attracted the attention of both George Whitefield and John Wesley in England, and with them the Evangelical movement in Scotland may be said to have begun in earnest. The Erskines remained in the Church of Scotland as long as they could, but opposition to them was strong and they were eventually forced into secession, taking some of their followers with them.[38] Others however remained in the established Church, where they gradually increased their numbers and influence as the century wore on.

The Church of Scotland was troubled by the *Marrow* controversy but its orthodox theological foundations were not seriously shaken. Thomas Blackwell (1660–1728) could write against it and it was later defended by Robert Riccaltoun (1691–1769), but both men remained well within the bounds of the Westminster Confession. Somewhat more adventurous was Thomas Halyburton (1674–1712), who engaged with John Locke and subscribed to a rationalistic approach that, with the benefit of hindsight, can be seen as preparing the way for the Scottish Enlightenment, but even he did not stray from the path of confessional orthodoxy.[39] For that we have to turn to John Simson (1668?–1740), who became a standard bearer of the so-called 'New Licht' theology, which placed considerable emphasis on rational enquiry as consistent with (and essential to) theology. Simson was accused of heresy and was tried by the General Assembly, which rendered its verdict against him on 14 May 1717.[40] Somewhat surprisingly, Simson was not deposed but merely cautioned, but

---

[37] D. C. Lachman, *The Marrow Controversy, 1718–1723: An Historical and Theological Analysis* (Edinburgh: Rutherford House, 1988); S. G. Myers, 'The *Marrow* Controversy: Boston, Erskine and Hadow', in D. Fergusson and M. K. Elliott (eds.), *The History of Scottish Theology*, 3 vols. (Oxford: Oxford University Press, 2019), 1:342–358.

[38] The secession occurred in two stages. In 1733 they formed an 'Associate Presbytery' on the margins of the Church of Scotland, but were not formally deposed from the latter's ministry until 1740.

[39] P. Helm, 'Between Orthodoxy and Enlightenment', in Fergusson and Elliott, *History of Scottish Theology*, 2:14–26.

[40] *Acts of the General Assembly of the Church of Scotland, 1638–1842* (Edinburgh: The Edinburgh Printing and Publishing Society, 1843), 518.

when the charges against him were renewed a decade later, he was suspended from teaching and preaching on 13 May 1729.[41] Simson left a number of disciples behind however, including Archibald Campbell (1691–1756), who like his master was accused of heresy for his rationalistic views but also escaped censure by the General Assembly when it considered the matter in 1736.[42]

Another influence in a rationalistic direction came from Francis Hutcheson (1694–1746), an Ulster Presbyterian who made his career in Scotland and is reported to have been the first professor at Glasgow to lecture in English instead of Latin. He was followed by one of his pupils, William Leechman (1706–85), who like Simson and Campbell was accused of heresy but managed to defend his orthodoxy to the satisfaction of the General Assembly.[43] The Scottish Church was having difficulty coming to terms with the challenge of rationalism, and it has to be said that the verdicts in favour of these men were concessions to the new way of thinking rather than vindications of traditional orthodoxy. Meanwhile a very different challenge was coming to the church in the form of Evangelicalism, which became a force to be reckoned with in the 1740s.

Scottish Evangelicalism was influenced to some degree by its English counterpart, but much of it was homegrown. There was a large-scale revival at Cambuslang and Kilsyth, near Glasgow, in 1741–2, which saw open-air preaching to crowds that numbered as many as 30,000, but it stayed within the established Church and there was little sign of the divisions that plagued the Evangelical movement south of the border. John Wesley visited the country, but was not on the same wavelength as the Erskines and his brand of Methodism never took root to any great extent. Scottish Evangelicals were overwhelmingly Calvinist in their theology and, if anything, more orthodox in their adherence to the Westminster Confession of Faith than their 'Moderate' brethren, as their opponents were known.[44] This orthodoxy allowed them to grow and even flourish within the established Church, although the Moderates did their best to keep them out of power. The problem with them was that they were pedestrian, in both their theology and pastoral practice. They did what was expected of them in the parishes but accepted the status quo in the church, even when, as in the case of patronage, there were reasons for objecting to it.

Evangelicals had the greatest opportunities in the Highlands and Islands, poor areas where many Moderate clergy were reluctant to go. Scottish parishes

---

[41] See C. Maurer, 'Early Enlightenment Shifts', in Fergusson and Elliott, *History of Scottish Theology*, 2:42–55.

[42] *Acts of the General Assembly*, 639 (21 May 1736).

[43] Ibid. 676–677.

[44] On the Moderates, who were similar to the Latitudinarians in England, see S. J. Brown, 'Moderate Theology and Preaching, c. 1750–1800', in Fergusson and Elliott, *History of Scottish Theology*, 2:69–83.

generally maintained high educational standards, with schooling both better and more widespread than in England, but the Gaelic areas were something of an exception. The Scottish SPCK, which worked within the established Church, did try to open schools in the Highlands, but insisted on teaching in English, which most of their pupils could not understand. The Evangelicals promoted the use of Gaelic and made headway in the evangelization of areas that had formerly been strongholds of episcopalianism and Roman Catholicism. By the end of the eighteenth century they had reduced both of these to a small minority and converted the Highlands into one of the staunchest and most conservatively presbyterian parts of the country. Even today, it is in these areas that traditionalist presbyterianism survives in a plethora of free presbyterian churches, internally divided over many secondary issues but appearing to the outside world as a bastion of conservatism. Even the use of instrumental music, which by the nineteenth century had conquered most of the church in the lowland areas, where it is now thoroughly domesticated, has been resisted in the Highlands, where the old a cappella style of singing the metrical psalter is still common. It gives Scottish Evangelicalism a flavour unknown elsewhere, although the preservation of the native language has been less successful than in Wales, perhaps because there is no corresponding hymn tradition to accompany it.

As the decades wore on, Evangelicals gradually increased in numbers.[45] Many of them left the established Church and set up independent, although almost always presbyterian, bodies, which naturally weakened their witness within the established Church. But in 1811, the very year in which English and Welsh Methodists were formally breaking with the Church of England, Thomas Chalmers (1780–1847), a minister of the Church of Scotland, was converted and advocated remaining within the Establishment and using it as the primary means of transforming the entire nation for Christ. Chalmers was a man of many parts, who combined in one man and his ministry a zeal for social reform, a commitment to education and a passion for the conversion of the people to Evangelical faith. He was a gifted orator, a brilliant organizer and a leader of men at a time when the church was ready for change. Inspired by him, many were either converted to Evangelicalism or prompted to offer themselves for the ministry. In 1832 the Evangelicals finally gained control of the General Assembly and retained it for the next decade. It looked very much as if change had come to stay and that real reform of the church, including the

---

[45] J. R. McIntosh, 'Eighteenth-Century Evangelicalism', in Fergusson and Elliott, *History of Scottish Theology*, 2:84–98.

abolition of the much-hated patronage system, was within reach. As it turned out however, it would be the egregious abuse of that very system that would lead to crisis, and instead of advancing in unity towards the evangelization of the nation, the Church of Scotland would split apart, with Chalmers and most of the Evangelicals seceding in what became the Great Disruption of 1843.

The Irish conundrum

As always, the religious situation in Ireland was very different from that in any part of Great Britain. The root of the difference lay in the fact that around 75% of the population remained loyal to the Church of Rome. This included virtually all of the Gaelic-speakers, but they did not dominate the Catholic community. Leadership was generally in the hands of the Anglo-Irish or 'Old English', who had always wanted to be accepted as English, on equal terms with their Protestant brethren. After 1690 the Irish Parliament, which by then was exclusively Protestant, did everything it could to discriminate against Catholics, confiscating most of their land and barring them from key professions such as the law. Their priests had to go to the European continent for training, and Irish colleges were set up in many places to cater for them. Somewhat ironically, they had the effect of making the Irish Catholic Church more Roman than it had ever been before. The Irish had once been the odd ones out as far as Rome was concerned, with married clergy and even abbots, but all that was now in the distant past. The remodelled Irish Catholic Church was thoroughly orthodox and mainstream, and loyalty to the pope became one of its central hallmarks. As time went on and Catholics in other countries were increasingly exposed to liberal ideas, the Irish appeared unusually conservative and traditional by comparison but, although that was appreciated in Rome, it did not lead to giving the Irish a greater role in the administration of the church. Valuable foot soldiers the Irish were; princes of the church they were not.

The penal laws enacted against Roman Catholics were designed to persuade them to convert to Protestantism in order to avoid the persecution that refusal would entail. Yet in the whole of the eighteenth century only about 6,000 Catholics became Protestants, a tiny proportion of the total number of Catholics in the country. We must assume that most of these converts were motivated by worldly considerations, but not all were insincere. The father of Edmund Burke (1729–97) became a Protestant in order to advance his career, but Edmund had a genuine Protestant faith and defended it throughout his life. That did not prevent him from becoming an advocate for Catholic relief, and indeed it might have spurred him on in that direction, since he understood better than many of his fellow co-religionists that spiritual ends cannot be achieved by purely political means, or justified by material rewards.[46]

In practice, persecution of Roman Catholics practically ceased in the early eighteenth century and the church was able to consolidate itself without much difficulty. Catholic laymen were free to become merchants in many of the most important towns, and by the 1760s they were dominant in places like Cork and Limerick. That gave them wealth and eventually political clout to agitate for reform, which they did. They understood that the route to change lay through the British Parliament, not the exclusively Protestant Irish one, and there Edmund Burke, who moved to England in mid-career, was one of their staunchest allies.

At the same time, the Irish Catholic Church acquired a series of reform-minded bishops who did their best to instil high standards of religious practice among their people. Rules for celebration of the sacraments were tightened, and greater discipline on both the clergy and the laity was imposed. In order to ensure that this new vigour would not be misinterpreted as sedition, Catholic priests were also enjoined to pray for the Royal Family and for the Protestant Lord Lieutenant of Ireland, which most of them did without question. Religious orders also began to take root in Ireland, providing personnel to staff the schools and charitable institutions until the late twentieth century.

Catholic emancipation eventually came to the whole of the UK 1829, but by then the damage in Ireland had been done. A charismatic Catholic layman, Daniel O'Connell (1775–1847), had led a clever campaign to force the British government to act, one that perforce depended on the cooperation of the Catholic clergy for its funding and eventual success. That concessions had to be extracted in this manner persuaded many that the union of Great Britain and Ireland was a failure, and before long Catholic voices were being raised for it to be repealed.

Protestant Ireland had a very different experience in the eighteenth and early nineteenth centuries. The Protestants were divided between members of the established Church of Ireland and the Presbyterians, most of whom were of Scottish descent and almost all of whom lived in the north-east (Ulster). Legally only members of the Church of Ireland could hold public office or serve in the Irish Parliament, and they constituted the 'political nation'. Never more than 15% of the total population, they were nonetheless very active and the best of them were a credit to their country. This was the age of Jonathan Swift and George Berkeley, a time when Dublin was the fashionable second city of

---

[46] See F. Lock, *Edmund Burke*, 2 vols. (Oxford: Clarendon Press, 1998–2006).

the expanding British Empire whose magnificent architecture still bears silent witness to an age of greatness. It was in Dublin that Handel's *Messiah* was first performed, and the elite of the capital were closely connected with the court in London and with English affairs generally. In 1711 the Irish Convocation even managed to enact a new set of canons to govern the church, something that was proposed in England but never got off the ground.[47]

The Church of Ireland used its wealth to build and refurbish churches and clergy houses all over the country, many of which are still standing, even if there is little or no congregation for them to serve. The casual visitor to Ireland may be surprised to discover that in many towns the city-centre church is a handsome Protestant building, even if services are few and far between. The leaders of the church, like the Moderates in Scotland, wanted peace and quiet above all else and were reluctant to risk that by reaching out to the nominally Catholic peasantry. The efforts of John Richardson (1669?–1747), a member of the Irish Convocation, to evangelize among the Gaelic-speaking population were discouraged and nothing came of them. Richardson knew that this could be Protestantism's last chance to convert the mass of the Irish people, but his pleas fell on deaf ears.[48]

The Church of Ireland's affairs were conducted, as in England, by the bishops, who were more active than their counterparts across the water. Diocesan administration was vastly improved, with the resurrection of the office of rural dean that had lapsed in the Middle Ages, and parsonage houses were built on a grand scale, allowing the clergy to reside on their benefices to a degree that had not previously been possible. Regular visitations were undertaken and deficiencies corrected with a zeal unknown in England at that time. The snag of course was that all this activity took place in a body that claimed to be the national church but that was almost non-existent in many parts of the south and west. Its weakness was not corruption or inefficiency but its unrepresentative nature, which it seemed to be incapable of changing.

Irish Presbyterians were in a kind of halfway house between the Establishment and the Catholics. They were Dissenters, and therefore excluded from the political nation, but they were also Protestants in a country that needed all the Protestants it could get. The Presbyterians remained closely tied to their brethren in Scotland and the divisions among them were similar. But because of their inferior political status, they were in some ways closer to English Dissenters,

---

47 Bray, *Records of Convocation*, 17:354–369, 374–375, 388–391, 419–422, 428; 18:178–182.

48 See ibid. 18:164–165; S. J. Connolly, *Religion, Law and Power: The Making of Protestant Ireland 1660–1760* (Oxford: Clarendon Press, 1992), 199–201; T. Barnard, *A New Anatomy of Ireland: The Irish Protestants, 1649–1770* (New Haven, Conn.: Yale University Press, 2003), 94.

whose causes they often supported. Their lay membership was also much more integrated into the life of the church than was the case with either the Church of Ireland or the Roman Catholics. This could sometimes cause embarrassments from what outside observers might call an 'excess of democracy', but it gave the church a solid base and staying power that would stand it in good stead.

The Evangelical Revival made good progress among the Protestants of Ireland, particularly within the established Church. In some places, like County Fermanagh, Methodism made a lasting impact but, as in Scotland, it met a solid wall of Calvinist resistance from the Presbyterians. Even so, there was a Presbyterian form of revivalism that complemented that of the Methodists in the Church of Ireland. The long-term effect of the Evangelical Revival was to create a conservative Protestant alliance in Ireland that transcended the denominational divisions that were otherwise dominant. The denominations did not disappear, but Protestants learned to cooperate across such boundaries, and in the early nineteenth century embarked on renewed efforts to convert the Roman Catholic population. Those efforts were more successful than is often recognized, as the ruins of Protestant chapels in the west of Ireland testify. For a few years in the early 1820s it seemed that Protestantism might make serious inroads into the Irish population, but Catholic priests were alive to the danger and organized resistance among their flocks. In the end Catholic emancipation, rising secularism and the devastating famine of 1845–51 brought these efforts to naught, and what has sometimes been called the Second Reformation in Ireland petered out with little to show for its efforts.

The dawn before the darkness?

An observer of the British scene in 1815 might have concluded that the country was living proof of the success of a Protestant state.[49] For most of the preceding twenty years it had been at war with France, but the defeat of Napoleon at Waterloo put an end to that power struggle, and the UK was clearly victorious. It is often forgotten, but the monument to Nelson in Trafalgar Square and Waterloo station in London are reminders of the immense sense of relief and achievement the nation felt at that time. The sense of triumph was worldwide. Columns to Nelson's victory were erected in Montreal, Bridgetown (Barbados) and Dublin, and the first is still standing.[50] New Zealand has cities named after

---

[49] For an overview of the period from 1815 to 1832, see S. J. Brown, *Providence and Empire 1815–1914* (London: Pearson Longman, 2008), 1–77.
[50] The Dublin pillar was blown up by nationalists on 8 March 1966. The Bridgetown one still survives but was moved to a museum on 16 November 2020 as part of an 'anticolonialist' drive.

Nelson and the Duke of Wellington, the victor of Waterloo. Britain was expanding to the four corners of the globe, and people noticed. Since 1789 several ancient states and institutions had disappeared. The 1,300-year-old French monarchy, although temporarily restored in 1814, was on its last legs. The Holy Roman Empire, a thousand years old, had vanished. The venerable Venetian Republic had been absorbed by Austria. The papacy had been humbled by Napoleon and had only just managed to survive, its prestige and power both severely damaged. The Spanish-American empire was tottering and in a few years would be gone. Brazil was effectively independent of Portugal and would soon go its own way as well. Even Poland had finally been partitioned by Austria, Prussia and Russia in 1795, erasing from the map what had been the largest European state. In this new dispensation the UK appeared to be going from strength to strength, and people wondered why. The idea that God had intervened on its behalf was easy to accept, and many people thought that the British Empire had been called to play a special role in the world. Specifically, it had been chosen to spread Protestant Christianity, Christian moral principles (like the abolition of slavery) and the material prosperity the Industrial Revolution was now bringing to Great Britain itself.

To all appearances, the British churches were also in good heart. The atheism of the French Revolution had been defeated and missionary activity both at home and abroad was expanding by leaps and bounds. In 1813 India had been opened to missionary activity, and some people were putting pressure on the British government to take measures to encourage the adoption of Christianity in that country. There could be no question of forced conversions, which went against the spirit of Protestantism, but it was felt that by the establishment of western-style schools teaching Christian principles, Indians would see the benefits for themselves and abandon their traditional beliefs. The abolition of *sati* gave them some hope of that, as did the success of English-language education among the upper classes. Indians would eventually accept other aspects of westernization, like the desirability of outlawing the caste system, but only a small minority would ever profess Christianity. Even at the time there was opposition in England to what seemed to be a utopian vision doomed to failure. In 1814 Thomas Middleton was consecrated in London as the first Bishop of Calcutta, but hostility to the project on the part of sceptical English observers ensured the event was not widely publicized.[51] It was a bad omen for the future.

More successful was the campaign against slavery. All through the Napoleonic Wars the British government had kept up the pressure to abolish the slave trade,

---

[51] See Brown, *Providence and Empire*, 38.

which it succeeded in doing in 1807. In the following year a project to resettle freed slaves in Africa was launched, and the new colony of Sierra Leone came into being. This led to a further push against the institution of slavery itself, which was increasingly denounced all over Britain as a stain on the empire's conscience. Scottish Presbyterians and English Dissenters joined with members of the Church of England to further the cause, drawing them closer together and giving their missionary zeal a practical focus. For much of the nineteenth century the ongoing need to stamp out slavery would fuel missionary efforts to penetrate the 'dark heart of Africa', from which most of the slaves came, and this crusade did much to justify imperial expansion in the minds of British Protestants.

On the home front, in 1818 and again in 1824, Parliament voted a subsidy for the building of new churches, made necessary by the urbanization accompanying the Industrial Revolution. After 1813 it was no longer possible to excommunicate Englishmen for non-payment of tithes, but the tithe regime was still in existence and the parish system to which it was linked remained unaltered. Baptisms, marriages and burials were still recorded by the clergy and most of what passed for poor relief and education was in the hands of the church as well. It was virtually impossible for anyone in the British Isles to escape the influence of the church, whatever form it took in the different kingdoms and Crown dependencies, and the likelihood of hearing the gospel preached with conviction was great, as the Evangelical Revival really started to take off. In 1815 the Evangelical Henry Ryder (1777–1836) became Bishop of Gloucester – the first in the Church of England. By happy accident, he was joined the following year by Power Le Poer Trench (1770–1839), Bishop of Elphin in the Church of Ireland, who was converted by the witness of his own archdeacon. These were small beginnings, but the citadel of the church hierarchy had been breached, and there was reason to hope that these men would not be the last of their kind to receive preferment.

Yet if we look back at the same scene from the vantage point of 1860, a generation or so after Waterloo, a very different picture emerges. The churches were still strong, Evangelical religion was familiar to most people and the numbers of men offering themselves for ordination was increasing year by year. Yet the structure of church–state relations had been altered almost beyond recognition, the voices of atheism and agnosticism were being heard more often, and even some church people were questioning the validity of their faith. Was the Bible really the Word of God? Was the Protestant Reformation a mistake that should have been avoided? Was there only one church, or did the proliferation of competing denominations suggest that nobody was in sole possession of the truth? Things that had been taken for granted only a few years before were now cast into doubt and the future seemed to promise only more of the same. What had happened to produce this situation?

To some extent the churches were the victims of their inability to adjust to the new social conditions the long war with France and the Industrial Revolution had produced. The Evangelical Revival burst the ancient parochial boundaries and led to widespread open-air preaching that the local clergy could not control. Those who were converted formed prayer cells that developed their own inner dynamic, which in turn led to the creation of a para-church network that could not be contained within the existing structures. As Evangelicals began to construct their own chapels, the state authorities insisted that they should be registered as dissenting places of worship, even if those who attended them had no intention of leaving the established Church. As a result, there was an explosion of 'dissent' that can be measured by the licensing of 54,804 chapels in England under the provisions of the Toleration Act of 1688 (1689). The statistics show that after an initial spurt in the late Stuart period, new licensings fell off until there was a massive revival from about 1771 that did not abate until toleration was granted to Dissenters in 1828:[52]

1688–90:	939
1691–1700:	1,279
1701–10:	1,360
1711–20:	896
1721–30:	475
1731–40:	448
1741–50:	529
1751–60:	759
1761–70:	786
1771–80:	1,136
1781–90:	1,470
1791–1800:	4,394
1801–10:	5,460
1811–20:	10,161
1821–30:	10,585
1831–40:	7,422
1841–50:	5,810
1851–52:	996

---

[52] *Twenty-Eighth Annual Report of the Registrar-General of Births, Deaths and Marriages in England* (London: Eyre & Spottiswoode, 1867), viii. The registration of chapels was discontinued in 1852.

The decades from 1811 to 1830 were the high point, although how many people attended these chapels is impossible to say for certain. There were at least 200,000 chapelgoers by 1820, but the true figure may be as high as a million or more, amounting to about 10% of the total population, and virtually all were highly committed to the Revival. How many were specifically opposed to the Church of England is unknown, and a good number retained at least a residual connection with the parish church, but that was no longer their spiritual home. The laws that prevented Dissenters from playing a full part in national life were called into question, and in 1828 were mostly abolished. Given the amorphous nature of dissent there was little resistance to this, even among supporters of the Establishment, although it was a different matter when Catholic emancipation was enacted in the following year. Few Protestants of any stripe were happy about that, fearing that it would lead to a gradual erosion of the religious liberty they associated with the Reformation and the Glorious Revolution of 1688–9.

Those fears were overblown, but the traditional bonds between church and state were inevitably weakened as the state found that it had to be more 'neutral' in its approach to religious questions. After 1824 there would be no more parliamentary grants for the building of new churches, nor would the government intervene in internal church affairs, which in the case of the Church of England meant that it would have no effective government at all. In the end 'neutrality' meant disengagement, which in turn meant secularization. The real beneficiaries of the new tolerance were not Dissenters or Catholics but atheists and agnostics, who could now profess their unbelief publicly and even recommend it as the best way to prevent religious strife. Defenders of the Establishment were not entirely wrong when they claimed that toleration opened the door to unbelief, and two centuries later few would dispute that unbelief was the real winner. The Christian faith takes many different forms but if it is institutionally divided, its impact on wider society is liable to suffer. That has certainly been the experience in Britain, even if it would be some time before the consequences became obvious to all.

Looking back now we can see that the years from 1815 to 1832 or so were a twilight that masqueraded as a kind of false dawn. The French Revolution had been defeated but the ideas that animated it had not disappeared. That was most obvious in France itself, where the restored Bourbon monarchy was overthrown in 1830 and finally abolished altogether in 1848, the last kings both seeking refuge in Britain.[53] Ideas and ideals of democracy, social justice

---

[53] Charles X (1824–30) arrived in 1830 and Louis-Philippe I (1830–48) came eighteen years later.

and religious freedom for all began to percolate everywhere, and not least in the British Isles, where many looked across the Atlantic to see how those principles were being worked out in the newly formed United States. British people were not particularly pro-American, but there was a steady stream of emigrants to that country, most of whom were seeking a better life and believed it could be found there. Others preferred to stay within the British Empire, going to Canada, Australia, South Africa and eventually New Zealand, but these new settler colonies were often just as egalitarian in outlook as America was and even more so in practice, certainly as long as slavery endured in the American south.

There was an underlying sense in the UK that things had to change, that social structures which had endured for centuries were now increasingly obsolete, and that if the nation's success was to continue, a different approach to just about everything had to be embraced. The churches and the Christian faith, so central to the established order, could not hope to escape from this. Change would be resisted, it would be delayed and it would often be half-hearted, but it would come; and when it did, the world of men like John Wesley and Charles Simeon would disappear for ever.

12

Faith in crisis (1832–60)

The death of the old order[1]

It is customary among historians to refer to the constitutional arrangements that prevailed in most of Europe from the mid-seventeenth to the late eighteenth century as the *ancien régime* (old order). It was a society in which the secular state was ruled by a powerful monarch who supported, and was supported by, an established church. In Catholic countries the church was theoretically governed by the pope, but much of his authority was delegated to various local rulers. Thus it was that in the Spanish and Portuguese realms the church was governed by a system known as the *patronato* (*padroado* in Portuguese), which allowed the king to nominate bishops and control the ecclesiastical administration. In France there was a General Assembly of the Église Gallicane similar to the English convocations, which voted subsidies to the king and pronounced on religious questions that the state was expected to act upon. While theoretically independent, in fact the elections to the Assemblies were carefully monitored by the court and seldom did anything that the king did not approve of.[2]

In Protestant countries the king was often regarded as the secular bishop, who governed the state church and to some extent determined its doctrine, which might be either Lutheran or 'Reformed' (Calvinist). The clergy were paid by the state and were expected to be loyal to it, which they usually were. The situation in the British Isles was somewhat different. There the three state churches were by and large financially independent of the state, and the Church of Scotland virtually governed itself. In England and Ireland the church was more closely controlled by Parliament, where bishops sat in the Upper House, but this made little difference in practice. The governing class in both countries

---

[1] See O. Chadwick, *The Victorian Church: Part One. 1829–1859*, 3rd edn (London: SCM Press, 1971); also S. J. Brown, *Providence and Empire 1815–1914* (London: Pearson Longman, 2008), 77–213.

[2] See P. Blet, *Le clergé du Grand Siècle en ses Assemblées 1615–1715* (Paris: Cerf, 1995); M. Cuillieron, *Les Assemblées du clergé et la société ecclésiastique sous le règne de Louis XVI* (Paris: Editions FAC 2000, 2002); J. McManners, *Church and Society in Eighteenth-Century France*, 2 vols. (Oxford: Clarendon Press, 1998), 1:141–173.

was small and closely knit, so there was little chance of state interference with the church – or vice versa. The Wesleys might have ruffled some feathers, but they were accepted as gentlemen, and nobody would have attacked the Countess of Huntingdon. It was normal for clergymen to have close friends and relatives in Parliament and so, for the most part, they were left alone.

But the political peace of the church came at the price of stagnation. By 1800 attentive churchmen could see that the parochial system was under strain, but there was little they could do about it. Rural dwellers moved into the urban industrial areas, which could not cope with such an influx of numbers. In England and Wales the bishops knew that the great discrepancies of wealth between one parish and another made it very difficult to ensure an equally efficient ministry across the country as a whole. Wealthy parsons could reside elsewhere and pay curates to take their duties, while residentiary canons in Westminster Abbey and many cathedrals had large incomes with few responsibilities.

There was no real ordination training, advowsons could be bought and sold to the highest bidder and bishops could appoint family members to lucrative positions in the ecclesiastical administration. Bowyer Edward Sparke, Bishop of Ely from 1812 to 1836, appointed his two sons as diocesan registrars in 1817. The elder became Diocesan Chancellor in 1824 and held the office until his death in 1870, along with a large number of benefices in the diocese. The younger son was only 12 years old when he was first appointed Registrar, but he remained in post until 1879 and, like his brother, accumulated several other offices and livings as well.[3] Nor were Sparke's appointments unique. Many bishops used their positions to advance their family members and there was nothing anyone could do about it. Others who were well connected to patrons could obtain lucrative benefices with only minimal qualifications, and there was almost no control over their activities once they were appointed. A few egregious examples of abuse came to light and were dealt with by the courts, but they were only the tip of a rather large iceberg. The most notorious case was that of Dr Edward Drax Free (1764–1843), Rector of Sutton, Bedfordshire, from 1808 to 1830, who had several bastard children by a succession of house-keepers, stole the lead from the roof of his church and sold it for scrap and was regularly more drunk than sober. None of these things was sufficient to remove him however. He was finally deprived of his living because he tried to fine one of his churchwardens for non-attendance at services. In the circumstances this

---

[3] For a list of these, see T. Park, *The Reform Bishops 1828–1840: A Biographical Study* (St Bees: St Bega Press, 2016), 143–144.

was one of his lesser misdemeanours, but it transgressed the social norms of his time and he suffered accordingly.[4] The absurdity of this situation infuriated many in the church who wanted to set higher standards for the clergy, particularly Evangelicals, who found it difficult to get livings because of their theological convictions but who were forced to look on helplessly as such immoral incumbents were being tolerated without apparent shame. Needless to say, Dissenters were even more incensed by this and used such examples as proof, if any were needed, that the state Establishment was irredeemably corrupt. Reform of some kind was increasingly urgent, but how it would be undertaken remained controversial and for a long time nothing much was done.

Another factor that came into play was a general change in attitude towards both Dissenters and Roman Catholics among the Establishment. By the early nineteenth century, dissent was either moribund or renewed by the Evangelical Revival. Some Evangelicals joined Baptist and Congregationalist churches, bringing those denominations back to life, but many more became Methodists, eventually starting a new denomination. But Evangelicals of all kinds worked together in organizations like the Bible Society, and the Dissenters among them were not feared by the Establishment in the way their seventeenth century forebears had been. The important role played by laymen in these societies and in other charitable works also lessened the barriers between church and dissent, where ecclesiological differences were often regarded as concerns of the clergy rather than of the laity.

Roman Catholics also appeared less threatening after the French Revolution, when the power of the pope was challenged and greatly reduced in many Catholic countries. Many persecuted French priests found refuge in England, where they made a good impression and attracted sympathy because of their suffering. That sympathy did not often extend to Irish Catholics, but the need to conciliate them, especially after the union of 1801, was widely felt. The opposition of George III was an obstacle, but George IV was less pious than his father had been and his reluctance to accept change was gradually overcome. In 1828 Dissenters were relieved of most of their disabilities and Catholic emancipation followed a year later. Efforts were made to cushion the impact of this, particularly in Ireland, where the franchise was limited in ways that benefited Protestants; but once the citadel of the old order was breached, there could be no going back. Parliament was no longer the exclusive preserve of the

---

[4] The story is well told by R. B. Outhwaite, *Scandal in the Church: Dr Edward Drax Free, 1764–1843* (London: Hambledon Press, 1997).

state churches, which now found themselves exposed to the danger that legislation for them could be drawn up and passed by people who were neither their members nor sympathetic to their concerns.

A major reform of parliamentary constituencies in 1832 reduced the power of the landed gentry and increased that of the industrial towns, a move that inevitably benefited Dissenters, who were well represented in the latter. Equally damaging to the established churches was the strong opposition of the bishops to parliamentary reform. The Church of England had always drawn its strength from the rural gentry and their obedient tenants, but as industrialization grew and cities expanded, it was becoming obvious that Parliament could no longer be dominated by the landed interest. Demonstrations in favour of reform turned violent, and for the first time in two centuries the bishops and clergy were singled out as 'enemies of the people'. Rioting in Bristol led to the destruction of the bishop's palace and most of the diocesan records, and up and down the country bishops were burnt in effigy. To make matters worse, there was a cholera epidemic at the same time, which led a group of Evangelical Members of Parliament to proclaim a National Day of Fasting on Wednesday 21 March 1832, just as the parliamentary reform bill was reaching its final stages.[5] Despite widespread popular support for the move, many people reacted to this gesture by calling it an act of hypocrisy, because they claimed that everyone knew that cholera had to be fought by improvements in hygiene and in medical care generally. To their minds, prayer and fasting were all very well, but they were no substitute for action based on scientific principles. Unfortunately some parliamentary supporters of the fast accused their critics of unbelief and atheism, creating a pseudo-conflict between science and religion that should have been avoided. When the panic finally subsided, it became apparent that the Evangelical social activists of an earlier generation had lost ground to the otherworldly pietists within their own ranks, an unfortunate development that was to have serious consequences for the future.

In Ireland, attempts to limit Catholic influence after emancipation were only partially successful and increased Catholic desire for 'justice', which they naturally interpreted as equal treatment for them. The British state was not yet ready to go that far, but appeasing the Catholic interest in Ireland was seen to be imperative, and one of the first measures the newly reformed parliament undertook was the partial disendowment of the Church of Ireland. As an

---

[5] See P. Williamson, A. Raffe, S. Taylor and N. Mears (eds.), *National Prayers: Special Worship Since the Reformation*, vol. 2: *General Fasts, Thanksgivings and Special Prayers in the British Isles, 1689–1870* (Woodbridge: Boydell & Brewer, 2017), 785–796. The fast was held a day later in Scotland because of a long-standing national tradition that fasts should be held on a Thursday.

inordinately wealthy church with a bloated hierarchy that had little to do, the Church of Ireland was an obvious target for would-be reformers, but churchmen did not see things that way. There was considerable resistance from bishops in both Ireland and England, who saw the reform as an attempt to rob the church of what rightfully belonged to it.

In the event the Church of Ireland was not disestablished in 1833 but lost a substantial portion of its income and the number of its bishops was cut in half. The ancient provinces of Cashel and Tuam were abolished and combined with Dublin and Armagh respectively, a move that had the unintended consequence of making the remaining bishops more frequent attenders in the House of Lords, since there were fewer of them to rotate.[6] There were suggestions that the ecclesiastical revenue of Ireland might be shared out among the Catholics and Presbyterians, as well as the established Church, but the practical difficulties of doing that proved to be too great. Would the Church of Ireland be expected to hand many of its buildings over to one of these other churches and, if so, to which one? Who would receive the tithe rent if it was paid by a Protestant landlord on behalf of his Catholic tenants? There was no satisfactory answer to questions like these, and the proposals never got off the ground, leaving the door open for a more radical solution in the next generation.

Meanwhile the would-be reformers of the church turned their attentions from Ireland, which to them was something of a sideshow, to the much more difficult case of the Church of England. Internal reform was catching on slowly, as the gradual re-establishment of rural deans after 1815 indicates, but progress was slow and in most places virtually imperceptible. The need was acute. The crunch came on 16 June 1835, when the newly established Ecclesiastical Commission, charged with the task of overhauling the church's finances and administration, which had been left virtually untouched since the Reformation 300 years earlier, reported its findings to Parliament. What it discovered made painful reading. The report revealed that there was no correlation between episcopal incomes and responsibilities, and that some bishops, notably Durham and Ely, were doing almost incredibly well out of the existing system. Table 12.1 demonstrates how lopsided things were. It lists the dioceses in order of episcopal stipends, followed by the population of the diocese and the number of benefices it contained, with the rank in the hierarchy indicated in parentheses.

---

[6] For a list of which Irish bishops attended Parliament from 1801 to 1870, see G. L. Bray (ed.), *Records of Convocation*, 20 vols. (Woodbridge: Boydell & Brewer, 2005–6), 18:251–253.

Table 12.1 English and Welsh dioceses in 1835: episcopal stipends

Diocese	Bishop's stipend (£)	Population	Benefices
Canterbury	19,182	405,272 (10)	343 (12)
Durham	19,066	469,933 (9)	175 (21)
London	13,989	1,722,685 (2)	577 (7)
York	12,629	1,496,538 (3)	828 (3)
Winchester	11,151	729,607 (7)	389 (11)
Ely	11,105	133,722 (26)	156 (23)
Worcester	6,569	272,607 (15)	232 (18)
St Asaph	6,301	191,156 (21)	160 (22)
Bath and Wells	5,946	403,795 (11)	440 (9)
Norwich	5,395	690,138 (8)	1,076 (2)
Lincoln	4,542	899,468 (5)	1,273 (1)
Bangor	4,464	163,712 (23)	131 (24)
Chichester	4,229	254,460 (16)	266 (16)
Salisbury	3,989	384,683 (12)	408 (10)
Lichfield	3,923 (+1,500)[a]	1,045,481 (4)	623 (4)
Chester	3,261 (+813)	1,883,958 (1)	616 (5)
Peterborough	3,103	194,339 (19)	305 (14)
Exeter	2,713 (+565)	795,416 (6)	604 (6)
Oxford	2,648 (+6,036)	140,700 (24)	208 (19)
Sodor and Man	2,555 (+978)	41,751 (27)	17 (27)
Hereford	2,516	206,327 (18)	326 (13)
Bristol	2,351 (+687)	232,026 (17)	255 (17)
Gloucester	2,282 (+2,125)	315,512 (14)	283 (15)
Carlisle	2,213 (+1,027)	135,062 (25)	128 (25)
St David's	1,897 (+3,266)	358,451 (13)	451 (8)
Rochester	1,459 (+2,840)	191,875 (20)	93 (26)
Llandaff	924 (+2,965)	181,244 (22)	194 (20)

a The figures in parentheses represent additional income derived from other sources that were attached to the see *in commendam*. See T. Park, *The Reform Bishops 1828–1840: A Biographical Study* (St Bees: St Bega Press, 2016), 366–367, for the details.

As a result of the report, a new diocese of Ripon was carved out of York, but this was balanced by the suppression of Bristol, which was united with Gloucester. In anticipation of future creations the number of bishops entitled to sit in the House of Lords was fixed at twenty-six. As new ones appeared, they would serve in rotation, apart from the senior sees of Canterbury, York, London, Durham and Winchester, which would always be represented. This arrangement persists to the present time, when there are now forty diocesan bishops potentially entitled to a place in the Upper House.[7] It was also determined, and passed into law in 1836, that in future the Archbishop of Canterbury would receive £15,000 a year, the Archbishop of York and the Bishop of London £10,000 each, the Bishop of Durham £8,000 and the Bishop of Winchester £7,000, the rest to be placed on a sliding scale ranging from £4,000 to £5,000 per annum. That was still very generous, with the minimum stipend worth about £400,000 in today's money, but it went at least some way towards equalizing the House of Bishops and set an example for the future reform of other clerical stipends, although that would not be finally achieved until the 1970s.

The ancient tithe regime was also commuted into cash payments that would be phased out over time. The intention was to relieve everyone of a burden that had become too great to bear and to remove one of the main objections Dissenters had to the church Establishment, but it did not work out that way. Tithe remained a problem for a further century, until it was finally abolished in 1936. In 1837 a system of civil registration for births, marriages and deaths was introduced, and for the first time the state also made provision for civil divorce. The clergy continued to act as registrars for practical purposes, so the change was not as apparent as it might otherwise have been, but they were now acting at the pleasure of the state and not purely within the confines of the church.

In 1838 the Pluralities Act tried to put an end to the non-residence of clergy on their benefices, but the fact that it was not retroactive meant that change was slow to take effect. Two years later, stipendiary canonries in the cathedrals were also abolished, although again only for new appointments, so that it was not for half a century that the reform was finally completed.[8] In the years that followed, the Ecclesiastical Commission managed to abolish most of the peculiar jurisdictions that had survived for centuries, a move that allowed for the consolidation of dioceses and a more effective administration, and plans were drawn up for creating new dioceses, although that took longer.

Another problem that had to be tackled was the emergence of overseas dioceses of the Church of England. Before the American Revolution there had been no colonial bishops, but from 1785 onwards appointments were made,

---

[7] The bishops of Gibraltar in Europe (Canterbury) and of Sodor and Man (York) serve outside England and are not entitled to sit in the House of Lords.

[8] The last of the traditional prebendaries was Richard Beadon, who died on 30 November 1890. He held the prebend of Wiveliscombe in Wells cathedral.

first in what is now Canada and then elsewhere in the British Empire. These bishops and their clergy were given official state support in the form of glebe lands that were meant to provide them with an income, and they enjoyed other privileges as part of the colonial Establishment. But state involvement of this kind was controversial, and before long the subsidies ceased and the privileges were curtailed. It was eventually decided that colonial bishoprics were not an integral part of the Church of England, and the way was opened for the creation of independent Anglican churches in other parts of the world. In the overseas empire Anglicans and Dissenters competed on equal terms, and the latter frequently outnumbered the former. This did not prevent the Church of England from sponsoring settlement in some places, notably on the South Island of New Zealand, where the city of Christchurch was founded in 1850 as an ostentatiously Anglican colony, although there was never a formal religious Establishment there. From that time onwards, a de facto separation of church and state became the norm almost everywhere overseas, although the presence of the Church of England (and to a lesser, but still significant, degree of the Church of Scotland) was a reminder that cultural hegemony did not depend on state support and remained palpable in many colonies as long as the empire lasted.

Cultural hegemony as well as centuries of habit ensured that traditional perceptions of the church remained in place for the remainder of the nineteenth century and for much of the twentieth, but for those with eyes to see the foundations of the old order were crumbling and a secular state was taking its place. The state churches retained their symbolic presence but they could no longer interfere in the lives of ordinary people, and freedom not to belong to them (or to any church) gradually became the norm, even if it was still assumed that all British people belonged to the state church unless they specifically opted out of it.

The incremental nature of ecclesiastical reform meant that by 1850 there were some things that still reflected the old order and which appeared to be increasingly anomalous in the new dispensation. The most obvious of these was the continuing existence of the ecclesiastical courts, which still controlled most of what we would now call 'family law'. This situation had to be tackled, which it eventually was. In 1855 the courts were deprived of their residual jurisdiction over defamation cases, which had already been practically inoperative for centuries. More significant was their loss of matrimonial and probate jurisdiction at the beginning of 1858, a change that affected the majority of the population one way or another. Ten years later it was the turn of church rates, a tax that had been levied on everyone for the upkeep of parish churches, but was felt to be unfair to those who did not attend them.[9] By then the ancient universities had been opened to non-Anglicans – Oxford in 1854 and Cambridge two years later.[10] Dissenters and others still could not read for theological degrees, nor could they become Fellows of the colleges, but even those restrictions were lifted in 1871 and the universities were secularized. The opening of the faculties of divinity to non-Anglicans was to have a significant effect, as they were no longer fully acceptable as seminaries for the training of Anglican clergy. Many felt that new arrangements had to be put in place, and this led to the widespread establishment of theological colleges to supplement the universities.

The need for such colleges had been felt for some time, and a few enterprising bishops and others had established them already, often in out-of-the-way places. One of their motives was to provide a route to ordination that did not involve going to university, which for many was too expensive and too educationally demanding. Others were founded to train men for overseas mission, which was not catered for in the ancient universities. Of the fifteen such establishments in existence in 1871, only one survives – Cuddesdon Theological College, established in 1853.[11] But between 1872 and 1909 a further twenty-seven were founded, of which six are still in existence.[12] These usually reflected one type of churchmanship, for the most part either Anglo-Catholic or Evangelical, although some were explicitly designed to be 'broad' and embrace the whole range of Anglican thought and practice. Only eleven colleges were started after the First World War, but three of them are still in operation, making a total of ten for the Church of England as a whole.[13] Of these, five are Evangelical, four are 'Catholic' in varying degrees and one (Queen's College, Birmingham) is ecumenical, being a joint venture with the Methodists.

Attendance at one of these colleges was voluntary until 1919, but then became virtually compulsory for intending clergymen. Other denominations had (and still have) their own colleges, although most of them are creations of their particular denominations and not independent foundations as the

---

[9] For the long-drawn-out controversy over church rates, see J. Ellens, *Religious Routes to Gladstonian Liberalism: The Church Rate Conflict in England and Wales, 1832–1868* (University Park, Pa.: Pennsylvania State University Press, 1994).

[10] Oxford had previously not allowed any non-Anglican students to matriculate, but Cambridge had permitted them to do so. However, even in Cambridge non-Anglican students could not graduate with a degree even if they had completed a recognized course of study.

[11] It merged with Ripon Theological College in 1975, but is still located at Cuddesdon.

[12] They are St Stephen's House, Oxford (1876), Wycliffe Hall, Oxford (1877), Ridley Hall, Cambridge (1881), Westcott House, Cambridge (1881), the College of the Resurrection, Mirfield (1903), and Cranmer Hall, Durham (1909).

[13] The three new colleges are the Queen's College, Birmingham (1923), based on a university department founded in 1850, Oak Hill College, London (1932), and Trinity College, Bristol (1971), which incorporates Tyndale Hall and Clifton Theological College, both of which were founded in 1925.

Anglican ones are. Economic considerations weigh heavily on their future, and it is likely that many, if not most, will close in the next few years. But there is no doubt that they have left their mark on the churches, and the faculties of divinity in Oxford, Cambridge and Durham depend on them for a significant proportion of their students, who continue to take courses at the universities but receive their spiritual and pastoral formation in their respective colleges.

Scottish exceptionalism

The wave of reform that swept over England was not replicated in Scotland, largely because the need for it there was less pressing. The church courts were secularized, but they had never been as restrictive as their English counterparts – notably over matrimonial questions – and so were less resented. Patronage, which had been a significant problem in Scotland, was eventually abolished, although in circumstances entirely unique and largely unhappy. The universities, which had never restricted entry to Presbyterians, continued to train the church's ministers, as they still do, despite increasing secularization and the loss of denominational exclusiveness.

Scotland was different from England in another way too. In England, Evangelical churchmen remained somewhat unwelcome outsiders, but in Scotland the Church's General Assembly acquired an Evangelical majority in 1832. The Evangelicals had a reform programme of their own, the centrepiece of which was the abolition of patronage. To get around the existing law, the General Assembly decided to pass a Chapels Act, which would allow the Church of Scotland to set up new parishes where they were needed without disturbing the ancient parochial system. It also passed a Veto Act, according to which the male heads of families in any parish could block the appointment of a minister whom they objected to. Thomas Chalmers wanted the state to subsidize the building of new churches, but he failed to obtain support for this, largely because Parliament was afraid that the much larger Church of England might make a similar request, and there was not enough money to go round. So instead, Chalmers launched a campaign that turned out to be remarkably successful. Ordinary Scottish people contributed alongside the wealthy, and within a few years sixty-four new churches were built. This was especially encouraging because there had been opposition to the original plan from a number of dissenting Presbyterians, who thought that the Church should not receive any state subsidy. By going directly to the people, Chalmers had demonstrated that the Establishment still had wide support and could expect the government to recognize that, although the most pressing question was whether the General Assembly had the right to legislate for the Church independently of Parliament.

Nobody worried much about the Chapels Act, but the Veto Act was something else altogether. In October 1834 the Earl of Kinoull appointed Robert Young to the parish of Auchterarder (Perthshire), but the heads of families rejected him – by 287 to 2. Young appealed to the General Assembly, which upheld the veto, but when the case was taken to the (secular) Court of Session, the decision was reversed. On 8 March 1838 it declared Young's appointment valid. The Church of Scotland appealed to the House of Lords but it too ruled in favour of Young. Shortly afterwards another problem arose, this time in the parish of Lethendy (Perthshire), where Thomas Clark had been presented and vetoed in much the same way as Young. However, in the Lethendy case the patron presented a second candidate, Andrew Kessen, who was accepted by the parish. Unfortunately the Court of Session intervened, declared the Veto Act to be illegal and voided Kessen's appointment. It also fined the presbytery of Dunkeld for having proceeded with Kessen's ordination in defiance of what it said was the law.

But the most serious crisis came when the Earl of Fife appointed John Edwards to the parish of Marnoch (Banffshire) in 1837. Edwards had already served as an assistant there, but he had been so unpopular that the heads of families had ordered his removal. When he was presented later on, they voted by 261 to 1 not to allow him into the church. In July 1839 the Court of Session ordered the presbytery to admit Edwards, which it agreed to do, in spite of pleas from the General Assembly not to. The parishioners walked out of the church during the ceremony, and in May 1841 the General Assembly deposed the seven members of the presbytery who had conducted the ordination. The problem was that those seven had obeyed the civil law but not that of the Church, which still maintained that its Veto Act had legal force. The Moderates in the Church supported Edwards, as did the government in London, but the Evangelicals in the General Assembly remained adamantly opposed. There was now no way out. At the General Assembly in May 1843, more than a third of the ordained clergy, and about half the lay membership of the Church, walked out and established the Free Church of Scotland.

To modern minds these events seem almost unbelievable. Who in his right mind would want to minister in a church where only one or two people supported him? Why would a patron be so blind to what was obviously the popular will? We react this way because we are used to democratic principles and would never dream of trying to force people to accept something like this by pulling rank, as it were. But social class was still a determining factor in the nineteenth century, especially in the affairs of the Church and even in Scotland, despite the fact that it was much more egalitarian than England. The result was a disaster for all concerned, and not least for the cause of the gospel in Scotland. A Church that had been making good progress with its evangelizing efforts was suddenly torn apart and it would never again regain the position it was forced to abandon.

This Great Disruption of 1843 split Scotland in two. Those parishes that joined the new Free Church were deprived of their property and had to build afresh, with the result that Scotland suddenly experienced a boom in church building. In many places the parish church was virtually deserted while new ones were erected nearby. By 1848 the Free Church had built no fewer than 730 new churches, 400 manses for the clergy and 500 primary schools – an incredible achievement. Meanwhile the state church was left as a minority body, claiming no more than about a third of the population as its adherents. It survived as the Establishment, but mainly because nobody knew what to do with it. Scotland was still overwhelmingly Presbyterian but no longer united in a single church, an odd situation for which there appeared to be no available remedy.

As usually happens in cases such as this, those who were committed to their faith tended to join the Free Church, while those who were nominal believers remained with the Establishment. That was not universally true of course, but the flavours of the two rival Presbyterian denominations were unmistakable. The Free Church was largely Evangelical and the state church was largely not. But over time the situation became more nuanced. The Free Church was less constrained by its official confession of faith than the Church of Scotland was, and as a result liberal theology penetrated the former more easily. It was also more subject to internal division – before long there was not one Free Church but many, which rivalled one another as much as the Establishment. Patronage was eventually abolished in 1874, removing the main grievance that had produced the Disruption in the first place, but by then positions were too entrenched to allow for easy reunion. Nevertheless the absurdity of having many equally presbyterian churches competing with one another did not go unnoticed, even among the Presbyterians themselves, and various reunions were attempted.

Initially these involved the Free Churches only, which managed to get together in 1900 as the United Free Church. Unfortunately not everyone went along with this, and a minority, based in the Gaelic-speaking Highlands, claimed continuity with the original Free Church – and thus regarded itself as the owner of all its property. The courts upheld them in this, with the result that a handful of people inherited a vast amount of real estate, including the theological college in Edinburgh. This lopsided judgment was eventually overturned, but the 'wee Frees' as they became known, remained independent, as they still are.[14] Meanwhile the United Free Church continued to seek re-union with the Church of Scotland, which was eventually achieved in 1929. The legacy of this sorry episode can now be seen in the large number of redundant church buildings in the northern kingdom, and in the unspoken, but often heartfelt, belief of many Scots that church quarrels are mostly about nothing.

Apocalypticism

One of the consequences of the social disruptions of the late eighteenth and early nineteenth centuries was a revival of interest in eschatology. Christianity is a future-orientated faith, looking forward to the return of Jesus Christ and the final culmination of all things, when evil will be abolished and divine justice, administered by the saints chosen by God, will reign over the earth. The early Christians often believed that the persecutions they had to endure were signs of the end times, and when Rome fell to a barbarian army in AD 410 they were convinced that those times had come. This misunderstanding was laid to rest by the great Augustine of Hippo (354–430), whose classic work *The City of God* became, and to a great extent has remained, the definitive word on the subject. Augustine interpreted the prophecies of the book of Revelation as essentially allegorical visions of the battle between good and evil that would continue to the end of time. In particular the millennium, or thousand-year reign of Christ, prophesied in Revelation 20:1–3, was to be interpreted not as a historical event that would occur sometime in the future but as a symbolic representation of the sovereignty of Christ over the forces of Satan.

Augustine's interpretation became the standard orthodoxy and was barely questioned for the next thousand years – a millennium in itself! There was a brief resurgence of the older view at the time of the Reformation in the sixteenth century, but it was clearly associated with extremists and never got very far. In 1553 Thomas Cranmer thought it dangerous enough to merit a condemnatory article in his Forty-two Articles of Religion, but when those Articles were revised ten years later, all reference to the millennium was dropped. Some of the Puritans got interested in it, but they were mostly eccentrics and were ignored by the mainstream. After that, not much more

---

[14] They continue to split over secondary matters – some traditions die hard.

was heard of it, although an exception must be made for the American Congregationalist Jonathan Edwards (1703–58), who believed that Christ would soon come again – oddly enough, to his home town of Northampton, Massachusetts.[15] This latent belief resurfaced among some British Evangelicals in the 1820s, with consequences that to some degree have endured to the present time. One of those influenced by it was Edward Irving (1792–1834), a Church of Scotland minister who attracted the attention of Thomas Chalmers and was his assistant in Glasgow for a brief period (1819–22). Irving was tempted to take the pulpit of a Scottish church in London, where his charismatic manner soon attracted attention, not least in high society. By 1827 he had built a new church in Regent Square and had a regular following. It did not last long, and in 1833 Irving was deposed from the Scottish ministry for heresy. He could not be silenced however, and went on to establish what he called the Catholic Apostolic Church before dying only a year later.

Irving believed that before the coming of Christ, an event he predicted would take place in 1868, there would be wars and tribulations of the kind mentioned in Revelation. Meanwhile, in order to prepare for this, the Holy Spirit would renew his extraordinary gifts to the church and guide the remnant of faithful believers by appointing twelve 'apostles' to rule over them. These apostles would in turn appoint 'angels' to supervise individual congregations as they waited expectantly for the coming end. Interestingly enough, Irving never claimed to be an 'apostle' himself and was content to remain an 'angel', which demonstrates a degree of humility unusual in the founder of a new religious movement. He was strongly supported by a wealthy English layman, Henry Drummond (1786–1860), who had a great interest in unfulfilled prophecies and organized conferences at which he proclaimed the imminent return of Christ, who would come to judge the wicked world in which they were then living. Drummond was no theologian and something of a crank, but he was well connected and even a Member of Parliament, which shows how influential Irving and his ideas could be.

Another Scot with millenarian tendencies was John MacLeod Campbell (1800–72), Minister of Rhu (Row) just outside Glasgow. Irving visited him there and two years later Rhu experienced a Spirit-filled revival, complete with speaking in tongues and claimed healings. Irving at first reacted negatively to this, but before long he was persuaded that the experiences were genuine and encouraged them in his own church in London. Meanwhile Campbell was

---

[15] Edwards is sometimes thought to have been one of the main influences on the growth of millenarianism in the USA, where its influence has been much stronger than in the UK.

deposed for heresy in 1831 and had to minister in an independent chapel, which he did until his health gave way in 1858. In his later years Campbell advanced a new theory of the atoning work of Christ, which has been very controversial. Campbell himself wanted to stay within the bounds of Reformed orthodoxy but he shifted the emphasis in Christ's vicarious death on the cross from the fulfilment of a legal obligation to the loving self-sacrifice of one who was both the Son of a gracious heavenly Father and the brother of sinful human beings. Opinion is still divided over whether this shift from a purely legal approach to the atonement towards a more relational one is a departure from official Reformed teaching or not. Perhaps the fairest judgment is to say that it is an emphasis that differs from what one normally expects to hear but that it does not amount to a heresy. At worst, and in the hands of some interpreters, it may lead to obscuring Christ's penal substitution on the cross, but although that is one possible interpretation of Campbell's teaching, it is not a necessary consequence of it.

Another very important figure in the revival of apocalyptic thinking was John Nelson Darby (1800–82), born in London to an Anglo-Irish family closely associated with Admiral Horatio Nelson, after whom he was named. Ordained in the Church of Ireland, Darby was drawn to circles in Dublin convinced that the world was coming to an end. Discouraged by the failure to convert Roman Catholics and by the apparent apostasy of the state in granting them tolerance, these Irish Protestants were all too ready to believe that Satan was being unleashed to do his worst. Darby gathered some of these men around him, resigned his orders and began a preaching and teaching ministry that would eventually take him around the world. His first port of call in England was Plymouth, from which his followers got the name of Plymouth Brethren. The Brethren were a close-knit, Bible-based group that had no hierarchy but practised closed (and regular) Communion – termed by them 'breaking of bread' – at a time when that was very rare outside the Roman Catholic Church.[16]

Darby's movement grew and in 1848 a split occurred between those who favoured a stricter internal discipline and those who were content to mingle more freely with others. The former became the Exclusive Brethren, and Darby sided with them, whereas the latter were (and are) known as the Open Brethren. Over the years they have exercised an influence in Evangelical circles out of all proportion to their numbers, not least because Darby developed a systematic

---

[16] F. R. Coad, *A History of the Brethren Movement: Its Origins, Its Worldwide Development and Its Significance for the Present Day* (Exeter: Paternoster Press, 1968); T. Grass, *Gathering in His Name: The Story of the Open Brethren in Britain and Ireland* (Milton Keynes: Paternoster Press, 2006).

understanding of premillenarianism, complete with detailed ideas of the tribulation and the rapture. Premillenarianism was not confined to the Brethren however. Many Evangelicals in the established churches were also persuaded by it, including important political figures like Anthony Ashley Cooper, the future seventh Earl of Shaftesbury (1801–85), who would become the standard bearer of Evangelical social action in the second half of the nineteenth century.[17] A deep interest in biblical prophecy led some of these mainstream Evangelicals to believe that the Jews would return to Palestine, where they would be converted to Christ shortly before his return. In 1846 they banded together across denominations to create the Evangelical Alliance, whose aims were to combat the spread of Roman Catholicism, to promote premillenarian beliefs and to evangelize the working classes, who might otherwise succumb to socialism or worse. Before long this combination of ideas was characteristic of conservative Evangelicals almost everywhere, and remained so for a century or more.[18] Today the Evangelical Alliance continues to promote interdenominational cooperation among Evangelicals, but its original anti-Catholic and premillenarian emphases have faded, if not completely disappeared.

In contrast to the premillenarians stood the majority of nineteenth-century Evangelicals, who interpreted the same concept in a completely different way. To them the millennium was the symbol of progress that God was bringing into the world with the spread of Protestant doctrine, natural science and free trade – the foundations of Britain's empire and its greatness as a nation. These 'post-millenarians', as they are called, were optimistic about the future and believed that the reverses they saw around them were temporary blips on what was otherwise an unstoppable movement forwards. To them, the gospel was all about breaking down barriers, whether of race, creed or general ignorance. They could even support such atrocities as the opium war with China in 1839–42, in which Britain forced the Chinese government to allow the import of a drug that was killing thousands of its citizens, because it opened the Middle Kingdom (China) to the benefits of free trade! It also led some to take an optimistic view of the great Irish potato famine of 1845–51, which they saw as the prelude to the much-needed reform of Irish agriculture and society. Many of them were disciples of Thomas Robert Malthus (1766–1834), an Evangelical clergyman and economist, and who in 1798 had predicted that the

---

17 See D. Furse-Roberts, *The Making of a Tory Evangelical: Lord Shaftesbury and the Evolving Character of Victorian Evangelicalism* (Eugene, Oreg.: Pickwick Publications, 2019).

18 A major influence in this was Alexander Haldane (1800–82), who bought the Evangelical newspaper *The Record*, in which he propagated millenarian views, along with anti-Catholicism and a strict biblical literalism. *The Record* began publication in 1828 (before Haldane acquired it) and ceased in 1949. See K. Hylson-Smith, *Evangelicals in the Church of England 1734–1984* (Edinburgh: T&T Clark, 1988), 96.

world's population would eventually outstrip its resources and that humanity would be forced into what Charles Darwin (1809–82) later called 'the survival of the fittest'.

The nineteenth century was the great age of the optimistic liberalism espoused by post-millenarians, and although post-millenarianism is no longer embraced by many Christians, it has proved to be remarkably resilient. Even after two world wars, mass genocides and the permanent threat of a nuclear holocaust, it is still the official doctrine of virtually all Western democracies, including those of the UK and Ireland. To suggest that humankind has not improved over time, that the world is not getting any better and that human achievements have their limitations is to fall into the secular heresy of our age, even though the evidence for such views is there for all to see. Premillenarianism might have been naive in its understanding of biblical prophecy, but its estimate of the total depravity of the human race, inherited from the Reformed theology of the seventeenth century, is surely closer to the truth. The saving message of Jesus Christ has not been made obsolete over time, and there has been no moral or spiritual progress to match the undoubted advances in science and technology. The world is a more dangerous place now than it was in the days of Irving and Darby, and warnings of impending doom, however unfashionable, are needed now just as much as they were back then.[19]

The assault on the churches

The reform movement of 1828–32 was an important turning point in British history, and it should not surprise us that it gave rise to a movement among secularists in the country for the abolition of the established churches, which were seen by them as props of the corrupt old order. The attack began in Edinburgh as early as 1833, when there was a movement for the non-payment of the so-called 'Annuity Tax', levied by the city on ratepayers for the support of the church's ministry.[20] The chief objection was that everybody had to pay it, whether they belonged to the church or not. The rebels did not say that they wanted to destroy the Church of Scotland, but many ministers drew that conclusion from the belief that if its income were to dry up, the Church would inevitably disappear. It would be twenty years before the Scottish Voluntary Association, so called because it wanted Church contributions to be voluntary,

---

[19] It is interesting to note that some of the strongest supporters of this view in modern times have been literary men – Fyodor Dostoyevsky, Franz Kafka, William Butler Yeats and William Golding – not professional theologians.

[20] The tax had been instituted in 1661 and was abolished in 1853.

would achieve its aims, and by then the Great Disruption had made its task much easier. In the meantime however, its example spread to England, where it was to have far-reaching effects.

As far back as 1818 the utilitarian Jeremy Bentham (1748–1832) had advocated the removal of the Church's endowments, which he believed would amount to its abolition. He was soon followed by the journalist Richard Carlile (1790–1843) and James Mill (1773–1836), both of whom regarded Christianity as inherently false and the Church as a parasite on society. It was left to Mill's son, John Stuart Mill (1806–73), to propose that the Church's endowments should be used to support a system of national education. Somewhat ironically, the message was heard by William Van Mildert (1765–1836), prince-Bishop of Durham from 1826, who realized that his assets would soon be stripped by the state and decided to forestall that by setting up a university in his cathedral city, which even now has a strong Anglican ethos and represents an outpost of gentility in what is otherwise an industrial wilderness.

The radical atheists were soon joined by the leaders of English dissent. These claimed that they had no desire to weaken the state church (of course not!) but that they wanted the remaining restrictions placed on Dissenters abolished. In particular they objected to compulsory church rates, the role of the Church of England in the registration of births, marriages and deaths, and the exclusion of nonconformists from the universities. Their demands seemed to be reasonable enough, but it soon became clear that they were merely a beginning. Behind the moderate leadership stood a more radical element that wanted to do away with the established Church altogether. Needless to say, this unholy alliance between atheism and dissent did not go unnoticed, and the Church of England closed ranks against them both. The setting up of the Ecclesiastical Commission was one result of this reaction, because everybody knew that the Church had to reorganize itself, and especially its finances, if it was to weather the onslaught.

No longer able to rely on state support, the Church set about raising the money to build new churches, managing to erect no fewer than 667 in the decade from 1831 to 1840. Laypeople, including women, were encouraged to devote themselves to pastoral care and visitation, and in 1836 some Evangelicals formed the Church Pastoral-Aid Society, which aimed to provide assistance, both lay and clerical, to the overworked clergy. Unfortunately the inclusion of the laity angered some High Churchmen, who felt obliged to set up the rival Additional Curates' Society in 1837, which sponsored only ordained men.[21]

---

[21] Both these societies still exist and are active within the Church of England.

Much of the impetus for High Church initiatives of this kind came from men close to John James Watson (1767–1839), Vicar and later Rector of Hackney, from which the group came to be known informally as the Hackney Phalanx.[22] Their insistence on maintaining a clerical caste distinct from (and by implication superior to) the laity was an example of the kind of silliness that was to plague the Church of England for the next 150 years and is still not entirely extinguished.

One area where state support for the church was still forthcoming was education, and in 1811 the Church of England set up a National Society, backed mainly by the Hackney Phalanx but supported by some Evangelicals, like William Wilberforce, with the aim of building schools. This was complemented by the British and Foreign Schools Society, sponsored by Dissenters but also receiving state subsidies. The results were highly satisfactory, especially for the National Society, which was soon running about three-quarters of the country's schools. There were however limits to what the Church could achieve. A proposal to regulate child labour in factories was presented to Parliament in 1843, with a clause that established educational provision for such children that would include religious instruction. It was assumed that the Church of England would take charge of this, but there was a furious reaction from Dissenters and radicals alike. Even the Methodists were coopted into the anti-Church campaign, which attracted support from nearly four million people. The proposal was accordingly withdrawn, but the result was the formation of the Anti-State Church Association, later renamed the Society for the Liberation of Religion from State Patronage and Control, which began to campaign for disestablishment. Any hope of a rapprochement between the Church and dissent was now abandoned and good relations between them would not be restored until the later twentieth century, by which time the problems surrounding establishment had either disappeared or taken on an entirely different complexion.[23]

Compulsory education, introduced in 1870, and subsequent reforms have reduced the impact of specifically Christian education, and Free Church schools are now very rare, but the Church of England (and of course the Roman Catholic Church) retains an extensive network of educational institutions. It is true that the level of Christian input into these schools is not always what it could (or should) be, but that is usually the fault of a neglectful Church. Today

---

[22] They were also called the Clapton Sect, in mock imitation of the Evangelical Clapham Sect.

[23] See G. I. T. Machin, *Politics and the Churches in Great Britain 1869 to 1921* (Oxford: Clarendon Press, 1987), who extends his study to cover the virtual disappearance of disestablishmentarianism in modern Britain.

'faith schools', as they have been rebranded, continue to attract a wide range of pupils and are not restricted to the children of Church members. They are still free to teach Christianity to everyone, including those who are specifically non-Christian, and they continue to excite the ire of secularists – a sure sign of their success.

The Oxford Movement

Of all the reverberations resulting from the reforms of 1828–32, none has been more widely studied, or more controversially debated, than the so-called 'Oxford Movement'.[24] This is one of the names given to the work of a group of Oxford men, most of them ordained Anglican clergymen, who reacted to those events with a programme of Church renewal that was intended to rescue it from what they perceived as the depredations of both dissent and radicalism.[25]

Some of the original members of the Oxford Movement came from an Evangelical background, and a few had been influenced by the apocalypticism of Edward Irving, but their main inspiration derived from the High Church Toryism that had emerged in the late seventeenth century and was now in deep crisis. Between 1688 and 1832, High Churchmen had weathered the storm of the Glorious Revolution, the temptations of Jacobitism and the challenge of the Evangelical Revival, which could claim High Church origins in the persons of the Wesleys. After the accession of George III in 1760, the state was more sympathetic to them and they were able to resist the progress of dissent more successfully than they might otherwise have done. But the abolition of religious tests for Dissenters and the emancipation of Roman Catholics cut the ground out from under them. The state might retain the trappings of an Anglican Establishment but it was now committed to a denominational pluralism that, in the eyes of High Churchmen, gave error equal rights with truth. Concessions to non-Anglicans could only weaken the Establishment because Parliament was the ultimate arbiter of the Church's doctrine and polity and it was now no longer equivalent to a lay synod of the Church of England.[26]

---

[24] The literature on this subject is vast and extremely varied in both approach and content. The best modern survey is S. J. Brown, B. Nockles and J. Pereiro (eds.), *The Oxford Handbook of the Oxford Movement* (Oxford: Oxford University Press, 2017).

[25] See O. Chadwick, *The Mind of the Oxford Movement* (London: Adam & Charles Black, 1960); B. Nockles, *The Oxford Movement in Context: Anglican High Churchmanship 1760–1857* (Cambridge: Cambridge University Press, 1994).

[26] Since the union of 1707, Parliament had also contained a contingent of Scottish Presbyterians, but as they were all members of the established Church of Scotland and not Dissenters, their presence was generally overlooked.

Until 1828, state control of the Church could be presented as lay control of the clergy, but that fiction was no longer tenable. Those who formed the Oxford Movement insisted that the Church of England was the direct descendant of the apostolic mission founded by Jesus himself, and passed on from one generation to the next by the laying on of the bishops' hands. Its doctrine, worship and ethos were all derived from an ancient Christendom that had been sundered in the sixteenth century but not broken. Not everything that had been handed down in this way was of equal importance, some things had been misused or corrupted and there were still theological questions that remained unresolved, but these were secondary considerations. The Reformation had tried to get the Church's priorities right, to weed out abuses and even to clarify the meaning of some doctrines like justification by faith, but it had not done violence to the body of Catholic tradition that the Church of England continued to share with Rome and the ancient churches of the East. The more optimistic members of the Movement could even suggest that the latter churches might look to the Church of England as a model for their own renewal!

The first stirrings of protest occurred in Oxford in 1829, when a High Church group managed to unseat Sir Robert Peel as the university's Member of Parliament, because he had voted for Catholic emancipation, which they opposed. But things really got going on 14 July 1833, when John Keble (1792–1866) preached a controversial assize sermon in Oxford in which he claimed that England had fallen victim to what he called 'national apostasy'. The precise effects of his sermon have been debated ever since, but later generations have looked back to it as the moment when the Oxford Movement came together, rather in the way that Protestants regard 31 October 1517, the day that Martin Luther supposedly nailed his ninety-five theses to the door of the church at Wittenberg, as the start of the Reformation.

What is undoubtedly true is that by the end of 1833 a series of 'tracts for the times' was starting to appear, and these became the chief vehicle for expressing the views of the new Movement. Until they were finally brought to a halt in 1841, ninety of them appeared and those who were associated with them came to be known as Tractarians. Twenty of the tracts were recycled from earlier High Church material, and of the remaining seventy, no fewer than twenty-nine (just over 40%) came from the pen of John Henry Newman (1801–90).[27] Newman may therefore rightly be regarded as the chief inspirer of the

---

[27] On Newman's theological development, see F. M. Turner, *John Henry Newman: The Challenge to Evangelical Religion* (New Haven, Conn.: Yale University Press, 2002). There is a vast literature on Newman, but much of it is hagiographical and must be read with caution.

Tractarians, even if the others cannot properly be described as his followers or disciples. Newman was the first among equals, as became apparent when he eventually moved away from his colleagues and entered the Roman Catholic Church. By then, the tracts were no longer being produced but the erstwhile Tractarians were still very much in existence and most of them remained active in the Church of England.

In general terms the Tractarians looked back to the early centuries of the undivided Church as their ideal, and glorified the Middle Ages, which until then had been regarded as a period of cultural and spiritual darkness. England was dotted with medieval churches and cathedrals, which the Tractarians now pointed to as evidence for their claim that this had been the great age of Christianity in the nation. In many cases they sought to restore these buildings to something like their medieval glory. The art of stained-glass-making was revived, medieval hymns were translated and sung in processions, and long-forgotten saints resurrected and given new honour with statues, windows and even church buildings dedicated to them. New buildings were erected in the neo-Gothic style, which was much in vogue in the mid-nineteenth century and had an appeal beyond that of the Oxford Movement, as the houses of Parliament in London so eloquently attest.

By itself, this antiquarian zeal need not have caused any lasting problem. Like other fads, it could come and go, leaving traces here and there without disturbing anything fundamental, and to some extent that is what happened. Many English parish churches still bear the marks of that period, but there is little sign that the parishioners have been deeply affected by it and most are probably unaware that what looks medieval to them is in fact a nineteenth-century recreation. Anyone who studies art and architecture can immediately distinguish what is truly medieval from what is not, and to purist minds the nineteenth-century imitations are usually decidedly inferior to their models. In many ways that does not matter, but the inability of imitators to recreate their originals in art or architecture is reflected in their theological recon-structions as well, and it is there that the controversies over the Oxford Movement really start to bite.

For the Oxford Movement was far from being a theological version of the UK television series *Antiques Roadshow*. It was a cultural vision, supposedly grounded in the writings of the ancient church Fathers but often closer in practice to the Roman Catholic Church, which was also plumbing the depths of its medieval past in search of recovery and renewal after the catastrophe of the French Revolution. That the Church of Rome (and the churches of the East) were just as different from their ancient prototypes as the Church of England was, albeit in other ways, was not always clear to the minds of those who were part of the Oxford Movement.

In fact their grasp of history was often shaky, as can be seen in the remarkable career of William Patrick Palmer (1803–85). Palmer developed what he called the 'branch theory' of the church, according to which there were three strands of authentic Christianity that went back to ancient times – the Eastern Orthodox, the Roman Catholic and the Anglican.[28] He even visited Russia in 1840 and 1841, hoping to persuade the Orthodox Church authorities there of the justice of his position, although without success. Nevertheless his theory attracted widespread support among the Tractarians and was defended by Newman, not only at the time but also many years later, long after his conversion to Rome.[29] By then Palmer's theory had been taken up in a slightly different form by the Russian philosopher Vladimir Solovyov (1853–1900), who suggested that the threefold division of Christendom was 'apostolic' in the sense that the Roman Catholic Church represented the tradition of Peter, the Protestant churches reflected the teaching of Paul and the Eastern Orthodox preserved the mind of John. This theory is sometimes still encountered in ecumenical dialogue, although it has never received official endorsement from any church and is usually regarded as a personal eccentricity, not unlike Palmer's view.[30]

To the extent that the Tractarians had a concept of historical development it was what Newman defined in his *Essay on the Development of Christian Doctrine*, which he wrote as an Anglican and published shortly after his conversion to Rome.[31] According to Newman, Catholic doctrines that had been proclaimed in later times – whether in the fourth or the sixteenth centuries – were the logical outworking of the mission of the Holy Spirit in preserving and extending the church. New challenges required new responses, and under divine guidance the popes and councils of the Middle Ages had been preserved from error as they sought to express eternal truths for a new situation. That this might have been true of the Church of England and of

---

[28] W. Palmer, *A Treatise on the Church of Christ*, 2nd rev. edn (London: C. & J. Rivington, 1842). The first edition had appeared in 1838.

[29] Newman edited Palmer's records of his Russian travels as late as 1882. See W. Palmer, *Notes of a Visit to the Russian Church in the Years 1840, 1841*, ed. J. H. Newman (London: Kegan Paul, 1882). In his introduction to this edition Newman stated that Palmer's position had been common to the Tractarians forty years previously. Palmer's grasp of reality may be judged by the fact that, after his father's death in 1865, he laid claim to a non-existent Irish baronetcy that he had supposedly inherited, and insisted on being addressed as Sir William Palmer.

[30] Solovyov (occasionally spelled as Soloviev or Solovyev) originally published his theory in French in 1889. His book was later translated into English as *Russia and the Universal Church* (London: G. Bles, 1948).

[31] It was republished in 1974 by Penguin, with an introduction by J. M. Cameron.

Protestantism more generally was something Newman either overlooked or discounted, because by breaking with the universal church men like Luther and Calvin had inevitably fallen into heresy. It should be said however that to many Catholic-minded people of the time, including William Palmer, Newman's theory of development came across as a liberal deviation from traditional orthodoxy because it accepted that the Catholic faith as it was professed in the mid-nineteenth century had been unknown in apostolic times.

The Oxford to which the Tractarians preached was still heavily clerical in composition, and most of the undergraduates were heading for parish ministry. The rise of dissent and the reform of the Church's appointments system unsettled them and they were ready to listen to those who emphasized the importance of the clergy as opposed to the laity. Men who could be persuaded that by having hands laid on them by a bishop they would enter into a higher order within the Church naturally found Tractarianism attractive, because it seemed to support their own sense of vocation. The Tractarians also stressed the importance of the visible Church and its sacraments at a time when the pull of inner, or vital, religion was strong and people were increasingly detached from the outward forms, even if they still made use of them from time to time. Almost everybody had been baptized in infancy, but the other rites of the Church were much less frequently observed. Holy Communion for example might be celebrated three or four times a year, or perhaps monthly in special cases, but seldom more frequently than that. Many children were never confirmed and there was no provision at all for penance or extreme unction, which had been dropped at the Reformation. Holy matrimony was celebrated in church, but only once in most people's lifetimes, and so it was hardly a frequent occurrence.

By developing a sacramental theology similar to that which had been abandoned at the Reformation, the Tractarians hoped to increase both the celebration of the sacraments and participation in them, and of course Holy Communion was central to that endeavour. Gradually many of them turned to questions of ceremonial and clerical dress, wanting to revive practices and vestments long discarded and that inevitably had a 'Roman' appearance to them, even though the Tractarians usually denied that. Before long however, the Romeward drift was inescapable and Newman's conversion in 1845 brought it into the open. At the same time, some of the Tractarians began publishing works explicitly hostile to the Reformation. One of their number, Richard Hurrell Froude (1803–36), had died young, leaving a pile of writings that expressed hatred for Protestantism. Newman and Keble edited them and published them two years after Froude's death.[32] In 1839 Tract 80 appeared, a work by Isaac Williams (1802–65) entitled *On Reserve in Communicating Religious Knowledge*, in which he advocated 'reserving' certain Christian teachings and not communicating them to the laity, an odd position that clearly exalted the clergy to a higher level of being and left the impression that laypeople were second-class members of the Church.

But the worst was still to come. In 1841 Newman published Tract 90, *Remarks on Certain Passages in the Thirty-nine Articles*, in which he argued that the Articles of Religion could be interpreted in a fully Catholic sense, something that nobody had ever tried to do before and that most people today would argue is impossible. The resulting storm led to a crackdown on Tractarian activity led by the 'heads of houses' (masters of colleges) at Oxford, which silenced Newman and encouraged him to resign his post as vicar of the university church in September 1843. By then the Romanizers among the Tractarians were publishing openly, and it was not long before Newman and some of his associates left the Church. Others, like Edward Bouverie Pusey (1800–82), were also silenced for a time, but they did not go over to Rome and remained within the Church of England, still hoping to Catholicize it from within.

The strength of opposition to the Oxford Movement is hard to imagine. Evangelicals were naturally incensed by it, as were many liberal members of the Church who thought its medievalism was particularly regressive. The Tractarians were relatively few in number – perhaps about 500 when Newman went over to Rome – but they were organized and determined. They also exploited the lax discipline of the Church of England. Once installed in a parish, they could introduce liturgical innovations without much fear of being deposed, and the few who did suffer did not hesitate to brand themselves as 'martyrs'. That anyone might be fined or put in prison for wearing a chasuble for example, seemed excessive to many people, who did not particularly care one way or the other, and gradually the Evangelicals and others who led such prosecutions were successfully portrayed as persecutors. That did not stop the more determined Evangelicals, some of whom remained active into the twentieth century, but it did encourage a spirit of 'live and let live', which in turn allowed a ritualistic Tractarianism to flourish and take root, not least in inner-city parishes where more respectable, middle-class Evangelicals were reluctant to go.

---

[32] J. H. Newman, J. Keble and J. B. Mozley (eds.), *Remains of the Late Richard Hurrell Froude* (London: J. G. & F. Rivington, 1838).

Perhaps the most significant, and certainly the most enduring, result of the anti-Tractarian movement was the Parker Society, founded in 1840 and dedicated to publishing the writings of the major English Reformers. More than fifty volumes were produced between 1841 and 1853, and some remain standard editions to the present day. A counterseries, the Library of Anglo-Catholic Theology, began publication about the same time and eventually stretched to ninety-five volumes (from twenty different authors), but it was broader in scope than the ideas of the Tractarians and included a number of works that would not normally be regarded as 'Anglo-Catholic'. Comparing the rival series, it must be said that the Parker Society one holds together as a recognizable unit, whereas the Anglo-Catholic Library series is more eclectic and includes a number of minor works from obscure authors. Placing them side by side, it is evident that the Parker Society collection better represents mainstream Church of England thought before the civil wars and is more deserving of serious scholarly attention.

One factor that made it easier for the Tractarians to undertake unpopular ministries was their increasing emphasis on celibacy. This was in direct imitation of Rome of course, but it took a peculiar twist in England. The Tractarians had a number of devoted female followers, some of whom they helped to form sisterhoods for their own spiritual development and for ministry in the parishes. Obviously, the sight of single men encouraging groups of women in this way was bound to raise comment of a salacious nature, and accusations of homosexuality were far from absent either. It is possible that Newman was a repressed homosexual and some of the Tractarians almost certainly were, although solid evidence is often lacking. In any case, whether they were guilty of sexual misconduct or not, the Tractarians were not always careful to prevent the appearance of evil, and their defiance of accepted social custom in the name of 'religion' merely helped to increase prejudice against them.

A moment of truth for the Tractarians came in 1847, when two quite unrelated events conspired to threaten their theological positions. One was the appointment of Renn Dickson Hampden (1793–1868) as Bishop of Hereford. Hampden was already well known in Oxford, where he had been a tutor at Oriel College since 1830 and Regius Professor of Divinity since 1836. He favoured the admission of Dissenters to the university and was rationalistic in his theology, although much of what he said was so obscure that nobody really understood it. He was a declared enemy of the Tractarians, and they protested loudly when the government of the day appointed him to Hereford, something that nobody in the Church could prevent. The other, and ultimately more serious, event was the refusal of the Bishop of Exeter to institute

George Cornelius Gorham (1787–1857) to the living of Brampford Speke in Devon. The main sticking point was that Gorham did not believe in baptismal regeneration; that is to say, the teaching that those who are baptized are *ipso facto* born again in Christ. The Bishop of Exeter believed the Book of Common Prayer taught that doctrine because its baptismal rite contains the words 'seeing therefore that this child is regenerate' after the actual baptism, but Gorham and the Evangelicals denied this. To their minds, the words of the baptismal service were to be understood in a conditional sense, meaning that if the baptized person received the sacramental gift in faith, then regeneration would be the natural consequence, but that no form of human words and no outward ceremony could possibly guarantee that that had happened in any individual case.

This question had never before been raised, and there were some High Churchmen who held to the idea of baptismal regeneration, despite its absurdity. To the modern mind, it is surely obvious that pouring water over someone, especially over an infant who is unaware of what is happening, cannot bring about spiritual rebirth, and few Protestants had ever believed that it could. In Reformed theology the efficacy of a sacrament depends upon what is called 'right reception by faith', and this was the generally held view among those who considered the question. It had the practical advantage of allowing Baptists and other Protestants to live together in peace, since neither side believed that the physical act of baptism made any spiritual difference to the recipient. The language of the Prayer Book that seems to say that a baptized child is 'regenerate' was therefore to be interpreted as a promise proclaimed by the sacrament, not as an established fact brought about by it.

Gorham took his case to the Court of Arches, the highest ecclesiastical court in the province of Canterbury, but lost. He then appealed to the Judicial Committee of the Privy Council, which on 9 March 1850 overturned the judgment of the Court of Arches and ordered the Bishop of Exeter to institute Gorham. It is often claimed that that decision prevented a mass exodus of Evangelicals from the Church of England, which would have created a situation similar to that in Scotland following the Great Disruption only a few years earlier. That must remain a matter of speculation, but it is certain that it did prompt a further exodus of Tractarians to Rome, including Henry Edward Manning (1808–92), who in 1865 would become the Catholic Archbishop of Westminster and build the Roman Catholic cathedral in that city.

At the time, many Tractarians consoled themselves by claiming that the Gorham judgment was an aberration that could be corrected later on, but that turned out to be wishful thinking. The doctrine of baptismal regeneration was always alien to the spirit of Reformation Anglicanism, and its rejection should come as no surprise. But the implications of the Gorham judgment went far beyond that. For High Churchmen the issue was one of authority – did a state tribunal have the right to pronounce on a matter of Church doctrine? For Evangelicals on the other hand the question was one of the nature of the church. Was it a visible institution capable of administering divine grace to its members, whether they believed in what was happening or not? Or was it an invisible company of the elect, present in the visible church but not coterminous with it? High Churchmen subscribed to the view that only Catholics (Roman or otherwise) were true Christians, whereas Dissenters were heretics to varying degrees. Evangelicals in contrast insisted that only God knows who the true Christians are, and that neither the Establishment nor dissent had any monopoly on belief. The true children of God would recognize one another and pay little attention to denominational labels, neither accepting nor rejecting anyone on that basis alone. Positions on both sides have mellowed somewhat over time, but the basic division brought out by the Gorham judgment still characterizes the different Church parties, making cooperation between them difficult and ruling out any genuine union of hearts and minds.

The revival of the convocations

One consequence of the strife of the late 1840s was the realization that the Church of England required some means of settling its internal affairs that would not be entirely dependent on Parliament. The convocations of Canterbury and York were still in existence and were duly chosen by the beneficed clergy at every parliamentary election. The Convocation of York did nothing more than that, not least because its bishops were attending Parliament in London, but the Canterbury one met, heard a sermon and voted a loyal address to the monarch before adjourning. Neither of them transacted any business, but it was not entirely clear whether this was by custom or by legal prohibition. In 1837 the Convocation of York took tentative steps to resolve this question, but did not get very far.[33] In 1852, however, the government allowed the Canterbury Convocation to meet for a few days to test the waters, as it were. The experiment was cautious but successful, and by the end of the decade the Convocation was fully functioning again.[34] The York Convocation was kept in abeyance because

---

[33] See D. A. Jennings, *The Revival of the Convocation of York, 1837–1861*, Borthwick Papers 47 (York: Borthwick Institute, 1975).

[34] For a detailed description of how this occurred, see Chadwick, *Victorian Church*, 1:309–324. See also *The Chronicle of Convocation 1847–57* (London: National Society's Depository, 1889).

its archbishop objected to the whole idea, and it was not until after his successor was appointed in 1861 that it followed suit.

The reactivation of the convocations was regarded by many High Churchmen as a positive development, but Evangelicals and others were suspicious of what they might do, or try to do. The main reason for that was that the convocations were no longer fit for purpose. They were originally provincial synods of the clergy that had been transformed into tax-granting bodies, and the membership was determined by the obligations of the clergy to pay taxes. Thus the bishops, deans of cathedrals and archdeacons were fully represented, whereas cathedral chapters elected one proctor and the beneficed clergy of each diocese two, to represent them. A number of peculiar jurisdictions also had representation, although as these were rapidly disappearing in the 1850s they could be ignored. The big problem was that there was no lay representation, and since Parliament could no longer be relied on to provide that, that was a serious defect. Many parliamentarians, including strong believers like Lord Shaftesbury, feared that they would be cut out of church discussions because they were laymen and without representation in the ecclesiastical synods. There were also two distinct convocations, which could lead to complications where legislation was concerned. What would happen if Canterbury passed new canons for example, but York rejected them? Could the Church of England function differently in the north of England from the south, or did it have to hold together, since it was legally constituted as the national Establishment?

Then too there was the problem of the Irish Convocation, which now became acute. When the Canterbury and York convocations were reactivated, the Irish portion of the United Church of England and Ireland suddenly discovered that it could play no part in deliberations that might affect it just as much as the English provinces, because its Convocation no longer met.[35] This was not merely a hypothetical question, since Canterbury and York proceeded to revise the baptismal canons in 1865 and it was not clear whether these applied to Ireland or not. The Irish clergy accordingly petitioned for the restoration of their Convocation, but its anomalous character as a national, rather than a provincial, body made that particularly difficult. There were many external reasons why the Church of Ireland was disestablished, but its inability to reactivate its Convocation was an internal cause that has not been properly recognized. Discussions on the matter proceeded through the 1860s but got nowhere, and in the end the government realized that disestablishment

---

[35] The Irish Convocation was last elected in 1727 but is not known to have met after 1714. See Bray, *Records of Convocation*, 18:198–203, for the details.

was the only viable solution. In that way the revival of the convocations contributed significantly to the dissolution of the United Church of England and Ireland and the ending of the state connection in the latter country.[36]

In the English context it was initially feared that the reactivation of the convocations would do no more than provide a public forum for the sorts of controversy stirred up by the Tractarians, but although there would be some of that, it was not the whole story. In fact, by providing a forum for discussion, the revived convocations allowed many questions of Church administration to be discussed and resolved with little acrimony, and a backlog of business dating back more than a century was cleared in a relatively short time. Virtually everyone understood that new canons would have to be drawn up for the Church and a commission was set up for that purpose, although its report was stillborn.[37] It would be some time before the problem of lay representation was resolved and serious canon law revision was undertaken, but the road map was clear and the convocations would never again sink back into the doldrums from which they had been rescued.

Tragedy in Ireland

The progressive disestablishment of the Church of Ireland was badly received in England, but reactions in the Emerald Isle itself were more complicated. Everyone knew that the Anglican Church had failed in the task of converting the bulk of the Irish population to Protestantism and that by the time it was united to the Church of England it had given up trying to do so. But events in the early nineteenth century seemed to be pointing towards the possibility that the Reformation might finally take root there. The papacy had suffered considerable loss of prestige during the French Revolution and the subsequent wars with France, and Britain's defeat of Napoleon struck many Protestants as the providential harbinger of a new age of evangelism that many believed would be the prelude to the second coming of Christ. Many Evangelicals believed there was no time to waste, and that the failure to win over the Irish needed to be put right without delay. A number of missionary societies began to work in the country, with some success. Roman Catholicism dominated in the lower middle classes, but beneath them was a large and desperately poor peasant community that few people, including Catholics, had bothered with. It was among these

---

[36] See ibid. 18:211–246.
[37] G. L. Bray (ed.), *The Anglican Canons, 1529–1947* (Woodbridge: Boydell & Brewer, 1998), 579–618.

people that the evangelists had their greatest success, and for a while it seemed that Protestantism might at last put down roots among the Gaelic Irish.[38]

In 1840 Alexander Robert Charles Dallas (1791–1869), an English Evangelical clergyman, visited Ireland and felt called to the work of evangelism in that country. He returned annually for several years and was able to raise a considerable amount of money to support his vision. Dallas was impatient with some of the more experienced missionaries, whom he thought were too cautious in their approach, and he was determined to press on full speed ahead. In August 1846 he set up his own organization and used the funds he had collected as a means of pressuring the existing missions into adopting a more aggressive approach. He could not have known that Ireland would soon be stricken with a serious famine that would last several years, but when it came he interpreted it as the providential judgment of God. For the next few years, as Irish peasants died in their thousands and many, including most of those who had converted to Protestantism, left the country in any way they could, Dallas went on preaching his message and persuaded his English supporters that hunger was driving many to find God through his ministry.

With spectacularly bad timing Dallas founded the Irish Church Missions in April 1849 and within a few years he had built twenty-one churches, forty-nine schoolhouses, twelve parsonages and four orphanages in Ireland. In other times that would have been a remarkable achievement, but in the circumstances it was doomed to failure. The people who were meant to benefit from this activity had disappeared, and the negative reactions from those who had survived were overwhelming. Many people, Protestants and Catholics alike, thought Dallas had taken advantage of a desperate situation and used it to preach an other-worldly salvation to people who were starving. Dallas's own pre-millenarian apocalypticism blinded him to the reality of what was happening, and he rashly persevered in his disastrous policies until he died, even though by then most of his supporters had deserted him.

The Dallas affair might have been swept under the carpet had it not been for another man of equally deep-seated and blind conviction. This was Paul Cullen (1803–78), the third son of prosperous Catholic tenant farmers, who was destined for the priesthood from an early age.[39] Unusually for the time, Cullen was sent to Rome for training and remained there for nearly three

---

[38] D. Bowen, *The Protestant Crusade in Ireland, 1800–1870* (Dublin: Gill & Macmillan, 1978).

[39] D. Bowen, *Paul Cardinal Cullen and the Shaping of Modern Irish Catholicism* (Dublin: Gill & Macmillan, 1983); E. Larkin, *The Making of the Roman Catholic Church in Ireland, 1850–1860* (Chapel Hill, N.C.: University of North Carolina Press, 1980); E. Larkin, *The Consolidation of the Roman Catholic Church in Ireland, 1860–1870* (Chapel Hill, N.C.: University of North Carolina Press, 1987).

decades. He fell in love with Italy and the papacy, to which he was devoted. In 1849, when the Papal States were in turmoil because of the 1848 revolutions on the Continent, Cullen was sent back to Ireland as Archbishop of Armagh. He had not been in the country during the famine and relied for much of his information on printed reports – including those sent by Protestant missionaries like Dallas, boasting of their famine converts.

Cullen lost no time in turning this to his advantage. He was not an Irish nationalist in the usual sense of the term, but he was a strong Catholic and saw it as his first duty to drive Protestants out of the country altogether.[40] His second duty, which he saw as being closely tied to the first, was to transform Irish Catholicism in the image of Rome by introducing devotional disciplines that he had learned in Italy and that he now regarded as far superior to normal Irish practice. He launched his programme at the Synod of Thurles in 1850, the first such gathering to be held in Ireland since 1690. Cullen had no idea that Protestants and Catholics had worked together to mitigate the effects of the famine, and he did not hesitate to attack his fellow clergy if he thought they were too friendly to those of a Reformed persuasion. One of his targets was the unfortunate Theobald Mathew (1790–1856), who was the leader of a remarkable temperance movement that attracted both Catholic and Protestant support.[41] Mathew was non-political and (by Irish standards) relatively non-sectarian, but Cullen could not abide that. He had little interest in Mathew's social work – what concerned him was the need to save Catholic souls, whether they were sober or not.

It was Cullen who picked up the Protestant propaganda about the conversion of starving peasants, and who more or less invented the myth that Protestants had connived with nature to de-Catholicize Ireland. The belief that ignorant peasants had sold their birthright for the soup that Protestant evangelists were supposedly distributing took hold and was soon widely believed, despite the lack of evidence to support it.[42] Cullen combined this kind of misrepresentation with an icy determination to keep Protestants and Catholics as far apart from each other as possible. Needless to say, convincing one side that the others were dangerous monsters served his purposes very well and played its inglorious part in creating the antagonism between the two traditions that would erupt after his death.

---

[40] M. Tanner, *Ireland's Holy Wars: The Struggle for a Nation's Soul 1500–2000* (New Haven, Conn.: Yale University Press, 2001), 247–252.

[41] M. Lysaght, *Father Theobald Mathew OFM Cap.: The Apostle of Temperance* (Blackrock: Four Courts Press, 1983); C. Kerrigan, *Father Mathew and the Irish Temperance Movement, 1838–1849* (Cork: Cork University Press, 1992).

[42] D. Bowen, *Souperism: Myth or Reality?* (Cork: Mercier Press, 1970).

On what might be seen as the positive side, Cullen succeeded in clearing out many of the folk traditions of the Irish peasantry in what came to be known as the 'Devotional Revolution'. True to his Roman orientation, Cullen emphasized the importance of the papacy for Catholics, just at the time when Pope Pius IX (1846–78) was moving towards a declaration of his own infallibility in matters of faith and morals. That in turn elevated the status of the bishops and priests, who were charged with inculcating the new devotional standards at parish level. Cullen was translated from Armagh to Dublin in 1852 and made a cardinal in 1866, after which time his authority over Irish Catholics was unchallenged. So successful was he, in fact, that his reforms remained essentially unchanged among Irish Catholics until the 1990s. In a very real sense the fear of Protestantism pushed the Catholic Church into a clergy-dominated system that in turn fuelled the worst Protestant nightmares about a 'priest-ridden' society, which would have seriously negative consequences in the political sphere. As many Irish people (including Protestants) pushed for greater autonomy within the UK, it was easy for Protestant opponents to come up with the slogan 'Home rule means Rome rule', a formula Cullen would have been only too happy to endorse.

The Irish famine was a tragedy by any standard, but the fallout in terms of Christian devotion and ecumenical understanding was equally severe, and has sadly proved to be much more long-lasting.

1859

In the middle years of the nineteenth century a profound change in the religious atmosphere of the British Isles was taking place. As with all such things, it was not immediately perceptible to most people but, looking back after more than 150 years, we can see that 1859 represented something of a tipping point. At the top end of the scale, that was the year in which the first changes were made to the 1662 Book of Common Prayer. The changes were peripheral, to be sure, but significant nonetheless. For nearly 200 years the Church of England had been obliged to commemorate three significant political events. The first and best-known of these was 5 November, the anniversary of the Gunpowder Plot in 1605. The second was 30 January, the day on which King Charles I had been beheaded in 1649, and the third was 29 May, the anniversary of the Restoration in 1660. To these the Church of Ireland had added 23 October, commemorating the foiling of the Catholic rebellion in Ulster in 1641, one of the seminal events that had led to the outbreak of civil war a few months later. The abolition of these services marked a stage in the progressive separation of church and state, but more importantly, it signified a growing detachment from the religious settlement of 1689 that had continued to shape the mindset of most British people, whether they were members of the established churches or not.[43] Today we may question whether those seventeenth-century events should ever have been officially commemorated, but taken together they undergirded the Protestant parliamentary monarchy that was widely held to be the key to Britain's successful rise to great power status. To abandon them could be seen as a loss of faith in the national mission, which was to spread British values across Europe and the rest of the world. If the mother country of representative democracy was losing its self-confidence, what hope was there for the nations that looked to it for inspiration?

The same year 1859 also saw the outbreak of religious revival in many parts of the British Isles. In one sense this was clearly harking back to the days of the Wesleys and Whitefield a century before, but in other ways it was significantly different. The eighteenth-century Revival had been led by clergymen of the established Church who had no intention of leaving it, and it was centred on England. The 1859 revival, largely the work of laypeople often only nominally connected to organized religion, was felt most keenly on the Celtic fringes. It was also inspired to some extent by a parallel movement in the USA, the first time (although by no means the last) that American influence could be detected on British Christianity rather than the other way around.

Revivalism struck a chord in Ulster, especially among Presbyterians, many of whom had drifted off into a rationalistic heterodoxy, not unlike the Unitarianism that had destroyed English Presbyterianism a century earlier.[44] A sense of impending crisis was aggravated by the growing confidence among Irish Catholics, who were experiencing a devotional revolution of their own. By 1859 the fire was ready to be lit; before long, strong Evangelical preaching was being heard across northern Ireland and in every Protestant denomination, including the established Church. The American influence was palpable and readily acknowledged. There were extended prayer meetings, open-air preaching sessions conducted by untrained laymen, and enthusiastic singing, all of which led to the 'altar call', the moment when doubters were invited to step forward and make a 'decision for Christ' as a mark of their conversion. Alongside all this came a new emphasis on emotional outbursts that often led to unusual behaviour. People fell to the ground weeping, some were overcome

---

[43] It may be added that 5 November doubled as the anniversary of William III's landing at Torbay in 1688, the start of the Glorious Revolution.

[44] F. Holmes, *The Presbyterian Church in Ireland: A Popular History* (Dublin: Columba Press, 2000), 108–113.

with fits of trembling and a few began to utter strange noises – not quite speaking in tongues but definitely moving in that direction. So remarkable was all this that it attracted widespread attention and divided public opinion across Britain. For some people the revival was the authentic restoration of biblical Christianity, whereas for others it was a hysterical delusion. It ended just about a year after it began, but it left lasting results in the churches, which saw a significant increase in membership and a renewed concern for religious experience as the true test of doctrinal orthodoxy. Ulster Protestantism became, and to a considerable degree has remained, more conservative than Protestantism elsewhere, and for that the ongoing inheritance of the 1859 revival can take much of the credit.

In Scotland the 1859 revival was also widespread, but it was more varied than in Ulster. Its base was in the Free Church of Scotland, where the fervour of the Disruption had started to cool, but it soon spread to the established Church as well. Its strong emphasis on lay preaching and leadership produced great results in outlying areas, where the clergy had been fewer and the influence of institutional religion less obvious. In the Highlands and islands a deeply conservative faith was entrenched among the laity, significant traces of which still remain. In the north-east there was a great expansion of the Plymouth Brethren, whose informality and lay leadership allowed them to establish a number of congregations, many of which have been active ever since.

In Wales the revival was largely confined to the Welsh-speaking areas and was heavily dominated by the Calvinistic Methodists. It had a particular impact on mining communities, some of which were converted en masse. Nonconformity had been strong in Wales since the time of Hywel Harris, but it was after 1859 that it really took over as the dominant form of Christianity in that country. The established Church was relatively untouched by the phenomenon, which merely increased the sense among many that it was an alien presence in Welsh society. Chapel religion, with its strong revivalist undertones, became the norm in much of Wales, and its impact would endure for the better part of a century. It has declined in recent years, but the scores of abandoned chapels that can be found throughout the principality are a silent reminder of a time when a high proportion of the inhabitants were on fire for the Lord.

In England the revival had noticeably less impact, but it was significant nonetheless and some of its results were to be lasting. As in the Celtic countries there was considerable American influence, although native English Evangelicals were noticeably more critical of what they saw as the Americans' slick professionalism than many of their Celtic brethren were. But that was not the whole story by any means. The revival gave a platform to William Booth (1829–1912), a Methodist lay preacher, and his remarkable wife Catherine (1829–90), both of whom felt called to preach to the poor of England's great cities, whom they regarded as just as needy as the most primitive savages in the Global South. Unable to work within the constraints of Methodism, they branched out on their own, founding a 'Christian Society' that they later transformed into the Salvation Army. Organized along quasi-military lines, complete with uniforms and brass bands, the Salvation Army made a great impact among slum dwellers, rescuing many from alcoholism, petty crime and prostitution. The Booths did not hesitate to advertise their mission among the middle classes, most of whom would never darken the door of a Salvation Army chapel, but many of whom came to appreciate their sincerity and beneficial social activities. To this day the Salvation Army, although in some respects a curious relic of Victorian England, retains the respect of people all over the world and receives charitable donations from many who have no idea what the Salvationists believe or practise. Lacking a clergy or sacraments, they are not a 'church' in the usual sense, but their impact is far greater than their numbers might suggest.[45]

Another outcome of the revival in England was the extraordinary growth of Nonconformist preaching, especially in the big cities. The most famous and influential of these preachers was the Baptist Charles Haddon Spurgeon (1834–92), whose Metropolitan Tabernacle in London became a place of pilgrimage for people from all over the country and the world, in addition to having a major impact on the capital itself. Spurgeon's influence was spread by his sermons, which were published in serial form until the supply finally ran out in 1917, a quarter of a century after his death. Scholars might quibble at some of his exegesis, particularly its strong predilection for allegory and other dubious kinds of exposition, but on the gospel message itself there could be no doubt. Spurgeon knew all about the horrors of sin and eternal damnation, the promise of salvation through the shed blood of Christ and the perseverance of the saints in a world of trials and suffering. To people who had little joy or hope in this life, he brought the message of the heavenly glory that awaited those who endured to the end, and his appeal did not fall on deaf ears. The Metropolitan Tabernacle is now a shadow of its former self but it is still there, and Spurgeon's College in south London stands as a reminder of the great man's commitment to the training of pastors and preachers for the spread of

---

[45] In 1882 Wilson Carlile (1847–1942) founded the Church Army, a Church of England counterpart to the Salvation Army. It still exists but operates on a much smaller scale and is little known outside church circles.

the gospel. For many, and especially for Baptists throughout the world, Spurgeon remains an inspiration and a challenge to those who continue to seek the blessing of revival.

Religious revival, a major theme of 1859 and widely recognized as such at the time, was not the only influence at work on the churches in Britain. Very different was the activity of a small number of intellectuals, working independently of one another, who were starting to question and even reject many of the premises Christians took for granted. At the time their doubtings appeared as little more than a cloud on the horizon, but it was a cloud that was set to grow, and from the vantage point of hindsight we can see that in the end it was to influence the course of Christianity in the British Isles at least as much as, and possibly more than, the revivals did. Typical of this approach are the comments of John Stuart Mill, who in 1859 wrote:

> What is boasted of at the present time as the revival of religion is always, in narrow and uncultivated minds, at least as much the revival of bigotry; and where there is the strong permanent leaven of intolerance in the feelings of a people, which at all times abides in the middle classes of this country, it needs but little to provoke them into persecuting those whom they have never ceased to think proper objects of persecution.[46]

Lest anyone find this criticism too vague to be applicable in any particular case, Mill added an explanatory note as follows:

> The ravings of fanatics or charlatans from the pulpit may be unworthy of notice; but the heads of the Evangelical party have announced as their principle for the government of Hindoos and Mahometans [in India], that no schools be supported by public money in which the Bible is not taught, and by necessary consequence that no public employment be given to any but real or pretended Christians . . . Who, after this imbecile display, can indulge the illusion that religious persecution has passed away, never to return?[47]

Mill's contempt for Evangelical Christianity could hardly be clearer, but even if he was right to think that Britain could not impose the faith on India in the manner he described, the Evangelical proposal regarding public

---

[46] S. Collini (ed.), *J. S. Mill 'On Liberty' and Other Writings* (Cambridge: Cambridge University Press, 1989), p. 33.
[47] Ibid. 33, n.

education cannot really be called 'persecution' of non-Christian religions. It seemed obvious to most British people then, and many would argue that it is still fairly clear now, that Indians would have been better off had they converted to Christianity in large numbers, even if we must agree that this can be accomplished only by the work of the Holy Spirit and not by some government policy.

Mill could write the way he did because he was tapping into a vein of scepticism that was growing bigger and more obvious by the day. There had always been those who scoffed at Christianity, but in the mid-nineteenth century objections to the faith took on a new and more challenging tone. More and more people from educated backgrounds were abandoning the beliefs of their youth, sometimes after considerable personal struggle. Stewart Brown lists the sample in Table 12.2 as representative of this tendency.[48]

Table 12.2 Examples of educated people who forsook their former beliefs, 1840–1860s

Date	Person	Occupation
1840	Mary Ann Evans (George Eliot) (1819–80)	Novelist
1840s	Herbert Spencer (1820–1908)	Philosopher
1849	James Anthony Froude (1818–94)	Former Tractarian
1849	Arthur Clough (1819–61)	Poet and friend of Florence Nightingale
1850	Francis Newman (1805–97)	Younger brother of John Henry Newman
1858	John Ruskin (1819–1900)	Art critic
1860s	Mark Pattison (1813–84)	Former Tractarian

It will not escape notice that at least two of these seven were former Tractarians, and Francis Newman, although not of that school himself, was the younger brother of its founder. This is of special significance because Tractarianism was supposed to be the antidote to the unbelief of the Victorian age, the answer of the Church to the infidelity of Protestantism and the assumed superficiality of its Evangelical variant in particular. It is fair to say that with the notable exception of George Eliot, these people and their objections to

---

[48] Brown, *Providence and Empire*, 227. Dates are those when the individual's unbelief became public knowledge.

Christianity are largely overlooked nowadays, even if their atheism is shared by many of our contemporaries. George Eliot stands out, partly because she was a woman in an age when women were treated as inferiors to men, which is one of the reasons why she wrote under a male pseudonym, but it may be asked whether her current reputation as one of the greatest English novelists would be what it is if the literary critics of our present age were spiritually sensitive to the faith she rejected and ridiculed. If they were, her anti-Christian views would now be just as forgotten as those of the others are.

But the name that will not go away belonged to by far the most influential of the nineteenth-century sceptics – Charles Darwin, whose epoch-making book *On the Origin of Species* first appeared in that fateful year of 1859. Darwin was not alone in his scepticism, nor did his ideas come out of the blue. Much of what he wrote had already been suggested by Robert Jameson (1774–1854), Professor of Natural History at Edinburgh, and by Sir Charles Lyell (1797–1875), author of *Principles of Geology*, which he published in 1830–33. Lyell argued that the earth was much older than the Genesis account would have us think and had undergone a series of mutations over the millennia. But it was Darwin's book that caught on and made the general public aware of the way that the study of natural science was evolving (no pun intended!). When and how Darwin lost his faith is a matter of controversy, but it probably had more to do with the untimely death of his daughter than with any of his biological theories.

But if his theories did not push Darwin himself into atheism, they had a considerable impact on many who read his work. He sketched out a plausible pattern of natural selection, according to which plants and animals are constantly mutating – for better or for worse. Most of the time it is for worse, and the mutations fail to reproduce. But sometimes it is for the better, and then one species will gradually evolve into another, more resilient, one. As Darwin saw it, nature is pitiless and the survival of the fittest is a brutal struggle for existence against overwhelming odds. And yet it was out of such struggles that the world as we know it has come into being. As long as this theory was confined to plants and the lower animals, nobody worried too much, but it was a different matter when it came to human beings. Did humankind evolve from some species of ape? If so, how, when and why did that happen? The discovery of so-called 'Neanderthal Man' in 1856 made this question acute, and Darwin's evolutionary hypothesis provided a possible answer to it. The connection was made by Thomas Henry Huxley (1825–95), who in 1863 published his important *Evidence of Man's Place in Nature*, in which he put flesh on the bones uncovered by Darwin. A few years later the work was carried further by

Edward Burnett Tylor (1832–1917), who developed the idea that religion emerged from the primitive fears of humankind, and that as evolution proceeded, these fears became fossilized in rituals. Tylor believed that in the next stage of evolution they would fade away altogether, an outcome he longed to see in his own lifetime. Thus we find that human and animal sacrifices were common in Old Testament times, mythologized in the supposed atoning sacrifice of Christ and are now (in the nineteenth century) on the point of losing all credibility. Christianity might be the highest form of religion ever to have evolved, but Tylor was convinced that it would soon evolve itself out of existence.

Theories like these could hardly go unchallenged, because they struck at the very heart of Christian belief, but the response of the Church was disappointing. Samuel Wilberforce (1805–73), son of the great William and a High Church Bishop of Oxford, tackled Darwin almost immediately, but it soon became apparent that the two men were living in different mental universes. Wilberforce's arguments, drawn largely from Scripture, were no match for Darwin's scientific evidence, and the only result of the conflict was to discredit Christianity in the eyes of many educated people. One way or another this argument is still going on, with not dissimilar results. The scientific Establishment clings to a belief in biological evolution, although the theory has developed considerably since Darwin's day, and the moral objections to a 'survival of the fittest' doctrine have largely faded away. On the other hand religious fundamentalists continue to advocate what they call 'creationism', believing that Genesis 1 – 3 is a reliable scientific account of the origins of the universe.

In fact, as many people have pointed out, 'evolutionists' and 'creationists' are talking past each other and no real dialogue between them is possible. All Christians are 'creationists' in some sense, but not all rule out biological evolution. It is possible to believe that evolution is a means used by God to perfect his creation without denying the largely symbolic account of human origins found in Genesis. This is a conflict that should never have arisen but that occurs because each side is blind to the most important affirmations of the other. The 'creationists' misinterpret Genesis 1 – 3, but the 'evolutionists' tend to rule God out of the picture entirely, concentrating on the process (the 'how') of human development rather than on the purpose (the 'why'), which God has revealed in his Word. In fairness there are many British scientists, often connected to the Victoria Institute, who have reconciled these two perspectives and defend orthodox Christian teaching, but unfortunately their voices tend to get drowned out by the extremists on either side and their syntheses go unnoticed outside the specialist circles in which these people move.[49]

The ability of the Church to respond to the challenges posed by Mill and Darwin was greatly hampered by what can only be called a revolt from within. Tractarians and Evangelicals were at odds on many things, but both agreed that the Bible was the infallible Word of God and that the orthodox tradition of the Church was a faithful interpretation of its meaning. There were however some people who questioned this, particularly within the Church of England. They were represented by men like Samuel Taylor Coleridge (1772–1834) and Thomas Arnold (1795–1842), the headmaster of Rugby School and a leading proponent of what later became known as 'muscular Christianity'. It was their belief that Christianity had to move with the times, embrace new ideas and adapt itself to a world that no longer thought in ways that were familiar to the biblical writers. They were not atheists or even sceptics in the usual sense of the term, but were relativists who believed that truth was not confined to one particular form of expression, and that it could be found even outside the bounds of traditional Christian faith. These men came to be lumped together as the 'Broad Church', although they never claimed that identity and seldom worked together in the way Anglo-Catholics and Evangelicals did.

There was however one notorious exception to this. In 1858 a group of Broad Churchmen got together to plan a series of essays that eventually appeared in April 1860. The essays were written at the same time as Mill and Darwin were publishing their theories, but appeared too soon afterwards to be regarded as answers to them. On the contrary, they are better regarded as supporting what the radicals were saying – or at least, that was the view taken by the orthodox within the Church. *Essays and Reviews*, as this symposium was called, created a stir that has still not entirely died down. Among its contributors were Frederick Temple (1821–1902), another headmaster of Rugby School, who argued for the development of doctrine throughout history, even to the point that the Church had now outgrown the need for Scripture and should be guided by reason and conscience alone. Then there was Rowland Williams (1817–70), who expressed his admiration for the kind of radical biblical criticism that was then

---

[49] The Victoria Institute was founded in 1865 in order to combat Darwinism and enjoyed considerable success for a generation or so. Its most distinguished president was Sir George Gabriel Stokes (1819–1903), Lucasian Professor of Mathematics at Cambridge (1849–1903), President of the Royal Society (1885–90) and Churchwarden of St Paul's Church, Cambridge, where there is a monument to him. It declined after Stokes's death but still exists and publishes occasional bulletins on the subject of the relationship between faith and science. On the impact of Darwinism in Scotland, see D. Fergusson, 'The Reception of Darwin', in D. Fergusson and M. K. Elliott (eds.), *The History of Scottish Theology*, 3 vols. (Oxford: Oxford University Press, 2019), 2:404–418.

emerging in Germany but had not yet made much of an impact in Britain. Baden Powell (1796–1860), the Professor of Geometry at Oxford, wrote a piece that denied the existence of miracles, and Henry Bristow Wilson (1803–88) claimed that parts of the Bible were mythological, that salvation could be obtained apart from Christ and that eternal punishment was an expendable doctrine. But the longest and most influential essay in the volume was the one by Benjamin Jowett (1817–93), who argued that the Bible should be examined and interpreted like any other piece of literature, thereby effectively sidelining any notion of divine inspiration.

The Church of England could hardly sit back and allow such an attack, launched by some of its own members, to go unchallenged. A charge of heresy was taken to the Court of Arches, where a mild judgment against the authors was passed. They were suspended from their posts for a year and ordered to pay the court costs, but that was all. An appeal to the Judicial Committee of the Privy Council was even more dissatisfying, as the judges ruled that none of the authors had explicitly denied any doctrines of the Church, even if they had questioned some and interpreted others in an unusually broad way. The Church itself was hardly appeased. Within weeks petitions against the essayists were circulating and gathering signatures – nearly half the ordained clergy formally expressed their dissent from this judgment. In June 1864 the newly revived Convocation of Canterbury flexed its muscles by condemning *Essays and Reviews*, although to no real effect.[50] People could protest all they liked, but in the end they had no power to exercise discipline over aberrant clergymen and the way was opened to the doctrinal pluralism – or some would say theological anarchy – that now characterizes almost all the mainstream churches in Britain and Ireland.

---

[50] E. S. Grindle, *Episcopal Inconsistency, or Convocation, the Bishops and Dr Temple: A Letter to the Archbishops and Bishops of the Church of England: Together with an Account of the Proceedings in Convocation with Regard to* Essays and Reviews, *and Extracts from the Speeches of the Bishops, Taken Verbatim from the* Chronicle of Convocation (London: Masters, 1869).

13
The Victorian mirage (1860–1914)

From faith to morality

From its beginnings in first-century Palestine, the basic message of the Christian Church has been that Jesus Christ came into the world in order to redeem his chosen people from sin and prepare them for eternal life with him in the kingdom of heaven. The Christian life is a blessed deliverance from the powers of evil that rule this present age, but those who have been set free know that they must struggle in a spiritual war against the world, the flesh and the devil.[1] This is true even when the institutional Church enjoys influence and privilege; indeed it is at those times when the temptation to turn away and deny the faith is stronger than ever. As the children of the Reformation and the subsequent revivals knew only too well, persecution of true believers is as likely to come from within the church as from outside it, and the faithful in every generation must be prepared to bear witness to the gospel of redemption that will prevail when Christ returns at the end of time.

In the mid-nineteenth century this message was being proclaimed from pulpits all over the British Isles. Churchmen, Dissenters and Roman Catholics were united in this belief, even though they expressed it in different ways and not infrequently clashed with one another because of that. Yet on the most fundamental things they were all agreed – life is short, this world is a place of pilgrimage and getting to heaven must be the primary goal and preoccupation of the Christian.

Sometime in the middle of the nineteenth century this vision and the world view that undergirded it began to be questioned, even by some who were officially sworn to uphold it.[2] One of these was Frederick Denison Maurice (1805–72), a man brought up as a Unitarian who converted to the Church of England, into whose ministry he was ordained in 1834. It might be thought

---

[1] See esp. Eph. 6:10–20.
[2] For a survey of the period, see B. M. G. Reardon, *From Coleridge to Gore* (London: Longman, 1971); repr. as *Religious Thought in the Victorian Age: A Survey from Coleridge to Gore* (London: Longman, 1980).

that someone who rejected a heretical background would have embraced a rigid and uncompromising orthodoxy, as often happens in such cases. But Maurice retained something of the free-thinking culture he had been brought up in, and this led him to see that much of the Christianity he knew was a middle-class religion that scarcely touched the poor or even the working classes of society. The Industrial Revolution and the urbanization that it had brought about made this failure even more obvious than it might otherwise have been, and widespread social unrest threatened to overturn not only the state but the all-too-complacent churches as well.

Britain avoided the upheavals that struck many European countries in the revolutionary year of 1848, but only just. On 10 April there was a massive demonstration in London by the so-called 'Chartists', a group that had composed a 'people's charter' advocating deep-seated social reform. The demonstrators wanted to challenge Parliament with a petition signed by more than two million people, but a combination of heavy rain (this was Britain, after all!) and the leaders' desire to prevent bloodshed at all costs blunted their efforts, leading to widespread disillusionment and frustration. On the evening of that fateful day, Maurice met with two of his colleagues and together they plotted out what they could do to meet the Chartists' demands without incurring the danger of revolution. What they came up with was what later came to be called 'Christian Socialism'. Maurice and his friends believed that the Church of England was the natural vehicle for uniting society in a common spiritual and moral purpose. That purpose would find its expression in a new deal between employers and workers that would make the former aware of their responsibility for the welfare of the latter and give the poor a fair share in the profits of trade and industry. Instead of being preoccupied with their own salvation, Christians should be concerned for the betterment of others.

Those with eyes to see had to admit that, rich although the UK was, it was far from being an equal or just society. In Ireland peasants were dying in their thousands because of the potato famine, and in Britain factory workers were only marginally better off. To move from a tenancy in the Irish countryside to a tenement in Manchester or Glasgow – as many did – was jumping from the frying pan into the fire, and it is not surprising that those who realized that were soon clamouring for action – Christians included. Men like William Booth and Lord Shaftesbury were soon in the vanguard of social reform, with lasting results. The Christian Socialists were less active, but they soon moved off in another direction. To them, the gospel of eternal salvation in heaven came to seem like a hypocritical excuse for avoiding the challenge of material improvement on earth. Heaven remained a theoretical goal – 'pie in the sky when you die' – but earth was real, and it was there that the churches were called to bear witness to the grace of God.

It soon became apparent to Maurice and others that the traditional picture of the saved as a persecuted remnant that had been rescued from eternal damnation did not fit with their vision of a more just social order. For Christian Socialism to work it had to be universal, and in orthodox Christian terms, universalism is heretical. Maurice therefore softened or abandoned many of the tenets of Christian orthodoxy, even to the point of believing that Christ was a great moral teacher whose message was valid for the whole of humankind, rather than the Saviour of an elect few. Somewhat surprisingly, perhaps, this message initially resonated on the foreign mission field more than it did in the British Isles. One of its leading advocates was John William Colenso (1814–83), an admirer of Maurice who was appointed missionary Bishop of Natal (South Africa) in 1853. Colenso did not confine his ministry to the white settlers there but went straight to the indigenous Zulus, with whose culture and cause he came to identify. Unlike most of his European contemporaries, he did not regard the Africans as benighted savages condemned to eternal darkness, but as children of God who needed to be set free from the bonds of social and economic oppression. He started translating the Bible into Zulu, a task that brought him face to face with the strangeness of much of the Old Testament. Asked by the Zulus to explain the miracles and extraordinary events recounted in the Hebrew Scriptures, Colenso was at a loss. He was not a biblical scholar but, like the higher critics in Germany who were saying much the same thing, he came to believe that the Scriptures were a collection of tribal myths that could not be taken at face value.

Rather than keep his doubts to himself, Colenso wrote them down and published them as *The Pentateuch and Book of Joshua Critically Examined*, which appeared in 1862 and immediately encountered a storm of opposition. Colenso was deposed from his bishopric but he continued to function in Natal, creating a schismatic church that endures to this day.[3] He moved away from an emphasis on Christian doctrine, where his position was weak, and focused instead on the moral demands of the gospel, which he believed could be introduced into African culture without difficulty. His advocacy of the Zulus naturally won him considerable support among them, but in time it also came to appeal to many in Britain who thought that missionary work was designed

---

[3] It came to be known as the Church of England in South Africa (CESA), though it has recently been rebranded as REACH-SA (Reformed Evangelical Anglican Church of South Africa). It has inherited Colenso's missionary legacy but rejects his theology and biblical criticism in favour of a strict Evangelical orthodoxy.

to impose an alien culture on indigenous peoples who were not morally or spiritually deficient, and who did not need to be told that their ancestors had been damned through their ignorance of Christian truth.

This liberal view soon spread to India, where Christian missions had been relatively unsuccessful in their attempts to convert the locals. Was this failure due to arrogance? What right did Christians have to condemn followers of other religions, many of whom had ethical ideals similar, or even superior, to their own? This line of thought was promoted by Brooke Foss Westcott (1825–1901), Regius Professor of Divinity at Cambridge. In 1876 he inspired the creation of the Cambridge University Missionary Brotherhood in Delhi, the aim of which was to foster dialogue with Hindus and Muslims as well as to engage in practical social work in the city's slums. At home a similar vision was promoted by men like Arthur Penrhyn Stanley (1815–81), who became Dean of Westminster in 1863 and used his influence to further the belief that Christianity was essentially a code of ethical behaviour all religions shared. According to Stanley, that code had been obscured by religious dogma and traditions that gave the different faiths the appearance of being mutually incompatible; but once these were removed, the common core would be revealed and universal agreement ensue. These men believed that progressive Christians of their own time were in the process of doing just that, and that the duty of missionaries was to encourage adherents of other religions to copy their example – converting them, in effect, to a doctrine of moral purity rather than to salvation in and by Jesus Christ alone.

The view that Christianity was essentially an uplifting message of morality was propagated by men like Matthew Arnold (1822–88), son of Thomas, who was well aware of the decline of traditional faith, which he proclaimed in his celebrated poem 'Dover Beach', published in 1867. Arnold was a vociferous advocate for a national church that would proclaim a unifying social ethic of 'sweetness and light', and he directed much of his ire against the Non-conformists, who in his view were trying to divide society by preaching an old-fashioned puritanical religion of sin and salvation. In this, Arnold was misreading his target, since many Nonconformists were coming around to much the same views as his, although without the attachment to the national church ideal.

Similar influences could be felt in Scotland, both in the established and in the Free Church. Whereas previously the former had been wedded to confessional orthodoxy in the form of the Westminster Confession and the latter had embraced revivalist Evangelicalism, the two drew closer together by the common attraction of liberal, non-dogmatic Christianity. This was particularly noticeable in the Free Church, where the higher criticism of the Old Testament was introduced by Andrew Bruce Davidson (1831–1902) and developed further by his pupil William Robertson Smith (1846–94). Davidson escaped censure but Smith was not so fortunate, in 1881 being deposed from his chair in Aberdeen. He was immediately snapped up by Cambridge, where he was appointed as Professor of Arabic, and his supporters in the Free Church did their utmost to ensure that freedom of thought, by which they meant acceptance of the new higher criticism, would become the norm in the Free Church.

Before long the citadels of traditional orthodoxy were collapsing and liberal theology was establishing itself in the universities, both in Scotland and in England, but the travel was not all in one direction. At Cambridge a trio of New Testament scholars, including the liberal Brooke Foss Westcott as well as Joseph Barber Lightfoot (1828–89) and Fenton John Anthony Hort (1828–92), were working to lay the foundations of a deeply conservative tradition of New Testament scholarship that has endured to the present day. Westcott and Hort produced an edition of the Greek New Testament that quickly became a classic, and Lightfoot demonstrated that the so-called 'Apostolic Fathers' of the early second century were authentic representatives of primitive Christianity and their witness substantiated the claims that the canonical texts were themselves a true record of Christian origins. Largely thanks to them, British biblical scholarship would never be as liberal as its German counterpart and a conservative reading of the Scriptures would always be acceptable in Britain to a degree that it would not be in Germany.

Disestablishment?

The rapid rise of Nonconformity in the early nineteenth century and the emancipation of Roman Catholics in 1829 created an unprecedented situation of religious pluralism in the British Isles, although all three kingdoms continued to have established churches that claimed the allegiance of their entire populations. The Irish situation was notoriously intractable. Everyone knew that the Church of Ireland represented a tiny proportion of the total population and that Roman Catholics constituted the vast majority, especially in the south and west, but nobody quite knew what to do about it. In Scotland the established Church had suffered the Disruption of 1843, which turned it into a minority, but as the Dissenters were almost all Presbyterians, it was hard to know whether they could really be called Nonconformists. Many people thought that in time the causes of the Disruption would be resolved and the churches would be reunited, as indeed happened in 1929, so the misfortunes of the Scottish Establishment might prove to be only temporary. In Wales Non-conformist chapels had taken over at least three-quarters of the population, including virtually all the native Welsh-speakers, making the Establishment seem like an alien occupation that would have to be rejected if Wales was to flourish as a nation. But the Church of England remained the largest single denomination in Wales, and its defenders resented any comparison with the situation of the Church of Ireland.

The English scene was the most complicated. The revivals had reinvigorated the so-called 'Old Dissenters', who dated from the seventeenth century, and had also created new denominations, but many people kept contact with the established Church, especially in the countryside. Church in the morning and chapel in the evening was a pattern that was not unusual, and in some places it still persists to a limited degree. Did this ambiguous situation give the Church of England a claim to state support? Many of its members thought so, and continued to press for parliamentary grants for the building of new churches, even though they knew that they were unlikely to succeed in their requests. To sort out who belonged where, the government decided to conduct a religious census in 1851, the only one ever attempted in the UK. Ireland was left out at this stage, but England, Wales and Scotland were all included.[4]

The results were astonishing, and deeply disconcerting. In a country where everyone was supposed to attend a church, only about 40% of the population had done so on census day. About half the remainder were absent for good reasons like poor health or necessary work, but that still left about 30% who had not gone at all. The majority of these were in urban areas, which fuelled the belief that the poor and the working classes, who were concentrated in the cities, were alienated from the churches. Furthermore, of the 40% who attended public worship, only slightly more than half went to the traditional parish church. It could therefore be claimed that the Church of England embraced less than a quarter of the total population, with Nonconformists making up nearly a fifth in England and a majority in both Wales and Scotland.

For the Church of England the results were traumatic. Nonconformists, whose numbers only a generation before had been almost negligible in many parts of the country, were now poised to take the lead, and had already done so in many places.[5] Reformers within the Establishment realized that unless they did something about it, the Church would soon decline into insignificance. The result was a determination to intensify the Church's presence in places

---

[4] A religious census was however held in Ireland (only) in 1861.

[5] See T. Larsen, *Friends of Religious Equality: Nonconformist Politics in Mid-Victorian England* (Milton Keynes: Paternoster Press, 1999).

where it was traditionally weak, and over the next half century remarkable results were achieved. New parishes were created, and each of them was equipped with a church and a clergyman to serve it. Very often there was also a church school to which most of the local children would go, and great effort was expended in this form of evangelism. It is impossible to say for sure whether the numbers of those regularly attending public worship increased accordingly, but whether people went to church or not, by 1900 the Church of England had re-established itself almost everywhere except in Wales, and even there there were signs that it was slowly improving its position.[6]

Another important development of this period was the creation of several new dioceses. After five had been established in 1540, following the dissolution of the monasteries, there had been no new creations until 1836. But then a remarkable change took place and over the following century no fewer than twenty new dioceses came into existence, raising the total from 24 to 44. Initially there was a heavy concentration on the northern province of York, although that declined in the twentieth century and in 2014 three of the new northern foundations were reduced to one (see Table 13.1, in which dioceses in the Province of York appear in italics).

Table 13.1 New dioceses created from 1836 to 1927

Dates	Dioceses
1836	*Ripon*[a]
1848	*Manchester*
1877	Saint Albans, Truro
1880	*Liverpool*
1882	*Newcastle*
1884	*Southwell*
1888	*Wakefield*[a]
1905	Birmingham, Southwark
1914	Chelmsford, Saint Edmundsbury and Ipswich, *Sheffield*
1918	Coventry
1919	*Bradford*[a]
1926	*Blackburn*, Leicester
1927	Derby, Guildford, Portsmouth

a Dissolved in 2014 when it became part of the new diocese of Leeds.

---

[6] On the survival of the Church of England at parish level in the nineteenth century, see F. Knight, *The Nineteenth-Century Church and English Society* (Cambridge: Cambridge University Press, 1995).

By any standard this was a remarkable performance, although the long-term effects of this expansion are hard to determine. What can be said with certainty is that a diocesan map of the Church of England now reflects its geographical spread more accurately than it once did and no longer looks like a curious survival of Roman Britain. But whether it has led to any significant increase in Church membership or attendance is another question, and it seems equally certain that whatever effects it has had, it has not led to a widespread revival of religion anywhere in the country.

Most of the new dioceses settled into the Church of England without much ado, but the creation of the diocese of Liverpool gave a public stage to John Charles Ryle (1816–1900), a staunch Evangelical who made a name for himself as a preacher and writer. Although largely ignored in the standard accounts of the Victorian church, Ryle is the only Anglican bishop of the nineteenth century whose works are still in print and widely read. His ministry has continued long after his death and he continues to be honoured, even by many Protestants who would never set foot inside an Anglican church.[7]

The Church of England was able to stave off calls for disestablishment by persuading those in power that it had an enduring link with the nation. The Church was also helped by the politicization of the issue among some Nonconformists who gave the impression that they were seeking revenge for the Great Ejection of 1662 as much as freedom of religion, which to all intents and purposes they already enjoyed. Much of the Nonconformist campaign was led by Robert William Dale (1829–95), a Congregational minister in Birmingham, but his belief that disestablishment would make England a more just society failed to carry much conviction.[8] When he and others objected to the provisions of the 1870 Education Act, which legislated for non-denominational religious instruction in schools, exasperation with the disestablishment campaign grew intense. Dale and his friends thought that the state school system would be skewed in favour of the Church of England, although there was no evidence to justify that belief, and parliamentary support for their cause faded away. Religious instruction in state schools remained fairly basic but it was provided, and there has never been much evidence that it has influenced pupils' faith decisions one way or the other. Christian education has given many people a

---

[7] It was originally intended that Liverpool should be part of the diocese of Sodor and Man, but neither the city nor the island wanted that. Instead Sodor and Man also received a strongly Evangelical bishop, Rowley Hill (1836–87), who transformed the diocese and established a tradition there that endured to 1966.

[8] Dale is remembered today mainly for *The Atonement* (London: Hodder & Stoughton, 1875), in which he argued for a more 'balanced' presentation of the penal substitutionary doctrine than had characterized traditional Evangelical theology. It was an early indication that Nonconformity was moving away from orthodoxy to a more liberal theological position.

grounding in the Bible that serves them in good stead if they are converted later on in life, but virtually nobody has ever claimed that their school religious education lessons led them to Christ, or (still less) to the Church of England.

Another problem faced by the Nonconformist supporters of disestablishment was that they found themselves allied with secularists and unbelievers against people who were supposed to be fellow Christians. Charles Spurgeon for example believed that disestablishment was a divinely ordained cause and did all he could to promote it, including inviting the Unitarian (and essentially atheist) Joseph Chamberlain (1836–1914) to speak in favour of it from the pulpit of the Metropolitan Tabernacle. Nobody was more surprised by this than Chamberlain himself, and the incongruity did not go unnoticed.[9] For many years Spurgeon continued to allow his chapel to be used for meetings of the Liberation Society, which was the main vehicle for disestablishment agitation, although he apparently cooled somewhat towards it when its basically anti-Christian character became too obvious to ignore.[10]

Ireland was another matter. The established Church there was an obvious anomaly and after the emancipation of Roman Catholics it was living on borrowed time.[11] The religious census of 1861 revealed that of the 5,768,967 people then living in Ireland, 4,505,265 (77.6%) were Roman Catholics and only 693,357 (11.9%) belonged to the Church of Ireland. Presbyterians, Methodists and other Protestants made up a further 10%, but they could not be counted on to support the Establishment.[12] Considered on its own merits and compared with the Church of England, the Irish Church had much to be proud of. The standards of its clergy were high, they took a real interest in their parishioners, including the Roman Catholics, and regular attendance at worship was in percentage terms much higher than it was in England. But whereas the Church of England operated against a background of religious indifference, the Church of Ireland was faced with an overwhelmingly hostile Roman Catholic population that was often more devout than Church of Ireland members were. Reconciling Ireland to the union with Great Britain was the urgent priority of the government, and for that to happen the privileged position of the Church of Ireland had to be sacrificed.

This was achieved by William Ewart Gladstone (1809–98), a devout High Churchman who had nevertheless embraced many tenets of Broad Church

---

[9] The incident occurred in 1876. See G. I. T. Machin, *Politics and the Churches in Great Britain 1869 to 1921* (Oxford: Clarendon Press, 1987), 95.

[10] Founded in 1844, the Liberation Society finally disbanded in 1958, its main object – the disestablishment of the Church of England – still unrealized.

[11] For the details, see M. H. Bell, *Disestablishment in Ireland and Wales* (London: SPCK, 1969).

[12] Ibid. 40–41.

theology and put political consensus ahead of doctrinal conviction. For him the struggle over the Irish Church was not a question of truth but of expediency. Catholic Irishmen were not going to be converted to Protestantism by theological arguments, and so the only solution was to accommodate the opinion of the majority, whether it was true or not. The Church of Ireland resisted as far as it could, but in the end had to give way and on 1 January 1871 it was disestablished.

The results of Irish disestablishment were ironic in many respects. The most deeply religious part of the UK was now the only one that had no official religion. It was meant to be a secular state, but the large Catholic majority, combined with the reactionary policies of the Roman Church under Pope Pius IX, ensured that in fact it gravitated towards an unofficial Catholic dictatorship. For the next hundred years or more, the Catholic Church in Ireland was in a position to tell the state what to do, and it did not hesitate to exercise that privilege whenever it could. On the other side, some Irish Protestants were so disillusioned by the way in which their cause had been sacrificed by English politicians that they began to turn against the Union. The Church of Ireland layman Isaac Butt (1813–79) founded a Home Government Association in 1870, dedicated to the proposition that Ireland should be free to govern itself. In 1873 the name was changed to the Home Rule League, which was initially led by Protestants but gradually moved much closer to the Catholic nationalist position. Perhaps only in Ireland could such an improbable association of people and ideas take place. To rub salt into the wound, the Catholic Archbishop of Dublin (Paul Cullen) ordered a *Te Deum* to be sung for the 'victory' of disestablishment even though many of his own laypeople advised him against it. Whatever else disestablishment might lead to, harmony among the different Christian denominations was not likely to emerge in its wake.

In Scotland the campaign for disestablishment was coloured by the fact that the three main actors were all presbyterian churches. In addition to the established Church and the Free Church, there was also the United Presbyterian Church, a collection of eighteenth-century dissenting movements that had banded together and were opposed to any church–state connection on principle. The difficulty was that sometimes the Free Church and the United Presbyterians would combine against the Establishment, but on other occasions the Free Church would side with the Church of Scotland, which it had only recently left. Members of the established Church thought that much of the difficulty could be resolved if patronage, one of the main causes of the Disruption, were to be abolished, and they achieved that aim in 1874. In theory that should have reconciled at least the Free Church to the Establishment, but it did not, because both it and the United Presbyterians interpreted the abolition as a clever move on the part of the Establishment to steal their members.

In 1851 the established Church of Scotland and the Free Church each represented about a third of the Scottish population, but by 1874 the former had increased its share to more than 40% while the latter had gone down to about a quarter. There thus appeared to be some substance to the Establishment's claims, although of course it was impossible to prove. In any case the removal of patronage made the different churches even more like each other than they had been before, and reunion began to look like a real possibility. Given the presbyterian polity of the established Church, its links with the state were less onerous than those of the Church of England, and it is not clear what difference disestablishment would have made. As a result, agitation for disestablishment declined due to lack of interest, and many people began to value the established Church as a symbol of Scotland's nationhood, which would have been eroded if it had been taken away – and to no obvious purpose.

The Catholic threat

Victorian Britain was a Protestant state that increasingly felt itself to be under siege from a Catholic resurgence it could not control. In Great Britain this threat was certainly exaggerated, as Catholics made up no more than 5% of the total population and were concentrated in areas of large Irish migration. In Ireland it was a different matter, and as time wore on, there was a fusion between Catholicism and nationalism that would last well into the twentieth century and eventually destroy the Union of 1801. There was however another 'Catholic' influence, this one from within the Church of England, that was also gaining in strength in the late nineteenth century and that posed a more subtle threat to the Protestant state. If the Church of England could be Catholicized from within, that state would effectively be overthrown, almost without anyone noticing.

Today many people find the anti-Catholicism of the Victorian era baffling and repulsive, but this is because we have forgotten the context in which it developed. After the anti-Catholicism of the French Revolution there was a reaction in much of Continental Europe and the papacy set itself firmly against all aspects of 'modernity', including democracy, free speech, workers' rights and so on. The popes still ruled most of central Italy and were therefore opposed to Italian unification, which many people elsewhere thought was a just and logical development, even though Italy had not been a single state since Roman times. In 1864 Pope Pius IX had issued a *Syllabus of Errors* in which many aspects of modern thought were condemned, and the *Index Librorum Prohibitorum* (*Index of Prohibited Books*), although it dated back to the sixteenth century, was considerably expanded. Among liberals everywhere, to be banned in Rome was something of a badge of honour, and few people had anything good to say about what was in fact a corrupt, inefficient and retrograde ecclesiastical government.

Yet this was the church that had attracted men like Newman and Manning, and this was the pope that many Irish Catholics vowed to defend on his throne against the rising forces of Italian democracy. Newman explained his position in his autobiographical work *Apologia pro Vita Sua*, which appeared in 1864 and was widely admired for its candour and obvious sincerity, and there was a steady trickle of aristocratic and other highly placed converts to Rome. Protestant opposition to this was not lacking however. It contained a strong dose of prejudice, to be sure, but it was based on facts that were hard to deny and British sympathy for the papacy was regarded in much the same way as the more recent sympathy of some well-meaning but naive idealists for the postwar Communist regimes in Eastern Europe. How anyone could reject the freedom and (relative) democracy of the UK for the totalitarianism of Rome was a mystery to many Protestant minds, but it was also a fact that had to be reckoned with – and combated. The declaration of papal infallibility at the First Vatican Council in 1870 sealed Protestant opposition to Rome, and for understandable reasons. Newman and Manning did their best to persuade the British public that the decree did not mean what they thought it did, but had limited success in their attempts. The carefully cultivated air of Catholics as urbane English gentlemen turned sour under the suspicion that such people were posing as secret agents trying to overturn the British state and, although tolerated, they were no longer admired as they had once been.

For Protestant activists, going to Rome to overthrow the pope was not a practical possibility, so the struggle had to be carried on closer to home – in Ireland, by renewed attempts at evangelism among Catholics, and in England by trying to suppress Catholicizing tendencies within the established Church. As Tractarianism entered its second generation, it transformed itself from being a doctrinally based High Church movement into a ritualistic tendency as much concerned with restoring medieval (and contemporary Roman Catholic) practices as it was with the theology that supposedly lay behind them. Whereas Newman and Manning, in their Anglican years, had not bothered with the niceties of clerical dress or with the manual acts that accompanied the Roman mass, the second generation showed a growing interest in such things. They reintroduced the wearing of stoles and gradually of chasubles and other eucharistic vestments that had been banned in 1549. They also put candles and crosses back on the Communion table, which they took to calling the 'altar', faced eastward for the celebration and indulged in such things as the 'elevation of the host', which was meant to signify the transubstantiation of the consecrated elements, even though the Church of England explicitly rejected that doctrine.

These innovations did not go unnoticed and in many cases parishioners (and others) voiced strong objections to them. In one notorious case George Anthony Denison (1805–96), Archdeacon of Wells, was prosecuted in 1856, not only for teaching the 'real presence' of Christ in the consecrated eucharistic elements, but also for insisting that ordinands in the diocese should profess belief that those who received the sacrament unworthily were receiving the true body and blood of Christ. Neither of these views was the doctrine of the Church, and those who took Denison to court were supported by the Evangelical Alliance and Lord Shaftesbury, among other prominent churchmen. Denison was duly convicted, but was spared deprivation on technicalities. The result of the affair was that Denison became popular among those who thought that he was being badly treated, but his opponents came to believe that legal action was both possible and necessary in order to prevent views like his from spreading.

In 1865 the Church Association was formed, with the express purpose of campaigning against ritualism in all of its forms. It soon acquired a large membership, mainly (although not exclusively) Evangelical and, along with other related bodies, was very active in promoting the Protestant cause.[13] Unfortunately for the Church Association, if the priest was properly instituted into his benefice there was little anyone could do to stop him from introducing such practices, apart from embarking on long and expensive court cases – which some people were prepared to do. It was bad publicity that the Church could ill afford and led to demands that Parliament should intervene. Eventually it did, and passed the Public Worship Regulation Act (1874). This Act did not expressly ban ritualistic practices but tried to buttress the traditional rites of the Church of England and set up a special court to try cases that contravened what was taken to be the law. The act was widely disregarded however, with the result that prosecutions continued. Among those affected was

---

[13] In 1950 the Church Association merged with the National Church League, founded in 1906, to create the Church Society, which still exists and is the main voice of Reformed Evangelicalism within the Church of England. It publishes the journal *Churchman*, originally founded in 1879.

Alexander Heriot Mackonochie (1825–87), who was widely regarded as the ringleader of the ritualists and was frequently suspended from his ministry, on one occasion for three years. Another was Arthur Tooth (1839–1931), who was sent to prison for his ritualism, as were one or two others of like mind. Needless to say, these people already had a martyr complex that was only fuelled by the way they were treated. Before long they were presenting themselves as godly victims of persecution by an infidel state and its Low Church supporters.[14] The latter remained active for many years, led by John Kensit (1853–1902), who founded the Protestant Truth Society in 1889. At first the Kensitites enjoyed considerable popular support, but as time went on and they became more extreme in their protests, sympathy for them ebbed away, and by the early years of the twentieth century even many Evangelicals were distancing themselves from them. They still exist, but their last significant protest was against the visit of Pope John Paul II in 1982, when they were mostly ignored by the wider public, and since then almost nothing has been heard from (or about) them.[15]

Many of the ritualist clergy were men of high moral and spiritual principles, and had independent means that enabled them to support themselves regardless of what the Church might do. They also had a certain aristocratic disdain for the law that allowed them to break it when it suited them to do so, and their grasp of Anglican ecclesiology was often weak, to put it mildly. One of their main ideologues was Edmund Gough de Salis Wood (1841–1932), whose book *The Regal Power of the Church, or the Fundamentals of the Canon Law: A Dissertation* became a major justification for their indiscipline.[16] Among other things, Wood argued that the Reformation settlement had been imposed by the state by muzzling the voice of the convocations, which he believed were the only legitimate authority in matters spiritual. Civil disobedience was therefore justified until such time as the Church was set free from state control. Wood's conclusion ignored the fact that in the sixteenth century, church and state were two aspects of a single Christian society, making the opposition he posited an anachronism. It was armed with such dubious interpretations of history that the ritualists went into battle against the very institutions they claimed to be upholding, driving a coach and horses through

---

[14] See M. Wellings, *Evangelicals Embattled: Responses of Evangelicals in the Church of England to Ritualism, Darwinism and Theological Liberalism 1890–1930* (Carlisle: Paternoster Press, 2003); J. C. Whisenant, *A Fragile Unity: Anti-Ritualism and the Division of Anglican Evangelicalism in the Nineteenth Century* (Carlisle: Paternoster Press, 2003).

[15] See N. Patterson, *Ecclesiastical Law, Clergy and Laity: A History of Legal Discipline and the Anglican Church* (Abingdon: Routledge, 2019), 59–102.

[16] (Cambridge: Macmillan and Bowes, 1887).

whatever remained of church discipline and ironically contributing to the anarchy that characterizes the Church of England.[17]

Today we can look back on the behaviour of these men and condemn it as ridiculous and ungodly, but their contemporaries were often impressed by their dedication and by personal qualities of pastoral care that many of them showed to the less fortunate members of society. Charles Lowder (1820–80), for example, was both a ritualist and a determined evangelist in east London, where he was particularly active during the cholera epidemic in 1866. In the end the authorities gave up trying to restrain men like him and ritualism flourished, even to the point of influencing a substantial section of the middle ground in the Church of England. It is no longer unusual to see clergymen wearing stoles and performing certain ritual acts that were once prohibited, although the use of incense is still rare and modern liturgical reforms have virtually abolished the eastward celebration that was such a mark of ritualism in the past. The ritualists have left their mark, not only on the Church of England but also on many Nonconformists, and even on the Church of Scotland. The passage of time has diluted much of what they fought for, but pockets of extreme ritualism can still be found here and there, and many overseas provinces of the Anglican Communion have been deeply marked by ritualism's missionaries, who have taught their converts that their tradition is nothing other than true Anglicanism.

One further consequence of Catholic renewal was the revival of religious communities, particularly for women. In the mid-nineteenth century there was an increasing number of women who wanted to adopt a consecrated way of life but there was little or no provision for them outside the Roman Catholic Church. John Henry Newman briefly established a community at Littlemore in 1842, but it did not survive his departure for Rome three years later. By then, a Sisterhood of Mercy had been founded at Christ Church, Albany Street (London) in 1844 and soon there were a number of imitators all over England. By 1900 there were over thirty of them, despite the strong opposition some of them had to face. Religious communities for men developed more slowly, with the first being the Society of St John the Evangelist, founded at Cowley (Oxford) in 1866. The Society of the Sacred Mission followed in 1891 and the Community of the Resurrection in 1892. The first of these established itself at Kelham in 1903 and the second at Mirfield in 1898, where it is still active and even supports a theological college for the training of Anglican clergy. But since the 1960s, religious orders have gone into serious decline in all the

---

[17] See Patterson, *Ecclesiastical Law*, 72–73.

churches, including the Roman Catholic Church, and some have closed altogether. It is still too early to say whether they will vanish completely, but their future does not look bright.

Evangelicals and Nonconformists did not take part in this movement, although the creation of an order of deaconesses in 1862, in imitation of a parallel Lutheran order that had been started in Germany in 1836, made it possible for non-High Church women to participate. By the end of the nineteenth century deaconesses had become common in the Church of England and women workers were also to be found in at least some of the Nonconformist churches. They continued to be active for two or three generations, but the ordination of women in the late twentieth century dealt them a severe blow and they are now in the process of disappearing altogether.[18]

The American Revolution

While controversy raged over ritualism, Darwinism and disestablishment, the grassroots of British Christianity witnessed the irruption of something quite different and relatively new. There had already been some American involvement in the revival of 1859 but that had been a largely British and Irish phenomenon. Fourteen years later things had changed. In June 1873 a pair of young Americans arrived in Liverpool, having been invited by two rich English Nonconformists who had agreed to sponsor them. But when they arrived, they discovered that both of their prospective hosts had died and that there was nobody to organize their tour. Lesser men would have turned around and gone home, but the two Americans were made of sterner stuff. They had an entrepreneurial spirit of the kind that says the difficult can be done immediately, but the impossible will take a little longer. Whether what they achieved was difficult or impossible must be left to historians to judge, but after their visit the churches in Britain were never quite the same again.

The first of these men was Dwight Lyman Moody (1837–99), a poorly educated Chicagoan who had become involved with the Young Men's Christian Association (YMCA), an Evangelical social organization that had been established for young working men by Sir George Williams (1821–1905) in 1844 and had spread to the major cities of the English-speaking world and beyond. Moody had honed his evangelistic skills during active service in the American Civil War and continued his preaching ministry afterwards. His

---

[18] In the Church of England for example the order of deaconesses was closed after 1992, when the ordination of women to the presbyterate was approved. No existing deaconess was forced to be ordained, but there are now only a few left, almost all of whom are retired.

partner, Ira David Sankey (1840–1908), came from a banking family in Phila-delphia. The two men met through the YMCA in 1870 and soon formed a team, with Moody preaching and Sankey leading the singing at the meetings they held.

Moody and Sankey began to tour parts of northern England but without much success until they were invited to Edinburgh by some Free Church ministers. There their simple, direct approach struck a chord and Edinburgh was taken by storm. Moody's message was simple and expressed as the 'three Rs' – ruin by sin, redemption by Christ and regeneration by the Holy Spirit. His addresses were short, simple and filled with homespun anecdotes and folk wisdom. Americans were still a novelty in Britain at that time, and their breezy, unaffected style appealed to people who were alienated by the stuffiness of so much British life, not least in the churches. They eschewed extraordinary manifestations – nobody fell on the floor weeping or started speaking in tongues – but they were direct and uncompromising. Those who heard their message were invited to respond by coming forward and staying on for further discussion and instruction, usually on a one-to-one basis.

Moody and Sankey trained volunteer counsellors to help with their work and their meetings were professionally organized. Oblivious to local con-troversies and standing outside the class system, they could preach the simple gospel to everyone without exception. They toured much of Scotland and Ireland in the course of 1874 and spent most of the following winter in the industrial cities of northern England. In March 1875 they finally arrived in London, where they became a sensation. Even Gladstone attended one of their meetings and was impressed by Moody's ability to hold an audience's attention. Needless to say, they were not universally popular and there was a lot of criti-cism from liberal churchmen and highly placed prelates. The Archbishop of Canterbury let it be known that he could not support them, and many clerics criticized their simplicity, their ignorance of modern theology and their com-plete disregard for ecclesiastical niceties. One is reminded of the sorts of opposition Jesus encountered during his earthly ministry, and the effect was much the same. While the learned scoffed, the simple folk responded. Moody and Sankey did not hesitate to take their message to the poor and underprivileged, believing that spiritual rebirth would be the prelude to moral and physical rehabilitation. The results spoke for themselves. Many people were solidly converted and a good number entered various forms of Christian ministry that would have a lasting impact both at home and abroad.

Moody and Sankey's tour coincided with a revival of interest in 'holiness', more specifically in the perfectionism that had been the hallmark of the later

John Wesley and that had always characterized a certain strand of Methodism. This undercurrent was brought to life by two other Americans, Robert Pearsall Smith (1827–98) and his wife Hannah Whitall Smith (1832–1911), who taught that it was both possible and necessary for Christians to lead a perfectly sinless life. This was the fruit of a second (spiritual) baptism, which led to the so-called 'higher life'. Unfortunately the Smiths themselves failed to live up to their message, and in 1875 Robert was caught trying to seduce a young lady in London. They were quickly sent back to America but the scandal was hushed up and their teaching survived. In July 1875 their supporters organized a meeting at Keswick in the Lake District, which they called a Convention for the Promotion of Practical Holiness. It became (and has remained) an annual event, promoting the 'higher life' teaching in its early days but now much more mainstream in its approach.[19]

Keswick had a particular impact in Cambridge, where the Cambridge Inter-Collegiate Christian Union (CICCU) was formed in 1877. It went on to encourage the establishment of other student Christian groups, which eventually gave birth to the Student Christian Movement (SCM). But when the SCM succumbed to liberal theology the CICCU resisted the trend and launched another organization, the Inter-Varsity Fellowship (IVF), which carries on its gospel witness to the present time. The original name is preserved in the Inter-Varsity Press (IVP), whose British branch merged with SPCK in 2015, and the student work is now undertaken by the renamed Universities and Colleges Christian Fellowship (UCCF). Other names are used in different countries, but the international network is linked by the International Fellowship of Evangelical Students (IFES), which has branches in most countries of the world.

In 1881 Charles Perry (1807–91), the retired Bishop of Melbourne, founded Ridley Hall in Cambridge as a training institute for Anglican ordinands and missionaries. The first Principal was Handley Carr Glyn Moule (1841–1920), who became Bishop of Durham in 1901. Moule was initially sceptical of Keswick but he was won over in 1884, and during his time at Ridley he prepared over 200 men for Christian service at home and abroad. These men were idealists and their standards of Christian conduct were often tinged with a somewhat uncharitable legalism towards those who did not measure up to them, but there can be no doubt that their lives and work made a major contribution to overseas missionary work and served to keep many in the home

---

[19] See 'The Keswick Convention and Anglican Evangelical Tensions in the Early Twentieth Century', in A. Atherstone and J. Maiden (eds.), *Evangelicalism and the Church of England in the Twentieth Century: Reform, Resistance and Renewal* (Woodbridge: Boydell Press, 2014), 89–108, for the history.

Church faithful to the gospel message they preached. The revivalist and Evangelical character of so much of the Global South's Christianity is eloquent testimony to the work of these dedicated men, who sacrificed everything, including their lives, for the sake of Christ's message of salvation.

The 'higher life' teaching of Keswick was strongly opposed by men like Bishop Ryle of Liverpool, who kept his distance from it, although in later life he reached out to some of its representatives and moderated his stance somewhat. Ryle was very concerned that Evangelicals were disunited among themselves and separatistic with regard to the mainstream churches to which most of them formally belonged. He believed that they should be willing to participate in the convocations of the Church of England and in the church congresses then being held on an annual basis. He was moderately successful in encouraging their involvement in these activities, but as the controversy surrounding Keswick demonstrates, genuine unity proved to be elusive. Time and again, Evangelicals failed to work together and so they lost influence to ritualists, liberals and others. As a result, their distinctive witness was pushed to the margins of church life, where it has remained ever since.

Before that happened however there was a last flowering of traditional nineteenth-century Evangelicalism that was to have some impact on future generations. The Evangelical Edmund Arbuthnott Knox (1847–1937) was Suffragan Bishop of Coventry (1894–1903) and then of Manchester (1903–21), where he tackled the inequities of clerical stipends by instituting a scheme that would ensure that all clergy received a comparable income, and took a lead in developing diocesan missions. Henry Wace (1836–1924) was Dean of Canterbury from 1903 to 1924 and one of the few Evangelicals who could hold his own with the intellectual giants of his day.[20] Perhaps the most influential of all was William Henry Griffith Thomas (1861–1924), who was Principal of Wycliffe Hall, Oxford (1905–10). By that time he had already published his classic work *The Catholic Faith*, which was written to answer the claims of Anglo-Catholicism and remains one of the most lucid expositions of Evangelical Anglicanism.[21] Griffith Thomas moved to Canada in 1910, where he became Principal of Wycliffe College, Toronto, and later went to the USA. In 1919 he helped to found Dallas Theological Seminary, which became and long remained a bastion of premillenarian dispensationalism. His British friends regretted his departure and missed him greatly, although perhaps we should be grateful that his millenarian theories never really caught on in the UK.

---

[20] He was Boyle Lecturer in 1874–5 and Bampton Lecturer in 1879, a rare honour for an Evangelical.

[21] W. H. Griffith Thomas, *The Catholic Faith: A Manual of Instruction for Members of the Church of England* (London: Hodder & Stoughton, 1904).

Politicization

In the last quarter of the nineteenth century British Christianity became politicized in a way and to a degree that it had not been since the seventeenth century. The UK was now the leading world power and its leaders felt a particular responsibility for the way in which they conducted its policies, both at home and abroad. The expanding empire was a matter for particular concern. What was Britain doing, occupying large portions of the globe that were either largely empty or else contained populations quite alien to the British way of life? In Canada, Australia and New Zealand, settlers quickly outnumbered the indigenous people, and Britain was able to create societies that more or less reflected the mother country. The fact that emigration from the Celtic fringe was stronger than from the English heartland produced countries in which Celtic churches – Presbyterian and Roman Catholic in particular – could compete with the exported Church of England on a more equal basis, and multidenominationalism was the norm. Initial attempts to endow the local Anglican churches were soon abandoned and a generic Protestantism of the kind that Broad Church people in England wanted to see at home became the dominant expression of Christianity in those places. Much the same was true in the USA as well, where there was a constitutional separation of church and state that did not exist in the British dominions.

British policies in Asia and Africa were more complicated. Pressure to use the imperial power as a means to further Christian evangelism was strongly resisted, not least by the imperial authorities themselves, although Christian missions were usually allowed to function without hindrance. In Africa there was the added incentive of seeking to root out the slave trade that still continued on the east coast, where it was dominated by Muslim Arabs. To forestall this, missionaries went out to different parts of the Continent – Bishop James Hannington (1847–85) to Uganda, where he was martyred for his faith, and Scottish Presbyterians to what is now Malawi. There they were able to create indigenous Christian societies that acknowledged the suzerainty of the British Crown, which protected them from the slavers but also allowed for local development. Across Africa, mission stations became centres of education and social welfare, which over time prepared an indigenous elite to take over the countries concerned when independence came, which it did two generations later. The missionaries were far from perfect, but it is generally acknowledged that they laid the foundations for a relatively peaceful and orderly progress to modern statehood, and the churches they founded continue to play an important role in states that are officially secular but in practice largely Christian.

In some places however things did not always go according to plan. One of these was South Africa, where the British found a European presence already implanted in the country when they took it over. This was the colony of Dutch settlers whom the British called the Boers (farmers) and who now call themselves Afrikaners. They were Calvinists in the Dutch Reformed sense of the word and fiercely independent. The nearest thing that Britain had to them was the Church of Scotland, which duly sent Andrew Murray (1794–1866) to minister to them. Murray was welcomed and integrated well into local Dutch society, but it was his son, another Andrew Murray (1828–1917), who would have the greatest impact. He was perfectly bilingual in Cape Dutch (now Afrikaans) and English and became a pastor of outstanding ability. He wrote many books, most of which are still in print, and in later life was a regular speaker at the Keswick Convention.

The Murrays tried to stay out of the tensions between the British and Cape Dutch, but that was not always easy. When Britain abolished slavery in 1833, many of the Cape Dutch were so incensed that they got up and left the Cape Colony, striking out for the interior, where they founded the Orange Free State and Transvaal. Britain did not recognize these two 'republics' and made periodic attempts to take them over, but without success. Finally, when gold and diamonds were discovered in large quantities in the Transvaal and English-speaking settlers poured in, the existence of these micro-states was inevitably called into question. The Boer War of 1899–1902 put an end to their independence, but Britain wanted to be generous to its erstwhile enemies and within ten years it had created the Union of South Africa, in which the British and Afrikaners were meant to live together in peace. It might have worked, had it not been for two factors that the British paid insufficient heed to. One was the resentment felt by the Calvinistic Dutch, who thought of themselves as God's chosen people and saw nothing wrong with discriminating against those who did not belong to their tribe. The other was the existence of large numbers of non-white people, black Africans for the most part, but also Indians who had migrated there for economic reasons, Malays (in the Cape) and mixed-race, or 'Coloured' people, most of whom were descendants of informal liaisons between Dutchmen and indigenous people.

The Union of South Africa was a state created for whites only, although there was a hope among some liberals that over time the rest of the population would be developed enough to take part in it as well. Christians in Britain were especially rosy-eyed about this, and many thought that this experiment in self-government would serve as a model for the rest of the Global South.

Unfortunately, as we know, it turned out to be a major embarrassment instead. Afrikaner nationalists gained control of the country in 1948 and within a few years had instituted a system of 'separate development' (apartheid), which they justified on Christian grounds. The Dutch Reformed churches provided it with theological ballast, most of it spurious, while the English-speaking churches were left wondering which way to turn. To its credit, the Anglican Church took the lead in opposing apartheid, which was eventually discredited and over-turned in 1994, but the liberation struggle became associated with a liberal theology that was only superficially related to traditional Christianity. There are still great reserves of faith in South Africa, but there can be no doubt that the message preached by the Murrays has been tarnished by its political associations and it is not yet clear when, or if, that can be reversed.

Another country where politics invaded the churches with harmful effects was Ireland. Irish grievances against Britain had a long history, but until the late nineteenth century Irish nationalism was not entirely defined by religion. That began to change after emancipation in 1829, especially when the home-rule movement used the Catholic parish network as a means of recruiting local support for its cause. But even as late as 1890 Irish nationalists were led by Protestants, notably Charles Stewart Parnell (1846–91), the 'uncrowned king of Ireland'. Unfortunately Parnell got involved with Kitty O'Shea, a married woman with whom he conducted an increasingly public affair. This scandalized both Catholics and Protestants, and Parnell was forced to resign his leadership. His fall from grace was dramatic, but it had two long-term effects. The first was that it ended significant Protestant involvement with Irish nationalism and the second was that it enabled the Roman Catholic Church to assert more influence over the latter. The Catholic hierarchy sensed that Irish nationalism was too powerful a force to be resisted, but attributed the Parnell fiasco to his Protestantism. In order to ensure that it retained the highest moral standards (as interpreted by the Vatican), the Catholic Church would have to assert its dominance in the nationalist movement, which it managed to do. By the early twentieth century Irish nationalism was a largely Catholic phenomenon (although by no means all Catholics were nationalists), whereas Protestants were increasingly distinguished by their loyalty to Britain. On both sides 'faith and fatherland' tended to merge into one, but the faith they professed and the fatherland to which they owed allegiance were not the same.

As Irish home rule drew closer to being realized, the Protestants banded together in protest. In 1912 virtually the entire adult male population of Prot-estant Ulster signed a Solemn League and Covenant – the term was taken from the Puritans of the seventeenth century – pledging to resist home rule (which they saw as 'Rome rule'; that is, control by the Vatican) with force if necessary. They backed up this threat by purchasing arms and organizing militia units, just in case they should be needed. It was not long before Catholics felt they had to follow suit, and by 1914 there was a serious risk of civil war in Ireland that was only avoided by the outbreak of the wider European conflict in August of that year.

In mainland Britain the most overt politicization of the church occurred in Wales, where it was deliberately fanned by David Lloyd George (1863–1945). Lloyd George came from a Welsh-speaking Baptist family and identified Nonconformity with disestablishment and the Liberal Party. By no stretch of the imagination could Lloyd George be regarded as a model Christian, but he could play on his Baptist roots and did so unscrupulously. Between 1886 and 1906 the Liberal Party was in power only briefly, but it dominated the Welsh seats and made disestablishment part of its programme. There was a chance between 1892 and 1894, during Gladstone's last administration, that Welsh disestablishment might make it on to the statute book, but Parliament was preoccupied with the Irish home-rule question and the Welsh were disappointed. It was not until the Liberals returned to power at the end of 1905 and won the following election by a landslide that Lloyd George was finally able to take advantage of the situation.

But just as that was happening, Wales was convulsed by something altogether different. A young man called Evan Roberts (1878–1951), who had narrowly escaped death in a mining explosion, suddenly started preaching to his fellows in a way that had an electrifying effect. Within a few months revival had broken out all over South Wales and at least 100,000 people, many of them miners, were converted. The Nonconformist churches, which had gone into relative decline, were suddenly reinvigorated. More than that, news of extraordinary occurrences, including speaking in tongues and reported healings, spread around the world and Roberts became an international celebrity. It was too much for him and he had a breakdown, withdrawing from public appearances and abandoning the revival to its own devices. Roberts never returned to the ministry, although he lived on for many years and retained a lively faith to the very end. By 1906 the revival was virtually over, but its effects were enough to give the Liberals the push they needed. Over the next few years they pressed on with their cause.[22] A Royal Commission in 1905 revealed the following church membership figures for Wales:

---

[22] See Bell, *Disestablishment*, 226–329, for the details.

Church of England	193,081
Congregationalists	175,147
Calvinistic Methodists	170,617
Wesleyans	40,811
Others	19,870

This gave a total of 743,361 regular adult churchgoers, out of a total population of 2,400,000. Allowance must be made for children who were not included in these figures, but even when that is done, churchgoers of all kinds were still less than half the population. A more accurate figure can be gained by looking at baptism and wedding figures. These show that the Church of England could claim about 30% of the population, and the Nonconformists (taken together) about 28%. But more than 37% married in registry offices and must therefore be regarded as unchurched, if not as outright unbelievers.

The political implications of this were potentially explosive. First of all, the figures demonstrated that the Nonconformist claim that they outnumbered the Establishment was not clear-cut. The Church of England was certainly a minority, but could claim that the unchurched were its responsibility, because it assumed that everyone belonged to the established Church unless they opted out of it. The Nonconformists knew that this was nonsense, but also knew that if they were asked, the unchurched might well identify themselves as 'C of E' out of habit, rather than out of conviction. If that were done, as the defenders of the Establishment wanted, the state Church might survive on the back of unbelievers, which was an outrage to the Nonconformists and an embarrassment to the Anglicans.

Discussions over disestablishment dragged on, complicated by the question of disendowment. Should the Church of England lose its property, as some of the more extreme Nonconformists wished? To whom did the cathedrals, churchyards and other land and property in Church hands really belong – the communicant parishioners or the nation? At this point the Liberals began to falter, because most of them wanted to secularize as much church property as they could, but many of their Nonconformist supporters were uneasy about that. The Nonconformists wanted to separate the Church from the state, but had no desire to see the state seizing what belonged to the Church. Separation was not the same thing as confiscation, and if the state could get away with appropriating the Church's revenues, what was to stop it from doing the same to the Nonconformists when it got the chance?

Rather late in the day, some Nonconformists woke up to the fact that disestablishment was not really a religious issue but a political one. Their support for the Liberals began to falter somewhat, although not enough to change the general direction of government policy. Welsh disestablishment was voted through Parliament in 1914, but the outbreak of war meant that its implementation was delayed. The Church continued to fight a rearguard action, with some success, and in 1919 the terms of disestablishment were slightly amended in its favour. Nevertheless the die had been cast, and on 31 March 1920 the four Welsh dioceses were separated from the Church of England and disestablished. By then the Liberal Party was broken beyond repair, Lloyd George's days as Prime Minister were numbered and Nonconformity was entering a decline that has continued uninterrupted to the present day. From being one of the more religious parts of the UK, Wales became and has remained the most secular, with less than 5% of the population having any connection with a church. The Church in Wales, as the disestablished body is officially known, is still the largest single denomination, but it too is in steep decline, with no more than 45,000 communicant members after a century of 'independence'.[23] The other churches – Baptist, Presbyterian (Calvinistic Methodist) and Roman Catholic – muster something between 25,000 and 30,000 members each, so the overall relationship between them and the former Establishment remains statistically the same as it was a century ago, but the 'unchurched', however they are to be described, have taken over the country while the churches struggle to survive.

One unforeseen result of Welsh disestablishment was that enthusiasm for repeating it in Scotland and in England virtually disappeared. The reunion of Scottish Presbyterians in 1929 was negotiated by removing most of the remaining traces of the state connection, but the Church of Scotland retained its status as the 'national Church', whatever that was supposed to mean. In practice it was free to do as it pleased and effectively moved out of the political sphere altogether.

Something similar happened to the Church of England, although it remained more closely tied to Parliament. A Royal Commission on Church–state relations recommended the setting up of a National Assembly that would combine the convocations and the houses of laity that had grown up alongside them but which lacked legal standing. Parliament would not allow the Church to govern itself if that meant the laity would have no voice, but it was not until 1885 (in Canterbury) and 1892 (in York) that a lay voice was established on a firm footing. As a result, Parliament passed the so-called 'Enabling Act' in

---

[23] See N. Doe (ed.), *A New History of the Church in Wales* (Cambridge: Cambridge University Press, 2020). Also D. C. Jones, 'Evangelical Resurgence in the Church in Wales in the Mid-Twentieth Century', in Atherstone and Maiden, *Evangelicalism*, 227–247.

1919, which allowed the Church to govern itself to a considerable degree, although the measures it passed would still require parliamentary approval. That was not guaranteed, but most of the time the system has worked smoothly and in 1970 it was incorporated into the new General Synod, which combined the convocations and the houses of laity into a single body. Church politics have thus moved from Parliament to the Synod, creating a situation in which the state does not normally interfere – a practical disestablishment that seems to have taken the question of a formal separation of church and state off the political agenda.

The Social Gospel

One important aspect of Victorian Christianity was its growing emphasis on social welfare. To some extent relieving the poor had always been part of the church's vocation, and the poor box was a regular feature of parish churches after the Reformation. But it was the Evangelical Revival, coupled with a growing awareness of the harm the Industrial Revolution was doing to the health and well-being of large segments of the population, that led to a concerted effort to improve living conditions across the board. Men like John Howard and the seventh Earl of Shaftesbury stand out, as of course do William and Catherine Booth, but there were many others and much of their work survives in one form or another to the present day. Thomas John Barnardo (1845–1905) for example, who set up his first children's home in 1866, George Müller (1805–98), a German immigrant who joined the Plymouth Brethren and established a network of orphanages, and Edward de Montjoie Rudolf (1852–1933), who founded what would eventually become the Church of England Children's Society, are all examples of this. To them may be added Josephine Butler (1828–1906), who was active in attempts to rescue and rehabilitate prostitutes.

Common to all these initiatives was a desire to put Christian principles into practice, although the extent to which they involved evangelism varied enormously. In general terms it may be said that the Evangelical foundations were more likely to be openly evangelistic and others less so, although it is hard to generalize and the situation varied considerably over time. By the late nineteenth century philanthropic work carried out by, or under the aegis of, the churches had become widespread but its character had changed from what had been common a century earlier. One of the main reasons for this was that in the course of the nineteenth century many middle-class people moved out of the inner cities and went to the suburbs, where they were no longer in daily contact with the working classes or the desperately poor. Those who knew what conditions were like in Bethnal Green or the Gorbals wrote books about the horrors they witnessed and these moved many prosperous people to donate funds to relief organizations, but this was not the same thing as personal involvement on a daily basis. Missions to the domestic poor were compared to missions in the heart of Africa, and the distance between donors and recipients was sometimes almost as great.

Nevertheless home missions were a feature of the nineteenth century and in some cases they are still active. Perhaps the most famous of them is the London City Mission, founded in 1835 and still going strong in the capital. The Mission is Evangelical and interdenominational and can be very flexible in its approach. It undertakes social welfare work where that is required, and in some places organizes worship services for those who are unable or unwilling to attend a local church. But it also cooperates with existing congregations and does not seek to duplicate or rival them.

High Churchmen also organized inner-city missions, although with mixed results. In 1877 Stewart Headlam (1847–1924), curate of St Matthew's, Bethnal Green, set up the Guild of St Matthew, which was designed to reach out to the unchurched in east London. Unfortunately Headlam was sympathetic to a number of people and groups that were either on the fringes of the Church or else outside it altogether. He befriended secularists, ritualists and actors on the London stage, who were widely thought to be promiscuously immoral. In 1882 he even became the education secretary of the National Secular Society, a very odd position for an Anglican clergyman to hold. His Guild suffered a crippling blow in 1895 when he decided to support Oscar Wilde, who was then facing criminal charges because of his homosexual liaison with Lord Alfred Douglas. It seems that Headlam was genuinely compassionate and wanted to help Wilde in his difficulties, but most people did not see matters that way and the Guild suffered a steep drop in membership. It survived for a few more years but was eventually wound up.

More successful was the so-called 'settlement movement', initiated by Samuel Barnett (1844–1913), Vicar of St Jude's, Whitechapel, and his wife Henrietta (1851–1936). They believed that the best way to influence the poor was to settle among them, and they pioneered residential accommodation for graduates of Oxford and Cambridge in deprived parts of London. Their first venture was Toynbee Hall, opened in 1884 in Whitechapel, and still in existence.[24] The experiment caught on and by 1914 there were forty-five such settlements in

---

[24] It was named after Arnold Toynbee, an Oxford economist who died in 1883 at the age of 30. This Toynbee was the posthumous uncle of another Arnold Toynbee (1889–1975), who became a noted historian and whose granddaughter Polly Toynbee (1946–) is a journalist and atheist campaigner.

the UK, including five in Scotland and one in Belfast. Thirteen of them had no religious affiliation at all, and none of them was evangelistic in the way that the London City Mission was. They did however offer important social services in their respective neighbourhoods and were particularly useful as conduits through which university-educated clergymen and others could experience inner-city deprivation first hand and be motivated to press for change. Some of these settlements are still active, although their social profile is much lower than it was in the years before the First World War.

The perceived distance between the world of most churchgoers and that of the underprivileged was problematic for the churches, not least because of what was happening at the same time in the middle-class suburbs. There church building was proceeding apace and on a scale never before seen in Britain. Between 1841 and 1911 the Church of England built no fewer than 5,358 churches and chapels, followed by the Baptists, who opened 5,163 between 1860 and 1901. In the latter period the Congregationalists put up 2,293 places of worship and the Roman Catholics 758. Even the Scottish Presbyterians, who already had a surplus of churches dating from the Disruption of 1843, managed to erect a further 332.[25] Some of these structures were fairly small, but many were huge and pretentious, capable of seating thousands of potential worshippers whom the churches were hoping to attract. The result was a vast oversupply that would soon become an albatross around the churches' neck, but even at the time it was something of an embarrassment. If people had the money to build such cavernous churches, could they not spend more on poor relief?

The perceived disconnect between middle-class respectability and the needs of a nation that professed Christianity without practising it in relation to the underprivileged was a source of scandal to many. Some church people realized this, but they could not control how individual congregations spent their money, nor would there have been enough to meet the need even if it could be collected. The result was that there was a growing number of people who drifted away from the churches and devoted themselves to social work instead. Some of those who took that path retained their Christian faith, but others did not, and it was the latter who made the biggest impression on contemporaries. Ex-Christians of various kinds derided what they saw as the hypocrisy of preaching heavenly rewards instead of relieving earthly sufferings, and some came to regard Christianity as a clever trick by which the rich dominated the poor and kept them in their place.

---

[25] S. J. Brown, *Providence and Empire 1815–1914* (London: Pearson Longman, 2008), 338–339.

What strikes us when we look back on this period is that many of those who rejected official Christianity looked and sounded like Evangelicals who had been secularized. Instead of preaching a gospel of eternal salvation they proclaimed a message of human improvement, which they thought they could bring about by their own efforts. Many of them were convinced that their moral standards were higher than those of Christians because they thought they were less selfish. Christians (in the rejecters' view) were helping the poor in the hope of obtaining an eternal reward for themselves, but the secularists said that they wanted nothing – their dedication to the poor was entirely altruistic, or so they claimed. What they often failed to see was that their beliefs were rooted in Christian principles and could not have existed otherwise. This was a point made by Gladstone and others, who sympathized with secularist concerns but thought that their rejection of Christian values was erroneous and ultimately dangerous, because they were undermining the foundation on which their philanthropy was built. It is therefore an exaggeration to say that an interest in social welfare went hand in hand with secularism, although the two things were increasingly connected in the popular mind.

One of the main reasons why social activism came to be associated with a rejection of Christianity was that the latter was misinterpreted by liberal thinkers, who professed sympathy with Christian principles without really understanding them. One of the chief culprits was Matthew Arnold, who thought of himself as a friend of the church but who saw its mission as teaching people to live moral lives and do their duty. This might be regarded as a form of salvation by works, except that Arnold did not believe in salvation as the church traditionally taught it. He claimed that the heart of Jesus' teaching was the proclamation of the 'kingdom of God', by which he meant social reform here on earth, not an eternal paradise in heaven. Arnold was right to state that Jesus proclaimed the kingdom of God, but wrong in the way he understood it.

Arnold's assertion that it was Jesus' disciples who spiritualized his message in order to preserve it in some form after their master's crucifixion is easily refuted, but proved to be surprisingly popular among those who heard it for the first time. After giving a public lecture on the subject on 22 February 1876, Arnold was surprised to discover how well it had been received, despite some opposition.[26] The reaction is well summed up by Stewart Brown:

---

[26] The lecture was published, first in *Macmillan's Magazine* 33 (April 1876), 481–494, and then in M. Arnold, *Last Essays on Church and Religion* (London: Smith Elder, 1877), 108–136.

In the view of those clergy who had rallied to the support of Arnold . . . the church must align itself with the progressive forces in society in order to work for practical social reforms. It must proclaim a 'social gospel'. It must seek to Christianise the social structures, relationships and attitudes in Britain's industrial state. It must strive, not only for the conversion and salvation of individuals in the life to come, but also for the establishment of a righteous Christian commonwealth in this world.[27]

For a time it seemed as though F. D. Maurice's brand of Christian Socialism might have a new lease of life, but many in the younger generation embraced the ideas (and ideals) of men like Karl Marx (1818–83), whose writings appeared to them to be a higher expression of Christian values than anything the churches were preaching.[28] Even so, the religious tone of many socialist meetings was unmistakable to those who were familiar with Evangelical revivals. There were personal testimonies of conversion to socialist values, lusty singing of socialist 'hymns', and calls to devote one's life to the service of social reform.[29]

The churches, and especially the Evangelical churches, were naturally hostile to this secularization of their message, but it was difficult to know how to respond to it. Social deprivation was a reality that could not be denied, and the churches were definitely strongest among the middle classes, where they set an example of 'respectability' that many people still associate with 'Victorian values'. To Christians, atheism and the rejection of an afterlife were worse than poverty for the simple reason that the goods of this world, however abundant, are given for a time, whereas salvation is for eternity. Unfortunately it was all too easy for that truth to become an excuse for doing nothing to tackle prevailing social injustices. Evangelical religion, which had been liberal and in many respects anti-Establishment in its early years, shifted towards a more conservative mindset that gradually came to dominate it. Even today there are many who assume that to be conservative in theology is to be conservative in politics as well, a stance that would have struck the Clapham Sect and even Lord Shaftesbury, who was himself a Tory grandee, as decidedly odd.

---

[27] Brown, *Providence and Empire*, 327.

[28] Marx lived and worked in London of course, but he wrote in German, so it was not until the late 1870s that translations made his writings better known to the English reading public.

[29] This resemblance has often been observed in Communist Party gatherings. Vladimir Lenin (1870–1924) is known to have looked favourably on Evangelical sects active in pre-revolutionary Russia, who were initially spared the persecution meted out to the 'parasitical' bourgeois churches after the Bolshevik Revolution. But communism's atheistic ideology eventually triumphed, and the Evangelicals suffered the consequences from about 1929 onwards, some years after Lenin's death.

What was true of the Church of England was equally true of English Nonconformity and of the churches in Wales and in Scotland, although less so of the churches in Ireland, where industrialization was more uneven and where other problems took precedence in the minds of most people. English Nonconformists set up their own organizations, like the Christian Socialist Society, which was established in 1886 but dissolved six years later because its members could not agree about what they meant by 'Christian'. In 1894 a Baptist preacher called John Clifford (1836–1923) founded the Christian Socialist League, which in 1898 became the Christian Social Brotherhood, and there were similar moves among the Methodists. In Scotland the various Presbyterian churches addressed the alienation of large numbers of working people, especially in Glasgow, where conditions were much the same as in London. Even the Roman Catholic Church got involved, spurred on by the papal encyclical *Rerum Novarum*, issued by Pope Leo XIII in 1891, which denounced the exploitation of workers and demanded fair treatment for them. Increasingly, and across the board, there was a growing sense that private initiatives could not meet the need and that the state would have to encourage a more collective sense of responsibility for the problems caused by industrialization. When that happened of course, the role of the churches decreased, although many Christians continued to be involved in social action and did much to prevent outbreaks of revolutionary violence like the ones that occurred periodically in other countries. Socialism might be a secularization of the gospel, but in its British forms never became as openly anti-Christian as it was elsewhere.

The dying of the light

Victorian Christianity reached its apogee sometime in the 1880s. By the end of that decade there were signs of retreat that were to cause increasing alarm as time went on. It had long been the custom for Members of Parliament to swear an oath 'on the true faith of a Christian', although Jews and Quakers were both excused from this – the former because they were not Christians and the latter because they had a conscientious objection to oath-taking. This arrangement was challenged in 1880, when Charles Bradlaugh (1833–91) was elected as the member from Northampton and refused to take the oath because he was a declared atheist. He was not allowed to take his seat until 1886, and then only because the speaker of the house decided to ignore the opposition to him. In 1888 the situation was regularized by the Affirmation Act, which allowed unbelievers to swear without mentioning any kind of faith. This seems innocuous to us now but it caused a storm at the time, because it was claimed that it opened the door of government to those who had no religious belief, and therefore threatened the Christian foundations of British society. Unfortunately for the protesters the Bradlaugh affair provoked a backlash that saw a huge increase in the number of professed secularists and created a climate in which many people, including some devout believers, started to think that religion should be kept out of politics altogether.

On a completely different plane, the churches were facing increased challenges to their faith from within. Liberal theology, kept at bay for most of the nineteenth century, suddenly began to make serious inroads into theological education, not least in Oxford and Cambridge. The results were not long in coming. Ordinations into the Church of England peaked in 1886 and then went into free fall. The Nonconformist churches lagged somewhat behind, but by 1900 all the Protestant denominations were short of recruits, and the quality of those coming forward for ordination was declining.[30] Losing one's faith became increasingly fashionable, and those who retained theirs found themselves more and more on the defensive. Their great enemy was what they called 'liberalism', an amorphous term that covers many different beliefs but in the late nineteenth century increasingly appeared to orthodox defenders of Christianity as a many-headed monster that threatened all the churches, including the Roman Catholic one, from within.

As far as the British Isles were concerned, this 'liberalism' first came to public notice in 1825, when Hugh James Rose (1795–1838) gave a series of lectures in Cambridge in which he claimed that the German Protestant churches were suffocating under a deluge of rationalism.[31] Rose's thesis was based on limited research (most of it in largely Catholic Bavaria) and was easily refuted, even by Edward Pusey, who in other respects shared much of Rose's outlook.[32] But however lopsided Rose's thesis might have been, it has left two legacies in the British mind that persist to the present day. The first is the belief that there was a development in early nineteenth-century thought that rejected traditional authority in religious matters in favour of private judgment, based not on divine revelation but on what the human mind was prepared to accept. The second is the conviction that this development originated in the German *Aufklärung* (Enlightenment) and entered Britain as a foreign import. Then as

---

[30] Brown, *Providence and Empire*, 401–402.

[31] H. J. Rose, *The State of the Protestant Religion in Germany; in a Series of Discourses Preached Before the University of Cambridge* (Cambridge: Deighton & Son, 1825).

[32] E. B. Pusey, *An Historical Enquiry into the Probable Causes of the Rationalist Character Lately Predominant in the Theology of Germany* (London: C. & J. Rivington, 1828).

now, few people understood that the Enlightenment has English roots going back to the seventeenth century, and that it spread to Germany largely thanks to the writings of the eighteenth-century French *philosophes*.[33] What is certainly true however is that the new 'liberalism' spread across Germany in the course of the nineteenth century but was little known in Britain. Incredible as it seems to us now, even as late as 1853 F. D. Maurice could be dismissed from his chair at King's College London for casting doubt on the doctrine of eternal damnation (of unbelievers, of course!).

There was however a growing recognition that between the pronounced Evangelicalism of what was coming to be identified with the traditional 'Low Church' and the Anglo-Catholicism of the opposing 'High Church' was a central mass of churchgoers who could not be placed in either category. William John Conybeare (1815–57) analysed the spectrum of church opinion as he saw it and labelled these people the 'Broad Church'.[34] According to Conybeare, the Broad Church was more liberal than either of the other church parties, as he called them. But while it is undoubtedly true that liberalism found its home among this Broad Church, it would be a mistake to regard the latter as either a defined 'party' or exclusively 'liberal'. What we have here is a spectrum of beliefs that included liberalism and that eventually became the default position of both the established and the Nonconformist churches, if only because it was relatively undefined and could serve as a compromise between the warring Low and High Church factions.[35]

One particularly unsettling event was the withdrawal of Charles Spurgeon and his Metropolitan Tabernacle from the Baptist Union in 1887. Spurgeon had become aware of liberal tendencies creeping into the Union and was determined to have nothing to do with what he termed the 'downgrading' of the Bible. Unfortunately the rest of the Baptist Union failed to take Spurgeon seriously and his withdrawal was ratified almost unanimously. The most famous Baptist preacher of his age was formally rejected by his own denomination, with consequences that unfolded over the next generation. The Baptist Union went into decline as people lost confidence in its doctrinal orthodoxy, and it would not be until after the Second World War that it would begin to regain something of its earlier reputation in the Nonconformist world.

---

[33] So little is this recognized that it prompted one German scholar to write a book to demonstrate it. See H. G. von Reventlow, *The Authority of the Bible and the Rise of the Modern World* (London: SCM Press, 1984).

[34] W. J. Conybeare, 'Church Parties', *Edinburgh Review* 200 (October 1853), 273–342.

[35] See R. A. Burns, 'W. J. Conybeare, "Church Parties"', in S. Taylor (ed.), *From Cranmer to Davidson: A Church of England Miscellany* (Woodbridge: Boydell & Brewer, 1999), 213–385.

But if liberalism was originally (and conventionally) associated with German Protestantism, there was also a liberal Catholic current on the European continent that was articulated above all in post-revolutionary France by men like Félicité de Lamennais (1782–1854), Charles de Montalembert (1810–70) and Jean Baptiste Lacordaire (1802–61), all of whom were determined to decouple the French Catholic Church from its traditional monarchist leanings, although they accepted the most conservative views of papal authority. They believed that the Roman Church's interests would best be served by a papacy that was not tied to secular rulers and that could exercise its moral and spiritual influence within a liberal democracy similar to what they found in the UK. But this kind of liberal Catholicism was alien to Britain (and even more so to Ireland) and had no real influence on British Christianity. When the papacy condemned it, as it did in 1864 and later, it disappeared from the British scene almost without trace, despite the sympathies of Lord John Acton (1834–1902), who remained its leading champion.

In Britain, and especially in England, 'liberal Catholicism' came to mean something else. It was not connected with Rome but with the third generation of the Tractarians. The mantle of Edward Pusey had fallen on Henry Parry Liddon (1829–90), Pusey's biographer and a theologian in the traditionalist Anglo-Catholic mould. One of Liddon's protégés however was Charles Gore (1853–1932), who would move off in quite a different direction. Gore always regarded himself as a Tractarian and played a part in Anglo-Catholic circles until his death, but his own theological outlook was a far cry from that of Pusey and horrified Liddon when he discovered what it was. Gore's genius – if that is the word for it – was to combine liberal (and largely Protestant) theology with ritualism, thereby helping to create the liberal Catholic ethos that in different forms has dominated the Church of England ever since and, for better or worse, influenced the course of British Christianity generally. What Liddon might not have appreciated was that Gore's philosophical outlook had been shaped by Thomas Hill Green (1836–82), an idealist whose approach to history and historical development reflected the influence of Georg Wilhelm Friedrich Hegel (1770–1831). Put simply, this was that progress over time was the result of a conflict of opposites (thesis and antithesis) that produced a synthesis, which in turn generated its opposite and continued the process still further. It was an attractive philosophy because it explained how conflict, which in one sense nobody desired, was necessary for development to occur and therefore ought to be welcomed.

As Warden of Pusey House in Oxford, Gore was a prominent Anglo-Catholic spokesman, but he was not alone in his thinking. Linked to him were several other Oxford men, including Henry Scott Holland (1847–1918), John Richardson Illingworth (1848–1915) and Edward Stuart Talbot (1844–1934). Like the first Tractarians, they met regularly to discuss their theology. True to their Hegelian antecedents, they wanted to combine what they saw as traditional Catholicism with then current trends in society and in biblical criticism. They came up with the belief that when Jesus Christ entered the world, he sanctified matter, overcoming the ancient division between the sacred and the profane, between the spiritual and the material, and between the religious and the secular. The conclusion they drew was that a true follower of Christ would work for the transformation of this world, using the powers of human reason, rather than merely promise a heavenly reward sometime in the future. It was a complete misunderstanding of the saving purpose of Christ's incarnation but it suited their philosophical outlook and appealed to people who thought that science could displace ancient myths about sin and judgment, and make the world a better place.

In 1889 Gore and his friends produced a symposium called *Lux Mundi: A Series of Studies in the Religion of the Incarnation*, which caused an immediate sensation. Critics, including Liddon and the old-school Puseyite Anglo-Catholics, denounced it as heretical and Evangelicals were equally appalled, if for somewhat different reasons. In his own contribution to the volume, Gore took up the challenge of biblical criticism. While he continued to affirm that the Bible had been inspired by the Holy Spirit, he saw it as a stage (or a series of stages) in the progressive revelation of God to humankind. In other words, when written it was positive and forward-looking but it had since been supplemented, if not superseded, by the Spirit's continuing work of sanctification, which could be seen in the advances of science and of social theory in his own time.

Gore sought to overcome the difficulties of a literal interpretation of the Bible, and especially of the Old Testament, by claiming that the text was concerned not with history as we now understand it but with theological principles that are essentially timeless. This approach was taken further by John Illingworth, who tried to demonstrate that orthodox creedal theology ought to be understood in that way. Thus for example the doctrine of the Trinity was not to be taken as literal truth but as a framework in which God's transcendence could be harmonized with his immanence (his presence in the world of time and space). Once again, we see the Hegelian notion of a synthesis of opposites being applied to the interpretation of traditional Christianity, which the authors of *Lux Mundi* (*Light of the World*) believed was the only way to rescue it in the face of contemporary challenges. After the initial reaction died down, the approach taken by Gore and his companions was gradually accepted in ever-widening circles of British (and especially English) theology, to the point where their incarnationalism came to be regarded as typically 'Anglican' and even admired as such outside the British Isles.[36] Gore was consecrated Bishop of Worcester in 1901 and rose rapidly in the hierarchy, becoming the first Bishop of Birmingham in 1905 and then Bishop of Oxford in 1911, where he remained until his retirement in 1919, after which he became something of a 'grand old man' in Anglo-Catholic circles. By the time he died his approach had become mainstream in the Church of England and had influenced a number of Nonconformists as well.

One of those affected by this was Reginald John Campbell (1867–1956). The son of a Methodist minister, he studied under Gore and his colleagues at Oxford and was briefly attracted to Anglo-Catholicism.[37] But his Nonconformist roots were too strong and in 1895 he became a Congregational minister in Brighton, where he was a popular and original preacher. Campbell combined the Hegelianism that he had imbibed at Oxford with an interest in the developing field of religious psychology, especially as exemplified by William James's classic work, *Varieties of Religious Experience*.[38] In 1903 Campbell became the Minister of the City Temple in London and it is said that 7,000 people attended his inaugural services there – an astonishingly high number, even for that time. Soon his pronounced socialist views and open acceptance of biblical criticism were causing considerable comment and landing him in controversy, which he attempted to address in a book entitled *The New Theology*, written somewhat hastily in 1907. In this book he offered a mystical understanding of Christian faith, emphasizing the presence of God in all creation, which he regarded as God's self-expression.

Campbell claimed that it was by introspection that a human being would discover his or her true self, and so realize that all humans are united with one another and with God. The biblical accounts of the fall and of salvation had to be understood psychologically. Adam 'fell' because he temporarily lost consciousness of the infinite, and sin was the failure of individuals to recognize the presence of the divine in themselves and in other people. Christ had come

---

[36] The German theologian Jürgen Moltmann (1926–) was particularly struck by this and based some of his own reflections on it – an unusual example of English influence on German theology rather than the other way around.

[37] Campbell was baptized as John Wesley Campbell but apparently changed his name during his student days at Oxford.

[38] William James (1842–1910) was an American psychologist and philosopher who expounded his ideas in a series of Gifford Lectures delivered at the University of Edinburgh in 1901–2, which were subsequently published in edited form as *The Varieties of Religious Experience: A Study in Human Nature* and are still in print more than a century later.

to restore this awareness, and his atonement had to be interpreted as the rediscovery of the fundamental unity of all creation. Needless to say, Jesus had not had any intention of founding a church. The existing churches were all mistaken, not merely in the message they preached but in their very existence. The true teaching of Christ was not to be found in them but in the rising socialist movement, which was the realization of the kingdom of God on earth.

Campbell's opinions were extreme and led to growing opposition, but he himself remained faithful to them until 1915, when a visit to the battlefields of war convinced him that his view of sin had been superficial and wrong. He renounced what he regarded as the Christ of liberal Protestantism and moved in a more Anglo-Catholic direction. By 1916 he had resigned his post at the City Temple and been received into the Church of England by none other than Charles Gore. He repudiated *The New Theology* but spent the rest of his life in relative obscurity, not wishing to stir up any more theological controversy. Campbell's personal spiritual journey was unusual, but other Nonconformists followed its broad outlines, particularly where socialism was concerned, and it was not long before the two currents began to merge, especially in places where the Nonconformists were strong. The modern Labour Party owes a considerable debt to this heritage, a debt that helped to prevent it from ever becoming overtly anticlerical or anti-Christian.[39]

At the beginning of the twentieth century, German liberal theology began to make a serious impact in Britain. A key figure in this was Adolf Harnack (1851–1930), professor at the University of Berlin and the recognized colossus of German Protestantism at that time.[40] His multivolume *History of Dogma* was translated into English in 1894–9, followed by a series of lectures, *What Is Christianity?*, he gave in 1899–1900, which were published.[41] In these seminal works Harnack developed his belief, already well established in the German-speaking world, that Christianity was a religion of spiritual feeling rather than of propositional doctrines, and that the development of the classical creeds of the church was a deviation from the original faith. It was an attractive thesis and, in one sense at least, appeared to be historically accurate, since the creeds were clearly composed several centuries after the events described in the New Testament. But the shift from the primacy of the mind to the emotions was bound to suggest that true Christianity was a spiritual experience that could

---

[39] See P. Catterall, *Labour and the Free Churches 1918–1939* (London: Bloomsbury, 2016).

[40] He became Adolf von Harnack in 1914, when he was ennobled by Kaiser Wilhelm II, an unusual honour for a theologian that testifies to his great influence.

[41] A. Harnack, *History of Dogma*, 7 vols. (London: Williams & Norgate, 1894–9); A. Harnack, *What Is Christianity? Sixteen Lectures Delivered in the University of Berlin During the Winter Term 1899–1900* (London: Williams & Norgate, 1901).

not be expressed properly in theological statements, a belief that inevitably undercut the teaching of the church.

Harnack's assertions were popular however because they appealed to the spirit of his time and offered a possible solution to the dilemma posed by scientific criticisms of the Bible. What did it matter whether Jesus was born of a virgin, as long as his Spirit was present in the heart of a Christian? His bodily resurrection was surely less important than his continuing moral and spiritual influence, and if someone accepted the latter why should the church insist on confessing the former as well? This approach attracted a number of younger scholars, including Burnett Hillman Streeter (1874–1937), who in 1912 edited a series of essays called *Foundations* that tried to do for its generation what *Essays and Reviews* and *Lux Mundi* had done for theirs. Ironically, it was too much for Charles Gore, who was not prepared to abandon the historicity of the Gospels and therefore came to be regarded as a 'conservative' – the fate of many aging radicals! But Harnack's views impressed William Temple (1881–1944), who was refused ordination in 1906 because of his sympathies with them, and Herbert Hensley Henson (1863–1947), whose preferment to the see of Hereford in 1918 caused considerable controversy for the same reason.[42]

Evangelicals tended to react against Harnack, but unfortunately they were often prejudiced against any form of scientific investigation of the origins of Christianity and dismissed biblical criticism as both ungodly and unnecessary. That inevitably led some of their number to adopt a more conciliatory position, and in 1905 three of them took the initiative to found what became known as the 'Group Brotherhood', an association of more open Evangelicals that wanted to come to terms with what they saw as the new learning. These men are largely forgotten, but were influential in their own time and did much to liberalize Evangelical thought in the first half of the twentieth century. Arthur James Tait (1872–1944) for example was Principal of St Aidan's College, Birkenhead (1901–7), and then of Ridley Hall, Cambridge (1907–27), where he was responsible for training several generations of ordinands. Charles Lisle Carr (1871–1942) became Bishop of Coventry in 1922 and of Hereford in 1931, resigning in 1941, only a few months before his death, and Frederic Sumpter Guy Warman (1872–1953) was Bishop of Truro (1919–23), Chelmsford (1923–9) and Manchester (1929–47). They and a number of like-minded colleagues met privately for many years, but in 1923 were finally moved to publish their own

---

[42] Henson soon became Bishop of Durham (1920–39) and had a major impact on the Church of England in the interwar period.

symposium, edited by Travers Guy Rogers (1876–1967), whose title could not have been clearer.[43]

The most prominent of these liberal Evangelicals was probably Vernon Faithful Storr (1869–1940), who acted as a spokesman for the Evangelical wing of the Church of England and was widely respected as such. Of him, Kenneth Hylson-Smith has written:

> Storr, and the other Liberal Evangelicals, emphasized that it was the mind of Christ and not the letter of holy scripture which was authoritative. They regarded the Bible as a literary product, in a class by itself among the national literatures of the world, but subject to the laws and principles which govern the growth of any literature. As a corollary to this, they considered some books and parts of the Bible as of more spiritual value than others. Most controversially, in the eyes of many Evangelicals, they also pronounced that the scriptures were not infallible.[44]

Also emerging at this time was a group of Broad Churchmen who in 1898 formed what they called the Churchmen's Union for the Advancement of Liberal Religious Thought. Like the Group Brotherhood, they were relatively quiet for a number of years, until a conference held at Girton College, Cambridge, in 1920, out of which came their own symposium, edited by Frederick John Foakes-Jackson (1855–1941) and Kirsopp Lake (1872–1946), called *The Beginnings of Christianity*.[45] By that time both men had emigrated to the USA, where they had distinguished academic careers, while the organization they left behind became the Modern Churchmen's Union in 1928.[46]

The attractions of modern thought were not confined to the Anglican and Nonconformist traditions however. The Roman Church was also affected, in particular by the movement known as 'modernism', which was condemned by Pope Pius X in 1907. Catholic modernism was not an exclusively British phenomenon of course, and most of its strength came from Germany and France, but it was represented in Britain and Ireland by George Tyrrell (1861–1909), an Irish Jesuit priest who played a leading part in it. Tyrrell was silenced,

---

[43] *Liberal Evangelicalism: An Interpretation by Members of the Church of England* (London: Hodder & Stoughton, 1923).

[44] K. Hylson-Smith, *Evangelicals in the Church of England 1734–1984* (Edinburgh: T&T Clark, 1988), 251.

[45] F. J. Foakes-Jackson, K. Lake and H. J. Cadbury (eds.), *The Beginnings of Christianity*, pt 1: *The Acts of the Apostles*, 5 vols. (London: Macmillan, 1920–33).

[46] Its journal had appeared since 1911 as *The Modern Churchman*. The Modern Churchmen's Union became the Modern Churchpeople's Union in 1986 and then simply Modern Church in 2010. Its president since 2014 has been the sociologist Linda Jane Pauline Woodhead (1964–).

along with the other modernists, and died soon afterwards, but his memory survived and in more recent times he has been hailed as a quasi-martyr in some liberal Catholic circles. Few Catholics read him now or share his ideas, but he stands out as an example of free thinking in a Church that in his day, and until fairly recently, had little or no time for that.[47]

Conservative reaction to these currents was strong on condemnation, which sometimes proved effective in the short term, but it was harder to produce a viable alternative. There were of course those who simply reiterated the traditional orthodoxy as if the new thinking did not exist, and this was a comfort to many whose consciences had been disturbed, even if it was not a long-term solution to the problems the 'new theology' was raising. None of the British churches, with the partial exception of the Church of Scotland, had much of a tradition of philosophical theology and there was little to be expected at that level. Where the British stood out was in their pragmatic approach to biblical studies, and it was here that the most effective conservative responses were to be found. One of the assumptions of nineteenth-century German liberalism was that ancient religious tales were largely 'myths' and not to be taken seriously as history. A famous example of this was the widespread dismissal of the Homeric poems, which portrayed a prehistoric conflict between Greece and Troy that had never taken place. Challenged by this, Heinrich Schliemann (1822–90), a German businessman and amateur archaeologist, set out to establish the 'truth'. In a thrilling series of discoveries he not only uncovered ancient Troy but also found substantial remains of the Mycenaean civilization of Greece. Of course that did not prove that the *Iliad* and the *Odyssey* were historical accounts, but it did place them in a genuine historical context, which made the scepticism prevalent in Germany at that time seem excessive at best and mistaken at worst.

British (and American) Christians took up the challenge with respect to the Bible, and in their hands a new discipline of 'biblical archaeology' came into being. Excavators went out and unearthed not only Babylon and Nineveh but also Ur of the Chaldees, the city from which the patriarch Abraham had originally come. Sites mentioned in the Bible now turned up on the archaeological map, but there was much more than this. The discovery and decipherment of ancient cuneiform texts, as well as of Egyptian hieroglyphics, brought the biblical world to life in unexpected ways. Law codes similar to those of the Hebrew Pentateuch were uncovered, as were stories of the flood. Even names similar to those of biblical characters were found on inscriptions, making the Old Testament records seem plausible even if they could not be directly

---

[47] See N. Sagovsky, *On God's Side: A Life of George Tyrrell* (Oxford: Clarendon Press, 1990).

confirmed. For a while it seemed that with enough time and effort the entire Bible would be supported by archaeological remains, but while this ambition was not to be realized in full, there is no doubt that archaeology had a restraining influence on the wilder theories put forward by the classical liberals and gave theological conservatives reason to think that their position could be supported by objective scientific investigation. Today we know far more about the ancient Near East than anyone in the nineteenth century did, and this has had a major impact on the way that we read the biblical narratives. Controversies about particular subjects continue – they always will – but the conservative position can no longer be dismissed as cavalierly as it once was. For this, British scholars can claim much of the credit, and it remains one of the lasting achievements of the pre-1914 period in the field of religious and theological research.[48]

Archaeological discoveries were encouraging to those who knew and cared about these things, but such people were a minority. For most, changes in lifestyle and expectations that began to multiply after about 1890 added to the conviction that science was replacing religion, and the result was a decline in church attendance and the influence that Christian leaders had on society. Incessant quarrelling about ritualism and increasing demands for money to finance unnecessary building projects did not help matters either. Towards the end of the nineteenth century, men, and in particular working-class men, were increasingly attracted to sporting clubs and events being organized in the main industrial centres. This was the era when the great football clubs we know today were founded and began to attract a mass following. Sunday remained for many the only day of leisure, and spending it in bed (or in a park) became more attractive than dressing up for long and often boring church services. Increasingly parents might send their children off to Sunday school and then enjoy some peace and quiet at home, and the children were not slow to notice that churchgoing was an activity that they would one day grow out of. The effects of this were masked for a generation or more because most people still owned a Bible, respected the churches as social institutions and turned to them at high points in their lives. Baptisms, weddings and burials were still overwhelmingly religious events practised by the majority of the population, and their support could usually be relied on at festival times. There was a large urban proletariat that never darkened the door of a church, but there was also a sense among many irregular churchgoers that respectable people ought to maintain some contact with religion, even if it was mainly to prevent being stigmatized as 'lower class'.

---

[48] See T. E. Levy, *Historical Biblical Archaeology and the Future: The New Pragmatism* (London: Routledge, 2017).

But beyond the general mass of the population was a growing number of people who were starting to look elsewhere for spiritual nourishment. In the early nineteenth century it would never have occurred to anyone in Britain to look to the non-Christian world for enlightenment, because it was obvious that the country's destiny was to bring light and civilization to the dark corners of the earth. By the dawn of the twentieth century many still thought that way, but there was a growing interest in Eastern mysticism, the occult and strange beliefs like reincarnation. Spiritualism, understood as the practice of trying to contact the dead, enjoyed a considerable vogue and many otherwise sensible people were taken in by the charlatans who practised it. The notion that all religions were fundamentally the same and that some had preserved a purity that had been lost by the industrialized Christianity of the West gained ground, and syncretisms of various kinds became popular.

One person who rode the crest of this new wave of interest was a Russian woman called Helena Petrovna Blavatskaya (1831–91), or Blavatsky, as she was known in the English-speaking world. Mme Blavatsky concocted a melange of Hinduism, Buddhism, Zoroastrianism and Christianity that she marketed as 'theosophy', which attracted such ne'er-do-wells as Annie Besant (1847–1933), who began her career as the wife of a Church of England vicar, abandoned him for atheism and socialism, and ended up as a disciple of theosophy. Improbable as it must seem, she became the first woman president of the Indian National Congress in 1917 and stated that the British Empire would soon become the vehicle for the transmission of Eastern wisdom to the lands of Christendom, something that she obviously thought was both desirable and long overdue. Such ideas attracted a number of popular writers like Rider Haggard (1856–1925), Bram Stoker (1847–1912), the author of *Dracula*, Arthur Conan Doyle (1859–1930), Rudyard Kipling (1865–1936) and William Butler Yeats (1865–1939), all of whom dabbled in mysticism of one kind or another and transmitted its aura of spiritual mystery to their readers. Even Irish nationalism, by this time increasingly dominated by the Roman Catholic Church, had more than its share of spiritualists, including the notorious Maude Gonne (1866–1953) and perhaps even Douglas Hyde (1860–1949), the son of a Church of Ireland clergyman and a leading light in the Gaelic revival that was supposed to 'de-anglicize' Ireland, at least in a spiritual sense.[49]

---

[49] Hyde's precise beliefs are hard to pin down. He was apolitical and when his Gaelic League was captured by nationalist politicians in 1915, he resigned from it. But in 1938 he became the first President of Ireland, chosen partly because of his Gaelic interests and partly because he was a token Protestant who could make it look as though heavily Catholic Ireland was really a tolerant, secular society!

Psychic research was taken seriously by men like Henry Sidgwick (1838–1900), who became Professor of Moral Philosophy at Cambridge in 1883 and was closely involved with the foundation of Newnham College for women, which was not part of the university and was specifically forbidden to have a Christian chapel, something almost unheard of in the city at that time.[50] One of the men he influenced was Arthur James Balfour (1848–1930), who would be Prime Minister from 1902 to 1905 and in 1917 would be responsible for issuing the famous 'Balfour Declaration' that committed the British government to allowing the establishment of a Jewish homeland in Palestine – a fateful decision that continues to have serious consequences.[51] Another psychic was William James (1842–1910), of whom Stewart Brown has perceptively written:

> His reflections on the varieties of religious experience led James to commend the fullest possible religious tolerance. Individuals had their own distinctive religious experiences. Most individuals interpreted their spiritual experiences according to the religious tradition and culture in which they had been raised. But each individual's experience yielded only a partial insight into 'human nature's total message', and none had the whole truth . . . James's *Varieties* did much to promote the psychological approach to religion in Britain. Religious faith, he suggested, was subjective and relative, a unique expression of the complex and multilayered individual self. Individuals should not be held culpable for having 'wrong' religious beliefs.[52]

Modern readers immediately recognize in this a clear statement of the way in which religious belief is usually portrayed. Everyone is entitled to his or her own opinion, based on experience, and all sincerely held views are equally valid. That this is diametrically opposed to true Christianity will immediately be obvious to anyone who has a genuine Christian faith, but any attempt to say that publicly is liable to call down condemnations of intolerance, bigotry and just plain ignorance. If any one person can be singled out as the chief inspirer of modern religious sensibility in the Western world, and especially

---

[50] Newnham College is now part of the University of Cambridge of course, but it still has no chapel, only a 'quiet room' set aside for private prayer and meditation. It is also the only college in Oxford or Cambridge that is still single-sex.

[51] In fairness to him Balfour did not envisage the displacement of the Palestinians, nor could he have had any knowledge of the terrible events of the Holocaust that would decimate European Jewry in the Second World War and make the establishment of a Jewish state of Israel in 1948 almost inevitable.

[52] Brown, *Providence and Empire*, 391.

in the British Isles, it must surely be William James, the seductive but deeply anti-Christian author of *The Varieties of Religious Experience*.

These then were the social and intellectual currents surfacing in British life in the early years of the twentieth century. To what extent were they perceived by contemporaries? This is a difficult question to answer. Statistical research shows that church membership peaked about 1905 in most denominations and went into decline after that, although nobody at the time could have known that the decline would be permanent. Nor was it evenly spread. English and Welsh Nonconformity suffered most, but Scottish church membership held up for another generation and the Roman Catholic Church did not begin to decline in a serious way until the 1980s. Smaller denominations, like the Pentecostals, may still be growing, as are individual congregations in the Church of England and elsewhere, but the overall trend is now unmistakable. However it is measured, church membership and, even more, church attendance have declined to a fraction of the levels they still enjoyed just over a century ago, and there is as yet no reason to suppose that this trend will be reversed anytime soon.

Having said that, the mood was buoyant in Edinburgh when the first world missionary conference was convened there in 1910. Protestant foreign missions had been the great success story of the nineteenth century, aided to some extent by European expansion but also critical of it, and by the efforts made to convert and educate indigenous peoples in the colonial world, sowing the seeds of the eventual destruction of the European empires that made such missionary efforts possible. The Edinburgh conference was determined to bring some order into this overseas expansion, not least by delimiting spheres of activity that were then assigned to particular missions and denominations. The purpose of that was to further the aim of winning the world for Christ 'in this generation'. No specific time limit was set for the completion of world evangelization, but many of the conference delegates assumed that it would come about in their lifetimes – perhaps by 1950 and certainly by 2000 at the very latest.

Looking back on this now we can only marvel at how blind they were to the future. Could any of them have imagined that in the generation they envisaged, Europe and the world would be ravaged by war – not once, but twice – that atheism would be proclaimed as the new creed in states that had previously been officially Christian and that more Christians would be persecuted for their faith in the twentieth century than in the entire history of the church? Could they have foreseen that in their own home countries, Christianity would be dethroned as the dominant belief (even if in places it would remain the state religion) and that it would be replaced by an often illiberal agnosticism that would try to ban any outward expression of faith? Would anyone have guessed that, far from Christianity converting the Muslim world, Muslims of different national origins would constitute a large and potentially hostile minority in their own homelands?

None of that could have been predicted in 1910, and none of it was. Yet only four years after the conference, the nations of Europe, so long accustomed to peace and prosperity, found themselves locked in a war to the death that would transform not only their continent but the entire world. As Sir Edward Grey, the British Foreign Secretary famously remarked when he saw the skies darkening in August 1914, 'The lamps are going out all over Europe; we shall not see them lit again in our lifetime.' The century of Enlightenment that was supposed to make warfare impossible disappeared in a cloud of gunsmoke, and those who had eyes to see realized that the Victorian age of progress and the apparently unstoppable progress of Christianity had all been a mirage. At first nobody could quite believe it, and many were convinced that it would all be over by Christmas. Indeed when that Christmas came, there was a truce on the Western Front during which German and British troops fraternized in a way that they had never done before. But it was an illusion, and the world that finally emerged from the carnage would never be the same again.

Today the ambiguous legacy of the Victorian age is most visible in the way that we celebrate Christmas. It had long been a religious festival, except in Scotland, which abolished it in the seventeenth century and did not revive it until 1958, but it was fairly low-key. Then, when Prince Albert arrived in Britain in 1840 he introduced the German custom of the Christmas tree, and before long the kind of Christmas we now recognize was taking shape. From being just one of the three major feasts of the Christian year (the other two being Easter and Pentecost) it became by far the most important – and also the most secular. Charles Dickens's A Christmas Carol is typical of this – it is a morality tale with no mention of Christ at all. Hymn writers produced saccharine Christmas carols that portrayed 'gentle Jesus meek and mild', the helpless baby in a manger whose image was quite different from that of the risen, ascended and glorified Lord of heaven and earth. Alongside these carols there have also grown up a number of Christmas songs that have little or nothing to do with Christianity, so much so in fact that 'put the Christ back into Christmas' has become something of a slogan in Christian circles. The largely non-religious Christmas holiday we know is a Victorian relic, a reminder to us of how that seemingly churchgoing age was in fact a time when the Christian faith was being hollowed out into a morality tinged with sentimentality, and not much else.

14

The decline and fall of 'Christian Britain' (1914–80)

The edge of the abyss

On 1 August 1914 the UK marked the bicentenary of the accession of George I of Hanover, the nation's first German monarch. For 200 years Britain and Germany were intimately linked in any number of ways. Its kings were electors (and later kings) of Hanover until 1837, when the succession passed to a male relative of Queen Victoria, who (as a woman) was unable to take the Hanoverian throne. But Victoria soon married Albert of Saxe-Coburg-Gotha, continuing the German connection into the next generation, and her eldest daughter Victoria married the Crown Prince of Prussia, who briefly became Emperor of Germany as Friedrich III in 1888. She was the mother of Wilhelm II (1859–1941), who is famously known to us simply as the 'Kaiser'. But only three days after the bicentenary, the UK declared war on Germany, and the once friendly relations between the two countries came to an end.

At first, nobody could quite believe what was happening. War between the two most prominent Protestant states of Europe seemed abnormal, and the British alliance with secular France, where a separation between Church and state had been decreed in 1905, and with tsarist Russia, with its obscurantist Orthodox Church, was incongruous, to say the least. Most people thought the conflict had no real cause and that it would be over by Christmas, but they were to be disappointed. The Germans quickly overran most of Belgium and, although they were halted just short of Paris, they were not repulsed. For four long years both sides dug themselves in across north-eastern France and scarcely budged. Now and again, one side or the other would attempt to advance and occasionally a few metres would be captured here and there, but for the most part it was a stalemate. There was more movement on the Eastern Front, but in 1917 the Russian Empire collapsed and the Ottomans were forced to retreat from most of their Arab lands. The entry of the USA into the war tipped the balance and after that it was only a matter of time before Germany and its allies would be forced to surrender in order to prevent starvation.

The Great War, as the 1914–18 conflict came to be called, was unlike anything before it. Of course there had been fighting for centuries and Britain was covered with monuments to the great struggle against Napoleon a hundred years earlier, but those battles had never touched the mass of the population. In the Great War almost everyone was involved one way or another. Young men went to the trenches, where they were slaughtered in their thousands. Women went to work in factories, taking jobs that the men had to leave behind, and in the process achieving a degree of financial independence and personal liberation that they had never previously known. Newspapers and the recently invented cinema made it possible for the entire population to follow what was going on, but at the same time made it harder to conceal bad news, of which there was plenty. When it was over, the entire nation breathed a collective sigh of relief, but there could be no going back to the innocent prewar time. New demons had been unleashed, and it would be a generation before real peace returned to Europe, albeit in conditions that made it a divided continent for a further forty years and more.

In 1914 none of that could have been foreseen. After the initial shock, men rushed to enlist, many of them persuaded by the strange belief that blood sacrifice was somehow going to cleanse what they perceived as the decadence of their society. This glorification of violence seems odd to us now, but there was a curious pseudo-militarism before the war that had echoes in church life. The Salvation Army, and its companion the Church Army, was one example of that. There was also the Boys Brigade, which had been founded in 1883 as an outlet for adolescent male testosterone, and a number of similar organizations, including the Boy Scouts, founded in 1908, and the Girl Guides, set up in 1910 as a female counterpart to them. The Boys Brigades were strong in Scotland and among Nonconformists in England, but there was also a Church Lads' Brigade for Anglicans (founded in 1891), not to mention a Catholic Boys' Brigade and even a Jewish Lads' Brigade, both of which were up and running by 1900. None of these bodies was militaristic in the usual sense of the term, but they all had their uniforms and taught their members to go on parade, often to and in the local churches. By 1914 there was a generation that had been primed for battle, even if unconsciously, and this may help to explain the euphoria that gripped so many when a real war finally broke out.

At first enlistment was not difficult, and the army had to turn people away, but as trench warfare consumed its victims a shortage developed, and conscription became the order of the day. The clergy often served as recruiting sergeants, especially in rural communities where they were still influential, and there was debate as to whether those in holy orders could (or should) enlist. The official line was that a clergyman could not serve as a soldier because of his higher calling to ministry, but this was not rigorously enforced and many curates took leave of absence and signed on. Many more became army chaplains, who were soon numbered in their thousands. Most came from the established churches, but there were plenty of Catholics and Nonconformists as well – in the crucible of war, theological differences were largely forgotten. The Chaplain-General was John Taylor Smith (1860–1938), who had briefly been Bishop of Sierra Leone (1897–1901) before being appointed to the army, where he served until his retirement in 1925. Taylor Smith was a strong Evangelical and initially blocked the appointment of Anglo-Catholics and others who did not share his outlook, but as the situation grew more desperate he was overruled, and clergy of many different shades of churchmanship were taken on.[1]

Although they did not see combat themselves, the chaplains were close enough to those who did to be able to share their lives. In the trenches they met men from backgrounds they (as largely middle-class university graduates) had not previously encountered, and came to realize just how alienated from the church and any form of religious practice so many of them were. They came face to face with indescribable suffering, with great heroism, with cowardice and with rebellion. They also came to appreciate the class gulf that separated the officers from their men, and could see for themselves how incompetent some of the commanders were. War is not an exact science and mistakes are bound to occur, but when the slaughter is on the industrial scale that prevailed from 1914 to 1918, there was more than the usual revulsion that such things stir up. It would be wrong to say that the chaplains became social revolutionaries, but they certainly acquired an awareness of the injustices that pervaded prewar Britain, from which they had been largely shielded in the past.[2] Socialism, preferably in a Christian form, acquired a new respectability among them and would help them navigate the political changes the post-war era would bring.

It is hard to evaluate what impact the experience of war had on the faith (or lack of it) of those who took part in it. Some certainly lost whatever belief they

---

[1] See J. Smyth, *In this Sign Conquer: The Story of the Army Chaplains* (London: Mowbray, 1968).

[2] Diaries and memoirs of chaplains are now being published here and there. See e.g. M. Snape (ed.), *The Back Parts of War: The YMCA Memoirs and Letters of Barclay Baron, 1915–1919* (Woodbridge: Boydell & Brewer, 2009); *The First World War Diaries of the Rt. Rev. Llewellyn Gwynne, July 1915 – July 1916* (Woodbridge: Boydell & Brewer, 2019).

had once had, but others gained it or had a renewed sense of God's providence at work in their lives. What is certain is that those who survived often experienced what we would now call 'survivor guilt' – they had been spared while their comrades had been taken, and they tried to come to terms with that awful reality. Here the chaplains and the churches faced a challenge that had never before presented itself on such a scale, and answers had to be found.

One of the first attempts to deal with this question appeared in the earliest stages of the war. What had initially appeared to be senseless was suddenly turned into a crusade for Christian civilization. The Germans and their allies, who until only a few months before had been regarded as spiritual equals, now came to be seen as diabolical. The German invasion of Belgium had met with unexpected resistance and they replied with the kind of cruelty military minds think will soften opposition and promote passive cooperation. The result was widespread destruction across the country, in particular at Louvain (Leuven), where the famous university library went up in flames. For British and French propagandists this was an unexpected gift, because it 'proved' to them that the Germans were barbarians – Huns who were out to destroy European culture. The secular French were reluctant to invoke the name of God but their British allies had no such qualms. They knew exactly whose side God was on, and why – and they did not hesitate to share this knowledge, either with the men under their command or with those on the home front.

After initially pleading for neutrality in the conflict, Henry Scott Holland was soon writing to a friend: 'every day reveals the black blind horror of Prussianism. It is the very devil. It has to be fought: and killed. It is the last word in iniquity. I could not have believed that men could be so diabolical.'[3]

Not to be outdone, Arthur Foley Winnington Ingram (1858–1946), Bishop of London (1901–39), preached a sermon on 6 September 1914 in which he said:

> this is an Holy War. We are on the side of Christianity against anti-Christ. We are on the side of the New Testament which respects the weak, and honours treaties, and dies for its friends, and looks upon war as a regrettable necessity . . . It is a Holy War, and to fight in a Holy War is an honour.[4]

In June 1915 he went even further, comparing the sacrifice of Britain's young men with that of Christ on Calvary:

---

[3] Quoted in A. Marrin, *The Last Crusade: The Church of England in the First World War* (Durham, N.C.: University of North Carolina Press, 1974), 86–87.

[4] Ibid. 79.

Christ died on Good Friday for Freedom, Honour and Chivalry, and our boys are dying for the same things. Having once realised that everything worth having in the world is at stake, the nation will not hesitate to allow itself to be mobilised. You ask for my advice in a sentence as to what the Church is to do. I answer MOBILISE THE NATION FOR A HOLY WAR.[5]

Nor was this sentiment confined to men on active duty. The judicial execution of Edith Louisa Cavell (1865–1915), a British nurse in occupied Belgium who helped soldiers on both sides escape capture and was shot by the Germans for her heroism, provoked an outpouring of pious grief that turned her into a latter-day martyr for her faith as well as for her country, even though she herself was anything but one-sided in her patriotism.

There were some voices that spoke out against such excesses, notably Charles Gore, who pointed out that the enemy were also human, that God loved them just as much as he loved the British, and that conscientious objectors to war had a right to have their view respected, even if it was not the majority opinion. Gore was not alone in seeking to redress the balance and, as time went on, more people began to see the need to work for a post-war reconciliation, but the voices of such men were largely drowned out at the time and only recalled years later, when it was safe to do so.[6]

As we might expect, the most extreme expression of this way of thinking came from Ireland, and for reasons that were only tangentially connected with the Great War. In 1914 Ireland was on the brink of civil war, with Protestants and Catholics both arming themselves and parading openly in the streets of Belfast and Dublin in anticipation of a great struggle for (or against) home rule for the island. The outbreak of war in Europe put a damper on this as the issue was postponed until hostilities should cease, and most Irishmen of both major confessions supported the British to one degree or another. But a small group of extremists believed that 'England's difficulty is Ireland's opportunity', as the saying went, and prepared themselves for a blood sacrifice that would drive a wedge between Britain and Ireland and make the latter independent, whether its people wanted that or not.[7]

---

5 Ibid.

6 Thus e.g. Gore's thoughts were first published for a wider readership by his biographer G. L. Prestige, *The Life of Charles Gore: A Great Englishman* (London: William Heinemann, 1935), 370.

7 See C. Townshend, *Easter 1916: The Irish Rebellion* (London: Penguin Books, 2005); *The Irish Uprising 1914–1921* (London: The Stationery Office, 2000). On the personalities and motives of the leading rebels themselves, see R. F. Foster, *Vivid Faces: The Revolutionary Generation in Ireland 1890–1923* (London: Penguin Books, 2014); R. Dudley Edwards, *The Seven: The Lives and Legacies of the Founding Fathers of the Irish Republic* (London: Oneworld, 2016). Both books detail the deep, if complex, relationship between Irish nationalism and Roman Catholicism.

These fanatics seized on the Christian theme of resurrection from the dead and prepared themselves to die so that the Irish nation (as they thought of it) would be reborn.[8] On Easter Monday (24 April) 1916 they seized the General Post Office in Dublin and began a revolt that caught the authorities unprepared, even though they had had ample warning of what was to come. The Easter Rising was hopeless from the start and after a week it was all over. The centre of Dublin was partially destroyed and the people turned against the rebels, but the harshness of the repression, which included the arrest and even the killing of innocent bystanders, was counterproductive. Within weeks the myth-makers of Irish history had turned a criminal act into a glorious struggle for freedom, and an enduring legend was born. The secularization of the central mystery of Christianity was total, but was confined entirely to the Catholic side and by no means to all of that. The separation of most of Ireland from Great Britain was duly achieved, but the aim of creating eternal enmity between the two islands backfired. What happened instead was that the enmity was largely confined to Ireland itself, with Protestants and Catholics permanently alienated from each other for reasons that had little to do with the Christianity that both of them officially confessed. Catholicism and Irish nationalism were now one and the same in Ireland and Protestants were unwelcome in the Free State, even if nobody said so openly. At the same time, Northern Ireland was carved out of Ulster as a Protestant province that was equally politicized, even if the link with Great Britain prevented it from becoming as openly pseudo-Christian as its southern counterpart would soon be. These events have left a residue of hatred that endures to the present day – a tragedy that so far no amount of preaching peace and reconciliation in the name of Christ has been able to overcome.

Elsewhere, and to a large extent in Ireland as well, the main legacy of the Great War was the emergence of a cult of the dead that has remained powerful for more than a century. Earlier wars were eventually forgotten – nobody now remembers who fell at Waterloo or Agincourt – but the casualties of 1914–18 were piously recorded on tablets placed in virtually every church, and every year since then, on 11 November (or the preceding Sunday), prayers have been said in the memory of the fallen. Members of the Royal British Legion who would otherwise never darken the door of a church turn up for the local parade, or line the streets of London near the Cenotaph, for the one occasion in the year when the nation collectively bows its head in prayer. Remembrance

---

[8] M. Laffan, *The Resurrection of Ireland: The Sinn Féin Party 1916–1923* (Cambridge: Cambridge University Press, 1999).

Sunday remains an overwhelmingly Christian event, at least in outward form, but like the war itself, its relationship to Christianity is controversial – and difficult even for the well-meaning to discern.

Waiting for God

The interwar years were a time of uncertainty when great hopes were entertained, only to be dashed on the hard rocks of reality. The Great War was supposed to have made the world safe for democracy, but instead it brought chaos to much of Europe and did little or nothing for the rest of the world. Four great empires – Germany, Austria-Hungary, Russia and Ottoman Turkey – were destroyed, but what took their place was hardly better, and in many cases worse. The British Empire was larger than ever but it was increasingly restless, and the UK no longer had the resources to support it indefinitely. It would survive to fight another day, but when that day was done it would collapse with breath-taking speed. A tradition of overseas expansion built up over four centuries vanished in a single generation, and fifty years after the armistice in 1918 Great Britain was reduced once again to what it had been in the early seventeenth century, or (if the loss of much of Ireland is taken into account) even less than that.

It was a huge psychological shock, and one from which neither the British people nor their churches have really recovered. Paradoxically, one of the reasons for that is the way in which Britain has clung to an emaciated notion of divine providence. For two centuries people had interpreted the nation's rise to power as God's will, and in the post-1918 chaos that belief seemed to be confirmed in a curious kind of way. The Tsar and the Kaiser were gone, but King George V was still on his throne. Whereas democracy might be struggling in Italy or Poland, it was alive and well at Westminster. Women had got the vote and Parliament was more representative of the people than it had ever been. The omens seemed good, but where was the nation headed? What was God planning to do with it next?

Different people had different answers to these questions. The Anglo-Catholic wing of the Church of England was convinced that its time had finally arrived. It was led by Charles Wood (1839–1934), Viscount Halifax from 1885 and President of the English Church Union from 1868 until 1919 (and again from 1927 until his death). Lord Halifax was strongly anti-Evangelical and even managed to persuade the Church of England to enter into negotiations with Rome, with the prospect of some form of reunion in the future, although there was never any real hope of that. The most he could do was pressure the

Church authorities into permitting Catholic forms of worship, an issue that was a permanent bone of contention with Evangelicals and others. In theory Anglo-Catholics had a high view of the Church and its authority, but in practice they treated the bishops with cavalier disregard when they failed to follow the Anglo-Catholic lead, and in the end they did little more than make clergy discipline in matters of worship a dead letter – the exact opposite of what they claimed to want.

In a curious way the mass slaughter of the war appeared to have strengthened the Anglo-Catholic position, because, like the Roman Catholic Church, it advocated prayers for the dead and requiem masses, which were repellent to other Protestants but could offer some comfort to those who had lost a loved one, of which there were many. Anglo-Catholicism also brought colour and drama to worship, and that had a certain appeal after years of wartime austerity. Army chaplains were addressed as 'padre', the Spanish and Italian word for 'father', which made it easier to continue the practice after the war's end. Their leaders lost little time in exploiting what they saw as a new mood in their favour. As early as 1920 they organized a congress at St Paul's Cathedral in London with the express aim of promoting their cause, which they identified with the evangelization of the country more generally. It was a great success, and four more were held at three- to four-year intervals, each of them larger than the one that had gone before (see Table 14.1).

Table 14.1 The Anglo-Catholic congresses, 1920–1933

Date	Attendees	Increase
1920	13,000	
1923	15,000	A 15.4% increase on 1920
1927	21,000	A 40% increase on 1923
1930	29,000	A 38% increase on 1927
1933	70,000	A 141% increase on 1930

The extraordinarily high number for 1933 may reflect the fact that it commemorated the centenary of the Oxford Movement and special efforts were made to make it a success but, however we look at the figures, it is clear that no other Christian group could have mustered so many participants, over such a long period, as the Anglo-Catholics could – and did – during these years. The congresses met over several days and included a solid diet of worship, teaching and fellowship. Speakers of high quality were invited and many participants were inspired by their addresses, although perhaps the greatest effect was simply meeting so many people in one spot, all dedicated to the same cause. Anglo-Catholics understandably went away thinking that they had the future of the Church in their hands, but did they?

A closer look at events may reveal some cause for doubts on that score. The Church of England had been nudged, largely by Anglo-Catholic pressure, into a lengthy process of liturgical revision that finally came to fruition in 1927. A revised Prayer Book was presented to the convocations and passed with substantial majorities, but when taken to Parliament failed to gain the necessary support in the House of Commons. A second attempt was soon made, with a slightly revised text, but it also failed, and more than a decade of work was suddenly redundant. The bishops tried to rescue the situation by authorizing the use of the revised services wherever they were acceptable to the local congregation, but this had limited success and raised doubts about the legality of the permission thus granted.

The trials of the 1928 Revised Prayer Book came from different quarters.[9] The Evangelicals were generally opposed to it because of what they perceived as its 'Romeward' tendencies; for example, in allowing the reservation of the sacrament for use in ministry to the sick. But many Anglo-Catholics also objected to it, often for the opposite reason. If the sacrament could be reserved for the sick, they argued, why could it not be reserved for more general purposes, including the sort of adoration practised by the Roman Church? Nonconformists also weighed into the discussion, and in the end they were the ones who tipped the balance in Parliament in favour of the Evangelical position. There had been conversations in Malines (Mechelen) between Anglicans and Roman Catholics, held with a view to promoting reunion of the churches, and it was clear to many that this was an anti-Protestant move.

Many people believed that if the Church of England's public liturgy moved in a Catholic direction, relations with other Protestant churches would deteriorate and the Protestant character of the nation would be imperilled. At the same time, Nonconformists were moving towards an ecumenical consensus, and many of them were exploring the possibility of union among themselves. They were also open to the possibility of reuniting with the Church of England, but if the latter moved in the opposite direction that avenue would be closed. Not much came of this, other than the merger of a number of Methodist bodies to form the United Methodist Church in 1932, but the ultimate goal was not abandoned. In fact, as we can now see, Nonconformity

---

[9] See D. Gray, *The 1927–28 Prayer Book Crisis*, Alcuin Club and The Group for Renewal of Worship Joint Liturgical Studies 60/61 (Norwich: SCM-Canterbury Press, 2005–6).

was in serious decline after 1918 and the gradual distancing of the established Church from the state brought the very existence of Nonconformity into question. How many people really understood why Methodists, Congregationalists and Presbyterians stayed apart when they looked the same to most outsiders? Scottish Presbyterians managed a reunion in 1929 that proved to be successful, so why could that not happen elsewhere?

The Baptists were different in that they rejected the practice of infant baptism, but that was never the Church-dividing issue it appeared to be on the surface. Evangelicals were not sacramentalists and believed in the necessity of personal conversion, so Baptists and others could claim to be at one on the essentials. Other Protestants were having doubts about the wisdom of baptizing large numbers of babies who did not then grow up to be church members, and there was an increasing sense that religious observance was ultimately a matter of personal choice, tendencies that favoured the Baptists. At the same time, almost everyone agreed that it was right for Christians to bring up their children 'in the knowledge and fear of the Lord', which put infant baptism in the proper covenant context and made it possible for Baptists and others to work together despite their difference over the sacrament.

The question remained a thorny one but there was widespread agreement in principle, if not in practice, and the hope was that with patience and good will the latter might eventually be brought into line with the former. There was a growing sense that matters like these were disputes for the clergy and theologians, not for ordinary people who were generally prepared to go along with whatever the local church decided. At a time when fewer people were going to church, arguing over details like these was for many a luxury that they could not afford and a distraction from the gospel message. The result was a greater willingness to participate in interdenominational evangelistic efforts and a general lessening of the Church–chapel tensions that had caused such division in the Victorian era.

Was God encouraging the churches to come together in order to present a united front against secularism and the rising atheistic ideologies of the day? Would church unity support the belief that Christianity was true and prove to be the harbinger of revival across the nation as a whole? It was a tempting suggestion and the need to connect with the large unchurched public was recognized on all sides, but reaching those who did not attend church was easier said than done. In effect it meant going outside the church buildings and the subculture they encouraged and meeting people where they were. Well before the end of the war there was a plan to do this in the National Mission of Repentance and Hope, which got underway in 1916. It was really an extension of the Christian Social Union and operated on the assumption that the conversion of individuals, while important, was not enough. Christian people had to learn to act in Christian ways, tailoring their behaviour to the requirements of their faith.

How successful the Mission was is impossible to say, but it led to the establishment of five committees that were designed to explore the issues more deeply. The last of these reported in December 1918 in a well-written and timely document entitled *Christianity and Industrial Problems*. It led to the creation of the Industrial Christian Fellowship (ICF), which conducted large open-air 'crusades' on street corners and in factories, and followed these up with correspondence courses and small study groups. The guiding spirit of the ICF was Geoffrey Anketell Studdert-Kennedy (1883–1929), an army chaplain popularly known as 'Woodbine Willie' because he distributed free cigarettes to the troops in the trenches. The ICF, which still exists, pioneered the practice of bringing Christianity into the workplace, and has been a model for several other groups of its kind. It achieved the remarkable feat of being effective outside the church and yet receiving the approval of bishops and other church authorities. It was necessarily ecumenical in practice and in recent years has even reached out to members of non-Christian faiths, despite the difficulties and controversies such a move is bound to cause. Most other bodies of this type have remained more distinctively Christian, perhaps because they are largely Evangelical in inspiration, and they do what they can to bring the gospel message to working people in an environment that seems natural and comfortable to them.

It is very hard to evaluate what organizations like the ICF achieve because they are means to an end and not ends in themselves. Many of those who belong to or associate with them are members of churches that may have little or no official contact with them, while others have little or nothing to do with the institutional Church but find companionship in bodies like these. What they have succeeded in doing is taking mission and evangelism outside the traditional church buildings and turning them into para-church activities. The complexities of institutional ecumenism are avoided, the essentials of the gospel take precedence over the distinctive features of particular denominations, and a fellowship of like-minded believers is created that transcends secondary divisions. Contemporary British Christianity has been deeply marked by these tendencies, for the most part positively. Today when we look back to the ritualist and Establishment controversies of the nineteenth century, we sense how alien they are to our modern experience, and for this we have to thank the para-church organizations that have shaped us more than anything else.

At the same time the dream of national revival has not materialized. Para-church groups are essentially private fellowships that avoid the limelight and so it is difficult to know how much influence they have. Probably the fairest thing to say is that they provide spiritual support to individuals who are trying to live a Christian life in a hostile environment and apply their principles to their work as much as they can. It is obviously easier for business owners and independent entrepreneurs to do this than it is for employees of large multinational corporations, where policy decisions may be taken at levels unpenetrated by most of the workforce, and there is still much to do to make Christian executives aware of their responsibilities. Yet business ethics and ethical investments are no longer the alien concepts they once were, and it seems reasonable to assume that Christian missions of this type have played at least some part in bringing them into the open.

The granting of full citizenship to women was also to have an impact on the churches, where women made up the majority of regular worshippers. Is God somehow closer to women than to men?[10] This question would have seemed bizarre to generations of Christians before the nineteenth century, and it is hard to deny that the church was male-dominated for most of its history. Jesus chose twelve men as his disciples, the overwhelming number of writers and theologians had been male and the ordained ministry was also a masculine preserve virtually everywhere. Some prominent women had been active from time to time, and they were never segregated from the men in the way they sometimes were in Judaism and Islam, but Christianity was definitely not a feminine (and still less a feminist) religion. That began to change in the Victorian era. Among Roman Catholics there was a revival of Marian devotion, symbolized by the apparitions claimed for her at Lourdes and a few years later at Knock, in the west of Ireland. In the Protestant world there was a greater focus on the presumed differences between men and women that supposedly made the latter more susceptible to spiritual values, and at the same time made them vitally important in curbing the vices of their menfolk. Women tended the home and kept order in the family, and the emphasis the Victorians placed on promoting middle-class respectability highlighted their role both in society and in the church.

The experience of war also contributed to changed perceptions of women in the church. There was a dearth of young marriageable males and many women were condemned to singleness whether they wanted it or not. The men who did survive were often marked by the horrors of warfare and found it

---

[10] See C. G. Brown, *Religion and Society in Twentieth-Century Britain* (London: Routledge, 2006), 69–73.

difficult to relate to those who had not been so exposed. The fact that clergymen had been exempted from active duty was also problematic because it contributed to the feeling in some quarters that they were not 'real men'. That feeling was unfair but, in the difficult emotional circumstances of the time, balanced judgments were not always made. What is certainly true is that after 1918 church congregations were made up mainly of women and children. This situation was not as dire as some contemporary observers portrayed it, but it was bad enough and the churches had to face that reality. What could they do to win back the men? Was it somehow natural, even inevitable, that women should predominate in the pews?

Most of the churches realized that they had to do something if they were going to attract large numbers of men, but few were able to grasp that the question had to be seen against a wider pattern of social change that was still only beginning in the 1920s. This was that the traditional role of women as mothers and homemakers was changing as younger ones went out to work and began to make careers for themselves. There were still plenty of women who were uncomfortable with that change and who remained bulwarks of their local congregations, so the question did not have to be confronted for a generation or more, but the writing was on the wall for those with eyes to see it. The steep decline of churchgoing in the 1960s and 1970s would be due to the mass departure of stay-at-home women at least as much, if not more, than to the relative absence of men.

How far and to what extent Christian principles dominated social life in the years after 1918 is hard to say. Was it God's will that the nation as a whole should pretend to be Christian, even if it was not, so that those who were could feel that their values were the ones officially approved? Or did God see this superficial piety as a kind of idolatry that had to be smashed so that true belief could be seen for what it was and not be confused with social conformity? A century ago most people in the British Isles paid lip service to Christian values and regarded deviations from them as reprehensible, even if they sometimes appeared to be almost unavoidable. It was generally accepted that a certain level of censorship was needed if publications, films and other means of mass communication were not to become channels for the spread of ideas and behaviour that were inconsistent with Christian values. Swear words were regularly edited out, anything to do with sex was carefully monitored and controlled, and the 'bad guys' always lost in the end. Nobody stopped to ask whether this was true to real life because the purpose of public discourse was to teach and uplift the population, not to reflect the proclivities of its baser elements.

Divorce was considered to be wrong, regardless of how prevalent it was, and even if it became easier to obtain. When King Edward VIII wanted to marry the twice-divorced Wallis Simpson in 1936, it was taken for granted that he could not do so and keep his throne, even if there was considerable private sympathy for him. The public standards of Christian morality had to be upheld and it was the Church of England that first brought the matter to public attention. Nobody complained and the king went because his conduct was not compatible with his office or with the teaching of the Church. There was certainly no call for disestablishment in order to remove any conflict between Church and state. In most people's eyes there was no such conflict, because what the Church taught was universally accepted as the required norm for public figures.

In this field the most consistent (and extreme) policy was that adopted by the newly created Irish Free State. One of the first actions it took after getting its independence in 1922 was to abolish divorce altogether. There were protests from individuals, notably from the Protestant William Butler Yeats, but not from the churches. The Roman Catholic Church saw it as the first step in imposing its own moral values on the state, and the Protestant churches disapproved of divorce just as much as the Catholic Church did, even if they would have preferred a different approach to the subject. The abolition of divorce was accompanied by a rigorous censorship of publications and, as time went on, by a series of other measures designed to keep out such things as birth control and abortion. The Free State was officially 'secular' and did not have an established Church, but the overwhelmingly Catholic majority of its population gave Irish lawmakers a popular mandate for their policies. Or to put it another way, the Roman Catholic Church was able to force politicians to adopt its moral code under threat of losing their seats in Parliament.

The Irish situation was mitigated in practice by the nearness of England, where those who wished to escape the constraints of the law at home could always go. In later years, as British laws were progressively liberalized, it became common for Irish people to escape in this way, leading to charges of gross hypocrisy in the framing and application of the laws in Ireland. But that was not how most Irish Catholics saw it. They had been taught that holy Ireland stood in sharp contrast to godless England and saw nothing odd in maintaining Catholic moral principles at home while allowing an escape valve for those who could not live up to them. Extreme defenders of this situation were even known to point out that Ireland was officially 'secular' in a way that Great Britain, with its two established churches, was not. Its 1937 constitution enshrined Catholic principles in law but accorded some recognition to other religious bodies as well, and even elected a Protestant, Douglas Hyde, as its first president. The appearance was one of liberalism and tolerance, but when Hyde died in 1949 the mask came off. He was buried in a Protestant church but no member of the government attended his funeral, because the Catholic Church told its members that they were not to go to Protestant worship services. That such bizarre behaviour was possible reveals what the true situation was, and of course it did nothing to reconcile Protestants and Catholics in Ireland. But for all its faults, it was an attempt to apply Christian principles consistently and for two generations it received popular support, which could not have been said quite so readily of similar attempts made in Great Britain.

What of the intellectual scene? Was God calling his people back to the orthodoxy of an earlier time by chastising them for their infidelity, or was he rather leading them on to a new way of thinking, unencumbered by the ignorance of the past? Before 1914 it had been almost universally assumed that God, or the 'Spirit of the universe', was blazing new trails of human knowledge and thought, an enterprise in which the liberal theologians and philosophers of Germany played a leading part. The war did much to turn British people off the Germans, but in the sphere of academic theology the impact was remarkably slight. If anything, German liberalism made deeper inroads into the British churches after 1918 than it had done before, and in the field of biblical studies it became dominant. This was in spite of the fact that British textual criticism remained relatively conservative, as did biblical archaeology. But these were practical disciplines largely unaffected by philosophical considerations. In the realm of systematic theology England had always been relatively weak, although the Scots had remained in closer contact with their Reformed colleagues on the Continent and, thanks to the influence of the Westminster Confession, were more attuned to systematics than most of their English contemporaries were.

The most significant new voice in German theology after 1918 was that of the Swiss-German Karl Barth (1886–1968), who caused a sensation by rejecting the teaching of his master Adolf von Harnack in favour of a neo-orthodoxy, which returned to the classic Reformed confessions of the sixteenth and seventeenth centuries. Barth did not reject the critical findings of modern liberal scholarship but he believed that they had to be integrated into a more traditional understanding of God, the human condition and the meaning of salvation. He rejected all forms of natural theology, which he regarded as typical of Catholicism, thereby earning the rebuke of both Roman Catholics and Anglo-Catholics, who accused him of having no doctrine of creation. But his strong emphasis on the incarnation of Christ, whom he believed was the full and final revelation of God to the world, gained him a wide following.

One of the first people in Britain to appreciate his importance was George Kennedy Allen Bell (1883–1958), Bishop of Chichester from 1929. Bell was one of the few Englishmen who took reconciliation with the defeated enemy seriously and who was both well known and widely travelled in Germany. When the German Confessing Church, under Barth's leadership, composed the Barmen Declaration in 1934, in which it repudiated the neo-pagan ideology of Nazism, Bell was the only British person who was present and who signed it. He never wavered in his opposition to Hitler, but his knowledge of Germany allowed him to see beyond him to the broader mass of the population, and in particular to the courageous stand of theologians like Dietrich Bonhoeffer (1906–45), who would lose his life as a martyr to Nazi rule. Throughout the Second World War, Bell resolutely opposed what he saw as the excessive destruction wrought by Allied forces on Germany and was one of the first to advocate a positive programme of rehabilitation for the defeated nation. This did not make him popular at the time, but he lived long enough to see his position vindicated, and died in the knowledge that British–German relations would only get better as time went on.[11]

In Scotland the impact of Barth was mediated mainly through the work of Thomas Forsyth Torrance (1913–2007), who had studied under him in the 1930s, and his younger brother James Bruce Torrance (1923–2003), who was also a distinguished Scottish divine of the late twentieth century. Thomas Torrance was a prolific writer who was widely influential in his native land, although little read elsewhere.[12] As Barthians, the Torrances were too conservative for many outside their own circles, but too liberal for the traditionally orthodox, who often did not know quite what to make of them. As a result they were widely honoured but not widely followed, and have not left behind a school of theology in Scotland or anywhere else.

The interwar years were a time of doubt and confusion in the British churches, but Christianity could still make a significant impact in certain places and in particular ways. The Nonconformist tradition of serious biblical preaching was in decline but it had not vanished, and Westminster Chapel in London provided a particularly important venue for those who wanted that.

---

[11] More than fifty years after his death, Bell's reputation was disgraced thanks to an anonymous accusation from a woman who claimed that he had groped her as a girl of five. Influenced by the belief that such accusations must be taken at face value, the Church authorities turned against Bell, even though there was no way of knowing the truth.

[12] D. Molnar, 'Thomas F. Torrance', in D. Fergusson and M. K. Elliott (eds.), *The History of Scottish Theology*, 3 vols. (Oxford: Oxford University Press, 2019), 3:227–241.

George Campbell Morgan (1863–1945) was a Welshman and when still a child was deeply impressed by Dwight Moody, and began to preach when still a teenager. From 1904 to 1919 he was the pastor at Westminster Chapel and, after spending time in the USA, returned there in 1932 for a further ten years. In 1943 he handed his pulpit over to Dafydd Martyn Lloyd-Jones (1899–1981), who preached there for twenty-five years and gave new depth and range to traditional expository sermons. Their subsequent publication has done much to ensure his ongoing influence, although the Chapel itself declined after his retirement in 1968 and, so far at least, no Nonconformist preacher has been able to take his place as an acknowledged master of biblical and pastoral preaching.[13]

At a completely different level, Christianity was drawing various members of the literary intelligentsia towards conversion. Among them was the Anglo-American poet Thomas Stearns Eliot (1888–1965), who is universally acknowledged as one of the greatest writers of the early twentieth century. Eliot made his name as a sharp critic of the emptiness of interwar society before going on to produce masterpieces of literature with a solid Christian theme.[14] Even more influential was Clive Staples Lewis (1898–1963), an Oxford don who became a prominent popular apologist for the Christian faith and whose writings are still a source of enlightenment and inspiration for many. Lewis achieved the unusual feat of being a 'mere Christian', neither Evangelical nor Anglo-Catholic, but in no sense liberal or 'modern' either. He has been claimed by all branches of the church as one of their own, living proof that Anglicanism at its best can be a bridge to otherwise incompatible parts of the traditional Christian world.

Other great names could be cited as well – John Betjeman (1906–84) and Wystan Hugh Auden (1907–73) were both brought up in an Anglo-Catholic tradition and reflected it in their writing. Rose Macaulay (1881–1958), Dorothy Sayers (1893–1957) and Barbara Pym (1913–80) added female voices to this choir, which were to be continued in the next generation by women like Phyllis Dorothy James (1920–2014). Susan Howatch (1940–) even endowed a theology chair at Cambridge with the profits she made from her remarkable Starbridge series of novels, in which she traced various aspects of Church of England history in the twentieth century. There was also a thriving musical tradition, built on the work of composers like Charles Villiers Stanford

---

[13] D. M. Lloyd-Jones, *An Exposition of Ephesians*, 8 vols. (Edinburgh: Banner of Truth Trust, 1972–82); *Romans 1:1–14:17*, 14 vols. (Edinburgh: Banner of Truth Trust, 1970–2003).

[14] See B. Spurr, 'The Twentieth-Century Literary Tradition', in S. J. Brown, B. Nockles and J. Pereiro (eds.), *The Oxford Handbook of the Oxford Movement* (Oxford: Oxford University Press, 2017), 544–546.

(1852–1924) and Sir Charles Hubert Hastings Parry (1848–1918). Parry's legacy was to be especially profound in the number of students he taught, among whom Ralph Vaughan Williams (1872–1958) stands out. It is a tradition that continues to this day in the work of composers like John Rutter (1945–) and in places like King's College, Cambridge, which has attained universal renown.

Post-war revival?

When the Second World War broke out in 1939 the reaction of the British churches was muted. Memories of 1914 were still fresh in the minds of many, as of course was the terrible disappointment when the war that was meant to end all wars turned out to be one of the causes of a second and even wider conflict. People went dutifully to war, but this time there was little sign of the crusading spirit and few thought that much good would come of it. In a sense this was ironic. In 1914 the war aims of the major powers were opaque, and the attribution of guilt to Germany in the peace treaty struck many people as unjust. This was of considerable benefit to Adolf Hitler in the 1930s, since he could exploit that sense of injustice to right the 'wrongs' that had been done, and got away with it for much longer than he should have done. But by 1939 it was clear to many people that the Nazi regime was infinitely worse than Imperial Germany had been before 1914, and by 1945, when it was all over, there could be no doubt at all. Whatever atrocities had been committed on the Allied side, and there were more than most people cared to admit, they paled by comparison with the mass murder of six million Jews and an equal number of others.[15] This time there could be no doubting Germany's guilt, but after the initial horror wore off, the response showed a depth of humanity and compassion that had not been seen in 1918. Germany was dismembered and rebuilt almost from scratch, and plans were laid for creating an integrated European economy that would make future conflict impossible. There was a drawback to this, in that most of central and Eastern Europe came under Russian sway as the Soviet Union created its own international empire and imposed what Winston Churchill dubbed an 'iron curtain' across the middle of the Continent, but the reconstruction of western Europe was an undoubted success.

These developments did not affect the British Isles directly, but their impact could not be ignored. Coventry Cathedral, which had been bombed in 1941,

---

[15] There was of course the murder of perhaps twenty million Soviet citizens by their own government, but that became known only many years later.

was rebuilt, partly with the help of volunteers from Germany, and became a symbol of reconciliation for many. In 1948 a World Council of Churches (WCC) was created and British churchmen of different denominations played a leading part in it. The WCC was not to live up to its initial promise and when it showed rather too much sympathy for violent liberation movements in the Global South and also for communism in Eastern Europe, its reputation was compromised, and after 1975 or so its influence declined. Nevertheless the impulse for closer integration of the churches, both at home and abroad, continued and bore fruit, especially in Asia, where the Church of South India was set up in 1947, embracing Anglicans and other Protestants in a single church. That example was followed later in North India, Pakistan, Bangladesh and Ceylon (Sri Lanka), although not without opposition from Anglo-Catholics, who saw it as a betrayal of their ecclesiastical principles.

Another significant development was the growing British interest in Christian affairs overseas. The introduction of apartheid in South Africa after 1948 provoked a strong reaction, and British churches were in the vanguard of international opposition to it. Anglicans were especially active in this, not least because their presence in South Africa made their intervention both easier and more significant. Richard Ambrose Reeves (1899–1980), an English Anglo-Catholic who was Bishop of Johannesburg from 1949 to 1960, was in the forefront of this movement, and was seconded by Trevor Huddleston (1913–98). Both men were forced to leave the country and Huddleston was accused of sexual misconduct with minors, but their stand against injustice was universally respected (at least outside white South Africa), and nobody could accuse the British churches of supporting an unjust social order in that country.

Someone else who left his mark was Michael Bourdeaux (1934–), who became aware of the Soviet repression of religion when on a student exchange in the late 1950s, and determined to do something about it. He founded an institute for the study of religion in Communist lands, which was initially based at Keston (Kent) before moving to Oxford. Keston College, as the institute is known, became an international centre for supporting Christians behind the Iron Curtain and was of immense help, not only in boosting the morale of persecuted believers but also in informing the British public of the true nature of the Soviet state and its satellites. Its work was largely accomplished when the Soviet Union collapsed in 1991, and in 2007 its massive archive was sent to Baylor University in Waco, Texas, but the Keston Institute (as it is now called) continues to exist and bear witness to a remarkable episode in the history of British Christianity.

Alongside the work of Keston, although only tangentially connected with it, was a renewed interest in the Eastern Orthodox churches. Relations with them had been occasional and sporadic before the twentieth century, but the Russian revolution and immigration of many Greek-Cypriots to the UK changed that considerably. The Russian diaspora contained a number of highly educated intellectuals who settled in various European capitals (and in the USA), where they presented an attractive face of Orthodoxy to a public largely ignorant of it. As a result, there was a small number of conversions to the Eastern Church, of whom the most notable was Timothy Ware (1934–), reborn as Bishop Kallistos of Diokleia and one of Orthodoxy's most respected interpreters in Great Britain. Bishop Kallistos joined the Greek Orthodox Church of Constantinople, at least partly for political reasons, but the Russians were ably represented in London by Bishop Anthony Bloom of Sourozh (1914–2003), who was well known and liked as a spiritual mentor and guide.

The Orthodox churches in Britain are still closely tied to their countries of origin and have never attracted more than a handful of British converts, many of them Anglo-Catholics looking for a conservative liturgical tradition, although a few Evangelical charismatics have also been attracted by the somewhat exotic and suprarational character of Orthodoxy.[16] There is a Fellowship of St Alban and St Sergius, dedicated to fostering a deeper rapport between Anglicans and the Orthodox, which publishes *Sobornost*, a journal that seeks to make Orthodoxy better known in Britain.[17]

On another front, post-war Christianity in Britain was greatly strengthened by the immigration of large numbers of West Indians, known in recent times as the *Windrush* generation, after the name of the ship (*Empire Windrush*) that brought so many of them to the country. They were not the only arrivals from the now rapidly vanishing empire but they were unusual in being both English-speaking and Christian, the biggest difference between them and their host country being one of skin colour (and to some extent of popular culture). The ease with which these new arrivals integrated into British society has been a matter of controversy, and there was certainly a good deal of racism in some quarters, but there is no doubt that congregational life in many urban centres was transformed by their presence. Some joined established churches, including the Church of England, while others formed independent ones. In

---

[16] It should also be said that the traffic is not all one way. Quite a few Greek Cypriots in London have joined the Church of England and become Anglican clergy.

[17] *Sobornost*, a Russian word meaning 'conciliarity', was more or less invented by Slavophile Russian Orthodox intellectuals in the nineteenth century, most of whom probably would not have approved of the ecumenical activities of the Fellowship of St Alban and St Sergius.

a number of instances failing city-centre chapels were effectively taken over by them and turned into hubs of Caribbean culture. Later on something similar happened when Christians from Africa began to arrive in significant numbers, and the 'black church' has become an important element on the Christian scene, particularly in London.

Among the home-grown population there was a significant revival of Evangelicalism, which had been relatively eclipsed in the first half of the twentieth century.[18] One sign of things to come was the wartime establishment of the London Bible College in 1943.[19] It was remarkably successful from the beginning and expanded rapidly after the end of the war. Over the years it has trained thousands of church workers, missionaries and teachers from many different denominations and provided a base for some outstanding biblical scholars, of whom Donald Guthrie (1916–92), Gilbert Walter Kirby (1914–2006) and Ralph Philip Martin (1925–2013) were especially notable.

Apart from that, there were Nonconformist chapels here and there, scattered Anglican parishes and various presbyterian groups in Scotland that had kept the tradition alive, but it was all but invisible in the public arena, with the exception of Northern Ireland, where it was often confused with sectarian politics and so misunderstood. In the universities a small but determined witness had been preserved through the work of the Inter-Varsity Fellowship and its Christian Unions, which gradually displaced the more liberal Student Christian Movement as the main Christian body in the tertiary sector. The Christian Unions were interdenominational and para-church fellowships that encouraged their members to join local congregations but did not usually specify any particular one. Over time they became a major feeding source for Evangelical clergy, especially in the Church of England. In 1944 their future general secretary, Oliver Rainsford Barclay (1919–2013), bought a house in Cambridge that belonged to one of his relatives and turned it into a study centre known as Tyndale House. It was connected with the Tyndale Fellowship for Biblical Research, which was sponsored by men like Martyn Lloyd-Jones and Frederick Fyvie Bruce (1910–90), who was of Scottish Plymouth Brethren background and a leading biblical scholar in the conservative British tradition. The Tyndale Fellowship had a strong Brethren presence, but it embraced all denominations and would have a significant impact across the board. The first

---

[18] See A. Atherstone and D. C. Jones (eds.), *The Routledge Research Companion to the History of Evangelicalism* (London: Routledge, 2019). Also A. Atherstone and J. Maiden (eds.), *Evangelicalism and the Church of England in the Twentieth Century: Reform, Resistance and Renewal* (Woodbridge: Boydell Press, 2014).

[19] It was renamed the London School of Theology in 2004.

librarian of Tyndale House was Henry Chadwick (1920–2008), who along with his older brother Owen (1916–2015) was to become one of the leading historians of Christianity in the Church of England.[20]

Without a doubt, one of the most prominent post-war Evangelical leaders was John Robert Walmsley Stott (1921–2011), who was converted as a schoolboy, ordained in 1945 and appointed Rector of All Souls' Church, Langham Place, in 1950. For twenty-five years he guided that parish and turned it into a major centre of Evangelical preaching and outreach in central London. His influence and example were soon to be felt across England, and a significant portion of the Evangelical wing of the established Church is indebted to him for its very existence. Stott was converted, as were many others, through the ministry of Eric John Hewitson Nash (1898–1982), affectionately known to his friends as 'Bash', who created an evangelistic strategy aimed at reaching boys in the top public (boarding) schools of England. 'Christ for the upper crust', as some called it, was remarkably successful, despite considerable opposition from the schools themselves and from some of the parents.

The boys would be taken on holiday to Iwerne Minster in Dorset, whence the name 'Iwerne' came to be used as shorthand for the movement as a whole. The Bash campers were taught to dedicate themselves to simple evangelism, to develop a disciplined devotional life and to look for opportunities for wider ministry, if possible as celibate clergy. They were strongly opposed to Anglo-Catholicism but, in this respect at least, they resembled their opponents more than they might have realized. Over the years a significant number of Bash campers fell away – to marriage, to less demanding forms of churchmanship, even to unbelief. But a solid core remained, and by the late 1930s it was starting to take a leading role in reviving Evangelicalism. For a generation after 1945 it constituted a kind of Evangelical freemasonry that, at its best, brought a new sense of drive and determination to the ordained ministry. In class-conscious England, 'Iwerne' was resented and admired at the same time, as those who could never belong to it nevertheless fell under its sway and were often deeply edified by it. Unfortunately it became tainted by scandal and in 2020 it was forced to close, but its impact will continue to be felt as long as its graduates are in ministry.[21]

John Stott, in some ways a model Bash camper and one of Bash's great success stories, first came to prominence in 1954, when he was involved in the

---

[20] On the history of Tyndale House, see T. A. Noble, *Tyndale House and Fellowship: The First Sixty Years* (Leicester: Inter-Varsity Press, 2006).

[21] The scandal has revealed homoerotic tendencies among some of the leaders, who have taken advantage of the boys in their care.

Billy Graham crusade, which took place over three months at Harringay. Hundreds of people were converted to Christ and many of them went on to full-time Christian service. Even thirty years later, the Church of England was still receiving ordinands who had been converted during the crusade.

Unfortunately, although not altogether surprisingly, Billy Graham (1918–2018) encountered significant opposition to his ministry, both from the liberal and from the Anglo-Catholic wings of the Church. Among the latter, Gabriel Hebert (1886–1963), a monk of the Society of the Sacred Mission based at Kelham, felt moved to write a full-length book against Graham and his message, which spurred another young Evangelical, James Innell Packer (1926–2020), to produce a substantial reply. Hebert's book is now justly forgotten, but Packer's is still in print and continues to influence new generations of Evangelical Christians around the world.[22]

This episode was the harbinger of much that was to come. It brought home the antipathy towards Evangelicals felt in many Anglo-Catholic and liberal circles, which had grown fiercer over the previous generation and which was to intensify still more as these two wings of the Church began increasingly to converge in the form of liberal Catholicism. At the same time, it also signalled that Evangelicalism was reviving, that it could (and did) produce scholars and theologians of high quality and that its approach, symbolized by the title of John Stott's bestseller *Basic Christianity*, was a force to be reckoned with.[23] But although Evangelicals were definitely making their mark, the higher echelons of both the Church and the academy remained more or less closed to them. The first Anglican bishop who can be linked to this post-war Evangelical revival was Maurice Arthur Ponsonby Wood (1916–2007), Principal of Oak Hill College (1961–71) and then Bishop of Norwich (1971–85). His consecration was met with opposition and he remained something of an outsider on the episcopal bench, but the tradition he represented could no longer be ignored quite as thoroughly as it had been up to then.

In Scotland there was a similar conservative revival, connected with clergymen like William Still (1911–97), who became the Minister of Gilcomston South Church in Aberdeen in 1945 and remained there until a few months before his death. During that time he transformed the parish into a hub of Evangelical faith and established the Crieff Brotherhood, which endeavoured to spread the message throughout the Church of Scotland and beyond. It enjoyed considerable success for a generation but declined after Reverend Still's

---

[22] G. Hebert, *Fundamentalism and the Church of God* (London: SCM Press, 1957); J. I. Packer, *'Fundamentalism' and the Word of God* (London: Inter-Varsity Fellowship, 1958).

[23] J. R. W. Stott, *Basic Christianity* (London: Inter-Varsity Fellowship, 1958).

death, and in 2013 his former parish left the national Church in protest at the latter's willingness to accept practising homosexual clergy. In Ireland both the Presbyterian Church and the Church of Ireland experienced a revival of Evangelicalism that has had a remarkable impact on both of them. The Presbyterian Church in Ireland is now mainly Evangelical and the Church of Ireland is increasingly so, especially in the north. It is estimated that about a third of the Protestants in Ireland are now Evangelicals, and that they are the majority of regular churchgoers in all the different denominations.

How real was the revival of religion after 1945? There was undoubtedly an increase in churchgoing when compared to the immediate prewar years, but this seldom if ever reached the levels current before 1914. Likewise, there was an increase in the numbers of men and women offering themselves for full-time ministry but, once again, these did not reach pre-1914 figures. Alongside the gains attributable to immigration and the revival of Evangelicalism must be set the decline of more traditional religious practice, which was especially noticeable among the working class. It is probably most accurate to say that the 'revival' slowed the pace of decline but did not reverse it, and when its effects started to wear off, the long-term collapse of Christianity as the national faith became apparent.

What really seems to have happened between 1945 and the early 1960s was that there was a coincidence of two tendencies that overlapped without being identical. On the one hand there was a genuine revival of faith among some who were exposed to the claims of the Christian gospel and responded to it. Many of those people had a chance to hear the message because they were churchgoers or were sent to Sunday school. Popular alternative entertainments were as yet underdeveloped, the impact of television was only beginning to be felt and mass attendance at rallies like the Billy Graham crusades was facilitated by a network of social organizations closely linked to local churches. People who might not have been regular worshippers were nevertheless connected to bodies like the Mothers' Union, the Boy Scouts or the Girl Guides, or even the Royal British Legion, all of which had ties to congregations that could encourage these 'fringe' elements to take an interest in special activities that in some cases might lead to conversion.

On the other hand there was still a general assumption in Establishment circles that Britain was a Christian nation and that this should be reflected in standards of public behaviour, especially in the rapidly developing media. The British Broadcasting Corporation was not an evangelistic body by any stretch of the imagination, but it had to make time for religious programming and maintain a corporate culture that respected Christian moral values. It was not (and could not be) used to promote an alternative world view or lifestyle, and the churches and the state cooperated to ensure that little or nothing that Christians might find offensive was allowed on air. This informal censorship created a cultural climate in which Christianity was assumed to be the norm, which in turn made it possible for preachers to strike a chord with those who knew that they ought to conform to that norm, whether they did so or not. A later generation would look back on this as collective hypocrisy, when the majority professed one thing but practised another, but that is a harsh judgment that is not entirely fair. Most people accepted that there ought to be a standard and that the standard ought to be Christian, whether they themselves subscribed to it or not. Dissent from this consensus existed but it was generally regarded as eccentric – the preserve of humanists, bohemians and criminals, all of whom were tiny minorities in society at large.

The ambiguity of the connection between faith and social behaviour is well illustrated by the Moral Re-Armament movement (MRA), founded by Frank Buchman (1878–1961) as a pressure group whose aim was to ensure that Christian values predominated in public life. Buchman was converted at Keswick in 1908 but did not found his organization until 1938, having spent much of the previous decades recruiting followers at different universities, and in particular at Oxford.[24] The MRA really got going in the post-war era, when it combined its moral crusade with strong anticommunism. It was not connected with any church and had no distinctive theology other than a strong emphasis on moral principles it regarded as foundational to the social order. It organized in cell groups that fostered a strong sense of commitment among the members, but it often gave the impression of being a closed society with an agenda not open to debate or criticism. Inevitably, as time went on, the specifically Christian element was obscured as the moral crusade took over, and church people of many different persuasions became increasingly sceptical of it. Nevertheless it was able to survive on the fringes of the institutional churches and many Christians were supportive of its aims, even if its somewhat secretive methods made them cautious about getting too involved with it.

It is hard to say what the impact of this combination of faith and morality was, but we know that the rate of illegitimate births for example fell during this period to a record low, which is at least some indication that the churches' teaching against extramarital sexual intercourse had an effect. Young men called up for national service often had no sexual experience either before or

---

[24] In some circles it was known as the 'Oxford Group' but is not to be confused with the 'Oxford Movement' of the previous century.

during their time in the armed forces, which was a considerable change on what had gone before and further evidence that the encouragement to remain chaste before marriage was having an effect on men as well as on women, who in this respect were more equal than they had ever been. This abstinence had no direct bearing on the Christian faith of the nation as a whole but, as that cannot be measured, it must serve as an indicator of what we may assume was a wider social trend. Christians loyal to church teaching would not be sexually promiscuous and so the evidence, imperfect as it is, is nevertheless strong enough to enable us to conclude that real faith and social conformity went hand in hand to produce the semblance of a Christian culture, even if its roots were to prove to be shallow when they were put to the test in the decades following.

The reckoning

It was sometime after 1960 that the structure loosely known as 'Christian Britain' began to give way and eventually to collapse almost entirely. It is hard to say exactly when it started, but 1963 seems to have been a turning point, and after that change was rapid and continuous, despite periodic attempts to hold back the tide and even reverse it. There were many different factors at work in this. One of them was the coming of age of a post-war generation that was the first in the twentieth century not to have known war or serious economic hardship. For those born after 1945 life seemed to be getting better all the time and there was no indication that prosperity would cease to be the norm for most people. Much of what had held the country together until that point was due to a culture of deference that allowed the Establishment to set the tone for the rest of society. The monarchy, the upper classes generally, the professions, the universities and churches were all seen as authorities that had a right and duty to maintain certain standards, and these were generally consistent with Christian principles.

But in the 1960s this deference began to give way to a new culture of mockery and satire, in which the traditional pillars of society were increasingly pilloried, sometimes affectionately but often with an ill-concealed sense of resentment. Those directly affected did not immediately realize what was going on and many people were initially shocked by the audacity displayed in the press, in the theatre and above all on the new medium of television, but this reaction soon wore off and people grew accustomed to hearing and seeing their inherited values disparaged by a generation that had nothing to put in their place. The proponents of this new 'permissiveness' spoke of freedom, but it was really the destruction of a moral and spiritual culture, which left a vacuum in its wake.

Another factor that contributed to this was the sudden availability of alternative forms of leisure and entertainment. People who had seldom ventured far from home and had had little to do at the weekend now bought cars that enabled them to travel more than they had ever done before. Package holidays abroad became more common, and students who went off in increasing numbers to universities far from home found that they were free to do more or less whatever they liked without parental supervision or the constraints of neighbourhood approval. Tales of premarital sex and drug taking have doubtless been exaggerated, but such things became possible to a degree that they had not been before and the voices of complaint were easily dismissed as intrusions into the business of others that an 'adult' society should not have to tolerate.

Increased mobility and personal 'freedom' soon led to pressures for allowing Sunday sport and shopping, which affected wide sectors of the population. There was also a growing demand for the greater availability of contraceptives and the decriminalization of both abortion and homosexuality, although for a while they were downplayed in the media and kept as far as possible out of sight. It would take a generation for these changes to be openly accepted and normalized in the public sphere, but the direction of travel was clear and attempts to stop it were generally thwarted, if not ridiculed by media personalities who were the avant-garde of the 'revolution'.

The churches were taken aback by all this and were mostly unprepared to face the consequences. There was a natural conservatism among them that tended to produce a backlash of sorts, but this was seldom effective and probably contributed to the increasing disengagement of the general public. Sunday schools and other church organizations still flourishing in 1960 went into serious decline and by 1980 were on the verge of disappearing altogether. The generation born and brought up in those years was the first in recorded British history to have virtually no contact with institutional Christianity, to which it was almost totally indifferent. There was little or no hostility to faith or religion as such, but it was increasingly ignored by the majority. Churchgoing became the preserve of the elderly and of a dedicated minority that increasingly came to see itself as a counterculture in secular Britain. Remoter parts of the country, in particular the Highlands of Scotland and most of Ireland, lagged behind but, as time would show, they either caught up with the rest or came to be regarded as alien cells in the body politic that were anomalous and (in the case of Northern Ireland especially) dangerous to the well-being of society as a whole.

Christian resistance to these trends was muted, not least because the churches were undergoing revolutionary changes of their own that made it difficult to mount a united front against them or to propose a viable alternative. One reason for this was that there was a growing sense in the churches that some form of modernization was necessary. For Protestants this began with new translations of the Bible. As late as 1960 virtually everyone still regarded the King James (Authorized) Version (kjv) as the English Bible par excellence. There had been an attempt to replace it as far back as 1881 in what was billed as the Revised Version (rv) – 'revised' because it was seen to stand in continuity with the kjv – but although it created a sensation at the time, it failed to catch on. Too many people were familiar with the traditional text, biblical criticism was still in its infancy (at least in the English-speaking world) and the literary style of the revision was so inferior that it stood little chance of success. Nothing much was done for another two generations, until John Bertram Phillips (1906–82) discovered that his youth group in London could not understand the kjv. Phillips then set about translating portions of the New Testament into colloquial English and began to publish them, with the encouragement of C. S. Lewis. The first portions of the Pauline Epistles came out in 1947 and the complete New Testament made its appearance in 1958. It proved to be popular with many and prepared the way for the acceptance of more far-reaching translation attempts.

In 1946 a group of British and American scholars began work on what was to become the Revised Standard Version (rsv), which made its appearance in 1952.[25] By then biblical criticism was far more advanced than it had been in 1881, but the kjv tradition was still strong, so the new translation was presented as a 'revision' of the kjv, even though it diverged from it at a number of points. In particular, passages of the New Testament that were of doubtful authenticity were sectioned off, either in parentheses or in footnotes, and a number of variant readings were proposed. Sometimes preference was given to the traditional interpretation but not always, and liberal theological influences led to the displacement of concepts like the 'wrath' of God on the dubious ground that such a thing was unworthy of the Deity.

The rsv did not disappear in the way that the rv had done, but it did not displace the kjv either. It was not until 1961, the year of the 350th anniversary of the kjv, that an entirely new translation appeared – the New Testament portion of what was to become the New English Bible. This was promoted with

---

[25] Disagreements on the committee led to the publication of a distinct American Standard Version as well.

great fanfare in the churches and for a while it remained the preferred translation of the authorities in most mainstream denominations, but its poor literary quality and liberalism in the choice of theological vocabulary eventually consigned it to oblivion.[26] By then however the principle that a new translation into modern English was needed was gaining general acceptance, and the way was opened to the plethora of versions that has appeared in the past generation. Ironically, the overall effect of this desire to make the Bible more accessible has probably been the opposite of what was intended. Awareness that a variety of different readings was often possible made people doubt what the true meaning was, and Bible-study groups were often reduced to debating the question in what was typically a sharing of ignorance and confusion more than anything else. New translations in everyday language were harder to memorize (or to recognize) and so few people bothered, with the result that the Bible was quoted less often than it had been in the past. Despite everything, it remained true that it was when people heard the KJV being read that its cadences and elevated style made them sense that this was the Word of God in a way that no revised replacement could replicate.

At the same time, the churches initiated changes to their worship that had an unsettling effect on many. The Church of England produced a series of experimental liturgies that culminated in the *Alternative Service Book* (1980) and entailed the virtual disappearance of the 1662 Book of Common Prayer, which had nourished the faith of generations of churchgoers. The *ASB* was more ecumenical in the sense that it incorporated texts shared to varying degrees by the main Nonconformist denominations, and even by the Roman Catholics, so that visitors to other churches could feel that everyone was on the same page (literally!), but there were so many possible liturgical options that the notion of genuinely 'common prayer' was hard to sustain. One result of this was that it became harder for a clergyman to take services in other churches because he had to familiarize himself with the local variations beforehand.

There was also the difficulty that this wealth of choice reflected a range of theological views that could be difficult to harmonize with traditional Protestant doctrine. The liturgical renewal of the twentieth century focused on the recovery of ancient liturgies that were supposed to be more authentically Christian (and ecumenical) than those that had been produced in the heat of sixteenth-century controversies. One of the most influential English contributors to this movement was Gregory Dix (1901–52), an Anglican Benedictine

---

[26] The present writer was given a copy of the NEB New Testament at his ordination in 1978 and of the entire Bible at his priesting a year later, but both have remained unopened on his shelf ever since.

monk openly hostile to the Reformation and critical of Thomas Cranmer's supposedly 'Zwinglian' views.[27] In 1945 he published *The Shape of the Liturgy*, in which he argued that it was not so much the words but the overall structure (or 'shape') of the worship service that mattered, and his view became highly influential in subsequent efforts at revision.[28] Critics of Dix have demonstrated that his approach was historically inaccurate and that his interpretation of Cranmer and traditional Anglican liturgy is false, but by the time that became clear the damage had been done. As with modern Bible translations, liturgical revision has sown confusion more than anything else and led to the demise of liturgy in general. Most congregations today do whatever they want, and if the different denominations resemble one another, it is more likely because they all use guitars instead of organs and sing the same spiritual songs, most of which are of variable theological content and of little durability.

The institutional churches undoubtedly drew closer together from the 1960s onwards, but with mixed results. On the one hand the traditional distinction (and occasional hostility) between the Establishment and Nonconformists was greatly reduced as the links between church and state were loosened and traditional Nonconformity was no longer defined in terms of dissent from an approved norm. As a sign of this, the word 'Nonconformist' gave way to the term 'Free Churches', which is now the preferred designation for non-Church of England or non-Church of Scotland Protestant denominations. Attempts at formal union were made but most got nowhere because those who cared about their denomination were usually opposed to seeing it disappear, and those who did not lacked the motivation to pursue institutional integration. The main exception to this was the union of the Presbyterian Church in England with the Congregationalists, which was consummated in 1972 as the United Reformed Church. The truth is that interdenominational cooperation, where it has occurred, has been driven by financial necessity more than by theological conviction, which is often hard to discern in any of the participating churches.

The Church of England experienced a major overhaul of its structures in the 1960s that made it more independent of the state (and therefore more like a 'Free Church') but which can hardly be said to have produced the kind of renewal that the proponents of change imagined would be the result. The canon law of the Church, which had remained basically unaltered since 1604 and was seriously out of date, was finally revised in 1964 and 1969, since which

---

[27] Dix's real name was George Eglinton Alston Dix; the 'Gregory' was his 'name in religion'.
[28] G. Dix, *The Shape of the Liturgy* (London: A&C Black, 1945).

time it has been in a constant state of flux.[29] Ecclesiastical law is now a major cottage industry, sponsored by the Ecclesiastical Law Society, which is heavily stacked with professional lawyers but it remains opaque and seemingly irrelevant to most churchgoers, many of whom have never heard of it. The General Synod, similar to that of the Church of Ireland, was created in 1970 and has since become the principal legislative body for the Church of England but it is still not taken seriously by many people, with the result that it tends to be dominated by radical pressure groups that profit from the apathy of most church members. The results have often been controversial, to put it mildly, and it remains to be seen whether a Synod that was intended to unite the Church and give it more of a corporate identity will end up dividing it still further, albeit on rather different lines from those that emerged in the mid-nineteenth century.

The Roman Catholic Church followed a different trajectory from that of the Protestant churches, but with similar long-term effects. The Second Vatican Council (Vatican II), which met from 1962 to 1965, was supposed to update the Church in a process known in Italian as *aggiornamento*, and it did in fact authorize a number of far-reaching changes, especially in everyday worship and practice. The language of the liturgy was changed from Latin to the vernacular, which in practice meant English throughout the British Isles – virtually nobody says or hears mass in Irish or Welsh for example, although Polish and other immigrants are often catered for in their mother tongue. Hymn singing became more common, a number of traditional devotions were downplayed or abandoned and even private confession to a priest, although still possible, has tended to give way to corporate confession (and absolution) in worship.

Communion in both kinds also began to spread, although it is still not universal. Other things, like clerical celibacy, were untouched, but the general impression left by Vatican II was that the Church had undergone a kind of Protestantization, even if few Protestants have recognized it as such. This was particularly unsettling for British and Irish Catholics, where opposition to Protestantism had been a major factor in creating their identity since the sixteenth century, and it was not long before the numbers of worshippers started falling off, sometimes faster than in most Protestant churches. As was the case with them, renewal in the Catholic Church led instead to decline, and the remaining traditionalists (like supporters of the Latin Mass) were relegated to the sidelines in spite of all the provisions made for them by Rome.

---

[29] For the details, see M. Hill, *Ecclesiastical Law*, 4th edn (Oxford: Oxford University Press, 2018).

The turmoil Vatican II caused in Roman Catholic circles was also felt to some extent among Anglo-Catholics, who had increasingly looked to Rome and to the possibility of reunion with it, unlikely though that was. Anglo-Catholicism was still capable of producing able theologians like Eric Lionel Mascall (1905–93), a defender of Neo-Thomism even after it went out of fashion, who introduced the thought of many Continental Roman Catholic theologians into England. Also a witty scourge of the 1960s radicals who wanted a 'religionless' Christianity, he did much to neuter their influence.[30] At a more popular level, he was ably seconded by Harry Blamires (1916–2017), who outlined the essential features of a Christian world view and demonstrated that Christianity's most dangerous opponents were not atheists and humanists who attacked it from outside but secularist churchmen who undermined it from within.[31]

Also of Anglo-Catholic leanings was the excellent church historian John Norman Davidson Kelly (1909–97), whose magisterial work on the early Christian creeds demolished the classical liberalism of nineteenth-century Germany, and remains the standard study of the subject.[32] But in spite of these individual achievements, Anglo-Catholicism as a whole was in decline. Its penchant for neo-medievalism was characteristic of the Victorian age and, as fashions changed, interest in it waned. Many of its ablest young people, like Alec Vidler (1899–1991) for example, gravitated to the liberal theology of the post-war era rather than to Neo-Thomism, which in any case was generally rejected by the leading voices at Vatican II. Anglo-Catholics had gained the freedom to worship more or less as they chose within the Church of England but they had not succeeded in converting the Church as a whole to their position, and for the most part continued to be a somewhat eccentric minority within it.

A major challenge for Catholics of all kinds was the so-called 'sexual revolution' of the 1960s. How much really changed at that time is a matter of dispute, but it is certain that things generally not talked about in public before were now increasingly being aired, and the social taboos surrounding much sexual activity were being overturned as never before. Catholics, with their emphasis on priestly celibacy and disapproval of artificial methods of birth control, were badly placed to deal with this, the more so because (as we now

---

[30] E. L. Mascall, *Up and Down in Adria* (London: Faith Press, 1963); *The Secularisation of Christianity* (London: Darton, Longman and Todd, 1965); *The Christian Universe* (London: Darton, Longman and Todd, 1966).

[31] H. Blamires, *The Christian Mind* (London: SPCK, 1963); *The Faith and Modern Error* (London: SPCK, 1965); *A Defence of Dogmatism* (London: SPCK, 1967).

[32] J. N. D. Kelly, *Early Christian Creeds*, 3rd edn (London: Longman, 1972). See also his *Early Christian Doctrines*, 5th edn (London: A&C Black, 1977), and *The Athanasian Creed* (London: A&C Black, 1964).

know) many of their clergy were engaged in illicit sexual activity themselves. Most of this was kept quiet for a long time, but rumours circulated among the faithful and the Church did not want to investigate matters too deeply, for fear of being exposed. This irresponsible behaviour would later come back to haunt them, and in the end their well-meaning attempts to conceal the facts would only make things worse, but in the 1970s that was still a disaster waiting to happen.

The situation of Protestant Evangelicals was rather different. After a low point in the mid-twentieth century they were once again on the move, and during the 1960s they appeared to be making great strides forward, not only in the established Church but in the Free Church world as well. There was a renewed interest in Puritan theology, sponsored by men like Martyn Lloyd-Jones and Jim Packer, who organized an annual conference to study it. The Banner of Truth Trust was founded in 1957 with the declared aim of bringing classical Puritan works back into print. Since none of them was in copyright this could be done quite cheaply and before long there was a steady stream of books large and small pouring off the press and into the studies of a rising generation of ministers. The Banner was astute enough to publish not only major collections like the works of John Owen, but also a number of shorter treatises, some with updated language, that were attractively presented, easy to read and cheap.

Unfortunately the Puritan revival gloried in the seventeenth century as the golden age of British theology (which it probably was) but was unable to be translated into a serious theological approach for the modern world. As a result, several young pastors became enamoured of the distant past and sought to replicate it, not least by preaching lengthy sermons that most people found impossible to absorb. Richard Baxter and Samuel Rutherford could stir the blood, but their practices and experiences could not be replicated in the television age, which required an entirely different kind of communication. Those who tried to imitate them, like Ian Paisley (1926–2014) in Northern Ireland, struck most hearers as either comic or slightly sinister rabble-rousers, and were often more successful in alienating audiences than in attracting them.

Another problem among Evangelicals that resurfaced in the 1960s was the great divide between the Establishment and the 'Free Churches', a divide that had originally appeared in the late eighteenth century. Martyn Lloyd-Jones, in particular, angered many Anglican Evangelicals when he called for them to quit the Church of England and join the Fellowship of Independent Evangelical Churches (FIEC). At a meeting of the National Evangelical Assembly on 18 October 1966, Lloyd-Jones made a dramatic speech, urging Evangelicals in mixed denominations to secede from them and make common cause with one another. He was answered by John Stott, who put the case for remaining in the established Church, and the battle lines were drawn. Lloyd-Jones feared that Evangelicals who remained in communion with others would lose their cutting edge and end up compromising their beliefs. Stott, on the other hand, feared that secession would lead to sectarianism and loss of evangelistic opportunities, especially when there were signs that the Church of England would soon be needing all the clergy it could get, including the despised Evangelicals.

The difficulty, as so often in these situations, was that both sides had a point. The FIEC, which had been established as far back as 1922, took on a new lease of life and established a network of thriving congregations, but it made no impression outside its own very limited circles. The younger generation of Anglican Evangelicals, on the other hand, decided to throw in their lot with the Church of England in ways that did in fact blunt their witness, both because it drew them away from their Free Church colleagues – the annual Puritan conferences for example broke up in 1969 – and because it forced them to engage in conversations with Roman Catholics and others in the search for an ecumenical consensus that was largely alien to Evangelical thinking. Some, it is true, were able to work with those of other traditions and managed to exercise considerable influence in limited spheres. Perhaps the most successful of these was Colin Ogilvie Buchanan (1934–), whose dedication to the Reformed view of the sacraments, and determination to preserve it through all the ups and downs of liturgical revision, enabled him to contain the wilder excesses of Anglo-Catholicism and make the new forms of worship acceptable to the broad mass of church people.[33]

Evangelicals stand out because they have taken to heart the apostle Paul's warning that 'we do not wrestle against flesh and blood, but against the rulers, against the authorities, against the cosmic powers over this present darkness, against the spiritual forces of evil in the heavenly places'.[34] But they have also discovered, sometimes to their cost, that these alien forces are present and active inside the Church, ready to deceive even the elect.[35] To cite but one prominent example, a generation ago Max Alexander Cunningham Warren (1904–77), General Secretary of the (Evangelical) Church Missionary Society (1942–63), was led astray by the Bishop of Woolwich, John Arthur Thomas

---

[33] For a concise overview, see C. Buchanan and T. Lloyd, *The Church of England Eucharist 1958–2012*, Alcuin Club and The Group for Renewal of Worship Joint Liturgical Studies 87/88 (Norwich: Hymns Ancient & Modern, 2019). See also D. Hebblethwaite, *Liturgical Revision in the Church of England 1984–2004: The Working of the Liturgical Commission*, Alcuin Club and The Group for Renewal of Worship Joint Liturgical Studies 57 (Cambridge: Grove Books, 2004).

[34] Eph. 6:12.

[35] Matt. 24:24.

Robinson (1919–83), to the point where he encouraged Robinson to publish *Honest to God*, a popular digest of liberal German theology that many ordinary people read as a repudiation of the Christian faith by someone who was publicly sworn to uphold it. Worse still, Warren joined in the fifth-anniversary celebrations of the book's appearance, although by then it was clear how disastrous it had been for the mission of the Church.[36] Evangelicals were dismayed by this at the time, but were not unduly discouraged, because back then it seemed as though the overall trend was working in their favour. By the 1970s roughly half the ordinands in the Church of England were being trained in Evangelical colleges, and Evangelicals assumed that in a generation they would take over the established Church and use it to influence the nation as a whole.[37]

What these optimists did not say, or did not realize, was that in the years from 1960 to 1990 the number of men being trained in residential theological colleges more or less halved. Nor did they appreciate that the shortfall would be made up by developing non-residential (and usually inferior) training courses designed to fill the churches with non-stipendiary ministers – part-timers or retired people, for the most part. Nor did they consider the effects of the ordination of women, who in twenty years would equal and even over-take the number of men. Opposition to the ordination of women has not been as strong among Evangelicals as it has been among Anglo-Catholics, but on the whole Evangelicals continue to prefer male pastors and are unenthusiastic about female clergy. Predictions are difficult, but it is unlikely that Evangelicals will look to ordained women for spiritual leadership anytime soon.[38]

The Evangelical optimists of the 1970s also failed to reckon with the fact that financial constraints were forcing parishes to amalgamate, particularly in the countryside. The traditional picture of the country parson who preached on Sunday and played cricket (or golf) during the week vanished during these years as the older generation retired or died off and was not replaced. Compulsory retirement at 68 was introduced in 1975, which speeded up this process. Once the awkward old gentlemen were out of the way, many of their parishes disappeared into 'united' benefices that could have as many as fourteen churches that needed to be served, often by a skeleton staff. Rural ministry became a nightmare, frequently leading to clergy burnout, and there

---

[36] See K. Hylson-Smith, *Evangelicals in the Church of England 1734–1984* (Edinburgh: T&T Clark, 1988), 305–306.

[37] The sense of optimism in Evangelical circles in the years around 1980 is best captured in R. Manwaring, *From Controversy to Co-Existence: Evangelicals in the Church of England 1914–1980* (Cambridge: Cambridge University Press, 1985). It makes embarrassing reading a generation later.

[38] However they are much more favourable towards the ministry of lay women, which is fully accepted by almost all Evangelical churches.

was no obvious way of remedying this apart from using non-stipendiary or retired volunteers.

In the intellectual sphere the impact of the revived Evangelicalism was mixed. It was felt most strongly in biblical studies, where a conservative approach, always latent in Britain, was accepted more readily than elsewhere. So much was this the case, in fact, that Evangelical biblical scholars were targeted by James Barr (1924–2006), who took the trouble to write an extensive – and grossly unfair – attack on them that even most of the liberal academy rejected as being too extreme.[39] Elsewhere the picture was less encouraging. In 1960 a group of Anglican Evangelicals had founded Latimer House in Oxford, which was intended to become a centre for theological studies not unlike the already well-established Anglo-Catholic Pusey House, but it never fulfilled its potential. Despite some encouragements at the beginning, internecine personal disputes and some poor decisions ensured that not much would be achieved and a substantial segment of the Evangelical wing of the Church would be alienated. Matters were not helped when John Stott stepped down as rector of All Souls', Langham Place, in 1975, in order to pursue a worldwide (and generally successful) ministry, nor when Jim Packer left Trinity College, Bristol, for Regent College, Vancouver, in 1979. At that time Trinity was the leading Evangelical theological college, a position it maintained until the retirement of John Alexander (Alec) Motyer (1924–2016) in 1982, after which it rapidly declined.

Evangelicals, never known for their intellectualism, faced a further challenge from what has come to be known as the 'charismatic movement'. This was a kind of latter-day Pentecostalism that erupted in the mainstream churches in the 1970s, not only among Protestants but in the Roman Catholic Church as well. Charismatics were noted for the emphasis they placed on speaking in tongues (glossolalia), which became their primary badge of identity, and for their unconventional worship style that included a good deal of physical contact ('laying on of hands', hugging, etc.) and modern popular music.

It was initially resisted by men like John Stott, who obliged those of his assistants who were attracted by the movement to resign their posts, but its progress could not be stopped. Its first vehicle was the Fountain Trust, created by Michael Claude Harper (1931–2010), who was one of those forced to resign from All Souls, Langham Place.[40] The Fountain Trust survived until the end of 1980, when it was wound up because by then its mission had been

---

[39] J. Barr, *Fundamentalism* (London: SCM Press, 1977).
[40] Harper left the Church of England in 1995 and joined the Antiochian Orthodox Church, which later ordained him as a priest.

accomplished. Charismatic worship had a recognized, if still somewhat contro-versial, status within the Church of England and to some extent in the Free Churches as well. It was completely non-denominational in its approach and sat lightly to the theology and traditions of the churches to which its members formally belonged. In that respect it was a genuine ecumenism, uniting Chris-tians of many different traditions by pushing traditional matters of contention into the background and emphasizing spiritual gifts and the 'baptism' of the Holy Spirit instead. It was not so much anti-intellectual as non-intellectual, and chimed in well with a wider social trend away from 'book learning' to more audio-visual means of communication. Theological education was side-lined and often felt to be unnecessary – those who were 'filled with the Spirit' being obviously closer to God than people who merely wrote and read books. That in turn did nothing to help the production of serious theological works, and many Christian publishers either shut down or merged with larger (and not always Christian) book companies. Christian bookstores also suffered, and by the early years of the twenty-first century most had gone out of business. Not all of this can be attributed to charismatic influence of course – the publishing industry has been ailing for a long time and decline seems set to continue – but it has to be said that in the 'happy clappy' world of the Spirit-filled there was little appetite for intellectual seriousness, even among university students who might be thought to have a particular interest in that.

By 1980 it was becoming increasingly obvious that Britain was no longer a Christian country, however that was understood. There were still some vestiges of an earlier era but, like the monarchy and House of Lords (where twenty-six Anglican bishops still sat), their presence was more symbolic than real. In the minds of the population, Christianity was rapidly receding and even the lip-service customarily paid to it disappeared. Slots on radio and television that had been set aside for religious programming were marginalized and made as innocuous as possible. Worship services could still be broadcast, especially on great Christian festivals like Christmas and Easter, but anything that might be regarded as proselytism had to be avoided. For Christians, this was an impossible dilemma. How can we express our faith without wanting to commend it to others? What is the point of religious pantomime if the beliefs underlying it have to remain unexpressed, and therefore undiscerned by anyone not directly involved? Religious education in schools (and daily worship), made compulsory by the 1944 Education Act, either vanished from the curriculum – illegally – or else became a series of multifaith lessons in which all beliefs and none were treated equally. This was justified to some extent by appealing to the considerable immigration of Muslims, Hindus,

Sikhs and others, who came to the country after 1945, but the opposition to teaching Christianity did not come from them. Rather it was a small group of atheistic humanists, who used these minorities as an excuse, who were mainly responsible for the change. Since virtually all of these came from nominally 'Christian' backgrounds their interventions often went unnoticed and were not regarded as alien intrusions on British society, as they probably would have been had they come from one of the religious minorities concerned.

The situation in Ireland presented a sharp contrast to that which prevailed in Great Britain, but its evident religiosity was hardly an attractive model to follow. In the Irish republic the Roman Catholic Church continued to exert its powerful sway, and it is estimated that in 1980 up to 90% of the population was still attending mass weekly. How many went out of genuine conviction as opposed to mere social habit is impossible to say, and probably the lines were blurred in many cases. But there is no doubt that the Catholic laity were kept in a subordinate position and the clergy ruled the roost, especially on matters relating to sex, about which they were hardly experts. Abortion, divorce and contraception were all ruled out and it was only the relative ease with which Irish people could travel to Britain for such things that helped keep the lid on. In Northern Ireland there was less churchgoing, especially among Protestants, but almost certainly greater conviction, as both Catholics and Protestants descended into a kind of civil war that lasted for thirty years and left nearly 4,000 people dead or maimed for life.

The churches were not directly responsible for the carnage of course, and from time to time religious leaders sought to distance themselves from the 'Troubles', as the war was somewhat euphemistically called, but despite high levels of church attendance and genuine commitment on the part of many, they were unable to change course or bring an end to the nightmare. 'Love your enemies and pray for those who persecute you' might be what Jesus said,[41] but those words failed to translate into reality in Northern Ireland and the churches lost credibility as a result, not least elsewhere in the British Isles, where the situation in Ulster was frequently held up as a prime example of the harm religion can do. In reality Christianity had long been secularized in Ireland, although in a very different way from the rest of Europe, and in time that would become apparent. The awful truth is that if peace and reconciliation are ever to come, churchgoing will probably plummet to levels known elsewhere and the harmony achieved will not be due to the triumph of the gospel. That day has not yet arrived, and perhaps it never will, but the prospects of a

---

[41] Matt. 5:44; Luke 6:27.

genuine religious revival in Ireland that will heal ancient divisions do not look good. Deep-seated prejudice has taken on a religious hue, and it is hard to see the one disappearing without taking the other along with it.

15

The rivers of Babylon (since 1980)

A tale of two cities

By the rivers of Babylon, there we sat down, yea, we wept, when we remembered Zion.[1]

In 1978 a little-known Caribbean singing group called Boney M made it to the top of the pop charts in the UK with a hit single 'Rivers of Babylon'. It stayed there for several weeks, becoming the second most popular song in the charts' history.[2] What is so unusual about this is that the words of the song are mainly taken from Psalm 137. It is the lament of the Jewish people who had been exiled to Babylon and were homesick for the country they had left behind. Their captors were not especially harsh, and hoped that the exiles would settle in their new home, as their own prophet Jeremiah encouraged them to do,[3] but there were some who could not rest in a foreign land. When the opportunity came to return to Jerusalem (Zion), those people went back and did what they could to re-establish the historic Jewish presence there.

Why did this psalm strike such a chord with the British public? Most of Boney M's fans had probably never heard it before, but did they sense that there was something prophetic in its words? Certainly the spiritual conflict between Zion and Babylon, symbols of good and evil respectively, has a long history. In the New Testament, 'Babylon' appears as a code name for Rome, the great heathen empire of its time.[4] It was under its hapless governor, Pontius Pilate, that Jesus Christ had lived, taught and been crucified. Three centuries later, the proud empire sought to save itself by adopting the faith of that Christ, but it failed. In August AD 410 the great city of Rome was captured and sacked by

---

[1] Ps. 137:1 (KJV).

[2] Even today it is still ranked among the top ten all-time hits.

[3] Jer. 29:1–23. Many took his advice, and the Jewish colony in Mesopotamia lasted from then until 1948, when the establishment of the state of Israel forced almost all of them to leave.

[4] Rev. 16:19; 17:5; 18:10, 21; probably also 1 Peter 5:13.

the armies of Alaric the Visigoth. In response to pagan taunts that Rome had fallen because it had rejected its ancient tutelary gods and embraced Christianity, Augustine of Hippo sat down and wrote one of the great books of Western civilization, *The City of God*. Redeploying the imagery of Scripture, Augustine portrayed the history of the world as a contest between the forces of evil, represented by the empire of Babylon, and those of good, manifested in the city of Jerusalem (Zion).

For many this came to be interpreted as the centuries-old struggle between church and state, but things were never that simple. At the time of the Reformation for example, the Protestant Reformers did not hesitate to adopt the imagery of the New Testament Apocalypse. They branded Rome and its papacy as 'the great whore of Babylon', and even those who were too circumspect to say so openly tacitly subscribed to this interpretation. The translators of the King James Bible, in their dedication to the king, claimed that his providential accession to the throne put paid to 'the expectation of many, who wished not well unto our Zion' that England would otherwise have lapsed into chaos on the demise of Queen Elizabeth I.[5] Nobody had to be told who these 'many' were. By the nineteenth century this confessional warfare was fading into the background, but a new kind of spiritual struggle had emerged. The forces of 'Babylon' were no longer overtly hostile to 'Zion' but they had developed a more subtle approach. Instead of attacking the Church directly, they now pretended that they too were Christian, that the values of the gospel were their charter also, and that the entire globe was a mission field open to the Bible and free trade, which they proclaimed were two sides of the same coin.

The Victorian pastiche of faith, morality and laissez-faire capitalism became 'Christianity' for at least two, and perhaps three, generations following the great queen's death, but it was a falsehood and eventually went the way of all flesh – quite literally in this case, as it was matters of the flesh that rose up and strangled it. One of the leading historians of religion in twentieth-century Britain, Callum Brown, has chronicled the sorry tale in a number of works, and traced the process of what he describes as de-Christianization in the years from 1945 to 1980.[6] As Dr Brown sees it, from 1945 to about 1965 the churches rode on a tide of goodwill, aided by a popular desire to return to normality after two world wars. For those twenty years, religious leaders were able to

---

[5] See G. L. Bray (ed.), *Documents of the English Reformation*, 3rd edn (Cambridge: James Clarke, 2019), 373.

[6] C. G. Brown, *The Battle for Christian Britain: Sex, Humanists and Secularisation, 1945–1980* (Cambridge: Cambridge University Press, 2019).

impose a strict moral censorship on many areas of British life, including the press, theatre and television. The censors believed that this was necessary in order to protect what they saw as society's Christian values, and they did not hesitate to prosecute those who fell short of their standards. What was true of Britain was even truer of Ireland, where the Roman Catholic Church imposed a cultural dictatorship that made the country one of the most devout on earth – at least on the surface.

Most of the issues the churches raised were connected to sexual behaviour – abortion, contraception and homosexuality in particular. This was not the whole story, and the censors were also vocal in their opposition to depictions of violence on film and to suggestions that euthanasia should be legalized, but questions related to sex dominated their imagination and consumed most of their time. With hindsight we can see that the best way of dealing with the growing sexualization of popular culture would have been to be utterly frank about the false glorification of the human body, the degrading nature of prostitution and the sad reality of homosexual life. But instead of exposing these things for what they are, the churches allowed themselves to be trapped in a warped sense of morality that obliged them to suppress all discussion of these evils, inevitably making them more attractive as the forbidden fruit that they became. The result, not surprisingly, was that in the end the whole artificial edifice blew up. The sexual 'permissiveness' we are now familiar with is at least partly a reaction to the misguided repression of the post-war years. But far from seeing this as a tragedy, Dr Brown and others like him hold it up as 'proof' that Christianity is a world-denying puritanism that ought to have no influence in the 'civilized' societies Britain and Ireland have supposedly become since these controls were abandoned.[7] The problem might have been correctly diagnosed, but it is arguable that the solutions proposed for it have made things worse than they were before.

How long this trend will last is impossible to say. There may be a counter-reaction as the consequences of 'permissiveness' become more apparent, but if so, it is still in the future. It is probably true that the public proclamation of permissiveness is greater than the reality, and that most people do not experience the sexual 'freedom' they are constantly exposed to in the media. Entertainment has always been a fantasy divorced from reality, and what we see on the screen and read about in the newspapers is a far cry from the comparatively dull lives most of us lead. But if the effects of the sexual revolution of the 1960s are less widespread than they have been made to

---

[7] Ibid. 287–295.

appear, there is no doubt that the 'permissive' decade saw the beginning of a continuous and at times steep decline in church membership and attendance. Christian education is also less common and less profound now than it was a generation ago, with the result that young people are often growing up with little or no knowledge of their country's ancestral faith. Their grandparents might have gone to Sunday school, but neither these young people nor their parents have ever darkened the door of a church and what goes on there is as alien to them as if it had just come from Mars.

Like the Jews in ancient Babylon, British and Irish Christians today are free to worship as they please, and many individual congregations are flourishing, but as far as the wider culture is concerned, we are in exile. A glance at the newspapers or a few hours in front of the television will soon tell us that we live in a world in which God does not exist. Traditional Christian morality may be less often mocked these days, but if so, that is mainly because few people try to uphold it publicly or even know what it is. Instead we are fed a steady diet of judgment-free sexuality. Even in so-called 'quality newspapers' like *The Times* or *The Guardian* it is common for columnists to talk about the joys of having premarital sex or an extramarital affair, as if these were the most natural things in the world. Dating sites feature homosexual as well as heterosexual couples without distinction. The right to a late-term abortion or to euthanasia is aggressively promoted, with few questions asked. In 2017 Ireland elected a practising homosexual as Prime Minister (*taoiseach*) and two years later the UK chose one who was not only a serial adulterer but who subsequently had a baby out of wedlock – in Downing Street! In neither case was there any discernible reaction from the churches, something that would have been unimaginable a generation ago.[8]

The open rejection of traditional Christian values at the centre of government brings into sharp relief how quickly the general acceptance that Britain and Ireland are 'Christian' societies has disappeared. That a crisis was brewing had been apparent for some time, as Donald Coggan (1909–2000), Archbishop of Canterbury (1975–80), signalled in his 'Call to the Nation', broadcast shortly after his enthronement in 1975:

> Many are realising that a materialistic answer is no real answer at all. There are moral and spiritual issues at stake. The truth is that we in Britain are without anchors. We are drifting. A common enemy in two

---

[8] However, it can be said that among the many congratulations that poured in after the baby's birth on 29 April 2020, none appeared to have come from religious leaders (or from the royal family).

world wars drew us together in united action – and we defeated him. Another enemy is at the gates today, and we keep silence.[9]

The response was overwhelming, with more than 28,000 letters sent to Lambeth Palace in support of the archbishop's remarks. For a brief moment it seemed that the Church of England might reclaim the spiritual high ground, but the archbishop had no idea of how to build on his apparent success and the positive effects of his intervention were soon forgotten. A generation later what surprises us most is that there was any significant response at all, since it is now almost impossible to imagine either an archbishop speaking so forthrightly or a groundswell of sympathy for his remarks.

Dr Coggan's statement had important political implications but he spoke without reference to any party or politician. Not since the retirement of William Gladstone in 1894 had a Prime Minister openly adopted Christian principles as an integral part of his programme, and for most of the twentieth century the question of a politician's private beliefs was never asked. In independent Ireland that hardly mattered, since legislators there were expected to do whatever the Roman Catholic Church wanted them to, whether they agreed with it or not.[10] In Britain most prime ministers and leading figures in government were at least nominal members of the Church of England, but the issue of personal faith almost never came up, perhaps because it was assumed that they would pay lip service to the prevailing Christian consensus. That pattern began to change when Margaret Thatcher became Prime Minister in 1979.[11] She was more open about her Christian beliefs than her predecessors had been, and in 1988 she even addressed the General Assembly of the Church of Scotland – an unprecedented event, and one popularly known as the 'Sermon on the Mound'.[12] Since then Christians have taken a greater interest in the Prime Minister's faith, perhaps because they have sensed that the former consensus can no longer be taken for granted. The picture that emerged after 1979 is as laid out in Table 15.1.

It turns out that while both Labour prime ministers have been active church members, only the female Conservative ones have been. This will surprise some, because there is a latent assumption in many Christian circles that the

---

[9] B. Jackson and R. Saunders (eds.), *Making Thatcher's Britain* (Cambridge: Cambridge University Press, 2012), 86.

[10] An exception to this was Éamon de Valera (1882–1975), who was a pious and practising Catholic, but also strong-willed and unafraid to stand up to the Church on occasion. He got away with it because he was 'too big to be touched'.

[11] See Jackson and Saunders, *Making Thatcher's Britain*, 85–93.

[12] This was because the Assembly meets on the Mound in Edinburgh.

Table 15.1 Church membership of UK prime ministers since 1979

Dates	Prime minister	Party	Denomination
1979–90	Margaret Thatcher	Conservative	Active Church of England
1990–97	John Major	Conservative	Nominal Church of England
1997–2007	Tony Blair	Labour	Active Church of England[a]
2007–10	Gordon Brown	Labour	Active Church of Scotland
2010–16	David Cameron	Conservative	Nominal Church of England
2016–19	Theresa May	Conservative	Active Church of England
2019–	Boris Johnson	Conservative	?

a He became a Roman Catholic after leaving office.

Conservatives are somehow more Christian than Labour, although that is not easy to demonstrate. Despite Mrs Thatcher's personal faith, secularization made great strides during her premiership. She presided over the loosening of the Sunday trading laws, which was an important step in the de-Christianization of the traditional day of rest. By contrast, Tony Blair's beliefs seem to have influenced his policies, at least to some extent. He inherited the ideals of Christian Socialism, which he tried to put into practice, and it may be that his introduction of civil partnerships for same-sex couples in 2005, instead of the same-sex marriage they were campaigning for, was at least partly because he wanted to protect the sanctity of traditional Christian marriage.[13]

On the other hand it was Mrs Thatcher's government that enacted section 28 of the Local Government Act (1988), which said that a local authority 'shall not intentionally promote homosexuality or publish material with the intention of promoting homosexuality' nor might it 'promote the teaching in any maintained school of the acceptability of homosexuality as a pretended family relationship'. The act became law in Great Britain on 24 May 1988, but it was repealed in Scotland on 21 June 2000 and in England and Wales on 18 November 2003 – in both cases by Labour governments.[14] Churches and other Christian organizations had supported section 28 but they lost out to a concerted campaign by homosexual activists, who had formed an alliance with some trade unions (and hence with influential elements in the Labour Party). Dr Brown has suggested that humanists also played an important role in this, as they have in many other actions against Christian influence on the law of the land.[15]

---

[13] Same-sex marriage was introduced under the Conservatives in 2013, although the churches were forbidden to perform such marriages.

[14] The Scottish legislation was one of the first acts passed by the newly established Scottish parliament.

[15] Brown, *Battle for Christian Britain*, 216–283.

Atheistic humanists have always been few in number, but for the past century they have been disproportionately represented in academia and more recently in broadcasting as well. Humanists typically base their case on certain assumptions that they regard as beyond dispute. They claim that the Christian churches have been guilty of repressing those who do not share their values and of imposing a moral standard on society without its consent. In the humanist view people should be free to make their own moral choices. They also insist that humanist values exalt humanity, whereas Christians supposedly seek to destroy personal freedom and restrict the meaning of what it is to be truly human. Evidence for these claims is patchy and in short supply, but this has not deterred the humanists, who merely assert them as true and assume that no Christian will dare to contradict them.[16]

The extent to which atheistic humanism now dominates the public sphere can be illustrated from two prominent examples, taken from different spheres of activity. The first is the way in which the Reverend Mr Michael Reiss (1960–), secretary of the Royal Society, was forced to resign in 2008 because he had suggested that it would be appropriate to debate the question of 'creationism' – the belief that Genesis 1 – 3 is a literal statement of historical fact and that the universe was made in six twenty-four-hour days. Mr Reiss made it clear that he did not believe that himself, but because the idea has some currency in conservative Christian circles, he thought it ought to be discussed (and presumably refuted). This innocuous suggestion was too much for Richard Dawkins (1941–), perhaps Britain's best-known atheist, who mounted a furious campaign that led to Mr Reiss's involuntary resignation. Many people complained about this at the time and it was generally admitted that Mr Reiss had been badly treated, but in spite of the widespread sympathy and support he received, he was not reinstated.

The second example is that of Tim Farron (1970–), a Liberal Democrat Member of Parliament and a declared Evangelical Christian, who was elected leader of the party in 2015. During the 2017 election he was savaged by elements of the press for his supposed homophobia (based on the belief that Evangelicals are opposed to homosexual practice). The attacks were unfair and irrelevant to the campaign, but they were pursued with an almost manic intensity and Mr Farron was eventually forced out of the party leadership. In his resignation speech he stated that it was impossible for a professing Christian to lead a

---

[16] It is perhaps not surprising that one of their most effective critics has been Terry Eagleton (1943–), a former Roman Catholic, who shares their humanist presuppositions but who also sees through the superficiality of their arguments. See e.g. T. Eagleton, *Culture and the Death of God* (New Haven, Conn.: Yale University Press, 2014).

political party in the UK, a view many shared. Humanists hailed his departure as a victory for them, whereas Christians recoiled in horror, but the most disturbing aspect of the affair was that no prominent church leader came to Mr Farron's defence, despite their oft-proclaimed readiness to stand up for truth and justice.

It is now apparent that those who profess the faith of Christ in Britain (and to a lesser, but increasing, extent also in Ireland) are not only a minority, but that they are under siege from the proponents of an aggressively secular society. It is no longer possible for a nurse or doctor to pray with or for a patient, unless the patient explicitly requests it without being prompted. Nor can a bed-and-breakfast owner turn away customers who do not conform to his or her moral standards, as some Christians have discovered when they have refused to accommodate same-sex couples. Even in conservative Northern Ireland, a Christian baker was fined in 2014 for refusing to make a wedding cake decorated with the words 'Support gay marriage', although his stance was eventually upheld by the Supreme Court in London.[17] Christian employees have even been dismissed for wearing a cross at work, although why anyone would regard a piece of jewellery as a form of proselytism is hard to say. Cases like these are petty in some ways, but it is their very banality that makes them so alarming. Does the conscientious profession of Christian belief have no place in modern Britain?

Some secularists have justified their opposition to public displays of Christianity by claiming that we now live in a 'multifaith' society. According to them, favouring one religion over another is not only discriminatory but potentially dangerous, since it might set one group of religious believers up against others. Militant Islam is cited as a constant threat, and it is claimed that only by ignoring all religious beliefs equally can problems like that be prevented. This argument has the appearance of fairness, but in fact it is deeply dishonest. There is no evidence that religious groups in Britain fight one another, despite their very different beliefs. Christians are usually quite happy to respect the customs of others and to defend them when they are attacked. For their part, Muslims, Hindus, Sikhs and others tend to share Christian values on matters of public morality and may be even more insistent on the need to protect them than many churches are. Christians evangelize among the entire population and rejoice when others repent and submit to the claims of Jesus Christ as their Saviour and Lord, but they make no attempt to suppress other religions and reject any form of coercion in matters of faith. Here it is

---

[17] The appeal was brought by Daniel and Amy McArthur of Ashers Baking Company, Belfast. On 10 October 2018 the Supreme Court unanimously overturned the ruling of the Northern Ireland Equalities Commission.

the secularists who try to force the issue, and they ought to have the honesty to admit it.

The secularization that has come over society in recent years has been so rapid and has gone so far that it is not surprising that Christians have not known how to react to it. With very few exceptions, church leaders have not spoken out in support of the Christian victims of unfair treatment. To talk of persecution is perhaps overblown – those who have suffered are not martyrs in the true sense of the word – but Christians have certainly been discriminated against because of their faith. They have been caught up in a social transformation that has seen their values publicly discarded, even though there are many individuals who still hold such values. Civil libertarians argue that religious believers are free to hold their own convictions as long as they do not impose them on others. That sounds good in theory, until it is interpreted to mean that those 'others' are under no obligation to show similar courtesy in return. In the secular world, tolerance is biased in favour of unbelief, and Christians suffer accordingly.

Carried into captivity

They that carried us away captive required of us a song.[18]

The real tragedy of the current situation is not that Christians have suffered discrimination because of their faith but that so many in the churches have acquiesced in it as an apparently inevitable consequence of secularization. Some church leaders, in particular those who continue to enjoy public recognition, like bishops of the Church of England and moderators of the Church of Scotland, carry on as though nothing has changed, believing that their social status gives them both a right and a duty to speak out on any number of subjects, and that their opinions will carry the weight of authority. Twenty-six bishops still sit in the House of Lords, and continue to play a decorative role on the public stage, but what they say is usually anodyne and almost never specifically Christian in content.[19] How long that will last is impossible to predict, but reform of the House of Lords is always somewhere on the political agenda and the survival of the 'lords spiritual' is by no means guaranteed.

---

18 Ps. 137:3 (KJV).

19 The role of the bishops in the House of Lords during Margaret Thatcher's premiership (1979–90) has been extensively analysed by Andrew Partington, *Church and State: The Contribution of the Church of England Bishops to the House of Lords During the Thatcher Years* (Milton Keynes: Paternoster Press, 2006). The author has shown that the bishops had virtually nothing to offer during that time and that if they had not been there, nobody would have noticed (or regretted) their absence.

In the 1980s the liberal Establishment in the churches was still very much in control and apparently deaf to the cries of those in the pews who sensed that the nation was fast slipping away from its Christian moorings. The nadir was reached in 1984, when David Jenkins (1925–2016) was consecrated in York Minster as Bishop of Durham. Jenkins was known for having denied the bodily resurrection of Jesus, and over 13,000 people signed a petition demanding that the consecration be halted. John Habgood (1927–2019), the Archbishop of York, ignored their protest and went ahead with the ceremony, but a few days later York Minster, where it had taken place, was struck by lightning – a sign, some thought, of divine disapproval. That could easily be dismissed as superstition, but worse was to come. It was the custom for *Crockford's Clerical Directory*, the official list of Anglican clergy throughout the British Isles, to contain an anonymous preface commenting, sometimes acerbically, on the state of the Church. Following the consecration of Dr Jenkins, this somewhat dubious honour fell on Gareth (Garry) Vaughan Bennett (1929–87), an Oxford academic of Anglo-Catholic leanings, who was unsparing in his criticism of what had transpired, and linked it to a number of events that to his mind signalled the apostasy of the Church of England. The Archbishop of York was incensed and lashed out somewhat intemperately at the anonymous writer, who then revealed himself by committing suicide. It was an unpleasant incident that brought credit on nobody, but it revealed a rottenness in the Church that made a bad impression on the public and forced the authorities to be more circumspect in the future, although whether it brought real or lasting change may be doubted.

Many church leaders have accepted secularization and believe that they must adapt to it order to remain 'relevant' to a society that rejects traditional Christianity. Having been captured by the prevailing culture and asked to sing its tune, they have complied, adjusting their theology and practices accordingly. To them, this is a form of evangelism consonant with the apostle Paul's statement that he became a Jew to the Jews and a Gentile to the Gentiles, in order to win them for Christ.[20] The difference is that Paul's would-be modern imitators do not make such adaptations in order to convert others. On the contrary, their view is that those who do not want Christ (or 'religion') must not be confronted with the gospel in any way. Some even argue that to fulfil its mission, the church has to stop talking about God altogether, since to mention him is liable to generate hostility or incomprehension in those to whom it is called to minister. For those who believe (as many who hold this

---

[20] 1 Cor. 9:19–23.

position do) that everyone is an 'anonymous Christian' who will be saved in the end, such self-effacement is understandable, but it is hard to see how it is compatible with the teaching of Jesus.

In support of the view that the church must adapt to the circumstances in which it finds itself, it can be argued that it has often done so before, and that great festivals like Christmas and Easter are replete with barely concealed pagan symbolism. That is certainly true, but there is an important difference between what happened in former times and what is going on now. In the past the Church took over pre-existing religious rites and symbols and gave them a Christian meaning, but what is being advocated today is the opposite of that. Christian beliefs are now being modified and reconfigured to suit current cultural norms, however alien to Christianity those norms may be. This approach can trace its roots to the eighteenth-century Enlightenment, which prided itself on having found alternative explanations to miracles and other supernatural phenomena in the Bible, but it was developed only in a nuanced and sophisticated way in the twentieth century by men like Rudolf Bultmann (1884–1976) in Germany. Bultmann and his followers portrayed the biblical writers as typical of their time, speaking of God in language and concepts their contemporaries would recognize and accept. But as modern science developed and the world views of the past were discarded, they claimed that the human race had 'come of age' and no longer needed or even under-stood the biblical imagery used to explain spiritual truths or to justify moral behaviour.

To those who had 'come of age', traditional religious language was held to be essentially 'mythological', talking of good and evil in terms of an imaginary heaven and hell, and so had to be 'demythologized' in order to make it com-prehensible to modern people. Demythologization was far more than the translation of ancient concepts into modern words however. It was a complete restructuring of the human mind, designed to abolish the 'supernatural' or 'metaphysical' entirely. Absolute truth is a metaphysical concept and therefore had to be abandoned – all truth is relative. According to this way of thinking, when Jesus told his disciples that he was the way, the truth and the life, and that nobody could come to God except through him, he might have been saying something meaningful to first-century Jews, but he was not stating a universal principle valid for every time and place.[21] If Jesus was to remain a model for 'modern man', it would not be because he is the only answer to the human quest for truth, but because he had the courage to tell his followers that

---

[21] See John 14:6.

they had to question their received wisdom and embark on a fresh and 'authentic' search for reality.

For Peter and Paul, that had meant rejecting Jewish traditional lore, but for 'modern man' it supposedly means abandoning inherited Christian concepts – Christianity being a construct deeply inimical to the teaching of Jesus himself, and thus to be rejected by those who would be his true disciples today. In particular, ethics could no longer be seen as applying the Ten Commandments in a straightforward manner, but was a choice that individuals must make according to the situation(s) in which they find themselves. As an antidote to false legalism this approach has some value, but its real purpose went much further than that. 'Situation ethics', as the new approach came to be called, wanted to legitimize forms of behaviour that traditional Christianity has always condemned. For example, the question 'Is it all right for me to sleep with someone I love, even if I am not married to him/her?' was given a positive answer, almost without qualification. The demands of 'love' were held to override the constraints of an artificially imposed morality. 'Love' became divorced from objective principles (law), and was reinterpreted in terms of subjective desire. Once that happened, it was only a matter of time before the constraints of faithfulness and commitment would be ignored and a new pattern of what constitutes acceptable behaviour would emerge.

For a variety of reasons, this way of thinking had little impact in the British Isles until the 1950s. By then, British Christians had grown used to arguments for and against the historicity of the scriptural narratives, but many of them were convinced that as archaeologists dug up places like Nineveh and Jericho, conservative interpretations of the Bible were becoming increasingly plausible. Never much inclined towards philosophical theology, questions of 'world view' were alien to them, making them ill-equipped to deal with the consequences of accepting ideas like 'demythologization'. Ever pragmatic in their approach, Christians in Britain scarcely noticed how their fundamental assumptions had been undermined, and were taken by surprise when they were confronted by challenges to the traditional moral order that few saw coming. As abortion was legalized and divorce made easier, the view that Christian teaching was out of step with the times became increasingly widespread and the churches did not know what to do about it. Innately conservative as they were, they initially resisted these novel ideas, but the pressures from civil society proved hard to oppose and by the early years of the twenty-first century they had largely capitulated to the secular trend, despite the vocal opposition of organizations like the Nationwide Festival of Light and the National Viewers' and Listeners' Association, championed by the redoubtable

Mary Whitehouse (1910–2001).[22] Mrs Whitehouse and her associates were cruelly mocked in the media, which resented their attempts to regulate them, but more telling was the failure of the churches to support their initiatives, of which many highly placed ecclesiastics silently disapproved and which a few openly ridiculed.[23]

The deeper consequences of this attitude were not immediately apparent however. For a long time it was tacitly assumed that the relaxation of traditional sexual mores applied only to heterosexuals, but eventually the question of homosexual relationships was raised and the churches were confronted with a fresh dilemma. The Bible has a consistently negative view of homosexual practice, but this was dismissed by those who regarded biblical teaching as 'culturally conditioned'. To their minds, how could an ancient document, conceived by and for a more 'primitive' society, be allowed to overrule the desires of a modern couple? They argued that if 'love' is the fulfilling of the law, surely any kind of behaviour that might be called 'love' is permissible.[24] By the same token, those who object to such logic must be standing in the way of God's will and therefore deserve condemnation for their 'unchristian' attitude. This is the thinking that underlies most of the revisionism in the churches today, and that explains why those who advocate the acceptance of things like same-sex marriage can believe they have the 'mind of Christ'.[25]

The belief that Christian doctrine has been determined by obsolete cultural contexts, and must therefore be replaced, is one of the greatest intellectual challenges the church has ever had to face. It is particularly serious when church leaders claim that their novel ideas proceed from the Holy Spirit. How do they know that? The only way we can know the mind of the Holy Spirit is by searching the Scriptures, but if the Scriptures are effectively neutered by a 'new hermeneutic', what good will that do? The great irony of our time is that although the Bible has never been more readily available, in a plethora of translations, ignorance of its contents and message has never been so extensive either. Like Israel in the time of the judges, everyone thinks what is right in his or her own eyes and there is no recognized authority to put them straight.[26]

---

22 Brown, *Battle for Christian Britain*, 169–178.

23 See M. Grimley, 'Anglican Evangelicals and Anti-Permissiveness: The Nationwide Festival of Light, 1971–1983', in A. Atherstone and J. Maiden (eds.), *Evangelicalism and the Church of England in the Twentieth Century: Reform, Resistance and Renewal* (Woodbridge: Boydell Press, 2014), 183–205.

24 See Rom. 13:10.

25 1 Cor. 2:16. For an expression of this view, see N. Patterson, *Ecclesiastical Law, Clergy and Laity: A History of Legal Discipline and the Anglican Church* (Abingdon: Routledge, 2019), 127–161.

26 Judg. 21:25.

The noxious effects of this have fallen most heavily on Evangelicals, who have been left trying to decide what they mean when they claim that the Bible is the Word of God. They have toyed with descriptive words designed to encapsulate this belief, like 'infallibility' and 'inerrancy', but although the former has had some currency in Britain, the latter has generally been avoided.[27] Most British Evangelicals are happy to agree that the Bible is infallible in the sense that it will not lead anybody astray, but are wary of saying that it is inerrant because of the difficulty in defining what constitutes an error.[28] In truth there has been very little discussion of hermeneutics among British Evangelicals, most of whom want to prevent the battles over this that have raged in the USA and few of whom have the philosophical inclination or interest that would be needed to address the subject in any depth.

Someone who has tried to do this is Anthony Charles Thiselton (1937–), an Evangelical who championed the 'new hermeneutic' in biblical interpretation, although he has not accepted the more radical conclusions that the theory was used to support. Put simply, the 'new hermeneutic' argues that there are two 'horizons' to any text – that of the writer and that of the reader. Whether, and to what extent, they might overlap is the job of the literary critic to work out.[29]

The wider problem with the new hermeneutic is that the more the antiquity of the Bible is emphasized, the less relevant it seems to modern life. If we stress the differences between the ancient world and now, rather than point out that human nature has not changed, the text will not speak to our generation. But the Bible's message is for every age, because everyone has sinned and fallen short of the glory of God.[30] It cannot be relegated to the time and place of its original composition, which in many cases is unknown to us. To interpret a book like Job in its original context is not only impossible (since we do not know what that context was) but it misses the point – the story has its own validity regardless of who wrote it (or why) and it has survived for that reason. Detailed information about the composition of a literary classic may be helpful in understanding it, but it cannot obscure or destroy its universal message. The ultimate effect of the new hermeneutic is to make the Bible inaccessible as an authority for Christian life and practice today. For a 'religion of the book', like Christianity, this is a serious problem and the new hermeneutic, which on the surface appears to be an adaptation of traditional beliefs and values

---

[27] For a detailed study of this, see R. Warner, *Reinventing English Evangelicalism, 1966–2001: A Theological and Sociological Study* (Milton Keynes: Paternoster Press, 2007), 192–233.

[28] In this respect most British Evangelicals are quite different from many of their American counterparts.

[29] A. C. Thiselton, *Thiselton on Hermeneutics: The Collected Works and New Essays* (Aldershot: Ashgate, 2006).

[30] Rom. 3:23.

designed to speak to the modern age, represents a surrender to the world that gravely compromises the eternal message of the gospel.

The intellectual weakness of Evangelicalism was seen most clearly in the appearance of so-called 'open' Evangelicals, who were happy to accommodate themselves to modern culture and to reinterpret the Bible accordingly. A dispute over this arose between the editorial board of the Evangelical journal *Churchman* and its proprietors, Church Society, who were of a more traditional persuasion. As a result, the board was reconstituted and in the Orwellian year 1984 a new 'progressive' journal was started – *Anvil* – which attempted to rival *Churchman*.[31] In 2003 another split occurred, when an open Evangelical organization called Fulcrum was founded to promote similar ideas. Like *Anvil*, Fulcrum enjoyed some initial success but interest gradually waned and it eventually became little more than an online chatroom.[32] It has to be concluded that open Evangelicalism is now moribund, if not completely dead. As evidence of this, the theological college that most readily embraced it, St John's Nottingham, was the largest in England in 1980, but subsequently declined to the point where in 2019 it finally closed for good.

The Evangelical world has also been challenged (yet again) on its understanding of the fundamental question of Christ's atonement. Evangelicals believe that the Bible teaches 'penal substitution'; that is to say, on the cross Jesus Christ took the place of sinners and paid the price for their sin.[33] This understanding of the atonement seems so obvious to Evangelicals that they are surprised anyone should question it, but it has been attacked from numerous angles. At one extreme a few have gone as far as to call it a form of 'cosmic child abuse', but this is a caricature and has generally been rejected.[34] More common has been a watering down of its meaning, often occasioned by a dislike of terms like 'the wrath of God' and/or the notion of 'substitution'. Objections of this kind are usually motivated by a desire to emphasize the love of a forgiving God in opposition to what is (wrongly) perceived as the vengeance of an offended heavenly Judge, but although they recur with disheartening frequency, they

---

[31] See A. Atherstone, *An Anglican Evangelical Identity Crisis: The* Churchman–Anvil *Affair of 1981–1984* (London: Latimer Trust, 2008).

[32] *Anvil* still survives, but in 2016 was taken over by the Church Mission (formerly Missionary) Society and now has a very different character from the one it had when first launched.

[33] D. C. Jones, 'Evangelicals and the Cross', in A. Atherstone and D. C. Jones (eds.), *The Routledge Research Companion to the History of Evangelicalism* (London: Routledge, 2019), 39–56, gives an excellent overview of the doctrine and its interpretation in the Evangelical world. For a classic exposition of this doctrine, see J. Denney, *The Death of Christ* (London: Hodder & Stoughton, 1902); J. R. W. Stott, *The Cross of Christ* (Leicester: Inter-Varsity Press, 1986). See also S. Jeffery, M. Ovey and A. Sach, *Pierced for Our Transgressions: Rediscovering the Glory of Penal Substitution* (Nottingham: Inter-Varsity Press, 2007).

[34] See S. Chalke, *The Lost Message of Jesus* (Grand Rapids, Mich.: Zondervan, 2003), 182.

have been regularly refuted, even by some who would not embrace the traditional Evangelical doctrine.[35]

A different but related challenge has come from theologians arguing for what has been called a 'new perspective on Paul'. The 'new perspective' is not a clearly defined movement, but those associated with it argue that Martin Luther misunderstood the apostle and imposed his own legalistic mindset on a New Testament that was written with other ends in view. In particular they claim that Luther was led into an anti-Jewish way of thinking that might have corresponded quite well to his own late medieval environment but which was diametrically opposed to what Paul was saying about justification by faith.[36]

The basic contention of the new perspective is that all Jews, and not just those who had accepted Jesus as the Messiah, believed that they were saved by grace through faith. By keeping the law of Moses they were maintaining their position inside the Abrahamic covenant and the promises of God made to Israel. In preaching the need to receive Christ, Paul was extending this covenantal understanding to Gentiles, and it was that to which the Jews objected more than anything else. According to proponents of the new perspective, baptism has replaced circumcision as a 'covenant marker' and Christians are called to work out the salvation they have received by their baptism by living a life of good works in conformity not to the letter of the law but to its spirit. The Christian life is therefore all about *staying* in a saving relationship with God, not about *entering* into one.

In essence the new perspective is an updated form of what used to be called 'hyper-Calvinism'. It is a scheme of salvation into which Christ fits but which existed without him in Judaism, making him less than essential to its outworking. The atonement is subtly reinterpreted, making Christ's 'once for all' death on the cross no longer central to it. It existed in the Old Testament in the form of the priestly sacrifices, and it continues to exist in the Church's Eucharist. Christ's death on the cross marks the transition from one dispensation to the other, but it does not fundamentally alter the believer's relationship with God.

Inevitably once Christ's sacrifice is relativized in this way, the traditional Evangelical emphasis on a personal union with him gives way to a vaguer idea of incorporation into his 'body', which is the church, and the focus shifts from

---

[35] See e.g. L. Morris, *The Atonement: Its Meaning and Significance* (Leicester: Inter-Varsity Press, 1983), 151–176, for a standard Evangelical critique of those who object to the notion of 'wrath', and C. E. Gunton, *The Actuality of Atonement: A Study of Metaphor, Rationality and the Christian Tradition* (Edinburgh: T&T Clark, 1988), 16–167, who defends 'substitution' from a conservative, though not obviously Evangelical, standpoint.

[36] See S. Westerholm, *Perspectives Old and New on Paul: The 'Lutheran' Paul and His Critics* (Grand Rapids, Mich.: Eerdmans, 2004).

the individual to the collective experience of the Christian community. That in turn leads to giving less importance to the conversion of individuals and more to the social witness of the 'people of God', something that Evangelicals are accused of having ignored in recent times. This approach became popular in the 1970s and later, leading some prominent Evangelicals to express their 'repentance' for having neglected social issues in the past and encouraging people to pour their time and money into relief agencies rather than support more traditional mission activities.

Catholics have also been deeply challenged by modernity but their encounter with it has followed a different path. The Second Vatican Council (1962–5) introduced a number of reforms that had an unsettling effect on many who had come to believe that the Roman Church never changed at all. The use of the vernacular in worship and the introduction of congregational hymn singing gave the Catholic mass a distinctly Protestant feel, even though its underlying doctrine did not change. More importantly, a number of liberal Catholics have used the freedom that they believed the Council gave them to introduce far-reaching changes, not just in liturgy but also in theology. Radical new ideas, some imported from the liberationist movements of Latin America and elsewhere, began to make their appearance, much to the chagrin of traditionalists. The sexual revolution of the 1960s also began to have its effect, and when Pope Paul VI condemned artificial birth control in his encyclical *Humanae Vitae* (1968), it was widely disregarded by lay Catholics, who were no longer prepared to have their sex lives controlled by a celibate male priesthood. British and Irish Catholicism were conservative by comparison with that of the Netherlands or France, but the wave of change was startling enough for those who were caught up in it. For many, obedience to the Pope and the Church hierarchy became a thing of the past, as they adopted what has been called a 'pick-and-mix' or 'cafeteria-style' Catholicism – taking what they wanted and ignoring or discarding the rest.

Anglo-Catholics, who, until Vatican II, had been hopeful of a growing rapprochement with Rome, were placed in an even more awkward position than Roman Catholics were. Those who had traditionally defended or promoted certain practices because they were standard in the Roman Catholic Church were undercut by the latter's reforms, and found it harder to argue their case on the basis of conformity to the 'universal Church'.[37] Sexual liberation, which in Rome was primarily a lay affair centred on issues of birth

---

[37] For the details, see C. Podmore, 'Afterword: The Oxford Movement Today. The Things that Remain', in S. J. Brown, B. Nockles and J. Pereiro (eds.), *The Oxford Handbook of the Oxford Movement* (Oxford: Oxford University Press, 2017), 622–631, esp. 625–631.

control and abortion, became among Anglo-Catholics an outlet for the promotion of homosexuality – discreet at first, but nevertheless widespread and destined to become more influential as time went on.

Although largely focused on getting closer to both Rome and the Eastern churches, some Anglo-Catholics were open to the idea of reunion with other Protestants, in particular with the Methodists. But they were a minority, and after the proposed scheme was defeated in 1972 little more was heard of it. One of the problems was that many of the Free Churches had ordained women, and this soon became an issue within the Church of England too. Before the arrival of the 'new hermeneutic', most people believed that although there was an important ministry for women in the Church, this did not include formal ordination to a preaching or teaching role, which the apostle Paul reserved for men.[38] But once it could be claimed that New Testament texts were products of their time that had to be reinterpreted in the light of a changed hermeneutical horizon, what appeared to be the plain teaching of the Bible could be set aside as the product of a 'patriarchal' culture that must be rejected in the name of modern gender equality. According to this way of thinking, what matters is not what the Scriptures say but the direction of travel in which they are supposedly headed – their so-called 'trajectory'. In other words although the Bible does not specifically endorse women's ordination, its assertion that men and women are equal in Christ is a principle that can be applied in that sense. Whether this is overturning the letter of the law by its spirit, as advocates of this method of interpretation think, or whether it is essentially a surrender to the spirit of the age, thus becomes a matter of dispute, or (perhaps) of what is now known as 'good disagreement'.

Whatever interpretation one prefers, the fact remains that when the Church of England's General Synod voted, on 11 November 1992, to proceed with the ordination of women to the presbyterate (priesthood), the Anglo-Catholic movement split down the middle. It is estimated that over the following decade about 440 priests left the Church of England, 227 to become Roman Catholics and about 30 to become Eastern Orthodox. The departure of that many conservative Anglo-Catholics left the field wide open for the liberals among them, who had already formed their own organization, Affirming Catholicism (1990). Affirming Catholics supported the ordination of women and the acceptance of homosexual practice, although they made considerable efforts to downplay these emphases by including them within a wider framework of objectives. According to their website:

---

[38] 1 Tim. 2:11–15.

We are a movement of inspiration and hope in the Anglican Communion, seeking to bring together and strengthen lay and ordained people who recognize the positive, inclusive and joyful currents in the Catholic tradition of Christianity. We are working to make the Catholic element within Anglicanism a positive force for the Gospel and a model for effective mission today. As reformed and reforming Catholics, we seek to renew the universal Church by including those with different perspectives and bearing witness in the world to Christ's healing and reconciling love.[39]

Those familiar with the jargon of modern 'progressive' thought will recognize what 'including those with different perspectives' means, but it is still too early to tell whether Affirming Catholicism will be successful in its aims. One of its early supporters was Rowan Douglas Williams (1950–), Archbishop of Canterbury (2002–12), but he does not appear to have done much in recent years to further its cause.[40] Even so its president, Stephen Geoffrey Cottrell (1958–), was elevated to the archbishopric of York in 2020, amid fears that he might use his position to promote a more liberal attitude towards homosexual practice. These fears are heightened by the fact that those pressing for change regard any compromise as a sell-out and are determined to press for more concessions. One case in point is that of the Reverend David Jeremy Christopher Davies (1946–), formerly a residentiary Canon of Salisbury cathedral, who in January 2006 entered into a civil partnership with his male lover of eighteen years. During that time he had been living in defiance of the Church of England's rules and, by his own admission, the Dean of Salisbury had called him out on it, although to no effect.[41]

In 2005 the English bishops decided to accept civil partnerships among the clergy, provided such clergy gave an assurance that their relationships would be 'celibate'. It was nonsense and was widely denounced as such at the time, but it was the sort of compromise the Anglican hierarchy delights in. At the time, Mr Davies gave the Bishop of Salisbury the necessary assurances about 'celibacy', but ten years later he said:

The whole process seems untruthful. Why should I collude with a dishonest intrusion into a private relationship? I don't see that a sexual

---

[39] As quoted by Podmore, 'Afterword', 629.

[40] For the views of Williams and the other supporters, see K. Hylson-Smith, *High Churchmanship in the Church of England from the Sixteenth Century to the Late Twentieth Century* (Edinburgh: T&T Clark, 1993), 361–366.

[41] The details of this story are taken from an interview published in *The Guardian* on 26 December 2015.

relationship is incompatible with a loving relationship, whether it's between people of the same gender or not. So in fact to give that assurance was, I think, colluding with the system. It shouldn't have happened.

By then retired, Jeremy Davies was planning to marry his partner and opined:

Why shouldn't two men or two women, who love each other and want to commit their lives to each other for ever, say these things? When the bishops said that clergy who enter into same-sex marriages are not modelling the teaching of the Church – yes, we are. It is embodied in that vow.

Here we come face to face with an interpretation of marriage that is incompatible with Christian teaching and where no compromise is possible. If a same-sex couple is 'modelling the teaching of the Church', as Jeremy Davies claims, then the 'Church' cannot stand idly by. This is the trap into which the would-be compromisers have fallen. When civil partnerships were extended to heterosexual couples, the true nature of such partnerships was revealed. On 20 January 2020 the bishops of the Church of England issued a statement in which they reminded people of the Church's official teaching that marriage is a permanent union of one man and one woman, sealed by a vow, and that neither civil partnerships nor same-sex marriage measured up to that. It should have surprised nobody, and the bishops sweetened the pill by saying (controversially) that the clergy were free to dispute the Church's official teaching and seek to change it, but the response was fierce. Not only did a large part of the media attack the bishops, but a significant section of the Church did as well, led by the Suffragan Bishop of Buckingham.

Anywhere else, someone who stepped out of line to that extent would have been expected to resign, but that did not happen. Instead the authority of the bishops was rejected by one of their own number – a renegade to Christians but a hero of sorts to those who will seize on anything to attack the Church. Will the bishops be forced to take a stand against such people or will they persist in trying to find solutions that neither radicals nor traditionalists can accept? The jury is still out on this one, but the fearful prospect looms of a world in which orthodox Christians will have to leave the mainstream churches in order to remain faithful to the gospel, and the future of Christian witness in Britain, Ireland and the world may hang on the outcome.

Situations like these have come about because those in authority have bought into the secular dictum that the Church must adapt its message to the society in which it lives. The idea that Christians are called to be 'a chosen race, a royal priesthood, a holy nation, a people for his own possession' in order to proclaim the God who has called them 'out of darkness into his marvellous light' is alien to their consciousness.[42] Would proponents of this view have erected statues of Marduk and Ishtar in the synagogues of ancient Babylon in order to reach out to the people around them? It is hard to say, but what they are doing in the modern church amounts to much the same thing.

In some cases the opposition of militantly secular groups puts the churches to shame. For example, transgenderism is criticized by ardent feminists who claim (among other things) that it is a way for men to pretend that they are women and enter all-female spaces with the intention of sexually assaulting others, but church leaders never mention that it is a denial of God's creation and ought to be resisted for that reason.[43] Astonishingly, while the Church of England continues to agonize over many aspects of sexuality, it does not seem to have any problem with transgenderism, and even declares on its official website that transgendered people are welcome to apply for the ordained ministry.

When women were first ordained as priests (in 1994), nobody foresaw that some men would take the opportunity to change sex and carry on in their ministry, but that is what has happened, and nobody has questioned it. In 2000 Peter James Stone (1954–2014), who was already twice-divorced and had an 18-year-old daughter, decided to apply for 'gender reassignment'. His bishop (Bristol) supported him in this and declared, 'There are no ethical or ecclesiastical legal reasons why the Rev. Carol Stone should not continue in the ministry of the Church of England.'[44] A more recent case is that of Rachel Mann (1970–), who transitioned to being female in 1995 and was later approved for ordination. She was subsequently made a minor Canon of Manchester Cathedral and in February 2018 was even elected to the house of clergy of the General Synod, where (needless to say) she is a vocal advocate of the full inclusion of practising homosexuals in the ranks of the clergy. In 2019 she was even shortlisted for the Michael Ramsey prize in theology, although she did not get it. Babylon could hardly get closer or be more threatening to Zion than this, but nobody has said a word about it. In fairness to them the readiness of the Church authorities to surrender to the prevailing zeitgeist on this and other matters is probably due to the legacy of the centuries in which church and

---

[42] 1 Peter 2:9.

[43] See V. Roberts, *Transgender* (Epsom: The Good Book Company, 2016).

[44] As reported by the British Broadcasting Corporation on 19 July 2000. He ministered in the same parish as 'Carol Ann Stone' until his death in 2014.

society were two sides of the same coin, or at least were thought to be. They cannot adjust to a world in which popular culture openly proclaims Satan's rebellion against Christ and the church is called to stand up and be counted. Instead they continue to behave as though they are the accredited religious representatives of the state and conform to its every wish. Not a few of them see their main task as dragooning unreconstructed believers into submission or, failing that, driving them out of the church altogether. Will faithful believers be able to make a stand against this before it is too late?

Singing the Lord's song in a strange land

How shall we sing the LORD's song in a strange land?[45]

The exiles in Babylon were tempted by its power and prosperity, but the psalmist knew it was wrong for the Jews to gain the whole world if they lost their soul by doing so – 'how shall we sing the LORD's song in a strange land?' For all its allurements, Babylon was not where God's people were meant to be. However desolate Zion was, it was the only place where they would ever feel at home. The New Testament writers shared the same outlook and reminded the early Christians that they were pilgrims and strangers on earth, looking for a heavenly city whose builder and maker is God.[46] Over the centuries the church has often wielded secular power or been coopted by the state, but in every generation there have been men and women who have resisted the seductive appeal of the present age. For them, faith has always been countercultural, whether it meant leaving the 'world' for a monastery, undertaking an uncertain and thankless ministry or going to the ends of the earth to preach the gospel. These are the true believers, the salt of the earth who have ensured that, however dark the social or political scene is, God has never been without a witness. Resident aliens in Babylon they may be, but they are the ones singing the Lord's song in a strange land. That is what defines their identity on earth and that is their passport to eternal life in heaven.

Who are these exiles? Where can they be found? How can we recognize them? Our first instinct is to turn to the church, and in the nature of things to look to its leaders for inspiration. But the sad fact is that resistance to the spirit of the age is unlikely to come from church hierarchies or bureaucracies. Most

---

[45] Ps. 137:4 (KJV).
[46] See 1 Peter 2:11–12; Heb. 11:10, 14–16; 12:22–24; Phil. 1:21–23.

Protestant churches do not have the kind of organization that allows individuals to stand out as denominational leaders, although there is a tradition of gifted preachers who have attracted a following, at least for the duration of their ministry. But as experience has shown, congregations formed in that way tend to disperse when their minister departs, leaving little lasting impact.[47] Even at the best of times, such model preachers are uncommon; and if they happen to fall from grace, the consequences may be particularly devastating. The Church of England, with its bishops and established status, enjoys a certain advantage, at least in theory, but it has to be said that its record has often been more embarrassing than edifying. Not even its staunchest supporters would claim that its prelates have been exemplary fathers in God, and bitter experience has had a negative impact on expectations. As Harry Blamires put it more than a generation ago:

> The Church as an institution is entangled in the weaknesses and deficiencies of human nature. Its earthly setup is necessarily corrupted by man's sinfulness and distorted by man's ignorance. But of course there is more to be said than that. For to think Christianly is to accept the fact that in God's eyes it may be more important to have a thoroughly holy, wise, instructed man as parish priest in a slum area than to have such a man as bishop of the diocese. If there are not enough good men to go round, it may well be a part of the divine economy to make sure that the weakest ones go where they can do the least damage – the episcopal bench, where their personal influence over the souls of the laity is reduced to a minimum ... God may have answered our prayers for the Church by putting the least promising human material into episcopal thrones, where the authority of the higher office will strengthen them and guide them in their ignorance, and where the responsibilities of status will operate to restrain their natural foolishness.[48]

Blamires was writing in 1963, but despite the many changes that have occurred in the Church since then, his portrait of the episcopate remains depressingly recognizable. The true strength of Christianity is not measured by the behaviour of those in the limelight but by the often-invisible faithfulness of humble people whose daily struggles go unnoticed by the wider public. As

---

[47] Two obvious cases in London are the Metropolitan Tabernacle, made famous by the ministry of C. H. Spurgeon, and Westminster Chapel, where Dr Martyn Lloyd-Jones held sway for many years. Both still exist, but neither enjoys much renown today.

[48] H. Blamires, *The Christian Mind* (London: SPCK, 1963), 54–55.

an Anglo-Catholic, Blamires quite naturally pointed to the largely anonymous parish priests, but he would doubtless have been prepared to extend his net to include the vast numbers of laypeople whose daily walk with God is known only to him. Who are they?

Trying to analyse a phenomenon that is largely unrecorded is an impossible task for mere mortals, and we are in no position to judge the secrets of the heart. All we can do is look at how the outward expression of committed Christian belief has been changing in recent years, and take that as a rough guide to where we should look to see God at work in our midst. A late-twentieth-century survey revealed that whereas in 1989 Catholics accounted for 39.4% of all churchgoers, by 1998 this had fallen to 26.4%, while Evangelicals went from 30.1% in 1989 to 37.4% in the same period. But this does not mean that large numbers of Catholics had become Evangelicals, because church-going of all kinds was going down. According to the same survey, Catholics had declined by 48%, 'Broad Church' people by 19%, 'liberals' by 11% and Evangelicals by 3%.[49]

To be fair, there were many factors keeping people away from church, and by no means all of them can be read as signs of growing unbelief. The intro-duction of Sunday trading in the 1980s, although resisted with partial success by campaigns like 'Keep Sunday Special', made it difficult for many shop workers to attend worship regularly and gave others an incentive to go shopping instead. Sporting activities on Sundays involved many young people, keeping them away from church. Then too, many people had to travel peri-odically on business, while weekend breaks away became common for many who were not free at any other time. Christmas and Easter services continued to attract large numbers, but more and more people took advantage of the days off to take a holiday abroad. In university cities, churches that were full of students in term time were often practically empty on those great feasts, but that says nothing about their spiritual health. Commuters who spent up to two hours on a train or bus journey found it difficult to get to midweek services or prayer meetings, which tended to die off as a result. Yet even when we make allowances for these factors, as well as for vagueness and inaccurate reporting of the numbers, the overall picture points in the same direction. Churchgoing was in decline, but those who had a well-defined personal faith commitment were more likely to resist the trend.

In such a situation it is no surprise to discover that Evangelicals have done better than most others. Personal commitment is the essence of their faith and

---

[49] Warner, *Reinventing English Evangelicalism*, 111–112.

they have never hesitated to preach this, often in non-traditional settings and in innovative ways. To the dismay of some, they have not hesitated to enter the world of popular music, producing songs that have enriched the worship of many who would not identify with them theologically. Composers like Graham Kendrick (1950–), Stuart Townend (1963–) and Matthew (Matt) Redman (1974–) have enjoyed widespread popularity, and several others have followed in their wake. No doubt many of their creations will prove to be ephemeral, but that was also true of the Wesleys. How many people realize that of the 10,000 or so hymns they wrote, only about 40 are still regularly sung, and even they are often modified or abridged? We shall not know for some time whether there will be lasting results from the current wave of hymn writing, but we can at least hope that it will bequeath a significant legacy to future generations.

Another aspect of this Evangelical investment in popular music has been the emergence of big bank-holiday festivals that bring together people from a wide range of church backgrounds. One of the first of these was Greenbelt, which began in 1974 and initially attracted a large following. It was fairly Evangelical to begin with, but it soon became broader in outlook and now embraces a wide range of opinions and activities. Numbers peaked in the late 1990s but have fallen off since then. Another festival of a similar kind is Spring Harvest, founded in 1979 and more obviously Evangelical than Greenbelt, although not exclusively so. In 2007 a subgroup called Word Alive split off from it, and has continued as a more clearly Evangelical (and evangelistic) gathering ever since. Before long, an entire subculture emerged that absorbed the energies of many (mostly Evangelical) Christians but at the same time ensured that they were not available for anything else. Very few got involved in social activities that would put them in contact with non-Christians, and only a handful entered politics. Zion was closing the gates and pulling up the drawbridge, determined to withstand the siege of the neo-Babylonians but unable to sally forth and defeat them. Rob Warner, who made a comprehensive survey of Spring Harvest in the late 1990s, had this to say about it:

> Spring Harvest constructed an evangelical village for a week. Isolation was both its strength and its limitation. Its strength because it provided a powerful, positive reinforcement of the plausibility structures, or 'sacred canopy' of evangelicalism: for a week, at least, evangelicals inhabited an essentially mono-cultural community where their convictions and customs prevailed. This reinforced the enthusiastically promulgated but

entirely implausible aspiration to move from a pluralistic society to an evangelical version of Christendom . . . the event was hermetically sealed from the host community . . . Spring Harvest talked about the need for engagement but provided a week-long experience of isolation . . . This looks less like a community gathering for advance than a remnant withdrawing into subcultural segregation.[50]

On a broader front, Evangelicals have spent vast sums of money on evangelistic campaigns, although these have never been more than moderately successful. Even so, the enthusiastic entrepreneurs who mount them have seldom been deterred by this apparent failure. They point to positive results in the USA and in the Global South, and claim that with the right approach they can achieve similar success in Britain. Again in Warner's words:

Ever amnesiac to past disappointments, they publicised and financed new programmes, confidently proclaiming that their latest initiative was sure to produce the assured advances in convertive piety they continued resolutely to expect. The conversionist–activist axis is remarkably resilient, but, in the context of secularization, shows evidence of delusional tendencies.[51]

Dispassionate analysis of the available statistics would appear to support Warner's pessimistic conclusions. There has been no overall growth of church attendance in the twenty-first century, additions acquired through evangelism being more than cancelled out by deaths among the elderly and desertions among the young. The expectations of widespread revival still continue to be fuelled by some, but even within the Evangelical community doubts have been expressed. In 2020 the British branch of the Billy Graham Evangelistic Association was still planning to hold a series of evangelistic meetings featuring Billy's very right-wing and politicized son Franklin, who was expected to draw crowds by playing on his father's name, although many in the Evangelical community were opposed to the venture and refused to cooperate in what they thought was a misconceived strategy.[52] The ensuing coronavirus pandemic put these plans on hold, but whether they have been abandoned altogether is still unclear.

---

[50] Ibid. 81–82.

[51] Ibid. 114.

[52] A number of secular venues cancelled Graham's appearances when they discovered what his views on certain controversial subjects were.

Whatever happens in the future, it seems safe to say that the rosy scenario painted by Evangelicals in the 1970s has failed to materialize. Men from an Evangelical background have been appointed to senior positions in the Church of England, but the overall effect of this has been disappointing. Many of them have explicitly distanced themselves from their erstwhile colleagues, and few Evangelicals see any reason why they should look to them for spiritual leadership. The Church of England has developed a managerial style geared to long-term retrenchment and decline and, on the whole, the Evangelicals who have been promoted within it conform to the prevailing mood and expectations.[53]

Convinced that they have to make themselves acceptable to the 'whole church', they have sometimes indulged in behaviour that an earlier generation would have found deeply heretical. For example, Maurice Wood, the staunchly Evangelical Bishop of Norwich, visited the Anglo-Catholic shrine of Walsingham as it was in his diocese, and was roundly criticized by other Evangelicals for doing so. Other Evangelical bishops have been more discreet, but there has been a general sense that they will not stand up for their supposed beliefs in the way Anglo-Catholic and liberal bishops have done. The accuracy of this perception was demonstrated when the General Synod of the Church of England voted for the ordination of women as priests and all six 'Evangelical' bishops went with the majority, even though a large number of their constituency was opposed. By then it had become clear that the wider Church had accommodated Evangelicals at the higher levels of its administration by choosing those who were most pliable to the wishes of the majority and expecting them to persuade the others to fall into line.

This suspicion was further confirmed when a large number of Evangelicals dissented and formed a network called Reform. As part of a diplomatic move to conciliate opponents of women priests, the Church had agreed to appoint non-diocesan bishops (the so-called 'flying' bishops) to minister to them, but when the Evangelicals asked for one they were turned down flat – by bishops who called themselves 'Evangelical' and who decreed that women's ordination was not an issue for them! It would not be until 2015 that Reform's wishes would finally be accommodated.[54] By then it was clear that nobody opposed

---

[53] There are however some exceptions to this pattern, notably Wallace Benn (1947–), the former Bishop of Lewes, Keith Sinclair (1952–), until 2021 the Suffragan Bishop of Birkenhead, and Julian Henderson (1954–), the Bishop of Blackburn, who have risked the opprobrium of their colleagues and stood up for their beliefs without flinching.

[54] On 23 September 2015 Roderick Charles Howell (Rod) Thomas, erstwhile president of Reform, was made the Suffragan Bishop of Maidstone (Canterbury) and other bishops were encouraged to allow him to minister in their dioceses, which many (though not all) of them did.

to the ordination of women would be made a diocesan bishop, despite assurances to the contrary made when women's ordination was first introduced, and the Church had little choice but to make some token provision for them.[55] These developments still lay some way in the future in 1980, but it was already clear, to those with eyes to see, what would happen when the crunch came. Everyone expected that the leading Evangelicals would conform to the majority view whether they personally agreed with it or not, and then try to keep their constituency united behind them. They would not be disappointed in this, although the constituency was not always as ready to go along with that kind of 'leadership' as most of the Establishment hoped it would be.

Lower down the ecclesiastical scale it is difficult to form an overall picture of ordained ministry in the different churches, because categories vary so much and statistics are hard to come by. But a sample from the diocese of Ely may help to put matters in perspective. In September 2020 Ely ordained twenty people, thirteen men and seven women. But of these, no fewer than fourteen (nine men and five women) were non-stipendiary ministers, which probably means that they were short-term, part-time or both. Only six (four men and two women) were stipendiary clergy likely to have a lifetime career in the Church of England. Of them, four (three men and one woman) were clearly Evangelicals, which perhaps indicates that they take the full-time ministry more seriously than others and are prepared to invest more in it. At least six of the non-stipendiaries (two men and four women) were also Evangelicals, making them half overall and equally divided between male and female. On the other hand none of the ordinands was obviously Anglo-Catholic, which highlights the current weakness of that wing of the Church and does not bode well for its future.[56]

The situation of the Church of Scotland and the Free Churches was just as dire, if not worse than that of the Church of England. The Church of Scotland lost about three-quarters of its official membership between 1980 and 2020. Many of them were purely nominal adherents of course, and some went to other denominations, but even when these factors are taken into account, the decline was spectacular. The traditional Free Churches tell a similar story, although rates of decline varied from one denomination to another. Many congregations merged or closed down because they could not afford to hire a

---

[55] Anglo-Catholics found themselves in much the same position, as was demonstrated by the career of Philip John North (1966–), who was nominated to the suffragan see of Whitby (York) in 2012 and to the diocese of Sheffield in 2017, but withdrew under pressure from those who opposed his stance on women's ordination. He was however made Suffragan Bishop of Burnley (Blackburn) in 2015.

[56] This information was gleaned from the diocesan website on 29 September 2020.

minister. Others joined in 'local ecumenical projects', frequently involving Anglicans as well, which operated more or less outside denominational structures. What happened to their members is hard to say for sure. Social surveys conducted between 2012 and 2016 suggest that significant numbers of people brought up as Presbyterians (43%), Methodists (44%), Baptists (37%) and 'Non-denominational' Christians (43%) now profess no religion at all. But whereas only 7% of Anglicans and 9% of Presbyterians have joined other churches, 23% of Methodists have done so and 36% of Baptists.[57]

But if the mainstream Protestant churches were in serious decline, the Free Church tradition was reinvigorated from an entirely new source. One of the most remarkable features of modern British Christianity has been the explosion of independent churches, almost all of which are Evangelical and often charismatic too. Some of these have come with immigrants who have established their own worshipping communities that have little or no connection with other Christian groups. There are large and vibrant gatherings of African and Caribbean believers whose very existence is unknown to more traditional churchgoers. The Fellowship of Independent Evangelical Churches (FIEC) now has more than 600 congregations and about 40,000 people connected to it, and (so far at least) seems to be resisting the overall pattern of decline.

The available statistics tell their own story of growth in the Free Churches. While Anglicans and Presbyterians have attracted relatively few members from outside their own ranks (6% of the current membership in both cases), 25% of non-denominational church members have come from elsewhere. Perhaps surprisingly, the same is also true of 20% of Methodists and fully 41% of Baptists. When compared with the percentages of Nonconformists who have joined other churches, we get a sense that there is something of a 'revolving door', with considerable numbers of people both coming and going, which suggests a relatively weak sense of denominational loyalty. But it must always be remembered that in every case those who have left the institutional churches altogether significantly outnumber those who have merely shifted from one congregation to another. When that is taken into account, we discover that for every person who joins a Presbyterian church seventeen leave, while the corresponding ratios for Anglicans and Methodists are 1:10 and 1:8 respectively. Baptists (1:4) and Non-denominational churches (1:3) come out much better, but the losses are still high, especially for churches that insist on a

---

[57] Surveys carried out by British Social Attitudes and cited in S. Bullivant, *Mass Exodus* (Oxford: Oxford University Press, 2019), 35.

personal profession of faith as the only valid basis for membership and so have few purely nominal members to begin with.[58]

The ability to sit loose to traditional structures is characteristic of the independent churches and is often a source of their vitality. Some are started by charismatic individuals who gather a following around them, while others are grounded in a collective enterprise to bring the gospel message to places inadequately served by the existing churches. A few have emerged from spiritual movements like the Vineyard churches, inspired by the ministry of the late John Wimber (1934–97), or New Wine, which embraces congregations in different denominations. There is even a group known as the Anglican Mission in England (AMiE), which has an ill-defined relationship to the established Church but operates as a separate organization and maintains close links with Anglican groups overseas that are not in communion with Canterbury.[59] In addition to these there are wholly independent congregations led by enthusiastic laypeople who are accepted as leaders whether they have any formal theological training or not. It is hard to generalize, but it is probably true to say that most of these churches are in cities, where they can attract congregations large enough to support them, and that their outreach is often limited to their local area.

In some ways the fluidity of the current scene is reminiscent of the late eighteenth century, when different kinds of 'Methodists' were emerging and the relationship between them and the established Church was unclear. Comparisons with that time would suggest that after the initial wave of enthusiasm subsides, things will settle down. Some of these new congregations will disappear. Others will regroup into what are effectively new denominations. Many will find their way back into the Establishment, but there will always be plenty who will prefer to go their own way. The familiar cycle of growth, decline, transformation and further renewal is likely to reassert itself as it has done in the past, and although the names will change, the underlying pattern will remain the same.

At the other end of the spectrum, the Roman Catholic Church, which had continued to grow for a few decades when Protestant churches were in decline, saw religious vocations falling off a cliff. By 1990 the number of men offering for the priesthood had dropped almost to vanishing point, even in Ireland, which had long provided so many clergy for the whole of the British Isles and overseas. In addition scandals came to light with increasing frequency. Several

---

58 British Social Attitudes survey cited in ibid. 38.

59 In 2020 AMiE apparently rebranded itself as the Anglican Mission in Europe, which includes England and the rest of the British Isles.

supposedly celibate priests, and even an Irish bishop, were unmasked as fathers of illegitimate children, whereas many others were closet homosexuals, and a few were even found guilty of paedophilia.[60]

That much of this was known to the Catholic Church hierarchy but had been kept quiet merely made matters worse, since suddenly *every* priest became suspect – who knew what was going on behind the closed doors of the presbytery? This was grossly unfair to the many loyal and blameless priests who were doing their best to serve increasingly sceptical congregations, but how could laypeople be expected to discern who was genuine and who was not? Mass attendance went down sharply, even if churchgoing was still higher than among most Protestants. The fall was all the more noticeable because of its suddenness and extent. In Ireland regular mass attendance was still well over 80% in the 1980s, but had dropped to 50% or less twenty years later, and has continued to decline since then. In Great Britain it was never as high as that, but it is now no more than 13%, with three times that number having left Christianity altogether. In other respects Roman Catholics parallel Anglicans, with only 6% of their members coming from other Christian denominations and the ratio of dropouts to converts being the same – 1:10.[61] Despite the reinforcements the Roman Catholic Church has received from immigration and the greater emphasis it places on the need to go to mass regularly, its attendance levels are now only marginally higher than those of the mainstream Protestant denominations and they look set to fall still further.

Can the Roman Catholic Church find the resources it needs for inner renewal? Many ordinary Catholics are distressed by the condition of their Church, but with no tradition of lay leadership to support them they do not know where to turn. The problem is an international one of course, and will be tackled successfully only on a worldwide basis. At the moment it seems that British and Irish Catholicism are most likely to be reinvigorated from overseas, not just by importing clergy but also by welcoming laypeople coming as immigrants. The Eastern Orthodox churches continue to rely on the latter, and tend to be concentrated in their traditional ethnic communities. For the moment this helps them to resist the social pressures affecting other churches, but what the future holds for them remains uncertain.

By their nature the established churches of England and Scotland find it difficult to speak with a common voice. They are often criticized by those who

---

[60] See T. Barrett, *Ireland: A History* (Cambridge: Cambridge University Press, 2010), 533–537.

[61] Bullivant, *Mass Exodus*, 38.

are frustrated by their lacklustre leadership and seeming inability to maintain orthodox doctrine and discipline, but these failings need to be weighed against the creative role that many of their clergy and laity play in the renewal of faith and devotion across the nation as a whole. Here the parallels with the eighteenth-century Evangelical revival are striking. Then too the lead was given by clergymen of the established churches and the movement spread out to reinvigorate the Free Churches as well.

In the Church of England, organizations like Proclamation Trust and the Evangelical Ministry Assembly do sterling work in training ministers to preach and teach their congregations and many independent churches have benefited enormously from them. These developments are the fruit of the ministry of Richard (Dick) Charles Lucas (1925–), rector of St Helen's, Bishopsgate, in the City of London from 1961 to 1998. Dick Lucas is also largely responsible for establishing the Cornhill Training Course (1991), which prepares young men and women for many different kinds of ministry. Participants come from every church background and serve in a wide variety of contexts.

Much the same can also be said for the Alpha Course, started by Charles Christopher Marnham (1951–) in 1977 and continued by Nicholas (Nicky) Glyn Paul Gumbel (1955–) from his base at Holy Trinity, Brompton, in west-central London. The Alpha Course is a new style of evangelistic outreach, designed to meet people where they are and minister to them on a one-to-one basis. In many ways its methods resemble those of 'Iwerne', although with a charismatic overlay that has proved controversial in some quarters. Alpha soared to extraordinary heights of popularity in the late 1990s and although it has settled down since then, it is still a major operation with outreach around the world. It is thoroughly ecumenical in approach and has managed to penetrate Roman Catholic and even some Eastern Orthodox circles, albeit in a modified form. Alpha has its critics, who have found it insufficiently theological, but it has also spawned a number of imitators, including the *Christianity Explored* course, which uses a similar format but without Alpha's charismatic emphasis.[62]

Another development that is essentially a spin-off from Alpha is a new theological college, St Mellitus (2007), which is pioneering an innovative kind of ministerial training. St Mellitus is non-residential, but has 'campuses' in London and (increasingly) in other parts of England, where instruction is given on a largely part-time basis. Like Alpha, it is basically Evangelical and

---

[62] See Warner, *Reinventing English Evangelicalism*, 115–137, for a detailed assessment of the Alpha Course and its impact.

charismatic in orientation but it seeks to operate beyond traditional church-manship boundaries and welcomes students of many different backgrounds and denominations in a spirit of what it calls 'generous orthodoxy'. This approach has attracted its critics, especially from non-charismatic Evangelicals, and the college may find it difficult to attract them. In July 2020 a number of dioceses in the north-west of England announced that they would be sponsoring a new theological college that would effectively supplant St Mellitus in that part of the country, although whether that will happen remains to be seen. Whatever its limitations may be, St Mellitus is pointing the way to a new type of theological training and doing what it can to supply the demand for knowledge that the churches' increasing reliance on lay and part-time ministers has created.

As far as creative theological thinking is concerned, British Christianity remains weaker than it ought to be, and the gap between the lecture theatre and pew seems to be widening into an ever-deeper chasm. On the one hand charismatic influences in the churches operate against serious intellectual inquiry, which some people fear is more likely to harm than promote faith. On the other hand systematic theology is often closer to modern philosophical trends than it is to the Bible, which simply reinforces the perception that it is subversive rather than edifying. Theologians churn out articles and books written in an academic language that non-specialists may find almost impossible to understand, and too many of them fear that if they try to simplify matters they will lose the respect of their colleagues. The result is that a small group of intellectuals talk to one another, while those outside their charmed circle – the vast majority of church members – pay no attention to them.

For the time being, theology departments continue to exist in many universities, and some are outstanding, although how long they will survive in the current secular climate is hard to say. In Scotland, where interest in theology has always been higher than in England, the Highland Theological College was founded in Dingwall in 1994 and has prospered, offering theological education as an integral part of the recently created University of the Highlands and Islands. The initiative came from ministers of the established Church of Scotland but the College reaches out to all denominations, and especially to the many breakaway Presbyterian churches that dot the Highland landscape. There are also good theology departments in the universities of Aberdeen and St Andrews that are exploring ways in which systematic theology and biblical studies can be brought together in the service of the pastoral ministry of the churches. In addition Rutherford House continues to foster theological orthodoxy both within the Church of Scotland and beyond it, as does the Crieff Fellowship, founded by the late William Still and continuing his preaching and teaching ministry.

In the current climate of opinion it seems unlikely the Christian churches will ever regain the public influence they enjoyed in the past, but that does not necessarily mean the voice of the gospel will be silenced. One of the more remarkable developments in recent years has been the way in which Queen Elizabeth II (1952–) has used her position to reaffirm the basic tenets of Christianity. Throughout her reign she has spoken to the nation and Commonwealth at Christmas, and on Maundy Thursday she has travelled across the UK to distribute money to the 'deserving poor' in a revival of an ancient ceremony meant to reflect the way Jesus washed his disciples' feet on the night he was betrayed. For a long time these rituals attracted little attention, but beginning in the millennial year 2000 a change of tone has been evident. Aware of the secularization of modern society, Her Majesty has not only called the nation back to its Christian roots but done something no other monarch has ever done – she has shared her own personal faith and proclaimed the gospel message in a brief and simple, but nevertheless powerful and moving, way. Whether her successors will continue to do this we cannot say, but as long as the head of the nation remains faithful there is hope for the healing of the body politic as a whole.

Above all, there is life in local congregations all over the British Isles. The sad pictures of abandoned churches and chapels must be balanced by the many flourishing communities where Christians are developing new forms of worship and witness. Some are bringing redundant buildings back to life, while others are exploring innovative ways of 'being church', whether in hired premises like schools or online. It is hard to gauge the impact of these things, but when *Songs of Praise* invited listeners in 2019 to nominate their favourite hymns, third place (after 'Jerusalem' and 'How great thou art') went to Stuart Townend's robustly orthodox 'In Christ Alone', composed in the millennial year 2000 and evidently already popular enough to rival the perennial favourites. If those who chose it really believe what it says, Christianity at the grassroots level has a rude health about it that bodes well for the future:

In Christ alone my hope is found
He is my light, my strength, my song
This cornerstone, this solid ground
Firm through the fiercest drought and storm!

What heights of love, what depths of peace
When fears are stilled, when strivings cease
My comforter, my all in all
Here in the love of Christ I stand.

In Christ alone, who took on flesh
Fulness of God in helpless babe
This gift of love and righteousness
Scorned by the ones he came to save
Till on that cross as Jesus died
The wrath of God was satisfied
For every sin on him was laid
Here in the death of Christ I live.

There in the ground his body lay
Light of the world by darkness slain
Then bursting forth in glorious day
Up from the grave he rose again
And as he stands in victory
Sin's curse has lost its grip on me
For I am his and he is mine
Bought with the precious blood of Christ.

No guilt in life, no fear in death
This is the power of Christ in me
From life's first cry, to final breath
Jesus commands my destiny
No power of hell, no scheme of man
Can ever pluck me from his hand
Till he returns or calls me home
Here in the power of Christ I'll stand.

Particularly impressive has been the greatly increased importance of online streaming for public worship. This was strikingly demonstrated in 2020, when the entire world was hit by the coronavirus pandemic, known universally as Covid-19.[63] From 22 March, which happened to be Mothering

---

[63] An abbreviation of 'Coronavirus disease–2019', so called because it first appeared in China in November 2019.

Sunday, places of worship in Britain and Ireland were closed, along with pubs, restaurants and leisure centres, all of which were considered to be 'non-essential' gathering places where the virus could easily spread. Easter celebrations were cancelled for the first time since 1214, when the country lay under a papal interdict. In 2020 there was no theological issue at stake, nor was the church being persecuted, but the effect was much the same and some opposition was expressed by those who thought that the state was imposing unacceptable restrictions on the church. Protests were muted however, because the danger to public health was obvious and most people thought that the churches should set an example to others of self-sacrifice for the common good. Initially it was believed that the restrictions would last only a few weeks, but it soon became apparent that they would continue for several months and that, in many respects, life would never be quite the same again.

The inability to meet together for public worship hit Catholics particularly hard, because access to the sacraments was effectively cut off. There were suggestions that some churches might be allowed to open for private prayer and small numbers might be allowed to share in the Eucharist, as long as proper social distancing measures were in place, but the practical difficulties were great. Catholic worship is heavily reliant on physical presence and participation, especially in the consecration of the sacred elements of bread and wine. The suggestion that laypeople might hold these up to the screen and have them virtually consecrated over the Internet seemed like an ingenious solution to some, but others quickly dismissed it as unworkable, even though there was no obvious alternative.

Protestants had less of a problem with this and Evangelicals in particular were well placed to deal with the changed circumstances. A number of Evangelical churches were already active online, and Covid-19 inspired them to expand their activities still further. Sermons could be preached, Bible lessons could be given and even singing was possible by a sophisticated use of modern technology.

It is hard to know what the long-term impact of all this will be, but it seems that during the lockdown more people were listening to worship services online than would typically go to church on Sundays. It has even been claimed that up to a third of young people, usually thought to be the ones most alienated from Christianity, were regular listeners. Technologically savvy as most of them are, they could organize singing and other musical activities, and there were some remarkable instances of choirs and even orchestras coming together to perform, despite their physical distance. It was not an ideal situation of course, but congregations adapted to what was possible within the limited options available to them. Although it must seem paradoxical, the effort required to link up meant that many people felt more involved in their church than they had been before.

Whether, or to what extent, this will continue for long after the pandemic is over is an open question. There will undoubtedly be some falling away as people return to their normal routine, and it is hard to see the churches suddenly filling up with worshippers who have never been near them before. But it is likely that online ministry has come to stay, and the gospel message will be communicated over the Internet to many who would not otherwise hear it. The residual attraction of Christianity was apparent on 1 August 2020, when the delayed Football Association Cup Final opened, as it always does, with the singing of 'Abide with me', the great hymn written by Henry Francis Lyte (1793–1847) only a few months before his death. As one commentator remarked at the time, the third and final verse was particularly poignant and appropriate, given the circumstances:

Hold thou thy cross before my dying eyes
Shine through the gloom and point me to the skies.
Heaven's morning breaks and earth's vain shadows flee
In life, in death, O Lord, abide with me.

Could this be a sign that hidden under the gloss of contemporary culture is a sleeping giant of faith waiting to stir back to life? Only time will tell.

At a deeper level, the pandemic has forced church leaders to think seriously about the future and consider how they will deal with it. It has long been understood that the gradual decline of the past century cannot go on for ever, that institutional structures are increasingly outmoded and unfit for purpose, and that online communication will play an increasingly important role in all aspects of church life. But the pandemic has forced people to accelerate the hitherto gradual process of change, with unforeseeable consequences. At the very least, it seems unlikely that Christians will go on pouring vast sums of money into unsuitable buildings, evangelistic literature and public rallies, especially now that we have seen that better results can be achieved free of charge on everyone's home computer. New ways of meeting and sharing will emerge, and even if they do not displace traditional gatherings they are very likely to play a greater part in church life generally. That in turn is almost bound to strengthen the ministry of the Word (Bible reading and preaching) and lessen the importance of the sacraments, which the pandemic has shown are more expendable than many people had previously thought. As with so much else, the longer-term impact of that realization must wait to be seen.

More fundamentally, the post-pandemic church will have to rethink the Christian message and the way it is presented. The crisis has revealed the underlying weakness of secular optimism and called into question the premises on which so much of it is based. People who never gave much thought to spiritual things before have suddenly been confronted with the emptiness of their own lives, the proximity of death and the vulnerability of even the strongest human beings to an invisible virus. The unrestricted freedom to say and do whatever one wants looks hollow when an entire population is placed in months-long confinement and the futility of so much of what we do is cruelly exposed. To the Christian of course, none of this is new:

> Vanity of vanities, says the Preacher,
>   vanity of vanities! All is vanity.
> What does man gain by all the toil
>   at which he toils under the sun?[64]

> All flesh is grass,
>   and all its beauty is like the flower of the field . . .
> The grass withers, the flower fades,
>   but the word of our God will stand for ever.[65]

The experience of a worldwide pandemic is a reminder of these things, an opportunity for Christians to unmask the materialism and atheism of our time for the deceptions they are. But it is not enough to resist the consequences to which modern humanism has led. We must tackle that at its root. 'Man' cannot replace God because man cannot be the measure of all things. The universe holds together because it has a Creator, Preserver and Redeemer – the God of the Bible. To put 'humanity' in his place is to exchange reality for fiction. The truth is that there is no such thing as man: there are only billions of human beings, each of whom is an individual. Which of them can set the standard or be the model for others?

Furthermore, human beings are not privileged because they have evolved from some 'lower' species. Our exalted place in the created order stems from

---

[64] Eccl. 1:2–3.
[65] Isa. 40:6, 8.

the fact that we are created in the image and likeness of God. Humanists have made the mistake of worshipping the image instead of the image-maker – a subtle but nevertheless fatal form of idolatry. The inevitable result is that the freedom and better life that humanists pretend will be the result of discarding belief in God turns out instead to be a message of death. It does not take much imagination to realize that abortion and euthanasia fall into that category. In a godless world suicide is the ultimate expression of human freedom, and so it is not surprising to find humanists advocating that we should extend it to those not yet born or not yet ready to die.

Homosexual practice is a less obvious form of death but, like transgenderism, it is a kind of sterilization that amounts to the same thing. In contrast to this Jesus said, 'I came that they may have life and have it abundantly.'[66] That is the Christian message. It is the promise held out to all who hear it, and the experience of all who believe. Certainly there are Christians who have failed to live up to their profession – in some ways, we all have. In the British Isles there are endemic plagues far more serious than the coronavirus that Christians have so far failed to tackle. England is riddled by class consciousness and in modern times the Church has been too closely associated with the middle and upper end of the spectrum. We must get to grips with this problem and overcome it. In Ireland, Christians have been tribalized in a sectarianism that has proved to be lethal, and the gospel message must bring healing to the wounds that have been inflicted if it is ever to be believed, either there or in Britain. It is sadly ironic that Northern Ireland, the part of the British Isles that has the highest level of church attendance and the greatest proportion of committed Christians, should also be the one place where blood is still being spilled in the name of Christ. Is it too much to hope that it may become the heartland of a new outpouring of God's Spirit that will heal old wounds and start a blaze that will spread to the rest of the country – and around the world?

Spiritual revival, when it comes, will have to grapple with these problems, but it will also encounter new challenges our forebears did not know. One of these is the presence of other religions in our midst. Christians will never try to coerce others into accepting their faith, but if large numbers of Muslims or Hindus start turning to Christ there is every chance that others in those communities will react against it. We must not forget that the preaching of the apostle Paul divided synagogues and sometimes led to violence, not from the Christians but from those who were opposed to them. Something similar

---

[66] John 10:10.

could happen again and we must be prepared to deal with it graciously, but without compromise.

We must also accept that British Christianity will not be able to develop in relative isolation from the rest of the world. No nation is an island – what we do and how we resolve our problems will send a message to the world that words alone cannot convey. Perhaps the pandemic will serve as the catalyst for new thinking and renewed efforts in these and other ways. It is possible that external influence will lead to a greater appreciation of Britain's Christian heritage than what we see at present. One sign of this is the appearance of an international version of the 1662 Book of Common Prayer, slightly modernized and expanded to accommodate the rest of the world, but otherwise faithful to the original.[67] Will this trend towards the traditional catch on at home? Once again, we can only wait and see.

For the moment, the captivity of the church to the power of atheistic humanism is likely to continue for the foreseeable future. The institutional Church appears to be in retreat, and we would be naive to think that the eternal battle between Babylon and Zion is coming to an end. The future will be as challenging as the past, and many will be tempted to despair. The forces ranged against us will always appear to be more formidable than they really are, and Christians will continue to wage spiritual warfare – within themselves, within the church and within the wider world. We must go on watching and praying, not knowing where our deliverance will come from, but confident that the Lord who has kept us for 2,000 years will not abandon us now. As Samuel Rutherford wrote to Robert Campbell when Rutherford was awaiting execution in Edinburgh for his part in the rebellion against Charles I:

> The Lord calleth you, dear brother, to be still 'steadfast, unmoveable and abounding in the work of the Lord.'[68] Our royal kingly Master is upon his journey, and will come, and will not tarry. And blessed is the servant who shall be found watching when he cometh. Fear not men, for the Lord is your light and salvation. It is true; it is somewhat sad and comfortless that you are alone. But so it was with our precious Master; nor are you alone, for the Father is with you. It is possible that I shall not be an eyewitness to it in the flesh, but I believe he cometh quickly who will remove our darkness, and shine gloriously in the Isle of Britain, as a

---

[67] S. L. Bray and D. L. Keane (eds.), *The 1662 Book of Common Prayer: International Edition* (Downers Grove, Ill.: Inter-Varsity Press, 2021).

[68] 1 Cor. 15:58.

crowned King, either in a formally sworn covenant, or in his own glorious way, which I leave to the determination of his infinite wisdom and goodness. And this is the hope and confidence of a dying man who is longing and fainting for the salvation of God.[69]

---

[69] T. Smith (ed.), *Letters of the Reverend Samuel Rutherford* (Edinburgh: Oliphant, Anderson and Ferrier, 1881), II, 70, 484. Rutherford died on 20 March 1661, before he could be executed.

Bibliography

Primary sources

General and England

Aelred of Rievaulx, *The Mirror of Charity*, tr. E. Connor; introduction and notes by C. Dumont (Kalamazoo, Mich.: Cistercian Publications, 1990).

Arnold, M., *Last Essays on Church and Religion* (London: Smith Elder, 1877).

Baker, D. N. (ed.), *The Showings of Julian of Norwich* (New York, N.Y.: W. W. Norton, 2004).

Baxter, R., *The Reformed Pastor* (London: Banner of Truth Trust, 1974).

Bede, *Ecclesiastical History of the English People* (London: Penguin Books, 1990).

Bennett, M., *Richard II and the Revolution of 1399* (Stroud: Sutton Publishing, 1999).

Black, J. L., *The Martin Marprelate Tracts: A Modernized and Annotated Edition* (Cambridge: Cambridge University Press, 2008).

Blamires, H., *The Christian Mind* (London: SPCK, 1963).

——, *A Defence of Dogmatism* (London: SPCK, 1967).

——, *The Faith and Modern Error* (London: SPCK, 1965).

The Book of Common Prayer: The Texts of 1549, 1559 and 1662 (Oxford: Oxford University Press, 2013).

Booty, J., *The Book of Common Prayer, 1559* (Washington, D.C.: Folger Books, 1976).

Bradford, P., and A. K. McHardy (eds.), *Proctors for Parliament: Clergy, Community and Politics c. 1248–1539 (The National Archives, Series SC 10)*, 2 vols. (Woodbridge: Canterbury and York Society and the Boydell Press), 2017–18.

Bray, G. L. (ed.), *The Anglican Canons, 1529–1947* (Woodbridge: Boydell & Brewer, 1998).

——, *The Books of Homilies: A Critical Edition* (Cambridge: James Clarke, 2015).

_____, *Documents of the English Reformation*, 3rd edn (Cambridge: James Clarke, 2019).

_____, *The Institution of a Christian Man* (Cambridge: James Clarke, 2018).

_____, *Records of Convocation*, 20 vols. (Woodbridge: Boydell & Brewer, 2005–6).

_____, *Tudor Church Reform* (Woodbridge: Boydell & Brewer, 2000).

Bray, S. L., and D. L. Keane (eds.), *The 1662 Book of Common Prayer: International Edition* (Downers Grove, Ill.: Inter-Varsity Press, 2021).

Brown, G. H., *A Companion to Bede* (Woodbridge: Boydell & Brewer, 2009).

Browne, R., *A Booke Which Sheweth the Life and Manners of All True Christians* (Middelburg: Richard Painter [R. Schilders], 1582).

Butler, J., *The Analogy of Religion* (London: J. M. Dent, 1906).

Cadbury, H. J. (ed.), *George Fox's 'Book of Miracles'* (Cambridge: Cambridge University Press, 2012).

Calendar of State Papers, Domestic 1634–5 (London: Her Majesty's Stationery Office, 1864).

Carlson, L. H., *The Writings of John Greenwood and Henry Barrow, 1591–1593* (London: Allen & Unwin, 1970).

Chaderton, L., *A Fruitfull Sermon upon the 3.4.5.6.7. & 8. Verses of the 12 Chapter of the Epistle of S. Paule to the Romans* (London: Robert Waldegrave, 1584).

Chalke, S., *The Lost Message of Jesus* (Grand Rapids, Mich.: Zondervan, 2003).

Chaucer, G., *The Canterbury Tales* (London: Flame Tree Publishing, 2019).

The Chronicle of Convocation 1847–57 (London: National Society's Depository, 1889).

Collini, S. (ed.), *J. S. Mill 'On Liberty' and Other Writings* (Cambridge: Cambridge University Press, 1989).

Conciliorum Oecumenicorum Decreta (Bologna: Istituto per le Scienze Religiose, 1973).

Conybeare, W. J., 'Church Parties', *Edinburgh Review* 200 (October 1853), 273–342.

Cosin, J., *Works*, 5 vols., ed. J. Sansom (Oxford: John Henry Parker, 1843–55).

Cronin, H. S. (ed.), *Rogeri Dymmok Liber contra XII Errores et Haereses Lollardorum* (London: Kegan Paul, Trench & Trübner, 1922).

Dale, R. W., *The Atonement* (London: Hodder & Stoughton, 1875).

Darbishire, H. (ed.), *The Poetical Works of John Milton* (London: Oxford University Press, 1958).

Denney, J., *The Death of Christ* (London: Hodder & Stoughton, 1902).

Dennison Jr, J. T. (ed.), *Reformed Confessions of the Sixteenth and Seventeenth Centuries in English Translation*, 4 vols. (Grand Rapids, Mich.: Reformation Heritage Books, 2008–14).

Dering, E., *A Sermon Preached Before the Queens Maiestie by Maister Edward Dering* (London: John Awdely, 1569 [1570]).

The Ecclesiastical Courts: Principles of Reconstruction, Being the Report of the Commission on Ecclesiastical Courts Set up by the Archbishops of Canterbury and York in 1951 at the Request of the Convocations (London: SPCK, 1954).

Elizabeth I: Collected Works, ed. L. S. Marcus, J. Mueller and M. B. Rose (Chicago, Ill.: University of Chicago Press, 2000).

Elton, G. R., *The Tudor Constitution*, 2nd edn (Cambridge: Cambridge University Press, 1982).

Fasti Ecclesiae Anglicanae 1066–1857, 3 series (London: Institute of Historical Research, 1962–2022).

Fawcett, T. J., *The Liturgy of Comprehension 1689: An Abortive Attempt to Revise the Book of Common Prayer* (Southend-on-Sea: Mayhew-McCrimmon, 1973).

Fincham, K., and S. Taylor, 'Vital Statistics: Episcopal Ordination and Ordinands in England, 1640–60', *English Historical Review* 126.519 (April 2011), 319–344.

The First World War Diaries of the Rt Rev. Llewellyn Gwynne, July 1915 – July 1916 (Woodbridge: Boydell & Brewer, 2019).

Fisher, E., *The Marrow of Modern Divinity* (Fearn: Christian Focus, 2009).

Foxe, J., *Actes and Monuments of These Latter and Perillous Dayes* (London: J. Day, 1563).

Fraenkel, P. (ed.), *Assertio Septem Sacramentorum Adversus Martinum Lutherum/Heinrich VIII* (Munich: Aschendorff, 1992).

Frere, W. H., and C. E. Douglas, *Puritan Manifestoes: A Study of the Origin of the Puritan Revolt* (London: SPCK, 1907).

Friedberg, E., *Corpus Iuris Canonici*, 2 vols. (Graz: Akademische Druck- und Verlagsanstalt, 1955).

Goodwin, T., *Of the Constitution, Right, Order, and Government of the Churches of Christ* (London: Thomas Snowden, 1696).

Goold, W. H. (ed.), *The Works of John Owen*, 23 vols. (London: Johnstone and Hunter, 1850–55; repr. London: Banner of Truth Trust, 1966).

Grindle, E. S., *Episcopal Inconsistency, or Convocation, the Bishops and Dr Temple: A Letter to the Archbishops and Bishops of the Church of England:*

Together with an Account of the Proceedings in Convocation with Regard to Essays and Reviews, *and Extracts from the Speeches of the Bishops, Taken* Verbatim *from the* Chronicle of Convocation (London: Masters, 1869).

Gunton, C. E., *The Actuality of Atonement: A Study of Metaphor, Rationality and the Christian Tradition* (Edinburgh: T&T Clark, 1988).

Haddan, A. W., and W. Stubbs, *Councils and Ecclesiastical Documents Relating to Great Britain and Ireland*, 3 vols. (Oxford: Clarendon Press, 1869–78).

Hall, D. W. (ed.), *Ius Divinum Regiminis Ecclesiastici, or The Divine Right of Church Government* (Dallas, Tex.: Naphtali Press, 1995).

Harding, T., *An Answer to Maister Juelles Chalenge* (Louvain: John Bogard, 1564).

Harnack, A., *History of Dogma*, 7 vols. (London: Williams & Norgate, 1894–9).

____, *What Is Christianity? Sixteen Lectures Delivered in the University of Berlin During the Winter Term 1899–1900* (London: Williams & Norgate, 1901).

Harrison, R., *A Little Treatise uppon the Firste Verse of the 122.Psalm, Stirring up unto Carefull Desiring a Dutifull Labouring for True Church Governement* (Middelburg: R. Schilders, 1583).

Hebert, G., *Fundamentalism and the Church of God* (London: SCM Press, 1957).

Hill, M., *Ecclesiastical Law*, 4th edn (Oxford: Oxford University Press, 2018).

Hill, W. S. (ed.), *The Folger Library Edition of the Works of Richard Hooker*, 7 vols., vols. 1–5 (Cambridge, Mass.: Belknap Press of Harvard University); vol. 6 (Binghamton, N.Y.: Medieval Texts and Renaissance Texts and Studies); vol. 7 (Tempe, Ariz.: Medieval Texts and Renaissance Studies, 1977–98).

Holcot, Robert, *Super Libros Sapientiae* (Haguenau, 1494; repr. Frankfurt, 1974).

Holt, J. C., *Magna Carta*, 2nd edn (Cambridge: Cambridge University Press, 1992).

Hornus, J.-M., *It Is Not Lawful for Me to Fight: Early Christian Attitudes Toward War, Violence and the State* (Scottdale, Pa.: Herald Press, 1980).

Jeffery, S., M. Ovey and A. Sach, *Pierced for Our Transgressions: Rediscovering the Glory of Penal Substitution* (Nottingham: Inter-Varsity Press, 2007).

Jewel, J., *Apologia Ecclesiae Anglicanae* (London: Reginald Wolfe, 1562).

Julian of Norwich, *Revelations of Divine Love* (London: Folio Press, 2017).

Kenyon, J. P., *The Stuart Constitution*, 2nd edn (Cambridge: Cambridge University Press, 1986).

Knowles, D., C. N. L. Brooke and V. C. M. London (eds.), *The Heads of Religious Houses: England and Wales I. 940–1216*, 2nd edn (Cambridge: Cambridge University Press, 2001).

Knowles, D., and R. N. Hadcock, *Medieval Religious Houses: England and Wales*, 2nd edn (London: Longman, 1971).

Lacey, T. A., *The King's Book or a Necessary Doctrine and Erudition for any Christian Man, 1543* (London: SPCK, 1932).

Letham, R., *The Westminster Assembly: Reading Its Theology in Context* (Phillipsburg, N.J.: Presbyterian and Reformed Publishing, 2009).

Lewis, D. M., *The Blackwell Dictionary of Evangelical Biography 1730–1860* (Oxford: Basil Blackwell, 1995).

Lloyd-Jones, D. M., *An Exposition of Ephesians*, 8 vols. (Edinburgh: Banner of Truth Trust, 1972–82).

———, *Romans 1:1–14:17*, 14 vols. (Edinburgh: Banner of Truth Trust, 1970–2003).

Logan, F. D., *The Medieval Court of Arches*, Canterbury and York Society, vol. 95 (Woodbridge: Boydell & Brewer, 2005).

Lombard, Peter, *The Sentences*, tr. G. Silano, 4 vols. (Toronto: Pontifical Institute of Mediaeval Studies, 2007–10).

Lumpkin, W. L, and B. J. Leonard, *Baptist Confessions of Faith*, 2nd edn (Valley Forge, Pa.: Judson Press, 2011).

Luther, Martin, *D. Martin Luthers Werke: Kritische Ausgabe. Briefwechsel*, 18 vols. (Weimar: Hermann Böhlaus Nachfolger, 1930–85).

Lyndwood, W., *Provinciale seu Constitutiones Angliae cui adiiciuntur Constitutiones Legatinae D. Othonis et D. Othoboni Cardinalium* (Oxford: Oxford University Press, 1679; repr. Farnborough: Gregg International Publishers, 1968).

MacLure, M., P. Pauls and J. C. Boswell (eds.), *Register of Sermons Preached at Paul's Cross 1534–1642* (Ottawa: Dovehouse Editions, 1989).

Mascall, E. L., *The Christian Universe* (London: Darton, Longman and Todd, 1966).

———, *The Secularisation of Christianity* (London: Darton, Longman and Todd, 1965).

———, *Up and Down in Adria* (London: Faith Press, 1963).

Miller, J., *James II* (New Haven, Conn.: Yale University Press, 2000).

Milton, A., *The British Delegation and the Synod of Dort (1618–1619)* (Woodbridge: Boydell & Brewer, 2005).

Milton, J., *The Works of John Milton*, 18 vols. (New York, N.Y.: Columbia University Press, 1931).

Morehouse, H. J. (ed.), *Extracts from the Diary of the Rev. Robert Meeke* (London: H. G. Bohn, 1874).

Morris, L., *The Atonement: Its Meaning and Significance* (Leicester: Inter-Varsity Press, 1983).

Murray, I. H., *The Reformation of the Church: A Collection of Reformed and Puritan Documents on Church Issues* (London: Banner of Truth Trust, 1965).

Newman, J. H., J. Keble and J. B. Mozley (eds.), *Remains of the Late Richard Hurrell Froude* (London: J. G. & F. Rivington, 1838).

Packer, J. I., *'Fundamentalism' and the Word of God* (London: Inter-Varsity Fellowship, 1958).

Palmer, W., *Notes of a Visit to the Russian Church in the Years 1840, 1841*, ed. J. H. Newman (London: Kegan Paul, 1882).

____, *A Treatise on the Church of Christ*, 2nd rev. edn (London: C. & J. Rivington, 1842).

Pantin, W. A., *The English Church in the Fourteenth Century* (Cambridge: Cambridge University Press, 1955).

Pauck, W. (ed.), *Melanchthon and Bucer* (Philadelphia, Pa.: Westminster Press, 1969).

Pearsall, D., *Piers Plowman* (Liverpool: Liverpool University Press, 2014).

Pelikan, J., and H. T. Lehmann, *Luther's Works*, 55 vols. (St. Louis, Mo.: Concordia Publishing House; Philadelphia, Pa.: Fortress Press, 1955–86).

Perkins, William, *The Works of William Perkins*, 10 vols. (Grand Rapids, Mich.: Reformation Heritage Books, 2014–20).

Powicke, F. M., and C. R. Cheney, *Councils and Synods with Other Documents Relating to the English Church II, A. D. 1205–1313*, 2 vols. (Oxford: Clarendon Press, 1964).

Pusey, E. B., *An Historical Enquiry into the Probable Causes of the Rationalist Character Lately Predominant in the Theology of Germany* (London: C. & J. Rivington, 1828).

Rex, R. (ed.), *Henry VIII Fid. Def., His Defence of the Faith and Its Seven Sacraments* (Sevenoaks: Fisher Press; London: Ducketts Booksellers, 2008).

Roberts, V., *Transgender* (Epsom: The Good Book Company, 2016).

Rose, H. J., *The State of the Protestant Religion in Germany; in a Series of Discourses Preached Before the University of Cambridge* (Cambridge: Deighton & Son, 1825).

Saint Victor, Richard of, 'On the Trinity', in B. T. Coolman and D. M. Coulter (eds.), *Trinity and Creation* (Hyde Park, N.Y.: New City Press, 2011), 195–382.

Schaff, P., *The Creeds of Christendom*, 3 vols. (New York, N.Y.: Harper & Row, 1931).

The Second Prayer Book of King Edward VI, 1552 (London: Church of England, 2015).

Selderhuis, H. J., *Marriage and Divorce in the Thought of Martin Bucer*, Sixteenth Century Essays and Studies 48 (Kirksville, Mo.: Thomas Jefferson University Press, 1999).

Shinners, J., and William J. Dohar (eds.), *Pastors and the Care of Souls in Medieval England* (Notre Dame, Ind.: University of Notre Dame Press, 1998).

Shirley, W. W. (ed.), *Fasciculi Zizianorum Magistri Iohannis Wyclif* (London: Longman, Brown, Green, Longmans, and Roberts, 1858).

Sibbes, R., *Complete Works of Richard Sibbes*, ed. A. B. Grosart, 7 vols. (Edinburgh: J. Nicol, 1862–4; repr. Edinburgh: Banner of Truth Trust, 1983).

Simeon, C., *Horae Homileticae*, 21 vols. (London: Holdsworth and Ball, 1832–3).

Smith, D. M., *The Heads of Religious Houses: England and Wales III. 1377–1540* (Cambridge: Cambridge University Press, 2008).

Smith, D. M., and V. C. M. London (eds.), *The Heads of Religious Houses: England and Wales II. 1216–1377* (Cambridge: Cambridge University Press, 2001).

Snape, M. (ed.), *The Back Parts of War: The YMCA Memoirs and Letters of Barclay Baron, 1915–1919* (Woodbridge: Boydell & Brewer, 2009).

Snoddy, R. (ed.), *James Ussher and a Reformed Episcopal Church: Sermons and Treatises on Ecclesiology* (Leesburg, Va.: Davenant Institute, 2018).

Sommerville, J. P. (ed.), *James VI and I: Political Writings* (Cambridge: Cambridge University Press, 1994).

Stott, J. R. W., *Basic Christianity* (London: Inter-Varsity Fellowship, 1958).

_____, *The Cross of Christ* (Leicester: Inter-Varsity Press, 1986).

Strype, J., *Ecclesiastical Memorials, Relating Chiefly to Religion, and the Reformation of It, and the Emergencies of the Church of England, Under King Henry VIII, King Edward VI, and Queen Mary I*, 3 vols. (Oxford: Clarendon Press, 1822).

Swanton, M., *The Anglo-Saxon Chronicle* (London: J. M. Dent, 1996).

Tanner, N. P., *Decrees of the Ecumenical Councils* (London: Sheed & Ward; Washington, D.C.: Georgetown University Press, 1990).

Taylor, S. (ed.), *From Cranmer to Davidson: A Church of England Miscellany* (Woodbridge: Boydell & Brewer, 1999).

Thiselton, A. C., *Thiselton on Hermeneutics: The Collected Works and New Essays* (Aldershot: Ashgate, 2006).

Thorpe, B. (tr.), *The Homilies of the Anglo-Saxon Church*, 2 vols. (Cambridge: Cambridge University Press, 2013).

Tocqueville, A. de, *The* Ancien Régime, tr. J. Bonner (London: J. M. Dent, 1988).

Trigg, T. D., *The Book of Margery Kempe* (Leominster: Gracewing, 2018).

Twenty-Eighth Annual Report of the Registrar-General of Births, Deaths and Marriages in England (London: Eyre & Spottiswoode, 1867).

Underwood, T. L. (ed.), *The Miscellaneous Works of John Bunyan*, vol. 4 (Oxford: Clarendon Press, 1989).

Van Dixhoorn, C. (ed.), *The Minutes and Papers of the Westminster Assembly 1643–1652*, 5 vols. (Oxford: Oxford University Press, 2012).

Wallis, F., *Bede: The Reckoning of Time* (Liverpool: Liverpool University Press, 1999).

Watson, N., and J. Jenkins (eds.), *The Writings of Julian of Norwich* (Turnhout: Brepols and University Park, Pa.: Pennsylvania State University Press, 2006).

Wendel, F. (ed.), *Martini Buceri Opera Latina XV: De Regno Christi* (Paris: Presses Universitaires de France; Gütersloh: C. Bertelsmann Verlag, 1955).

Wenzel, S., *Preaching in the Age of Chaucer: Selected Sermons in Translation* (Washington, D.C.: Catholic University of America Press, 2008).

Wesley, J., *The Journal of John Wesley*, ed. N. Curnock, 8 vols. (London: Epworth Press, 1931).

Whitelock, D., M. Brett and C. N. L. Brooke (eds.), *Councils and Synods with Other Documents Relating to the English Church I, A. D. 871–1204*, 2 vols. (Oxford: Clarendon Press, 1981).

Wilkins, D., *Concilia Magnae Britanniae et Hiberniae*, 4 vols. (London: Various presses, 1737).

Williamson, P., A. Raffe, S. Taylor and N. Mears (eds.), *National Prayers: Special Worship Since the Reformation*, 3 vols. (Woodbridge: Boydell & Brewer, 2015–20).

Wolfe, D. M. (ed.), *Complete Prose Works of John Milton*, 8 vols. in 10 (New Haven, Conn.: Yale University Press, 1953–82).

Wood, Edmund Gough de Salis, *The Regal Power of the Church, or the Fundamentals of the Canon Law: A Dissertation* (Cambridge: Macmillan and Bowes, 1887).

Woolley, R. M., *The York* Provinciale, *Put Forth by Thomas Wolsey, Archbishop of York, in the Year 1518* (London: Faith Press, 1931).

Wulfstan, *Die* Institutes of Polity, Civil and Ecclesiastical, *ein Werk Erzbischof Wulfstans von York*, ed. K. Jost, 2 vols. (Bern: Francke, 1959).

Ireland

Annála Ríoghachta Éireann = Annals of the Kingdom of Ireland by the Four Masters, from the Earliest Period to the Year 1616, 2nd edn (Dublin: Hodges, Smith, 1856).

Barnard, T., *A New Anatomy of Ireland: The Irish Protestants, 1649–1770* (New Haven, Conn.: Yale University Press, 2003).

Gwynn, A., and R. N. Hadcock, *Medieval Religious Houses: Ireland* (London: Longman, 1970).

The Irish Uprising 1914–1921 (London: The Stationery Office, 2000).

Keating, G., *Foras Feasa ar Éirinn: The History of Ireland*, 4 vols., ed. and tr. D. Comyn and P. S. Dinneen (London: Irish Texts Society, 1902–14).

Kenney, J. F., *The Sources for the Early History of Ireland: Ecclesiastical*, 2nd edn (New York, N.Y.: Columbia University Press, 1968; repr. Dublin: Four Courts Press, 1997).

O'Loughlin, T., *St Patrick: The Man and His Works* (London: SPCK, 1999).

Simms, J. G., *Jacobite Ireland* (London: Routledge & Kegan Paul, 1969; reissued Dublin: Four Courts Press, 2000).

Scotland

Acts and Proceedings of the General Assemblies of the Kirk of Scotland from the Year 1560 Collected from the Most Authentic Manuscripts, Part Third (1593–1618) (Edinburgh: Church of Scotland, 1845).

Acts of the General Assembly of the Church of Scotland, 1638–1842 (Edinburgh: The Edinburgh Printing and Publishing Society, 1843).

Bertie, D. M. B., *Scottish Episcopal Clergy 1689–2000* (Edinburgh: T&T Clark, 2000).

Burns, C., *Calendar of Papal Letters to Scotland of Clement VII of Avignon, 1378–1394* (Edinburgh: Scottish History Society, 1976).

Calderwood, D., *The History of the Church of Scotland from the Beginning of the Reformation, unto the end of the Reign of King James VI* (n.p., 1678).

Cameron, J. K. (ed.), *The First Book of Discipline* (Edinburgh: St Andrew Press, 1972).

Donaldson, G., *Scottish Historical Documents*, corrected edn (Glasgow: Neil Wilson Publishing, 1974).

Easson, D. E., *Medieval Religious Houses: Scotland* (London: Longman, 1957).

Hume, D., *Dialogues Concerning Natural Religion*, ed. N. Kemp-Smith (Oxford: Oxford University Press, 1935).

James VI, *Basilikon Doron* (Edinburgh: Robert Waldegrave, 1599).

Kirk, J., *The Second Book of Discipline* (Edinburgh: St Andrew Press, 1980).

Laing, D. (ed.), *The Works of John Knox*, 6 vols. (Edinburgh: Woodrow Society, 1846–64; repr. Edinburgh: Banner of Truth Trust, 2014).

McMillan, S. (ed.), *The Whole Works of the Late Reverend Thomas Boston*, 12 vols. (Aberdeen: G. & R. King, 1848–52); repr. as *The Complete Works of Thomas Boston*, 12 vols. (Wheaton, Ill.: Richard Owen Roberts, 1980).

Mann, A. J., *James VII: Duke and King of Scots, 1633–1701* (Edinburgh: John Donald, 2014).

Patrick, D., *Statutes of the Scottish Church 1225–1559* (Edinburgh: Edinburgh University Press, 1907).

Smith, T. (ed.), *Letters of the Reverend Samuel Rutherford* (Edinburgh: Oliphant, Anderson and Ferrier, 1881).

Wales

Winterbottom, M., *Gildas: The Ruin of Britain and Other Works* (London: Phillimore, 1978).

Secondary sources

General and England

Allison, C. F., *The Rise of Moralism: The Proclamation of the Gospel from Hooker to Baxter* (London: SPCK, 1966).

Arens, J., A. Buckle, G. Campbell and T. Stratford, *The Richard III Reinterment Liturgies*, Alcuin Club and The Group for Renewal of Worship Joint Liturgical Studies 81 (Norwich: Hymns Ancient & Modern, 2016).

Aston, M., *Lollards and Reformers: Images and Literacy in Late Medieval Religion* (London: The Hambledon Press, 1984).

Atherstone, A., *An Anglican Evangelical Identity Crisis: The* Churchman–Anvil *Affair of 1981–1984* (London: Latimer Trust, 2008).

_____, *Charles Simeon on* The Excellency of the Liturgy, Alcuin Club and The Group for Renewal of Worship Joint Liturgical Studies 72 (Norwich: Hymns Ancient & Modern, 2011).

Atherstone, A., and D. C. Jones (eds.), *The Routledge Research Companion to the History of Evangelicalism* (London: Routledge, 2019).

Atherstone, A., and J. Maiden (eds.), *Evangelicalism and the Church of England in the Twentieth Century: Reform, Resistance and Renewal* (Woodbridge: Boydell Press, 2014).

Atkinson, N., *Richard Hooker and the Authority of Scripture, Tradition and Reason* (Carlisle: Paternoster Press, 1997).

Aubrun, M., *La paroisse en France des origines au XVe siècle* (Paris: Picard, 1988).

Babbage, S. B., *Puritanism and Richard Bancroft* (London: SPCK, 1962).

Barber, M., *The Trial of the Templars* (Cambridge: Cambridge University Press, 1978).

Barker, W., *Puritan Profiles: 54 Influential Puritans at the Time When the Westminster Confession of Faith Was Written* (Fearn: Mentor, 1996).

Barlow, F., *Durham Jurisdictional Peculiars* (London: Geoffrey Cumberledge for Oxford University Press, 1950).

———, *Edward the Confessor* (Berkeley and Los Angeles, Calif.: University of California Press, 1970).

Barr, J., *Fundamentalism* (London: SCM Press, 1977).

Bavin, L., and R. Rees, *Margery Kempe of Lynn* (Peterborough: Upfront Publishing, 2019).

Bell, P. M. H., *Disestablishment in Ireland and Wales* (London: SPCK, 1969).

Bellinger, D. A., and S. Fletcher, *Princes of the Church: A History of the English Cardinals* (Stroud: Sutton Publishing, 2001).

Bennett, G. W., *The Tory Crisis in Church and State 1688–1730: The Career of Francis Atterbury, Bishop of Rochester* (Oxford: Clarendon Press, 1975).

Bernard, G. W., *The King's Reformation* (New Haven, Conn.: Yale University Press, 2005).

———, *The Late Medieval English Church: Vitality and Vulnerability Before the Break with Rome* (New Haven, Conn.: Yale University Press, 2012).

Beza, T., *The Judgement of a Most Reverend and Learned Man from Beyond the Seas, Concerning a Threefold Order of Bishops* (London, 1585?).

Blair, P. H., *The World of Bede* (Cambridge: Cambridge University Press, 1970).

Blet, P., *Le clergé du Grand Siècle en ses Assemblées 1615–1715* (Paris: Cerf, 1995).

Bosher, R. S., *The Making of the Restoration Settlement: The Influence of the Laudians 1649–1662* (London: Dacre Press; Adam & Charles Black, 1951).

Brigden, S., *London and the Reformation*, rev. edn (Oxford: Clarendon Press, 1991).

Brooke, Z. N., *The English Church and the Papacy from the Conquest to the Reign of John*, 2nd edn (Cambridge: Cambridge University Press, 1989).

Brown, C. G., *The Battle for Christian Britain: Sex, Humanists and Secularisation, 1945–1980* (Cambridge: Cambridge University Press, 2019).

＿＿, *Religion and Society in Twentieth-Century Britain* (London: Routledge, 2006).

Brown, G. H., *A Companion to Bede* (Woodbridge: Boydell & Brewer, 2009).

Brown, R., *Church and State in Modern Britain* (London: Routledge, 1991).

Brown, S. J., *Providence and Empire 1815–1914* (London: Pearson Longman, 2008).

Brown, S. J., P. B. Nockles and J. Pereiro (eds.), *The Oxford Handbook of the Oxford Movement* (Oxford: Oxford University Press, 2017).

Brundage, J. A., *Medieval Canon Law* (London: Longman, 1995).

Brydon, M., *The Evolving Reputation of Richard Hooker: An Examination of Responses 1600–1714* (Oxford: Oxford University Press, 2006).

Buchanan, C., *The Hampton Court Conference and the 1604 Book of Common Prayer*, Alcuin Club and The Group for Renewal of Worship Joint Liturgical Studies 68 (Norwich: Hymns Ancient & Modern, 2009).

＿＿, *The Savoy Conference Revisited*, Alcuin Club and The Group for Renewal of Worship Joint Liturgical Studies 54 (Cambridge: Grove Books, 2002).

Buchanan, C., and T. Lloyd, *The Church of England Eucharist 1958–2012*, Alcuin Club and The Group for Renewal of Worship Joint Liturgical Studies 87/88 (Norwich: Hymns Ancient & Modern, 2019).

Buckley, M. J., *At the Origins of Modern Atheism* (New Haven, Conn.: Yale University Press, 1987).

Bullivant, S., *Mass Exodus* (Oxford: Oxford University Press, 2019).

Campbell, W. H., *The Landscape of Pastoral Care in Thirteenth-Century England* (Cambridge: Cambridge University Press, 2018).

Cannadine, D. (ed.), *Westminster Abbey: A Church in History* (London: Paul Mellon Centre and Yale University Press, 2019).

Capp, B. S., *The Fifth Monarchy Men: A Study in Seventeenth-Century English Millenarianism* (London: Faber, 1972).

Carlton, C., *Charles I: The Personal Monarch* (London: Routledge & Kegan Paul, 1983).

Catterall, P., *Labour and the Free Churches 1918–1939* (London: Bloomsbury, 2016).

Chadwick, O., *The Mind of the Oxford Movement* (London: Adam & Charles Black, 1960).

——, *The Victorian Church: Part One. 1829–1859*, 2 vols., 3rd edn (London: SCM Press, 1971).

Cheney, C. R., *From Becket to Langton: English Church Government 1170–1213* (Manchester: Manchester University Press, 1956).

Chibi, A. A., *Henry VIII's Bishops: Diplomats, Administrators, Scholars and Shepherds* (Cambridge: James Clarke, 2003).

Chrimes, S. B., *Henry VII* (New Haven, Conn.: Yale University Press, 1972).

Clifford, A. C., *Atonement and Justification: English Evangelical Theology 1640–1790 – An Evaluation* (Oxford: Clarendon Press, 1990).

Coad, F. R., *A History of the Brethren Movement: Its Origins, Its Worldwide Development and Its Significance for the Present Day* (Exeter: Paternoster Press, 1968).

Coffey, J., *Politics, Religion and the British Revolutions: The Mind of Samuel Rutherford* (Cambridge: Cambridge University Press, 1997).

Cole, A., and A. Galloway, *The Cambridge Companion to Piers Plowman* (Cambridge: Cambridge University Press, 2014).

Collinson, P., *Archbishop Grindal 1519–83: The Struggle for a Reformed Church* (London: Jonathan Cape, 1979).

——, *The Elizabethan Puritan Movement* (London: Jonathan Cape, 1967; Oxford: Clarendon Press, 1990).

——, *The Religion of Protestants: The Church in English Society 1559–1625* (Oxford: Oxford University Press, 1982).

Coppack, G., and M. Aston, *God's Poor Men: The Carthusians in England* (Stroud: Tempus, 2002).

Crawford, A., *The Yorkists: The History of a Dynasty* (London: Continuum, 2007).

Cressy, D., *Charles I and the People of England* (Oxford: Oxford University Press, 2015).

Crosby, E. U., *Bishop and Chapter in Twelfth-Century England: A Study of the* Mensa Episcopalis (Cambridge: Cambridge University Press, 1994).

Cross, R., *Duns Scotus* (Oxford: Oxford University Press, 1999).

Cuillieron, M., *Les Assemblées du clergé et la société ecclésiastique sous le règne de Louis XVI* (Paris: Editions FAC 2000, 2002).

Cust, R., *Charles I: A Political Life* (London: Pearson Longman, 2005).

Daniell, D., *The Bible in English* (New Haven, Conn.: Yale University Press, 2003).

_____, *William Tyndale: A Biography* (New Haven, Conn.: Yale University Press, 1994).

Davies, J., *The Caroline Captivity of the Church: Charles I and the Remoulding of Anglicanism* (Oxford: Clarendon Press, 1992).

Dawley, P. M., *John Whitgift and the English Reformation* (New York, N.Y.: Charles Scribner's Sons, 1954).

DeGregorio, S., *The Cambridge Companion to Bede* (Cambridge: Cambridge University Press, 2010).

Dever, M., *Richard Sibbes: Puritanism and Calvinism in Late Elizabethan and Early Stuart England* (Macon, Ga.: Mercer University Press, 2000).

Dickens, A. G., *The English Reformation*, 2nd edn (London: B. T. Batsford, 1989).

_____, *Late Monasticism and the Reformation* (London: Hambledon Press, 1994).

_____, *Lollards and Protestants in the Diocese of York* (London: The Hambledon Press, 1982).

Dix, G., *The Shape of the Liturgy* (London: A&C Black, 1945).

Dobson, E. J., *The Origins of the* Ancrene Wisse (Oxford: Oxford University Press, 1976).

Dominiak, P. A., *Richard Hooker: The Architecture of Participation* (London: T&T Clark, 2020).

Duffy, E., *The Stripping of the Altars* (New Haven, Conn.: Yale University Press, 1992).

Duggan, A., *Thomas Becket* (London: Bloomsbury Academic, 2004).

Eagleton, T., *Culture and the Death of God* (New Haven, Conn.: Yale University Press, 2014).

Edwards, J., *Mary I: England's Catholic Queen* (New Haven, Conn.: Yale University Press, 2011).

Ellens, J. P., *Religious Routes to Gladstonian Liberalism: The Church Rate Conflict in England and Wales, 1832–1868* (University Park, Pa.: Pennsylvania State University Press, 1994).

Evans, G. R., *John Wyclif: Myth and Reality* (Oxford: Lion Hudson, 2005).

_____, 'Thomas of Chobham on Preaching and Exegesis', *Recherches de Théologie Ancienne et Médiévale* 52 (1985), 159–170.

Everett, H., P. Bradshaw and C. Buchanan, *Coronations Past, Present and Future*, Alcuin Club and The Group for Renewal of Worship Joint Liturgical Studies 38 (Cambridge: Grove Books, 1997).

Faulkner, R. K., *Richard Hooker and the Politics of a Christian England* (Berkeley, Calif.: University of California Press, 1981).

Fincham, K., *Prelate as Pastor: The Episcopate of James I* (Oxford: Clarendon Press, 1990).

——, 'The Restoration of the Altars in the 1630s', *Historical Journal* 44.4 (2001), 919–940.

Flint, B., *Edith the Fair: Visionary of Walsingham* (Leominster: Gracewing Press, 2015).

Foakes-Jackson, F. J., K. Lake and H. J. Cadbury (eds.), *The Beginnings of Christianity*, pt 1: *The Acts of the Apostles*, 5 vols. (London: Macmillan, 1920–33).

Foot, S., *Athelstan: The First King of England* (New Haven, Conn.: Yale University Press, 2011).

Furse-Roberts, D., *The Making of a Tory Evangelical: Lord Shaftesbury and the Evolving Character of Victorian Evangelicalism* (Eugene, Oreg.: Pickwick Publications, 2019).

Gant, A., *'O Sing unto the Lord': A History of English Church Music* (London: Profile Books, 2015).

Gay, P., *The Enlightenment: An Interpretation*, 2 vols. (New York, N.Y.: Norton, 1966).

Gibson, W., *James II and the Trial of the Seven Bishops* (Basingstoke: Palgrave Macmillan, 2009).

Gibson, W., and J. Begiato, *Sex and the Church in the Long Eighteenth Century* (London: I. B. Tauris, 2017).

Gradon, M., *The Making of Piers Plowman* (London: Longman, 1990).

Grass, T., *Gathering in His Name: The Story of the Open Brethren in Britain and Ireland* (Milton Keynes: Paternoster Press, 2006).

Gray, D., *The 1927–28 Prayer Book Crisis*, Alcuin Club and The Group for Renewal of Worship Joint Liturgical Studies 60 and 61 (Norwich: SCM-Canterbury Press, 2005–6).

Gribben, C., *An Introduction to John Owen: A Christian Vision for Every Stage of Life* (Wheaton, Ill.: Crossway, 2020).

——, *John Owen and English Puritanism: Experiences of Defeat* (Oxford: Oxford University Press, 2016).

——, *The Puritan Millennium: Literature and Theology 1550–1682*, rev. edn (Carlisle: Paternoster Press, 2008).

Griffith Thomas, W. H., *The Catholic Faith: A Manual of Instruction for Members of the Church of England* (London: Hodder & Stoughton, 1904).

Gruenter, C. A., *Piers Plowman and the Poetics of Enigma* (Notre Dame, Ind.: University of Notre Dame Press, 2017).

Gunther, K., *Reformation Unbound: Protestant Visions of Reform in England, 1525–1590* (Cambridge: Cambridge University Press, 2014).

Guy, J., *Thomas More: A Very Brief History* (London: SPCK, 2017).

Gwyn, P., *The King's Cardinal: The Rise and Fall of Thomas Wolsey* (London: Barrie & Jenkins, 1990).

Haag, M., *The Templars: History and Myth* (London: Profile Books, 2008).

Hadjiantoniou, G. A., *Protestant Patriarch* (Richmond, Va.: John Knox Press, 1961).

Hamlin, H. (ed.), *The Cambridge Companion to Shakespeare and Religion* (Cambridge: Cambridge University Press, 2019).

Hampton, S., *Anti-Arminians: The Anglican Reformed Tradition from Charles II to George I* (Oxford: Oxford University Press, 2008).

Hanley, C., *Matilda: Empress, Queen, Warrior* (New Haven, Conn.: Yale University Press, 2019).

Hazard, P., *The European Mind 1680–1715* (London: Hollis & Carter, 1953).

Heal, F., *Reformation in Britain and Ireland* (Oxford: Oxford University Press, 2003).

Hebblethwaite, D., *Liturgical Revision in the Church of England 1984–2004: The Working of the Liturgical Commission*, Alcuin Club and The Group for Renewal of Worship Joint Liturgical Studies 57 (Cambridge: Grove Books, 2004).

Helmholz, R. H., *The* ius commune *in England: Four Studies* (Oxford: Oxford University Press, 2001).

———, *The Oxford History of the Laws of England*, vol. 1: *The Canon Law and Ecclesiastical Jurisdiction from 597 to the 1640s* (Oxford: Oxford University Press, 2004).

———, *The Spirit of Classical Canon Law* (Athens, Ga.: University of Georgia Press, 1996).

Hill, C., *Economic Problems of the Church from Archbishop Whitgift to the Long Parliament* (Oxford: Clarendon Press, 1956).

———, *The Experience of Defeat: Milton and Some Contemporaries* (London: Faber & Faber, 1984).

———, *Milton and the English Revolution* (London: Faber & Faber, 1977).

———, *Society and Puritanism in Pre-Revolutionary England* (London: Secker & Warburg, 1964).

———, *A Turbulent, Seditious and Factious People: John Bunyan and His Church* (Oxford: Clarendon Press, 1988).

Hill, C., B. Reay and W. M. Lamont, *The World of the Muggletonians* (London: Temple Smith, 1983).

Hill, M., *Ecclesiastical Law*, 4th edn (Oxford: Oxford University Press, 2018).

Hilton, B., *The Age of Atonement: The Influence of Evangelicalism on Social and Economic Thought 1795–1865* (Oxford: Clarendon Press, 1991).

Hindmarsh, D. B., *The Evangelical Conversion Narrative: Spiritual Autobiography in Early Modern England* (Oxford: Oxford University Press, 2005).

——, *John Newton and the English Evangelical Tradition* (Oxford: Clarendon Press, 1996).

——, *The Spirit of Early Evangelicalism: True Religion in a Modern World* (Oxford: Oxford University Press, 2018).

Hinnebusch, W. A., *A History of the Dominican Order*, 2 vols. (New York, N.Y.: Alba House, 1966–72).

Hooykaas, R., *Religion and the Rise of Modern Science* (Edinburgh: Scottish Academic Press, 1973).

Horst, I. B., *Radical Brethren: Anabaptists and the English Revolution to 1558* (Nieuwkoop: B. De Graaf, 1972).

Houlbrooke, R., *Church Courts and the People During the English Reformation 1520–1570* (Oxford: Oxford University Press, 1979).

Hudson, A., *The Premature Reformation: Wycliffite Tracts and Lollard History* (Oxford: Oxford University Press, 1988).

Hughes, P. E., *Theology of the English Reformers*, 3rd edn (Abington, Pa.: Horseradish, 1997).

Hylson-Smith, K., *Evangelicals in the Church of England 1734–1984* (Edinburgh: T&T Clark, 1988).

——, *High Churchmanship in the Church of England from the Sixteenth Century to the Late Twentieth Century* (Edinburgh: T&T Clark, 1993).

Israel, J. I., *The Enlightenment That Failed: Ideas, Revolution and Democratic Defeat, 1748–1830* (Oxford: Oxford University Press, 2019).

——, *Radical Enlightenment: Philosophy and the Making of Modernity 1650–1750* (Oxford: Oxford University Press, 2001).

Jackson, B., and R. Saunders (eds.), *Making Thatcher's Britain* (Cambridge: Cambridge University Press, 2012).

Jacobs, H. E., *The Lutheran Movement in England During the Reigns of Henry VIII and Edward VI and Its Literary Monuments* (Philadelphia, Pa.: Frederick, 1890).

Jarrett, B., *The English Dominicans* (London: Burns, Oates & Washbourne, 1921).

Jeanes, G. P., *Signs of God's Promise: Thomas Cranmer's Sacramental Theology and the Book of Common Prayer* (London: T&T Clark, 2008).

Jenkins, G. W., *John Jewel and the English National Church: The Dilemmas of an Erastian Reformer* (Aldershot: Ashgate, 2006).

Jennings, D. A., *The Revival of the Convocation of York, 1837–1861*, Borthwick Papers 47 (York: Borthwick Institute, 1975).

Kay, B., *Trinitarian Spirituality: John Owen and the Doctrine of God in Western Devotion* (Milton Keynes: Paternoster Press, 2007).

Kelly, J. N. D., *The Athanasian Creed* (London: A&C Black, 1964).

_____, *Early Christian Creeds*, 3rd edn (London: Longman, 1972).

_____, *Early Christian Doctrines*, 5th edn (London: A&C Black, 1977).

Kenyon, J. P., *The Popish Plot* (London: William Heinemann, 1972; repr. London: Phoenix Press, 2000).

Killeen, K., H. Smith and R. Willie (eds.), *The Oxford History of the Bible in Early Modern England, c. 1530–1700* (Oxford: Oxford University Press, 2015).

King, E., *King Stephen* (New Haven, Conn.: Yale University Press, 2010).

Knight, F., *The Nineteenth-Century Church and English Society* (Cambridge: Cambridge University Press, 1995).

Lahey, S. E., *John Wyclif* (Oxford: Oxford University Press, 2009).

Lake, P., *Anglicans and Puritans? Presbyterianism and English Conformist Thought from Whitgift to Hooker* (London: Allen & Unwin, 1988).

_____, *Moderate Puritans and the Elizabethan Church* (Cambridge: Cambridge University Press, 1982).

Lamont, W., *Last Witnesses: The Muggletonian History 1652–1979* (London: Routledge, 2006).

_____, *Puritanism and Historical Controversy* (London: University College London Press, 1996).

Lane, J. (E. Dakers), *Titus Oates* (London: A. Dakers, 1949; repr. London: Greenwood Press, 1971).

Larsen, T., *Friends of Religious Equality: Nonconformist Politics in Mid-Victorian England* (Milton Keynes: Paternoster Press, 1999).

Lawrence, C. H., *The Friars: The Impact of the Early Mendicant Movement on Western Society* (London: Longman, 1994).

_____ (ed.), *The English Church and the Papacy in the Middle Ages*, rev. edn (Stroud: Sutton Publishing, 1999).

Le Goff, J., *The Birth of Purgatory* (Chicago, Ill.: University of Chicago Press, 1984).

Lehmberg, S., *The Reformation Parliament 1529–1536* (Cambridge: Cambridge University Press, 1970).

Levy, T., *Historical Biblical Archaeology and the Future: The New Pragmatism* (London: Routledge, 2017).

Lionarons, J. T., *The Homiletic Writings of Archbishop Wulfstan: A Critical Study* (Woodbridge: Boydell & Brewer, 2010).

Littlejohn, W. B., *The Peril and Promise of Christian Liberty: Richard Hooker, the Puritans, and Protestant Political Theology* (Grand Rapids, Mich.: Eerdmans, 2017).

Littlejohn, W. B., and S. N. Kindred-Barnes, *Richard Hooker and Reformed Orthodoxy* (Göttingen: Vandenhoeck & Ruprecht, 2017).

Liu, T., *Discord in Zion: The Puritan Divines and the Puritan Revolution 1640–1660* (Den Haag: Nijhoff, 1973).

Loades, D. M., *The Oxford Martyrs* (London: B. T. Batsford, 1970).

Long, R. J., and M. O'Carroll, *The Life and Works of Richard Fishacre, OP: Prolegomena to the Edition of His Commentary on the Sentences* (Munich: Verlag der Bayerischen Akademie der Wissenschaften, 1999).

Lossky, N., *Lancelot Andrewes the Preacher (1555–1626): The Origins of the Mystical Theology of the Church of England* (Oxford: Clarendon Press, 1991).

Loyn, H. R., *The English Church 940–1154* (Harlow: Longman, 2000).

Maas, K. D., *The Reformation and Robert Barnes* (Woodbridge: Boydell & Brewer, 2010).

MacCulloch, D., *Thomas Cranmer*, rev. edn (New Haven, Conn.: Yale University Press, 2016).

_____, *Thomas Cromwell: A Life* (London: Allen Lane, 2018).

_____, *Tudor Church Militant: Edward VI and the Protestant Reformation* (London: Penguin Books, 1999).

Macek, E. A., *The Loyal Opposition: Tudor Traditionalist Polemics, 1535–1558* (New York, N.Y.: Peter Lang, 1996).

McEntegart, R., *Henry VIII, the League of Schmalkalden, and the English Reformation* (London: Royal Historical Society, 2002).

McEntire, S. J., *Margery Kempe: A Book of Essays* (London: Routledge, 2019).

McEvoy, J., *Robert Grosseteste* (Oxford: Oxford University Press, 2000).

McGowan, A. T. B., *The Federal Theology of Thomas Boston* (Carlisle: Paternoster Press, 1997).

McGregor, J. F., and B. Reay (eds.), *Radical Religion in the English Revolution* (Oxford: Oxford University Press, 1984).

Machin, G. I. T., *Politics and the Churches in Great Britain 1869 to 1921* (Oxford: Clarendon Press, 1987).

McManners, J., *Church and Society in Eighteenth-Century France*, 2 vols. (Oxford: Clarendon Press, 1998).

McNiven, P., *Heresy and Politics in the Reign of Henry IV: The Burning of John Badby* (Woodbridge: Boydell Press, 1987).

Maltby, J., *Prayer Book and People in Elizabethan and Early Stuart England* (Cambridge: Cambridge University Press, 1998).

Manning, R. R., and M. Byrne (eds.), *Science and Religion in the Twenty-first Century: The Boyle Lectures 2004–2013* (London: SCM Press, 2013).

Manwaring, R., *From Controversy to Co-Existence: Evangelicals in the Church of England 1914–1980* (Cambridge: Cambridge University Press, 1985).

Marchant, R. A., *The Church Under the Law: Justice, Administration and Discipline in the Diocese of York 1560–1640* (Cambridge: Cambridge University Press, 1969).

Marrin, A., *The Last Crusade: The Church of England in the First World War* (Durham, N.C.: University of North Carolina Press, 1974).

Marsh, C. W., *The Family of Love in English Society, 1550–1630* (Cambridge: Cambridge University Press, 1994).

Marshall, P., *Heretics and Believers* (New Haven, Conn.: Yale University Press, 2017).

Martin, R. P., *A Guide to the Puritans* (Edinburgh: Banner of Truth Trust, 1997).

Mayer, T. F., *Reginald Pole: Prince and Prophet* (Cambridge: Cambridge University Press, 2000).

Mayr-Harting, H., *Religion, Politics and Society in Britain 1066–1272* (Harlow: Pearson, 2011).

Milton, A., *Laudian and Royalist Polemic in Seventeenth-Century England: The Career and Writings of Peter Heylyn* (Manchester: Manchester University Press, 2007).

Moore, J. D., *English Hypothetical Universalism: John Preston and the Softening of Reformed Theology* (Grand Rapids, Mich.: Eerdmans, 2007).

Moorman, J. R. H., *A History of the Church in England*, 3rd edn (London: A&C Black, 1973).

———, *A History of the Franciscan Order* (Oxford: Clarendon Press, 1968).

Morgan, J., *Godly Learning: Puritan Attitudes Towards Reason, Learning and Education, 1560–1640* (Cambridge: Cambridge University Press, 1986).

Mortimer, I., *The Fears of Henry IV: The Life of England's Self-Made King* (London: Jonathan Cape, 2007).

Mortimer, S., *Reason and Religion in the English Revolution: The Challenge of Socinianism* (Cambridge: Cambridge University Press, 2010).

Mühling, A., and P. Opitz (eds.), *Reformierte Bekenntnisschriften*, 3 vols. in 8 (Neukirchen-Vluyn: Neukirchener Verlag, 2002–16).

Muller, R. A., *Grace and Freedom: William Perkins and the Early Modern Reformed Understanding of Free Choice and Divine Grace* (Oxford: Oxford University Press, 2020).

Noble, T. A., *Tyndale House and Fellowship: The First Sixty Years* (Leicester: Inter-Varsity Press, 2006).

Nockles, P. B., *The Oxford Movement in Context: Anglican High Churchmanship 1760–1857* (Cambridge: Cambridge University Press, 1994).

Norton, D., *A Textual History of the King James Version* (Cambridge: Cambridge University Press, 2005).

Null, A., *Thomas Cranmer's Doctrine of Repentance* (Oxford: Oxford University Press, 2000).

Oberman, H. A., *Luther: Man Between God and the Devil* (London: Fontana, 1993).

Orchard, S., and J. H. Y. Briggs, *The Sunday School Movement: Studies in the Growth and Decline of Sunday Schools* (Milton Keynes: Paternoster Press, 2007).

Outhwaite, R. B., *The Rise and Fall of the English Ecclesiastical Courts, 1500–1860* (Cambridge: Cambridge University Press, 2006).

———, *Scandal in the Church: Dr Edward Drax Free, 1764–1843* (London: Hambledon Press, 1997).

Park, T., *The Reform Bishops 1828–1840: A Biographical Study* (St Bees: St Bega Press, 2016).

Partington, A., *Church and State: The Contribution of the Church of England Bishops to the House of Lords During the Thatcher Years* (Milton Keynes: Paternoster Press, 2006).

Patterson, N., *Ecclesiastical Law, Clergy and Laity: A History of Legal Discipline and the Anglican Church* (Abingdon: Routledge, 2019).

Patterson, W. B., *King James VI and I and the Reunion of Christendom* (Cambridge: Cambridge University Press, 1997).

———, *William Perkins and the Making of a Protestant England* (Oxford: Oxford University Press, 2014).

Paul, R. S., *The Assembly of the Lord* (Edinburgh: T&T Clark, 1985).

Pearson, A. F. S., *Thomas Cartwright and Elizabethan Puritanism 1535–1603* (Cambridge: Cambridge University Press, 1966).

Pettegree, A., *Foreign Protestant Communities in Sixteenth-Century London* (Oxford: Oxford University Press, 1986).

Pfaff, R. W., *The Liturgy in Medieval England: A History* (Cambridge: Cambridge University Press, 2009).

Phillips, H., *Chaucer and Religion* (Woodbridge: Boydell & Brewer, 2010).

Pierce, W., *An Historical Introduction to the Marprelate Tracts: A Chapter in the Evolution of Religious and Civil Liberty in England* (New York, N.Y.: E. P. Dutton, 1909).

Pounds, N. J. G., *A History of the English Parish* (Cambridge: Cambridge University Press, 2000).

Powicke, F. M., *Stephen Langton* (Oxford: Clarendon Press, 1928).

Prestige, G. L., *The Life of Charles Gore: A Great Englishman* (London: William Heinemann, 1935).

Raedts, P., *Richard Rufus of Cornwall and the Tradition of Oxford Theology* (Oxford: Clarendon Press, 1987).

Ramirez, J., *Julian of Norwich: A Very Brief History* (London: SPCK, 2016).

Reardon, B. M. G., *From Coleridge to Gore* (London: Longman, 1971; repr. as *Religious Thought in the Victorian Age: A Survey from Coleridge to Gore* (London: Longman, 1980).

Redgate, A. E., *Religion, Politics and Society in Britain, 800–1066* (Abingdon: Routledge, 2014).

Redworth, G., *In Defence of the Church Catholic: The Life of Stephen Gardiner* (Oxford: Basil Blackwell, 1990).

Reeves, A., *Religious Education in Thirteenth-Century England* (Leiden: Brill, 2015).

Reilly, T., *Cromwell: An Honourable Enemy. The Untold Story of the Cromwellian Invasion of Ireland* (London: Phoenix Press, 1999).

Reventlow, H. G. von, *The Authority of the Bible and the Rise of the Modern World* (London: SCM Press, 1984).

Rex, R., *The Lollards* (Basingstoke: Palgrave, 2002).

———, *The Theology of John Fisher* (Cambridge: Cambridge University Press, 1991).

Robins, W., *Sacred and Profane in Chaucer and Late Medieval Literature* (Toronto: University of Toronto Press, 2010).

Rogers, T. G., *Liberal Evangelicalism: An Interpretation by Members of the Church of England* (London: Hodder & Stoughton, 1923).

Roper, L., *Martin Luther: Renegade and Prophet* (London: The Bodley Head, 2016).

Rosemann, P. W., *Peter Lombard* (Oxford: Oxford University Press, 2004).

Rubin, M., *Corpus Christi: The Eucharist in Late Medieval Culture* (Cambridge: Cambridge University Press, 1991).

Runciman, S., *The Great Church in Captivity* (Cambridge: Cambridge University Press, 1968).

Rupp, E. G., *Religion in England 1688–1791* (Oxford: Clarendon Press, 1986).

Ryrie, A., *The Age of Reformation: The Tudor and Stewart Realms 1485–1603*, 2nd edn (London: Routledge, 2017).

―――, *The Gospel and Henry VIII: Evangelicals in the Early English Reformation* (Cambridge: Cambridge University Press, 2003).

Sagovsky, N., *On God's Side: A Life of George Tyrrell* (Oxford: Clarendon Press, 1990).

Sayers, J. E., *Papal Judges Delegate in the Province of Canterbury 1198–1254* (Oxford: Oxford University Press, 1971).

Scarisbrick, J. J., *Henry VIII* (New Haven, Conn.: Yale University Press, 1997).

Scase, W., *Piers Plowman and the New Anticlericalism* (Cambridge: Cambridge University Press, 1989).

Seaward, P., *The Cavalier Parliament and the Reconstruction of the Old Regime 1661–1667* (Cambridge: Cambridge University Press, 1989).

Secor, P. B., *Richard Hooker, Prophet of Anglicanism* (London: Burns & Oates, 1999).

Shagan, E., *The Birth of Modern Belief: Faith and Judgment from the Middle Ages to the Enlightenment* (Princeton, N.J.: Princeton University Press, 2019).

Sharpe, K., *The Personal Rule of Charles I* (New Haven, Conn.: Yale University Press, 1992).

Shuffelton, F., *Thomas Hooker (1586–1647)* (Princeton, N.J.: Princeton University Press, 1977).

Smalley, B., *English Friars and Antiquity in the Early Fourteenth Century* (Oxford: Oxford University Press, 1960).

―――, *The Study of the Bible in the Middle Ages*, 3rd edn (Oxford: Basil Blackwell, 1984).

Smith, J. D., *The Eucharistic Doctrine of the Later Non-Jurors: A Revisionist View of the Eighteenth-Century Usages Controversy*, Alcuin Club and The Group for Renewal of Worship Joint Liturgical Studies 46 (Cambridge: Grove Books, 2000).

Smith, M. G., *The Church Courts 1680–1840: From Canon to Ecclesiastical Law* (Lewiston, N.Y.: Edwin Mellen Press, 2006).

Smith, W., *The Use of Hereford: A Medieval Diocesan Rite Reconsidered*, Alcuin Club and The Group for Renewal of Worship Joint Liturgical Studies 89 (Norwich: Hymns Ancient & Modern, 2020).

Smyth, A. P., *Alfred the Great* (Oxford: Oxford University Press, 1995).

Smyth, J., *In this Sign Conquer: The Story of the Army Chaplains* (London: Mowbray, 1968).

Southern, R. W., *Robert Grosseteste: The Growth of an English Mind in Medieval Europe*, 2nd edn (Oxford: Clarendon Press, 1992).

Spurlock, R. S., *Cromwell and Scotland: Conquest and Religion 1650–1660* (Edinburgh: John Donald, 2007).

Spurr, J., *English Puritanism 1603–1689* (Basingstoke: Macmillan, 1998).

_____, *The Post-Reformation 1603–1714* (Harlow: Pearson, 2006).

_____, *The Restoration Church of England 1646–1689* (New Haven, Conn.: Yale University Press, 1991).

Squibb, G. D., *Doctors' Commons: A History of the College of Advocates and Doctors of Law* (Oxford: Clarendon Press, 1977).

Starkie, A., *The Church of England and the Bangorian Controversy, 1716–1721* (Woodbridge: Boydell & Brewer, 2007).

Swanson, R. N., *Church and Society in Late Medieval England* (Oxford: Basil Blackwell, 1989).

Tapsell, G. (ed.), *The Later Stuart Church 1660–1714* (Manchester: Manchester University Press, 2012).

Thomas, A., *Piers Plowman and the Reinvention of Church Law in the Middle Ages* (Toronto: University of Toronto Press, 2019).

Thomas, K., *Religion and the Decline of Magic* (London: Weidenfeld & Nicolson, 1971).

Thompson, A. H., *The English Clergy and Their Organization in the Later Middle Ages* (Oxford: Clarendon Press, 1947).

Till, B., *York Against Durham: The Guardianship of the Spiritualities in the Diocese of Durham*, Sede Vacante, Borthwick Papers 84 (York: Borthwick Institute, 1993).

Toon, P., *God's Statesman: The Life and Work of John Owen* (Exeter: Paternoster Press, 1971).

Townend, M. (ed.), *Wulfstan, Archbishop of York: The Proceedings of the Second Alcuin Conference* (Turnhout: Brepols, 2004).

Trevor-Roper, H., *Archbishop Laud 1573–1645*, 3rd edn (Basingstoke: Macmillan, 1988).

Trueman, C. R., *The Claims of Truth: John Owen's Trinitarian Theology* (Carlisle: Paternoster Press, 1998).

_____, *Luther's Legacy: Salvation and the English Reformers, 1525–1556* (Oxford: Oxford University Press, 1994).

Turner, F. M., *John Henry Newman: The Challenge to Evangelical Religion* (New Haven, Conn.: Yale University Press, 2002).

Tyacke, N., *Anti-Calvinists: The Rise of English Arminianism c. 1590–1640* (Oxford: Clarendon Press, 1987).

Usher, R. G., *The Rise and Fall of the High Commission* (Oxford: Clarendon Press, 1913).

Van Nieuwenhove, R., *An Introduction to Medieval Theology* (Cambridge: Cambridge University Press, 2012).

Voak, N., *Richard Hooker and Reformed Theology: A Study of Reason, Will and Grace* (Oxford: Oxford University Press, 2003).

Waldron, J., *God, Locke, and Equality: Christian Foundations in Locke's Political Thought* (Cambridge: Cambridge University Press, 2002).

Wallace-Hadrill, J. M., *Bede's Ecclesiastical History of the English People: A Historical Commentary* (Oxford: Clarendon Press, 1988).

Walsh, K., *A Fourteenth-Century Scholar and Primate: Richard FitzRalph in Oxford, Avignon and Armagh* (Oxford: Clarendon Press, 1981).

Walsham, A., *Church Papists: Catholicism, Conformity and Confessional Polemic in Early Modern England* (Woodbridge: Boydell & Brewer, 1993).

———, *Providence in Early Modern England* (Oxford: Oxford University Press, 1999).

———, *The Reformation of the Landscape: Religion, Identity and Memory in Early Modern Britain and Ireland* (Oxford: Oxford University Press, 2011).

Ward, B., *The Venerable Bede* (London: Geoffrey Chapman, 1990).

Ward, W. R., *Early Evangelicalism: A Global Intellectual History, 1670–1789* (Cambridge: Cambridge University Press, 2006).

Warner, R., *Reinventing English Evangelicalism, 1966–2001: A Theological and Sociological Study* (Milton Keynes: Paternoster Press, 2007).

Wellings, M., *Evangelicals Embattled: Responses of Evangelicals in the Church of England to Ritualism, Darwinism and Theological Liberalism 1890–1930* (Carlisle: Paternoster Press, 2003).

Westerholm, S., *Perspectives Old and New on Paul: The 'Lutheran' Paul and His Critics* (Grand Rapids, Mich.: Eerdmans, 2004).

Whisenant, J. C., *A Fragile Unity: Anti-Ritualism and the Division of Anglican Evangelicalism in the Nineteenth Century* (Carlisle: Paternoster Press, 2003).

Whiting, M. S., *Luther in English: The Influence of His Theology of Law and Gospel on Early English Evangelicals (1525–35)* (Eugene, Oreg.: Pickwick Press, 2010).

Yates, N., *Eighteenth-Century Britain 1714–1815* (Harlow: Pearson Education, 2008).

Yorke, B., *The Conversion of Britain 600–800* (Harlow: Pearson, 2006).

Young, M. B., *Charles I* (Basingstoke: Macmillan, 1997).

Ireland

Barnard, T. C., *Cromwellian Ireland: English Government and Reform in Ireland 1649–1660* (Oxford: Clarendon Press, 1975).

Barrett, T., *Ireland: A History* (Cambridge: Cambridge University Press, 2010).

Bowen, D., *Paul Cardinal Cullen and the Shaping of Modern Irish Catholicism* (Dublin: Gill & Macmillan, 1983).

_____, *The Protestant Crusade in Ireland, 1800–1870* (Dublin: Gill & Macmillan, 1978).

_____, *Souperism: Myth or Reality?* (Cork: Mercier Press, 1970).

Brady, C., *The Chief Governors: The Rise and Fall of Reform Government in Tudor Ireland, 1536–1588* (Cambridge: Cambridge University Press, 1994).

Burke, W. P., *The Irish Priests in the Penal Times (1660–1760)* (Shannon: Irish University Press, 1969).

Cahill, T., *How the Irish Saved Civilization* (London: Hodder & Stoughton, 1996).

Canny, N., *Making Ireland British 1580–1650* (Oxford: Oxford University Press, 2001).

Carney, J., *The Problem of St Patrick* (Dublin: Dublin Institute for Advanced Studies, 1973).

Charles-Edwards, T., *Early Christian Ireland* (Cambridge: Cambridge University Press, 2000).

Clarke, A., *The Old English in Ireland, 1625–42* (Dublin: Four Courts Press, 2000).

Connolly, S. J., *Contested Island: Ireland 1460–1630* (Oxford: Oxford University Press, 2007).

_____, *Divided Kingdom* (Oxford: Oxford University Press, 2008).

_____, *Religion, Law and Power: The Making of Protestant Ireland 1660–1760* (Oxford: Clarendon Press, 1992).

Crawford, J. G., *Anglicizing the Government of Ireland: The Irish Privy Council and the Expansion of Tudor Rule, 1556–1578* (Dublin: Irish Academic Press, 1993).

_____, *A Star Chamber Court in Ireland: The Court of Castle Chamber, 1571–1641* (Dublin: Four Courts Press, 2005).

Cunningham, B., *The Annals of the Four Masters: Irish History, Kingship and Society in the Early Seventeenth Century* (Dublin: Four Courts Press, 2010).

_____, *The World of Geoffrey Keating: History, Myth and Religion in Seventeenth-Century Ireland* (Dublin: Four Courts Press, 2000).

Downham, C., *Medieval Ireland* (Cambridge: Cambridge University Press, 2018).

Dudley Edwards, R., *The Seven: The Lives and Legacies of the Founding Fathers of the Irish Republic* (London: Oneworld, 2016).

Ellis, S. G., *Ireland in the Age of the Tudors, 1447–1603* (London: Longman, 1998).

Fauske, C. J., *Jonathan Swift and the Church of Ireland 1710–1724* (Dublin: Irish Academic Press, 2002).

FitzPatrick, E., and R. Gillespie, *The Parish in Medieval and Early Modern Ireland: Community, Territory and Building* (Dublin: Four Courts Press, 2006).

Flanagan, M. T., *The Transformation of the Irish Church in the Twelfth Century* (Woodbridge: Boydell Press, 2010).

Flechner, R., *St Patrick Retold: The Legend and History of Ireland's Patron Saint* (Princeton, N.J.: Princeton University Press, 2019).

Ford, A., *James Ussher: Theology, History and Politics in Early Modern Ireland and England* (Oxford: Oxford University Press, 2007).

_____, *The Protestant Reformation in Ireland 1590–1641* (Dublin: Four Courts Press, 1997).

Ford, A., and J. McCafferty (eds.), *The Origins of Sectarianism in Early Modern Ireland* (Cambridge: Cambridge University Press, 2005).

Forrestal, A., *Catholic Synods in Ireland, 1600–1690* (Dublin: Four Courts Press, 1998).

Foster, R. F., *Vivid Faces: The Revolutionary Generation in Ireland 1890–1923* (London: Penguin Books, 2014).

Gougaud, L., *Christianity in Celtic Lands: A History of the Churches of the Celts, Their Origin, Their Development, Influence and Mutual Relations* (Dublin: Four Courts Press, 1992).

Gribben, C., *God's Irishmen: Theological Debates in Cromwellian Ireland* (Oxford: Oxford University Press, 2007).

_____, *The Irish Puritans: James Ussher and the Reformation of the Church* (Auburn, Mass.: Evangelical Press USA, 2003).

Gwynn, A., *The Irish Church in the Eleventh and Twelfth Centuries* (Dublin: Four Courts Press, 1992).

Gwynn, A., and R. N. Hadcock, *Medieval Religious Houses: Ireland* (London: Longman, 1970).

Hanson, R. P. C., *St Patrick: His Origins and Career* (Oxford: Clarendon Press, 1968).

Holmes, F., *The Presbyterian Church in Ireland: A Popular History* (Dublin: Columba Press, 2000).

Jefferies, H. A., *Priests and Prelates of Armagh in the Age of Reformations 1518–1558* (Dublin: Four Courts Press, 1997).

Kearney, H., *Strafford in Ireland 1633–41: A Study in Absolutism* (Cambridge: Cambridge University Press, 1959).

Kerrigan, C., *Father Mathew and the Irish Temperance Movement, 1838–1849* (Cork: Cork University Press, 1992).

Knox, R. B., *James Ussher Archbishop of Armagh* (Cardiff: University of Wales Press, 1967).

Laffan, M., *The Resurrection of Ireland: The Sinn Féin Party 1916–1923* (Cambridge: Cambridge University Press, 1999).

Larkin, E., *The Consolidation of the Roman Catholic Church in Ireland, 1860–1870* (Chapel Hill, N.C.: University of North Carolina Press, 1987).

——, *The Making of the Roman Catholic Church in Ireland, 1850–1860* (Chapel Hill, N.C.: University of North Carolina Press, 1980).

Lenihan, P., *Consolidating Conquest: Ireland 1603–1727* (London: Routledge, 2008).

Lock, F. P., *Edmund Burke*, 2 vols. (Oxford: Clarendon Press, 1998–2006).

Lydon, J., *The Lordship of Ireland in the Middle Ages*, 2nd edn (Dublin: Four Courts Press, 2003).

Lysaght, M., *Father Theobald Mathew OFM Cap.: The Apostle of Temperance* (Blackrock: Four Courts Press, 1983).

McCafferty, J., *The Reconstruction of the Church of Ireland: Bishop Bramhall and the Laudian Reforms, 1633–1641* (Cambridge: Cambridge University Press, 2007).

MacCarthy-Morrogh, M., *The Munster Plantation: English Migration to Southern Ireland 1583–1641* (Oxford: Oxford University Press, 1986).

Nicholls, K. W., *Gaelic and Gaelicized Ireland in the Middle Ages*, 2nd edn (Dublin: Lilliput Press, 2003).

Ó Cróinín, D., *Early Modern Ireland 400–1200* (Harlow: Longman, 1995).

Ó Siochrú, M., *Confederate Ireland 1642–1649: A Constitutional and Political Analysis* (Dublin: Four Courts Press, 1999).

——, *God's Executioner: Oliver Cromwell and the Conquest of Ireland* (London: Faber & Faber, 2008).

Richardson, H. G., and G. O. Sayles, *The Irish Parliament in the Middle Ages*, 2nd edn (Philadelphia, Pa.: University of Pennsylvania Press, 1962).

Seymour, St J. D., *The Puritans in Ireland (1647–1661)* (Oxford: Clarendon Press, 1921).

Snoddy, R., *The Soteriology of James Ussher: The Act and Object of Saving Faith* (Oxford: Oxford University Press, 2014).

Tanner, M., *Ireland's Holy Wars: The Struggle for a Nation's Soul 1500–2000* (New Haven, Conn.: Yale University Press, 2001).

Townshend, C., *Easter 1916: The Irish Rebellion* (London: Penguin Books, 2005).

Watt, J., *The Church in Medieval Ireland* (Dublin: University College Dublin Press, 1998).

Isle of Man

Dugdale, D. S., *Manx Church Origins* (Lampeter: Llanerch, 1998).

Gelling, J. D., *A History of the Manx Church (1698–1911)* (Douglas: Manx Heritage Foundation, 1998).

McDonald, R. A., *The Sea Kings: The Late Norse Kingdoms of Man and the Isles, c. 1066–1275* (Edinburgh: John Donald, 2019).

Scotland

Burleigh, J. H. S., *A Church History of Scotland* (London: Oxford University Press, 1960).

Clarkson, T., *The Picts: A History*, rev. edn (Edinburgh: Birlinn, 2010).

Dawson, J. E. A., *John Knox* (New Haven, Conn.: Yale University Press, 2015).

_____, *Scotland Re-formed 1488–1587* (Edinburgh: Edinburgh University Press, 2007).

Donaldson, G., *The Scottish Reformation* (Cambridge: Cambridge University Press, 1960).

Fergusson, D., and M. K. Elliott (eds.), *The History of Scottish Theology*, 3 vols. (Oxford: Oxford University Press, 2019).

Fissel, M. C., *The Bishops' Wars: Charles I's Campaigns Against Scotland, 1638–1640* (Cambridge: Cambridge University Press, 1994).

Fraser, J. E., *From Caledonia to Pictland: Scotland to 795* (Edinburgh: Edinburgh University Press, 2009).

Gougaud, L., *Christianity in Celtic Lands: A History of the Churches of the Celts, Their Origin, Their Development, Influence and Mutual Relations* (Dublin: Four Courts Press, 1992).

Lachman, D. C., *The Marrow Controversy, 1718–1723: An Historical and Theological Analysis* (Edinburgh: Rutherford House, 1988).

Marshall, R. K., *John Knox* (Edinburgh: Birlinn, 2000).

Oram, R., *Domination and Lordship: Scotland 1070–1230* (Edinburgh: Edinburgh University Press, 2011).

Ryrie, A., *The Origins of the Scottish Reformation* (Manchester: Manchester University Press, 2006).

Whytock, J. C., *Continental Calvinian Influences on the Scottish Reformation: The First Book of Discipline (1560)* (Lewiston, N.Y.: Edwin Mellen Press, 2009).

_____, 'An Educated Clergy': Scottish Theological Education and Training in the Kirk and Secession, 1560–1850* (Milton Keynes: Paternoster Press, 2007).

Wales

Doe, N. (ed.), *A New History of the Church in Wales* (Cambridge: Cambridge University Press, 2020).

Gougaud, L., *Christianity in Celtic Lands: A History of the Churches of the Celts, Their Origin, Their Development, Influence and Mutual Relations* (Dublin: Four Courts Press, 1992).

Victory, S., *The Celtic Church in Wales* (London: SPCK, 1977).

White, E., *The Welsh Bible* (Stroud: Tempus, 2007).

Williams, G., *Renewal and Reformation Wales c. 1415–1642* (Oxford: Oxford University Press, 1993).

_____, Wales and the Reformation* (Cardiff: University of Wales Press, 1999).

Index of names and places

Monarchs, popes and archbishops are grouped together under their respective jurisdictions.

Abercorn 76

Aberdeen xii, 76, 106, 15, 228, 282n,
  317–318, 508, 571, 620
  Gilcomston South Church 571–572

Abernethy 76

Achonry 72, 109, 295

Acton, Lord John Emerich Edward
  Dalberg 537

Adelfius 3

Aelfric 51

Aelle 23

Aelred of Rievaulx 166

Aethelbert, king of Kent 24–25

Aethelwold 48

Africa
  Central 444, 523
  East 444, 523
  North 5
  see also South Africa

Agilbert 28–29

Aidan, St 28, 34, 42

Ainsworth, Henry 255

Alaric 5, 589

Alban, St 2–3

Albert, Prince 548–549

Alchfled 29

Alcuin of York 37, 43–44

Alexander, Cecil (Mrs) xv, 17

Alfred the Great, king of Wessex 47–48, 53

Allen, William 258, 260

Allestree, Richard 368

America
  Latin 457

North xviii, 19, 214, 291, 303, 328, 404,
  422

Amyraut, Moise 301

Andrew, St xvi

Andrew of St Victor 83

Andrewes, Lancelot 288–290

Angelos, Christopher 286

Angus 234

Annaghdown 73, 109

Aquinas, Thomas 94–95, 124

Ardagh 72, 109, 313, 382

Ardcarn 72

Ardfert 72, 109

Ardmore 72

Argyll 76–77

Argyll, Earl of 233

Aristotle 90, 94, 124, 127, 355, 391

Arius 400

Arles 3–4, 13, 24–26

Armagh 70–73, 109–111, 142, 156–157,
  225–227, 298n, 300, 324, 378, 466,
  493–494

Armagh, archbishops of
  Dowdall, George 226–227
  FitzRalph, Richard 142
  Goodacre, Hugh 226
  Loftus, Adam 296–297
  Plunkett, Oliver (Catholic) 378
  Ussher, James 300–302, 312–314, 324,
    362, 369

Arminius, Jacob 283, 306, 427

Arminius of Lincoln 3

Arnold, Matthew 507, 532–533

Arnold, Thomas 502, 507
Arthur, King 15–16
Arthur, Prince 16, 178–179
Atterbury, Francis 400–402
Auchterarder 449, 472
Auden, Wystan Hugh 565
Augustine of Hippo 5, 24, 58, 78, 163, 195, 218, 365, 432, 474, 589
Australasia, Australia xviii, 460, 523
Austria 104, 283, 457, 555
Avalon 16
Avignon 115, 118, 124, 126, 134–135, 141–144
Ayrshire 234

Babylon 543, 588–628
Bach, Johann Sebastian 435
Badby, John 148
Bainbridge, Christopher 121
Bala 439
Bale, John 226
Balfour, Arthur John 546
Balmerino, Lord 315
Balsham 254
Bancroft, Richard 261–263, 277
Bangladesh 567
Bangor (County Down) 70
Bangor (Wales) 67, 169, 212n, 288, 402, 467
Barclay, Oliver Rainsford 569
Barebone, Praise-God 361
Barlow, William 288–289
Barnardo, Thomas John 529
Barnes, Robert 191, 198–199
Barnett, Henrietta 530
Barnett, Samuel 530
Barr, James 584
Barrow, Henry 254
Barth, Karl 563–564
Basil of Caesarea 167
Bastwick, John 310–311

Bath 33, 61, 172, 199, 212n, 248n, 289n, 381n, 383, 441, 446, 467
see also Wells
Baxter, Richard 362, 372, 404, 406, 414–415, 581
Bayly, Lewis 288
Beadon, Richard 468n
Beaton, David 121, 229–230
Beaufort, Henry 121
Beaufort, Lady Margaret 170, 177
Bede 21–25, 27–28, 34, 36–38, 40–41, 43, 60, 77, 83, 163, 257
Bedell, William 313–314, 368
Bedford 257, 365, 367, 443
Belfast 531, 553, 595n
Belgium 11, 549, 552–553
Bell, George Kennedy Allen 564
Benedict of Nursia 33, 48, 57
Benn, Wallace 614n
Bennett, Gareth (Gary) Vaughan 597
Bentham, Jeremy 479
Bentley, Richard 418
Berkeley, George 418, 454
Bernard of Clairvaux 58, 71
Bernham, David 107
Bertha, queen of Kent 25
Berwick-upon-Tweed 204, 318
Besant, Annie 545
Betjeman, John 565
Beverley Minster 32, 121
Beza (de Bèze), Theodore 214, 250–251, 260, 356
Bilney, Thomas 183–184
Birinus 28
Birkenhead 614n; St Aidan's College 541
Birmingham 470, 510–511, 539
Blackburn 510, 614n, 615n
Blackwell, Thomas 450
Blair, Tony 593
Blake, William 352

Blamires, Harry 580, 610–611
Blavatskaya (Blavatsky), Helena Petrovna 545
Bloom, Anthony 568
Boethius 48
Bohemia xvii, 91, 149, 283
Bolingbroke, Viscount *see* Henry St John
Bologna 98
Bonhoeffer, Dietrich 564
Boniface, St *see* Wynfrith of Crediton
Bonner, Edmund 137, 204–205, 209
Booth, Catherine 497, 529
Booth, William 497, 505, 529
Bosher, Robert 375
Boso, disciple of Anselm 79
Boston (Lincolnshire) 307
Boston (Massachusetts) 307–308
Boston, Thomas 449–450
Bothwell, Earl of *see* Hepburn, James
Bouchier, Thomas 121
Bourdeaux, Michael 567
Bourke (de Burgo), Richard 295
Bowring, John xvii
Boyd, Lady 330–331
Boyle, Robert 397
Bradford 510
Bradlaugh, Charles 534–535
Bramhall, John 312–313
Brampford Speke 458
Bray, Thomas 393, 397, 420, 426
Brazil 457
Brechin 75–76
Brecon 67n
Bréifne 72
Brendan of Birr 9
Brendan of Clonfert 9
Bridgetown (Barbados) 456
Brighton 441, 540
Bristol 199, 212n, 248, 349, 380n, 429, 465, 467, 470n, 584, 608
    Trinity College 470n, 584

Brittany 11, 177
Brontë, Charlotte 445
Brown, Callum 589–590, 593
Brown, Gordon 593
Brown, Stewart 499, 532, 546
Browne, Robert 253–255
Bruce, Edward 114
Bruce, Frederick Fyvie 569
Bruno of Cologne 154
Bucer, Martin 204, 333
Buchanan, Colin Ogilvie 582
Buchman, Frank 573
Buckingham, Suffragan Bishop of 607
Bullinger, Heinrich 201
Bultmann, Rudolf 598
Bunyan, John xx, 257, 365–367, 372, 406
Burke, Edmund 453–454
Burnet, Gilbert 374, 416
Burnley 615n
Burton, Henry 310–311
Bury St Edmunds 60
    see also St Edmundsbury and Ipswich
Butler, Joseph 417–418, 430
Butler, Josephine 529
Butt, Isaac 513
Byzantine Empire 78

Caerleon 12
Caithness 76
Calais 76, 215
Calcutta 456n
Calvin, John 84, 213–215, 223, 235, 250–251, 283, 334, 350, 485
Cambridge 32, 42, 63, 65, 85, 130, 138, 152, 155, 166, 182–183, 185, 190, 204, 224, 248–249, 251, 257, 270, 277, 289, 293, 324, 364, 378, 399, 443n, 446, 470–471, 502n, 507–508, 521, 530, 535, 546, 565–566
    Christ's College 265
    Clare College 248

Cambridge (*cont.*)
  Corpus Christi College 217
  Emmanuel College 252
  Girton College 542
  Holy Trinity Church 446
  King's College 161, 446
  Magdalene College 419
  Newnham College 546
  Pembroke College 248
  Peterhouse 130, 248
  Queens' College 443n
  Ridley Hall 470n, 521, 541
  Round Church (Holy Sepulchre) 104
  St Andrew the Great 265
  St John's College 248, 270
  St Paul's Church 502n
  Trinity College 249, 286, 418
  Tyndale House 569–570
  Westcott House 470n
Cambridge (Massachusetts) 308
Cambuslang 451
Camelot 16
Cameron, David 593
Cameron, John 301
Cameron, Richard 409
Campbell, Archibald 451
Campbell, John MacLeod 475–476
Campbell, Reginald John 539–540
Campbell, Robert 627–628
Canada 377n, 423n, 461, 469, 522–523
Canice of Aghaboe 9
Canterbury 18, 25, 29–30, 33–34, 40, 49, 60, 67, 69, 77, 83–84, 86–87, 98, 100, 106, 139–140, 146, 151n, 156–157, 159, 168, 178n, 186, 188, 208, 212n, 315n, 267, 388, 467–468, 488, 490, 522, 528, 614, 617
Canterbury, archbishops of
  Abbot, George 286, 288
  Anselm, St 69, 77–80, 83
  Arundel, Thomas 145–148
  Augustine, St 24–28, 35, 40, 77
  Bancroft, Richard 261, 263, 277
  Beckett, Thomas 85–87, 159, 334
  Bradwardine, Thomas 126–127, 129
  Coggan, Donald 591–592
  Courtenay, William 159
  Cranmer, Thomas 49n, 189, 192n, 193–195, 197–199, 201–209, 212, 221, 246, 474, 578
  Dunstan, St 48–49
  Grindal, Edmund 247–248, 269
  Justus 27
  Lanfranc of Bec 59–60, 69, 83
  Langham, John 131
  Langton, Stephen 83–85, 104
  Laud, William 289, 310, 314–316, 318, 320–321, 331, 370, 386, 427
  Laurence 27
  Mellitus, St 27–29, 40
  Parker, Matthew 217, 247
  Peckham, John 112–114, 139
  Pole, Reginald 121, 210–212, 215
  Sancroft, William 380
  Tait, Arthur James 541
  Temple, William 541
  Tenison, Thomas 373
  Theodore of Tarsus 34–36, 286
  Tillotson, John 373, 388
  Wake, William 373, 388, 401
  Warham, William 186
  Whitgift, John 248–250, 253, 256–257, 262–263, 270, 277–278, 305
  Williams, Rowan Douglas 606
Carey, William 445
Carlile, Richard 479
Carlile, Wilson 497n
Carlisle 33, 59, 61, 66, 75, 111, 212n, 288, 421, 467
Carmarthen 268
Carolinas (USA) 384n

Carr, Charles Lisle 541
Carrick-on-Suir 298
Carstares, William 410–411
Cartwright, Thomas 248–250, 252
Cary, Lucius, Viscount Falkland 358–359
Cashel 69–73, 109–111, 156, 295, 298, 466
Cassiodorus 5
Cavell, Edith Louisa 553
Cedd, St 29
Celsus, abbot of Armagh 70
Ceredig (Coroticus) 20
Cerne 52
Chad, St 34
Chaderton, Laurence 252
Chadwick, Henry 570
Chadwick, Owen 570
Challoner, Richard 261n, 422
Chalmers, Thomas 452–453, 471, 475
Chamberlain, Joseph 512
Channel Islands 178
Chapuis, Pierre 98
Charlemagne (Charles the Great) 37, 44, 47, 78
Charles, Thomas 439
Charles V, Holy Roman emperor 180–181, 190, 200
Chartres 165
Chatton, Walter 126
Chaucer, Geoffrey 172–173
Chelmsford 510, 541
Cheltenham xii, 446
Chester 19, 30, 42, 44, 61, 199, 212n, 248n, 381n, 467
Chester-le-Street 28, 30, 61
Chichester 19, 30, 44, 61, 167, 208, 212n, 248n, 288n, 289, 306, 380n, 381n, 467, 564
Chillingworth, William 359
China xvii, 444, 477, 622n
Christchurch (New Zealand) 469

Chrysostom, John 167
Churchill, Sir Winston xvii, 566
Ciarán of Saighir 9
Clarendon, Earl of see Hyde, Edward
Clark, Thomas 472
Clarke, Samuel 399–400, 416–417
Clifton, Richard 290, 292
Clogher 72, 109, 156, 157n
Clonfert 9, 72, 109, 295
Clonmacnois 72, 109
Clough, Arthur 499
Clovesho 35
Clovis, king of the Franks 37
Cloyne 72, 109, 418
Cluny 53–54, 58
Colenso, John William 506
Coleridge, Samuel Taylor 502
Colet, John 185
Colman, Bishop 31–32
Cologne 94, 154
Columba (Crimthann) of Iona xv, 9, 20, 22, 69
Columba of Terryglas 9
Columbanus 37
Columbus, Christopher 9, 178
Compton, Henry 380, 388
Connecticut 291, 308, 429
Connor 70, 72, 109–110, 295, 368
Constantinople 5, 35–36, 286, 568
Conybeare, William John 536
Cooke, Robert 236
Cooper, Anthony Ashley, third earl of Shaftesbury 399
Cooper, Anthony Ashley, seventh earl of Shaftesbury 477, 490, 505, 516, 529, 533
Cork xii, 72, 109, 397, 454
Cornwall 1n, 2, 10–13, 30, 94
Cosin, John 288
Cotton, John 307–308, 329
Coutances 178

Coventry 33, 61, 152–153, 199, 212n, 510, 522, 541, 566–567
Coverdale, Miles 196, 208, 214, 237–240
Cowper, William 437–438
Cox, Richard 213, 216, 248–249
Crayke 66
Crediton xvii, 37, 61
Cromwell, Oliver 302, 324–328, 343, 350–352, 360–361, 363, 368–369
Cromwell, Richard 369
Cromwell, Thomas 188–189, 195–198, 324
Cudworth, Ralph 265
Cumbria 10–11, 75
Cuthbert 28, 41, 44

Dál Ríata 20
Dale, Robert William 511
Dallas, Alexander Robert Charles 492–493
Damian, Peter 95
Danelaw 44, 47, 50
Daniel, William 296
Daniell, David 260
Darby, John Nelson 476–478
Darnley, Lord 241
Darwin, Charles 478, 500–502
Davenant, John 301
Davenport, John 329n
David of Wales, St xvi, 12
Davidson, Andrew Bruce 508
Davies, David Jeremy Christopher 606–607
Davies, Richard 268–269
Davies, Thomas 268
Davies of Mallwyd, John 271
Dawkins, Richard 594
Day, George 208
Deira 23
Delhi 507
Denison, George Anthony 516
Denmark 10, 385

Derby 510
Dering, Edward 251–252
Derry (Londonderry) xv–xvi, xix, 20, 72, 109, 295, 297, 312
Dickens, Charles 548
Dingwall 45, 620
Dix, Gregory 577–578
Dominic de Guzmán 92, 153
Donkan (Donegan), John 143–144
Donngus, bishop of Dublin 69
Dorchester 28–30, 61
Dort (Dordrecht) 283–290, 300–301, 356
Dostoyevsky, Fyodor 478n
Douai (Douay) 219–220, 258, 261, 305, 422
Douglas, Lord Alfred 530
Down 71–72, 109–110, 295, 368
Downham, Clare 14–15
Downpatrick 7
Doyle, Arthur Conan 545
Drogheda 110, 327–328
Dromore 72, 109
Drummond, Henry 475
Dry Drayton 253
Dublin 45, 69, 71–73, 108–111, 156, 224–226, 295–299, 326–327, 383, 426, 454–456, 466, 476, 494, 513, 553–554
   Christ Church (Holy Trinity) 111
   General Post Office 554
   Public Record Office 328
   St Patrick's Cathedral 111, 418
   Trinity College 31, 44, 250n, 296, 300, 313, 329n
Dublin, archbishops of
   Bicknor, Alexander 141
   Cullen, Paul (Catholic) 492–494, 513
Dudley, John, duke of Northumberland 205, 207–208
Duleek 72
Dunan (Donatus), bishop of Dublin 69
Dunbar 324

Dunblane 76

Dundee 232

Dunkeld 76, 472

Duns Scotus, John 94–95, 123–124

Dunstable (Dunstaple), John 166

Dunwich 30

Durham 28, 32n, 33, 44, 61, 64, 66, 102,
107, 121, 159n, 167, 186, 205, 212n,
288, 309n, 320, 323, 466–468, 470n,
471, 479, 521, 541n, 597

Dymock, Roger 145–146

Eagleton, Terry 594n

Earconbert, king of Kent 29

East Anglia 29, 42, 44, 60, 128

Easton, Adam 121

Ebba, St 42

Eborius 3

Echternach 37

Edinburgh 77n, 143, 156, 233–234, 277,
315–317, 319, 324–325, 411, 445, 478,
520, 539n, 547, 592n, 627
Greyfriars Kirk 317
St Giles Cathedral 234, 316

Edmund, St 60

Edward, Prince of Wales (the Black
Prince) 118

Edward the Elder, king of Wessex 48

Edwards, John 472

Edwards, Jonathan 475

Edwin, king of Northumbria 28, 40

Egric, king of East Anglia 29

Eliot, Thomas Stearns 87, 129, 565

Elizabeth of the Palatinate 283, 385

Elkins, John 309

Elmham 30

Elphin 72, 109, 458

Elton, Sir Geoffrey 220

Ely 33, 42, 49–50, 61, 65, 130, 183, 212n,
216, 248–249, 270n, 288n, 380n, 381n,
463, 466–467, 615

Emly 72, 109

England xvi–xix, 11–12, 18, 22–66,
74–75, 77, 80–88, 93, 96, 99–106,
112–123, 130–140, 145–154, 161,
167–174, 176–224, 243–266, 277–282,
287–294, 303–314, 320, 323–326, 342,
355, 358, 360–389, 392–412, 420–421,
428–429, 433–434, 442–444, 459,
462–471, 478–491, 494–503, 509–512,
521–522, 529–534, 537–540, 550,
555–559, 569–571, 577–579, 589, 591,
593, 597, 605–609, 614–615, 617,
619–620

England, kings and queens of
Anne of Bohemia 149
Anne Boleyn 191, 215
Athelstan 48, 57
Catherine of Aragón 178–180, 182,
189, 191, 208
Cnut 50, 52–53
Edgar 49, 52
Edith 43
Edward I 55, 112–114, 140, 143
Edward II 114, 118, 142
Edward III 116, 119–120, 126,
133–134, 151, 177
Edward IV 177–178
Edward V 177–178
Edward VI 202, 205–209, 213, 221,
226–227, 271, 279, 333
Edward the Confessor 53–54
Elizabeth I 215–224, 227, 232–233,
241, 243, 248–252, 254–255,
257–258, 260–261, 263–264, 267,
277, 279, 287, 295–297, 305, 589
Emma 53
Ethelred the Unready 50, 53
Harold II 43, 54
Henry I 59, 75, 81, 179, 208
Henry II 73, 76, 85–87, 97, 104, 116,
154, 179n, 225

England, kings and queens of (*cont.*)
  Henry III 105, 110
  Henry IV 146, 148–149, 151, 176
  Henry V 148, 151, 176
  Henry VI 151, 161, 173–174, 176–178
  Henry VII 16, 149, 154, 170, 174,
    176–180, 224, 227, 310
  Henry VIII 16, 82, 87, 99, 174, 176n,
    179–184, 186–202, 204, 208–210,
    215, 217, 225–227, 255n, 267, 287,
    394
  Jane Grey 178n, 208–209, 217
  Jane Seymour 205n
  John 84, 104–105
  Mary I 179, 208–210, 212, 214–217,
    226–227, 248, 257, 266–267, 376
  Matilda 81, 179, 208
  Philip (II of Spain) 212, 227, 260, 266
  Richard I 104
  Richard II 133–135, 145–146,
    148–149, 151, 176
  Richard III 177
  Stephen 81, 85, 208
  William I 54
  William II 77, 80, 167
Epworth 395, 421
Erasmus of Rotterdam 182, 184–185,
  188, 194, 214
Ernst Augustus of Braunschweig-
  Lüneburg 283
Erskine, Ebenezer 450
Erskine, John 233
Erskine, Ralph 450
Etheldreda, St 42
Etherius 24–25
Eton 166, 446
Eustace, Prince 81
Evans, Mary Ann (George Eliot) 499–500
Exeter 13, 19, 30, 61, 168, 208, 212n, 467,
  487–488
Eynsham 52

Falkland, Viscount *see* Cary, Lucius
Falmouth 304n
Faroe Islands 9
Farron, Tim 594–595
Fawkes, Guy 261
Ferdinand of Aragón 178
Fermanagh 456
Ferns 72, 109
Ferrar, Nicholas 129, 293–294
Ferrara 121
Field, John 247, 251
Fife 233–234
Fife, Earl of 472
Fillingham 131
Fincham, Kenneth 288–289
Finnian of Movilla *see* Ninian, St
Fishacre, Richard 94
Fisher, Edward 448–449
Fisher, John 121, 188
Flew, Antony 419
Foakes-Jackson, Frederick John 542
Forbes, William 315
Forrestal, Alison 299
Fountains Abbey 58
Fox, George 324, 346, 349, 353, 363
Foxe, Edward 191, 193
Foxe, John 216–217, 246
France 37, 45, 58, 80, 83–85, 88, 104,
  115–116, 119, 135, 149–150, 154–155,
  164–165, 170, 176–177, 190, 204,
  215–216, 222, 227, 230, 232, 241, 250,
  266, 274–275, 295, 303–304, 326, 376,
  378–379, 381, 383, 385, 394, 401n, 402,
  418–419, 422, 456, 459–460, 462, 491,
  537, 542, 549, 604
France, kings and queens of
  Charles X 460n
  Francis II 241
  Henry II 232
  Henry IV 304
  Louis VII 86

Louis XII 178
Louis XIII 304
Louis XIV 376, 378–379, 384, 394
Louis-Philippe I 460n
Mary, wife of Louis XII 178
Philip IV 115–116
Francis of Assisi 92–93, 153
Frankfurt 213, 248, 250
Franklin, Benjamin 429
Frederick V, elector Palatine of the Rhine
283
Free, Edward Drax 463–464
Frideswide, St 42
Friel, Brian 158
Friesland 37
Frith, John 184
Froude, James Anthony 499
Froude, Richard Hurrell 485

Gainsborough 290
Galileo Galilei 355
Gallus, St Gallen 37
Galway 112
Gardiner, Stephen 204, 209
Garnier, Arnald 133
Gaul 14, 22, 24, 26, 28–29
Geddes, Jenny 316
Geneva xvii, 213–215, 223, 235, 236n,
249–251, 258, 266, 279, 356
Genoa 28
George, David Lloyd 526, 528
George, St xvi
George of Denmark, Prince 385
Germanus of Auxerre 5–6, 13
Germany xvii, 10, 37, 180, 182, 191, 193,
200, 210, 255, 342, 351, 376, 378,
424–425, 435, 503, 506, 508, 519, 536,
542–543, 549–550, 555, 563–564,
566–567, 580, 598
Germany, emperors and empresses of
Friedrich III 549

Victoria 549
Wilhelm II 540n, 549
Gibraltar 394, 468n
Gibson, Edmund 401, 430
Gilbert, bishop of Limerick 70
Gilbert of Sempringham 59
Gildas 10, 16–17, 52
Gladstone, William Ewart 512–513, 520,
532, 592
Glasgow 75–77, 155, 228, 274, 317, 421,
451, 475, 505, 534
Glastonbury 1, 48, 159
Glendalough 72
Gloucester 199, 208, 212n, 221, 288,
381n, 388, 458, 467
Golding, William 478n
Gonne, Maud 545
Goodwin, Thomas 332n
Gordon, Lord George 422, 424
Gore, Charles 537–539, 553
Gorham, George Cornelius 488–489
Graham, Billy 571–572
Graham, Franklin 613
Gratian, canonist 98
Great Britain, kings and queens of
Charles I 289, 293, 303–325, 327, 341,
360, 370, 377, 401, 494, 627
Charles II 318, 325, 369–370, 375–379,
385
Henrietta Maria 304, 326
James I/VI of Scotland 227, 242–243,
253, 261, 264, 273–283, 287,
297–298, 303–304, 306, 309n, 317,
324, 385
James II/VII of Scotland xv, 373,
376–386, 400, 408, 426
Mary II 380–381, 384–385
Mary of Modena 376, 380
William III/II of Scotland xviii,
380–385, 392–394, 401, 410, 426,
495n

Green, Thomas Hill 537

Greenham, Richard 253

Greenland 9, 43

Greenshields, James 411

Greenwood, John 254–255

Grey, Sir Edward 548

Gribben, Crawford 314

Groote, Gerhard 137, 170

Grosseteste, Robert 88–89, 93, 132

Guildford 510

Gumbel, Nicholas (Nicky) Glyn Paul
 619

Gundulf of Rochester 60

Guthrie, Donald 569

Guthrie, James 335

Guzmán, Dominic de 92, 153

Haggard, Rider 545

Haldane, Alexander 477n

Halle 425

Halifax, Viscount see Wood, Charles

Halyburton, Thomas 450

Hamilton, John 230, 242

Hamilton, Marquess of 317–318

Hamilton, Patrick 228

Hampden, Renn Dickson 487

Hampton Court 277–279

Handel (Händel), Georg Friedrich xviii,
 435, 455

Hannington, James 523

Hanover 283, 385, 400, 435, 549

Hanson, Richard 7

Harding, Thomas 257

Harley, John 208

Harnack, Adolf (von) 540–541, 563

Harper, Michael Claude 584

Harris, Hywel (Howell) 427, 431, 441,
 496

Harrison, Robert 253–254

Harsnett, Samuel 289

Harvard, John 308

Hastings, Selina, countess of Huntingdon
 441–442, 446, 463

Hatfield 35

Hawksmoor, Nicholas 398

Haymo of Faversham 93

Headlam, Stewart 530

Hebert, Gabriel 571

Hebrides 20, 45, 143–144

Hegel, Georg Friedrich Wilhelm 537

Heigham, John 305–306

Helwys, Thomas 292–293, 342

Henry, duke of Lancaster 118

Henry of Blois 81

Henry St John, Viscount Bolingbroke 419

Henson, Herbert Hensley 541

Hepburn, James, earl of Bothwell 241

Herbert, George 293–294

Hereford 30, 168, 191, 208, 212n, 402n,
 467, 487, 541

Hereman 167n

Herrnhut 425–426

Hertford 35

Hexham 30, 41

Heylyn, Peter 321

Hilda, St 41–42

Hildesley, Mark 447

Hill, Christopher 354

Hill, Rowley 511n

Hilton, Walter 138

Hitler, Adolf 564, 566

Hoadly, Benjamin 402, 416

Hog, James 449–450

Holcot, Robert 127–129

Holgate, Robert 209

Holland, Henry Scott 538, 552

Holy Roman Empire 80, 180–181, 283,
 303, 457

Hong Kong xvii

Hooker, Richard 249–250, 262–263, 266

Hooker, Thomas 329n

Hooper, John 208–209, 221

Horsley, Samuel 403
Hort, Fenton John Anthony 508
Howard, John 443, 529
Howatch, Susan 565
Howden 66
Hoyle, Joshua 329n
Huddersfield 389
Huddleston, Trevor 567
Hume, David 417
Hunne, Richard 185, 187
Huntingdon, Countess of *see* Hastings, Selina
Hus, Jan 149, 425
Hutcheson, Francis 451
Hutchinson, John 403
Huxley, Thomas Henry 500
Hyde, Anne 376
Hyde, Douglas 545, 563
Hyde, Edward, earl of Clarendon 374, 376
Hylson-Smith, Kenneth 542

Iceland 9, 15, 43
Illingworth, John Richardson 538
India 444–445, 457, 498–499, 507, 545, 567
Ingram, Arthur Foley Winnington 552–553
Inis Pátraic 71
Inishboffin 31–32
Iona xv, 9, 20–22, 28, 31, 43–44, 74–76, 143
Ireland xv–xvi, xvii, 1n, 6–9, 11, 13–15, 17–18, 20–21, 31–32, 37, 44–45, 48, 68–77, 101, 108–112, 120–121, 140–143, 156–157, 224–227, 243–244, 295–303, 305, 311–314, 321–322, 326–329, 368, 375–377, 383–384, 386, 392n, 408–409, 422–424, 453–456, 464–466, 477, 490–496, 505, 508, 509n, 512–513, 515, 525–526, 545, 553–554,

562–563, 575, 579, 586–587, 590–592, 618, 626
see also Northern Ireland; Ulster
Irving, Edward 475, 478, 481
Isabella of Castile 178
Isham 309
Isidore of Seville 147n
Isle of Man 45, 143–144, 426, 447
see also Sodor and Man
Isle of Wight 29
Isles, diocese of the 45, 76
Italy 14, 22, 38, 45–46, 54, 76–78, 154, 164, 357, 399, 493, 514–515, 555
Iwerne Minster 570, 619

Jacob, Henry 290–291
Jacobs, Henry Eyster 191
James III/VIII (Old Pretender) 380, 385, 393–394, 400–402, 411
James, Phyllis Dorothy 565
James, William 539, 546–547
Jameson, Robert 500
Jane, William 388
Jarrow 36–37
Jaruman 29
Jean de Pouilly 142
Jenkins, David 159n, 597
Jericho 599
Jerome 5
Jersey 178n, 218
Jerusalem xv, 1, 16, 104, 115, 351–353, 429, 588–589, 621
see also Zion
Jesus Christ xi–xiii, xv–xx, 1, 4–5, 16, 23, 36, 42, 51, 78, 99, 103, 139, 147, 158, 163, 203, 218n, 223–224, 285, 309, 335, 337, 353, 357–358, 363, 391, 436, 474, 478, 482, 504, 507, 520, 532, 538, 540–541, 548, 560, 586, 588, 595, 597–599, 602–603, 621–622, 626–628
Jewel, John 216, 257

Joan of Arc 170
Jocelin de Bohun 167
Jocelin, bishop of Glasgow 76
John of Gaunt 133–135
John of Reading 124, 126
Johnson, Boris 533
Johnson, Francis 255, 290, 292
Jones, Mary 439
Joseph of Arimathea 1, 3
Jowett, Benjamin 503
Julian of Norwich 170
Julius Caesar 1

Kafka, Franz 478n
Keating, Geoffrey 321–322
Keble, John 482, 485
Kelham 518, 571
Kells 31, 44, 71–72
Kelly, John Norman Davidson 580
Kelso 228
Kemp, John 121
Kempe, Margery 170
Kempis, Thomas à 170
Ken, Thomas 383
Kendrick, Graham 612
Kenmure, Lady 330
Kennett, White 401
Kensit, John 517
Kenstec 12
Kent 22, 24–25, 27, 29, 34, 42, 139, 354, 567
Kenya 444
Kessen, Andrew 472
Keswick 521–522, 524, 573
Kidderminster 362
Kildare 8, 72, 109, 224, 314n, 382
Kildare, Earl of 224–225
Kilfenora 72, 109
Kilkenny 8, 226, 298n, 299, 326
Killala 72, 109, 295
Killaloe 72, 109

Kilmacduagh 72, 109
Kilmore 73, 109, 313
Kilsyth 451
Kingarth 76
Kingston-upon-Hull 443
Kingswood 429
Kinsale 297
Kipling, Rudyard xix, 545
Kirby, Gilbert Walter 569
Knock 560
Knox, Edmund Arbuthnott 522
Knox, John, reformer 204, 213–215, 229–230, 232–237, 240–243, 248, 250, 271, 275, 281
Konopios, Nathanael 286
Kritopoulos, Metrophanes 286

Lacordaire, Jean Baptiste 537
Laisrén of Munster 9
Lake, Kirsopp 542
Lamennais, Félicité de 567
Langham, Simon 121
Langland, William 171–172
Lapthorne, Anthony 308–309
Łaski, Jan 204
Latimer, Hugh 198, 212
Law, William 383
Leamington Spa 446
Ledrede, Richard 142
Leechman, William 451
Leicester 30, 177, 510
Leiden 290
Leighlin 72, 108–109
Leith 233
Lenin, Vladimir 533n
Lesley, John 231–232
Lethendy 472
Leutherius 29
Lever, Thomas 248
Leveson, William 267
Lewis, Clive Staples 565, 576

Lichfield 30, 33–34, 61, 152–153, 199, 212n, 467
Liddon, Henry Parry 537–538
Lightfoot, Joseph Barber 508
Limerick 70, 72, 109–110, 156, 454
Lincoln 3, 19, 30, 61, 65, 88, 121, 148, 169, 199, 209, 212n, 289n, 290, 467
Lindisfarne 28–31, 33, 43–44
Lindsey 30
Lisbon 121
Lismore (Ireland) 71–72, 109–110
Lismore (Scotland) 68n
Lithgow 317n
Little Gidding 129, 293
Littlejohn, Bradford 262
Liudhard 25
Liverpool 510–511, 519, 522
Llandaff 67, 212n, 467
Llanddewi Brefi 12
Llanrhaeadr ym Mochnant 270
Lloyd-Jones, Dafydd Martyn 565, 569, 581–582, 610n
Llysfaen 268
Locke, John 384, 399, 450
Lombard, Peter 88–89, 94, 113, 250
London (Londinium) 2–3, 18, 22, 27–30, 44–45, 48, 50, 59, 66, 81, 86n, 94, 102, 104, 122n, 133, 137, 145, 148, 159, 168, 177, 181–182, 184–185, 190, 198, 204–205, 209, 212–213, 225, 244, 249, 253, 255, 261–262, 269, 275, 277, 287, 289, 293n, 297, 300, 315, 318, 320, 323–324, 330, 331n, 333n, 354, 361, 373, 378, 380–381, 387–388, 392–394, 399–401, 428–429, 435, 441, 455–457, 467–468, 470n, 472, 475–476, 483, 489, 497, 505, 518, 520–521, 530, 534, 536, 539, 552, 554, 556, 564, 568–570, 576, 595, 610n, 619
    Aldersgate Street Chapel 428
    All Souls, Langham Place 570, 584
    Christ Church, Albany Street 518
    Christ Church, Spitalfields 398
    City Temple 539–540
    Clapham 443, 480n, 533
    Hackney 480
    Holy Trinity, Brompton 619
    Islington 446
    King's College 536
    Lambeth 18, 134, 592
    Metropolitan Tabernacle 497, 512, 536, 610n
    Paul's Cross 261
    St Anne's, Limehouse 398
    St Clement Danes 45
    St Helen's, Bishopsgate 619
    St Jude's, Whitechapel 530
    St Martin-in-the-Fields 373
    St Mary-le-Bow 66
    St Mary Woolnoth 398
    St Matthew's, Bethnal Green 530
    St Paul's Cathedral 102, 182, 185, 261, 394, 401, 556
    St Peter, Cornhill 2–3
    Temple Church 104, 249
    Westminster Chapel 564–565, 610n
    see also Tower of London
Lough Derg 142
Louth (Ireland) 110, 224
Louvain (Leuven) 219, 258, 322, 552
Lowder, Charles 518
Lucas, Richard ('Dick') Charles 619
Ludgershall 131
Ludwig IV, duke of Bavaria 126
Lukaris, Cyril 286
Lund 45
Lundie, Archibald 410n
Luther, Martin 79, 93n, 149, 172, 180–184, 190–195, 200–201, 210, 214n, 228, 251, 252n, 425, 429, 482, 485, 603

Lutterworth 131, 135
Luxembourg 37
Lyell, Sir Charles 500
Lyndwood, William 100–101, 186
Lyte, Henry Francis 624

McArthur, Amy 595n
McArthur, Daniel 595n
Macaulay, Rose 565
Macaulay, Zachary 443
McGregor, J. F. 344, 347–348
Mackenzie, Charles Frederick 445n
Mackonochie, Alexander Heriot 517
Magrath, Miler 295
Mainz 180
Mair, John 155
Major, John 593
Malawi 523
Malines (Mechelen) 557
Malthus, Thomas Robert 477–478
Manchester 505, 510, 522, 541, 608
Mann, Rachel 608–609
Manning, Henry Edward 488, 515
Marnham, Charles Christopher 619
Marnoch 472
Marsilius of Padua 123
Martin, Gregory 260
Martin, Ralph Philip 569
Martyn, Henry 445
Marx, Karl 533
Mary, mother of Jesus 42, 95, 158, 163, 166, 228, 260–261, 334n
Maryborough 227
Maryland 393
Mascall, Eric Lionel 580
Massachusetts 291, 308, 404, 475
Mathew, Theobald 493
Maucteus (Mochta) 8n
Maurice, Frederick Denison 504–506, 533, 536
May, Theresa 593

Maynooth 423
Mayo 32, 73
Mayr-Harting, Henry 58
Meath 72, 108–110, 142, 224, 300, 312
Meeke, Robert 389
Mellifont 71
Melrose 228
Melville, Andrew 274–276
Mercia 29–30, 35, 42, 44
Michael of Northgate 139
Middelburg 253–254
Middleton, Thomas 457
Mill, James 479
Mill, John Stuart 479, 498
Milton, John 332–333, 354, 364–365
Mirfield 470n, 518
Mobhi of Glasnevin 9
Moltmann, Jürgen 539n
Monmouth 67n
Mont, Christopher 191
Montreal 456
Montagu, Richard 305–306
Montalembert, Charles de 537
Moody, Dwight Lyman 519–520, 565
Moray 76, 228
More, Hannah 441, 443
More, Sir Thomas 184, 188
Morgan, George Campbell 565
Morgan, William 270–271
Mortlach 76
Morton, John 121
Motyer, John Alexander (Alec) 584
Moule, Handley Carr Glyn 521
Mount Badon 15

Muggleton, Lodowicke 353–354
Müller, George 529
Munster 9, 69n, 70, 295–296
Murray, Andrew (junior) 524
Murray, Andrew (senior) 524

Napoleon 456–457, 491, 550
Nash, Eric John Hewitson ('Bash') 570
Nayler, James 349, 363
Nelson, Horatio 456–457, 476
Netherlands xviii, 10, 37, 253–255, 257, 260, 269, 283, 287, 290, 342, 378, 384, 410, 604
New Zealand 456–457, 460, 469, 523
Newburn 320
Newcastle-upon-Tyne 204, 510
Newfoundland 16, 43
Newman, Francis 499
Newman, John Henry 482–487, 499, 515, 518
Newton, Isaac 417
Newton, John 437, 439, 441
Nicholls, Kenneth W. 141
Niclaes, Hendrick 254
Nineveh 543, 599
Ninian, St 21
Ninnidh of Lough Erne 9
Noakes, Philip 354
Normandy 45, 54, 59, 62, 88, 104
North, Philip John 615n
North Carolina 384n
Northampton 199, 534
Northampton (Massachusetts) 475
Northern Ireland xvi, 339n, 554, 575, 581, 586, 595
    see also Ulster
Northumberland, Duke of see Dudley, John
Northumbria, Northumberland 21–24, 28–29, 34, 37, 40, 44
Norwich 33, 61, 170, 184, 212n, 253, 289, 306n, 381n, 467, 571, 614
    St Andrew's Church 289

O Dúnáin, Maol Muire 70
Oates, Titus 377–378
O'Brien, Turlough 69n

O'Cleary, Michael 322
O'Connell, Daniel 454
Offaly, Lord 'Silken Thomas' 225
O'Gallagher, Redmond 295
O'Harte, Eugene 295
Oldcastle, Sir John 148
Olivers, Thomas 437
Olney 437, 439
O'Neill, Owen Roe 327
Origen 2
Orkney 45, 76
O'Shea, Kitty 525
Osmund, bishop of Salisbury 167
Osney 84
Ossory 73, 108–109, 142, 226
Oswald, king of Northumbria 28, 40–41
Oswy, king of Northumbria 29
Otho, Cardinal 101, 106, 210
Othobon, Cardinal 101, 107, 210
Overall, John 278–279, 287
Owen, John 364–365, 368, 372, 427n, 581
Oxford 32, 42, 59, 63, 85, 87–89, 93–94, 124–127, 130–132, 135, 137–138, 142, 146–148, 152, 166, 183, 186, 190, 199, 204, 212–213, 224, 248, 257–258, 286, 309n, 364, 398, 403, 428, 467, 470–471, 481–489, 501, 503, 518, 522, 530, 535, 537–539, 546n, 565, 567, 573, 584, 597
    All Souls College 398
    Balliol College 131, 286
    Canterbury College 130–131
    Christ Church 42, 59, 130, 186, 199
    Durham College 130
    Exeter College 130, 309n
    Jesus College 131
    Latimer House 584
    Lincoln College 130
    Merton College 131
    New College 131
    Oriel College 258, 487
    Pusey House 537, 584

Oxford (*cont.*)
Queen's College 131
St Aldate's 59
St Ebbe's 59
St Frideswide's 42, 59
St John's College 130–131
St Stephen's House 470n
Trinity College 131
Worcester College 130
Wycliffe Hall 470n, 522

Packer, James Innell 571, 581, 584
Paisley, Ian 581
Pakistan 567
Palestine 5, 78, 93n, 306n, 477, 504, 546
Paley, William 419
Palladius 6–9
Palmer, William Patrick 484–485
Paparo, John 75
Paris 28, 71, 83–88, 93–94, 137, 155, 196, 228, 304, 549
Parnell, Charles Stewart 525
Parry, Sir Charles Hubert Hastings 566
Parry, Richard 271
Patrick, bishop of Dublin 69
Patrick, St xvi, 6–9, 16–18, 20–21, 70
Patrick, Simon 373
Pattison, Mark 499
Paul, St 1–2, 40, 119n, 163, 306n, 437, 484, 597, 599, 603, 605, 626
Peada 29
Peak Forest, Derbyshire 304n
Peel, Sir Robert 482
Pelagius 4–6, 12, 16, 195
Pembrokeshire 12
Penda, king of Mercia 29
Penn, William 406
Pennsylvania 406
Penry, John 253
Pentreath, Dolly 13n
Perkins, William 265–266

Perth 233, 281–282, 315, 317n
Perry, Charles 521
Peter, St xvi, 171, 484, 599
Peter the Chanter 84
Peterborough 49, 199, 212n, 380n, 381n, 467
Petronilla of Meath 142
Philipstown 227
Phillips, John Bertram 576
Plymouth 476
Plymouth (Massachusetts) 291
Poland 357, 457, 555
Ponet, John 209
Poore, Richard 107, 167–168
Portsmouth 510
Portugal 457, 462
Potters Bar 304n
Powell, Baden 503
Poynings, Sir Edward 224n
Prague 283
Preston, John 289, 301
Price, Ellis 268
Pride, Thomas 360
Prussia 457, 549
Prynne, William 310–311
Puleston, Hugh 268
Pusey, Edward Bouverie 486, 535, 537
Pym, Barbara 565

Queen's College (Birmingham) 470

Raikes, Robert 442
Ráith Bressail 70
Ramsbury 61
Raphoe 72, 109, 297n
Rathlurensis 73
Redman, Matthew (Matt) 612
Reeve, John 353
Reeves, Richard Ambrose 567
Regensburg 229
Reims (Rheims) 258, 260, 261n, 422

Reiss, Michael 594
Repingdon, Philip 148
Restitutus 3
Rhode Island 291–292
Rhu 475
Riccaltoun, Robert 450
Richard of St Victor 83, 87n
Richardson, John 455
Richeldis 42–43
Richmond (York) 199
Ridley, Nicholas 209, 212
Rievaulx Abbey 58, 166
Rinuccini, Giovanni Battista 326–327
Ripon 30, 320, 467, 470n, 510
Rizzio, David 241
Roberts, Evan 526
Robin Hood 64
Robinson, John 290–291
Robinson, John Arthur Thomas 582–583
Rochester 27–28, 30, 33, 60, 131, 188,
    212n, 289, 381, 400, 445, 467
Roger le Poer 167
Rogers, Travers Guy 542
Rolle, Richard 137–138, 170
Roman Empire, emperors of
  Claudius 1
  Decius 3
  Diocletian 3
  Justinian I 56
  see also Julius Caesar
Romania 11
Rome 13, 22–23, 28–29, 34, 36, 47, 49,
    53–54, 69, 71, 74, 76, 80–82, 87, 96,
    101, 106, 119, 134–135, 146, 155–156,
    173, 181, 188, 190, 195–196, 200, 208,
    210–211, 216, 220, 225–226, 228, 241,
    249, 258, 261n, 269, 280, 282, 288, 295,
    305–306, 316, 326–327, 339, 351, 384,
    403, 421, 453, 474, 482–488, 492–494,
    515, 518, 526, 537, 579–580, 588–589,
    604–605

Rome, popes of
  Alexander III 76
  Alexander V 143
  Boniface VIII 98
  Boniface IX 146
  Celestine III 76
  Clement V 98, 115
  Clement VII, antipope 134
  Gregory I 22–27, 48, 70
  Gregory II 163
  Gregory IX 98, 147n
  Gregory XI 134
  Hadrian IV (Nicholas Breakspear) 73,
    82, 225
  Hadrian V see Othobon, Cardinal
  Innocent XI 384
  John XXII 98, 123, 125, 133, 142
  John Paul II 517
  Julius III 211
  Leo XIII 534
  Marcellus II 211
  Martin IV 95
  Nicholas IV 95, 112, 189
  Paul IV 211–212
  Pius V 219, 223
  Pius IX 513, 515
  Pius X 542
  Urban VI 134
Roscrea 73
Rose, Hugh James 534
Ross (Ireland) 73, 109
Ross (Scotland) 76, 231
Rous, Francis 237–240
Rowland, Daniel 427
Ruadháin of Lorrha 9
Rudolf, Edward de Montjoie 529
Rufianus 27
Rufus, Richard 94
Ruskin, John 499
Russia 43, 122n, 457, 484, 533n, 549, 555,
    566

Rutherford, Samuel 330–331, 335, 581, 627–628
Rutter, John 566
Ryder, Henry 458
Ryle, John Charles 511, 522
Ryrie, Alec 199

Sacheverell, Henry 401
St Albans 3, 510
St Andrews 75–77, 107, 143, 146, 155, 157, 228, 230, 232–234, 242, 274–275, 315, 317n, 620
St Asaph 67, 212n, 268, 467
St Clement 45
St David's 12, 67, 75, 100, 106, 168n, 212n, 289n, 380n, 467
St Edmundsbury and Ipswich 510
    see also Bury St Edmunds
St John's College (Nottingham) 602
Salesbury, William 268–269
Salisbury (Sarum) 30, 61, 84, 86n, 107, 111, 167–168, 178, 199, 212n, 216, 248n, 402n, 467, 606
Saltoun 410n
Sankey, Ira David 520
Santiago de Compostela 159
Sarum see Salisbury
Saumur 301
Sayers, Dorothy 565
Scattery Island 73
Schliemann, Heinrich 543
Scotland xi, xvi, xviii–xix, 1n, 18, 20–22, 38, 44–45, 48, 53, 62, 67, 68n, 74–77, 100–101, 106–107, 112, 114, 119n, 120–121, 130, 135, 143–144, 146n, 154–156, 168, 178, 204, 214, 216, 227–243, 248, 251, 253–254, 261, 264, 271–282, 284–285, 287, 290, 297n, 298, 303, 311, 313–320, 323, 325–326, 328, 330, 335, 341, 349, 362, 375–376, 381–383, 385, 387, 398, 404, 408–414, 420–422, 424, 431, 438, 448–453, 455–456, 462, 465n, 469, 471–475, 481n, 488, 496, 502n, 507–509, 513–514, 518, 520, 524, 528, 531, 534, 548, 550, 564, 569, 571, 575, 578, 592–593, 596, 615, 618, 620–621, 627–628
Scotland, kings and queens of
    David I 74–75
    James III 228
    James IV 178, 227
    James V 227–229, 233
    Macbeth 74
    Macbeth, Lady 74
    Malcolm III 74
    Margaret 74
    Margaret, wife of James IV 178, 227
    Marie de Guise 232–233
    Mary I 216, 227, 230, 232, 234, 241–242, 252, 258, 272, 314, 325
    Robert I Bruce (de Brus) 114
Scrooby 290
Sebastopol 122
Sedan 275
Sedgefield 309n
Selsey 30
Selymbria 122
Senan of Inis Cathaigh 9
Sexburga, St 42
Seymour, Edward, duke of Somerset 205
Seymour, St John D. 328
Shaftesbury, earls of see Cooper, Anthony Ashley
Shakespeare, William 214
Sheffield 510, 615n
Sherborne 30, 61, 167n
Sherwood Forest 64
Sibbes, Richard 266
Sicily 45, 54, 76
Sidgwick, Henry 546
Sierra Leone 458, 551

Sigbert, king of East Anglia 29
Simeon, Charles 446–447, 461
Simnel, Lambert 224
Simons, Menno 292
Simson, John 450–451
Sitric, king of Dublin 69
Skye 76
Smith, Hannah Whitall 521
Smith, John Taylor 551
Smith, Miles 288
Smith, Robert Pearsall 521
Smith, William Robertson 508
Smyth, John 290, 292
Sodor and Man 45, 143–144, 199, 212n,
 426–427, 447, 467, 468n, 511n
 see also Isle of Man
Solovyov, Vladimir 484
Somerset, Duke of see Seymour, Edward
Sophia of Hanover 283, 385, 400
Sourozh 122n, 568
South Africa xviii, 444, 461, 506,
 524–525, 567
South Carolina 384n
Southcott, Joanna 433
Southwark 254, 290, 293, 510
Southwell 510
Sozzini, Fausto 319n, 357
Sozzini, Lelio 357
Spain 2, 22, 159, 178–180, 190, 211–212,
 215, 260, 266, 295–296, 298, 326, 330,
 376, 422, 462
Sparke, Bowyer Edward 463
Spencer, Herbert 499
Spurgeon, Charles Haddon 497–498,
 512, 536, 610n
Spurr, John 388
Sri Lanka (Ceylon) 567
Stanford, Charles Villiers 565–566
Stanley, Arthur Penrhyn 507
Stapleton, Thomas 257
Stephen, James 443

Sternhold, Thomas 237–239
Stewart, James 233, 242
Still, William 571–572, 621
Stillingfleet, Edward 373
Stirling 232, 335
Stoker, Bram 545
Stokes, Sir George Gabriel 502n
Stone, Peter James (Carol) 608
Storr, Vernon Faithful 542
Stott, John Robert Walmsley 570–571,
 582, 584
Strafford, Earl of see Wentworth, Sir
 Thomas
Strathclyde 20–21
Streeter, Burnett Hillman 541
Strype, John 236
Stuart, Charles (Young Pretender) 383
Studdert-Kennedy, Geoffrey Anketell
 559
Suetonius 1
Suisse Romande 11
Sutton 463
Swansea xii, 67n
Swanson, Robert 151–152
Swift, Jonathan 418–419, 454
Switzerland 11, 37, 201, 229, 249, 255,
 336, 351

Talbot, Edward Stuart 538
Tanzania 445n
Taylor, Jeremy 368
Taylor, John, bishop of Lincoln
 208–209
Teignmouth, James Shore, baron 443
Temple, Frederick 502
Termonfeckin 110
Tertullian 2
Thatcher, Margaret 372, 592–593
Thiselton, Anthony Thomas 601
Thomas, Roderick (Rod) Charles Howell
 614n

Thomas, William Henry Griffith 522
Thomas of Chobham 84
Thorney 49
Thornton, Henry 443
Throckmorton, Job 252
Thurles 493
Thyatira 122n
Tindal, Matthew 398
Tocqueville, Alexis de 419
Toland, John 392, 417
Toledo 22
Tone, Wolfe 423
Tooth, Arthur 517
Toplady, Augustus 436–438
Torbay 381, 401, 495n
Toronto 522
Torrance, James Bruce 564
Torrance, Thomas Forsyth 564
Tours 11
Tower of London 177, 198, 275, 320,
   380–381, 387
Townend, Stuart 612, 621
Toynbee, Arnold I 530n
Toynbee, Arnold II 530n
Toynbee, Polly 530n
Travers, Walter 249–250, 252
Trench, Power Le Poer 458
Tretire with Michaelchurch 308–309
Trimmer, Sarah 442
Trondheim 45
Truro 13, 510, 541
Tuam 71–73, 109–110, 156, 298n, 466
Tunbridge Wells 441
Tunstall, Cuthbert 181, 184, 205
Tylor, Edward Burnett 501
Tyndale, William 182–183, 188, 196, 214,
   259, 270, 280, 334
Tyrrell, George 542–543

Uganda 444, 523
Uinniau see Ninian, St

Ulster 229n, 296–298, 321, 323, 422, 451,
   454, 494–496, 525, 554, 586
   see also Northern Ireland
United Kingdom (UK) xii, xv–xvi, xviii,
   377n, 385, 394, 412, 454, 456–457, 461,
   475n, 478, 483, 494, 505, 509, 513, 515,
   522–523, 528, 531, 537, 549, 588, 591,
   593, 595, 621
United Kingdom, kings and queens of
   Anne 283, 385, 394, 399–400, 411
   Edward VIII 562
   Elizabeth II 621
   George I 283, 400–401, 411, 416,
      549
   George II 435
   George III 423, 464, 481
   George IV 412, 464
   George V 555
   Victoria xix, 549
United States of America (USA) 158,
   291, 377n, 409n, 424n, 461, 475n,
   495, 522–523, 542, 549, 565, 568, 601,
   613
Ur of the Chaldees 543

Valera, Éamon de 592n
Van Dixhoorn, Chad 331
Van Mildert, William 479
Vannes 11
Venice, Venetian Republic 457
Venn, Henry (junior) 443, 445
Venn, Henry (senior) 443
Venn, John I 443n
Venn, John II 443n
Venn, John Archibald 443n
Vermigli, Pietro Martire 204, 207
Verulamium 3
Vidler, Alexander (Alec) Roper 580
Virginia 260–261, 291
Vittel, Christopher 254
Vortigern 9

Wace, Henry 522

Waco 567

Wakefield 510

Walachia 11

Waldegrave, Robert 252–253, 276

Wales xi, xvi–xix, 1n, 10–13, 28, 33n, 48, 53, 62, 67, 106, 119–120, 122, 140, 148, 151, 168, 212n, 243–244, 267–271, 342, 362, 414, 421, 425, 438–441, 452, 463, 496, 509–510, 526–528, 534, 593

Wallonia 11

Walpole, Horace 429

Walsingham 42–43, 159, 614

Waltham Abbey 54n

Warbeck, Perkin 224

Ward, Samuel 301

Ware, Timothy (Kallistos) 568

Warman, Frederic Sumpter Guy 541

Warner, Robert (Rob) 612–613

Warren, Max Alexander Cunningham 582–583

Waterford 72, 327

Waterland 292

Waterland, Daniel 419

Waterloo 456–458, 554

Watson, John James 480

Watts, Isaac 406–407

Wearmouth 36, 121

Wellington, Duke of 457

Wells 33, 61, 199, 212n, 248n, 289n, 380n, 381n, 383, 467, 468n, 516
  see also Bath

Welschschweiz 11

Wentworth, Sir Thomas, earl of Strafford 311–313, 318, 320–321

Werburgh, St 42

Wesley, Charles 395, 428–429, 435

Wesley, John 393, 395, 412, 427–430, 435, 450–451, 461, 521

Wesley, Samuel 395, 427

Wesley, Susannah 421

Wessex 44, 47

Westbury-on-Trym (Bristol) 131

Westcott, Brooke Foss 507–508

Westminster 81, 199, 329–342, 356, 488, 507, 555

Westminster Abbey 53, 134, 199, 302, 401n, 463

Wexford 45, 327–328

Whiston, William 399, 416–417

Whitby 31, 34, 42, 163, 615n

White, Francis 288

Whitefield, George 427–431, 441, 450, 495

Whitehouse, Mary 600

Whithorn 21, 30, 74–76

Whittingham, William 237–239

Wilberforce, Samuel 501

Wilberforce, William 443, 480

Wilcox, Thomas 247

Wilde, Oscar 530

William, bishop of London 59

William of Ockham 124–127, 130, 132

William of Pagula, 138

Williams, Sir George 519

Williams, Glanmor 268

Williams, Isaac 486

Williams, Ralph Vaughan 566

Williams, Rowland 502

Williams, William (Pantycelyn) 439–440

Willibrord 37

Wilson, Daniel 446n

Wilson, Henry Bristow 503

Wilson, Thomas 426–427, 446–447

Wimber, John 617

Wimborne Minster 32

Winchester 29–30, 33, 47–48, 52, 60, 81, 131, 166, 178, 204, 209, 212n, 288n, 402n, 467–468

Winram, John 234

Wishart, George 229–230

Wittenberg xvii, 180, 183, 191, 192n, 202, 204
Wodeham, Adam 126
Wood, Charles, Viscount Halifax 555–556
Wood, Maurice Arthur Ponsonby 571, 614
Woodhead, Linda Jane Pauline 542n
Worcester 30, 33, 49–50, 60, 69, 178, 198–199, 208, 212n, 248n, 270, 381n, 467, 539
Worms 180
Wrexham 268
Wulfstan II, bishop of Worcester 60
Wyclif (Wycliffe), John xvii, 130–137, 142–149, 153, 159
Wynfrid 35
Wynfrith of Crediton (Boniface) xvii, 37

Yeats, William Butler 478n, 545, 562
York (Eboracum) 3, 18, 21–22, 24, 27–28, 30, 33, 36–37, 41, 43–44, 49–50, 60, 66, 69, 74–77, 83, 86n, 98, 100–101, 121, 139, 144, 149, 151n, 155–156, 159n, 168, 186–188, 199, 209, 212n, 248n, 264, 273, 278, 289, 379, 381, 401, 467–468, 489–490, 510, 528, 597, 606, 615n
York, archbishops of
   Cottrell, Stephen Geoffrey 606
   Habgood, John 597
   Heath, Nicholas 191
   John of Hexham 41
   Neile, Richard 288, 310
   Oswald 49
   Paulinus 27–28
   Scrope, Richard 149
   Sharp, John 381
   Thoresby, John 139
   Wilfrid 29, 33–34, 36
   Wolsey, Thomas 121, 186–188
   Wulfstan 50–51
Young, Robert 472

Zanzibar 444
Zinzendorf, Count Nikolaus von 425–426, 429
Zion 588–628
   see also Jerusalem
Zurich xvii, 201, 248
Zwingli, Huldrych 201, 578

Index of subjects

abortion 562, 575, 586, 590–591, 599, 605, 626

Additional Curates' Society 479

adiaphora 184, 221

advowsons 63, 86, 96, 119, 123, 246, 446, 463

Affirmation Act (1888) 534–535

Affirming Catholicism 605–606

alien priories 121, 153–154

Alpha Course 619

Anabaptism, Anabaptists 207, 236, 254–255, 292, 330, 337, 342–343, 425

Ancrene Wisse (*Ancrene Riwle*) 85

Anglican Communion 333, 426, 518, 606

Anglican Mission in England 617

Anglicanism xvii, xix, 262–263, 489, 518, 522, 565, 606

Anglo-Catholicism 470, 487, 502, 514–519, 522, 536–540, 551, 555–557, 567, 570, 580, 582, 584, 597, 604–606, 611, 614–615

Anti-State Church Association 450

Antichrist 123, 171, 214, 339, 351

Anvil 602

apartheid 525, 567

apocalypticism 350, 361, 474–478, 481, 492

Apostles' Creed 18, 113, 139, 193–194, 206, 341

archaeology 390, 543–544, 563

archdeacons, archdeaconries 51, 61, 65, 105n, 150, 199, 231, 490

Arianism 22, 396, 399

Arminianism 285, 305–307, 405, 427, 430, 436, 438, 447

Articuli Cleri 98

Athanasian Creed 206

atheism xvii, 391, 419, 457–458, 460, 465, 479, 500, 512, 530n, 533–534, 545, 547, 558, 586, 594

atonement 79, 236, 259, 285n, 300–301, 342, 357, 427, 476, 511n, 540, 602–603, 625, 627

limited 236, 284, 285n, 300, 427

Augsburg Confession 190–192, 197, 205

Augustinian canons/friars 33, 58–59, 71, 93n, 111, 138

Balfour Declaration 546

Bampton Lectures 522n

Banner of Truth Trust 581

banns of marriage 100, 264, 421

baptism 18, 25–27, 55, 64, 89, 114, 125–126, 160, 192, 200, 204, 206, 207n, 236, 254, 277, 281, 292–293, 309, 313, 339, 342, 344, 346–347, 367, 386–387, 404–405, 412, 488–489, 521, 527, 558, 585, 603

baptismal regeneration 488–489

Baptist Union 536

Baptists xviii–xix, 293, 326, 328, 333, 342–347, 367, 379, 387, 405–406, 434, 464, 488, 497–498, 526, 528, 531, 534, 536, 558, 616

First London Confession 293n

Second London Confession 333n

see also General Baptists; Particular Baptists

681

Barebone's Parliament 351, 361
Barmen Declaration 564
Baylor University 567
Benedictines 33, 48–49, 57–58, 577
benefices 96–97, 116–123, 151–153, 155,
    189, 211, 230, 246, 264, 272, 275, 277,
    281, 371, 314, 420, 455, 463, 466–468,
    516, 583
Beowulf 15, 38
Bible 10, 13n, 14, 52, 79, 83n, 88, 91, 113,
    125–126, 132–137, 145, 147, 164,
    182–183, 188, 190, 196, 198, 202, 206,
    209, 214, 218, 229, 232, 236, 243, 245,
    250–251, 253, 258, 260, 267–271,
    279–280, 286, 297, 313, 333–334, 336,
    339–341, 348, 351, 355–356, 358–359,
    367, 390, 399, 416, 421–422, 431,
    434–435, 437–438, 445, 447, 458, 476,
    498, 502–503, 506, 512, 536, 538,
    541–544, 569, 576–578, 589, 598–605,
    620, 623–624
    American Standard Version 576n
    Authorized (King James) Version 260,
        270–271, 279–280, 422, 435, 447,
        576–577, 589
    Bishops' 279
    canon of the 218
    Douai-Reims 258, 260, 422
    Geneva 214, 258, 279
    Great 198, 202, 214, 279
    inerrancy of the 601
    infallibility of the 502, 601
    interpretation of 502–503, 538,
        598–604
    Irish (Gaelic) 297, 313
    Lollard 137
    Manx 447–448
    Old English 47
    New English 279n, 576–577
    Revised Standard Version 576
    Revised Version 576

    translation of the 182–183, 188, 190,
        196, 258–260, 445, 447, 576, 578
    Welsh 243, 268–271, 438–439
Bible Society 439, 443, 464
Billy Graham Evangelistic Association
    613
bishops 3–4, 12–13, 26, 28, 35, 37, 40,
    49–52, 59–60, 62, 65–69, 74–75, 80–81,
    86, 91, 100, 105, 107–108, 110, 114,
    116–118, 121–122, 130, 133–134,
    140–144, 149–150, 152, 156, 166, 185,
    187, 193–195, 197–198, 202n, 204, 208,
    211, 217, 219, 222, 226, 228, 231,
    234–235, 247–248, 251, 257, 267–268,
    270–273, 275–277, 279, 281, 287–288,
    298, 304–305, 308, 310–311, 316–319,
    324–325, 369, 371–373, 379–383, 387,
    394–395, 400–402, 419–421, 423, 431,
    445, 454–455, 462–463, 465–470, 482,
    489–490, 494, 556–557, 559, 585, 596,
    606–607, 610, 614
    suffragan 110, 122, 140, 150, 380, 387
Bishops' Book 193–195
'black church' 568–569
Black Death 128–130, 137, 152–153, 174
black rubric 213, 281
blasphemy 147, 206, 218, 349, 392
Boney M 588
Book of Common Order 235
Book of Common Prayer
    1549 168, 203, 205, 211, 217, 316
    1552 203–205, 207, 213, 217, 226, 281
    1559 213n, 217, 219, 245, 247
    1604 217, 289, 302, 305, 308, 331, 369
    1637 316–317
    1662 203, 213n, 217, 237, 240, 307n,
        370, 380, 382, 386, 411, 413, 432,
        434–435, 446n, 488, 494, 577, 627
    1928 205n, 557
    Irish (Gaelic) 297
    Welsh 268–271

Book of Discipline (English) 250

Books of Discipline (Scottish) *see* First Book of Discipline; Second Book of Discipline

Book of Sports 291, 310, 371

Boy Scouts 550, 572

Boyle Lectures 397n, 399, 522n

British Broadcasting Corporation (BBC) 572–573, 608n

British Parliament 397–398, 402, 411–412, 421, 423, 440, 442–443, 454, 458, 462–463, 465–466, 471–472, 475, 480–483, 489–490, 505, 516, 526, 528–529, 534–535, 555, 557, 562, 594

Calvinism 250–251, 257, 282, 285–290, 292, 300–301, 305–306, 310, 342, 405, 427, 430, 436–438, 441, 447, 451, 456, 462, 524, 603

Calvinistic Methodists 439, 496, 527

Cambridge Inter-Collegiate Christian Union (CICCU) 521

Cambridge University Missionary Brotherhood 507

canon law 84, 97–102, 114, 119, 133, 138, 179, 186, 189–190, 205, 207, 209, 211, 246–247, 263–264, 277–278, 300, 305, 312–319, 390, 455, 491, 517, 578–579

cardinals 101, 115, 121, 134, 210

Carmelites 93n

Carthusians 58, 154

cathedrals 30, 32–33, 60–62, 65, 67, 71, 102, 105n, 111, 114, 116–117, 119, 122, 151n, 153, 165, 199, 248, 287, 434, 463, 468, 483, 490, 527

Catholic Apostolic Church 475

Catholic Boys' Brigade 550

Catholic emancipation 420, 423, 454, 456, 460, 464–465, 481–482, 508, 512, 525

Catholicism *see* Roman Catholic Church, Roman Catholics

céli Dé (Culdees) 75

celibacy 64, 69–70, 90, 99, 190, 198, 207, 230, 487, 579–580, 606

Celtic church xvii, 13–15, 75

census, religious 509, 512

chantries 153, 161, 412

Chartism, Chartists 505

Christian Social Brotherhood 534

Christian socialism 504–506, 533, 593

Christian Socialist League 534

Christian Socialist Society 534

Christianity Explored 619

Christmas 103, 158, 166, 219, 281, 309, 413, 548, 585, 598, 611, 621

Church Army 497n, 550

Church Association 516

church councils

    Chalcedon 35

    Constance 148

    Constantinople I 35

    Constantinople II 35

    Constantinople III 35–36

    Ephesus I 35

    Lateran (649) 35

    Lateran I 64, 80, 99

    Lateran II 71, 80

    Lateran III 108n

    Lateran IV 96, 100, 113, 138, 142, 147n, 398, 421n

    Nicaea I 13, 35, 399–400

    Trent 200–201, 210, 231–232, 241, 257, 259, 298

    Vatican I 515

    Vatican II 579–580, 604

church discipline 207, 245, 247, 277, 324, 330, 332, 339–340, 362, 371, 387, 389, 404, 518

Church Lads' Brigade 550

Church Missionary Society (CMS) 443–444, 582

Church of England xvii, xix, 12, 32, 60, 63,
    66, 77, 99–100, 101n, 113–114, 123,
    144, 147–148, 185–187, 200–204, 208,
    210, 216–217, 219n, 221–222, 236, 240,
    244, 246, 250, 252–254, 257–258,
    260–271, 279–280, 286–303, 305–306,
    308, 311–312, 318, 333, 343–344,
    346–347, 350–351, 358, 364, 370,
    372–375, 377, 379, 381, 384–388,
    393–394, 398, 400–403, 406, 408, 412,
    415–416, 419–428, 433–435, 439–440,
    442–443, 446–447, 452, 458, 460,
    465–466, 468–471, 479–484, 486–491,
    494, 497n, 502–506, 509–512, 514,
    516–519, 522–523, 527–529, 531,
    534–537, 539–542, 545, 547, 555, 557,
    562, 565, 568–571, 577–585, 596–597,
    605, 607–608, 610, 614–615, 619
  Alternative Service Book (1980) 577
  Children's Society 529
  General Synod 529, 579, 605, 608, 614
  National Assembly 528–529
Church of Ireland 73, 156n, 299–300,
    312–313, 368, 375, 422–424, 454–456,
    458, 465–466, 476, 490–491, 494,
    508–509, 512–513, 545, 572, 579
Church of Norway 121
Church of Scotland xix, 45, 75, 214, 243,
    274, 276, 282, 287, 315–317, 337, 385,
    409, 411–412, 420, 449–450, 452–453,
    462, 469, 472–475, 478, 481n, 513–514,
    518, 524, 528, 543, 571, 578, 592–593,
    598, 615, 620–621, 627–628
  Annuity Tax 478
  Chapels Act 471–472
  Evangelicals 448–453, 471
  General Assembly 271–276, 281–282,
    282n, 315, 317, 319, 341, 378,
    409–410, 449–452, 471–472, 592
  Great Disruption 453, 473, 479, 488,
    531

  Marrow controversy 448–450
  Moderates 448–453, 455, 472
  'New Licht' 450
  superintendents 235, 272–273
  Veto Act 471–472
church papists 222, 243, 268
Church Pastoral Aid Society (CPAS) 479
church rates 414, 469, 470n, 479
Church Society 516n, 602
Churchman 602
Churchmen's Union for the Advancement
    of Religious Thought 542
Cistercians 58, 71, 111
civil magistrate 207, 219, 236, 263, 339,
    345
civil partnerships 593, 606–607
Clapham Sect 443, 480n, 533
Clapton Sect 450n
Clarendon Code 374
clergy
  benefit of 57, 85
  non-stipendiary 405, 583–584, 615
Clericis Laicos 115
Clifton Theological College 470n
Cloud of Unknowing 138
coarbs 68
Codex Alexandrinus 286
Codex Bezae 251
collegiate churches 65, 248, 287, 434
Community of the Resurrection 470, 518
comprehension, religious 380, 386–388
Confederation of Kilkenny 326–327
confession (to a priest) 89, 142, 198, 579
confirmation 70, 89, 114, 200, 281, 344
conformity, occasional 372
Congregationalists 302, 308, 326,
    331–333, 343, 367, 387, 404–405, 464,
    475, 527, 531, 540, 558, 578
Conservative Party 377n, 593
    see also Tories
Constitutions of Clarendon 85–87

Conventicle Act 374

convocation(s) 105, 106n, 110, 118, 147n, 151, 155, 186–188, 199–200, 210, 300, 307, 317–318, 388n, 401, 426n, 462, 517, 522, 528–529, 557
    Ireland 299–300, 422, 455, 490–491
    Sodor and Man 426–427

Convocation of Canterbury 105, 147, 183, 186, 188, 193, 195, 199–200, 207, 246, 263–264, 277–278, 318–319, 370, 379, 388, 393–402, 416, 420, 489–491, 503

Convocation of York 105, 186, 188, 199, 278, 379, 489–491

Cornhill Training Course 619

Corporation Act 374

courts, ecclesiastical 55–57, 66, 97–102, 119, 150, 173, 185, 190, 221, 231, 277–278, 307–308, 310, 317, 379–380, 386, 410, 421, 469, 471, 488

covenant theology 333–340, 367

Covid-19 pandemic 613, 622–625

Cranmer Hall, Durham 470n

creed see Apostles' Creed; Athanasian Creed; Nicene Creed

Crieff Brotherhood 571, 621

Crockford's Clerical Directory 597

Crusades 78, 82, 103–104, 107, 115, 150, 162

Cuddesdon Theological College 470

Dallas Theological Seminary 522

de-Christianization 589, 593

De Haeretico Comburendo 146–147

deaconesses 519

deacons 90n, 152, 219, 251, 405

Declaration of Indulgence 380, 383

defamation 97, 469

Defender of the Faith (royal title) 181

deism, deists 392–393, 399, 418, 424

Devotional Revolution (Ireland) 494–495

Diet of Augsburg 190

dioceses 29–30, 33, 45, 60–61, 63, 65–67, 70–77, 102, 106, 108–111, 113, 122, 130–131, 140, 150, 155, 186, 199, 209, 211, 212n, 267, 271–272, 287, 445n, 466–468, 510–511, 528, 614n, 620

disestablishment 67, 77, 440, 480, 490–491, 508–514, 519, 526–529, 562

Dissenters see Nonconformists

divine right of episcopacy 261, 279

divine right of kings 276, 279, 304, 316

divorce 35, 56, 99–100, 179, 207, 333, 339, 421, 468, 562, 586, 599
    annulment 99–100, 179–181, 187, 189–191, 264
    separation 99–100, 264

Doctors' Commons 190

Dominicans 93–94, 127, 145

Donatism 3–5

Dream of the Rood 38–40

Easter xvi, 103, 143, 159, 165, 219, 259, 281, 309, 413, 548, 585, 598, 611, 623
    date of 3–4, 13, 29, 31, 34–36, 43

Easter Rising (Ireland) 554

Eastern Orthodox Churches 122n, 163, 167, 174n, 280, 285–287, 425, 482–484, 549, 568, 584n, 605, 618–619

Ecclesiastical Commission (1686) 379–381

Ecclesiastical Commission (1835) 466, 468, 479

Edict of Nantes 303–304, 378–379

Education Act (1870) 511

Education Act (1944) 585

election, unconditional 284

Elizabethan Settlement 215–224, 244, 246, 248–249, 257, 262–263, 266, 269, 307

Enabling Act (1919) 528–529

English Church Union 555

English Parliament 67, 105, 119,
      145–146, 186–191, 197–198, 200, 205,
      207, 209, 213, 247, 249, 252, 261,
      267–268, 273–274, 278, 306–308, 311,
      318–332, 340–343, 349–351, 360–361,
      369–370, 374, 377, 380–381

Enlightenment 359, 391–392, 403, 418,
      424, 450, 535–536, 548, 598

erenachs 68, 156

Essays and Reviews 502–503, 541

Eucharist see Holy Communion

Evangelical Alliance 477, 516

Evangelical Ministry Assembly 619

Evangelicalism, Evangelicals 405,
      424–453, 459, 464–465, 470–472, 475,
      477, 479–480, 486, 488–492, 495–498,
      502, 507, 516–517, 519–522, 529–530,
      532–533, 536, 538, 541–542, 551,
      556–558, 569–572, 581–585, 594,
      601–604, 611–615, 620, 623

Exclusive Brethren 476

excommunication 101–102, 106, 180,
      207, 219–220, 231, 264, 269, 277, 295,
      319

extra-parochial areas 64–65

extreme unction 89–90, 114, 160, 485

Family of Love 254

Fellowship of Independent Evangelical
      Churches (FIEC) 581–582, 616

Fellowship of St Alban and St Sergius
      568

Fifth Monarchists 346, 351–352, 360–361

Filioque 79

First Book of Discipline 235, 240

First Book of Homilies 199, 202, 204,
      207, 245, 247, 250n

First Scottish Confession 234–236

First World War 470, 531, 549–553,
      555

Five Articles of Perth 281–282, 315

Five-Mile Act 374

football 225, 291, 544, 624

Forty-two Articles (1553) 205–207,
      217–218, 236n, 340, 474

Fountain Trust 584–585

Franciscans 93–94, 124, 126, 133, 142,
      157, 322

Free Church of Scotland 409n, 472–474,
      496, 507–508, 513–514, 520

Free Churches 409, 473, 578, 581, 585,
      605, 615–617, 619
      see also Nonconformists

French Revolution 420, 423, 457, 460,
      464, 483, 491, 514

friars 92–95, 111–112, 131, 135, 142–143,
      145, 157, 169, 172–173, 313, 322

Friars of the Sack 93n

Fulcrum 602

General Baptists 292–293, 342–344, 346,
      405

German Confessing Church 564

Girl Guides 550, 572

Glorious Revolution 383–384, 386, 399,
      408, 410, 420, 460, 481, 495n

grace xii, 5, 55–56, 90–91, 94, 113, 128,
      160, 162, 171–172, 180, 193–194, 206,
      223, 239, 256–257, 263, 282, 285, 335,
      337–338, 343, 345, 347, 429, 432,
      436–438, 448–449, 489, 506, 603
      irresistible 257, 285

graduates, university 152, 155–156, 265,
      443n, 530, 551

Grand Remonstrance 320

Great Ejection 370–372, 381, 404, 511

Great Tew circle 358–359

Great War see First World War

Greenbelt 612

Group Brotherhood 541–542

Guild of St Matthew 530

Hackney Phalanx 480

heresy 5–6, 22, 31, 33, 35, 90, 115, 128, 133–134, 142, 145–149, 159, 170, 184, 196, 199, 212, 215n, 219, 226, 228–231, 290, 292, 319n, 353, 355, 358, 395–398, 400, 416, 431, 450–451, 475–476, 478, 489, 505–506, 538, 614

High Commission courts 221, 278, 289, 307–310, 317

Highland Theological College 620

Hinduism, Hindus 507, 545, 585–586, 595, 626

Holy Communion 89–92, 103, 124, 127, 135, 160–161, 164–165, 172, 192, 201–203, 213, 217, 246, 413–414, 551, 603, 623

holy orders 57, 90, 113–114, 120, 125, 167, 206, 236, 264, 281, 309, 339, 382, 403, 432, 446, 485, 551

home-rule movement (Ireland) 494, 513, 525–526, 553

homilies, Bishop Bonner's 209, 211

homosexuality 378, 487, 530, 572, 575, 590–591, 593–594, 600, 605–608, 618, 626

Honest to God 583

House of Commons 105, 187, 247, 306–307, 318, 323, 331–332, 340, 360, 400, 557

House of Lords 105, 187, 246, 323–325, 381, 401–402, 411, 466–467, 468n, 472, 585, 596

Huguenots 378–379, 384, 416

Humanae Vitae 604

humanists (atheistic) 573, 580, 586, 593–595, 626

hymns, hymnody xviii, 163, 240, 294, 366, 405–406, 434–439, 483, 533, 612, 621

Ignorantia Sacerdotum 112–114, 139

Indian National Congress 545

indulgences 140, 161, 174–175, 180, 182

Industrial Christian Fellowship (ICF) 559

Industrial Revolution 457–459, 505, 529

interdict 104, 623

International Fellowship of Evangelical Students (IFES) 521

Inter-Varsity Fellowship (IVF) 521, 569

Inter-Varsity Press (IVP) 521

Ireland

    Gaelic 110–112, 140–141, 156–157, 225, 243, 296–298, 321–322, 375, 453, 455, 492, 545

    New English in 243, 296, 322–323

    Old English in 243, 295–296, 300, 305, 311–313, 321–322, 326–327, 375, 453

Irish Articles 299–300, 306, 312, 329

Irish Church Missions 492

Irish Parliament 110–111, 224–226, 300, 312–313, 414, 423, 453–454, 462

Islam, Muslims 122, 163, 178, 286–287, 507, 523, 548, 560, 585–586, 595, 626

Islington Clerical Conference 446n

Jacobitism, Jacobites 400–402, 410, 420, 481

Jewish Lads' Brigade 550

Jews, Judaism 1, 55, 147, 218, 259, 316, 353, 421–422, 437, 477, 534, 546, 550, 560, 566, 588, 591, 597–599, 603, 609

justification by faith (alone) 184, 192–194, 203, 210, 229, 338

Keston College 567

Keswick Convention 521–522, 524, 573

King's Book 195, 209

Labour Party 430, 540, 593

Lambeth Articles 256, 278, 299, 306

languages
  Afrikaans 524
  Arabic 508
  Assamese 445
  Bengali 445
  Cornish 13
  English xviii, 10n, 11, 17n, 21, 38, 42,
    44–45, 47–48, 50n, 52, 58n, 70n, 77,
    84n, 85, 87n, 119n, 123, 136–139,
    141, 165–166, 168–170, 183, 186n,
    190, 192n, 200, 201n, 203, 210n, 214,
    220n, 223, 229, 237, 250–251, 256n,
    258–261, 265, 267=268, 270, 280,
    290, 313n, 321n, 322, 333, 364, 368,
    376, 393, 400, 406, 435, 437,
    439–440, 451–452, 457, 484n, 519,
    524–525, 540, 576–577, 579
  French 11, 85, 96, 138–139, 165, 223,
    250–251, 419n, 484n
  Gaelic 229, 297n, 313, 321–322, 438,
    447, 452, 473
  German 58n, 182–183, 250n, 533n
  Greek 88, 168, 185, 214, 218, 223, 251,
    259, 279–280, 334n, 508
  Hebrew 83, 214, 237, 259, 279–280,
    403
  Hindi 445
  Irish 17, 20, 68n, 70n, 110–112, 141,
    244, 297, 313–314, 321–322, 368,
    438, 453, 455, 579
  Italian 223, 556, 579
  Latin xviii, 2n, 5–6, 8, 14, 20–21, 23,
    25, 32, 48, 52, 63, 67, 78–79, 84n, 85,
    91–92, 97, 103, 106, 119, 136–139,
    164–169, 185, 190, 200, 209, 210n,
    220n, 223, 235n, 250n, 251, 256n,
    258–260, 267, 306n, 313n, 451,
    579
  Manx 393, 426, 447–448
  Marathi 445
  Odia (Oriya) 445

  Persian 445
  Polish 579
  Sanskrit 445
  Scots 229, 235n
  Spanish 223, 556
  Urdu 445
  Welsh 67, 106, 243, 267–271, 393,
    438–441, 447, 496, 509, 526, 579
  Zulu 506
Latitudinarians 373–374, 401
League of Schmalkalden 190
lectureships (Puritan) 249, 265–266, 290,
  446
legates, papal 70–71, 81, 100–101, 107,
  186, 210
Levellers 345
liberal Catholicism (Anglican) 537–539,
  571
Liberal Democratic Party 594
Liberal Party 377n, 526, 528
  see also Whigs
liberalism, theological 535–543, 563
Library of Anglo-Catholic Theology
  487
litany 200, 268
liturgy 14, 34, 58, 70, 78, 92, 162, 165,
  168, 203–204, 208, 217, 267, 302, 330,
  380, 386–389, 557, 577–579, 604
Lollards 136–137, 140, 143, 145–149,
  153, 157, 170, 173, 182, 185, 228
London Bible College 569
London City Mission 530–531
London Confessions see Baptists
London Missionary Society 444
Lord Chancellor 63, 131, 145, 188, 315,
  374
Lord's Supper see Holy Communion
Lutheranism 181–182, 184, 190–203,
  210, 218, 228–229, 246, 250n, 284, 385,
  400, 424–425, 435, 444, 462, 519
Lux Mundi 538, 541

Purgatory 90, 140, 160–162, 174–175, 180, 184, 192, 206, 236

Puritanism, Puritans 213n, 215, 221–222, 243–257, 261–266, 271, 276–280, 285, 287–291, 293–294, 300, 305–308, 310–314, 319, 321–323, 325, 328–329, 334–335, 344–348, 350–351, 356–357, 359–371, 372–373, 376, 395, 401–402, 404–405, 413–415, 425–427, 429, 474, 526, 581, 582

Quakers 324, 326, 328, 346–350, 363, 379, 387, 405–406, 421, 534

quarter days 158

Queen Anne's Bounty 394

Ranters 350, 353

recusants 220, 243, 254, 269, 295, 307, 407–408

Reform (organization) 614–615

Reformatio Legum Ecclesiasticarum 246–247, 334

Reformation, Protestant 8, 42, 68n, 77, 91–92, 98, 102, 106, 108, 111, 113, 118, 120–121, 125, 128, 131, 137, 144, 148–149, 153–157, 170, 174, 178, 181, 183, 189, 191, 194, 196–209, 213, 214n, 215, 217, 226, 228–244, 246, 251, 253, 257, 260, 266–274, 286, 296, 298, 300, 314–316, 330, 333, 338, 342, 346, 350, 374–377, 407, 410, 412, 434, 447, 458, 460, 465–466, 474, 482, 485, 489, 491, 504, 517, 529, 578, 589

regium donum 409

Regnans in Excelsis (papal bull) 219–220, 223, 258

Regnans in Excelsis (papal decretal) 143

religious communities 518

see also monasteries, monasticism

Religious Tract Society 441

Remonstrants 283–284, 290

Representation of Religion 394–398

Rerum Novarum 534

Roman Catholic Church, Roman Catholics xi, xv, xviii–xix, 95, 98, 100, 149n, 158, 174n, 188, 199–201, 204, 206, 208–220, 223, 226, 227n, 229, 231–235, 240–243, 250, 254, 257–263, 267–269, 274, 280, 285, 287, 295–299, 302–306, 311, 314, 316, 319–322, 324, 326–329, 339n, 346–347, 351, 353, 355, 357–359, 368, 370, 375–381, 383–384, 386, 390, 393, 396, 403, 408–409, 414–416, 420–426, 448, 453–456, 460, 462, 464–466, 470, 476–477, 481–485, 488–489, 491–495, 504, 508, 512–516, 518–519, 523, 525–526, 528, 531, 534–535, 537, 542–543, 545, 547, 550–551, 553–554, 556–557, 560, 562–563, 577, 579–582, 584, 586, 590, 592–593, 594n, 604–605, 611–615, 617–618

Royal British Legion 554, 572

Royal Society 502n

Rump Parliament 360–361, 369

rural deaneries 65–66, 150, 455, 466

Sabbatarianism 265, 544, 611

sacraments, sacramental theology 87–92, 113–114, 200, 204

St Martin's Day (Martinmas) 158

St Mellitus College 619–620

'St Patrick's Breastplate' 17–18

St Swithun's Day 158

saints

canonized 42, 49, 52, 60, 68, 142, 158–159, 165, 173, 184, 192, 334, 483

relics of 41, 44, 142, 159, 196, 313

Salvation Army xvii, 497, 550

same-sex marriage 593, 595, 600, 606–607

Sarum Rite 111, 167–169, 203, 211

scholasticism 79, 87–95, 123–128, 209
Scottish Confession *see* First Scottish Confession; Second Scottish Confession
Scottish Episcopal Church 382, 385
Scottish Parliament 155, 228–229, 232, 234–235, 237, 272–273, 275–276, 315–317, 319, 385, 410, 593n
Scottish Voluntary Association 478–479
Second Book of Discipline 274–275
Second Book of Homilies 219, 245, 247, 250n
Second Helvetic Confession 336
Second Scottish Confession 274, 316
Second World War 149n, 354, 536, 546n, 564, 566
secularization 460, 471, 532–534, 554, 593, 596–597, 613, 621
Seekers 330, 346–348, 350
sexual matters and behaviour 26–27, 59, 107, 344, 487, 561, 567, 573, 580–581, 586, 590, 593, 595, 600, 604, 606–607
Sikhs 585–586, 595
sinecures 116–118, 121, 211
Sion College, London 331n
Sisterhood of Mercy 518
situation ethics 599
Six Articles (1539) 197–198
slavery 334, 443–444, 457–458, 461, 524
societies for the reformation of manners 397, 420, 441
Society for the Liberation of the Church from State Control 480, 512
Society for the Promotion of Christian Knowledge (SPCK) 393, 412
Society for the Propagation of the Gospel (SPG) 393
Society of Jesus (Jesuits) 210, 378, 542
Society of St John the Evangelist 518
Society of the Sacred Mission 518, 571
Socinianism 319, 357–358, 390

Solemn League and Covenant (1643) 323, 329, 374
Solemn League and Covenant (1912) 525–526
Songs of Praise 434, 621
spiritualism 545
Spring Harvest 612–613
Spurgeon's College 497
Star Chamber 310–311
stipendiary chaplains 117, 122
Student Christian Movement (SCM) 521, 569
subdeacons 51, 152
Sunday schools 442, 544, 572, 575, 581
superstition 158–162, 196, 244, 277, 299, 355, 390, 396, 418, 597
supremacy (royal) 195, 262, 282, 313n, 316, 319
Supreme Court 595
synods, provincial 12, 66, 98, 100–101, 105–106, 110, 147, 156, 183, 186, 224–225, 298, 490

taxation
    clerical 95, 104–107, 110, 112, 116, 133, 151, 189, 318, 379, 401
    papal 81–82, 115
Ten Articles (1536) 192–195, 202, 205
Test Act 374, 379
Thanksgiving (holiday) 291
Thirty-nine Articles (1563, 1571) 162n, 218, 236, 245–246, 299, 306, 312, 329, 340, 350, 374, 400, 431, 486
tithe 49–50, 95–97, 101, 106, 110, 123, 153, 246, 275, 314, 328, 345, 352, 361, 414, 458, 466, 468
toleration, religious 292–293, 303–305, 311, 321, 345, 370, 378–379, 384, 386–387, 389, 403–404, 408, 411, 420, 459–460
Toleration Act 389n, 459

Tories 374, 377–379, 387–388, 393–394, 400–401, 411, 430, 533
  see also Conservative Party
total depravity 14, 285, 432, 478
Toynbee Hall 530
Tractarianism, Tractarians 482–488, 491, 499, 502, 537–538
transgenderism 608–609, 626
transubstantiation 91–92, 124–127, 135, 148, 184, 197, 201, 203, 299, 355–356, 391
Triers, parliamentary 361–362, 371
Trinity Sunday 87
Tyndale Fellowship for Biblical Research 569–570
Tyndale Hall 470n

Unitarianism, Unitarians xvii, 404, 495, 504, 512
United Free Church of Scotland 473–474
United Presbyterian Church of Scotland 513–514
United Reformed Church 578
universalism 207, 506
  hypothetical 300–301
universities 42, 63, 85, 87–89, 93–94, 113, 117, 128, 130, 154–155, 209, 224, 229, 245, 306, 398, 470–471, 479, 508, 569, 573, 620
Universities and Colleges Christian Fellowship (UCCF) 521
Universities' Mission to Central Africa (UMCA) 445n
unworthy reception (of communion) 201, 246, 369
Utraquism 91, 149

Valor Ecclesiasticus 189
vestments, vestiarian controversy 165, 221, 224, 244, 277, 288, 315, 485, 516
via media 202, 204

vicars-general 150
Victoria Institute 501, 502n

Wesleyans 433, 439, 527
Westminster Assembly 309n, 323, 329–342, 356
Westminster Confession of Faith 333–341, 350–351, 369, 404, 431, 450–451, 507, 563
Westminster Larger Catechism 341
Westminster Shorter Catechism 341
Whigs 377, 379, 401–402
  see also Liberal Party
Whole Duty of Man, The 368, 446
wills, last (testaments) 64, 97, 106, 152, 185, 207, 231
Windrush generation 568–569
witches, witchcraft 142, 159, 170, 313, 355
Wittenberg Articles 192n
women xvii, 16, 26–27, 41–43, 59, 85, 99, 137–138, 159, 170–171, 353, 420–421, 441–442, 479, 487, 500, 518–519, 546, 550, 555, 560–561
  ordination of 519, 583, 605, 608, 614–615
Word Alive 612
World Council of Churches (WCC) 567
World Missionary Conference 445, 547
worship 14, 25, 50, 61, 63–64, 92, 103, 106, 111, 162–170, 173, 190, 197, 200, 204–206, 211, 213, 217, 223, 232, 235, 240, 245, 247, 263, 265, 268, 271, 273, 277–278, 281–282, 305, 313, 324, 326, 331, 333, 338–339, 353, 366, 368–369, 372–374, 382, 386–387, 389, 396, 404, 406, 411–412, 431–432, 434–435, 439, 459, 482, 509–510, 512, 516, 530–531, 556, 563, 577–580, 582, 584–585, 591, 604, 611–612, 621–623

Young Men's Christian Association (YMCA) 519–520